HA'WAY/HOWAY THE LADS

Alan Candlish

SPORTS
BOOKS

Published in Great Britain by
SportsBooks Limited
PO Box 422
Cheltenham
GL50 2YN
Tel: 01242 256755
Fax: 01242 254694
email: info@sportsbooks.ltd.uk
www.sportsbooks.ltd.uk

Front cover designed by Kath Northam.
Front cover photograph: Actionimages.

A catalogue record for this book is available from
the British Library.

ISBN 1 899807 39 X

Printed by Cromwell Press

CONTENTS

BIBLIOGRAPHY

Newspapers
Newcastle Evening Chronicle
Newcastle Evening Chronicle (Football/Cricket Edition, Sports Edition
& The Pink)
Evening Mail
Evening World
Journal
Newcastle Daily Chronicle
Newcastle Daily Leader
North Mail
Northern Echo
Sunday Sun
Sunderland (Daily) Echo
Sunderland Echo (Football/Sports Echo)

Books
Football League Players' Records: 1888 – 1939 (Michael Joyce)
Football League Players' Records; 1946 – 1992 (Barry J Hugman)
Soccer at War: 1939 – 1946 (Jack Rollin)
Rothmans Book of Football Records (Jack Rollin)
Rothmans/Sky Sports Football Yearbooks
Newcastle United FC Official Handbooks
Newcastle United – A Complete Record (Paul Jounnou)
A Black 'N' White Alphabet (Paul Joannou)
Sunderland – The Complete Record (Rob Mason)
The History of Sunderland (Bob Graham)
Sunderland AFC – The Official History (Ed. by John Hudson & Paul Callaghan)
Newcastle Utd v Sunderland – History of Great Football Rivalry (Brett & Clark)
Hotbed of Soccer (Arthur Appleton)
Through the Turnstiles (Brian Tabner)
Soccer's Golden Nursery (John Gibson)
Clown Prince of Soccer (Len Shackleton)
Return of the Clown Prince (Len Shackleton)
United We Stand (Bob Moncur)
Sporting World of Bryan 'Pop' Robson (Bryan Robson)

ACKNOWLEDGEMENTS

IN MAKING my acknowledgements for help with this book I must express my gratitude to a significant number of people, many of who are anonymous. First and foremost are the football reporters who have reported Tyne-Wear derbies for over a century of sporting conflict. A considerable number of newspaper reports have been consulted during the compilation of the match details in this book. As many as five match reports for each game have been examined and, it must be admitted, occasionally it seemed as if different games were being described. Nevertheless, only by obtaining such diverse perspectives can a consensus be obtained. In the early days of sporting journalism, many reports were issued under nom de plumes and occasionally different individuals may have used the same pen names. So the true names of all of the reporters are not known. It is therefore as a group that I acknowledge their invaluable contribution.

Considerable use has been made of the archive facilities in the main public libraries in the North East. I therefore gratefully acknowledge the assistance given by the Local Studies staff in the Newcastle Central Library (which must have one of the most wide-ranging local newspaper archives in the country), Sunderland Central Library (for the *Sunderland Echo* and *Football/Sports Echo*) and Darlington Library (*Northern Echo*). Work at these premises has been supplemented by occasional use of the facilities at the British Newspaper Library in Colindale, North London.

Much of the minutiae in this book has been due to the willing co-operation of club historians. A particular debt is owed to Paul Joannou, the official Newcastle United club historian, and Sunderland AFC historian Mike Gibson. Their patience in answering my queries is much appreciated. They have also generously supplied the photographs from their own personal collections for the player profiles appended to each chapter of the book.

Randall Northam, of Sportsbooks, has also helped with some of the suggestions for the book. Both his support for the publication and the ideas he contributed have been very welcome.

Last, but most definitely not least, I must mention my wife Margaret. Not only has she shown commendable patience during the eight years research that went into the book but helped enormously with the checking of much of the statistical detail. She is one in a million (I just hope she doesn't find out about the other 999,999!)

Alan Candlish

DEDICATION

This book is dedicated to the memory of my father – who first took me to both Roker Park and St James' Park and taught me about the pride and passion of Tyne-Wear derbies. He also made me appreciate that, whether you are a Mackem or a Magpie, football is in your blood.

INTRODUCTION

JACKIE ASHURST, Sunderland defender of the 1970s, once observed that if a Third World War broke out during a Tyne-Wear derby, the fans would not notice until after the final whistle! Andy Cole said something similar when he suggested that if the bomb was dropped, all that the supporters would worry about was whether the buses would be running by Saturday or whether they would have to walk to the match. As epigrams, the comments are on a par with Bill Shankly's famous view that football was not a matter of life or death – it was much more important. Such is the passion for the game in the outpost known as the Hotbed of Soccer.

There is also an element of truth in it because nowhere in the country does a local derby carry as much pride and passion. Perhaps the antagonism and bitterness of the Old Firm games in Glasgow, fuelled by national fervour and sectarian bigotry, is greater. But nowhere in England is there so much delight or despair depending upon the result; certainly not on Merseyside, Manchester, London or the Midlands. In all of those places, defeat by the local rivals hurts. But within a month or so the pain begins to ease as other local games take place. But the geographic remoteness of the North East prevents this from happening. Middlesbrough is the only other local 'big' team and fans on both Tyne and Wear do not really regard games against the Teessiders as derbies. No, defeat by the Geordies/Mackems (depending upon their persuasion) gnaws at supporters' souls until the next meeting.

Ruud Gullit did not realise this. He could not understand how a game between teams from two different cities (albeit only 12 miles or so apart) could be regarded as a derby. He did not understand the psyche of supporters in the North East. It cost him ultimately his job.

Romantics with an historical inclination like to point out that there has always been rivalry between Newcastle and Sunderland. Even as far back as the English Civil War when the former declared for the Crown but the latter sided with Parliament.

But this book is about sporting rivalry and football in particular. Although a number of clubs based on Tyneside and Wearside came into existence (and many exist today), we are mainly concerned with Newcastle United and Sunderland. However, for the sake of completeness, clashes also involving two other clubs, not directly part of the Black Cats or the Magpies but related to them, are included.

These two clubs are Newcastle West End and Sunderland Albion. The former were the tenants of St James' Park immediately prior to Newcastle (who were then called East End) moving in. West End folded in 1892 but East End not only recruited a few of their players and co-opted some of their directors on to their board, but also signed on the complete West End Reserve side. It was little wonder that, when East End changed its name to Newcastle United a few months later, many regarded the newly named team as a merger between East and West. Legally, however, it wasn't. As a club, West End simply ceased to exist.

The reverse happened on Wearside where a group of players broke away from the parent club in 1888 and formed a rival club. As the rebel players were Scotsmen, the new club was consequently named Sunderland Albion. They quickly became a force to be reckoned with on Wearside. If the rivalry between East End and West End in Newcastle was strong, it was nothing compared to the acrimonious struggle for survival that developed in Sunderland. The present Sunderland club emerged victorious. Co-incidentally, by some quirk of fate, it was formally presented with the League Championship on the same day in 1892 that Albion folded. But it was a close run thing for a while.

Therefore, for completeness, the results between both West End and Albion themselves and with the main Tyne-Wear clubs are included.

Readers unacquainted with the North East may wonder at the title of the book. "Ha'way (the Sunderland spelling) or Howay (the Newcastle spelling) the Lads" is the exhortation of supporters for their favourites to strive harder. It effectively means "Come on Boys".

But why "Ha'way/Howay"? It seems that the term originated in the regional pitmatic dialect (ie idiomatic to pit villages). Miners in the North East pits would call down the shaft for the cage to come half way up ("Half way, lads").˙ So the Sunderland spelling is nearer to the origins of the phrase. For years, however, the accepted spelling was 'Howway' and some Geordies still spell it that way. The phrase became a popular expression in the Geordie dialect which relates more correctly to Tyneside than Wearside but both sets of fans have the right to use and spell it whichever way they prefer. As it is a vernacular expression, there is no right way or wrong way to spell it.

So the scene is set. Every competitive game between Newcastle and Sunderland is detailed in the following pages. Every goal is described; the key incidents recorded; every hero and villain is there. The referee is poised with the whistle to his lips. He blows. Let battle commence.

HA'WAY/HOWAY THE LADS!

*There are different derivations of the phrase. Rev. Oliver Heslop in his Glossary of Northumberland (& Tyneside) Words (1893-94) similarly defines "Howay" – "Howay, in a pit, means lower the cage half way down, or quicken its movement if it is already being lowered. In North Northumberland the call "Haway" is given to the farm hands by the woman-steward at starting or yoking time, so that the women all start together". All definitions still mean "Come on!".

EXPLANATORY NOTES

Alphabetical Order

'Sensitive' is an adjective that very few (if any) North East football supporters would use to describe themselves. Yet that is precisely what they are as
far as their football teams are concerned. For that reason, this book needs an
explanatory note.

Many Newcastle fans could take umbrage that, in the title of the book,
the word "Ha'way" (the Wearside spelling) precedes "Howay" (the Tyneside
spelling). Conversely, Sunderland supporters will not be too happy when I
refer to Newcastle/Sunderland derbies. But this sequence is purely because, to
avoid any bias, I have adopted alphabetical order. So we have Roker Park/St
James' Park and Black Cats/Magpies as well as Geordies/Mackems and Tyne/
Wear (until the latter became unacceptable in recent years for games played
on Wearside).

Conflicting Statistical Information

Official club records for the early years of football are often sketchy (at best)
and non-existent (at worst). Much of the statistical information shown in
many record books is the result of research carried out by present day football
historians from sources that are contemporary to the time under review.

Unfortunately some of the sources disagree. Press match reports from the
Victorian and Edwardian eras, for instance, occasionally give different goalscorers in a few games. A typical example is the first game detailed in this book,
an FA Cup tie between Sunderland and East End in November 1888. The *Sunderland Daily Echo* attributes Sunderland's second goal to Peacock. But other
local newspapers like the *Daily Chronicle, Daily Leader* and the *Journal* all
credit the goal to Jobling. In these cases of conflicting information, I have
accepted the majority opinion but have recorded in the details of the match
report that there are different views. For each match report detailed in the
following pages, I have examined at least three different newspaper reports
(some times as many as five) to obtain a consensus view.

Differences in goal scoring details, fortunately, are few. This is not so
for match attendance figures – the bane of football historians' lives. Prior
to 1925, attendance figures for league games were largely based on press
estimates. These often varied dramatically. However, from 1925, clubs were
obliged by the Football League to notify them of their attendances. But the
figures shown in most record books prior to that year are based on press
estimates at the time.

Occasionally, precise 'official' figures did slip out. But even these are open to doubt, even after 1925. The 'official' attendance quoted was usually allied to the gate receipts and based on turnstile figures, excluding season ticket holders or guests admitted free to the directors' enclosure. Once again, a consensus view is shown in this book with ticket holders figures taken into consideration where known.

Symbols Legend

The team listings shown in each match report have symbols and annotations against certain players. The meanings are as follows:

*	= Booked
**	= Double booking
#(36)	= Sent off (with time of dismissal)
inj (72)	= Off injured (with time of withdrawal). NB where players were withdrawn injured but replaced by a substitute, this is shown merely as a substitution (see following entry).
(D Elliott 45)	= Name of substitute (and time introduced)
[47, 83]	= Times of goals

CHAPTER 1

19th Century Sunderland Supreme

ASSOCIATION FOOTBALL arrived on Tyneside before Wearside, but Sunderland were formed before Newcastle (although both clubs have to bow to Middlesbrough as the oldest of the 'big three' in the North East). Sunderland actually appeared at St James' Park (then merely an enclosed field) before the present Newcastle club was even formed when they faced Newcastle Rangers, the original tenants of the enclosure, in a Northumberland & Durham FA Cup tie in 1881. Tyneside drew first blood in this encounter, winning 5-0.

But Sunderland had a two year start on the club that eventually became Newcastle United and the Wearsiders soon became firmly established as the premier club in the North East. Certainly they were the stronger of the two clubs by the time they first met in a friendly fixture in 1883, when Newcastle played under its East End banner. Sunderland were also the first club in the North East to join the Football League (1890), three years before Newcastle were eventually elected to the Second Division.

Although they were in different divisions, the two clubs met on a fairly regular basis in friendly games, usually on Tyneside as Sunderland were the greater attraction. In most cases the Wearsiders won – and when they didn't, they usually met again soon afterwards to gain revenge.

The first major competitive meeting between the two clubs was in 1888 in the FA Cup and Sunderland, holders of the Northumberland and Durham Challenge Cup, emerged successful. But the Wearsiders had already met Newcastle West End twice in this competition, losing in 1886 (after a protest by the Tyneside club) but gaining revenge in the following year.

There was a gap of ten years before Tyne met Wear in the league. By this time West End had folded and East End had changed its name to United. By the time they met Sunderland on an equal footing in 1898, the Magpies had spent five years as a Second Division club and Sunderland had won the League Championship three times, clearly marking themselves as the supreme club in the North East.

They were still Cocks of the North as the 19th century came to an end but Newcastle were not far behind. Indeed, both clubs were in the top five in the country by 1900 and the scene was set for a new century of rivalry when fortunes would wax and wane for both sides.

League Meetings (4)
At Newcastle:	Newcastle	Won 0	Drew 0	Lost 2
At Sunderland:	Sunderland	Won 0	Drew 0	Lost 2

FA Cup Meetings (1)
At Sunderland:	Sunderland	Won 1

FA Cup
3rd Qualifying Round
Sunderland 2 Newcastle East End 0 (HT: 0-0)
17th November 1888
Newcastle Road
5,000

Sunderland: W Kirkley*, J Oliver, P Ford, W Gibson, H McLaughlan, J Spain, A Davison [**60**], R McDermid, J N Breconridge*, A Peacock, J Jobling [**80**]
East End: D Henderson, R Creilly, J Miller, W Young, J Raylstone, W Caldwell, J Collins, J Smith, M Mulvey, T Hoban, A Muir
Referee: F Hardisty (Middlesbrough FC)

THIS WAS the first major competitive meeting between the two clubs who were destined to become the soccer giants in the North East. At the time neither played league football although Sunderland, holders of the Northumberland & Durham Challenge Cup by virtue of a victory over Newcastle West End at St James' Park in April, were recognised as the strongest side in the region (although East End had a slightly better record so far this season).

But there was conflict on Wearside with the creation of the breakaway Sunderland Albion club and it was Albion, and not any Tyneside team, who were regarded as Sunderland's greatest rivals. Indeed, to-date, Albion had a 100% record, something even Sunderland could not boast. East End had their own rivals in Newcastle in West End but these teams had different origins and the bitter acrimony which existed between the Wearside clubs far exceeded that on Tyneside.

Sunderland had been disqualified from the FA Cup during the previous season following a protest by Middlesbrough about fielding three ineligible players. They were keen to make their mark in the tournament this year and had already knocked out another Newcastle club, Elswick Rangers, in the previous round. East End were also doing reasonably well and had disposed of Port Clarence and Stockton in earlier rounds but, ominously, had lost to Elswick Rangers a mere two weeks ago. Sunderland were forced to field a slightly weakened team while East End were at full-strength so an intriguing cup tie beckoned.

Tommy Hoban won the toss for East End and chose to defend the top goal, taking advantage of a strong wind that blew from one end of the pitch to the other. Although the day was generally fine, squally showers made it uncomfortable for the spectators. East End mounted the early attacks and goalkeeper William Kirkley was soon in action. Twice Ford blocked goalbound shots as the Tynesiders took the game to Sunderland, forcing a series of corners. But over-eagerness on the part of the visitors saw most of their shots go over the bar. The Wearsiders did manage to mount some attacks of their own and Henderson was forced to fist away at one point but soon it was East End back on the attack again. Three times Oliver had to head clear from his goalmouth and both Hoban and Collins went close. But when the half-time whistle went, the scoreline was still blank.

Although Sunderland had the elements in their favour in the second half, it was East End who once again took up the attack. This time, however, they could not maintain it and Sunderland soon forced them back on defence. The Wearsiders gained a free kick for a handling offence and Oliver took it, beating Henderson with his shot but, as no-one touched the ball from the free kick (a requirement at the time), the goal was not allowed. By now Sunderland were well on top and it was no surprise when they eventually breached the East Enders' defence after 60 minutes.

Arnie Davison gained possession in the middle of the pitch and ran down the middle, straight at the visitors' defence who stood off. Once he was close enough, he tried a shot and comprehensively beat Henderson. His success met with extraordinary scenes of enthusiasm, unusual at the time.

Bob McDermid, a former Newcastle West End player, nearly made it 2-0 soon afterwards, his shot just grazing the top of the crossbar. Sunderland sustained their attacks and for a long time play was in front of the visitors' goal. The Wearsiders forced numerous corners and it was from one of these, after 80 minutes, that they increased their lead.

Jobling took the corner and his cross led to an exciting scrimmage in front of the posts. He ran in to join the fray and, as he did so, the ball broke to him and he shot through the melee between the posts. Some reports attribute this goal to Peacock but most credit Jobling.

Sunderland had now won but they maintained their attacks. To their credit, East End fought to keep the score respectable with both full backs, Creilly and Miller, outstanding. But it was their central defender, Raylstone, who was the real hero. He was the best player on the pitch although, with Sunderland encamped in the Tyneside half, he had plenty of opportunities to impress. Sunderland forced several more corners in the last quarter of an hour and Gibson clipped the top of the Tynesiders' bar but East End held out to prevent any further scoring.

Even in the 19th century passions usually ran high in cup games. On this occasion, however, the press were at pains to emphasise the sporting nature of this tie. It was stressed that both teams deserved credit for the "exceedingly friendly manner in which the contest was waged".

It was acknowledged that it had been a hard fought game but without any bad feeling shown on either side. Sunderland deserved to go through but East End had done themselves proud, showing that the gap between the Wearsiders and themselves was not as great as many thought it was.

But the draw for the next round brought with it controversy. Sunderland were matched with arch-rivals Sunderland Albion. The latter, formed by dissenting Scottish Sunderland players, had now played 12 games and had won them all. Sunderland were determined to starve the embryonic club out of existence by denying them the undoubted cash windfall that the local tie would bring them. So, rather than face them, Sunderland resigned from the competition! Thus for the second year running, Sunderland dropped out of the FA Cup without losing a game. Later they similarly withdrew from the Durham Cup after they were, once again, paired with Albion.

NB. *The precise times of the goals in this game have never been reported. The times shown above are approximations indicated by the various match reports.*

The surname of William Kirkley for many years was recorded as Kirtley (and, indeed, was shown as such in contemporary match reports). Recent research, however, has shown that his name was really Kirkley. Breconridge's surname was also published as Breckonridge or Breckonbridge in press reports. I have, once again, adopted the spelling shown in Sunderland – The Complete Record

---

Football League
Division 1
Sunderland 2 Newcastle United 3 (HT: 1-2)
24th December 1898
Roker Park
30,000

Sunderland: J E Doig, P Bach, R McNeil, M Ferguson, A McAllister, R Jackson, J Crawford, J Leslie [**15, 70**], W Raisbeck, H Wilson, C McLatchie
Newcastle: M Kingsley, W Lindsay, J Jackson, T Ghee, J Ostler, J Stott, J Rogers, J Stevenson, J Peddie [**28, 50**], A Aitken, W Wardrope [**18**]
Referee: John Lewis (Blackburn)

PAST TYNE-WEAR Derbies had, with the odd exception, been restricted to friendly encounters with Sunderland invariably the senior team in the North East. Now Newcastle travelled to Wearside on an equal footing although behind their neighbours in the league. Both sides had finished as runners-up in their respective divisions in the previous season. Sunderland were criticised for increasing their admission prices for this game.

The North Eastern Railway Co was also criticised for not supplying enough trains and for delays en route although 8,000 enthusiasts went by train. Overall it was estimated that United had almost as many supporters at the game as the home side.

Newcastle were in a relegation position (17th out of 18) after failing to win any of their first 10 games. But their results had improved recently while Sunderland had lost their last three matches. The Wearsiders were also suffering from injury problems and were forced to field a somewhat weakened team. Nevertheless they were 4-6 favourites to win and the Newcastle hierarchy acknowledged the Wearside superiority by saying before the match, "If we lick Sunderland today, we shall stamp the word 'class' upon our men's jerseys".

League Positions

	Pos	Pl	Pts		Pos	Pl	Pts
Before: Sunderland	10th	16	16	Newcastle	17th	17	11
After: Sunderland	11th	17	16	Newcastle	17th	18	13

The opening exchanges were fairly even with both sides relying heavily on wing play and Sunderland were the first to go close when a Wilson shot rebounded off Lindsay on the goal line.

The home side made the breakthrough after 15 minutes with Hugh Wilson and Colin McLatchie dribbling their way into the corner from where the latter centred. The Newcastle defence hesitated, allowing Jim Leslie to nip in and turn the ball into the net. As the press reported, 'the Sunderland section of the crowd went delirious with joy, and the players shook hands with each other all round'.

But the goal drove on Newcastle. They took the game to Sunderland and equalised three minutes later. Good play by Jimmy Stevenson out on the right ended with him crossing to Andy Aitken who touched the ball forward for Willie Wardrope to rush towards the bye-line three yards wide of the goal. Unexpectedly, when he was a foot from the line, he fired in a shot from the most acute of angles, giving Doig no chance. Experienced referee John Lewis described it as one of the most remarkable goals he had ever seen.

Newcastle kept up the pressure with quick passing moves and Sunderland were almost run off their feet.

The Magpies took the lead after 28 minutes with a goal out of nothing. A huge kick upfield by Jimmy Jackson found Jock Peddie who burst forward before blasting a shot past Doig. Sunderland were shocked to be behind. Tension built up although referee Mr Lewis (described in the press as 'the soundest and firmest tootler in the country') kept tight control and ensured that the game was played in a sporting spirit. Many rated this as the best game seen at Roker this season. Jim Crawford grazed the visitors' bar at one point but United deserved their lead at half-time.

Newcastle, two goals up, fell back on defence in the second half but

Sunderland seemed subdued and failed to take advantage. United relied on breakaways and one of these saw them increase their lead after 50 minutes. Wardrope won possession out on the wing and supplied Andy Aitken who crossed for Jock Peddie to shrug off the challenge of Wilson and rifle the ball into the net; 1-3.

The goal acted as a spur to Sunderland who at last threw off their lethargy. Excitement reached fever pitch as the Rokermen forced three corners in quick succession and then twice went close with efforts at goal. But Newcastle continued to look dangerous on breakaways.

Sunderland eventually pulled a goal back after 70 minutes when Wilson and McLatchie again combined to create an opening. A Crawford shot was blocked but Jim Leslie pounced to score a similar goal to his earlier one. Some reports suggest that Raisbeck may have been the scorer.

Sunderland bombarded the Newcastle goal in search of the equaliser but the United rearguard held firm and by the closing stages they were back on top and emerged as deserved, if somewhat surprising, winners.

This was only Sunderland's second home defeat of the season and Newcastle's first away win in the top division. But no-one on Wearside begrudged United their success. In fact the sporting Sunderland public admitted that the better team had won on the day although it must have been an unusual sight (and somewhat galling) to see masses of overjoyed visiting supporters wend their way to Sunderland's Central Station to catch their trains home.

Yet the Wearsiders were to recover from this shock defeat and were to lose just two of their next ten league games. Newcastle, conversely, were to fail to win any of their next four although four successive wins after that were to lift them away from the relegation zone.

Football League
Division 1
Newcastle United 0 Sunderland 1 (HT: 0-0)
22nd April 1899
St James' Park
25,000

Newcastle: M Kingsley, W Lindsay, J Jackson, T Ghee, W Higgins, A Aitken, J Rogers, J Stevenson, J Peddie, A Macfarlane, T Niblo
Sunderland: J E Doig, A McCombie, R McNeil, H Wilson, A McAllister, W Raisbeck, J Crawford, J Leslie, J W Farquhar, W Fulton, C McLatchie [74]
Referee: John Lewis (Blackburn)

THE MATCH at St James' came at the very end of the season but it was a major attraction nonetheless. Newcastle had already defeated Sunderland in the league at Roker and had won one and drawn one of the two friendlies played during the season. They were eager to confirm their perceived position as 'Cock of the North' despite the fact the Sunderland were above them in the league.

The ground was full an hour before kick-off and several hundred men climbed over the railings to get in. Spectators swarmed on to the roof of the directors' stand putting the occupants below in real danger. Balconies on the houses in Leazes Terrace overlooking the ground were similarly packed and one man perilously stood on the chimney pots of a four storied house in St James' Street.

League Positions

		Pos	Pl	Pts		Pos	Pl	Pts
Before:	Sunderland	9th	32	32	Newcastle	13th	33	30
After:	Sunderland	10th	33	34	Newcastle	13th	34	30

Newcastle won the toss and chose to kick up the hill towards the Leazes, a decision that gave the initiative to Sunderland in the opening stages. United gradually gained the upper hand and routed many of their attacks through Rogers on the right wing but Bob McNeil generally marked him well. Both Andy Aitken and Bill Lindsay netted with free kicks but as the ball had not touched a player in either case (a requirement at the time) the goals were disallowed. Although play was end-to-end, both sets of full backs and 'keepers were alert and neither side seemed likely to break the deadlock.

It was expected that Newcastle would dominate the second half with the notorious slope in their favour so it was a surprise when Sunderland began to control play with their renowned passing game. United eventually began to mount attacks but Peddie was ineffective at centre forward. Both Lindsay and Macfarlane went lame in the second half and Newcastle began to struggle.

After 74 minutes a half clearance by Kingsley was picked up by Jim Leslie (some reports credit Bill Fulton or Jim Crawford) and he sent over a pass to the far post where the unmarked Colin McLatchie was able to shoot home.

Newcastle mounted some determined attacks to try and rescue the game but were unable to breach the indomitable Wearside defence and Sunderland deservedly held on to win.

Victory confirmed Sunderland's position as the leading club in the North East and they went on to win their last league game to finish in a respectable seventh position. Newcastle were not too despondent with their final 13th place, having shown that they could compete in the top division of the league.

Big changes were to take place at St James' Park during the summer when work was carried out to level the notorious sloping pitch.

Football League
Division 1
Newcastle United 2 Sunderland 4 (HT: 2-1)
23rd December 1899
St James' Park
21,000

Newcastle: M Kingsley, W Lindsay, D Gardner, A Aitken, W Higgins, J Carr, J Rogers, J Stevenson, A Gardner [42], A Macfarlane [20], J Fraser
Sunderland: JE Doig, A McCombie, R McNeil, M Ferguson, A McAllister, W Raisbeck, W Hogg, J Leslie, R Hogg [12, 55, 61], T Becton [57], C McLatchie
Referee: J Fox (Sheffield)

SUNDERLAND TRAVELLED to St James' riding high in the league. Although they were ten points behind leaders Sheffield United and five behind second placed Aston Villa, the Wearsiders had three games in hand on both. Newcastle, on the other hand, were five points above second bottom Glossop (a relegation position). United had won just one of their previous nine matches and were unable to field a full-strength team.

The referee carried out a pitch inspection on the morning of the match and declared it playable despite a thin covering of snow. The pitch markings were made in red.

League Positions		Pos	Pl	Pts		Pos	Pl	Pts
Before:	Sunderland	3rd	15	20	Newcastle	9th	15	15
After:	Sunderland	3rd	16	22	Newcastle	10th	16	15

Exchanges were rather tentative in the early stages with Newcastle having slightly the better of things. So it was a bit of a surprise when Sunderland opened the scoring with a break-away goal after 12 minutes.

Colin McLatchie started the attack and there was not a move out of place until the ball reached Bobby Hogg and he made no mistake, scoring with a lightning shot.

The goal acted as a jolt to Newcastle who pressurised Doig's goal. The veteran 'keeper did well to keep them out but he was eventually beaten some eight minutes later. Sandy Macfarlane took full advantage of a well worked opening 20 yards out, sending in a raking ground shot that went in just inside a post.

End-to-end play followed with Newcastle gradually forcing their visitors back. United eventually grabbed the lead three minutes before half-time. A Joe Rogers' pass led to scrimmage in front of the Sunderland posts and both Alex Gardner and Jimmy Stevenson forced the ball over the line, the former eventually getting the credit for the goal. It was a scrappy affair but it counted nonetheless.

The light was fading as the game was resumed. Sunderland were determined to make amends and it was soon Newcastle's turn to defend. But after 55 minutes the Wearsiders grabbed an equaliser although this goal, like Newcastle's second, was scrappy. Kingsley managed to parry a free kick and Bobby Hogg turned the rebound into the net from another scrimmage in front of the posts.

Encouraged by the goal, Sunderland continued to push forward and United found themselves over-run. It took the visitors just another couple of minutes to take the lead and this goal was a much more spectacular effort. A quick raid on the Newcastle goal ended with Tommy Becton in possession within shooting distance. His drive at goal was powerful enough but Kingsley should have saved it. Instead the ball sailed over the 'keeper's arms into the net. Some sources credited the goal to Colin McLatchie but the majority of contemporary reports attribute it to Becton.

Newcastle had hardly recovered from this shock when, four minutes later, they found themselves two down, a neat header by Bobby Hogg doing the trick, his third goal of the game.

By now it was all Sunderland and McLatchie nearly made it five when he rattled the Newcastle bar with a rasping shot. United were forced to hang on for a while although they managed to survive. They eventually launched a few attacks of their own and Billy Higgins was particularly unlucky when he shook the Wearside bar with a well-directed shot. But they flattered to deceive although Sunderland were guilty of time-wasting in the closing minutes when their full backs resorted to kicking the ball out of the ground at every opportunity. Nevertheless, they emerged as comfortable and, in view of their second half performance, deserved winners.

The official attendance at the match was 19,129 but this did not include approximately 2,000 season ticket holders which brought the crowd up to about 21,000.

The win confirmed Sunderland's third position in the league. In fact they closed the gap slightly on Sheffield United who had managed only to draw. Newcastle slipped a place and looked as if they had a battle for survival in front of them. However they soon turned the corner and began to climb to safety.

Football League
Division 1
Sunderland 1 Newcastle United 2 (HT: 1-2)
28th April 1900
Roker Park
22,000

Sunderland: JE Doig, A McCombie, R McNeil, M Ferguson, A McAllister, W Raisbeck, W Hogg, J Leslie, R Hogg, W Fulton [44], C McLatchie
Newcastle: M Kingsley, W Lindsay, D Gardner, T Ghee, A Aitken, J Carr, J Rogers, A Gardner [20], J Peddie, A Macfarlane, J Fraser [8]
Referee: J B Stott (Rawtenstall)

THE LOCAL derby at Roker was the last game of the season for the North East rivals. Sunderland were still close to the top of the league following three successive wins. They were in third place which is where they were guaranteed to finish as they were nine points behind leaders Aston Villa and seven behind Sheffield United. Wolverhampton Wanderers were fourth but they could not catch the Roker men.

Apart from local pride, Newcastle had slightly more to play for because a top six finish would guarantee them £10 bonus per man. They came into the game following four successive draws. They had massive support at Roker with every train to Sunderland packed to capacity. Despite their respective league positions, the local press billed the game as "The Championship of the North".

League Positions		Pos	Pl	Pts		Pos	Pl	Pts
Before:	Sunderland	3rd	33	41	Newcastle	6th	33	34
After:	Sunderland	3rd	34	41	Newcastle	5th	34	36

McAllister lost the toss and Sunderland were asked to kick-off into the sun and the breeze. Consequently Newcastle showed up in attack first and it did not take them long to open the scoring.

After eight minutes the ball was played into the home goalmouth and although Doig caught it, he was not able to clear. Jack Fraser dashed in to gain possession and deftly dribble his way into the net; 0-1.

Sunderland retaliated by mounting some attacks of their own only to be forced back by the determined Tynesiders. Rogers forced Doig to concede a corner as United went for a second goal.

McNeil handled just outside the home penalty line after 20 minutes and Billy Lindsay quickly touched the ball to Alex Gardner who, seeing Doig dazzled by the sun, banged the ball first time past the surprised 'keeper. The Sunderland players surrounded the referee, appealing for offside, but there seemed nothing wrong with the goal and it was allowed to stand.

Newcastle soon had the ball in the home net again but this one was disallowed for offside. Newcastle were easily the better side with Sunderland strangely lethargic. Yet it was Sunderland who reduced the deficit, somewhat against the run of play, a minute before half-time.

Billy Fulton and the two Hoggs combined in a break towards the Tyneside goal. Lindsay dashed over to try and cut them out but he ended up on the floor, leaving Fulton with an open goal and he blasted the ball home.

Sunderland had recovered from a half-time deficit at St James' earlier in the season to win by two clear goals so the Wearside supporters were by no means dispirited when the second half began. Indeed, the early stages of this session gave them cause for optimism as their favourites went on the attack. Unfortunately for them, their finishing was feeble. McAllister and Aitken clashed heads at one point with the Sunderland man coming off decidedly the worse, having to go off for treatment and eventually emerging with a gigantic plaster on his forehead.

Surprisingly both sets of rival supporters cheered the opposing goalkeepers for good saves but gradually play deteriorated with both sides indulging in long, aimless kicks upfield – much to the ire of the spectators.

Newcastle did not endear themselves to the Wearside supporters by booting the ball into touch whenever the home side threatened either. This had the desired effect of nullifying most of Sunderland's attacks although neither side looked like scoring as the game petered out to an inauspicious finish.

A third place finish for Sunderland indicated a good season. Newcastle also had cause to be happy about their campaign as well – their fifth position was their best to-date. But the game had been a typical end of season affair. In fact the highlight had been a stray dog that had somehow got on to the pitch during the game (seemingly a regular occurrence at Roker Park this season!). For five minutes, the referee, his linesmen and all 22 players entertained the crowd with their Keystone Cops antics as they tried to catch it. Contemporary press reports claimed that this was the most entertaining part of the day!

Ace 'Keeper

Jimmy Lawrence holds the record for most penalty saves in the history of Tyne-Wear derbies (4). No other 'keeper has saved more than one. He was only beaten once from the spot (Jackie Mordue on March 17, 1913).

Player of the Decade
19th Century

John Middleton Campbell

EACH GENERATION has its own goal scoring heroes. Similarly, each rival faction can put forward plausible arguments as to why their particular favourite is the best of his time. One thing is indisputable, however, is the identity of the North East's first ace goalscoring marksman – John Middleton Campbell.

Like many of the top men of his time, Johnny Campbell was a Scot. Born and bred in Renton near Dumbarton, he made his name with his home town club and was an immediate success, winning a Scottish FA Cup Winners' medal as an 18 year old when Renton hammered Cambuslang 6 – 1 in the final of 1888. When it is considered that Cambuslang thrashed Sunderland 11 – 0 on Wearside that year, it can be appreciated that Renton were more than a decent team.

Johnny's goalscoring exploits quickly brought him to the attention of the more prosperous clubs south of the border, among them Sunderland. Throughout the summer of 1889, Wearside saw an influx of players from Scotland, including no fewer than three from Renton – outside right John Harvie, outside left David Hannah and centre forward Johnny Campbell.

Sunderland had the avowed aim of election into the Football League and they pursued this ambition by playing a series of friendly matches against the top teams of the day. A game against Aston Villa, runners-up to Proud Preston in the inaugural Football League season a year earlier, has gone down in folklore. The Wearsiders thrashed the Villans 7-2 (Campbell netting two of the goals) and elicited the famous view from one of the visitors' officials, William McGregor (the principal founder of the Football League), that Sunderland had a talented man in every position. So the 'Team of all the Talents' was born.

Sunderland were duly elected to the league that year and Johnny Campbell led their forward line with fire and determination. He was short and stocky ('sturdy' may be a better way of describing him) and liked nothing better than to run through the middle at the opposition's defence – often from his own half of the field – frequently with devastating effect.

He was the club's top scorer in Sunderland's first three seasons in the Football League as he set the benchmark for all other goalscoring forwards to follow. Admittedly, the Wearsiders only finished in mid-table in their first season as a league club but what followed has gone down in legend. The Red'n Whites had an unparalleled run of success (for the time) in the league, finishing as Champions, Champions, Runners-up and Champions in the next four seasons, thus clearly establishing themselves as the top team in the country. And in the three years that they won the title, Johnny Campbell was the top scorer, not only at Sunderland, but also in the Football League.

His scoring record was phenomenal. He set a pace in goalscoring that few could match. Up until Christmas during Sunderland's first championship winning campaign (1891-92), he scored in no fewer than 12 out of the club's 15 games. The following year he did even better, again scoring in 12 of the first 15 (including three hat tricks) but one of the games where he did not score, he was not even playing!

It was during this time (April – December 1892) that he achieved the incredible sequence of scoring in 13 out of 14 successive league matches that he appeared in (28 goals). Such basic statistics leave modern day football supporters gasping in amazement and admiration.

Yet he somehow failed to impress the Scottish national selectors. It is a travesty that Johnny was never capped for his country. Yet perhaps this is not so surprising as the selectors rarely looked south of the border in picking their teams. Indeed, during Johnny's peak years with Sunderland (1890-95), Scotland played 15 international games and fielded over 40 different forwards. Not one of them was an Anglo-Scot.

Goalscoring was Sunderland's forte during their glory years. In their first championship winning season they scored an incredible 93 goals in only 26 matches (29 of them thanks to Campbell) and then chalked up the magic 100 (in 30 games) in the following campaign (28 from Johnny). No other club was to reach the magical century of goals in the top league until after the First World War.

But the first sign of a decline in our hero's goalscoring ability showed during the 1895-96 season when he was 'only' able to net 16 times in 28 league appearances. But his goal scoring touch really deserted him during the following year when a mere four goals is all that he could muster. Sunderland only managed to score 34 goals in total in the league that season and finished second bottom, suffering the ignominy of having to take part in the Test Matches to survive in the First Division.

They succeeded but the Team of all the Talents was now virtually a thing of the past and Campbell was soon to be on his way. He did not travel far, only as far as Tyneside to join Newcastle. The Magpies reasoned that while he may not now be able to grab the goals at the top level, the Second Division was a different matter and he may just be the man to shoot them into the First. They just managed to pip Dundee for his signature with the Tayside club's representative journeying to Sunderland in the hope of persuading Johnny to return north of the border.

Instead he made the short journey to St James' along with fellow Scot Johnny Harvie, both of them joining United for a £40 transfer fee each. They both received a £10 signing on fee with a weekly wage of £3 a week at a time when many top players in the First Division were earning £4 and, reputedly, as much as £4 10s 0d at some clubs.

His brief time with the Magpies was a success albeit a qualified one. He did not regain his goalden touch of yesteryear but nine league goals (from 21 appearances) was a reasonable return and helped United to runners-up spot in the league and a place in the end of season Test Matches.

This was the last season of this type of 'play-offs'. They were scrapped amidst controversy and suggestions of match fixing although Newcastle were eventually elected into an extended First Division. Johnny had the satisfaction of scoring for United in the league, cup and test matches that year bringing his total to twelve.

So, in September 1898, both Johnny Campbell and Johnny Harvie lined up for Newcastle for their first game in the top flight, just as they had done for Sunderland eight years earlier. But Campbell's career was almost over as he was soon to fall foul of club regulations.

He realised that a sporting career cannot last forever and, with one eye on the future, he took over as mine host at the Darnell public house in New Mills, just off Barrack Road, virtually a stone's throw away from St James' Park. This, however, was in direct contravention of club rules and the directors immediately suspended him. The public was blissfully unaware of what was happening behind the scenes as the press informed them that the club was experimenting with new forwards and triallists. Just over a month later, Johnny's contract was terminated and his playing career was cut short at the tender age of 28.

He stayed on Tyneside for two or three years but his heart was still on Wearside and when the opportunity arose for him to take over the Turf Hotel in Bedford Street, Sunderland, he took it. And it was as mine host there that he spent the remainder of his years although, sadly, there were not to be many of them. He suffered ill health and, after a long illness (from which he seemed to be recovering), he died in April 1906. He was only 36.

"Small time, but in that small so greatly lived this star" – so wrote William Shakespeare. The Bard was writing about Henry V but his verse could equally apply to Johnny Campbell – a talented man in a Team of all the Talents.

Record

Sunderland	(Summer 1889 – May 1897)	
Football League	186 apps	136 gls
Test Matches	4 apps	0 gls
FA Cup	25 apps	18 gls
Total	215 apps	154 gls
Newcastle	(May 1897 – Oct 1898)	
Football League	23 apps	9 gls
Test Matches	3 apps	1 gl
FA Cup	3 apps	2 gls
Total	29 apps	12 gls

CHAPTER 2

1900s
Newcastle Glory Years

JUST AS the 1890s had been Sunderland's decade, the 1900s belonged to Newcastle – perhaps even more so. While the Wearsiders' 'Team of all the Talents' had won three league championships in their prime, they had to bow to Aston Villa (five league titles and two Cup wins) as the top team in the country. Newcastle, however, could claim the elite crown for themselves in the 1900s with not only three league championships (more than any other club) but also four FA Cup Final appearances (although they won only one).

Yet it was Sunderland who looked as if they were going to continue with their earlier successes as the new century began. The first three years saw them finish second, first and third in the league and it could have been even better as they missed out on the title by just one point (and goal average) in 1903. Gradually, however, Newcastle were emerging as a power in the land. They finished a creditable third when Sunderland won the championship in 1902 and, although a poor season immediately followed, they displaced the Wearsiders as Cocks of the North in 1904 by finishing in fourth place. They were never to finish below that position for the rest of the decade.

This was an era of star players for both sides with Sunderland fielding the likes of Jimmy Millar, Billy Hogg, Jimmy Gemmell, Arthur Bridgett, Bobby Hogg, George Holley, Alf Common and Charlie Thomson. But Newcastle more than matched them with legends such as Alex Gardner, Andy Aitken, Bob McColl, Bill McCracken, Colin Veitch, Peter McWilliam, Jackie Rutherford, James Howie and Jimmy Lawrence. Never were Tyne and Wear to field such a galaxy of stars. A Select XI taken from both clubs could probably have defeated any team in the world.

But this was a time when Tyne-Wear rivalry reached unprecedented levels, culminating in the infamous St James' Park riot in 1901. A Sunderland fan even took Newcastle to court (unsuccessfully) for the refund of entrance monies.

Yet although the decade belonged to Newcastle, in terms of Tyne-Wear derbies Sunderland were the top dogs. They lost just five of the twenty league meetings between the teams (although the Magpies came out on top in cup ties). More importantly (as far as Wearside is concerned), there was one game which ensured that Sunderland could look back on this period with more than pride and satisfaction. It was on 5th December 1908 that Sunderland chalked up the record derby victory for either team when they demolished United at St James' Park. Newcastle went on to win the title but it is the amazing 9-1 score-line that is remembered today thus proving conclusively that derby results can be more important than trophies.

League Meetings (20)
At Newcastle:Newcastle – won 3 drew 1 lost 6
At Sunderland:Sunderland – won 4 drew 4 lost 2
Cup Meetings (3)
At Newcastle:Newcastle – won 1 drew 1 lost 0
At Sunderland:Sunderland – won 0 drew 0 lost 1

Football League
Division 1
Sunderland 1 Newcastle United 1 (HT: 0-1)
6th October 1900
Roker Park
28,688

Sunderland: J E Doig, A McCombie, J Watson, M Ferguson, A McAllister, J W Farquhar, W Hogg, A Common, J Millar, G Livingstone [60], C McLatchie
Newcastle: M Kingsley, C Burgess, D Gardner, T Ghee, A Aitken, J Carr, T Niblo, A Gardner, J Peddie, A Macfarlane, J Fraser (og A McCombie [43])
Referee: A J Barker (Hanley)

ALTHOUGH IT was still early in the season, both sides came into this game undefeated. Aston Villa topped the league, three points above Newcastle, but the Midlanders had played two games more. United were optimistic. Their defence had conceded just one goal in their opening five games and the Mag-pies had won both of their league games at Roker Park since they had been elevated to the top flight.

Sunderland, however, were by no means overawed. They were just one point behind their neighbours and could field a full-strength team, including their three new recruits – Jimmy Millar, George Livingstone and Alf Common.

League Positions		Pos	Pl	Pts		Pos	Pl	Pts
Before:	Newcastle	2nd	5	8	Sunderland	5th	5	7
After:	Newcastle	5th	6	9	Sunderland	7th	6	8

Pouring rain did not deter the masses from turning up, the crowd of 28,688 being the second highest at Roker so far. There were major criticisms of the North Eastern Railway Company which was castigated as being inefficient and slow. Their trains were also appallingly overcrowded with 20 to 22 people crammed into compartments meant for six to eight!

Sunderland wore white jerseys for a game where expectations and feelings were high. Play was fast, furious and full of excitement. In fact it was reminiscent of a cup-tie. Newcastle initially forced Sunderland back on defence with the home side attacking only occasionally although they looked more dangerous near goal. It took a great save by Matt Kingsley to keep out Common. The Wearsiders gained the upper hand as the half progressed and the visiting defence had to work hard. Then, near the interval, United began to push forward and it was Teddy Doig's turn to keep the ball out, saving a stinging shot by Macfarlane. The opening goal came from an unexpected source. After 43 minutes a cross by Jack Fraser out on Newcastle's left caused panic in the Sunderland defence and McCombie, under pressure from Jock Peddie, turned the ball into his own net. The Novocastrians in the crowd went wild with delight.

Play was fairly even in the second half although scientific football was at a premium. When it wasn't kick and rush, it was rush and kick! Gradually Sunderland forced Newcastle back but, once again, their defence looked equal to the task until, on the hour, Jimmy Millar picked up the ball from a crowd of players and played it to George Livingstone who, with just Kingsley to beat, deftly headed in the equaliser. The Roker Roar rang out loud and clear as the Wearside supporters celebrated.

With the scores level, both sides pushed for the winner and play swept from end-to-end. Both sides went close to grabbing the winner, Newcastle hitting a Sunderland post and McLatchie heading over the top at the other end. But the scores were still level at the final whistle – a fair result.

Both sides were lauded in the press as a credit to the North East. The draw meant that honours were even in more ways than one with both sides retaining their unbeaten records. On the other hand, the loss of a point meant that both slipped in the league.

Newcastle were to lose just one of their next eight games and climb to second position by mid-season although they were subsequently to fall away with a bad run during the winter months. Sunderland, on the other hand, were to win just one of their next four matches to slip down the league – at least initially. But their winter form was to be the antitheses of Newcastle's as they embarked on an unbeaten run of 11 league games which was to take them to the top of the league by the time they met United again at the end of the season.

Football League
Division 1
Newcastle United - Sunderland -
5th April 1901
St James' Park
45,000

Newcastle: M Kingsley, C Burgess, D Gardner, T Ghee, A Aitken, J Carr, A Gardner, A Macfarlane, J Peddie, F Heywood, T Niblo
Sunderland: J E Doig, A McCombie, J Watson, M Ferguson, A McAllister, R Jackson, W Hogg, J Leslie, J Millar, G Livingstone, C McLatchie
Referee: J Stott (Rawtenstall)

THIS WAS the game that never was. With just four games to go, Sunderland came into this Good Friday match top of the league and with a very real chance of winning the Championship. They were two points ahead of second placed Nottingham Forest (who had a game in hand) and five ahead of third placed Liverpool (who had two games in hand). In those days there were two points for a win and one for a draw.

With so much at stake, Newcastle anticipated an exceptionally large crowd and arranged for 25 policemen to be on duty as well as their own officials. But numbers exceeded even their highest expectations with an estimated 70,000 turning up at the ground. The capacity at the time was approximately 30,000!

When it became evident that they could not be admitted, many forced their way in by wrenching away the iron railings around the ground (which were topped with barbed wire) and pouring in. So many broke in that no-one knew how many were there altogether. At the time, recorded crowds were based on press estimates. These varied from 30,000 to 50,000. Frank Watt, the Newcastle club secretary guessed that there were about 45,000 inside the ground.

About 5,000 swarmed on to the pitch. First the Newcastle team came out, forcing their way through the throng that gathered around them like flies around a honey pot. Sunderland then appeared and received a similar welcome. Neither side was able to begin their customary practice warm up and referee Mr Stott had no option but to take the players off the field back to the dressing rooms. All efforts to clear the playing area failed and some 45 minutes after taking the players off, the referee announced that the match was abandoned.

The crowd still refused to leave the pitch. Initially they were good humoured but after about another hour, their mood changed. Most of the spectators outside the ropes surrounding the playing area and those in the 'stands waited with commendable patience. Not so those on the pitch itself where impromptu 'pitch and toss' gambling schools took place, soon followed by 'fistic encounters'.

Then matters deteriorated. The club flag was torn down and ripped into shreds. The mob (which is what it now was) decided to tear down the goalposts and the nets at the bottom end of the ground. This was defended successfully by a small group of policemen – but the top goal was undefended. Off the rioters charged towards their new target. A single constable held them at bay, brandishing one of the net poles, but he was soon overcome by weight of numbers.

The goal was smashed to pieces and the nets ripped. It was now a full scale riot as the mob turned their attention back to the bottom goal. A Sergeant Potts was in command of the police and he grouped most of his men (15 to 20 of them) in front of the goal. He decided that matters had now got totally out of hand and ordered a baton charge to clear the field.

An intense battle now ensued with bottles and other missiles being thrown indiscriminately. The constabulary waded into the crowd and the ensuing melee was vicious and bloody. One policeman was seen wielding a wooden stake as a weapon. Sergeant Potts was described in the contemporary press as "a fine general" and his concerted tactics, coupled with the fact that reinforcements arrived to supplement his meagre force, won the day. The ground was gradually cleared some two hours after the mayhem had started but it was a miracle that no-one was killed. Nevertheless, serious injuries were sustained with various people incurring broken arms, broken legs, cuts, bruises, and sprains.

There were to be repercussions for Newcastle. Their directors were worried about any possible Football Association action against them because of the riot. This was despite the fact that they had taken special precautions for an exceptionally big crowd and that the referee, in his report to the governing body, had stated that, in his opinion, the club had taken adequate measures to effect crowd control.

According to rule, clubs were entitled to a half share of the gate receipts for postponed matches. Newcastle held a management meeting at the Hotel Metropole to decide what to do with the receipts and cagely dangled a carrot in front of the FA by declaring that they would donate their share of the receipts to local charities, provided the FA took no action against them.

But the consequences did not end there. R H Bell, a Sunderland resident, called a meeting to discuss the possibility of bringing a court action against the Newcastle club for a refund of entrance monies from the postponed game. A mere handful of people turned up but a Mr Frater (a solicitor) was delegated to try and sue the Newcastle directors. He duly lost his test case in the County Court and had to pay £39 17s 6d costs.

An FA Commission held an inquiry into the riot in the Station Hotel, Newcastle, at the beginning of May when three witnesses were called: William Neasham (Chairman of Newcastle United), William Bramwell (Honorary Treasurer) and Sergeant Potts (in charge of the police on the day of the match).

The Commission found that the club had taken reasonable precautions but owing to inefficient fencing and the unusually large crowd of spectators, the arrangements had broken down. Certain recommendations were made for better fencing and an increased number of police. The Commission agreed to the proposal to distribute United's share of the gate to charities. The club also had to pay the expenses of the inquiry.

League Positions	Pos	Pl	Pts		Pos	Pl	Pts
Before: Sunderland	1st	30	39	Newcastle	7th	27	30

Football League
Division 1
Newcastle United 0 Sunderland 2 (HT: 0-1)
24th April 1901
St James' Park
18,694

Newcastle: M Kingsley, C Burgess, D Gardner, T Ghee, A Aitken, J Carr, A Gardner, T Niblo, J Peddie, F Heywood, J Fraser
Sunderland: J E Doig, A McCombie, J Watson, M Ferguson, A McAllister, R Jackson, W Hogg [25], R Hogg [70], J Millar, G Livingstone, C McLatchie
Referee: J Stott (Rawtenstall)

THIS WAS Sunderland's last game of the season and they came into it in pole position. A win would be a major step towards the Championship although Liverpool, who were just behind them on goal average and had a game in hand, could still pip them for the title. Newcastle had little to play for apart from local pride – but in a North East derby, this was enough.

There was a heavy police presence following the Good Friday riot. Officers were stationed at short intervals all around the perimeter of the pitch and mounted policemen patrolled outside the ground to prevent crowds from scaling the railings. The authorities were taking no chances.

League Positions	Pos	Pl	Pts		Pos	Pl	Pts
Before: Sunderland	1st	33	41	Newcastle	7th	32	37
After: Sunderland	1st	34	43	Newcastle	7th	33	37

Sunderland won the toss and elected to play down the hill, with a slight breeze behind them and even the sun in their favour. But it was Newcastle who launched themselves forward on attack, determined to prove themselves equal to their championship seeking neighbours. Sunderland were forced to defend but they held firm with Andy McCombie particularly catching the eye.

The opening goal after 25 minutes came largely against the run of play during a Sunderland counter attack. Jimmy Millar fired in a daisy-cutter that Matt Kingsley managed to block, diving full length, but was unable to clear. Billy Hogg was lying, handily placed, just five yards away and he blasted the ball into the net – a simple goal. United continued to attack but were unable to break through a sound Wearside defence. Nevertheless, the Magpies could regard themselves as unfortunate to be behind at the interval.

The second half began in much the same way that the first had ended – with Newcastle forcing the play. Once again the visitors' rearguard was equal to the task although they had luck on their side when a tremendous shot by Jock Peddie rattled the Sunderland crossbar with Doig well beaten. United were by far the better team at this stage and were running their visitors off their feet. But Andy McCombie and Jim Watson performed heroics and gradually United seemed to run out of ideas. This meant that the Rokermen came into the game more and after 70 minutes, Sunderland grabbed the clinching second goal when a weak clearance by Burgess saw Jimmy Millar return the ball back into the goalmouth. Dave Gardner tried to head it away but Millar headed it on to Bobby Hogg out wide of the goal. The angle was very tight but his shot was hard and accurate and caught Kingsley by surprise.

The second goal disheartened Newcastle and they never really threatened again. In fact Sunderland took up the running and United were forced to defend in the closing stages when Kingsley made a couple of good saves. At the final whistle, the Sunderland supporters celebrated. Victory had probably given them the championship – or so they thought.

Any Sunderland celebrations were tinged with caution. They knew that Liverpool could pip them for the title if they could collect three points from their last two games (two points for a win, one for a draw). The Merseysiders duly won their home game against Nottingham Forest and had to travel to bottom placed (and already relegated) West Bromwich Albion, knowing that a draw would suffice. They won 1-0 and the league title went to Merseyside rather than Wearside. Newcastle? They finished in a creditable sixth place. Their glory years were still a little way ahead.

The Turnstiles Click

The first time that turnstiles were ever used at St James' Park was on November 21, 1891 when West End played Sunderland Albion.

Football League
Division 1
Newcastle United 0 Sunderland 1 (HT: 0-1)
28th September 1901
St James' Park
25,000

Newcastle: M Kingsley, D Gardner, T Davidson, T Ghee, A Aitken, J Carr, A Gardner, A Macfarlane, T Niblo, R Orr, R Roberts
Sunderland: J E Doig, A McCombie, J Watson, M Ferguson, A McAllister, R Jackson, W Hogg, R Hogg, J Millar, J Gemmell [26], C McLatchie
Referee: John Lewis (Blackburn)

DESPITE HAVING played only three games, Newcastle were one of just three unbeaten teams in the First Division. Sunderland, on the other hand, were a mere one point behind leaders Everton and Wolverhampton Wanderers and had the same number of points as third placed Derby County. But the Wearside attack had been particularly poor in their last two games against Wolves and a weakened Liverpool team. The directors, therefore, made changes for the derby match.

To avoid a repetition of the previous year's riot, Newcastle had 60 policemen on duty plus six mounted constables patrolling outside the ground to prevent anyone from scaling the gates and railings. The gates were opened at 1.00pm for a 3.00pm kick-off but the ground filled quickly and they were locked 40 minutes before the scheduled start time. Many hundreds turned up to find that they could not get in. Some 23, 330 paid for admission and these, together with ticket holders, put the crowd around the 25,000 mark. It was not exactly a full house but the authorities were not taking any chances after the Good Friday riot.

League Positions		Pos	Pl	Pts		Pos	Pl	Pts
Before:	Sunderland	5th	4	5	Newcastle	6th	3	4
After:	Sunderland	2nd	5	7	Newcastle	13th	4	4

John Lewis, the referee, missed his train connection at York on the way to the match and arrived at the ground just minutes before the game was due to start.

Sunderland were slightly the better side in the opening exchanges but soon Newcastle forced them back and end-to-end play followed. The game was played at a fast pace but was spoilt to a large extent by excessive fouling (by both sides) and the referee was quick to whistle up for any and every infringement. Newcastle looked more likely to break the deadlock and it was something of a surprise (or a shock, depending upon your viewpoint) that it was Sunderland who eventually did so against the general run of play.

There seemed to be little danger after 26 minutes when Jimmy Gemmell sent in a cross from 30 yards out on the left wing. Perhaps Kingsley was dazzled by the sunlight or perhaps he just totally misjudged the flight of the ball but it curled in at the far corner of the goal and dropped into the net. Once again, descriptions of the goal depended upon an individual's viewpoint – it was either a goal of sheer quality or pure luck!

The goal acted as a spur to Newcastle and they pressed forward in search of the equaliser. They almost grabbed it when an Andy Aitken daisy-cutter nearly caught out Teddy Doig but the 'keeper reacted well to block the ball on the line with his foot. The half ended with Sunderland hanging on.

Sunderland stormed into the attack at the start of the second half and only a great save by Matt Kingsley denied Billy Hogg. Newcastle sustained a major handicap when they lost their captain, Dave Gardner, in the 52nd minute. He hobbled off for treatment and United had to adjust their line-up, Ghee dropping back to full back and Macfarlane into the half-back line. Sunderland should have gone two up when Billy Hogg intercepted a pass on the half-way line. He outpaced Aitken as he raced for goal and his angled shot completely beat Kingsley. It looked a goal all of the way until Gemmell, rushing in to make sure, inexplicably helped the ball on its way into the net with his fist. Obviously, the goal was disallowed.

Gardner returned after seven minutes but Sunderland retained the upper hand. Gradually, towards the end, tiredness began to affect both sides and United came back into the game. It was Sunderland's turn to defend but, with Ferguson dropping back to take up a third back role, they held on and collected both points. Newcastle's attack had been disappointing and the visitors were deserved winners.

Victory lifted Sunderland to second place while defeat left Newcastle just one point above second bottom Bolton Wanderers. The Rokermen were to win their next three games and take over the league leadership. It was the first step towards the championship.

Newcastle were not to worry about relegation as they soon began consolidate themselves in mid-table. Amazingly, the result meant that neither Newcastle nor Sunderland had won in the league against each other on their own pitches.

FA Cup
2nd round
Newcastle United 1 Sunderland 0 (HT: 0-0)

12th February 1902
St James' Park
23,000

Newcastle: M Kingsley, R Bennie, T Davidson, A Caie, A Aitken, J Carr, W Stewart, R Orr [89], A Gardner, J Peddie, R Roberts
Sunderland: J E Doig, A McCombie, J Watson, M Ferguson, A McAllister, R Jackson, W Hogg, R Hogg, J Millar, J Gemmell, C McLatchie
Referee: John Lewis (Blackburn)

THIS TIE should have been played on Saturday, 8th February, but heavy snow began to fall at 5.00am on the day of the match. By late morning, the snow was four to five inches deep. Newcastle recruited more than 100 men to try and shift it but a steady snowstorm forced John Lewis, the match referee, to call off the game at 1.45pm although 10,000 spectators had already turned up. Instead it was staged on the following Wednesday afternoon although Sunderland had to postpone a league game against Stoke scheduled for midweek.

There was still two inches of snow on the pitch when the game eventually took place. As this was before the advent of floodlights, the game had an afternoon kick-off and there was a mass exodus from the factories, shipyards and pits as supporters flocked to Gallowgate. Hawthorn, Leslie & Co, Stephenson & Co and the Elswick Arsenal were particularly affected.

The North Eastern Railway put on thirty special excursion trains and by 2.15pm (for a 3.00pm kick-off) all seats in the covered stand were taken. Within a further quarter of an hour, the terraces were almost packed – and this was despite Newcastle doubling their prices!

United underwent special cup tie preparations at Alnmouth but were handicapped by the absence of Bob McColl (who had an abscess behind his left knee) and Colin Veitch. The postponement of the original tie had left the latter in a dilemma. He had just established himself as a regular in the first team this season but there was still an element of doubt as to whether he would make a full time career in the game. He had an important examination scheduled for the same day as the re-arranged tie and opted for an academic future at this stage in his career.

Sunderland were top of the league, four points clear of second placed Everton, and at full-strength. Surprisingly, although fancied by many to achieve a league and cup double this season, Sunderland seemed affected by the tense atmosphere and looked nervous. Newcastle, on the other hand, were composed and confident with their right wing partnership of Willie Stewart and Ronald Orr in fine form.

Sunderland had their own hero in centre half Sandy McAllister who stood out like a beacon in the middle of their defence. Nevertheless, both sides started at a terrific pace and a great match ensued despite the slippery conditions. The tie was reported in the press at the time as "a game worthy of the highest traditions of the sport".

Newcastle had slightly the better of the opening exchanges but found the visiting full backs, Andy McCombie and Jim Watson, in top form. Sunderland soon came into the game themselves but the Newcastle half-backs tackled vigorously to crowd the renowned passing movements of the visiting forwards. The Wearsiders had the better of play in the later stages of the half but Tom Davidson stood out in the Tyneside defence and the interval arrived with the scoreline blank

Newcastle came out for the second half revitalised and the increasingly erratic visitors were soon penned back in defence. Doig was a shade lucky to deflect a Peddie shot just past a post. This was a prelude to a series of sustained attacks on the Sunderland goal which, at times, seemed to bear a charmed life. But the Wearside backs still stood firm and the visitors survived. When the flag was taken down to indicate that there were only ten minutes to go, United redoubled their efforts. Teddy Doig saved brilliantly from Peddie before Matt Kingsley was at last called into action, superbly defying Jimmy Millar and Billy Hogg in quick succession. But soon the siege continued at the other end. A Roberts' shot a couple of minutes from time looked like a certain goal until Jim Watson somehow managed to deflect it over the bar with his head. The reprieve, however, was only temporary as the resultant corner led to the breakthrough a minute from full time.

A poor corner kick saw the ball played out to Bob Bennie who put it straight back into the goalmouth. It was cleared again but this time only as far as Richard Roberts. He quickly tipped the ball to Ronald Orr who shot first time, giving Doig no chance. Hats, caps and sticks were waved aloft as the crowd went wild.

Sunderland attacked immediately upon the resumption but virtually within seconds the whistle was blown and their interest in the Cup was ended for another year as prolonged celebrations took place among the Tyneside adherents on the terraces.

Although Newcastle had left it very late to win the game, they received virtually all of the accolades following the match. This was possibly because, until now, Sunderland had won every competitive game that they had played against United at St James' Park.

It would be trite to say that Sunderland could now concentrate on the league. In truth, they had hopes of going for a league and cup double but that dream was now over for this season. They returned to their league campaign while Newcastle went back to Alnmouth. They had another home fixture, against Sheffield United, in the Third Round (quarter-final) and announced that they would double their prices for that game as well!

The Sunderland supporters could only wait for the two teams to meet again at Roker Park, seven weeks hence, in a league fixture. Revenge would be sweet – they hoped! By that time, Newcastle's interest in the cup would be over as well, although it would take a replay for the Blades to put them to the sword.

Football League
Division 1
Sunderland 0 Newcastle United 0 (HT: 0-0)
31st March 1902
Roker Park
34,819

Sunderland: J E Doig, R Jackson, J Watson, M Ferguson, A McAllister, J W Farquhar, W Hogg, R Hogg, J Millar, J Hewitt, J Craggs
Newcastle: M Kingsley, R Bennie, T Davidson, A Gardner, A Aitken, J Carr, W Stewart, R Orr, R S McColl, J Rutherford, R Roberts
Referee: Mr Boldison (Stockton)

THE LOCAL rivals came into this Easter Monday game in elevated positions in the league. Sunderland were the leaders, three points ahead of second placed Everton but with two games in hand, with Newcastle not far behind in fourth place – a little bit adrift and not really in contention for the title. But neither team had done well in their previous games. United had lost away to Grimsby Town on Good Friday while, on the Saturday, Sunderland had managed only to draw at home to Small Heath.

Both were also handicapped by a number of injuries. Sunderland suffered with both McCombie and McLatchie ruled out for the rest of the season and Gemmell missing after taking rather bad kick in the head on the Saturday. Newcastle had both Veitch and Dave Gardner missing from their line-up, the former suffering from bronchitis and the latter injured at Grimsby. Peddie was also a longer term absentee.

Sunderland had prepared for the game at their special training headquarters at Seaton Carew and the Newcastle team travelled to Roker on a horse-drawn brake to avoid the horrendous railway traffic.

League Positions		Pos	Pl	Pts		Pos	Pl	Pts
Before:	Sunderland	1st	28	39	Newcastle	4th	29	32
After:	Sunderland	1st	29	40	Newcastle	5th	30	33

The huge crowd set a new Roker record, comfortably beating the 31,500 against Aston Villa in September 1900. The scheduled referee, John Lewis (known as 'the Prince of Referees'), yet again missed his train connection (this time at Harrogate) and telegraphed a fellow referee, Mr Boldison of Stockton, to take charge of the game. This he did, apparently most satisfactorily.

Sunderland wore white shirts instead of their usual red and white stripes. Newcastle won the toss and played with the wind and sun in their favour but were forced back on defence. Davidson had a chance with a header but cleared the bar. The Wearsiders forced a series of corners but United defended well with Matt Kingsley giving a magnificent display between the posts. Newcastle mounted a series of attacks but these were mainly spasmodic. Carr fell back to help out his full backs as United were forced into a rearguard action. Towards the interval, however, they managed to put pressure on the home goal and it was Teddy Doig's turn to show his goalkeeping skills.

Kingsley was soon back in action at the start of the second half although a breakaway attack by the Tynesiders nearly resulted in a goal. Jack Carr banged in a free kick and the ball struck Doig's legs, bouncing up to rattle the crossbar. McColl latched on to the rebound and blasted in a shot that thumped against Doig's chest without the 'keeper knowing very much about it.

The incident encouraged Newcastle and the home defence soon found themselves hard pressed for a while. But it was not sustained and they were soon back on the attack. Only a fine tip over by Kingsley kept out a rasping shot by Hewitt as a prelude to three quick successive corners to Sunderland. Soon it was Newcastle's turn to have Lady Luck smile on them. Jim Watson took a free kick and it looked as if the ball would go directly into the net without touching another player (the laws of the time did not allow for goals to be scored directly from such kicks) but it hit the bar and dropped into the goalmouth. An almighty scrimmage ensued before United eventually scrambled the ball away. But it was not for long and another Sunderland corner saw McAllister head against the Newcastle bar. The lowering of the ten minute flag was the signal for both sides to go for the winner but with Sunderland clearly the better team. Kingsley had four times the work to do than Doig and it was thanks to their 'keeper that United escaped with a point. Overall it was only a mediocre game although the consensus of opinion was that Newcastle were lucky.

The failure to win meant that Sunderland had now played three successive games at home (including a friendly against Third Lanark) and had failed to win – an unusual occurrence for a club who had emerged as champions-elect.

But the loss of this home point was just a stumble in their march to the title. They were now two points ahead of Everton with two games in hand but the Toffees had only three games left. Sunderland were actually to lose three of their last five matches but, such was their lead in the league, that they were to be crowned League Champions by three clear points over the Merseysiders. This was their fourth title win during an 11 year period that had also seen them finish as runners-up three times – a real golden era for 'The Team of all the Talents'.

However, it was coming to an end and they were to be replaced as top dogs by their neighbours from Tyneside. This season, Newcastle were also to lose two of their last four matches but were still to finish in a very encouraging third position, their best season yet in the league. Their golden era lay just around the corner.

Football League
Division 1
Sunderland 0 Newcastle United 0 (HT: 0-0)
27th December 1902
Roker Park
28,000

Sunderland: JE Doig, A McCombie, J Watson, JW Farquhar, A McAllister, R Jackson, W Hogg, J Millar, J Gemmell, G Harper, J Hewitt
Newcastle: M Kingsley, W Wilson, W Agnew, A Caie, A Aitken, J Carr, H Stenhouse, C Veitch, Alex Gardner, J Rutherford, E Birnie
Referee: John Lewis (Blackburn)

ALTHOUGH NEITHER team was in a particularly high position in the league, Sunderland were one of the in-form teams in the country. So far, that December, they had won three and drawn one of their four games – with three of them away from home. Although they were in eighth, they were only five points behind league leaders Derby County and Notts County.

Newcastle, on the other hand, had lost three of their last four games and were badly hit by injuries and illnesses. McColl, Orr, Roberts, Stewart and Bennie were all conspicuous by their absence. There were just four teams below United in the league, with the bottom two automatically relegated. The Magpies were seven points clear of second bottom Grimsby Town. It was little wonder that their supporters travelled to Wearside with little hope and even less expectation.

League Positions		Pos	Pl	Pts		Pos	Pl	Pts
Before:	Sunderland	8th	17	19	Newcastle	14th	16	15
After:	Sunderland	8th	18	20	Newcastle	14th	17	16

The game was played at a tremendous pace with smart football from both sides. Newcastle showed up first and a long range effort by Alex Gardner was adroitly tipped over the bar by Teddy Doig. Sunderland did most of the attacking but rarely troubled Kingsley until Jimmy Millar sent in a rasping shot that the 'keeper had difficulty in clearing. United then took up the running and the Wearsiders were lucky not to concede a penalty following rough work by McAllister. The best chance of the first half came just before half-time when

Millar was presented with an opportunity bang in front of the visitors' goal. He could not manage a clean shot and the ball rolled to Hogg but he banged his effort wide.

Newcastle did the early attacking in the second half but their forwards were rather dilatory in front of goal. Stenhouse nearly broke the deadlock but missed the target by inches. Defences were generally on top for both sides although Birnie should have opened the scoring 20 minutes from time when he was left in possession right in front of goal but he hurried his shot and sent it wide. Sunderland made a final aggressive push forward in the last 10 minutes but Newcastle held firm.

There was one final chance near the end when the Rokermen were awarded a free kick a couple of yards outside the Newcastle penalty line. Jim Watson's shot was on target but Matt Kingsley was well placed to collect and he booted his clearance clean over the grandstand and out of the ground.

The draw meant that Sunderland had now gone six games without defeat, albeit half of them were draws. But the new year was to see them climb the league and challenge for the championship as they embarked upon a further sequence of seven league games unbeaten, this time chalking up six wins. A solitary defeat in the cup by Aston Villa was to be their only setback.

Newcastle, on the other hand, were to win only one of their next ten matches (including elimination from the cup) and were to slide down the league, eventually slipping to second bottom (a relegation position) before climbing to safety.

Football League
Division 1
Newcastle United 1 Sunderland 0 (HT: 0-0)
25th April 1903
St James' Park
26,562

Newcastle: C Watts, A Aitken, W B Agnew, P McWilliam, C Veitch, J Carr, A Turner, Alex Gardner, R S McColl [49], W Appleyard, R Templeton
Sunderland: J E Doig, J Watson, E Rhodes, J W Farquhar, A Barrie, R Jackson, W Hogg, R Robinson, J Millar, J Hewitt, A Bridgett
Referee: John Lewis (Blackburn)

THIS GAME was arguably the most important Tyne-Wear derby ever. This was the last match of the season and Sunderland came into it in second position in the league, only one point behind leaders Sheffield Wednesday who had completed their fixtures.

The Owls had a slightly better goal average so the Wearsiders knew that only a win would see them lift the title. Any other result would mean that Wednesday would finish as Champions. In their favour, Sunderland had won every league game that they had played at St James' Park. They had even played a 'home' fixture there a week earlier when Roker Park had been closed for disciplinary reasons (spectator misbehaviour) and they had defeated Middlesbrough 2-1. So Gallowgate held no fears for them despite the fact that two of their key defenders, Andy McCombie and Sandy McAllister, were ruled out with injuries sustained against Boro'.

Newcastle were also affected by injury with goalkeeper Matt Kingsley missing. But United came into the game with renewed confidence having pulled away from the relegation zone by winning their last five home games to reach 15th.

League Positions		Pos	Pl	Pts		Pos	Pl	Pts
Before:	Sunderland	2nd	33	41	Newcastle	15th	33	30
After:	Sunderland	2nd	34	41	Newcastle	14th	34	32

A large contingent of Sheffield supporters (estimated at 500-600) made the journey to Tyneside to cheer on Newcastle. The FA were worried that United would lie down and let their neighbours win the title so they sent invigilators to monitor the game. Silly FA! As if either of the North East teams would lie down for the other. The Sunderland v Middlesbrough game had attracted 26,000 to Gallowgate, which had been the biggest crowd of the season there so far. But even this was broken for a game that became the championship decider.

Sunderland won the toss and played towards the Leazes. Charlie Watts was the first 'keeper to be called into action, saving well from Hewitt and Hogg. Newcastle counter-attacked but were whistled up when Templeton bundled Teddy Doig into the net after the goalie had cleared the ball. A weak clearance by the Sunderland 'keeper barely cleared the 18 yard line and went straight to McColl who was taken by surprise. He managed a shot at goal but Doig cleared comfortably. It was a close game. Play went from end-to-end without any side really threatening. Sunderland enjoyed most of the possession but the Newcastle half-back line played well. Just before the interval the visitors went close twice in quick succession but first Watts fisted the ball away and then, seconds later, gathered it comfortably.

Newcastle made a slight change to their forward line at half-time, moving new signing Bill Appleyard to centre forward and this paid dividends within four minutes. Colin Veitch started the move. He won possession from Millar and took the ball 20 yards before transferring it to Appleyard. The former Grimsby man tipped it to Alex Gardner who went past two defenders before returning it to the burly forward. An astute pass inside to Bob McColl left the Scottish international with only Doig to beat although the angle was narrow. He made no mistake, much to the delight of the Newcastle and Sheffield supporters and the despair of those from Wearside.

With the spectre of the championship being snatched from their grasp, Sunderland redoubled their efforts and laid siege to the home goal. Newcastle's attempts to relieve it were short-lived as the Wearsiders began to dominate play. Watts had to go full length to scoop the ball away from Hogg who then sent in a second shot only for Veitch to clear off the line when a goal looked certain. But on the rare occasions that United managed to break away, they looked dangerous. Appleyard hit the Sunderland crossbar at one point as the visitors were forced back. They had to concede three corners in rapid succession but Newcastle just could not force the ball through for a second, decisive goal.

Sunderland began to adopt a one back game to play an offside trap. This brought them much criticism after the match, with many regarding it as "unsportsmanlike" and "a contravention of the true spirit of football and code of honour". During the match, however, it certainly bamboozled Newcastle who found themselves penned in their own half. But they held firm with Veitch outstanding and Aitken and Watts not far behind. The Sunderland forwards swarmed around the Newcastle goal but frustration began to creep into their play and they resorted to strong arm tactics to try and hammer United into submission. The home goalmouth was packed with players while Doig stood as a forlorn, isolated figure at the other end. But the Geordies held firm and still led by the solitary goal at the final whistle which saw the Sheffield supporters go wild. A brass band struck up "Cock 'o the North" for the Magpies followed by "Auld Lang Syne" for the heart-broken Wearsiders.

Sunderland's first ever league defeat on Tyneside not only meant that they had lost the championship but they did not even have the prestige and satisfaction of finishing as runners-up. Aston Villa eventually squeezed in front of them with a better goal average. The fact that Sunderland had been the better team for the bulk of the game and had deserved at least a point (if not two) was no consolation.

It was a classic case of so near, yet so far. Never in the history of Tyne-Wear derbies had so much been at stake and been lost.

Most Consecutive Clean Sheets

Newcastle		Sunderland	
4	12 Feb 1902 – 25 Apr 1903	2	On six separate occasions
3	24 Feb 2002 – 26 Apr 2003		

Football League
Division 1
Newcastle United 1 Sunderland 3 (HT: 0-2)
26th December 1903
St James' Park
30,000

Newcastle: M Kingsley, J Tildesley, T Wills, A Gardner, C Veitch, A Aitken, A Turner, J Rutherford [87], W Appleyard, R S McColl, R Templeton
Sunderland: JE Doig, A McCombie, J Watson, JW Farquhar, A McAllister, R Jackson, J Craggs, A Bridgett [23], W Hogg, J Gemmell, HR Buckle [21, 89]
Referee: John Lewis (Blackburn) [initially Fred Dennis (Middlesbrough)]

BOTH TEAMS were more or less level in the league and doing quite well. Sunderland located themselves at Seaton Carew for special training and came into the match in tip-top condition. Crucially, they also had a free day on Christmas Day while Newcastle had undergone a gruelling game away to Sheffield United. The Magpies were also handicapped by an injury to star man Jimmy Howie against the Blades.

Thousands flocked to Gallowgate from all parts of the north of England with massive support for Sunderland. A total of 28,797 supporters paid for admission before the gates were closed with another 5,000 to 6,000 still outside. With ticket holders, this brought the total to around 30,000.

But when the 2.00pm kick-off time arrived, the referee hadn't. Mr Lewis had missed his train connection from Blackburn and didn't arrive at St James' until 20 minutes after the start. Both clubs agreed to Mr Dennis of Middlesbrough taking charge until the nominated referee arrived and the deputy match official reportedly did his job admirably.

League Positions		Pos	Pl	Pts		Pos	Pl	Pts
Before:	Newcastle	5th	18	21	Sunderland	6th	17	20
After:	Sunderland	5th	18	22	Newcastle	7th	19	21

Sunderland set off at a wonderful pace on the heavy ground and seldom relaxed their efforts. Their energy and superiority were soon obvious. In striking contrast, apart from one or two spasmodic raids, Newcastle showed nothing of their usual brilliance and never seemed to get into their stride. United were probably affected by their exertions on the previous day but the Wearsiders were clearly the better team and outplayed the out of sorts Magpies. The football was not of the highest standard in the early stages but it lacked nothing in excitement to keep the capacity crowd enthralled.

It was no surprise when Sunderland eventually took the lead after 21 minutes. Harry Buckle and Jimmy Gemmell worked the ball into the centre within the 18 yard line. Wills, with his back to the goal, attempted to clear but Buckle stole up and, gathering the ball, promptly placed it beyond the reach of Kingsley. Many people thought (and most reports stated) that it was an own goal by Wills but the referee and linesmen later confirmed that Buckle was the scorer.

Two minutes later Sunderland increased their lead. Buckle, Gemmell and Hogg all combined in an impressive manoeuvre up the left wing before playing the ball in to Arthur Bridgett who was totally unmarked in the middle and able to score an easy second goal.

Newcastle had chances to reduce the deficit with Appleyard looking particularly dangerous. But the nearest to another goal came just before half-time and fell to Bridgett who let fly with the best shot of the game only for Matt Kingsley to save and kick clear.

Sunderland were also on top in the second half and at times ran rings around a tired Newcastle side. Fortunately for the Tynesiders, their defence was equal to all of their visitors' efforts apart from a disallowed goal scored by Craggs that was ruled offside. As the game reached its closing stages, however, United suddenly began to force the Rokerites back and it became Sunderland's turn to hang on.

United's late pressure eventually paid dividends when Bob McColl supplied Bobby Templeton who dashed past McCombie to the goal line. His cross into the goalmouth found Jackie Rutherford right in front of the posts and his header gave Doig no chance. That was with three minutes left but, with a minute to go, just when it was thought that Newcastle's belated grandstand finish might steal a point, Sunderland grabbed a crucial third goal. It came as a result of a terrible blunder by Tildesley who allowed Harry Buckle to brush past him and, finding himself clean through, notch a final goal that gave the scoreline a more realistic look.

There is no doubt that Sunderland were worthy winners. In fact with more steadiness in front of goal they may have won even more comfortably. The win saw them leap-frog over Newcastle in the league.

United's supporters pointed to the arduous game on Christmas Day and the absence of star man Howie as the obvious causes of their lack lustre performance. They convinced themselves that the return game at Roker on New Year's Day would see a different Newcastle. Adherents of both Tyne and Wear could hardly wait for the game.

Football League
Division 1
Sunderland 1 Newcastle United 1 (HT: 0-0)
1st January 1904
Roker Park
37,000

Sunderland: JE Doig, A McCombie [83 (pen)], J Watson, JW Farquhar, A McAllister,
R Jackson, J Craggs, A Bridgett, W Hogg, J Gemmell, HR Buckle
Newcastle: C Watts, J Tildesley, T Wills, A Gardner, A Aitken, C Veitch, J Rutherford,
R Orr [50], W Appleyard, RS McColl, R Templeton
Referee: John Lewis (Blackburn)

NOT SURPRISINGLY, considering their comfortable success at St James'
Park on Boxing Day, Sunderland fielded an unchanged side for the return
fixture at Roker. Newcastle, however, rang the changes. Charlie Watts took
over in goal from Matt Kingsley who was carrying an injury. In fact, a chain of
events (injury, sickness, loss of form and eventually conflict with the club) had
begun which meant that Kingsley, Newcastle's first ever international player,
had played his last game for the club. Other changes saw Ronald Orr come
into the United line-up at inside right and Jackie Rutherford switching out to
the right wing and Turner dropping out.

The result at Gallowgate ensured that another bumper crowd turned out
with packed trains arriving on Wearside from 10.00am onwards. In the end,
a new attendance record for Roker Park was set up with 37,000 (at least one
estimate gave the crowd as 40,000) inside the ground, comfortably beating the
34, 819 that had attended the derby game two years earlier.

The kick-off was scheduled for 2.00pm but, with the gates locked, the game
started ten minutes early.

League Positions		Pos	Pl	Pts		Pos	Pl	Pts
Before:	Sunderland	5th	18	22	Newcastle	7th	19	21
After:	Sunderland	5th	19	23	Newcastle	6th	20	22

After a cautious start, the massive crowd were entertained by a superb
game of football. Incident followed incident although it was Sunderland who
did most of the attacking in the first half. But they found Charlie Watts in fine
form between the posts for Newcastle. One tip over the bar from a Gemmell
shot and a fist out from a Bridgett effort were particularly impressive. Even an
astute back-header by Buckle failed to catch out United's reserve goalkeeper.
United relied largely on breakaway attacks and it was from one of these that
Jackie Rutherford hit the side netting with a long distance pot shot at goal.

Sunderland started off the second half determined to make the break-through. Arthur Bridgett went desperately close when he struck the outside of one of the Newcastle posts. But after 50 minutes Newcastle immediately launched a counter-attack up their left wing where Bobby Templeton and Bob McColl proved too much for the home defence. It was the former who centred the ball for Ronald Orr, without hesitation, to hammer in a first time shot at goal. Doig did well to block the effort but Orr was in like a flash to rattle the rebound home, much to the wild delight of the Tyneside adherents in the crowd.

Newcastle looked a different team after their success and took control of the game. Yet Sunderland redoubled their efforts and Watts had to be on his toes time and time again. But most of the action was around the Sunderland goal and by the time the flag was lowered to indicate that there were only ten minutes to go, the Wearsiders were virtually under siege.

But then seven minutes from time Lady Luck (or, to be more precise, referee John Lewis) smiled on the Rokermen. During a by now isolated Sunderland attack, Jim Watson played a free kick inside the Newcastle 12 yard line. McAllister, head down, charged in, apparently intent on butting Aitken only for the Newcastle captain to neatly brush past him and clear the danger. The referee blew his whistle and everyone, including the Sunderland players who immediately retreated towards the half-way line, assumed that he was penalising McAllister for rough play.

Incredibly, however, Mr Lewis pointed to the penalty spot. Not a single person in the press box knew why and none of the spectators probably knew either. But Andy McCombie was not going to look a gift horse in the mouth and he sent in a low, hard shot past Watts to make the scores level. Mr Lewis later explained that he thought that Aitken had held McAllister, something that the Newcastle captain emphatically denied.

Sunderland kept up a heavy attack in the closing minutes to try and snatch both points but Newcastle held out.

The draw consolidated both teams in their positions in the top of half of the league. It had been a tremendous game with both sets of players lauded for their sporting attitude. There were also no reports of trouble among the rival supporters even though it took two hours for the crowds to disperse. Monkwearmouth and Sunderland stations were crammed as the spectators set off home.

The draw gave Newcastle confidence and they were to lose just three more league games before the end of season, climbing to second place at one point before slipping back to finish fourth. Sunderland were not to do quite as well. Indeed, they were to lose two of their next three games although they were eventually to finish in a highly respectable sixth position.

Football League
Division 1
Sunderland 3 Newcastle United 1 (HT: 2-1)
24th December 1904
Roker Park
29,500

Sunderland: I Webb, E Rhodes, J Watson, J W Farquhar, W Fullerton, R Jackson [**30** secs, **62**], W Hogg, A Bridgett, A Common, J Gemmell, H R Buckle [**38**]
Newcastle: J Lawrence, A McCombie, J Carr, A Gardner, C Veitch, P McWilliam [**29**], J Rutherford, J Howie, W Appleyard, R Orr, A Gosnell
Referee: Fred Kirkham (Burslem)

NEWCASTLE MUST have been confident coming into this game. They were top of the league and had won their last seven games. Even history was on their side – they had never lost a league game at Roker Park. But Sunderland were not doing too badly themselves and were five points and three positions behind the high flying Magpies. However there had been major upheavals behind the scenes at Roker with an FA enquiry into illicit payments resulting in mass suspensions of their directors and administrative personnel. The player who had primarily (although inadvertently) been at the root of the enquiry, Andy McCombie, was now on Newcastle's books to give added spice to an already volatile fixture.

More than 7,000 train tickets were sold from Newcastle plus thousands more from Gateshead, South Shields and all stations between Tyneside to Wearside to ensure another massive Roker crowd.

League Positions		Pos	Pl	Pts		Pos	Pl	Pts
Before:	Newcastle	1st	16	24	Sunderland	4th	16	19
After:	Newcastle	1st	17	24	Sunderland	4th	17	21

Gardner won the toss and asked Sunderland to kick-off – a fatal mistake with the Rokermen scoring virtually straight from the start.

Straight from the kick off Sunderland launched a raid down the right wing that Carr managed to stop only by fouling Bridgett. Ernie Rhodes sent the free kick into the Newcastle penalty area where Dicky Jackson just managed to get his head to the ball in front of McCombie (some reports gave the goal to the full back but the consensus was that he never touched the ball). Lawrence's first touch was to pick the ball out of the back of the net.

Sunderland adapted much better than Newcastle to the greasy, treacherous playing surface. The Wearsiders' choice of leather studs in preference to United's rubber studded boots was a deciding factor. The Newcastle players slithered and slipped all over the place and Sunderland, mainly by their aggressive play in attack, had the visitors' defence struggling. Gradually, however, Newcastle began to realise that the footing was firmer on the wings and they soon forced the Wearsiders back on defence.

But the equaliser came out of the blue a minute before the half hour. Peter McWilliam decided to try a pot at goal from out near the touchline. There was little power and even less threat in his shot but Webb, making his home debut for the Red and Whites, slipped and missed the ball completely. He could only lie in the mud and watch helplessly as the ball trundled over the line into the net.

The goal encouraged Newcastle and they pressed Sunderland back. Yet in one breakaway attack Hogg took the ball around Lawrence to face an open goal only for Jack Carr to dash back and block his shot.

Sunderland broke away again and scored completely against the run of play after 38 minutes. Harry Buckle sent Billy Hogg away with a long pass and he ran on to blast a rasping shot at goal. Lawrence saved it but as he tried to throw the ball out, he slipped in the mud and lost possession. Buckle was up in support and he rushed in to score a gift of a goal much to the delight of his fellow players and the home supporters.

Newcastle redoubled their efforts and Sunderland were hanging on when, just before the interval, Jackie Rutherford broke through and looked a certain scorer when Watson took his legs away. The offence was inside the penalty line and it was an obvious penalty. Up stepped Appleyard to take it. His shot was hard enough but atrociously wide (anywhere between two and 20 yards according to contemporary match reports!). Sunderland were distinctly lucky to be ahead at the break.

Newcastle launched themselves into the attack straight from the restart with the burly Bill Appleyard causing all kinds of trouble to the Sunderland defence. Both sides mounted attacks as they went for the crucial next goal with Sunderland looking increasingly dangerous as the game progressed.

They went further ahead after 62 minutes when Veitch and Orr dallied in looking to clear the ball, waiting for each other to boot it clear. Dicky Jackson saw the hesitation and rushed in to hook a shot at goal that went over Lawrence and his defenders into the net.

Newcastle were discouraged by this third goal and Sunderland went all out to rub it in. McCombie and Carr had their work cut out. The Wearsiders now had much the better of the play and should really have scored a hat full. With anything like decent marksmanship, they would have done so but chance after chance went begging with Common particularly at fault. In the end, however, they were still comfortable winners.

The state of the pitch undoubtedly had a big bearing on the game. Sunderland definitely made the right choice with their leather studs for a pitch that was soft and greasy for the first two inches but rock hard below the surface. It was like a ploughed field by the end of the match.

McCombie was booed throughout by the Roker supporters but did not let it affect him. At the end, Newcastle were still top of the league but Sunderland had at last defeated their neighbours in a league game at Roker.

Sunderland returned to Harrogate for special training. Newcastle returned to Tyneside and winning ways as they continued their quest for the league championship.

Football League
Division 1
Newcastle United 1 Sunderland 3 (HT: 1-2)
22nd April 1905
St James' Park
30,000

Newcastle: J Lawrence, A McCombie, J Carr, A Gardner (inj 25), A Aitken, P McWilliam, J Rutherford, J Howie, W Appleyard, C Veitch [**30** pen], A Gosnell
Sunderland: I Webb, E Rhodes, J Watson, D Willis, A Barrie, R Jackson, W Hogg, G Holley [**20, 83**], J Gemmell, A Bridgett, HR Buckle [**26**]
Referee: Fred Kirkham (Burslem)

NEWCASTLE HAD high hopes of winning the League Championship for the first time. They were in second place, a point behind leaders Everton but with a game in hand. United also had a game in hand over third placed Manchester City who were behind the Magpies only on goal average. Victory over Sunderland was even more important than usual. Two years earlier, victory for the Magpies over their neighbours in the last game of the season at St James' had deprived the Rokermen of the championship. Now it was the Wearsiders' chance to return the compliment.

Despite wind and rain sweeping the North East, the crowds hoping to get into St James' far exceeded the ground capacity. Officially 28,493 paid for admission before the gates were locked. With approximately another 1,500 season ticket holders, it brought the crowd up to 30,000. Perhaps the gates were closed too early. Approximately a further 2,000 scaled the fences to get in but 20,000 were left locked outside.

League Positions		Pos	Pl	Pts			Pos	Pl	Pts
Before:	Newcastle	2nd	31	44	Sunderland		7th	32	36
After:	Newcastle	2nd	32	44	Sunderland		7th	33	38

Newcastle started well and for the opening 20 minutes virtually outclassed the Wearsiders. But they did not turn their superiority into goals and paid the consequences after 20 minutes when Sunderland shocked St James' by grabbing a goal totally against the run of play.

To make matters worse, it was the softest goals conceded at Gallowgate this season. The Rokermen were awarded a free kick when Aitken fouled Gemmell. The resultant cross-shot did not look as if it was going to trouble the Newcastle defence with Carr shepherding the ball out of play. Until, that is, George Holley darted around him to take possession and try a shot at goal. There was no power in his effort and all Lawrence really had to do was pick it up – but it went straight through his legs into the net! Shock, horror – Newcastle 0 Sunderland 1.

If this goal was not bad enough, United suffered a major handicap when Gardner was forced to retire from the game five minutes later with a leg injury. Veitch dropped back to cover for him.

Within a minute, Sunderland increased their lead. Harry Buckle caught both McCombie and Veitch unawares as he dodged past them to score with a high but deceptive shot.

Newcastle were now furious. They had dominated the game but were now two goals down with only ten men. They were very unlucky not to pull a goal back almost immediately when Aitken volleyed in from a Gosnell flag kick. His shot looked a goal all of the way before it touched Appleyard on its way into the net. He was in an offside position so, naturally, the effort was disallowed. They did pull a goal back on the half hour. James Howie went past two defenders before transferring the ball to Bill Appleyard who made a bee-line for goal. He was well inside the Sunderland penalty line when he was brought down by Rhodes. Up stepped Colin Veitch to blast the spot kick low past Webb's left hand.

Newcastle should then have equalised when Howie threaded his way through before presenting Rutherford with an ideal opening right in front of the posts but he somehow mulled it. United continued to battle valiantly to try and get on level terms. They played some superb football in the second half and just as in the first half dominated the first 20 minutes. Appleyard (twice) and Rutherford both went close before the latter wasted another great chance after being set up by Gosnell. The Sunderland backs tackled robustly, kicking the ball into touch at every opportunity. The heavy going eventually began to take its toll and soon both sides were tottering on the brink of exhaustion when, seven minutes from time, Sunderland grabbed the crucial final goal. George Holley looked well off-side when he took a pass from Jimmy Gemmell but the flag stayed down and he was allowed to go on unchallenged to make it 3-1.

The injury to Gardner undoubtedly affected Newcastle but they were also beginning to look stale. It was commonly accepted that Sunderland overstepped the mark with their robust play, committing 22 fouls compared to only eight by Newcastle. But as far as they were concerned, the end justified the means. They were worthy winners. Yet defeat for United could have been much worse because league leaders Everton had also lost at Woolwich Arsenal and Manchester City had not played. Far from dispiriting Newcastle, the loss against Sunderland spurred them on and they won their last two games, both away from home, pipping the Toffees to the League Championship by one point.

Football League
Division 1
Sunderland 3 Newcastle United 2 (HT: 1-1)
2nd September 1905
Roker Park
30,000

Sunderland: T Naisby, E Rhodes, J Watson, J W Farquhar, A Barrie, D Willis, W Hogg, G Holley, J Gemmell [**68**], A Bridgett [**3, 48**], HR Buckle
Newcastle: J Lawrence, A McCombie, J Carr, A Gardner, A Aitken, C Veitch, J Rutherford, J Howie [**14**], H W Hardinge, R Orr [**72**], A Gosnell
Referee: G B Capes (Burton)

WHAT A way to start the season – the League Champions playing away to their arch-rivals. Changes had taken place at both clubs during the close season. For Sunderland, their long serving wing-half Dicky Jackson had joined Portsmouth and, compared to the previous Tyne-Wear Derby at St James' at the end of the previous campaign, Tom Naisby had taken over from Ike Webb in goal (although the latter was still at the club). Newcastle were lacking their burly centre forward Bill Appleyard who was out with an injured foot. Kent county cricketer Harry Hardinge, a close season recruit from Maidstone United, took his place at centre forward.

It was estimated that two-thirds of the spectators travelled to Roker by train with 6,000 coming from Newcastle Central Station alone. Once again, the gates were locked with thousands still outside.

League Positions		Pos	Pl	Pts		Pos	Pl	Pts
After:	Sunderland	6th	1	2	Newcastle	15th	1	0

Aitken won the toss and took advantage of a stiff breeze in the first half. But it was Sunderland who mounted the early attacks and shocked their visitors by grabbing the lead after just three minutes.

Billy Hogg and George Holley worked the ball up the right wing past Veitch and Aitken. When it was crossed into the middle, Arthur Bridgett was perfectly placed to crack in a low shot past Lawrence.

The goal spurred Newcastle into life and a cross by Rutherford looked dangerous until Tom Naisby dived among a crowd of players to fist the ball clear. Newcastle persevered and were eventually rewarded with the equaliser just before the quarter hour mark. Rhodes fouled Hardinge and Jack Carr sent the free kick into the Sunderland goalmouth. Rhodes managed to get his head to it but was able just to head it on to where James Howie had the simple task of tapping it home.

United continued to push forward. Jack Rutherford cleverly beat both Watson and Rhodes before scoring a brilliant goal only to have it disallowed for offside – a very dubious decision by all accounts. Sunderland managed to force Newcastle back as half-time approached and when Lawrence was able only to partially clear a shot by Holley, Jack Carr came to the rescue by booting clear.

Sunderland started the second half in the same way that they had the first but by this time the elements had worsened and Newcastle had to face a cold, fierce wind. As in the first half, the Wearsiders had an early success. Three minutes had gone when again Arthur Bridgett did the damage, raking in a low shot that flew past Lawrence's outstretched hand into the net.

Sunderland had a period of ascendancy but never really threatened before Rutherford put in a dangerous shot at the other end that Jim Watson cleverly turned away. But it was mainly Sunderland and the Newcastle defence was hard pressed to keep them out with Jimmy Lawrence distinguishing himself with a series of outstanding saves.

He was eventually beaten again after 68 minutes when skilful work by Buckle and Bridgett created the opening for Jimmy Gemmell to net number three with apparent ease. United's forwards rallied within four minutes and Ronald Orr raised the hopes of their supporters when he cleverly turned the ball out of the reach of Naisby to make it 3-2.

Newcastle briefly threatened to grab another equaliser but they soon fell away and it was their defence who had to work hardest. Jimmy Lawrence was their hero and he brought the house down with a series of breath-taking saves in the later stages to keep the score respectable.

The elements certainly affected the game but Sunderland were worthy winners. They looked fitter than their Tyneside counterparts. But it was a false dawn for Wearside as their favourites proceeded to pick up only one point from their next seven games.

Newcastle had a similar undistinguished start to the campaign but a run of six successive wins in October and November soon put them in contention for the title again.

First Use of Floodlights in a Derby Game

22 December 1956 – St James' Park.
Floodlights had not been permitted for league games prior to 1956.
Indeed, the first use of them had only been made a few months earlier at Fratton Park (Portsmouth v Newcastle – 22nd April 1956).

Football League
Division 1
Newcastle United 1 Sunderland 1 (HT: 1-1)
30th December 1905
St James' Park
56,000

Newcastle: J Lawrence, A McCombie, J Carr, A Aitken, C Veitch, P McWilliam, J Rutherford, A Gardner, J McClarence, R Orr [**26**], A Gosnell
Sunderland: T Naisby, E Bell, J Watson, JW Farquhar, A Barrie, D Willis, W Hogg [**9**], D O'Donnell, J Gemmell, G Holley, A Bridgett
Referee: F Kirkham (Preston)

NEWCASTLE WERE doing quite well in the league, lying fifth, four points behind leaders Aston Villa and Sheffield Wednesday with a game in hand. Sunderland on the other hand were in a rather precarious position, 17th out of 20, and ahead of second and third bottom clubs, Bury and Middlesbrough, only on goal average. The one thing in their favour was their record in the league at St James' Park – it was their lucky ground with six wins out of seven games there so far. Another advantage for the Wearsiders was that Newcastle had injury problems with McCracken, Howie and Appleyard all ruled out. Sunderland had no such problems. With the exception of Bell for Rhodes at right back, they were able to field their strongest team.

United had spent £20,000 on ground improvements and extensions at St James', and such was the clamour to see the game that a new record attendance was set up for a Football League match with 56,000 people paying £1,600, easily beating the previous best – 41,357 (gate receipts £1,588) at Villa Park in April 1899.

League Positions		Pos	Pl	Pts		Pos	Pl	Pts
Before:	Newcastle	5th	20	23	Sunderland	17th	19	14
After:	Newcastle	6th	21	24	Sunderland	16th	20	15

Newcastle mounted the early attacks with Rutherford causing problems on their right wing. Willis continually fouled the winger but Jackie almost took revenge when his centre was met by McClarence who sent a header over Naisby against the crossbar.

Sunderland made the most of their reprieve and grabbed the opener after nine minutes. Jimmy Gemmell gained possession in midfield and passed the ball to Arthur Bridgett who outstripped Aitken. Carr partially cleared the Sunderland winger's centre but only sent it to the opposite wing where Billy Hogg picked it up. He cut inside, dribbling past Carr and Veitch before cracking in a low hard drive through a crowd of players with Lawrence unsighted.

Lady Luck now smiled on Newcastle as Bridgett, on the Sunderland left wing, cracked a great shot past Lawrence but saw it hit a post. Rutherford continued to torment the Wearside rearguard, at one time beating four defenders in a magnificent dribbling run before volleying in a terrific shot that Tom Naisby saved well at the foot of a post. Sunderland were speedy and alert but Newcastle played the more scientific football and slowly gained control, thanks mainly to the prompting of Peter McWilliam. Rutherford fired in a low, hard shot that Naisby saved but, in helping his goalie to clear, Willis clearly handled the ball. Fortunately for him the referee failed to spot the offence.

Newcastle's equaliser came as a result of the best move of the game after 26 minutes. Andy Aitken cleverly pushed the ball forward to Alex Gardner who transferred it to Joe McClarence. He was just on the point of trying a shot at goal when he noticed Ronald Orr in a better position and unselfishly allowed Newcastle's pocket Hercules to score with a fast low shot.

Now Newcastle had their tails up and they were unlucky not to take the lead when Rutherford took a pass from Gardner and beat Naisby only to have his effort disallowed for offside – a dubious decision. Lawrence saved a rasping shot by Bridgett but most of the action was at the other end where Sunderland were hanging on when the half-time whistle came.

The second half saw Sunderland concentrating on defence, hoping to hold out for a draw. Their half-backs and inside forwards dropped back to help pack their defence, leaving Willie Hogg isolated up front. Their breakaway attacks were few and far between and rarely troubled Newcastle. The second half consisted almost entirely of persistent United attacks. Watson and Bell tackled robustly but time-wasted at every opportunity and the rest of their team soon followed. Newcastle were by far the better side but Sunderland deserved credit for their determination and stamina. It was still stalemate at the final whistle.

Although Newcastle had dominated most of the game, they had badly missed James Howie. They were undoubtedly a better side than Sunderland but the Wearsiders could point out that they had dropped just one point to the Magpies this season.

As the season wore on, Tyneside became engrossed on progress in the FA Cup (where they reached the final) rather than the league where they did quite well but never really challenged for the title despite finishing in a very respectable fourth position. Sunderland were to climb the league after the new year, winning seven out of their next nine games, only to fall away and finish in a mediocre 14th place.

Football League
Division 1
Newcastle United 4 Sunderland 2 (HT: 1-0)
1st September 1906
St James' Park
56,875

Newcastle: J Lawrence, A McCombie, J Carr, A Aitken, C Veitch, P McWilliam, J Rutherford [**77, 82**], J Howie [**87**], W Appleyard [**27**], R Orr, A Gosnell
Sunderland: T Naisby, E Rhodes, J Watson, TS Tait, A Barrie, D Willis, W Hogg, J Gemmell, Jos Shaw, M Hall, A Bridgett [**51, 69**]
Referee: TP Campbell (Blackburn)

AS USUAL, both sides came into this, the first game of the season, with optimism. Newcastle had enjoyed a fairly successful season last year, finishing fourth in the league and reaching the Cup Final, and were favourites to win. Sunderland, on the other hand, had a very good record at St James' and were determined to improve on last season when they had collected three points out of four from the derbies.

United had a team selection dilemma, whether to play Andy Aitken or Alex Gardner at right half. The former gained the nod although Alex was to make the position his own not long afterwards. Sunderland fielded two new signings, centre half Tom Tait from Bristol Rovers and Matthew Hall, an inside left from St Mirren.

Glorious weather attracted a bumper record crowd to Gallowgate with massive gate receipts (£1,575). Newcastle turned out in white jerseys "to make better distinction".

League Positions	Pos	Pl	Pts		Pos	Pl	Pts
After: Newcastle	3rd	1	2	Sunderland	14th	1	0

The tropical heat did not prevent both teams from serving up superb football. Newcastle were handicapped early on when Aitken took a bad kick on his right knee from Bridgett. In fact a small bone had been fractured but he courageously insisted on playing on. Despite the handicap, Newcastle looked the better side in the early stages.

They grabbed the lead after 27 minutes when Bill Appleyard gained possession 25 yards out. Both Rhodes and Watson stood off as he bustled his way between them to try a low shot at goal. It was not particularly hard but was well placed with Naisby, despite going full length, just failing to reach it.

Newcastle were temporarily reduced to ten men when McWilliam took a kick in the face from Gemmell resulting in a very heavy nose bleed. He was forced to go off for treatment but soon resumed. The injuries to Andy and

Peter gave the impression that this was a dirty game but nothing could be further from the truth; both sides played enthusiastically but sportingly in a game that was packed with incidents.

Sunderland came out for the second half determined to get on level terms and did so after six minutes. A brilliant goal by Arthur Bridgett did the trick. Receiving the ball in midfield he first went past Aitken and then McCombie and Carr before cracking in a shot that Lawrence had no chance of saving.

Encouraged by their success, Sunderland pushed forward and suddenly Newcastle found themselves under pressure. Twice the Wearsiders rattled the United crossbar from melees in front of the home goal. The Rokermen even scored at one point but had the effort disallowed for a foul on Lawrence. The infringement was not obvious with the goalmouth packed with players so the Magpies had a lucky escape.

Sunderland worked hard and gained their reward with another goal from the irrepressible Bridgett after 69 minutes. A raid down their right wing saw Billy Hogg play the ball to Jimmy Gemmell who placed his pass right in front of Bridgett who once again gave Lawrence no chance. The Wearsiders looked as if they were heading for victory. But Newcastle refused to give up and suddenly, with quarter of an hour to go, realised that Sunderland were tiring.

A scrappy goal 13 minutes from time brought United back on level terms. Naisby managed to stop an effort from Howie but was unable to get rid of the ball. Appleyard tried to force it home but his shot came out to Jackie Rutherford. It was a difficult chance but he succeeded where his team mates had failed.

Sunderland had shot their bolt and a rejuvenated Newcastle looked a different class. The Wearsiders were soon hanging on, praying for the final whistle. It was not to be. In the 82nd minute Bert Gosnell worked a fine opening as he went past Rhodes, leaving the full back on the deck, before sending a perfect pass to Rutherford who confidently stuck the ball past Naisby. The final nail in the Rokerites' coffin came three minutes from time when James Howie coolly dribbled his way through the dispirited visitors' defence to net United's fourth goal.

Newcastle probably deserved to win because they had been the better footballing side but Sunderland had given them a shock until the closing stages. Long serving Andy Aitken's injury was a bad one and he was to be out of action for six weeks, returning for only two more games before joining Middlesbrough as player/manager.

The win over Sunderland gave United a great start to a season that was to end with them lifting the league title.

The referee, T P Campbell, had been so impressed by the sporting attitude of both teams that he wrote to the Newcastle secretary, Frank Watt, asking him to pass on his appreciation to the players of both clubs. He said that their conduct called for the highest praise and that it was the very best and enjoyable match that he had ever refereed. He singled out James Howie for his exemplary conduct. No wonder he was nicknamed 'Gentleman Jim'.

Football League
Division 1
Sunderland 2 Newcastle United 0 (HT: 0-0)
20th March 1907
Roker Park
32,000

Sunderland: R Ward, E Rhodes, T Daykin, T S Tait, J McGhie, E McConnell, J E Raine, W Hogg [77], A McIntosh, G Holley [85], A Bridgett
Newcastle: W Kelsey, W McCracken (inj 84), A McCombie, A Gardner, F Speedie, P McWilliam, J Rutherford, J Howie, W Appleyard, H Brown, A Gosnell
Referee: T P Campbell (Blackburn)

NEWCASTLE WERE top of the league, five points clear of second placed Everton, but they went to Roker with team selection problems. Goalkeeper Lawrence and full back Carr had been injured in the previous league game against Aston Villa. There was a more than able deputy for Jack in Andy Mc-Combie but a replacement for the 'keeper was a different matter. United had to call on the inexperienced teenager Billy Kelsey, a recent signing from Boldon Star, as cover. It was the youngster's league debut – a baptism under fire if ever there was one. Sunderland had no such problems and were able to field a full-strength team.

Once again, extra trains were put on to provide almost a shuttle service between Newcastle and South Shields to Sunderland and Monkwearmouth stations but Newcastle, in view of their past difficulties, decided to take no chances with rail travel and went to Roker by road.

League Positions		Pos	Pl	Pts		Pos	Pl	Pts
Before:	Newcastle	1st	30	44	Sunderland	14th	27	27
After:	Newcastle	1st	31	44	Sunderland	11th	28	29

Appleyard started the game, playing towards the Fulwell End in bright, dazzling sunshine. Both sides set off at a hot pace and the best chance early on fell to Bridgett but he lifted his shot over the bar from six yards with only Kelsey to beat. Soon afterwards the Newcastle 'keeper did well to block a McIntosh shot but he fumbled the ball. McIntosh pounced again but Kelsey managed to scramble the ball away. Sunderland did most of the attacking with Newcastle relying on breakaways. Bert Gosnell threatened at times with runs down his wings and Brown should have done better when he sliced one shot wide with the home goal at his mercy. It was all square at half-time – probably a fair score.

Sunderland laid siege to the Newcastle goal when the game resumed and United had some narrow and lucky escapes. Some credit had to go to young

Billy Kelsey for keeping the Wearsiders at bay. The Magpies continued to look dangerous on the break and should have scored when James Howie played in Rutherford. The flying winger made a bee-line for goal and was almost through when McConnell brought him down. It was a blatant penalty. Up stepped McCracken to take it but, amidst mingled shouts of delight and groans of disappointment, he shot well wide.

United stayed level until 13 minutes to go. Raine did well on Sunderland's right wing and it was he who created the opening for George Holley to hit the crossbar from among a crowd of players. The ball flew straight up and everyone waited for it to come down into the crowded goalmouth. When it did so, Willie Hogg was there first and he gave Kelsey no chance. Some reports credited the goal to Angus McIntosh.

Newcastle threw everything on attack but the home defence restricted them to a string of corners – all fruitless. It was just not McCracken's day. He injured himself in tackling Holley six minutes from time and had to be carried off, Speedie going to full back.

A minute later Sunderland assured themselves of victory with a second goal. It came from an all out attack involving all five of the home forwards. George Holley had a comparatively simple task in scoring.

Sunderland were content to play out the closing minutes and, for their second half performance alone, were worthy winners. With better shooting, they would have won by a more comfortable margin.

Despite the defeat, Newcastle were still strong favourites to win the championship. Their finish to the campaign was no more than average with three wins, a draw and three defeats from their remaining seven games. But they were still to win the title by three points over Bristol City.

Having beaten Newcastle, Sunderland seemed to think that their season was over. They were to lose six of their next eight games although they were to finish with a couple of victories. These were enough to see them finish in a mid-table 10th position.

But spare a thought for Newcastle's young goalkeeper, Billy Kelsey. He was to make only one more league appearance (another defeat, 1-4 at Liverpool, in United's next match) in his entire career. Yet he had played quite well against Sunderland.

Football League
Division 1
Sunderland 2 Newcastle United 4 (HT: 2-3)
21st December 1907
Roker Park
30,000

Sunderland: R Ward, R Bonthron, T Daykin, T S Tait, H Low, E McConnell, W Hogg [**7**], G Holley, J Foster, S Raybould, A Bridgett [**29**]
Newcastle: J Lawrence, W McCracken, R Pudan, A Gardner, C Veitch [**9**], P McWilliam, J Rutherford [**4**], A Higgins, W Appleyard, F Speedie, G Wilson [**24, 89**]
Referee: A Hargreaves (Blackpool)

THE LOCAL rivals were encountering widely differing fortunes. Newcastle were high in the league, just three points behind second placed Sheffield Wednesday although eight adrift of runaway leaders Manchester United, and reaping a rich harvest of points. But Sunderland had fallen upon evil days and the shadow of relegation was looming. They had won only one game at home since early October and were now in second bottom place, three points above Birmingham although one only behind Sheffield United, Nottingham Forest and Middlesbrough.

United had won their last game 5-1 away to Liverpool and naturally fielded an unchanged side. They prepared for the derby at Redcar and travelled from there to Roker on the morning of the match.

Thus they avoided the chaos on the trains from Tyneside when thousands squeezed into the coaches, smashing windows as they crammed on board. Problems continued during the journey and when one train came to a halt half a mile from Monkwearmouth Station, the passengers' eagerness and enthusiasm got the better of them and they jumped off the train en masse and set off on a direct line for Roker Park.

League Positions	Pos	Pl	Pts		Pos	Pl	Pts
Before: Newcastle	3rd	17	21	Sunderland	19th	17	12
After: Newcastle	3rd	18	23	Sunderland	19th	18	12

The game lived up to expectations despite the heavy conditions. For Sunderland, victory was essential to try and ward off the growing threat of relegation. The opening minutes had the crowd breathless with excitement with both sides grabbing early goals.

After four minutes Peter McWilliam played a ball inside the Sunderland 18 yard line from 40 yards out. Daykin tried to let it run on to his 'keeper but Jackie Rutherford anticipated his ploy and darted forward between the two Sunderland men to score with a fine shot.

Three minutes later the Sunderland forwards all combined to bring the ball forward. A pass was played to Billy Hogg who scored with a fast angled shot with Lawrence partially unsighted. Newcastle retaliated within two minutes with an attack down their right wing. Alex Gardner beat Daykin before centring from the touchline. Higgins and Speedie let the ball run on and Appleyard left it to Colin Veitch who blasted home a first time shot from 25 yards.

Newcastle opened up a gap in the scoreline with a third goal after 24 minutes when Jackie Rutherford dribbled in, leaving both McConnell and Daykin behind before lifting an astute ball over a cluster of heads to George Wilson who headed home.

But Sunderland would not lie down and five minutes later they pulled a goal back again. Billy Hogg and George Holley combined to beat McWilliam and Pudan before crossing to Arthur Bridgett who volleyed into the far corner of the net from 20 yards.

There was just one goal between the teams at half-time but Newcastle had been the better team and deservedly held the lead. The scoreline, if anything, flattered Sunderland.

If Newcastle had been the better team in the first half, Sunderland held the upper hand in the second with Bridgett, Hogg and Holley all impressing. The United goal seemed to bear a charmed life with the home side coming close to equalising time and again. Low, Holley and Bridgett should all have scored and if Hogg had received better service, he would have undoubtedly have done so. But the Tyneside defence was resolute. United's attacks were few and far between although Higgins should have put the game beyond Sunderland's reach when he broke through only to try and walk the ball into the Sunderland net and was dispossessed.

There were only seconds remaining when a crucial final goal was scored and it was Newcastle who grabbed it. Some enterprising play by Sandy Higgins cunningly deceived the home defence before he laid off a pass to George Wilson who scored a similar goal to Bridgett's. Final score: 2-4.

The scoreline flattered Newcastle. Sunderland deserved at least a point for their second half performance alone. Defeat was a serious blow to them. It meant that they were now just one point ahead of bottom placed Birmingham and two behind third bottom Chelsea with the last two teams in the league relegated. A long, hard battle lay ahead.

The win for Newcastle meant that they closed the gap on second placed Sheffield Wednesday to one point but they were still eight adrift of leaders Manchester United. The Magpies were to lose only one of their next 13 league games but, incredibly, to draw nine of the other 12. This ensured that they were never to make any impression on the league leaders.

Football League
Division 1
Newcastle United 1 Sunderland 3 (HT: 0-1)
18th April 1908
St James' Park
50,000

Newcastle: J Lawrence, A McCombie, J Carr, A Gardner, C Veitch, D Willis, A S Duncan, J Howie [80], W Appleyard, F Speedie, A Gosnell
Sunderland: L R Roose, E A Marples, H Forster, T S Tait, H Low [57], G Jarvie, A McIntosh, W Hogg, S Raybould, G Holley [40], A Bridgett [65]
Referee: A Hargreaves (Blackpool)

THIS GAME took place on Easter Saturday and its timing could not have been worse for Newcastle – one week before they were due to face Wolverhampton Wanderers in the Cup Final. Although second top of the league, United were well adrift of Manchester United who were already champions.

There were doubts as to whether the Newcastle directors would adopt a 'safety first' approach in their team selection and exclude most of their first team players. Both United and Sunderland delayed naming their teams until after their Good Friday games. Sunderland made only one change, actually strengthening their team by bringing in Angus McIntosh in place of Hurdman on the right wing.

Newcastle protected quite a few of their players, making four changes to their line-up. In fact only six of the team that were to appear in the Cup Final faced Sunderland in the local derby.

League Positions		Pos	Pl	Pts		Pos	Pl	Pts
Before:	Newcastle	2nd	36	42	Sunderland	13th	36	33
After:	Newcastle	2nd	37	42	Sunderland	11th	37	35

The game lacked the usual competitive edge largely because Newcastle fielded a weakened team. Those who turned out for the Magpies seemed as much concerned with avoiding injury rather than putting wholehearted effort into their games. The Rokermen could afford to devote their entire combined attentions towards victory in this match – and it showed. A gale force wind blew the length of the field and did not help matters but Sunderland seemed to deal with the conditions without too much trouble. Surprisingly, both sides played better facing the elements. Appleyard, Howie and Duncan were a menace for Newcastle but Tait, Low, Marples and Forster were equal to everything thrown at them and Roose was seldom troubled. For Sunderland, George Holley was their star player. He was a real thorn in the side of the home defence.

It looked like the first half was going to be goalless when Sunderland grabbed the lead five minutes before the interval. Willie Hogg and Sam Raybould combined to bring the ball forward before it went to Holley. He broke past McCombie to create an opening before blasting a glorious drive that gave Lawrence no chance.

Sunderland had the gale in their favour in the second half and it looked as if they were going to run away with the match when they went two up after 57 minutes.

A melee in the Newcastle goal area ended with McCombie heading out only for the ball to fall to Harry Low who cracked a shot at goal from distance. He was credited with the goal but the ball may have gained a deflection off Arthur Bridgett before flying past Lawrence.

Newcastle tried to hit back and both Howie and Gosnell wasted opportunities before Sunderland struck again. The goal was a brilliant solo effort by Arthur Bridgett who raced past McCombie before touching it wide of the advancing Lawrence and tucking it away; 0-3 after 65 minutes.

With the game obviously won, Sunderland could afford to ease off and Newcastle came into it more. This did not stop Raybould from scoring another but he was clearly offside.

James Howie similarly looked well offside (about three yards according to some reports) when he scored United's consolation goal from right in front of the posts with ten minutes remaining. Roose managed to get a touch as the ball flew past him but was unable to keep it out. Nevertheless, everyone was surprised when the referee allowed the goal to stand.

Newcastle were well on top at the final whistle but Sunderland were worthy winners. The two points virtually guaranteed Sunderland's survival in the league. They could even afford to lose their last game away to Bristol City and still finish two points clear of the drop.

The very end of the season turned sour for Newcastle. Not only did they lose this Tyne-Wear derby but they also lost away to Middlesbrough in their final league game as well as succumbing to Second Division Wolverhampton Wanderers in the Cup Final. Although they had been second top of the league since before Christmas, defeat in their last two league games saw Aston Villa and Manchester City sneak past them and they finished fourth. A classic case of so near yet so far.

Football League
Division 1
Newcastle United 1 Sunderland 9 (HT: 1-1)
5th December 1908
St James' Park
56,000

Newcastle: J Lawrence, A Whitson (inj 70), R Pudan, R Liddell, C Veitch, D Willis, A S Duncan (inj 85), A Higgins, A Shepherd [**44** pen], G Wilson, A Gosnell
Sunderland: L R Roose, H Forster, A Milton, T Daykin, C Thomson, H Low, J Mordue [**73**], W Hogg [**8, 58, 77**], A S Brown, G Holley [**47, 62, 67**], A Bridgett [**69, 71**]
Referee: A E Farrant (Bristol)

NEWCASTLE, LYING second in the league, had surprisingly lost to Aston Villa in their previous home game two weeks earlier. Controversially, the directors had dropped half of their stars for the following game away to Nottingham Forest and the reserves brought in had done themselves proud with a 4-0 win. The directors decided to rely on this inexperienced team for the crucial local derby match that attracted a record crowd to St James' Park.

Thousands were locked out. It was not until the teams appeared that it was realised how much bigger physically the Sunderland players were than their Tyneside opponents. "A striking disparity in the stature and weight of the opposing teams" reported the press at the time. Newcastle played in their change strip of white shirts with black cuffs and collars.

League Positions		Pos	Pl	Pts		Pos	Pl	Pts
Before:	Newcastle	2nd	15	21	Sunderland	6th	15	16
After:	Newcastle	2nd	16	21	Sunderland	6th	16	18

The record crowd saw some sparkling football in a first half that was full of pace, spirit and incident, with Sunderland scoring in their first meaningful attack after eight minutes. Jackie Mordue beat Pudan on the wing and slipped the ball to Billy Hogg who advanced on goal as Lawrence rushed out and drove the ball low into the net.

The rest of the first half was close with both sides creating scoring chances and little indication of what was to come. The crucial moment came when Thomson sent Shepherd (making his home debut) flying on to the cinder track surrounding the pitch. The centre forward had to leave the pitch for treatment and the Sunderland defender was warned by the referee. But when he returned, Shepherd was limping badly and was virtually a passenger after that. Liddell was also injured in the opening half and was left hobbling for the rest of the game.

Newcastle equalised with a debatable penalty a minute before the interval when the Sunderland captain, Charlie Thomson, was adjudged to have handled in the penalty area. The referee consulted his linesman before awarding the spot kick which Albert Shepherd confidently converted. The level scoreline was probably a fair reflection of play in the first half.

It was evident that Newcastle were handicapped as the second half started with Shepherd limping painfully and Liddell also struggling. Sunderland made another great start. Two minutes had gone when Arthur Bridgett and George Holley combined in a break away before the latter unleashed a long drive that left Lawrence helpless.

Newcastle laid siege to the Sunderland goal but were further handicapped when Whitson was badly hurt ten minutes into the half. He could hardly walk after that and, with their wing halves outpaced and Pudan grossly overworked, Newcastle collapsed. Holley almost made it 3-1 when he broke away again only to hit a post. Then came the avalanche.

After 58 minutes Jackie Mordue easily evaded a half-hearted tackle from Pudan before creating the opening for Hogg to score Sunderland's third.

By now those Newcastle players who were not struggling with injury were dispirited and United fell to pieces. Sunderland were completely on top and it soon became a question of 'how many?' United, and their supporters, were soon to find out.

Four minutes later Holley raced between the Newcastle backs to make it 4-1 from close range. Then came four goals in ten minutes. Newcastle were being over-run and Holley soon completed his hat-trick, converting a Mordue centre. It was becoming too easy.

Then Arthur Bridgett ghosted past the distressed Whitson to score the sixth. By this time the South African born full back could hardly walk and he hobbled off the field to the dressing room. Veitch dropped back to full back but this meant that United's midfield, already handicapped by Liddell's injury, lost what little bite they had.

The goals continued to come fast and furious. Bridgett grabbed the seventh with a cracking shot from distance. Almost everything Sunderland tried succeeded.

After 73 minutes Jackie Mordue got on the scoresheet, beating the exhausted Pudan before making it 8-1.

Finally, after 77 minutes, Billy Hogg completed his hat-trick and the rout when he scored Sunderland's ninth.

Scott Duncan was knocked out in the closing stages and carried off to the dressing room on the back of the trainer. By now it was not so much 'men against boys' but rather 'giants against pygmies' (and depleted pygmies at that) and hundreds of Newcastle supporters were leaving the ground. When the final whistle was blown, Newcastle's day of disaster was complete and their seven 'fit' men (now near to exhaustion) and their two badly injured colleagues staggered off the field to leave the spoils of victory to their arch-rivals.

This was undoubtedly the most amazing result in Tyne-Wear football history. Rival factions alternately criticised and defended the Newcastle directors for their team selection. The press at the time reported that this was Newcastle's record defeat. But it wasn't. They had lost 9-0 away to Burton Wanderers in the Second Division back in 1895 – but that would have been scant consolation for the Newcastle supporters even if they had been aware of it.

But Sunderland were to get a little taste of their own medicine later in the season, losing 8-1 to Blackburn Rovers. Newcastle, to their credit, recovered from this setback to regain top spot in the league and eventually win the championship. They also reached the semi-final of the Cup, eliminating Sunderland on the way. But these achievements would be largely forgotten with the passage of time; the 9-1 defeat at St James' would never be.

FA Cup
4th round
Newcastle United 2 Sunderland 2 (HT: 2-2)
6th March 1909
St James' Park
53,353

Newcastle: J Lawrence, W McCracken, A Whitson, J Howie, C Veitch, P McWilliam, J Rutherford [**14**], A Higgins, A Shepherd, G Wilson [**33**], A Anderson
Sunderland: L R Roose, H Forster, A Milton, T S Tait, C Thomson, H Low, W Hogg, G Holley, A S Brown [**32**], A Bridgett, J Mordue [**15**]
Referee: J Mason (Burslem)

SURPRISINGLY, CONSIDERING that Newcastle were top of the league, Sunderland were the more fancied side to win the tie. This was probably due to their emphatic win at St James' in the league earlier in the season coupled with the fact that United had not looked too impressive in eliminating Second Division Blackpool and non-league West Ham in their earlier rounds. But Sunderland had won each of their previous three ties only by the odd goal although they had all been away from home.

Persistent sleet and snow did not deter supporters from queuing from 10.00am at the 6d enclosure gates. Although they were drenched, the massive crowd was in good humour. Despite a liberal covering of sand, the pitch was very heavy.

Although the playing conditions were appalling, both teams served up a classic cup tie, described at the time as one of the best matches ever seen – hard and determined, with no little skill, and played with a sporting attitude by both sides. Newcastle adapted quicker to the conditions and gained the upper hand before opening the scoring after 14 minutes. Colin Veitch sent a free kick into the Sunderland penalty area where Milton blocked it only for Jackie Rutherford to pounce and flash a shot across Roose into the net.

The Newcastle supporters' joy was short-lived as within a minute Arthur Bridgett and Jackie Mordue immediately counter attacked up their wing. Mordue centred from 40 yards and Whitson left it for Lawrence to collect. The 'keeper was mortified to see the ball slip through his hands and roll through his legs into the net.

A hard and fast game ensued with both sides attacking at every opportunity. Sunderland were generally on top but Newcastle created the better chances with Sandy Higgins grazing the Sunderland bar.

But it was Sunderland who went in front after 32 minutes. Billy Hogg centred and Arthur Brown ran in to blast a shot goalwards. Lawrence saved but could not hold the ball and Brown, following up, netted the rebound to score the best goal of the match.

But now it was Newcastle's turn to retaliate immediately. George Wilson won possession from the hesitant Sunderland backs and equalised as Roose ran out in vain to try and block him. Newcastle were the main aggressors from then until the interval.

Both sides continued to throw everything into attack after the break although the pace of the first half could not be maintained. Anderson twisted his knee and had to leave the field for treatment. He eventually returned but he was clearly labouring and by this time Rutherford was also limping badly. With both wingers injured, Newcastle's forward line was nowhere near as effective as it had been in the first half and Sunderland were on top until the final whistle.

Both sides left Gallowgate apparently satisfied with the result. Newcastle were pleased to have survived despite playing part of the game with two passengers. Sunderland were delighted to take their neighbours back to Roker. The Sunderland public deserved to see a cup tie at home after being drawn away in all four rounds so far this season. Although the crowd at St James' was not a record, the gate receipts (£2,521) were.

The Fastest Sub

Michael Chopra's goal for Newcastle on April 17th 2006 was timed at 13 seconds after coming on to the pitch and is the fastest goal by a substitute in Wear-Tyne derbies. It is also believed to be the quickest goal by a substitute in Premier League history.

FA Cup
4th round replay
Sunderland 0 Newcastle United 3 (HT: 0-1)
10th March 1909
Roker Park
27,512

Sunderland: L R Roose, H Forster, H Low, T S Tait, C Thomson, G Jarvie, W Hogg, G Holley, A S Brown, A Bridgett, J Mordue
Newcastle: J Lawrence, W McCracken, A Whitson, J Howie, C Veitch, P McWilliam, A S Duncan, A Higgins, A Shepherd [**79, 88**], J Stewart, G Wilson [**7**]
Referee: J T Ibbotson (Derby)

SLEET AND rain had fallen virtually without a break since the first game and the replay was also played in appalling conditions.

Sunderland were heavily criticised for doubling their admission prices to a maximum of 5s 0d for seats and a minimum of 1s 0d for a place on the terraces. The club explained that they were heavily in debt and needed the money. Their policy paid dividends with new record gate receipts of £1,979 – a full £732 above the previous record.

Hundreds of unemployed men were recruited to stop spectators breaking into the ground but a large number stormed the barricades and gained admittance, seriously injuring a policeman and over a dozen other people in the process.

Merciless rain and sleet drenched most of the crowd but Newcastle adapted immediately to the conditions and took the game to the Wearsiders.

Albert Shepherd did the spadework for George Wilson to score the first goal after seven minutes although the winger had to take the ball around Forster before shooting low past Roose from a narrow angle.

Newcastle clearly had the upper hand for the rest of the first half and the one surprising thing was that they failed to increase their lead before the interval.

Sunderland rearranged their front line by switching their inside forwards and wingers on both flanks. This strengthened their attack considerably and the Tynesiders were forced to defend in depth for long periods.

The turning point came with 20 minutes left. The Rokermen were awarded a penalty when McCracken clearly pushed Arthur Brown inside the penalty box as he was breaking through. The centre forward took the spot kick himself but Jimmy Lawrence saved well.

Within nine minutes Jimmy Stewart played a fine forward pass to Albert Shepherd who set off on a foray up front from within his own half. He beat Forster and outpaced Low before blasting a shot past Roose from only eight yards.

Sunderland tired dramatically and with two minutes left, Shepherd broke away again from the half-way line. He once more held off Low's attempts to challenge as he converged on goal before tucking his shot just inside an upright.

Newcastle were worthy winners, a fact readily acknowledged by the Sunderland players who accepted their defeat 'in a manner becoming true sportsmen'. They wished Newcastle (who were now through to the semi-final) every success in their efforts to bring the FA Cup to the North East for the first time.

The referee, Mr Ibbotson, came in for special praise. Neither team wanted a change of referee for the replay. Both clubs had asked for Mr Mason, the referee who officiated in the first game, but his employers would not release him from work.

Hundreds of supporters crowded Newcastle Central Station to welcome their team when they arrived home at 8.30pm. Newcastle, however, would have to wait for another year for cup final success. They went out this season in the semi-final, defeated by the only goal of the match by eventual cup winners Manchester United.

Football League
Division 1
Sunderland 3 Newcastle United 1 (HT: 0-1)
10th April 1909
Roker Park
27,493

Sunderland: L R Roose, H Forster, A Milton, T S Tait, C Thomson, G Jarvie, J Mordue, H Low, A S Brown [47, 50], G Holley [73], A Bridgett
Newcastle: J Lawrence, W McCracken, A Whitson, J Howie, C Veitch, P McWilliam, J Rutherford, J Stewart, A Shepherd [1] (inj 45), G Wilson, A Anderson
Referee: D Hammond (Heywood)

NEWCASTLE HAD an impressive unbeaten sequence in the league behind them – since December. Indeed, their one defeat in their last 19 matches had been that narrow 1-0 slip up against Manchester United in the semi-final of the Cup.

But Sunderland were also a good side as their third place in the league testified. They were just two places behind the Magpies but, with only four games to go and two points for a win, they knew that they could not catch their neighbours. However, local pride was a big enough incentive to perform.

League Positions		Pos	Pl	Pts		Pos	Pl	Pts
Before:	Newcastle	1st	32	49	Sunderland	3rd	34	38
After:	Newcastle	1st	33	49	Sunderland	3rd	35	40

The game was played in brilliant sunshine, conditions more suitable for cricket than football and Newcastle's start was just as perfect.

In the first minute, Albert Shepherd gained possession near the half-way line and set off for the Sunderland goal closely pursued by Jarvie. However the centre forward could not be caught and, although Roose dived full length to try and stop his shot, he failed to gauge the fight of the ball and it ended in the net.

But the goal was to prove disastrous for both Newcastle and Shepherd who was badly hurt in scoring. He was carried off for treatment and, although he returned after five minutes, he was clearly struggling with his injury. Both sides had chances but the score remained unchanged until half-time.

Shepherd was unable to come out for the second half and ten men Newcastle soon found themselves in arrears.

After two minutes Jackie Mordue gave the ball to Arthur Brown who tried a hard shot at goal from outside the penalty area. Lawrence got his hands to the ball but could not hold it and it ended in the net.

Three minutes later a Sunderland corner found Arthur Bridgett who touched the ball off to Brown and he drove it hard and sharp into the net for his second goal.

A great run by Brown after 73 minutes saw him beat Howie and McCracken near the half-way line. He reached the Newcastle penalty area but was tripped by Whitson as he tried to go around him. Holley took the resultant penalty kick and, although Lawrence managed to block it, George followed up to net the rebound.

Sunderland continued to have the upper hand in the closing stages and actually had a goal disallowed a couple of minutes from time when Brown netted again only to be ruled offside. As he had run almost 50 yards before the whistle had been blown, he had reason to feel aggrieved at having his hat-trick goal ruled out.

Sunderland had reason to celebrate completing a league double over their neighbours although Newcastle felt, with some justification, that Shepherd's critical injury had a great deal to do with the Wearside successes.

Consolation was swift for United. On Easter Monday, two days after the Roker game, they met second top Everton at St James' Park and clinched the League Championship by virtue of a 3-0 win. Sunderland finished in a highly respectable third place.

Football League
Division 1
Sunderland 0 Newcastle United 2 (HT: 0-1)
18th September 1909
Roker Park
40,000

Sunderland: L R Roose, H Forster, A Milton, T S Tait, C Thomson, G Jarvie, J W Thompson, G Holley, A S Brown, J Mordue, A Bridgett
Newcastle: J Lawrence, W McCracken, A Whitson, G Jobey, C Veitch, W Low, J Rutherford, J Stewart [14], A Shepherd [88], G Wilson, A Gosnell
Referee: J Mason (Burslem)

BOTH SIDES had made quite good starts to the season. Newcastle may have been higher in the league but Sunderland were hot on their heels with a couple of games in hand – and they were unbeaten as well.

Not unnaturally, the Wearsiders were unchanged. In fact they had fielded the same team in all of their games so far. Newcastle made one change to their side that had lost at home to Nottingham Forest in their last game, James 'Tadger' Stewart coming in for James Howie. United had been criticised for their lack of fitness against Forest but this had largely been due to the fact that they had just returned from their 'Lancashire tour' when they had played three league games in four days.

A record crowd turned up at Roker and there was feeling that the attendance was dangerously over capacity. The terraces were so crammed that the spectators were forced on to the playing area time and time again. This seriously hampered play and tempers became frayed when the police tried to force the crowd back. More than once conflict with the constabulary threatened to break out.

League Positions		Pos	Pl	Pts		Pos	Pl	Pts
Before:	Newcastle	4th	5	6	Sunderland	5th	3	5
After:	Newcastle	1st	6	8	Sunderland	10th	4	5

Sunderland attacked first and both Holley and Thompson launched themselves at a cross by Mordue in front of the posts and both ended up in the net – but the ball didn't. Jackie Rutherford gave the Wearsiders a warning with a volley that merely cleared their bar by inches.

Just before the quarter hour Bert Gosnell centred and Milton miskicked an attempted clearance. Albert Shepherd and Dick Roose raced for the ball, the Newcastle centre forward just getting there first. His shot on the run cannoned off the 'keeper's legs and rebounded straight to Jimmy Stewart who calmly lobbed it into the untenanted net.

Both sides pushed forward and Sunderland came desperately close to grabbing an equaliser when both Arthur Bridgett (who was carrying a knee injury) and Jackie Mordue tried volleys at goal only to see their efforts come back off a Newcastle upright. United forced a series of corners and when Gosnell took his, a lane had to be cleared in the crowd to allow him to run up.

After half an hour the game was stopped for ten minutes to allow the police to force the crowd back off the pitch. One particularly large spectator overstepped the mark in his resistance and was forcibly led away by two policemen. This enraged a certain section of the crowd and mounted police were brought out to subdue them. Eventually they were driven back but not before one of the police horses was reportedly stabbed!

Newcastle took control when the game resumed with Rutherford and Stewart both causing problems for the Roker rearguard.

So much time had been wasted in the first half due to crowd encroachment, that the referee refused to let the band come on at half-time but merely instructed the teams to change ends and resume the game. Newcastle were well on top early in this half when Shepherd went close on a couple of occasions. But during a Sunderland counter-attack Lawrence was penalised for taking too many steps with the ball. George Holley took the free kick and blasted the ball home. Unfortunately for him, his goal was disallowed because it was an indirect kick and no-one touched the ball before it went in. When Roose was similarly penalised for the same offence soon afterwards, Rutherford took the kick and merely tapped it to Stewart. His shot beat Roose but whizzed past a post. Despite their superiority, Newcastle were still ahead only 1-0 until two minutes before the end.

Then George Wilson started a move that ended with Bert Gosnell transferring the ball to Albert Shepherd who dribbled past three defenders before scoring with a low, hard shot.

There had undoubtedly been too many people allowed in to Roker Park and the overcrowding was just asking for trouble. The police were naturally concerned that one of their horses had been stabbed and they offered £5 reward to try and identify the culprit. On Wearside after the match, however, it was asserted that the wound or scar could have been accidentally caused by the horse scraping against something sharp like a metal railing. In either case the horse was not badly hurt.

As regards the game itself, Newcastle were worthy winners and the 2-0 scoreline certainly did not flatter them. The win lifted them to the top of the league but it was to be a solitary visit to such heady heights this season. They were soon to slip down, winning just one of their next four league games. They were not to have a bad league campaign but their glory lay in the cup (at last!). Sunderland were to have a similar season league season of mixed fortunes – reasonable, but not good enough to challenge for honours.

Football League
Division 1
Newcastle United 1 Sunderland 0 (HT: 0-0)
13th April 1910
St James' Park
40,000

Newcastle: J Lawrence, W McCracken, J Carr, C Veitch, W Low, J Finlay, A S Duncan, J Howie, A Shepherd, A Higgins [86], G Wilson
Sunderland: T Allan, W Troughear, H Forster, T S Tait, C Thomson, G Jarvie, J Mordue, W Clark, H Low, G Holley, A Bridgett
Referee: W C Clover (Leicester)

THIS WAS a game that had been postponed in January when St James' Park had been icebound. It was a second benefit match for acting skipper Colin Veitch who was filling the captain's role since Alex Gardner had been injured over a year earlier. Colin was guaranteed a minimum of £500.

Newcastle went into the game with half an eye on the Cup Final against Barnsley which was only ten days away. Although United were fourth in the league and had games in hand, Aston Villa were nine points clear at the top and a League-Cup double was not a realistic target.

An unusual feature of the game was that Harry Low, normally a central defender, led the attack for Sunderland and was in direct opposition to his brother Wilf, centre half for Newcastle. Sunderland had only local pride to play for. They were just one point behind the Magpies and a win would see them leapfrog their neighbours. That was enough incentive.

Promises of uncertain weather on the afternoon of the match affected the gate. Although the attendance of 40,000 was respectable enough, it was a long way short from the massive crowds of recent seasons. It so happened that the weather stayed fine and those who stayed away missed a classic – hard and fast with plenty of excitement.

League Positions		Pos	Pl	Pts		Pos	Pl	Pts
Before:	Newcastle	4th	33	40	Sunderland	8th	34	39
After:	Newcastle	3rd	34	42	Sunderland	8th	35	39

There was plenty of lusty charging but it was all of a legitimate character. Press reports commented upon the sportsmanlike nature of the game. Sunderland started off stronger and held the upper hand for the first 20 minutes but Newcastle held them out and came into the game more after that. The clash between the Low brothers was a closely fought affair but the Newcastle man generally came out on top. United went closest to scoring in a goalless opening session when a scorching drive by Sandy Higgins hit the Sunderland crossbar. The rebound went straight to James Howie who also tried a shot only to see it deflected for a corner. Play flowed from end-to-end although goalscoring chances were at a premium and half-time arrived with the scoresheet blank.

Newcastle took up the running after the interval and it was Sunderland's turn to fall back on defence. Shots rained in on Allan's goal and Howie struck a post early in the half. United's greater pace and endurance gradually wore the Rokermen down. Shepherd and Higgins combined to create an opening for Sandy to score but the roar of the crowd was silenced when they realised that the whistle had already gone for offside. It soon became a matter of whether Sunderland could hang on until the final whistle. Just when it seemed that they might, Newcastle scored with four minutes left.

Albert Shepherd broke away up the right wing and, after a tussle with Forster, whipped in a short, sharp cross from the bye-line. It was too fast for Allan and Sandy Higgins, who was standing unmarked in the middle, had time to control the ball before tucking it away – a comparatively simple goal.

As they say, it had been a game of two halves with little to choose between the sides before the interval but Newcastle had been clearly the better side late on. The final score was a fair one.

This was the first time that Newcastle had completed a league double over their Wearside rivals so there was extra reason for the Geordie supporters to celebrate. They had even greater reason to enjoy themselves a couple of weeks later when United lifted the FA Cup for the first time, albeit after a replay against Barnsley. They were to finish only fourth in the league but the fact that they picked up seven points out of eight from their North East derby games (v Sunderland and Middlesbrough) was good enough for most supporters.

Sunderland finished in a respectable eighth position but this seemed like failure compared to United's successes.

Home from Home

In April 1903, Roker Park was closed by the FA for crowd misbehaviour. So Sunderland, who were challenging for the league title, played their last 'home' game of the season at St James' Park, defeating Middlesbrough, 2-1. The Rokermen had just one game left to play – away to Newcastle. A win would have given them the league title but they lost 1-0.

Player of the Decade 1900s

Andrew McCombie

THERE ARE certain sporting records that will last for all time. While most are there to be broken, someone who achieves something for the first time attains a level of immortality in the record books. Roger Bannister, for instance, was the first man to break the four minute mile barrier. There have been many athletes who have now done this, most of them a good deal faster than the doctor. But his name will live forever more in sporting annals.

Similarly Floyd Patterson was the first man to regain the heavyweight championship of the world. Few (if any) would regard him as the greatest heavyweight boxer of all time and others have repeated his feat (Muhammad Ali regained the title twice). But Patterson was the first to do it and no-one can take that away from him.

So it is with Andy McCombie. He was the first man to be capped for his country while playing for both Sunderland and Newcastle United. Others have received the same distinction but he was the first. For good measure, he won the league title with both clubs as well and that is a unique achievement.

But rarely can a player at one stage in his career have been so reviled in one camp and yet revered in the other. To understand how this came about, we have to look back over his career. It was Sunderland who spotted his talents in 1898. At 22 years of age, he was beginning to gain a bit of a reputation as a skilful yet powerful full back with his home town team of Inverness Thistle. Sunderland saw him as a player who could develop into a top class defender and help bolster a team that had finished as runners-up to Sheffield United the previous season but were seemingly unable to build on that fine achievement.

He was not the finished article when he came to Sunderland's new ground at Roker Park. Indeed, he did not make his debut until he had been on Wearside for a couple of months, only getting his initial run-out away to Sheffield Wednesday because his predecessor, Phil Bach, was playing for England against Ireland in the first international to be played at Roker. This was to be the only cap of Phil's career but a 13-2 win was not a bad way to mark it!

By the end of the season, McCombie was the first choice right back and Sunderland were so confident in his abilities that they felt able to let Bach join local rivals Middlesbrough.

Their confidence was well founded as Andy was to serve the club with distinction over the next five years, gaining recognition from Scotland in 1903 when he was capped against Wales and England. The Scots won both games and they were both away from home! The North East connections with the team that beat

England are amazing. Not only did the Scottish side include the Sunderland rear-guard of Teddy Doig, McCombie and Jimmy Watson but also Andy Aitken and Bobby Templeton from Newcastle as well as Finlay Speedie who was later to join the Magpies.

But more important as far as the Sunderland supporters were concerned was the fact that this Scottish defensive trio, along with centre half Sandy McAllister (another Scottish international), formed the foundation of the side that delivered the league title to Roker during the 1901-02 season.

Everything in the garden looked rosy until an incident happened that shook the Wearside club to its very foundations – and Andy McCombie was at the heart of it. Incredibly, the root cause of the problem came about because of the generosity of the Sunderland directors. In the summer of 1903 they gave McCombie £100 to help him to purchase stock for a pianoforte business that he was starting. Unfortunately Andy came to regard this as a gift but the club meant it to be a loan. After completing five years with the club, he was granted a benefit (which was usual at the time) and made a handsome profit. The club expected the 'loan' to be repaid from this sum. He was not expecting them to ask for it back and refused to pay!

The matter came to a head at the end of January 1904 when Andy was dropped from the team that travelled to Blackburn Rovers for a league game. More importantly, he was excluded from the squad that underwent special training at Seaton Carew in preparation for a cup tie away to Manchester City on the following weekend. The rift between the player and the club quickly developed into a chasm and it quickly became apparent that McCombie's days at Roker were numbered. Clubs immediately queued up to procure the signature of a player who was now regarded as one of the best full backs in the country. The likes of Aston Villa, Derby County, Liverpool and Everton all lined up to sign him, as did Glasgow giants, Rangers and Celtic. So it was somewhat galling for the Wearside supporters when he opted to make the short journey up the road to St James' Park. The problem was that he had been made so welcome in the North East, he just did not want to leave the region. Newcastle had to fork out a world record transfer fee of £700 to get him but it was to be money well spent.

The 'loan/gift' dispute eventually ended up in the courts where it was ruled that the money was indeed a loan and not a gift. Not only did McCombie have to repay the money but he also had to pay the £76 legal costs.

Both parties were to lose in the end because the Football Association were far from happy with the decision or the situation. The ruling body expressed sympathy with McCombie and decided to investigate Sunderland's books. Defalcations were discovered with the club found to have made illicit payments to their players in terms of re-signing fees and win/draw bonuses. McCombie understood that the £100 had been such a payment.

Sunderland were hit with a hefty fine (for the day) of £250 and six of their directors were suspended for two-and-a-half years. In addition, financial secretary Alex Watson was suspended for eighteen months and team manager Alec Mackie for three. As a consequence, the club was plunged into crisis and, reputedly, it very nearly went under. However, as history shows, it survived and eventually recovered. But McCombie was widely blamed on Wearside for the situation. Meanwhile, at St James' Park, Newcastle went from strength to strength and Andy was one of the stars of a team in the ascendancy. He was a defensive stalwart at Gallowgate during United's league championship successes of 1904-05 and 1906-07 as well as playing in two FA Cup Finals (1905 & 1906). He also played a minor part when the club won the league title in 1908-09 but by then he was no longer a first choice player.

By that time, however, he had added another couple of caps to his collection, playing for Scotland against Wales and England in 1905. It was strange that all of his international appearances came in away games.

His last first team league appearance for Newcastle was in April 1910 and he retired as a player at the end of that season. But that was not the end of his career at Gallowgate. He went on to serve the club in various capacities, including that of trainer for a while in the 1920s, until he eventually retired in 1950 when he was approaching his 74th birthday. He died on his adopted Tyneside two years later.

In his prime, Andrew McCombie was not only one of the best full backs in the country but he was also a supreme team player, forming brilliantly effective defensive partnerships with Jim Watson at Sunderland and both Jack Carr and Bill McCracken at Newcastle. United also discovered how versatile he was and that he could be equally at home on the left flank as on the right.

When they paid a record transfer fee for him, Newcastle easily received value for money. Sunderland's loss was Newcastle's gain. One just wonders what would have happened if the Wearside directors had not been so generous with their loan – or perhaps had been clearer when the gift had been given. We will never know.

Record

Sunderland	December 1898 – February 1904	
Football League	157 apps	6 gls
FA Cup	7 apps	0 gls
Others	1 app	0 gls
Total	165 apps	6 gls

Newcastle	February 1904 – April 1910	
Football League	113 apps	0 gls
FA Cup	18 apps	0 gls
Total	131 apps	0 gls

The Successful Part Timer

Shola Ameobi has appeared in six Tyne-Wear derbies and has never lost. But he has never played the full 90 minutes in any of these games.

CHAPTER 3

1910s
Changing Fortunes

WITH THE end of the Edwardian Era, Newcastle's Golden Age similarly came to a close. It had reached its zenith with eventual success in the FA Cup in 1910 and, although they reached the final again in the following year and, indeed, finished third in the league in 1912, gradual decline set in.

Sunderland soon took over as the Cocks of the North and enjoyed their most successful season of the century in 1913 when they finished as League Champions and almost won the Cup as well, losing only to a single Aston Villa goal in the final. Perhaps it was fate that the goal should have been scored by North East born Tommy Barber.

But there was to be no Golden Age for Sunderland. Indeed, both the Tyne and Wear rivals had to give way to Middlesbrough as the regional top dogs in the 1913-14 season, the first time that the 'big two' had failed to live up to their self-perceived status.

Although Sunderland were clearly the best team in the North East during the half decade before the world slipped into the tragedy of Armageddon, it was Newcastle who came out on top in head-to-head meetings with their neighbours, winning five and losing three of the ten league encounters. Sunderland, however, emerged victorious in an epic three-game tie in the FA Cup.

Sadly, many players from both sides had their football careers decimated by the First World War. Tragically some failed to survive the conflict, paying the supreme sacrifice in a world seemingly gone mad.

When competitive football resumed at the end of the War, there were naturally many changes at both clubs. They were both to enjoy the heady delights of a top five place when they met in back to back encounters in 1919 although a league double success for Sunderland quickly brought the Geordies down to earth. Nevertheless there was optimism on both Tyneside and Wearside that happy days lay ahead as a new era began.

League Meetings (10)

At Newcastle:	Newcastle – won 2	Drew 2	Lost 2
At Sunderland:	Sunderland – won 3	Drew 0	Lost 3

Cup Meetings (3)

At Newcastle:	Newcastle – won 0	Drew 1	Lost 1
At Sunderland:	Sunderland – won 0	Drew 1	Lost 0

Football League
Division 1
Sunderland 2 Newcastle United 1 (HT: 1-0)
1st September 1910
Roker Park
30,000

Sunderland: L R Roose, W Troughear, A Milton, T S Tait, C Thomson, H Low, J Mordue, J G Coleman [**87**], G Holley [**32**], J Gemmell, A Bridgett
Newcastle: J Lawrence, W McCracken, A Whitson, C Veitch, W Low, P McWilliam, J Rutherford, J Stewart, A Shepherd [**80** pen], A Higgins, G Wilson
Referee: T P Campbell (Blackburn)

THIS WAS the first game of the season which, for competitive games, was not allowed to start before the beginning of September. Consequently the match was staged on a Thursday evening with a 5.30pm kick-off (gates opened at 4.30). Thousands of begrimed workmen turned up straight from work.

The game was played against a background of controversy. The Players' Union had been established for only a year and was trying to 'encourage' all players to join it. The Union applied to the Football League for permission for its members to wear armbands during games bearing the words "Players' Union". The League Executive refused as it was felt that the action could intimidate those players who were not members. The players defiantly went ahead and wore the armbands anyway.

The derby game also saw an innovation – the introduction of a rubber ball. The design was the same as a leather one but the casing was rubber with a base of linen or cotton fabric (a bit like a bicycle tyre). Such a ball was supposed to be impervious to water and, unlike leather balls in wet conditions that became heavier as the game went on, the weight of the new ball would remain unaltered.

League Positions		Pos	Pl	Pts		Pos	Pl	Pts
After	Sunderland	4th	1	2	Newcastle	15th	1	0

Play was fairly even although Sunderland gradually gained the upper hand by making more use of their wing men. Yet United went closest to scoring early on. They forced the first corner of the match and Sandy Higgins rattled a Sunderland post following a scramble in front the Wearside goal. Newcastle relied very heavily on Albert Shepherd up front and the home defenders marked him closely throughout. The elusive Jackie Mordue was the Wearside danger man. Once he centred with such force from out near the corner flag that the ball flew straight through the side netting into the net. Both defences were generally on top.

But after 32 minutes a ball into the middle by Charlie Thomson was just too high for Whitson who could do no more than help it on its way with his head to Mordue. The winger raced on unchallenged to the bye-line before squaring a pass inside for George Holley who never broke stride as he rushed in and blasted a shot so hard into the net that Lawrence hardly saw it. Both sides had chances to score before the interval but Holley's goal was the only one to separate them at the break.

Newcastle pushed forward at the start of the second half and they thought that they had equalised, but Higgins' shot went just wide into the side netting. Billy Troughear and Albert Milton defended well and Dick Roose was seldom troubled despite United doing most of the attacking. Bill McCracken and Wilf Low excelled in the Newcastle defence although Jimmy Lawrence had to be on his toes to pull off some good saves. Newcastle could easily have been awarded a penalty when Shepherd was blatantly body checked by Thomson inside the Sunderland penalty area but the referee waved play on.

Ten minutes from time Newcastle equalised. Jackie Rutherford centred the ball into the Sunderland area and, in the ensuing tussle, Troughear deliberately handled. It seemed an obvious penalty but the referee consulted both of his linesmen before awarding a spot kick. Albert Shepherd made no mistake when he eventually took it.

Newcastle seemed to settle for a point and surrendered the initiative to Sunderland who became the more forceful side in the closing minutes and United suffered the consequences when the Red'n Whites forced a corner three minutes from time. Arthur Bridgett's flag kick was perfect for 'Tim' Coleman to head into the far top corner. Lawrence managed to get his fingertips to it but was unable to keep it out.

The game had been close but Sunderland had been worthy winners. The referee expressed surprise at how fit both sets of players were so early in the season.

There were repercussions following the players' action in wearing armbands. The Football League Committee avoided immediate confrontation by deciding to take no action against the players on this occasion. But they decreed that "If any player wears such badges on the field of play in future, the Committee instructs all clubs that such players must immediately be suspended after the match and reported to the league".

Football League
Division 1
Newcastle United 1 Sunderland 1 (HT: 1-1)
19th November 1910
St James' Park
59,416

Newcastle: J Lawrence, W McCracken, A Whitson, C Veitch, W Low, P McWilliam, J Rutherford, J Howie, A Shepherd [16], J Stewart, A Anderson
Sunderland: L R Roose (inj 75), W Troughear, H Forster, T S Tait, C Thomson, H Low, J Mordue, J G Coleman [19], J Cowell, G Holley, A Bridgett (in goal 75)
Referee: T P Campbell (Blackburn)

TABLE TOPPING Sunderland travelled to Gallowgate unbeaten and full of confidence, eager to complete a league double over Newcastle having defeated United at Roker Park at the very beginning of the season. They attracted a new attendance record at St James', comfortably exceeding the 53,353 who had watched the Cup tie between the two rivals a couple of years earlier. Some 57,416 paid at the gates but there were a further 2,000 ticket holders on top of this.

The size of the crowd on this occasion was a bit of a surprise considering that there was a lock-out of boilermakers in the shipbuilding and engineering industries. The ground was jam-packed full half an hour before the scheduled kick-off time (2.30pm) with thousands still outside clamouring to get in. The referee decided to start the game at 2.24pm as the gates were locked.

League Positions		Pos	Pl	Pts		Pos	Pl	Pts
Before	Sunderland	1st	12	19	Newcastle	10th	12	11
After:	Sunderland	1st	13	20	Newcastle	9th	13	12

This was a classic encounter between two closely matched sides with both teams demonstrating fine sportsmanship throughout and playing an open, attacking game. Sunderland attacked first with Coleman breaking through with only Lawrence to beat but his shot from wide on the wing went right across the penalty area for a goal kick. If anyone had been up in support, a goal would have been a certainty. Soon it was United's turn to push forward and a Howie effort ended up in the side netting.

It was United who drew first blood after 16 minutes. Jimmy Lawrence punted a long ball upfield to Albert Shepherd midway inside the Wearside half. As Forster hesitated, the Newcastle centre forward burst past him and let fly from fully 30 yards with a shot that sailed past Roose into the net

Newcastle did not have long to bask in the luxury of their lead because Sunderland retaliated within three minutes. Their goal was almost a copy of

Newcastle's. George Holley supplied Tim Coleman out on the left wing and, as McCracken hesitated, the inside forward slammed in a raking shot from distance. Lawrence managed to get a hand to it but not enough to keep it out.

From that point onwards the spectators were treated to a hard game – clean, fast and remarkably even. The visitors went desperately close to grabbing the lead when Lawrence advanced out of his goal to face Cowell who had broken away up the Sunderland left wing. The centre forward put the ball past the 'keeper only for Tony Whitson to breast it off the goal line. The Sunderland players appealed that it had crossed the line before it was cleared but the referee was up with play and waved their protests aside. United also went close when Tadger Stewart hit the crossbar so the 1-1 half-time scoreline was about right.

Newcastle were the more aggressive side in the second half. The Sunderland defence was superb although they had luck on their side with both Albert Shepherd and Tadger Stewart striking the bar. The corner that resulted from the latter effort resulted in an unfortunate accident. It occurred in the 75th minute. Roose and Rutherford collided as they went for the ball with the 'keeper falling awkwardly when he landed. After treatment, he had to be helped off the field. His wrist was broken. Arthur Bridgett took over the 'keeper's jersey and, although he kept a clean sheet, it was hardly surprising that Sunderland never threatened after Roose's departure. They held out largely because they packed their defence to protect their emergency custodian. They were more than satisfied to return to Wearside with a point and their unbeaten record intact.

After the game there was a general impression that the referee had signalled the end of play too early, not adding any time on for Roose's injury. The time taken to treat the 'keeper, bind his arm and help him from the field of play was not less than four minutes but Mr Campbell appeared to make no allowance for it at all. The 'keeper's injury was a bad one, effectively finishing his Sunderland career. It ruled him out of action for the rest of the season and he was never to play for them again.

It was felt that Newcastle had not closed the gates early enough and had allowed too many spectators into the ground. The crush barriers on the Popular Side had snapped like reeds when the crowd had surged forward and it was a miracle that no-one was injured. The crowd was praised by the police for their exemplary behaviour except for one incident. A sergeant of infantry from the nearby barracks had his bayonet stolen from its scabbard in the crush. The club thought that this was taken as a joke and that it would be returned either to the club secretary, Frank Watt, or direct to the barracks. Quite what the sergeant was doing carrying a bayonet into a football match is another matter. It was probably regarded as part of his uniform!

Football League
Division 1
Sunderland 1 Newcastle United 2 (HT: 0-1)
14th October 1911
Roker Park
30,000

Sunderland: W Scott, W Troughear, A Milton, T S Tait, C Thomson, W Cringan, R Best, C Buchan, G Holley [47], J Gemmell, J Mordue
Newcastle: J Lawrence, W McCracken [43 pen], T Whitson, D Willis, W Low, J Hay, A S Duncan, J Stewart, A Higgins, G Wilson, J G Scott [87]
Referee: A Adams (Nottingham)

RAIL EXCURSIONS from Berwick in the north, Carlisle in the west and Darlington in the south all gravitated towards Roker, thus illustrating the hold that Tyne-Wear derbies had over football enthusiasts throughout the far north of England.

It was commonly accepted before the game that Sunderland's attack was superior to Newcastle's largely because of Albert Shepherd's long term injury that was to rule him out of action for the entire season. United's defence, on the other hand, was regarded as the stronger of the two.

The Tynesiders spent the week before the game trying to sign Billy Hibbert from Bury but negotiations were not finalised until after the derby. The Newcastle board of directors even approached Bill McCracken to see if he would lead the attack at Roker. The Irish full back sensibly declined the invitation.

Sunderland had to make one change to the side that had won at Aston Villa in their previous game, bringing back Charles Buchan in place of Richard Healey who opted to turn out for his parent club, Bishop Auckland, in an FA Cup tie against Spennymoor. Healey was not to play for Sunderland again. There was little between the teams in the league (just one point) with Sunderland only two points adrift of three teams at the top.

League Positions		Pos	Pl	Pts		Pos	Pl	Pts
Before	Sunderland	5th	7	8	Newcastle	12th	7	7
After:	Newcastle	8th	8	9	Sunderland	11th	8	8

Newcastle threw everything that they had into the game straight from the kick-off and the Sunderland defence was on the rack for the first 20 minutes. But Charlie Thomson and Billy Troughear were in top form and they held out. Gradually the Roker men came into the game more with Bobby Best particularly impressing with some scorching raids up the wing. Bill McCracken was United's defensive hero but both the Sunderland players and supporters were convinced that he used his hands when he blocked a shot by George Holley and appealed for a penalty.

The referee played on but incurred the wrath of Wearside when he later awarded United a controversial spot kick two minutes before halt time. A cross from Scott Duncan dropped between Higgins and Wilson. Higgins was forcing his way through when Troughear tackled him. The ball bounced off the Newcastle man and the Sunderland full back handled – a penalty. Bill McCracken took it and although Scott made a determined effort to save, the Irishman scored.

The Sunderland players, convinced that the hand ball was accidental, were far from happy with the penalty decision. The Newcastle men were equally convinced that it was deliberate. It was certainly a contentious decision and Roker Park was buzzing as the players left the field at half-time.

Sunderland attacked straight from the start and grabbed the equaliser within a couple of minutes. McCracken should have cleared but dallied on the ball allowing Jackie Mordue to run in and dispossess him. He squared it into the centre to Bobby Best who was only a yard out but unable to shoot goalwards. Instead he smartly turned it back to George Holley who hooked it home.

Both sides went for the winner and an action packed game ensued. The one surprise was that neither side was able to push their attack home. Holley was unlucky with a shot that hit the crossbar as Sunderland mounted increasing pressure. It looked a matter of whether Newcastle could hold out for a draw or whether the Rokermen could grab the winner when United broke away on a last ditch attack.

Sandy Higgins broke clear to run half the length of the field with Jack Scott up in support. Troughear gamely pursued him and slid the ball away from him inside the penalty area. The Sunderland 'keeper dashed out but Scott got there first. Showing amazing calmness for a reserve, he proceeded to take the ball around Milton before chipping a shot in just under the bar. There were just three minutes left.

It was an exciting finish to an amazing game that would long remain in the memories of supporters of both sides.

This had been one of the most strenuous games ever witnessed at Roker Park. Every player had thrown every ounce of effort and energy into his game and they were all exhausted by the end. So was the crowd. The Newcastle supporters were elated with the victory and argued that their team had won because they had deserved to, forgetting the contentious penalty decision. In truth, neither team had deserved to lose after serving up such magnificent entertainment.

James Hay had joined Newcastle from Celtic just over a month earlier. The former captain of the green half of Glasgow and Scotland expressed astonishment at the tension in the North East over the game. He had encountered nothing like it, even in Glasgow – the city of football. He admitted that even he had been affected by nerves – but it didn't show in his performance.

Football League
Division 1
Newcastle United 3 Sunderland 1 (HT: 1-0)
17th February 1912
St James' Park
45,000

Newcastle: S Blake, W McCracken, F Hudspeth, D Willis, W Low, J Hay, J Rutherford, T Lowes [3], J Stewart [81], G Wilson, A Anderson [48]
Sunderland: W Scott, W Troughear, A Milton, F Cuggy, C Thomson, I G Martin, R Best, D R McCulloch, H Low [88 pen], T Hall, A Bridgett
Referee: A Adams (Nottingham)

THE NORTH EAST rivals were still in contention for the league title when they met in mid-February. Newcastle were four points behind leaders Blackburn Rovers with a game in hand and two points behind second placed Everton (level games). Sunderland were fourth, a place adrift.

Rumours swept Tyneside during the week before the derby that Newcastle were about to sign Jock McTavish of Tottenham Hotspur. The press even quoted a fee of £1,500 (dismissed by United as "ridiculous"). He was eventually to join the Magpies later in the season although at less than half the price quoted.

United were badly hit with their team selection with Lawrence unavailable and both Higgins and McWilliam not yet recovered from injury. On top of that Hibbert was chosen to play for the Football League in a inter-league match at Ayresome Park. But Sunderland were affected much more in that respect with Buchan, Holley and Mordue all called upon to play on Teesside. So both sides brought in inexperienced local youngsters, Newcastle in the shape of Walker-born Tommy Lowes and Sunderland with Bob McCulloch from Gateshead. It was to be the latter's only first team appearance during his two years at Roker.

League Positions		Pos	Pl	Pts		Pos	Pl	Pts
Before	Newcastle	3rd	25	30	Sunderland	4th	26	29
After:	Newcastle	2nd	26	32	Sunderland	5th	27	29

Despite its unusual set up, the Newcastle forward line linked together well and soon had Sunderland back on defence. After three minutes Jackie Rutherford took the ball to the Sunderland left wing corner flag before slinging over a cross that the 'keeper managed to touch on to the bar only for Tommy Lowes to take control and fire in a first time shot from a narrow angle that gave goalkeeper Walter Scott no chance.

The goal seemed to dishearten Sunderland. They looked strangely lethargic while Newcastle were full of vigour and enthusiasm, attacking first down one wing and then the other. However their finishing left something to be desired and that, coupled with some debatable offside decisions, prevented them from rattling up a big score. Somehow Sunderland reached the refuge of the interval just one goal in arrears.

The second half continued in a similar vein to the first and, once again, United made an early breakthrough. Once again the move emanated from Jackie Rutherford on United's right wing. Tommy Lowes sent him forward and he took the ball into the penalty area before crossing it into the middle. Stewart missed the cross but Andy Anderson dashed in behind him to crash the ball past Scott.

Sunderland seemed to surrender meekly (which was very unusual for a derby match) and never looked like getting into the game. Most of their best players were in defence although Bob McCulloch caught the eye as he tried to push forward. He did not let anyone down.

Newcastle went three ahead in the 81st minute when Rutherford, having a field day, left Milton standing as he raced in before centring to Tadger Stewart who did not have to break stride as he blasted the ball past the helpless Sunderland 'keeper. It was the goal of the match.

Surprisingly Sunderland seemed to rally after this although it was a classic case of too little, too late. Nevertheless they scored a consolation goal a couple of minutes from time – although it needed a spot kick to do it. Hudspeth was adjudged to have handled the ball, something he strenuously denied. Harry Low took the penalty and made no mistake from the spot.

The win pushed Newcastle above Everton on goal average although they were still four points adrift of leaders Blackburn with a game in hand. But that was as close as their title challenge went with them losing three of their next four games. They eventually finished in a highly respectable third place but their great Edwardian era was now behind them.

Sunderland slowly slipped down the league to finish a disappointing eighth. But their glory season, one of the greatest in their history, was just around the corner.

A (not so) Merry Christmas

Two Tyne-Wear derbies have taken place on Christmas Day.
Strangely, on each occasion the away team won by three clear goals
– Sunderland, 5-2, in 1914 and Newcastle, 4-1, in 1951.

Football League
Division 1
Newcastle United 1 Sunderland 1 (HT: 1-0)

7th September 1912
St James' Park
54,200

Newcastle: J Lawrence, W McCracken, F Hudspeth, C Veitch, W Low, J Hay, J Rutherford, J McTavish, A Shepherd [11], W Hibbert, J McDonald
Sunderland: W Scott, W Troughear, H Ness, F Cuggy, C Thomson, H Low, J Mordue [52], C Buchan, J Richardson, G Holley, H Martin
Referee: J T Howcroft (Bolton)

THIS GAME took place very early in the season which was not allowed to start before September. The 1st had been a Sunday so most clubs began their league campaign on the Monday.

Newcastle fielded the team that had won their first game (against Bolton). Sunderland were one of four First Division teams that did not start their league season until the first Saturday of the month. Newcastle issued advice to their supporters in the press, "Applicants for season tickets are advised to secure their tickets at the office before 12 noon on Saturday in order to avoid disappointment".

Sunderland were forced to make a team change from their expected first choice side when Albert Milton broke his collar bone in a practice match. Harry Ness took his place at left back. There was one new recruit in the Roker ranks – James Richardson, a centre forward signed from Huddersfield Town.

League Positions		Pos	Pl	Pts		Pos	Pl	Pts
Before	Newcastle	6th	1	2	Sunderland	10th	0	0
After:	Newcastle	7th	2	3	Sunderland	10th	1	1

McCracken won the toss and played with the slope in his favour in the first half. Sunderland looked the livelier side in the opening stages as Newcastle struggled to get into their stride so it was a bit of a surprise when it was United who opened the scoring.

After 11 minutes, John McDonald, a recent recruit from Liverpool, was sent away up the left wing by Hay. He managed luckily to get around Cuggy and warded off a challenge by Troughear before slipping the ball to Billy Hibbert. The pass was short and Scott advanced but the Newcastle man just managed to reach it first to hook it back to Albert Shepherd who blasted in a shot that went into the net off the crossbar.

Newcastle were generally on top for most of the first half but their wing play left something to be desired. Although they did not see as much of the ball, Sunderland looked more dangerous when they pushed forward.

Fortunately for Newcastle, their defence stood firm with Frank Hudspeth, Jimmy Hay and Jimmy Lawrence particularly strong. United probably merited their one goal half-time lead.

But it was a different story in the second half when Sunderland took up the running. Jackie Mordue should have levelled the scores early in the half but he missed a sitter. However he soon made amends with a delightful goal after 52 minutes. Hudspeth allowed him to get to the ball first and the Sunderland winger showed the full back a clean pair of heels as he tore forward and raced towards the Newcastle goal. Low and Hay tried to close in on him but he drove a shot, hard and low, across Lawrence into the net at the far post.

Once level, Sunderland dominated play and had the home defence at full stretch. But over-eagerness seemed to be the visitors' downfall. They were decidedly faster than their neighbours but their finishing left a lot to be desired. Charles Buchan created an absolute gift of a chance for Holley but he dawdled and allowed Lawrence to fall on the ball and smother it. Wilf Low and Colin Veitch stood out for Newcastle during this prolonged onslaught. It was by no means a dazzling game with both sides relying more on individual skills than team work.

The scores were still level at the final whistle and a draw was probably a fair result although most Wearside supporters felt that their team's second half dominance deserved more.

The attendance at St James' Park was more than twice that anywhere else in the First Division with the exception of Old Trafford (39,000) and White Hart Lane (30,000). There were ten games played in the First Division that day and half of them ended as draws!

Sunderland were to lose five of their next six games (drawing the other one) but then were to complete one of the most amazing recoveries in the history of league football (as we shall see). Newcastle were to do the exact opposite, losing just one of their opening eleven matches only to fall away badly before the two North East rivals were to meet again in mid-season.

Biggest Derby Wins (by four goals or more)

Newcastle		Sunderland	
9 Oct 1920	6-1 (H)	5 Dec 1908	9-1 (A)
26 Dec 1955	6-1 (A)	22 Nov 1930	5-0 (H)
22 Dec 1956	6-2 (H)		

Football League
Division 1
Sunderland 2 Newcastle United 0 (HT: 1-0)
28th December 1912
Roker Park
35,000

Sunderland: J Butler, C Gladwin, A Milton, F Cuggy, C Thomson, H Low, J Mordue, C Buchan, J Richardson, G Holley [**34, 86**], H Martin
Newcastle: J Lawrence, W McCracken, R Little, R Hewison, W Low, J Hay, A S Duncan, J McTavish, A Higgins, G Wilson, W Hibbert
Referee: J T Howcroft (Bolton)

ALTHOUGH NINTH in the league, Sunderland were only three points behind three teams who were at the top at this, the half-way point in the season – Aston Villa, West Bromwich Albion and Sheffield Wednesday.

Both of the North East rivals had undergone a gruelling Christmas holiday programme with Sunderland the more successful, having won two of their three games in the previous week. Unfortunately their one defeat had been at home against joint leaders Sheffield Wednesday (although they had beaten the Owls at Hillsborough on Christmas Day).

Newcastle had done appallingly by comparison, having lost all three of their games. In fact they had lost their last four games and had seen the Wearsiders overtake them in the league. They came into this game with low expectations, their team badly affected by injuries. Hudspeth, Whitson, Rutherford, McDonald and Peart were all out. Sunderland were clear favourites to win.

League Positions

		Pos	Pl	Pts		Pos	Pl	Pts
Before	Sunderland	9th	20	22	Newcastle	11th	20	20
After:	Sunderland	7th	21	24	Newcastle	13th	21	20

Three spins of the coin were necessary before it landed flat in the muddy ground. McCracken won the toss and played with the breeze. Newcastle peppered the Sunderland goal straight from the kick-off to try and seize the initiative but the Rokermen withstood the early onslaught and soon took command. They forced United back, mainly with raids down the right wing, and the visitors had to concede a string of corners. Both Charles Buchan and Jackie Mordue struck the woodwork and Frank Cuggy rattled a shot into the sidenetting when perhaps he should have done better. Newcastle's best chance was when goalkeeper Joe Butler did well to beat the ball down following a George Wilson shot but McTavish put the loose ball over the top.

Sunderland eventually took the lead that their play deserved after 34 minutes. Jimmy Richardson broke away on attack and, when Hay slipped, he played in a pass to set up George Holley. Lawrence did well to block his first effort but, despite a McCracken tackle, the Sunderland man whipped the ball into the net.

Newcastle were soon reduced to ten men with Little badly winded when a shot from Buchan was blasted into him and had to go off the field to recover. Up against a depleted side, Sunderland were easily better than the lack-lustre Tynesiders.

Back to full-strength after the resumption, Newcastle managed to have a fair share of the offensive work but they tended to over-elaborate when a willingness to try a few shots might have been a better option. They should have taken a leaf out of Charlie Gladwin's book. At least he tried a shot from distance and nearly scored, hitting the United crossbar. But Newcastle were still in with a chance – until, that is, the last five minutes.

Then, four minutes from time, Charlie Thomson intercepted a clearance from Wilf Low and neatly dribbled forward before laying the ball off to Jimmy Richardson. He tapped it to George Holley who could not miss – and he didn't.

Sunderland were deserved winners. Indeed, the scoreline probably flattered Newcastle considering that Buchan, Mordue and Gladwin had hit the woodwork. However the game could have gone either way until the 86th minute.

Incredibly, the Rokerites were to embark on a magnificent run of results, losing just one of their remaining 17 league games, to lift the league title. This was one of the greatest recoveries in the history of the Football League (arguably 'the greatest') when it is considered that they failed to win any of their opening seven games, picking up only two points out of their first 14! They also went desperately close to completing a league and cup double, reaching the final of the latter only to lose by the only goal of the match to Aston Villa.

Newcastle, in contrast, slipped into mediocrity to finish in the bottom half of the league. Their season was only rescued by an encouraging cup run. But even that was spoiled by the fact that they were to eventually to lose to Sunderland at the quarter-final stage.

Another Nine Goals

It is common knowledge that Sunderland defeated Newcastle 9-1 in December 1908 but it less well known that they have netted nine times at St James' Park in more recent times. In September 1979, the clubs met over two legs in the Second Round of the Football League Cup. They drew 2-2 in both games so the second match, at St James' Park, went to a penalty shoot-out. Sunderland won 7-6 and so scored nine goals at St James' for a second time!

FA Cup
4th round (quarter-final)
Sunderland 0 Newcastle United 0 (HT: 0-0)
8th March 1913
Roker Park
29,111

Sunderland: J Butler, C Gladwin, A Milton, F Cuggy, C Thomson, H Low, J Mordue, C Buchan, J Richardson, G Holley, H Martin
Newcastle: J Lawrence, W McCracken, F Hudspeth, C Veitch, W Low, J Hay, J Rutherford, J Stewart, W Hibbert, G Wilson, J McDonald
Referee: H H Taylor (Altrincham)

THIS WAS a crucial game for both teams – the quarter-final of the FA Cup. Sunderland, riding high in the league and with a real chance of a league and cup double, were clear favourites. It was commonly accepted that they were one of the best teams (probably the best) in the country with brilliant forwards, consistently good half-backs and a steady defence.

In comparison Newcastle were no more than a middle of the table team who relied heavily on a solid defence. On top of that, they had injury problems with both Higgins and Shepherd ruled out of the tie.

United underwent special cup training at Saltburn while Sunderland remained on Wearside. At the time Roker Park had 2,450 seats but these were sold out well in advance. United were the largest group purchasers with 150 of them for directors, players and friends. Sunderland doubled the admission prices but there was still tremendous demand with thousands of supporters assembled outside the ground by noon although the kick-off was not until 3.30pm.

The North Eastern Railway Company made provision to convey 5,000 people from Newcastle and intermediate stations with the first 'special' leaving Newcastle Central at 11.25. Although there was a good crowd, everyone who wanted to go the match got in and there was no need to lock the gates.

Surprisingly there was little between the teams in a grim struggle. Defences dominated with Sunderland's much vaunted forwards virtually subdued. The half-back lines of both sides shone and, with both sets of full backs in top form, the goalkeepers had a fairly easy time of it. The best that could be said of the attacks was that they were persistent. Harry Martin's speed on the Sunderland left wing forced a number of corners but as far as tactics went, he met his master in Bill McCracken.

The Wearsiders did most of what attacking there was in the opening half hour when they had the wind and the sun in their favour but they seemed to tire after that. Newcastle went closest to scoring when George Wilson tried a swerving shot that had Butler beaten only for Albert Milton to divert on to the crossbar and safety. The best that Sunderland could offer was a Richardson effort that was directed straight at Lawrence.

Newcastle suffered a setback when Gladwin and Stewart collided. Both were stunned but Stewart had to go off and United had to play the last 15 minutes of the half with ten men. Yet they still went closest to scoring in that time.

A corner kick left Hibbert in possession just three yards out from the Sunderland goal line but, taken unawares, he was only able to hit a post. He later flashed a shot just wide of the target with Butler well beaten. Overall, Newcastle could regard themselves as unfortunate not to be ahead at the interval.

Stewart resumed after the break but was obviously still feeling the effects of his concussion. Newcastle did most of the attacking, mainly down their left flank, although Sunderland went close on a couple of occasions when McCracken had to concede corners. It was evident that Mordue was not fully fit and perhaps he should not have played. The goalkeepers were rarely troubled and it gradually became apparent that a goalless draw was in the offing. Sunderland made a strong finish to try and snatch victory but it was too little, too late. The final whistle came with the scoreline blank. There would have to be a replay and the advantage swung Tyneside's way.

Charlie Thomson, who was Sunderland's captain and best player in this game, admitted that Newcastle probably deserved to win. But there was a feeling that United had played above themselves. Whether they could do that again, even in front of their own supporters, was open to doubt especially with Stewart highly doubtful for the replay when it was hoped a better game would be served up.

Jimmy Hay had been a revelation and had clearly been the best half-back on the field. Even the Wearside supporters applauded his skills. Perhaps, overall, excitement and flair were lacking in the Roker game but no-one could criticise the commitment and determination of both teams.

Only One Miss

Technically, Sunderland have only ever missed one penalty against Newcastle (when Bobby Best shot wide on December 26, 1914). The other eight spot kicks where they have failed to score have all been saved.

FA Cup
4th round second replay
Newcastle United 2 Sunderland 2 (HT:1-1) [aet]
12th March 1913
St James' Park
56,717

Newcastle: J Lawrence, W McCracken, F Hudspeth, C Veitch [**88**], W Low, J Hay, J McTavish [**17**], W Hibbert, A Shepherd, G Wilson, J McDonald
Sunderland: J Butler, C Gladwin, A Milton, F Cuggy, C Thomson, H Low, J Mordue, C Buchan [**86**], J Richardson, G Holley [**28**], H Martin
Referee: J Baker (Nantwich)

DESPITE BEING held to a draw at Roker Park in the first game, Sunderland were still favourites to go through. Not only were they a bigger team in terms of height and weight but Newcastle were handicapped with injuries to Stewart (shoulder) and Rutherford (ankle). So United were forced to field a weakened team although Shepherd was brought back into the starting line-up.

The pull of the FA Cup and the fact this was a local derby, attracted a magnificent crowd of 56,717 to St James' (receipts totalling £2,547 12s 1d) with a further 15,000 locked outside.

Both sides threw everything that they had into their play, perhaps too desperately at times. The game was played at a cracking pace with end-to-end football although the light, bouncing ball gave problems. Once again the Newcastle full backs and half-backs subdued Sunderland's star forward line. The Magpies did most of the early attacking and it was they who eventually opened the scoring.

After 17 minutes John McDonald started a move by plying Billy Hibbert who hooked the ball into the middle along the goal line. Gladwin was caught ball watching as Jock McTavish rushed in to breast it past Butler. The goal gave United confidence and they looked as if they were going to build on their lead – until Sunderland struck back eleven minutes later. Jimmy Richardson dashed through the middle before playing the ball high into the Newcastle penalty area. Both of the Newcastle backs went up for it but neither succeeded and Richardson, running in, nudged the ball forward with his elbow, an offence seen seemingly by everyone except the match officials. To make matters worse for the Magpies, the ball broke to George Holley who looked as if he was offside. But the whistle never came and he tucked the ball away as Lawrence advanced to cut down the angle. To say that the goal was a lucky one was an understatement – at least to Tyneside eyes.

The game was fairly even until, just before the break, an incident occurred that was to have a profound effect on the game. Shepherd was breaking through when he was body-checked by Milton and sustained a serious thigh injury.

The seriousness of the injury soon became apparent and, with no substitutes in those days, he was forced to switch to the wing where he hobbled for the rest of the game. Both teams continued to play at pace but neither seemed likely to gain the upper hand until the closing stages when Sunderland began to push back their opponents.

They forced two corners in quick succession five minutes from time and it was from the second of these that they gained the lead. Jackie Mordue sent the ball in to the middle where Charles Buchan headed in. Hay tried to clear but the ball glanced off his head and was deflected past the committed Lawrence.

If Sunderland thought it was all over, they were wrong. Newcastle were awarded a free kick for hands near the visitors' penalty area and Wilf Low touched the ball forward to Colin Veitch. His shot through a crowd of players was low and hard. Gladwin managed to get a finest of touches but succeeded only in helping it past Butler. There would have to be half-an-hour's extra time.

Both teams were at full stretch in the added half hour with both goals having narrow escapes, Lawrence saving well by going full length to stop a Buchan effort and McTavish sending a shot just over the top. Sunderland were on top at the end but the scores were still level at the final whistle.

If Newcastle had probably just deserved to win the first game at Roker, Sunderland could regard themselves as unfortunate not to have won the replay. Their skipper, Charlie Thomson, had won the toss at the start of the game but Newcastle club secretary Frank Watt won it after the final whistle for the choice of venue for the second replay. Naturally, he chose St James' Park. But the cup saga was telling its toll on Newcastle with injuries. McDonald also sustained an injury near the end of this game and neither he nor Shepherd would be available for the second replay.

FA Cup
4th round 2nd replay
Newcastle United 0 Sunderland 3 (HT: 0-2)
17th March 1913
St James' Park
49,354

Newcastle: J Lawrence, W McCracken, F Hudspeth, C Veitch, W Low, J Hay, A S Duncan, J McTavish, W Hibbert, J Stewart, G Wilson
Sunderland: J Butler, C Gladwin, A Milton, F Cuggy, C Thomson, H Low, J Mordue [**40** (pen), **75**], C Buchan, J Richardson, G Holley [**8**], H Martin
Referee: J Baker (Nantwich)

BY THE time this second replay was played, more than 135,000 supporters had seen the North East rivals in this round alone, bringing in total gate receipts of £6,648 – a small fortune at the time.

Both sides had fielded weakened league teams on the previous Saturday, keeping their big guns for the cup tie. Sunderland had still been strong enough to defeat Manchester United away despite the absence of Mordue, Low and Thomson. Charlie Thomson and Harry Low had been selected for the Scotland squad to face Ireland in Dublin on the Saturday before the second replay (which took place on the Monday) but they both withdrew to play in the cup instead. This was particularly unfortunate for Harry as he was never to receive an international cap. Sunderland also petitioned the Football Association to have George Holley released by England (who were due to play Wales). Newcastle supported the application which was successful. So Sunderland were able to field the team that had turned out throughout their cup run and were at full-strength.

The situation at Newcastle was considerably different. They had fielded almost a reserve side at home to Blackburn Rovers and had lost. But their cup selection was still severely curtailed by injuries. With Rutherford, Shepherd and McDonald all ruled out injured, they were forced to play Wilf Low despite the fact that he was ill and doubtful right until the kick-off. At least Stewart was fit to return but this was small consolation.

The Tyneside masses feared the worst. Sunderland, now only one point behind Aston Villa in the league, had their eyes on a league and cup double.

Sunderland captain Charlie Thomson, who had won the toss in both of the earlier cup games, took one look at the gale blowing the length of the Gallowgate pitch and the gathering storm clouds and declared that whoever won the toss this time would win the game. Both his call and his prediction were spot on. Newcastle, to their credit, held their own early on in the teeth of the gale but once the snow and hail began to fall, they succumbed both to the elements and to Sunderland.

There was an element of misfortune about the opening goal as far as Newcastle were concerned. Jim Richardson bored his way through before playing a pass forward to George Holley. Lawrence advanced out of his goal while Hudspeth ran across to try and kick clear. He merely shot against the Sunderland man and the ball rebounded high over the 'keeper's head into the net.

Sunderland exerted all the pressure, forcing a number of corners but Newcastle defended well. Until, that is, McCracken sustained a bad knee injury in a collision with Buchan and struggled for the rest of the game. Holley and Richardson combined again to force the ball into the net but the point was disallowed for a handling offence by the former who vigorously denied it. But after 40 minutes Harry Low forced his way through towards the Newcastle goal only to be tripped by Veitch. Jackie Mordue made no mistake with the penalty, sending a rising shot into the net just under the bar.

Ominously for Newcastle, the snow and hail storm had stopped before half-time. Now, to make matters worse, the gale eased and all Sunderland had to contend with was a fairly strong breeze. This was no real handicap to the effervescent Wearsiders who were by now well on top although most of the play was in their half of the field. United pushed men forward but found Joe Butler in top form in the Sunderland goal. Three times he pulled off top class saves while his team mates looked increasingly dangerous on breakaway attacks.

The goal after 75 minutes that put the tie beyond United's reach was a beauty. Charles Buchan and Mordue combined to slice open the Newcastle defence before Jackie showed skills of the highest order as he beat three men before calmly slipping the ball past Lawrence as the 'keeper rushed out. It was a goal worthy of winning any game.

This was one of Sunderlandis best performances of the season and they undoubtedly deserved to win but the elements and injuries had a lot to do with it. The Newcastle players and directors were good enough sportsmen to congratulate the victors and honestly wish them good luck in the semi-final where they were to meet Burnley.

Whether the Newcastle supporters expressed similar wishes is open to conjecture. Sunderland went on to the final where they met Aston Villa at Crystal Palace in front of a massive crowd of 120,081. Sunderland were to win the league this year but failed to do the league and cup double, losing 1-0 in the final, the only goal being scored by Tommy Barber – a Geordie!

Football League
Division 1
Sunderland 1 Newcastle United 2 (HT: 1-1)
6th September 1913
Roker Park
45,000

Sunderland: J Butler, C Gladwin, H Ness, W Cringan, F Cuggy, H Low, R Best, C Buchan, J Richardson, G Holley [7], H Martin
Newcastle: J Lawrence, W McCracken, F Hudspeth, J Hay, W Low, J Finlay, E Cooper, J King [82], T Hall [44], W Hibbert, J McDonald
Referee: H Taylor (Altrincham)

COMPETITIVE FOOTBALL was prohibited before September and six teams had yet to start their league season although both Newcastle and Sunderland had managed to play. Both had comparatively poor results with Sunderland picking up a point away to Preston and Newcastle crashing 3-0 at Blackburn.

Now facing a trip to Roker, United could not have had a harder start to the season by playing away to the last two League Champions in their first two games. Their attack had been particularly weak at Ewood Park and three changes were made to the forward line for the derby game including the selection of Tommy Hall, recently signed from Sunderland.

The Sunderland line up looked a little strange with skipper Charlie Thomson and Jackie Mordue (who had been injured at Preston) missing.

An innovation at Roker Park for this game was the provision of catering at the various entrances by Messrs Boyd & Co. It proved to be a great success.

A collection was taken at the ground for the widow of Mr F W Robson who had been drowned at Roker on the August Bank Holiday weekend while attempting to rescue someone.

League Positions

		Pos	Pl	Pts		Pos	Pl	Pts
Before	Sunderland	4th	1	1	Newcastle	12th	1	0
After	Newcastle	11th	2	2	Sunderland	14th	2	1

Newcastle were clearly the underdogs but both sides showed determination and eagerness in a keenly contested match. They were rather anxious in the early stages and it was the League Champions who broke through first after seven minutes. George Holley and Harry Martin interchanged passes before the former burst past McCracken. Both backs converged on him but he shook them off before firing home. It was a top class goal by any standards.

Spurred on by this early success, Sunderland took control. They displayed some beautiful footwork in midfield and played with plenty of dash up front. But a change of tactics by the Newcastle half-backs changed the game. Instead of plying their inside trio, they began to spray passes out to their wingers. Both Ed Cooper and John McDonald swept over some tantalising centres and, although the Wearside rearguard defended well, United looked more and more likely to score.

Their goal came when Tommy Hall set off on a determined run just before half-time. Gladwin and Ness hesitated with their tackles, allowing their former team mate to steady himself before shooting. Even then, goalkeeper Butler probably should have saved the effort but he dived far too early and the ball ended up in the net.

Sunderland still had plenty of confidence as they started the second half with their forwards dominating play. Twice they were foiled by the illegal tactics of the Tyneside defenders and on the second occasion a penalty kick was awarded. Harry Low took it but was foiled by Jimmy Lawrence who pulled off a magnificent save. This seemed to dispirit the Wearsiders and Newcastle came more into the game. Only the Sunderland centre forward Jimmy Richardson, looked likely to break through with some exciting bursts upfield. A draw seemed the most likely (and fairest) result but Newcastle shocked the Roker masses by grabbing a late winner.

With eight minutes remaining Jimmy Hay swung a pass to John McDonald on the left wing. His cross into the middle was accurate enough but there did not seem to be too much danger until Gladwin failed to cut it out. John King saw the opportunity in a flash and dashed between Cuggy and Ness to drive the ball past Butler and give Newcastle victory.

The win was a major upset although the Magpies were a shade lucky to collect both points. They were the better balanced side and their defence was steadier than the home team's. A drawback for Sunderland was the failure of the artistic Buchan to link up with Best.

But the Wearsiders were soon to recover in the league. They were to lose their next match but were to lose only a couple more before Christmas (16 games). Newcastle were almost to do the opposite, winning only five of their 17 games before the return derby match with Sunderland at the end of the year.

Football League
Division 1
Newcastle United 2 Sunderland 1 (HT: 0-0)
27th December 1913
St James' Park
50,000

Newcastle: J Lawrence, W McCracken, F Hudspeth, R Hewison, W Low, J Hay, A Douglas, W Hibbert [73], T Hall, G Wilson, T Goodwill [53]
Sunderland: J Butler, B Hobson, H Ness, F Cuggy, C Thomson, W Cringan, R Best, C Buchan [89], J Waugh, G Holley, H Martin
Referee: H Taylor (Altrincham)

THE SIDES came into the game with totally contrasting fortunes. Newcastle had won just one of their last seven games and had scored only twice in the last five (one of them was a penalty!) and eight in the last 12. Relegation was becoming a real threat.

Sunderland, on the other hand, had recently enjoyed a superb run, losing only once since early October. Now they were just two points behind league leaders Blackburn Rovers and were nicely placed for a bid to retain the championship.

Harry Low had been injured in the previous game against Burnley so they gave a debut to recent signing John Waugh at centre forward. It was to be his one league appearance for them (and, indeed, in his entire career). But the Wearsiders were acknowledged to have one of the best defences in the country and their confidence was high.

However, Newcastle's position was becoming desperate and they had a habit of rising to the occasion when all seemed lost. This gave the Magpies' supporters hope.

John Middleton Campbell. *(courtesy Paul Joannou)*

Andrew McCombie. *(courtesy Paul Joannou)*

David Lalty Willis. (courtesy Paul Joannou)

Thomas Urwin. *(courtesy Paul Joannou)*

Albert McInroy. *(courtesy Paul Joannou)*

Leonard Francis Shackleton. *(courtesy Sunderland Evening Echo)*

Stanley Anderson. *(courtesy Sunderland Evening Echo)*

Robert Moncur. *(courtesy Paul Joannou)*

Bryan Stanley Robson. *(courtesy Sunderland Evening Echo)*

Jeffrey Derrick Clarke. *(courtesy Mike Gibson)*

Paul Bracewell. *(courtesy Paul Joannou)*

Stephen Caldwell. *(courtesy Sunderland Evening Echo)*

Gary Rowell scores his third goal at St James' Park in February 1979 from the penalty spot. It is the only Sunderland hat-trick against Newcastle since the First World War. *(courtesy Sunderland Evening Echo)*

Marco Gabbiadini clinches the 1990 play-off semi-final victory for
Sunderland at St James' Park despite a lunge from Mark Stimson.
(courtesy Sunderland Evening Echo)

Liam O'Brien celebrates his equaliser at Roker in November 1991 as a disconsolate Sunderland skipper Paul Bracewell looks on. *(Newcastle Chronicle)*

Alan Shearer scores the last goal of his career in the 4-1 defeat of Sunderland at the Stadium of Light in April 2006. Also in the picture are (left to right) are Justin Hoyte (half obscured), Dean Whitehead, Charles N'Zogbia & Celestine Babayaro (Newcastle United FC)

League Positions

		Pos	Pl	Pts		Pos	Pl	Pts
Before	Sunderland	2nd	20	26	Newcastle	18th	19	16
After:	Sunderland	2nd	21	26	Newcastle	17th	20	18

This was an amazing game as Newcastle produced their best performance of the season. It was they who looked like championship contenders as they penned Sunderland back in their own half. But credit had to go to the visitors' defence who stood firm despite intense pressure.

The Magpies fired in shots from every conceivable angle. Wilson missed two good chances but the nearest United came to scoring was when a Frank Hudspeth free kick from well outside the area comprehensively beat Butler but struck the bar and rebounded back into play. It was still goalless at half-time.

Newcastle once again attacked as the second half got under way. Tommy Goodwill should have opened the scoring soon after the resumption when a shot by Tom Hall came back off the crossbar and left him with an open goal only six yards out but he fired wide.

He soon made amends. After 53 minutes a free kick into the middle by Bobby Hewison found the Newcastle left winger who took the ball past Hobson before scoring with a low shot from close range. It was Goodwill's first goal for Newcastle.

With the wind behind them in the second half, the Wearsiders came into the game more but Newcastle were still generally on top. Best and Buchan were well supplied by their half-backs but they could make little headway against Wilson, Hay and Hudspeth.

Newcastle virtually made certain of victory with a second goal after 73 minutes. George Wilson shook himself clear of Thomson and sent Angus Douglas off down the right wing. He drew the Sunderland defence out of position before crossing the ball into the middle where Billy Hibbert glanced a header wide of Butler.

Sunderland tried to fight back as Newcastle decided to merely contain them. The Rokermen did, however, manage to score a consolation goal with virtually the last kick of the match. Harry Martin sent over the ball from a corner kick and a Charles Buchan header did the trick – but it was too little, too late.

Newcastle had been a revelation although Sunderland's efforts in the closing minutes had deserved the goal they scored. But the final scoreline undoubtedly flattered the Wearsiders. On the balance of play Newcastle should have won by three or four goals. Only a combination of poor finishing and resolute Sunderland defending prevented them from doing so.

The defeat seemed to affect Sunderland's confidence in the league. Although they were still second after the match, they were to slip away badly in the second half of the season and finished a mediocre seventh.

The reverse happened to Newcastle. Their victory seemed to be a catalyst for improvement as they climbed away from the relegation zone to eventually finish in mid-table, only three points behind their neighbours.

Football League
Division 1
Newcastle United 2 Sunderland 5 (HT: 0-3)
25th December 1914
St James' Park
40,000

Newcastle: J Lawrence, W McCracken, F Hudspeth, R Hewison, W Low, J Hay,
A Douglas, J King, W Hibbert, T Hall, T Goodwill (ogs Scott [**73**], Ness [**75**])
Sunderland: L Scott, B Hobson, H Ness, F Cuggy, C Thomson, W Cringan, J Mordue,
C Buchan [**44**], R Best [**8, 31, 49**], G Philip [**69**], H Martin
Referee: J T Howcroft (Bolton)

THERE WAS little between the teams with both beginning to show signs of
improvement after bad times. The public eagerly looked forward to the two
Christmas games to help take their minds off the war. Soldiers, sailors and
women were admitted at half price.

The referee inspected the pitch on the morning of the match and initially
declared it unfit for play largely because it was frozen solid. Surprisingly, despite no apparent improvement, he then let the game go ahead. The slight
sprinkling of sand that was scattered over the surface made little difference.
The consensus view was that it should never have taken place.

League Positions

		Pos	Pl	Pts		Pos	Pl	Pts
Before	Sunderland	11th	17	17	Newcastle	14th	18	15
After:	Sunderland	10th	18	19	Newcastle	14th	19	15

The Christmas crowd witnessed a farce of pantomime football with players
slithering and sliding all over the pitch. But Sunderland adapted quicker to the
conditions and their first time passing game was much more effective than
Newcastle's insistence on dribbling.

After eight minutes George Philip took the ball to the Newcastle bye-line
before pulling it back for Sunderland's Tyneside-born centre forward Bobby
Best who made no mistake with a hard shot although, perhaps, Lawrence
should have saved it.

Newcastle should have equalised after 20 minutes when Angus Douglas
was brought down by Cringan inside the Sunderland penalty area. Hudspeth,
normally so deadly from the spot, stook the resultant penalty but shot wide.

Bobby Best got his second just after the half hour, beating the hesitant King
and Hibbert before sliding the ball home. Then, a minute before half-time,
Charles Buchan made the score 0-3, tapping the ball between two defenders
before stroking it into the middle of the net as Lawrence helplessly slithered
about as he tried to stop it.

Sunderland continued with their shoot on sight policy and it soon paid further dividends. Four minutes after the interval Bobby Best completed his hat-trick (his first in the league), ending a clever dribble that opened up the Newcastle defence with another hard shot that caught Lawrence by surprise and ended in the right hand corner of the net.

The pitch remained frozen on the flanks and ensured that most of the play was concentrated in the middle. Sunderland took the score to 5-0 with 21 minutes left. Harry Martin and George Philip took the ball upfield and George helped the ball into the net. To compound Newcastle's misery, there were still more than 20 minutes to go and spectral visions of a repeat of the 1-9 thrashing of six years earlier arose for the Newcastle supporters. But after 73 minutes a corner taken by Tom Goodwill caught out Scott in the Sunderland goal and the all the 'keeper could do was fist the ball into his own net. Goals could not be scored direct from a corner before 1924 so this was officially an 'own goal'.

Two minutes later a second 'own goal' followed, with Ness, 20 yards out, firing rather than lobbing the ball back to his goalie who had advanced off his line to collect it. It was perhaps fitting that this pantomime of a game should end with such a farcical goal.

Strangely, considering that they scored all seven goals, the scoreline flattered Sunderland. Newcastle had enjoyed more possession but their game had fallen apart whenever they reached the Sunderland penalty area. Whereas the visitors' defence had been strong and solid, the home rearguard had been hesitant in the slippery conditions. The Rokermen consequently had taken full advantage.

Defeat meant that Newcastle had now dropped 13 points out of 22 at home so far this season and were only four points above relegation. But the casualty lists from France, growing by the day, put events on the football field into perspective.

Sunderland Mags!

When Sunderland met Southampton at Roker Park in the Fourth Round of the FA Cup in January 1951, they found that they had a colour clash. So they borrowed a set of Newcastle's black and white shirts – and won 2-0!

Football League
Division 1
Sunderland 2 Newcastle United 4 (HT: 2-2)
26th December 1914
Roker Park
20,000

Sunderland: L Scott, B Hobson, H Ness, F Cuggy, C Thomson, W Cringan, J Mordue [10], C Buchan [20], R Best, G Philip, H Martin
Newcastle: W Mellor, W McCracken, F Hudspeth [5], R Hewison, W Low, J Hay, A Douglas, W Hibbert [75, 78], R Pailor, A Higgins [16] (inj 49), G Wilson
Referee: J T Howcroft (Bolton)

ON THE morning of the match the Sunderland Fire Brigade was called to put out a fire in the south east corner of Roker Park. It had broken out near the club secretary's office and billiard room (which were housed in wooden premises) but it was soon extinguished and the game went ahead as planned.

The day marked the half-way point in the season for most clubs. Not unexpectedly, Sunderland fielded the same eleven which had won so handsomely at St James' on Christmas Day and were favourites to complete a holiday double over their neighbours. Newcastle, on the other hand, made four team changes, three of them in the forward line where Bob Pailor, Sandy Higgins and George Wilson came in for King, Hall and Goodwill. Bill Mellor took over from Lawrence in goal for the other change.

League Positions		Pos	Pl	Pts		Pos	Pl	Pts
Before	Sunderland	10th	18	19	Newcastle	14th	19	15
After:	Sunderland	10th	19	19	Newcastle	13th	20	17

The soft and heavy pitch mitigated against good football and played tricks on both teams although Sunderland seemed to suffer more than Newcastle. The home side showed better individual skills but the nippy United forwards constantly had the cumbersome Wearside defence in trouble.

The opener came after just five minutes when George Wilson sent over a dangerous corner. The home defence managed to clear it but only as far as Frank Hudspeth 40 yards out. He blasted in a full blooded volley that swerved away from Scott high into the net.

Sunderland quickly retaliated and were level within five minutes. Charlie Thomson sent in a cross for Jackie Mordue who, running in past Hudspeth, cracked in a low shot out of Mellor's reach.

Newcastle' hit back six minutes later. Angus Douglas rode two crunching tackles on the wing before centring for Sandy Higgins to drive home a fine shot to restore the Geordies' lead.

Sunderland should have levelled within a couple of minutes when they were awarded a penalty for a handling offence, Low illegally saving a shot by George Philip that caught Mellor out of his goal. The Newcastle 'keeper, however, made amends when he blocked Mordue's spot kick.

But Newcastle hardly had time to celebrate their escape when Sunderland scored again. A Mordue corner was perfectly placed for Charles Buchan to net the equaliser.

Newcastle dominated play until the interval with Bobby Hewison hitting a Sunderland post and Harry Ness clearing a shot off the line when a goal seemed certain but the scores were still level at the break.

Fatigue began to set in due to the heavy ground, made worse for United when they lost Sandy Higgins due to a thigh strain early in the half. But the end-to-end football and deluge of shots delighted the crowd and either side could have taken the lead. Sunderland wasted a great chance to do so when they were awarded a second penalty, this time for a body-check by Hay on Mordue. Best was entrusted with the kick on this occasion but he blasted wide.

Newcastle gained the breakthrough with 15 minutes left, Angus Douglas setting up Billy Hibbert who was left unmarked with only the goalkeeper to beat from 15 yards. He made no mistake. Three minutes later United assured themselves of victory with a crucial fourth. Hibbert was on the spot again, this time to meet a cross from George Wilson from out on the left and neatly steer a header home.

Just as the Christmas Day scoreline had flattered Sunderland, this time the result flattered Newcastle. But any team that wastes two penalties doesn't deserve to win.

After the derbies, Sunderland had quite a good run in to the end of the season and finished in a respectable eighth position. Newcastle, however, despite a good cup run, faded in the league to finish a disappointing 15th before football was suspended for the rest of the war.

Most Consecutive Scoring Games

Newcastle	Sunderland
16 9 Oct 1948/27 Dec 1955	14 22 Aug 1953/13 Oct 1962
17 Nov 1991/17 Apr 2006	
(On-going)	

Football League
Division 1
Sunderland 2 Newcastle United 0 (HT: 1-0)
22nd November 1919
Roker Park
47,148

Sunderland: T Allen, B Hobson, R Young, F Cuggy, J Kasher, J Poole, R Best,
C Buchan [**17, 48**], B Travers, J Mordue, H Martin
Newcastle: W Bradley, W McCracken, F Hudspeth, T Curry, W Low, J Finlay,
R Robinson, E S Dixon, W Hibbert, C Booth, A Ramsay
Referee: L N Fletcher (Bury)

NEWCASTLE WERE on the back of a ten-match unbeaten run with wins
in their last six games. They were unchanged although Jimmy Lawrence was
still out injured. They had 'enjoyed' an enforced rest on the previous weekend
when their game against Middlesbrough had been snowed off. As it turned
out, this break disrupted their momentum.

Sunderland had also made a good start to the season and were pleased
to welcome back Charles Buchan and Jackie Mordue to field their strongest
eleven for the derby. But their plans were thwarted at the last minute when
first choice 'keeper Leslie Scott (who had been back from injury for just one
game) broke a small bone in his wrist in practice and Tom Allen took over
again in goal.

First class travel was suspended on trains from Tyneside to Wearside as the
railway company tried to squeeze as many passengers as possible into every
train. One guard's van reportedly had 80 people crammed into it.

The Roker Park gates were locked half an hour before the kick-off with between 5,000 and 10,000 still outside. Many remained there to follow the game
by the cheers and groans of those lucky enough to get in.

League Positions		Pos	Pl	Pts		Pos	Pl	Pts
Before:	Newcastle	1st	14	21	Sunderland	5th	14	16
After:	Newcastle	1st	15	21	Sunderland	5th	15	18

This was a fast and exciting game with both teams contributing towards
the entertainment. The opening stages were fairly even but it was Sunderland
who broke the deadlock when, after 17 minutes, Jackie Mordue sent Harry
Martin on a run up the left wing and he centred for Charles Buchan to head
firmly past Bradley.

Newcastle fought back well and had the upper hand for a while but soon
Sunderland were back on the attack. Buchan continued to look dangerous but
Bill Bradley was in excellent form in the United goal and pulled off a couple of

outstanding saves. Half-time arrived with the Wearsiders still one goal ahead, probably deservedly so if only because they had looked sharper in front of goal.

It did not take them long to increase their lead although there was an element of luck about the goal. McCracken tried to clear the ball during an early Sunderland attack with a hefty kick upfield. Unfortunately for him he merely succeeded in blasting the ball against Barney Travers and the rebound fell straight to Charles Buchan who was close in. His shot hit the foot of a Newcastle post and ricocheted against Bradley who went down to try and collect the ball. However the spin proved too much for him and it squirmed out of his grasp and crept over the line in the narrow gap between the 'keeper and a post.

Now two goals ahead, Sunderland quickly adopted the one-back game and ensnared Newcastle in the offside trap, much to the delight of the Roker faithful. United went desperately close to pulling a goal back when Ray Robinson met a Booth cross and rocketed a shot against an upright with Allen well beaten. The game ended with Newcastle pressing strongly but the Sunderland rearguard held firm.

Strangely, the top three teams in the league all lost with Burnley and West Bromwich Albion (second and third respectively) also going down away from home. But the fourth placed side (Manchester United) won so Sunderland merely closed the points gap at the top of the league without climbing any higher. But Newcastle, although still top, were now within their reach.

Most Times Substituted

Newcastle	Sunderland
Nolberto Solano – 3	Charlie Hurley – 2
Gary Nicholson – 2	Peter Davenport – 2
Darren Bradshaw – 2	David Rush – 2
Les Ferdinand – 2	Paul Stewart – 2
Robert Lee – 2	Niall Quinn – 2
Clarence Acuna – 2	Stefan Schwarz – 2
Laurent Robert – 2	
Shola Ameobi – 2	
Alan Shearer – 2	

Football League
Division 1
Newcastle United 2 Sunderland 3 (HT: 2-0)
29th November 1919
St James' Park
61,761

Newcastle: W Bradley, W McCracken, F Hudspeth, T Curry, W Low, J Finlay, R Robinson [43], E S Dixon, W Hibbert [38], T Hall, A Ramsey
Sunderland: T Allen, B Hobson, R Young, F Cuggy, J Kasher, J Poole, J Mordue [62], C Buchan, B Travers [75, 85], C Crossley, H Martin
Referee: L N Fletcher (Bury)

WITH NEWCASTLE the league leaders and obviously determined to gain revenge for their defeat at Roker a week earlier, a massive crowd was anticipated at St James'. Special trains ran every 10 minutes from Sunderland to Newcastle commencing at 10.00am.

Like Sunderland, Newcastle also closed the boys' gate, ostensibly for safety reasons but also perhaps to maximise income. Gates were opened at 1.00pm for a 2.20pm kick-off but they were closed before 2.00pm for everyone but ticket holders. However. they were not all closed at the same time and thousands of supporters rushed frantically from one gate to another as each one was shut.

Newcastle made one change to the side beaten at Roker, bringing in Tom Hall (who had been out injured since September) for Curtis Booth. Sunderland intended to field an unchanged side but Bobby Best had spent two days in bed with a sore throat so they shuffled their forward line and brought in Charley Crossley at inside left.

League Positions		Pos	Pl	Pts		Pos	Pl	Pts
Before:	Newcastle	1st	15	21	Sunderland	5th	15	18
After:	Newcastle	3rd	16	21	Sunderland	4th	16	20

Sunderland attacked from the kick-off but Newcastle withstood the early onslaught to mount a few attacks of their own. Tom Allen saved brilliantly from Robinson, diving to the foot of a post to turn the ball for a corner. Charles Buchan managed to 'score' with a header but the whistle had already gone, the referee spotting his foul on Finlay. It was end-to-end football and surprisingly skilful considering the treacherous playing surface.

Newcastle grabbed the lead seven minutes from half-time when Allen managed to punch the ball away following a corner but only as far as Wilf Low. He returned it into the goalmouth where Allen gathered it only to drop it under pressure from Billy Hibbert who tapped it into the net.

Five minutes later the Newcastle supporters must have thought that they were home and dry. Good work by Tom Hall created the opening for Ray Robinson who banged in a beauty.

United deserved their interval lead and held the upper hand for the first quarter of an hour of the second half. Gradually, however, they were forced back on defence and increasingly had to rely on breakaway attacks.

Yet it was a Sunderland break up their left wing that saw them open their account after 62 minutes. Harry Martin was the architect, crossing into the middle with pace. It proved to be too fast for Hudspeth but not for Jackie Mordue who rushed in and had time to steady himself before shooting past Bradley.

Sunderland, looking particularly strong on their left wing, began to look more and more dangerous and it was no surprise when they equalised with a quarter of an hour to go although the move came from their right flank. Frank Cuggy started it and his centre was inch perfect for Barney Travers who met the ball in his stride to blast an unstoppable shot past Bradley.

Both sides now went for the winner and the game could have gone either way. But it was Sunderland who snatched the points and it was Travers who became the toast of Wearside. He decided to go through on his own and managed to get in a tremendous shot despite a last ditch tackle by McCracken. The ball flew into the corner of the net to give the Wearsiders the victory and send their supporters wild.

A draw would probably have been a fairer result but Sunderland deserved credit for their resilience. Victory saw them crowned as undoubted Cocks of the North, especially as Newcastle picked up three points out of four against Middlesbrough in games on either side of the Tyne-Wear derbies (Sunderland were to gain a similar reward against the Teessiders later in the season).

The two defeats against the Rokermen saw United lose the league leadership. They were to gradually slip down the league to finish in a moderate eighth position, three places behind the Wearsiders. It was certainly Sunderland's year as far the North East was concerned.

Deadly From the Spot

No player has missed more than one penalty kick in the entire history of Tyne-Wear derbies. Only three players have scored more than one penalty – Albert Shepherd, Bobby Mitchell and Ollie Burton (all Newcastle). Pop Robson (Sunderland) and Alan Shoulder (Newcastle) could be added to this list if the 1979 League Cup penalty shoot-out was included.

Player of the Decade 1910s

David Lalty Willis

IT IS highly unlikely that any Sunderland or Newcastle supporters would regard David Willis as one of their all-time greats. In fact most fans have probably never heard of him. But, as a player who spent two periods on Wearside and helped Newcastle to a league championship success as well as winning a Charity Shield medal with them (and therefore being a member of a select band indeed), he deserves at least to be remembered.

Davy was born in Byker in the east end of Newcastle in 1881, the same year that Stanley AFC (Newcastle's original name) played their first games there. He first made his name as a footballer while playing for Jarrow in the Northern Alliance. This was the league that both Sunderland 'A' and Newcastle 'A' teams (the reserves) played in and it was the Wearsiders who first spotted the potential of the young wing half.

Joining the Roker Park club in 1901, Davy initially spent most of his time there playing in the Alliance for Sunderland's second string. His first appearance for the 'A' team at Roker saw him take part in a 7-2 win over his former club, Jarrow. Debuts don't come much better than that. During his first period on Wearside he made one solitary appearance in the league for the first team. It was during his second season there that he deputised at right half for Jim Farquhar away to Derby County. A 5-2 defeat was not the best way to mark a league debut.

He left Roker at the end of that season to try his luck at Reading for a year. When he returned to Wearside for his second stint in the summer of 1904 he was, at 22, a more experienced and better player.

Consequently, this time he made a much greater impact and by the end of his first season back at Roker he had forced his way into the first team. In 1905-06 he did even better and established himself as the club's first choice left half. During the following campaign, however, he had a fight on his hands to hold down his place in the team as he vied with Irish international English McConnell for the coveted first team shirt.

It looked like the Irishman had won the battle when Davy left Sunderland at the end of the 1906-07 season and joined his home town team for a nominal £100 fee. But McConnell was to make only a few more league appearances for Sunderland as both Gavin Jarvie and Harry Low (the brother of Newcastle's Wilf) forced him out of the first team picture and he eventually moved on himself (to Sheffield Wednesday) at the end of the following campaign.

The turnover in playing personnel at both of the Tyne and Wear clubs at this time was incredible. During the 1907 close season, Newcastle either released or made available for transfer no fewer than 34 players, retaining 45 (this obviously included players at all levels in the club). Sunderland did something similar, releasing 35 while retaining 21. Down the road at Middlesbrough, the turnover was even greater with 49 players released and only 18 retained!

Meanwhile, at St James' during the 1907-08 season, Davy Willis had a fight on his hands to gain a first team spot in a side that had just won the league championship. Initially he had to prove his worth in the 'A' team who now played in the North Eastern League. It was here that he showed his versatility, turning out at both right half and left half with equal facility. He could even play at centre half when the occasion demanded.

He managed to play a few first team games quite early in the season as injuries began to take their toll at Gallowgate but it was not until the glut of fixtures over the Christmas/New Year period that he managed to force his way into the team as a regular. Even then, he played right across the half-back line before the season ended.

He was a bit unfortunate not to get an FA Cup Final medal that year. He played in all except one of the league games from the turn of the year until the final and even turned out in the semi-final (a 6-0 win over Fulham). He was in the Cup Final party that travelled to Crystal Palace but not in the team itself. Red hot favourites Newcastle suffered a shock defeat (3-1) at the hands of Second Division Wolverhampton Wanderers but still enormous crowds gathered on the streets of Newcastle to welcome the return of their 'heroes' at the Central Station. In the event, only four players had the courage to return to Newcastle with the official party. The rest stayed in London to return by a later train rather than face their public. The real 'heroes' who returned to Tyneside (to a genuinely warm welcome) were Jimmy Lawrence, Peter McWilliam, skipper Alex Gardner and Davy Willis.

Perhaps Davy's versatility was his main enemy. Although he played in most of the league games for the first team during the 1908-09 season – when Newcastle won the league for the third time in five campaigns – he never made one particular position his own. The fact that, once again, he turned out in all three half-back positions (albeit only once as centre half) illustrates the point.

However he was included in the Newcastle side that took on Southern League Champions Northampton Town at Stamford Bridge for the FA Charity Shield in April 1909. It was then that, for the only time in their history, United won the trophy, a 2-0 win over the Cobblers doing the trick. Davy's medal may not have been as valuable as an FA Cup medal but, for Newcastle, it was a good deal rarer.

For the next two campaigns, Davy was more a supporting player, turning out a fair number of times for the first team, but never enough to be regarded as a regular. He missed out when United eventually won the Cup in 1910 but at least gained a long-awaited finalist's medal the following year when the Magpies lost 1-0 to Bradford City in a replay at Old Trafford.

City had finished higher than United in the league that year so this was not such a shock as it seems today. Davy played in both of the 1911 Cup Final games although he was deputising for the injured Peter McWilliam.

By 1911-12, United's glory years were behind them. So it was somewhat ironic that it was then that Davy firmly established himself as a first choice regular at

St James'. He made 33 appearance (in 38 games) in the league that year – all of them at right half.

But by now he was approaching his 31st birthday and he knew that his best days were behind him. He made only a couple of first team appearances during the following year and he left Gallowgate as soon as the season ended, returning to Elm Park to rejoin Reading in the Southern League.

He was not finished with North East football, however, and he returned to Tyneside a couple of years later in 1915 to see out his playing career with Palmers (Jarrow).

But his career in sport was most definitely not over. In fact, arguably, his best days were ahead of him as he became a respected and successful trainer/coach, initially with Raith Rovers before settling in the Midlands to train Nottingham Forest and Derby County. His biggest success in this phase of his career was training the Rams to FA Cup success in 1946.

He retired from football a year later but eventually took up the role of masseur with the Derbyshire County Cricket Club. It was following Derbyshire's game against Surrey at the Oval in 1949 that Davy passed away at the home of his son-in-law, the great Alex James, in North London.

Sadly his passing went virtually unnoticed back in his native North East. He had belonged to a different era and had really largely missed out in the pre-First World War haul of honours on both Wearside and Tyneside (although players at both clubs in the post-Second World War era would hardly call league championship success 'missing out'). He was almost a forgotten man.

Perhaps David Willis was not one of the 'greats'. But he was undoubtedly versatile, always gave 100% effort and made his mark in both the red'n white and black'n white colours of Sunderland and Newcastle. For that he deserves to be remembered

Record

Sunderland	October 1901 – May 1903;May 1904 – May 1907	
Football League	48 apps	2 gls
FA Cup	4 apps	0 gls
Total	52 apps	2 gls

Newcastle	May 1907 – May 1913	
Football League	95 apps	0 gls
FA Cup	12 apps	1 gl
Others	1 app	0 gls
Total	108 apps	4 gls

CHAPTER 4

*1920s
Tyneside Success*

WITH BOTH a league and cup trophy to their credit, Newcastle could be regarded as more successful than Sunderland in the 1920s. However the Rokermen also had some memorable seasons, managing to finish in the top four in the league no fewer than five times. But it seemed as if it was always a case of so near yet so far. The title invariably eluded them. Newcastle managed a top four finish just twice – but they won the championship in the second of these (1927).

On the other hand, Newcastle finished in the bottom half of the league just once compared to three times by Sunderland. But in United's one occasion (1930), they went desperately close to relegation, finishing just one point above relegated Burnley.

In terms of frequency, honours were evenly divided with Sunderland finishing above their neighbours five times but behind them on an equal number of occasions. United also managed to have a slight advantage in head-to-head meetings, winning eight of their 20 meetings compared to Sunderland's six.

But the decade was also notable for the appearance of two of the greatest goalscorers in Tyne-Wear football history – Hughie Gallacher and Dave Halliday. They both came to the North East from Scotland in 1925 and stayed for almost five years before seeking the bright lights of London. Co-incidentally, they had both played for Queen of the South Wanderers in their younger days but Dave joined Sunderland from Dundee while Hughie came to Tyneside from Airdrieonians. The little Newcastle man was always held in higher regard, gaining no fewer than 20 caps during an era when full internationals were limited to the home countries. It was Dave's misfortune that he was a contemporary of the volatile (yet talented) Hughie and was never capped.

Yet, statistically, Halliday's goalscoring record was better than Gallacher's during their time in the North East as he rattled in an incredible 165 goals in 175 league and cup appearances for Sunderland – a goalscoring percentage of 94.3%! However Hughie's rate of 82.2% (143 goals in 174 games) was also impressive and he had the distinction of captaining United to the league title as well. Both players created new seasonal league goalscoring records for their respective clubs with Hughie notching 36 on his way to the league title in 1926-27 and Dave amassing 43 two years later.

Dave never missed a Tyne-Wear derby during his time at Sunderland and enjoyed/suffered success and failure in equal measure with three wins, three defeats and three draws. International duties meant that Hughie missed quite a few derbies although he had more success in head-to-head encounters, winning three and losing only one of the four games that he played. The wee man also had a better goalscoring ratio in these games, finding the net three times compared to Dave's four in nine matches.

A number of other great players also graced both clubs during the decade. Men such as Bob Thomson, Bob McKay, Tommy Urwin and Albert McInroy wore both red'n white or black'n white (or green in the case of Albert who was a goalkeeper). Tommy had the rare distinction of receiving a benefit from both clubs and, indeed, also from Middlesbrough for whom he had played before joining United. But it was Albert, who served Sunderland so well and was capped for England while with the Wearsiders, who seemed to excel during derby games. Perhaps the passion of the matches ensured that he always had plenty of opportunities to shine.

League Meetings (20)

At Newcastle:	Newcastle – won 7	Drew 2	Lost 1
At Sunderland:	Sunderland – won 5	Drew 4	Lost 1

Penalties Scored (excluding penalty shoot-outs)

Newcastle – 17	Sunderland – 8
C Veitch – 22 Apr 1905	A McCombie – 1 Jan 1904
A Shepherd – 5 Dec 1908	H Low – 17 Feb 1912
A Shepherd – 1 Sep 1910	J Mordue – 17 Mar 1913
W McCracken – 14 Oct 1911	H Shaw – 3 Mar 1934
N Harris – 9 Oct 1920	W Elliott – 1 Feb 1958
H Gallacher – 9 Mar 1929	G Rowell – 24 Feb 1979
J Milburn – 26 Dec 1951	B Robson – 29 Aug 1979
R Mitchell – 22 Aug 1953	M Scott – 4 Sep 1996
R Mitchell – 9 Oct 1954	
T Casey – 22 Dec 1956	
R McGarry – 14 Mar 1964	
A Burton – 20 Dec 1967 (2 pens)	
A Shoulder – 1 Jan 1980	
P Beardsley – 1 Jan 1985	
N Solano – 26 Apr 2003	
A Shearer – 17 Apr 2006	

Football League
Division 1
Newcastle United 6 Sunderland 1 (HT: 2-0)
9th October 1920
St James' Park
61,000

Newcastle: J Lawrence, W McCracken, W Hampson, R McIntosh, W Low, J Finlay, W Aitken, E Ward [**88**], N Harris [**43** (pen), **48**], A Smailes [**33, 57**], G S Seymour [**53**]
Sunderland: L Scott, B Hobson, E England, F Cuggy, J Kasher, J Poole, R Best, C Buchan [**50**], B Travers, A V Shore, H Martin
Referee: J T Howcroft (Bolton)

THIS WAS an eagerly awaited fixture and a close match was anticipated; a question of Newcastle's exuberant attack against Sunderland's renowned defence. The Rokermen came to Gallowgate with only one defeat behind them – away to Blackburn. They were just two points behind league championship pacesetters Everton and Aston Villa with Newcastle not far behind. In fact, with both of the North East rivals near the top of the First Division and South Shields actually top of the Second, this was a good time for local football.

Despite wins in their last games, both sides made changes, some voluntary but at least one that was not. Newcastle brought back Low and Harris in place of Mooney and Pyke to field a full-strength line-up while Sunderland similarly recalled fit again Cuggy and Best for George and Foster. One change that they probably would not have made if it had not been forced upon them was the selection of Shore at inside left in place of the injured Moore.

A bumper crowd was anticipated with Newcastle announcing, "The ground has been reconstructed so that 70,000 spectators can be housed provided that, on the Popular Side, they do not congest the gangways and pack closely". Presumably they were expected to breath in permanently as well!

Despite this optimism, queues began to form at the gates by 10.00am – and they were not due to open until three hours later for the 3.00pm kick-off. By 1.30pm the main entrances to the 'stand were closed and all gates were shut an hour later. The game began 20 minutes early.

League Positions		Pos	Pl	Pts		Pos	Pl	Pts
Before:	Sunderland	4th	8	11	Newcastle	7th	8	10
After:	Newcastle	3rd	9	12	Sunderland	6th	9	11

Jock Finlay won the toss and decided to defend the town goal (Gallowgate End). Sunderland did the early attacking but soon fell foul of Newcastle's offside trap. Soon United took up the offensive but somehow Smailes and Seymour missed easy chances to score. For once Sunderland sprang McCracken's offside trap and Martin broke clear to look a certain scorer until McCracken brought him down to concede a penalty. Hobson blasted the spot kick straight at Lawrence who blocked it with Hampson turning the loose ball for a corner. Undeterred, McCracken was soon up to his offside ploy again and twice foiled Wearside attacks.

The opening goal could have gone either way but it was Newcastle who scored it after 33 minutes. Stan Seymour rounded the visitors' defence and came within two yards of the goal line before crossing to Andy Smailes who blasted in a great shot from an acute angle that rattled the underside of the crossbar before ending up in the far corner of the net.

Sunderland launched an onslaught with Best, Buchan and Travers working hard. But Newcastle's defenders were up to everything thrown at them and, at the other end, their forwards showed the visitors how to score goals.

Ten minutes after they had taken the lead Newcastle scored again. Leslie Scott produced a great save from Aitken but the ball came out to McIntosh. Rather than shoot at the crowd of Sunderland players blocking the goalmouth, he played a pass out to the unmarked Seymour. Stan hit the ball first time at the unattended target but was foiled by Kasher who threw himself to block the shot with his hands. Neil Harris took the spot kick and gave Scott no chance; 2-0 at half-time.

Sunderland again attacked straight from the kick-off but were made to pay within three minutes for throwing too many players upfield. They tried to play an offside trap of their own but failed as Stan Seymour raced up the wing. His centre was perfect for Neil Harris who snapped up the cross to comprehensively beat Scott.

It took Sunderland only two minutes to reduce the leeway and it was a fair reward for a veritable siege on the Newcastle goal. A hasty clearance by the United defence went out to Harry Martin who crossed the ball into the middle. Charles Buchan showed sublime anticipation as he rounded two Newcastle defenders to reach the ball first and head into the net.

Hardly had the excitement died down than Scott had to be on his toes to keep out Ward. But his partial clearance only reached Bob McIntosh who plied Stan Seymour. The winger's ball control was perfect as he took the pass in his stride and confidently shot home.

Sunderland tried to strike back but it was now a lost cause and it was United who soon increased their lead to 5-1. A Seymour corner was met by Andy Smailes and he deflected a header past Scott.

Newcastle sensed a massacre and went for it as Sunderland were forced to defend desperately. Seymour and Smailes particularly caused havoc although, fortunately for the Wearsiders, their finishing was not very accurate.

But another goal had to come and two minutes from time Wilf Low started a move that was carried on by Billy Aitken. He cut inside before trying a shot from 10 yards. Scott did well to save but was unable to hold the ball which rolled from his grasp. Ted Ward and Seymour were lurking nearby and it was the inside forward who got there first to complete the scoring.

This was a big win for Newcastle in more ways than one. They had systematically out-generalled and then outplayed Sunderland although, to the Wearsiders' credit, they had given as good as they had received in the first half hour. But by the end the 6-1 scoreline probably flattered them.

This was the first time that Newcastle had beaten Sunderland by more than two goals and after suffering a double defeat at the hands of their local rivals last season, revenge was sweet. But for how long? The return fixture at Roker was only a week away.

Football League
Division 1
Sunderland 0 Newcastle United 2 (HT: 0-0)
16th October 1920
Roker Park
40,000

Sunderland: L Scott, B Hobson, E England, W George, J Kasher, J Poole, R Best, C Buchan, B Travers, F R Cooke, H Martin
Newcastle: J Lawrence, W McCracken, W Hampson, R McIntosh, W Low, J Finlay, W Aitken, E Ward, N Harris [58], A Smailes, G S Seymour [47]
Referee: J T Howcroft (Bolton)

HOT ON the heels of their 6-1 win over the Wearsiders a week earlier, Newcastle naturally took an unchanged side to Roker for the return fixture. Sunderland had a 100 percent home record this season but their confidence had been severely dented by their defeat at Gallowgate. Possible changes to their side were limited with their reserve team comprised largely of untried players. In the event, just two alterations were made – Bill George coming in for only his second (and last) first team league appearance along with Bob Cooke in place of Cuggy and Shore.

Although queues began to form outside the ground at 10.30am with the gates opening at 1.00pm, the crowd was a little below that expected. A pit strike and the heavy defeat at St James' a week earlier both had an impact but the atmosphere was still intense at kick-off time.

League Positions		Pos	Pl	Pts		Pos	Pl	Pts
Before:	Newcastle	3rd	9	12	Sunderland	6th	9	11
After:	Newcastle	3rd	10	14	Sunderland	10th	10	11

Newcastle were on top for the first 20 minutes but the nearest that they came to scoring was when Scott fisted away a Seymour shot for a corner. Sunderland, however, came into the game more midway through the half. The Sunderland supporters reminded their Tyneside visitors that their six goals a week earlier was not a Tyne-Wear record by chanting the numbers one to nine, reminding the Geordies of the 1908 game at Gallowgate.

Neither team were able to gain the upper hand before the interval although it was apparent that Sunderland relied heavily on their captain, Charles Buchan. The whole team looked up to him and depended on him. United's skipper, Jock Finlay, became aware of this and realised that if Buchan could be marked out of the game, Sunderland could be beaten. Nevertheless, the goalless scoreline at half-time was fitting tribute to two solid defences.

Newcastle attacked straight from the restart and opened their account within two minutes. Bob McIntosh played the ball up the wing to Billy Aitken and the winger's accurate cross into the middle was met by Stan Seymour whose stooping header from right in front of the posts gave Scott no chance.

Sunderland tried to force their way back into the game with both Buchan and Best going close but Newcastle soon took control again and it was no surprise when they increased their lead. McIntosh again started the move, taking the ball from the feet of Cooke to ply Aitken with another superb pass. The winger took the ball forward before slipping a pass through for Neil Harris who darted between Hobson and England to crack a shot home.

The second goal silenced the bell-ringing home crowd and disheartened their team, particularly their half-back line who began to struggle badly. Yet United fell back on defence for long periods, seemingly content with their two goal lead. It was enough and that was the way it stayed until the final whistle. No-one could deny that they were worthy winners.

This was only Sunderland's second home defeat in 10 months but it shattered their confidence. They failed to win any of their next seven games, including home and away defeats against their other North East First Division neighbours, Middlesbrough. They plunged down the league but staged a bit of recovery later in the season to finish in mid-table.

The Tyne-Wear double victory established Newcastle as championship contenders, only two points behind leaders Everton with two games in hand. They soon climbed to second place and held that position for quite a while, even briefly topping the league at the end of October. But just two wins in their last eight games saw them slip to finish a disappointing fifth.

Football League
Division 1
Newcastle United 2 Sunderland 2 (HT: 2-0)
19th November 1921
St James' Park
49,000

Newcastle: J Lawrence, R Roxburgh, F Hudspeth, R McIntosh [3], W Low, T Curry, W Aitken, A Hagan, E S Dixon, T McDonald [7], T Mitchell
Sunderland: L Scott, B Hobson, E England, C Parker, J Kasher, J Poole, R Best, J Stephenson, C Buchan [51], R Marshall [56], H Martin
Referee: J Cahill (Liverpool)

HIGH-FLYING SUNDERLAND were just behind both Burnley and Liverpool on goal average in the league. They were also able to field their strongest team with both Bobby Best and Harry Martin returning from a two week absence due to a chill and injury respectively. These were the only changes to the side that had lost away to Oldham a week earlier.

Newcastle, on the other hand, had a number of injuries and illnesses with no fewer than seven probable first team starters missing: McCracken, Finlay, Mooney, Hampson, Harris, Smailes and Seymour. Their directors delayed team selection until an hour before the kick-off to give any of their experienced players time to recover but to no avail. They eventually gambled by making two changes to the side that had lost at home to Tottenham, bringing in Stan Dixon (for his first game of the season) and Alf Hagan (for only his ninth game in over two years) into the attack. Expectations in the Gallowgate camp were not high.

League Positions

		Pos	Pl	Pts		Pos	Pl	Pts
Before:	Sunderland	3rd	14	19	Newcastle	9th	14	16
After:	Sunderland	3rd	15	20	Newcastle	9th	15	17

Bad weather kept the crowd below that expected and Buchan started the game, playing against the wind, 10 minutes before the appointed time. Newcastle launched the first attack and soon broke through the Sunderland rearguard. After just three minutes Tom Mitchell forced a corner off Hobson and took the resultant flag kick himself, placing the ball for Bob McIntosh to head a fine goal. He was to score just two goals in over 100 games for the Magpies and this was his first.

United stormed straight back on to the attack and had a good claim for a penalty turned down when Stan Dixon was felled inside the area. They were full of confidence and it was no surprise when they increased their lead within four minutes. A clever run to the goal line by Billy Aitken saw him loop a

115

short, dropping centre into the penalty area where Tommy McDonald applied the finishing touch.

So far it had been all Newcastle but Sunderland gradually began to play their way back into the game. However, with Tom Curry giving a magnificent display, United's forwards were soon back on the attack. Their free-flowing open football created a number of openings but Leslie Scott in the Sunderland goal was in top form. One tip over the top from a Dixon shot was superb.

Play was stopped after 34 minutes when Parker received a blow on his nose from Mitchell's boot as the Sunderland man went in with a tackle. Charlie had to leave the field and it was learned that his nose was broken. He was still absent when the teams reappeared for the second half but he returned within a couple of minutes.

The visitors' persistence finally paid off when they reduced the deficit early in the half. Harry Martin easily beat Roxburgh out on the left wing to centre for Charles Buchan to shoot. Lawrence almost kept it out but the ball entered the net low down.

It took the Rokerites only five more minutes to level the scores and this included two periods of treatment to players who were injured as play became rather hectic. Buchan, who had largely been well held by Low, broke clear with a rare burst of speed and eye-catching footwork that took him to the bye-line where he just managed to cross for Bobby Marshall to snap up the equaliser.

Within a minute, Newcastle had the ball in the Sunderland net again following a scramble under their crossbar – but the effort was disallowed. United once again began to dominate the game but Leslie Scott was unbeatable in the Sunderland goal. The visitors were confined in their own half for prolonged periods, relying on spasmodic break-aways. A final burst through the middle by Aitken in the dying minutes looked likely to produce the winner but Scott rushed out to foil Newcastle yet again. It was all square at the final whistle following a hard game although the consensus of opinion from both camps was that Sunderland were lucky to escape with a point.

The result saw no change in either team's league position. Sunderland were still third but were now a point adrift of Liverpool and still behind Burnley on goal average. The injury to Parker made him a major doubt for the return fixture at Roker Park a week later by which time Newcastle hoped to have a couple of their injured players available. Whether they would change a side that had generally outplayed the Wearsiders, however, was a different matter.

Football League
Division 1
Sunderland 0 Newcastle United 0 (HT: 0-0)
26th November 1921
Roker Park
49,483

Sunderland: L Scott, B Hobson, E England, J Mitton, J Kasher, J Poole, R Best, J Stephenson, C Buchan, R Marshall, H Martin
Newcastle: W Bradley, R Roxburgh, F Hudspeth, R McIntosh, W Low, T Curry, W Aitken, A Hagan, N Harris, T McDonald, T Mitchell
Referee: J Cahill (Liverpool)

SUNDERLAND WERE forced to make one team change from the side that had drawn at St James' a week earlier. Charlie Parker had broken his nose in that game but still wanted to play at Roker only for the club doctor to rule otherwise. Jack Mitton therefore came in to take his place.

Newcastle had been forced to field a weakened side in the Gallowgate game and most of their missing stars were still absent. There was one exception – Neil Harris was now fit. He was going to return to lead the attack with Alf Hagan dropping out but an injury to Stan Dixon saw Alf gain a reprieve. Bill Bradley was preferred to Jimmy Lawrence in goal. It was a topic for debate at the time as to who was the better goalkeeper.

As usual, the fixture attracted a bumper crowd with the stands full an hour before the scheduled 2.15pm kick-off.

League Positions		*Pos*	*Pl*	*Pts*		*Pos*	*Pl*	*Pts*
Before:	Sunderland	3rd	15	20	Newcastle	9th	15	17
After:	Sunderland	3rd	16	21	Newcastle	9th	16	18

This was a hard and strenuous game but both sides played fair. Sunderland applied pressure early on but the Newcastle defence was sound and reliable. Both sides had narrow escapes as United came into the game more. Tommy McDonald showed up well in the visitors' attack and went very close with a shot that skimmed the bar. Neil Harris felt that he was hard done by when he broke past both of the Sunderland backs and had only Scott to beat when the referee blew his whistle and brought play back to restart it with a bounced ball. Bobby Marshall looked dangerous for Sunderland and forced Bill Bradley into an impressive full length save. Buchan and Low were involved in a battle royal. The Newcastle pivot never had the same control of the Sunderland leader that he had the previous week but still had a slight advantage. The first half ended goalless but the consensus of opinion was that this was one of the best games seen at Roker Park this season.

Both sides created chances early in the second half but both 'keepers saved well. A great fight was developing between two very good teams. But Aitken was soon limping on the Newcastle right wing and this badly hampered his movement. Sunderland's best chance of the match came 27 minutes into the half. Harry Martin out-manoeuvred the Newcastle defence and advanced towards their area. Bradley was caught in two minds as he advanced to cut down the angle but then retreated when he realised that Buchan was unmarked in the middle. Martin centred perfectly but Buchan headed over the top with a gaping goal in front of him.

Soon afterwards came the best shot of the match. Curry and Harris combined to send in Tommy McDonald who ran clear of all opposition to beat Scott comprehensively with a shot that came out off the foot of an upright. Newcastle pressurised the Wearsiders in the closing stages when Harris, too anxious, shot wide from close range and McDonald shot straight into Scott's hands. Newcastle probably enjoyed a slight edge on the overall play by virtue of creating the better openings but neither team deserved to lose an entertaining game.

The back to back derby matches ended with Newcastle still more or less in mid-table and Sunderland still in third place, one point adrift of leaders Burnley and just behind Liverpool on goal average. However the Rokermen were not able to maintain their momentum and were to lose nine of their next dozen games and slip down the league to finish in mid-table, six points and five places behind seventh placed Newcastle.

Football League
Division 1
Newcastle United 2 Sunderland 1 (HT: 1-0)
4th November 1922
St James' Park
60,000

Newcastle: W Bradley, W Hampson, F Hudspeth, T Curry, W Low, E Mooney, J Low, W Aitken [35], N Harris, T McDonald [76], G S Seymour
Sunderland: E Robson, W Cresswell, E England, G Hunter, C Parker, J Poole, A Donaldson, C Buchan [57], J Paterson, A Hawes, W Ellis
Referee: G N Watson (Nottingham)

SUNDERLAND HAD emerged as early season championship contenders and were behind leaders Liverpool only on goal average. It was not surprising they were unchanged for a fifth consecutive game. It was a good time for North East football with Middlesbrough in third place, just one point behind the Rokermen.

Newcastle were slightly adrift, due largely to a bad injury situation. First team regulars McCracken and McIntosh were both out as were possible deputies Russell and Roxburgh along with Mutch, Dixon and Richardson. Team selection was delayed until the morning of the match.

Sunderland's success so far raised enthusiasm on Wearside with between 600 and 700 of the town's unemployed lining up to march en masse to Newcastle. About another 1,000 supporters also walked with many travelling by char-a-banc and nearly 5,000 queuing up at Sunderland Central Station to travel by train.

League Positions

		Pos	Pl	Pts		Pos	Pl	Pts
Before:	Sunderland	2nd	12	16	Newcastle	8th	12	13
After:	Sunderland	4th	13	16	Newcastle	5th	13	15

This turned out to be one of the hardest games ever between these two earnest rivals. Newcastle started by playing a close controlled game, possibly too close at times, while Sunderland swung the ball around, adopting more open tactics. United were the more aggressive with Mooney closely shadowing Buchan. Seymour was the first to threaten, sending a shot just over the bar. Once Newcastle began to open out their play more, they soon breached the Wearside rearguard. Jimmy Low was allowed a run unattended down the wing and his cross was met perfectly by Neil Harris but as he shot into the net, the whistle went for offside. But Newcastle were not to be denied and the next time that they scored, the goal counted.

After 35 minutes, a Stan Seymour corner was met by Harris who headed the ball in to Billy Aitken. Standing almost on the goal line, Aitken could hardly miss and he headed home.

Newcastle deserved their lead and, with their wingers always dangerous on the flanks, they pushed back Sunderland. Jimmy Low beat Robson in the Sunderland goal with a cross-shot that went inches outside the far post. Then Warney Cresswell cleared a great shot by Harris from under the bar as the Rokerites hung on. United were easily the better side in the first half and clearly deserved their half-time lead.

But Sunderland were a totally different proposition after the interval. They set up the early attacks and it was Newcastle's turn to defend. Mooney failed to clear a Billy Ellis cross and Wilf Low had to be sharp to clear off his line. United played some impressive defensive football with Billy Hampson and Frank Hudspeth outstanding. But Sunderland were undeterred and, 12 minutes after half-time, Alex Donaldson put Charles Buchan in possession. For once, he found himself with space and he made the most of the opportunity, giving Bradley no chance with a great shot.

Encouraged by their success, Sunderland pushed forward and Buchan went close again with a shot that flew just past a post. But Newcastle weathered the storm to regain the lead, albeit against the run of play with just under a quarter of an hour remaining. Tommy McDonald scored the goal, running in to meet a Jimmy Low pass and lift his shot into the roof the net from an acute angle.

Sunderland attacked again and Newcastle had to battle to hang on before coming back in the closing stages. Yet it was the visitors who went closest to scoring again. There were just five minutes to go when Hawes seemed clean through only for Hudspeth to come to United's rescue, robbing him just as he seemed about to score.

Both sets of players were exhausted at the end of a monumental battle that Newcastle just about deserved to win. The members of the St John Ambulance Brigade were also pretty tired. They had worked virtually non-stop, removing injured spectators from the crowd. They helped 50 people in all, although just one had a serious injury (crushed ribs).

The defeat saw Sunderland slip to fourth place, now two points behind leaders Liverpool and one behind second placed Middlesbrough. With Newcastle climbing to fifth, this meant that all three of the North East's 'Big Three' were in the top five.

Football League
Division 1
Sunderland 2 Newcastle United 0 (HT: 0-0)
11th November 1922
Roker Park
47,000

Sunderland: E Robson, W Cresswell, E England, G Hunter, C Parker, J Poole, A Donaldson, C Buchan, J Paterson [57], A Hawes [47], W Ellis
Newcastle: W Bradley, W Hampson, F Hudspeth, T Curry, W Low, E Mooney (inj 34), J Low, W Aitken, N Harris, T McDonald, G S Seymour
Referee: G N Watson (Nottingham)

BOTH SIDES relied on the players who had fought out the momentous struggle at St James' Park a week earlier.

Once again a bumper crowd turned up. Attendances for league games were unofficial at the time and were based on press estimates. The crowd for this game was variously quoted as 'well over 40,000', 47,000 and 50,000 although it was also stated that the crowd was some thousands less than the previous year (49,483). It was also estimated that 4,500 travelled to Wearside from Newcastle by train. Expectations were high in both camps.

League Positions		Pos	Pl	Pts		Pos	Pl	Pts
Before:	Sunderland	4th	13	16	Newcastle	5th	13	15
After:	Sunderland	2nd	14	18	Newcastle	9th	14	15

As the teams appeared the ground was bathed in sunshine except where the stand cast its shadow. Sunderland stormed into the attack straight from the kick-off and a great Charles Buchan shot tested Bill Bradley who managed to clear the ball at the second attempt. Alex Donaldson then sent a great drive inches over the bar.

Soon Newcastle were on the attack and Ed Robson had to be on his toes to save from an Aitken header. The 'keeper did even better to clear a Tommy McDonald shot soon afterwards. Then it was Stan Seymour's turn to test him as Cresswell and England struggled to keep out the Tyneside wingers.

But the home side also threatened and efforts by Hunter and Hawes were both blocked by defenders. It was enthralling end-to-end stuff. But an incident in the 34th minute changed the whole complexion of the game. Mooney and Hunter both went for the ball together and both ended in a heap. Hunter was quickly to his feet but Mooney never moved. He was carried off and took no further part in the game. Up to this point he had kept Buchan under close control but, although McDonald moved back from the forward line to bolster midfield, Charlie now found that he had some freedom. He made the most of it as Sunderland took command of the game. The rest of the play was generally a Tyneside rearguard action. Fortunately for them, Bill Bradley was in top form as were his full backs, Billy Hampson and Frank Hudspeth, and United held out until the interval.

But it took Sunderland just a couple of minutes after the resumption to break through. It was a simple goal. Alex Donaldson swung in a centre that was misjudged by Bradley. The ball went over him to Arthur Hawes who had a simple task to nod home from right in front of the posts.

Newcastle struggled gamely but soon found themselves further behind and it was a great move by Charles Buchan that set up the goal. He raced up the middle of the field and drew the defence before slipping a perfect pass into the path of Jock Paterson. The centre forward did not even have to break stride as he shot past the helpless Bradley.

Newcastle did manage to mount the occasional raid and Stan Seymour nearly scored at one point, Robson blocking (but failing to hold) his shot and scrambling the ball away at the last second. Generally, however, Sunderland were well on top and laid siege to the United goal. Only heroics by the visiting 'keeper and his defenders kept them at bay. Bill Bradley was superb as he foiled Buchan, Parker and Ellis in quick succession but this just kept the score down to a respectable level as the Wearsiders emerged comfortable winners.

Sunderland collected both of the points but most of the accolades after the match went to the Newcastle defence. Mooney (who had received a bad kick in the stomach/groin) was to be out of action for three weeks. He sportingly insisted that the injury had been an accident and absolved Hunter of any blame. Until his retirement, it had been anybody's game.

The victory lifted Sunderland back into second place, just one point behind

Liverpool with Middlesbrough a further point behind in third place. The win was the beginning of a 16 game unbeaten run for the Rokermen in the league as they mounted a serious title challenge. But a poor finish, in which they lost seven of their last 13 games, saw them finish six points adrift of Liverpool although still in second place.

Newcastle were to finish a respectable fourth although Middlesbrough failed to maintain their pace and slipped to finish close to a relegation spot (18th).

Football League
Division 1
Sunderland 3 Newcastle United 2 (HT: 3-2)
15th December 1923
Roker Park
45,000

Sunderland: A McInroy, J E Oakley, E England, W Clunas, C Parker, A Andrews, W Grimshaw, C Buchan, J Paterson [**19**], A Hawes [**22, 24**], W Ellis
Newcastle: W Bradley, W Hampson, F Hudspeth, T Curry, E Mooney, W Gibson, W Aitken, W Cowan, N Harris [**7**], T McDonald, G S Seymour [**42**]
Referee: A Ward (Kirkham)

THERE WAS little between the two sides when they met at Roker with United ahead only on goal average – 0.2 of a goal!

The Magpies had defeated Burnley a week earlier and fielded an unchanged side. Sunderland, however, with a defeat at Huddersfield behind them, made two changes, one by choice and one by necessity. Marshall was dropped and replaced by Jock Paterson in a re-arranged forward line but a potentially serious accident to Cresswell forced a change in defence. It had happened on the Thursday before the game. The players were in the communal bath when Mitton tried to close a skylight window. It crashed down and broke, part of the falling glass striking Warney behind his left shoulder. The cut required two stitches but it could have been much worse. As it was, he was ruled out of the Newcastle game and Oakley deputised. It was rare run out for the reserve full back – just his second first team game since he had joined the club from Blyth Spartans 18 months earlier.

One of the linesmen did not turn up in time for the kick-off and Wilf Low (now Newcastle's reserve centre half) ran the line for the first ten minutes when, to his obvious relief, the official arrived.

League Positions		Pos	Pl	Pts		Pos	Pl	Pts
Before:	Newcastle	7th	19	22	Sunderland	8th	19	22
After:	Sunderland	6th	20	24	Newcastle	8th	20	22

An exciting game provided fine entertainment for the Roker Park enthusiasts. Sunderland created the first opening but Buchan, of all people, shot over the top with a yawning goal in front of him. Newcastle made the Rokermen pay for this miss by storming into an early lead after seven minutes. Neil Harris played a beautiful return pass with Stan Seymour out on the left before neatly wheeling around England and blasting a shot past McInroy into the roof of the net.

Sunderland immediately tried to hit back, plying their wingers and stretching the Tyneside defence and it was no surprise when they equalised after 19 minutes. Billy Grimshaw raced in from the wing to try a shot at goal. This was blocked on the line by Hampson but, before it could be cleared, Jock Paterson, following up, managed to touch it home.

Sunderland maintained this momentum and went ahead three minutes later. The ball came out to Charlie Parker who pushed it forward to Arthur Hawes and the inside man coolly placed a shot wide of Bradley into the corner of the net.

The Newcastle defence were now a shambles and the Rokermen increased their lead a couple of minutes later. Grimshaw, once again, dashed down the right wing before sending over a dropping centre to the unmarked Hawes who steered a header well away from Bradley.

Three goals in five minutes had sent the Roker crowd into ecstasy and, with the visiting defenders looking totally dejected, visions of a repeat of the 9-1 debacle of 15 years earlier were conjured up. But, to their credit, the Newcastle defenders rallied, stopped the rot and threw back the home attacks. Gradually United came more and more into the game. The referee was forced to suspend play for a time to get the crowd, which had encroached over the touchline, off the pitch. The Magpies had a goal disallowed when the scorer, Stan Seymour, was ruled offside but they still pushed forward, eventually gaining just reward for their endeavours three minutes before the break when Billy Aitken raced down the right and sent over a pass to Seymour and Stan was able to volley home a first time shot that easily beat McInroy.

No sooner was the game restarted than Cowan went down injured following a collision with England and was carried off with an injured knee. The game was back in the melting pot but much depended upon how badly Cowan was injured.

There was doubt whether he would resume – but he did, albeit hobbling on the wing. Newcastle maintained their pressure, even when they were temporarily reduced to ten men after Mooney fell heavily and was missing for five minutes receiving treatment. They nearly equalised when Seymour set up a chance for Harris in front of goal but Albert McInroy pulled off an instinctive save to foil the centre forward from point blank range. There was no love lost between Hudspeth and Buchan who seemed to regard this game as a personal duel. Sunderland looked the more likely scorers in the closing stages but Bill Bradley did well to keep out a rasping shot by Paterson. The game ended with the Wearsiders back on defence, content to hold out with their one goal advantage.

Sunderland collected both of the points but the general consensus of opinion was that Newcastle had deserved at least a share of them. Indeed, more than a few spectators felt that the Magpies could have won if Cowan had not been injured. England was criticised for his reckless tackle on the Newcastle man which would rule him out of the return meeting at St James' a week later.

Football League
Division 1
Newcastle United 0 Sunderland 2 (HT: 0-1)
22nd December 1923
St James' Park
49,000

Newcastle: A Mutch, W Hampson, F Hudspeth, T Curry, W Low, W Gibson, W Aitken, J R Clark, N Harris, T McDonald, G S Seymour
Sunderland: A McInroy, W Cresswell, E England, W Clunas, C Parker, A Andrews, W Grimshaw, C Buchan, J Paterson [**25, 71**], A Hawes, W Ellis
Referee: A Ward (Kirkham)

NEWCASTLE HAD injury problems as they went into the return game. Bradley, Cowan and Mooney, all injured at Roker a week earlier, were ruled out so Sandy Mutch (making his first appearance of the season), young Bob Clark (making only his second) and veteran Wilf Low filled their respective berths.

Sunderland made one change, Cresswell returning in place of Oakley. The latter, who had excelled in last week's game, was unlucky to lose his place but Warney was one of Sunderland's stars.

League Positions		Pos	Pl	Pts		Pos	Pl	Pts
Before:	Sunderland	6th	20	24	Newcastle	8th	20	22
After:	Sunderland	5th	21	26	Newcastle	9th	21	22

Sunderland, with the wind in their favour, did the early attacking but rarely got within shooting distance and it was Newcastle who threatened first through Harris. The game was played at a cracking pace with Sunderland looking the better side so it was no surprise when they grabbed the first goal.

After 25 minutes Hudspeth failed to intercept a long ball into the Newcastle half and Charles Buchan raced away, taking the ball almost to the goal line before crossing. It was no more than a gentle lob but it went straight to Jock Paterson who nodded it against the underside of the crossbar, the ball bouncing into the net.

Both Buchan and Harris tried long shots at goal, each time their efforts going just wide. Newcastle fought their way back into the game and there was soon very little between the sides. As the interval approached, however, United began to create chances. Warney Cresswell cleared from a Neil Harris header with McInroy beaten and a Tommy McDonald shot from the rebound cannoned off another defender. But it was still 0-1 at the interval.

Newcastle were clearly on top for the first 25 minutes of the second half but Warney Cresswell and Ernie England played superbly in the Wearside defence. Sunderland were penned in their half but a mixture of bad luck, bad finishing and heroic defending kept the Magpies out. With Billy Gibson having Buchan in a tight grip, the Rokermen rarely looked dangerous. A Seymour drive from out on the wing looked as if it as going to dip under the bar but Albert McInroy tipped it over the top. Then Sunderland scored a breakaway goal totally against the run of play with 19 minutes left.

Hampson was caught in possession after receiving from a Mutch throw and Charlie Parker dashed in to play the ball forward to Arthur Hawes. His shot was charged down but the ball was promptly swung over to Jock Paterson who shot past Mutch into the net.

This goal virtually settled the issue although Newcastle kept pushing forward. Albert McInroy twice saved well following Hudspeth free kicks. Then, near the end, the 'keeper was beaten by a shot from Tommy McDonald only for the crossbar to come to his aid. Newcastle knew that this was just not going to be their day.

This was Newcastle's first home defeat of the season. The consensus of opinion was that Sunderland probably deserved to win although the scoreline flattered them.

Having completed the 'double' over their neighbours, Sunderland used the win as a springboard to a fairly successful season. They were to finish third in the league, just four points behind the top two, Huddersfield and Cardiff.

Newcastle went on to have a moderate league season, finishing in a respectable ninth place. But their glory lay in the Cup and they were to end the season with the ultimate knock out trophy, defeating Aston Villa in the second ever Wembley final. Most Newcastle supporters were more than happy with that.

Football League
Division 1
Sunderland 1 Newcastle United 1 (HT: 1-1)
18th October 1924
Roker Park
55,642

Sunderland: A McInroy, W Cresswell, E England, W Clunas, C Parker, A Andrews, W Grimshaw, R Marshall [26], C Buchan, A Hawes, W Death
Newcastle: W Bradley, S Russell, F Hudspeth, E Mooney, C Spencer, W Gibson, T Urwin, J R Clark [9], N Harris, T McDonald, G S Seymour
Referee: H Hopkinson (Rochdale)

SUNDERLAND WERE a point behind leaders Huddersfield Town and second placed West Bromwich Albion when they welcomed Newcastle to Roker. The Rokerites, who had won four of their five home games so far this season, fielded the same starting eleven that had won their last game away to Everton.

United, who had drawn four of their five away games, made a couple of changes to their side that had drawn at home to Liverpool a week earlier. Cowan had been injured against the Merseysiders so Bob Clark took his place. Peter Mooney also returned after a three week absence and replaced Curry who went along as a reserve. The Newcastle players travelled to Wearside by motor car.

Sunderland were favourites to win in front of a record Roker Park attendance which was 6,000 above the previous best set in a Burnley cup tie in 1920. Many of the gates were closed a full hour before kick-off time and the ambulance men were kept busy carrying injured spectators away long before the match started.

League Positions		Pos	Pl	Pts		Pos	Pl	Pts
Before:	Sunderland	3rd	9	13	Newcastle	7th	11	11
After:	Sunderland	4th	10	14	Newcastle	8th	12	12

The game was played at a fast and furious pace with never a dull moment. Newcastle struck first after nine minutes. A centre from Stan Seymour out on the left sailed into the home penalty area and, as the Wearside defence watched United's danger man Neil Harris, Bob Clark stole in almost unnoticed to give McInroy no chance with a superb header.

Clark had a very good game on his return to the first team and he looked Newcastle's most effective forward, although Tommy McDonald ran him close. Sunderland suffered a setback when Clunas sustained a strained muscle at the base of his spine. He had to go off for treatment but returned after just five minutes to play on. Many were unaware of his handicap and it was not long after he resumed that Sunderland equalised.

126

A corner kick by Billy Death in the 26th minute was placed with pin-point accuracy on to the head of Charles Buchan who immediately played it on to Bob Marshall who tipped it away from Bradley into the net.

The game continued at breakneck speed after this with little advantage either way. Newcastle's first attack after half-time nearly resulted in a goal but Harris headed just over the bar following a Seymour centre. Soon, however, Sunderland were back on the attack and the Newcastle defence was made to work hard. Frank Hudspeth shone when the Rokermen pushed forward but Ernie England was just as good when play switched to the other end. The teams tended to cancel each other out with Charlie Parker shackling Harris and Charlie Spencer subduing Buchan.

Defences were to the fore although Sunderland were further handicapped when Death, whose pace had caused Newcastle problems in the first half, sustained a leg injury which made him virtually a passenger for much of the second. Buchan created an opening for himself but shot straight at Bradley and Seymour raced on to a pass from Harris only to see Albert McInroy tip his effort over the bar. But these were isolated incidents in a game generally dominated by defences and a draw was a fair result.

The result confirmed Newcastle as draw specialists. They had now drawn eight of their 12 games so far this season. They were to eventually learn how to turn some draws into wins and were to climb the table before the return game with Sunderland in February.

For the Wearsiders, the injury to Clunas was to turn out to be not too serious and he was to miss just one game. Death, however, was to be ruled out for a month although he was normally second choice left winger to Ellis at this time. Sunderland were also to enjoy a reasonably comfortable season although they were to gradually slip below Newcastle in the league.

Football League
Division 1
Newcastle United 2 Sunderland 0 (HT: 0-0)
21st February 1925
St James' Park
52,000

Newcastle: W Bradley, W Hampson, F Hudspeth, R McKenzie, C Spencer, W Gibson, T Urwin [59], W Cowan [64], N Harris, T McDonald, G S Seymour
Sunderland: A McInroy, W Cresswell, J Oakley, W Clunas, C Parker, A Andrews, J Prior, R Marshall, J Rogers, W Ellis, W Death
Referee: J V Pennington (Bury)

NEWCASTLE HAD just established a tremendous sequence of results. They had lost just one game out of the previous 14 (since mid-December) and that had been in the cup. They had climbed the league in spectacular fashion and were now three points behind leaders West Bromwich Albion and two behind second placed Huddersfield (although both teams had a couple of games in hand). Injuries had forced United to field a weakened team in their last match (a game away to Liverpool that was marred by violence) but they returned to full-strength for the derby.

Sunderland had hoped to field the side that had beaten Everton at Roker a week earlier but Buchan failed a fitness test on an injured leg on the day before the Gallowgate game so they were forced to make changes. Their reserve forward, John Rogers, was drafted in to make a rare first team appearance in a reshuffled forward line.

League Positions		Pos	Pl	Pts		Pos	Pl	Pts
Before:	Newcastle	3rd	31	37	Sunderland	7th	30	34
After:	Newcastle	3rd	32	39	Sunderland	7th	31	34

The game was hard, keen and clean but it lacked the finer skills many had hoped to see. Strenuous effort came to the fore in their place and both sides exploited offside tactics although it was still an exciting match.

Newcastle launched the early attacks without really threatening. Sunderland had the wind in their favour but were often forced back in defence with the home half-back line of McKenzie, Spencer and Gibson dominating midfield. But Albert McInroy was in top form for the Wearsiders and a wonderful save from a Cowan shot even impressed the Newcastle supporters. He was well supported by Cresswell and Oakley as the Rokermen were forced to adopt a rearguard action. Billy Cowan found the net with a header following a Stan Seymour corner but his goal was chalked off for a foul by Harris on the 'keeper. Sunderland mounted a few attacks of their own but their finishing left a lot to be desired.

Sunderland tried to add some bite up front by switching Death into the middle with Ellis going out on the wing at the start of the second half – but to no avail.

Newcastle eventually breached the Wearside defence just before the hour when Neil Harris and Tommy Urwin briefly switched places. The former took the ball up the wing and Tommy was in position to take his centre and shoot wide of McInroy's right hand into the net.

Five minutes later United made sure of the points with a second goal. Seymour attacked down the left and recovered the ball after losing possession to Clunas. His dropping centre was perfect for Billy Cowan who gave McInroy no chance with a full volley.

Again McInroy distinguished himself with a fine save from Cowan but by now Newcastle had the game well in hand. Sunderland's attacks were spasmodic, with a Prior shot, comfortably saved by Bradley, being their best effort. The trouble was that their forward line played as individuals rather than as a unit and Newcastle were worthy winners.

Not only did the win confirm Newcastle as the Cocks of the North with three points from the Tyne/Wear derbies but it also closed the gap at the top of the league. They were now just one point behind leaders West Bromwich and Huddersfield. But United had played more games than both and a mediocre finish saw them slip to sixth by the end of the season.

They were almost caught by Sunderland who lost only one of their remaining 11 games. They ended seventh, just behind Newcastle on goal average. An aftermath of the derby game was that there were calls for McInroy to be capped by England. But for some reason he was disregarded and three new goalkeepers were to be given a chance before Albert was awarded his one and only cap some 18 months later. Charlie Spencer was a bit more fortunate. His display against Sunderland convinced the national selectors to pick him and a week later he gained his second cap, away to Wales.

Football League
Division 1
Newcastle United 0 Sunderland 0 (HT: 0-0)
17th October 1925
St James' Park
52,000

Newcastle: W Wilson, A Chandler, F Hudspeth, R McKenzie, C Spencer, E Mooney, T Urwin, W Cowan, N Harris, T McDonald, G S Seymour
Sunderland: A McInroy, W Cresswell, E England, I M McGorian, C Parker, A Andrews, J Prior, R Marshall, D Halliday, S Ramsay, W Death
Referee: H V Stott (Tamworth)

SUNDERLAND HAD made an excellent start to the season having won eight of their 11 games so far. They topped the league, two points clear of Aston Villa (who had a game in hand), Huddersfield Town (two in hand and unbeaten to-date) and Tottenham. Most of Newcastle's team had gone to Roker on the previous Wednesday to see their neighbours beat Bury. Billy Clunas had missed that game due to illness and had still not recovered for the derby match.

Sunderland sprang a surprise, however, by bringing in a local youngster, Isaac McGorian, in place of Ditchburn who had deputised against Bury. Billy Death also stood in for the absent Ellis on the visitors' left wing.

Mid-table Newcastle had no such injury problems with a fit again Peter Mooney recovering and returning to the side in place of Curry.

League Positions		Pos	Pl	Pts		Pos	Pl	Pts
Before:	Sunderland	1st	11	16	Newcastle	11th	10	10
After:	Sunderland	1st	12	17	Newcastle	11th	11	11

This was a fast and thrilling game but the emphasis was on frenzy rather than football. Newcastle had a strong wind behind them in the first half and, roared on by the massive crowd, took the game to the powerful Roker outfit. The crucial moment came after a quarter of an hour. A lob by Urwin was gathered by McInroy and Harris shoulder charged him, bundling him backwards. There were strong appeals that the 'keeper had stepped back over the line but the views of those present depended upon whether they were black and white or red and white. The Newcastle supporters were adamant it was a goal but the referee, who was up with the play, sided with the Wearsiders and waved play on despite volatile protests both on the pitch and from the terraces.

It wasn't all Newcastle. Willie Wilson distinguished himself with a clever save from Death and Frank Hudspeth made a great clearance from the toes of Prior. But the most impressive full back on the field was Warney Cresswell. He was magnificent.

Newcastle enjoyed a greater share of possession in the first half and they also saw more of the ball in the second. But territorial advantage does not necessarily result in goals. In fact, Sunderland came the nearest to scoring but both Halliday and Marshall failed to take a cross from Death and then Prior ran in to shoot into the side netting. It was Wilson who pulled off the save of the match when he blocked Ramsay's strong shot. Both sides lacked a cool head in front of goal and, despite the exhortations of the masses on the terraces, the game ended goalless.

The loss of a point did not knock Sunderland off the top of the table but they were now just one point ahead of Huddersfield who still had two games in hand. Arsenal, Tottenham and Aston Villa were a point further behind.

Newcastle remained ensconced in mid-table but their supporters were just happy to take a point off the league leaders.

You Can't Bribe Me

In November 1922, Charles Buchan received a letter offering him £1,000 if Sunderland lost their game away to Newcastle. He immediately reported it to the Chief Constable of Sunderland, asking him to investigate it. It was eventually traced to an inmate of an asylum in Bristol. Newcastle won the game anyway, 2-1 but Charlie scored Sunderland's goal.

Football League
Division 1
Sunderland 2 Newcastle United 2 (HT: 1-1)
27th February 1926
Roker Park
36,000

Sunderland: A McInroy, W Cresswell, E England, W Clunas, C Parker,
I M McGorian, J Prior, R Kelly, D Halliday [69], R Marshall, W Death [10]
Newcastle: W Wilson, A Chandler, F Hudspeth, R McKenzie, O Park, W Gibson,
T Urwin [50], J R Clark, T Mordue [5], W Cowan, T Mitchell
Referee: H V Stott (Tamworth)

SUNDERLAND WERE challenging for the championship, a point behind
leaders Huddersfield Town and two ahead of third placed Arsenal. But they
had lost in a FA Cup replay away to Manchester United on the preceding
Wednesday. Nevertheless, with Arthur Andrews still injured, Isaac McGorian
kept his place in the team. Otherwise the Roker men were at full-strength.

Newcastle were not in such a happy position. They had lost their last three
league and cup games (all away from home) and had a number of injuries. Yet
they still released Hughie Gallacher to play for Scotland against Ireland. United delayed team selection until the last minute and took 14 players to Roker.
In the event, they drafted in five new men for the clash with Sunderland, three
of them (Ossie Park, Tucker Mordue and Tom Mitchell) were regular members of the reserve side.

League Positions

		Pos	Pl	Pts		Pos	Pl	Pts
Before:	Sunderland	2nd	30	37	Newcastle	10th	29	30
After:	Sunderland	2nd	31	38	Newcastle	10th	30	31

The meeting between the two rivals at St James' Park earlier in the season
can best be summed up in one word – 'insipid'. The return meeting at Roker
Park was exactly the opposite – all fire and sparkle and one of the best ever
Tyne-Wear derbies. The first half was fairly even. Newcastle hardly missed
Gallacher with Mordue proving himself an effective leader of the attack in
every sense.

It was his quickness of thought and movement that brought about the
opener after five minutes. Mitchell seemed to pull his centre behind his supporting forwards but Urwin sent it back for Cowan to spoon a shot into the
air off a defender. But Tucker Mordue showed commendable anticipation as
he dashed in to send a header beyond McInroy's reach.

It did not take Sunderland long to strike back. Wilson leapt well to take a
cross by Prior but failed to hold the ball as he hit the deck. Half a dozen players

131

kicked out in a goalmouth melee and the ball fell to Billy Death who initially struggled to control it before shooting home. The Newcastle defenders were convinced that he had handled but their protests went unheeded.

There could have been a lot more goals before the interval but both defences played well and the nearest to a goal came when Cowan broke clear for Newcastle, chasing a through-pass from Urwin. But the ball came awkwardly to his wrong foot and he screwed his shot just wide of the target.

Sunderland were clearly on top for the first 20 minutes of the second half. So it was a bit of a surprise when United regained the lead in a rare attack five minutes into the half. A lob into the middle was intended for Urwin but either Cresswell or England could have cleared. As they hesitated Tommy nipped in to take the ball off the former and score with a cleverly placed shot that clipped the inside of an upright and glanced into the net.

That was the last seen of Newcastle as an attacking force for quite a while as Sunderland suddenly seemed to realise that this weakened United side were capable of producing a shock result. The Roker men poured forward and the Magpies were forced to draft men back to keep them at bay. Young Ossie Park stood out in the centre of an inspired visitors' defence as the Rokerites laid siege to the visitors' goal.

A goal had to come and it was unfortunate for Wilson (who made a number of outstanding saves) that both of the Sunderland goals came as a result of his mistakes. This time, after 69 minutes, he totally missed a corner from Death and left Dave Halliday with the simplest of chances to nod the ball down into the net.

Sunderland kept coming forward to try and grab the winner and dominated the game for a while. Eventually, however, United began to mount a few attacks of their own. Albert McInroy saved well from Mordue and Mitchell and then Clark sent rasping drives just wide as Newcastle finished stronger than the tiring Wearsiders. But it was Sunderland who almost snatched victory with the very last kick of the game. A cracking shot by Charlie Parker rattled the visitors' crossbar and went over the top for a goal kick. The whistle went to end this scintillating match before the kick could be taken and the spoils were shared – a fair result.

The combination of a gruelling midweek cup-tie and the heavy ground had resulted in Sunderland tiring badly in the closing stages. Newcastle supporters could only wonder what difference Hughie Gallacher, who scored a hat-trick for Scotland against Ireland that day, would have made. But they had to agree that his deputy, Tucker Mordue, had enjoyed his best game yet in the Magpie colours.

The draw saw no change in either team's league position although Sunderland were now two points behind Huddersfield (who still had a game in hand). Arsenal were still two points behind in third place but they were to finish stronger than the Rokermen towards the end of the season and were to end up as runners-up ahead of the Wearsiders although Sunderland were a very respectable third.

Football League
Division 1
Sunderland 2 Newcastle United 0 (HT: 1-0)
30th October 1926
Roker Park
31,152

Sunderland: A McInroy, W Cresswell, E England, I M McGorian, G Henderson, A Andrews, W Grimshaw, R Kelly, D Halliday [**34**], R Gurney, W Death [**71**]
Newcastle: W Wilson, A Maitland, F Hudspeth, R McKenzie, C Spencer, W Gibson, T Urwin, J R Clark, J Loughlin, T McDonald, G S Seymour
Referee: A E Fogg (Bolton)

NEWCASTLE WERE unbeaten in nine games dating back to 4th September although there was little to choose between the sides. A telegram was pinned up in United's dressing room which said, "Best of luck to the lads – Hughie". It was from Hughie Gallacher who was at Ibrox helping Scotland to beat Wales. United sent a similar message to Glasgow but they would have preferred to have their captain at Roker particularly with Sunderland boasting such a powerful defence and half-backs.

The Roker selectors made a big selection surprise when they brought in Isaac McGorian in place of Clunas in the half-back line. However they were pleased to see Dave Halliday return to fitness to lead the attack after missing their last game, away to Cardiff. Coglin stepped down from the forward line to allow his return.

League Positions		Pos	Pl	Pts		Pos	Pl	Pts
Before:	Newcastle	2nd	12	16	Sunderland	6th	14	15
After:	Sunderland	2nd	15	17	Newcastle	5th	13	16

Newcastle swept forward from the kick-off and, with their half-backs pushing up in support, they threatened to over-run Sunderland. But every attack broke down when it reached Albert McInroy who was magnificent in the Wearside goal. One of his saves from a Loughlin rocket was international class. A great header by Tommy McDonald scraped the home bar as the Roker-men were pushed back on defence. A melee in the home penalty area saw the Tyneside forwards try to force the ball home through a packed defence until Clark managed to get in a header. But McInroy parried it away. Eventually Sunderland began to counter-attack and Billy Death's dashes down their left wing began to trouble the visitors' defence. The Red'n Whites went desperately close when Billy Grimshaw rounded Hudspeth only for Wilson, rooted to his line, to push his effort away. Then a dropping drive by Death wide on the left almost caught out Wilson as Sunderland gained the upper hand.

It was they who broke the deadlock ten or so minutes before half-time. Kelly and Grimshaw combined for the latter to centre to the unattended Dave Halliday. He took the ball in his stride and advanced a couple of yards before blasting a tremendous shot past Wilson.

The goal initially inspired Sunderland but they were soon forced back on defence again as Newcastle once again took up the attack. It was thanks to McInroy that the home side kept their lead until the interval.

There was no sign of any slackening in the pace when play resumed and the crowd were kept on their toes as they roared their favourites on with thrills piled upon thrills. Once again Albert McInroy was the hero although he had luck on his side when he knocked the ball in the air from an Urwin centre only for McDonald to return it into the goalmouth. It seemed to be in the net but it hit a post instead and the 'keeper took a kick in the head as flung himself at Seymour's feet.

Yet it was Sunderland who increased their lead after 71 minutes. Newcastle's 'keeper Wilson hesitated briefly but fatally before advancing to meet a long through-pass to Billy Death allowing the winger to reach it first to shoot home.

United kept pushing forward but it became an increasingly forlorn task with McInroy and his resolute full backs in top form. The goalkeeper deservedly left the field to a standing ovation.

Victory saw Sunderland leapfrog over Newcastle into second position, one point behind leaders Burnley.

Newcastle had undoubtedly missed Gallacher (who had scored for Scotland at Ibrox) and felt that they could have won comfortably with their diminutive leader in their team although this view hardly seemed fair on his deputy, Jimmy Loughlin, who had enjoyed a reasonable game. Although they had slipped back to fifth place, United still had two games in hand over their neighbours and, with a long way to go in the league, were not too disheartened.

This game marked the start of an incredible run of goalscoring by Sunderland's ace goalscorer, Dave Halliday. In the 10 games up until the turn of the year, he was to score in all but one of them, rattling in 13 goals in the process. He even continued his form into the new year, scoring nine in the eight league and cup games up to mid-February. Yet the Scottish selectors still preferred Hughie Gallacher as leader of their attack and Dave was never capped.

Football League
Division 1
Newcastle United 1 Sunderland 0 (HT: 1-0)
19th March 1927
St James' Park
67,211

Newcastle: W Wilson, A Maitland, F Hudspeth, R McKenzie, C Spencer, W Gibson, J Low, R McKay, H Gallacher [32], T McDonald, G S Seymour
Sunderland: A McInroy, J Oakley, E England, W Clunas, C Parker, A Andrews, A Wilks, R Marshall, D Halliday, S Ramsay, W Ellis
Referee: A E Fogg (Bolton)

LEAGUE LEADERS Newcastle were clear favourites and, although Sunderland were flying high in the league themselves, even the most optimistic Red'n White supporter believed that the best that they could hope for would be a draw. The departure of Warney Cresswell and Bob Kelly in the previous month undoubtedly affected their team and Sunderland supporters had mixed views about new signing Allwyn Wilks.

This was to be Hughie Gallacher's first taste of a Tyne-Wear derby although Newcastle felt that the absence of Tommy Urwin (playing for the Football League against the Scottish League) slightly weakened their team. Jimmy Low, however, was a capable deputy.

A total of 28 special trains were laid on to take supporters to Newcastle. The gates were opened at 12.10pm and the turnstiles clicked merrily away until a new record crowd was crammed into the Gallowgate enclosures, comfortably beating the previous record by 4,000.

League Positions

		Pos	Pl	Pts		Pos	Pl	Pts
Before:	Newcastle	1st	31	43	Sunderland	3rd	33	38
After:	Newcastle	1st	32	45	Sunderland	5th	34	38

Both sets of supporters and teams knew the result would have a direct bearing on the destination of the championship. Consequently the atmosphere was electric and over-anxiety showed in the play of both sides on many occasions, particularly among the forwards who missed a number of chances. It was a fast, pulsating match of contrasting styles with Newcastle's short passing game radically different from Sunderland's tactics of playing long balls down the wings. But their wing play was not always successful. United's half-back line of McKenzie, Spencer and Gibson soon began to control midfield although Albert McInroy was once again in magnificent form, repulsing everything that Newcastle threw at him. Sunderland actually had the ball in the Newcastle net at one point when Wilson saved a header from Halliday but was bundled over the line by Marshall. But the referee rightly ruled that the 'keeper had been charged before he had caught the ball.

The crucial goal came just after the half-hour from an attack down Newcastle's left flank. Tommy McDonald played the ball across the penalty area to Jimmy Low who quickly returned it into the middle to Hughie Gallacher who wheeled around and struck a shot towards the bottom corner of the net. The little centre forward's luck was in as the ball struck the foot of an upright before rolling over the line into the net.

Newcastle, still controlling midfield thanks to their half-back line, had the upper hand in the second half, but only just. The crowd was enthralled although most agreed that there was more fervour than football on the pitch. The game was played at an unrelenting pace with United better in attack but Sunderland more impressive in defence where Ernie England staunchly supported McInroy. Bob McKay managed to beat the Wearside 'keeper at one point but his effort came off the crossbar. Strangely both of the last named players were to join their respective derby opponents later in their careers.

Although they still had eight games to go, defeat against the league leaders effectively killed off any aspirations that Sunderland had for the Championship. Nevertheless, they managed to finish in a highly creditable third place just two points behind runners-up Huddersfield but seven adrift of champions Newcastle.

To make it an excellent year in the league for the North East, Middlesbrough also won the Second Division. Hughie Gallacher's goal against Sunderland established a new seasonal league goalscoring record for United, passing Albert Shepherd's 28 in 1909-10. Hughie went on to chalk up 36 in the league (plus three in the cup) before the season was over. Dave Halliday was not far behind with 36 league and cup goals for Sunderland, a total that he was surpass in three out of the four seasons he spent on Wearside.

Incredibly, however, neither Dave nor Hughie were the top goalscorers in the North East this season. George Camsell rattled in 63 goals (59 in the league) as Middlesbrough stormed to the Second Division title. His 59 goals set up a new league record but, even more amazingly, it was to last just for a year, Dixie Dean netting an astounding 60 for Everton in 1927-28.

But in 1926-27, the North East's 'big three' top goalscorers amassed an unbelievable 138 goals between them. It was no wonder that the crowds flocked through the gates in the Hotbed of Soccer.

Football League
Division 1
Newcastle United 3 Sunderland 1 (HT: 1-1)
5th November 1927
St James' Park
45,000

Newcastle: W Wilson, A Maitland, F Hudspeth, T Curry, C Spencer, J Harris,
T Urwin, R McKay [**81**], H Gallacher, T McDonald [**7**], G S Seymour [**69**]
Sunderland: J C Bell, W Murray, E England, C Parker, A Allan, A Andrews, A Wilks,
R Marshall [**11**], D Halliday, D Wright, L Hargreaves
Referee: A Josephs (South Shields)

LEAGUE CHAMPIONS Newcastle were making a strong effort to retain their
title. They came into the game a point behind leaders Everton and were able to
field almost a full-strength side, with the indisposed McKenzie the one absentee. They also had the advantage of having a settled team so it was no wonder
that they were clear favourites to win against a struggling Sunderland eleven.

The Wearsiders had been experimenting since the start of the season to
try and find their most effective line-up. They decided on a 'safety first' team
for their trip to St James' although, having chalked up a comfortable win over
high-flying Huddersfield Town in their last game, many people questioned
why they changed a winning side. They were stuck among a group of teams
just two points above a relegation spot. Dave Halliday had been acting as captain but he asked that Charlie Parker should take over the role whenever he
was in the side. The directors agreed to his request.

An innovation for this match was community singing, sponsored by the
North Mail newspaper, both before the game and at half-time. This was a big
success.

League Positions

		Pos	Pl	Pts		Pos	Pl	Pts
Before:	Newcastle	2nd	12	16	Sunderland	17th	12	10
After:	Newcastle	2nd	13	18	Sunderland	19th	13	10

Typical for a Tyne-Wear derby, both sides threw everything into the game.
It was Newcastle who drew first blood with a goal after seven minutes. Bob
McKay sold a dummy to McDonald but he found his route to goal blocked
and played the ball wide to Tommy Urwin on the right wing. His centre was
carried by the wind back to McDonald and Tom's first time shot flew low past
Bell's despairing dive just inside an upright.

It took Sunderland just four minutes to pull level. They forced a right
wing corner and Wilson was badly hampered as he went up to punch Wilks'
flag kick clear. He succeeded only in weakly fisting the ball as far as Bobby

Marshall who coolly sent in a lob over the massed heads of the home defenders. The ball hit underside of the crossbar before ending up in the net.

Sunderland had massive support, virtually half of the crowd, and they roared on their favourites. They had the wind in their favour and looked the more dangerous side but Newcastle played more controlled football. Halliday should have scored when he latched on to a Maitland back-heeler but Willie Wilson smothered his shot. The home 'keeper was in top form.

The miss of the first half came at the other end. Gallacher was brought down by Allan inside the visitors' penalty area and up stepped McDonald to take the spot kick. He had a 100% record with penalties for the first team but lost this proud boast on this occasion, shooting wide of the goal after apparently being put off by the back-chat of the Sunderland players.

United's quality shone through after the interval with Bob McKay displaying his ample ball-skills and almost stealing the show. Hughie Gallacher was also impressive and clearly showed that he was a different class to his Sunderland counter-part, Dave Halliday. But, in mitigation, the Sunderland man received poor support.

The Wearsiders had their own star man – their goalkeeper Jack Bell. He was magnificent and held United at bay almost single handed. But even he was eventually beaten midway through the second half.

The move started with a Frank Hudspeth free kick dropped right in front of the posts. For the one time in the match, Bell was not quick enough to whip the ball away from Hughie Gallacher's head and the little forward looped a header over him. The crossbar came to the Rokerites' aid but it was a momentary respite because Stan Seymour anticipated the rebound and nipped in to shoot into the empty net.

Now Newcastle were clearly on top and they confirmed their superiority with a final goal nine minutes from time, the best of the match. It was a great solo effort by Bob McKay. He set off on a mazy dribble right across the penalty area, leaving half a dozen men in his wake, before unleashing a great cross shot that gave Bell no chance.

The game was now won but Sunderland should have made the scoreline closer two minutes from time when Len Hargreaves opened up the Newcastle defence but first Halliday and then Wilks missed easy chances.

Despite the win, Newcastle remained one point adrift of Everton at the top of the league – and the Toffees had a much superior goal average. Defeat for Sunderland looked ominous. They were now just one point ahead of second bottom Derby County. But even the Newcastle supporters admitted that the Wearsiders did not look like relegation material. They just had to find a settled line-up. Too much chopping and changing was proving a handicap and, on reflection, leaving out Cresswell and Ramsay for this game was a mistake. But it was easy to be wise after the event.

The disappointing thing as far as Newcastle was concerned was the size of the crowd – a mere 45,000 when they really expected nearer 60,000. Then it was realised that the match had been broadcast on the 'wireless' and the press suggested this could have affected the gate. It was not to be the last time that a fall-off in attendances would be blamed on the broadcasting media.

Football League
Division 1
Sunderland 1 Newcastle United 1 (HT: 1-1)
17th March 1928
Roker Park
40,071

Sunderland: A McInroy, W Murray, R Thomson, W Clunas, C Parker, W Whelan, A Wilks, R Gurney, D Halliday [**12**], D Wright, L Hargreaves
Newcastle: W Wilson, A Maitland, T Evans, J Harris, O Park, W Gibson, T Urwin, R McKay, J Wilkinson, T McDonald [**29**], G S Seymour
Referee: A Josephs (South Shields)

THE LNER ran 18 additional trains from Newcastle to Sunderland for this match – plus a further nine from South Shields, all of them stopping at 'the football platform at Sunderland'.

Sunderland came into the game fresh from a magnificent 5-1 win over Arsenal in midweek, when Bobby Gurney had played his first league game for a year and had celebrated with a hat-trick. Newcastle had signed Billy Chalmers from Rangers during the week before the game, just before deadline day, but did not select him for Roker. However, they welcomed back Bob McKay from injury to strengthen their side. But there was little doubt that they would miss Hughie Gallacher who was just finishing two months suspension. There was little between the sides going into the game and both seemed confident.

League Positions

		Pos	Pl	Pts		Pos	Pl	Pts
Before:	Newcastle	7th	31	33	Sunderland	9th	30	31
After:	Newcastle	7th	32	34	Sunderland	9th	31	32

The crowd at Roker saw a hard, fast but clean game with plenty of thrills. Sunderland were clearly in top in the first half. They could have scored as early as the opening minute when Dave Wright sent in a terrific shot from an awkward angle that Willie Wilson did well to keep out. It was no surprise when Sunderland eventually opened the scoring after 12 minutes.

Bob Thomson lobbed the ball into the Newcastle penalty area from near the half-way line. Wilson came out for it, but totally mistimed his advance and Dave Halliday reached it first to head over the 'keeper's outstretched hands. Bobby Gurney dashed in to add the finishing touch but the ball was already over the line. It was unfortunate for the Newcastle 'keeper because this error marred an otherwise fine display.

Sunderland continued to control play and really should have increased their lead before half-time with both Halliday and Gurney having goalbound shots charged down. For some reason the Rokermen virtually starved the speedy Wilks on the right wing in the first half and this contributed to their failure to build on their lead.

Park started shakily but soon gained confidence as he stuck closely to Halliday. Hargreaves was dominated by Maitland but was still terribly unlucky when he blasted a shot against the inside of the far post. The ball may even have spun into the net but Evans dashed in to clear it off the line. Whenever Newcastle attacked, they came across a barrier in Albert McInroy who had a superb game in the Sunderland goal. It was just unfortunate for him that, like Wilson, his one error in the game resulted in a goal.

The move started with a fine save by McInroy just before the half hour. He punched out a shot from Harris but failed to clear the ball properly. He rushed forward to punch it a second time but failed to notice he had advanced just outside the penalty area. Referee Josephs did not and promptly awarded a free kick for a hand ball. This was such an unusual occurrence at the time that most of the players did not know whether it was a direct free kick or not. Mr Josephs, for some reason, apparently would not tell them. Tommy McDonald took the kick and decided to fire a low shot at goal. The ball flew through a forest of legs past an unsighted McInroy into the net.

If Sunderland were the better side in the first half, roles were reversed after the interval when Newcastle took up the running. But they, like Sunderland earlier, could not turn their advantage into goals. This was due almost entirely to one man – Albert McInroy. He produced an inspired display of goalkeeping and, try as they did, United just could not find a way past him.

Wilks saw more of the ball on the Sunderland wing in the second half and did enough for supporters to wonder what the outcome of the game would have been if he had not been starved of possession before the interval. The Roker cause was not helped when Halliday pulled a leg muscle but a similar accident befell Seymour for Newcastle.

It was clearly a game of two halves and a draw was a fair result. The share of the points meant that it was a case of 'no change' in the league.

But Newcastle were to lose their next three games (and, indeed, win just one of their next eight) and were to plummet down the table before recovering to finish just above mid-way. Sunderland were to suffer an even worse finish to the campaign and were to lose four of their last five games to end up one point above a relegation position. Their good goal average saw them finish in a flattering 15th position – not very good but much better than neighbours Middlesbrough who were relegated in bottom place.

Football League
Division 1
Sunderland 5 Newcastle United 2 (HT: 3-1)
27th October 1928
Roker Park
50,519

Sunderland: A McInroy, W Murray, E England, W Clunas, C Parker, A Andrews, A McLean, R McKay [**12, 82**], D Halliday [**15, 80**], T McInally, L Hargreaves [**25**]
Newcastle: W Wilson, A Maitland, R Thomson, R McKenzie [**48**], J Hill, T McDonald, J Boyd [**20**], W Chalmers, J Wilkinson, J McCurley, T Lang
Referee: S H Harris (York)

DURING THE week before the game, Burnley let it be known that they were willing to listen to offers for their international centre half Jack Hill. Newcastle and Sunderland both went in for him and delayed their team selections, hoping to include him in their respective sides. United were in a relegation position in the league although there was a long way to go and there were just two points between the sides. Nevertheless the Geordie supporters were pessimistic about the local derby, especially with Hughie Gallacher missing on international duty. There were even fears that, without Hill in the Newcastle defence, Sunderland could break their 9-1 record win. United signed Hill on the Friday before the game and he made his debut.

This made Sunderland even more determined to win the game. There was added spice by the fact that both sides included players who had recently swapped clubs in a player-exchange transfer deal – Bob Thomson to Newcastle and Bob McKay to Sunderland.

League Positions		Pos	Pl	Pts		Pos	Pl	Pts
Before:	Sunderland	13th	11	10	Newcastle	21st	12	8
After:	Sunderland	11th	12	12	Newcastle	21st	13	8

Newcastle adopted the maxim that the best form of defence is attack and tore at Sunderland straight from the kick-off. The home side was forced back as United enjoyed territorial advantage early on but two goals in quick succession set the Magpies back on their heels.

After 12 minutes Bob McKay gave the Newcastle directors cause to regret their decision to transfer him by opening the scoring. Outside left Len Hargreaves created the opening, leaving Maitland standing before centring for McKay to hook in a cracker.

Three minutes later the Newcastle defenders made the fatal mistake of stopping and appealing optimistically for offside against Dave Halliday. Their claims fell on deaf ears and he was left unchallenged as he ran calmly on to score.

Yet Newcastle refused to be disheartened by these setbacks against the run of play and they soon pulled a goal back. After 20 minutes Monty Wilkinson was unlucky with a shot that beat McInroy but came back off a post. Fortunately for Newcastle Jimmy Boyd was there to tuck away the rebound.

But five minutes later the visitors' defence again let themselves down, once more stopping to appeal for offside although this time it seemed that their claims were justified. The player in question, Len Hargreaves, looked well offside and even stopped playing himself. But he quickly realised that the referee was not going to blow for an infringement and he ran on to place the ball past Wilson.

Play continued to fluctuate, but the score remained unaltered until the break when Newcastle could regard themselves as distinctly unfortunate to be behind.

They began the second half where they had left off and soon blasted themselves back into contention. Tommy Lang crossed the ball into the middle but pulled it too far back, well behind his forwards. He was lucky that Roddy McKenzie was up in support and he raced in to crash a low drive from fully 25 yards that flew just inside a post.

Sunderland realised that their slender lead was too close for comfort and they now took up the running with Bob McKay orchestrating play. He looked better than all of the Newcastle forwards put together as he sprayed passes out to his wingmen and spoon-fed Halliday. Newcastle's forwards were enthusiastic but were too lightweight and inexperienced to bother a sound Roker rearguard. Soon only Newcastle's half-backs stood up to the pressure. McKenzie and Hill stood out but the former's rough tactics left a lot to be desired. Clunas hit the visitors' crossbar and Halliday then had the ball in the net again but the referee disallowed it after consulting a linesman. But the Wearsiders' ace centre forward was not to be denied and he made the score 4-2 with 10 minutes to go. Len Hargreaves again created the opening with a fine pass. Dave Halliday may have been ponderous compared to the other forwards on the pitch but he knew how to put the ball away and he made no mistake with this chance. From that point onwards, Newcastle were a beaten team.

Two minutes later McKay rubbed salt in the wounds of his former teammates with a fifth goal. Yet again the Tyneside defence failed with their offside trap, this time against McLean and, once again, they paid the consequences. They left Hargreaves alone in front of goal only for him to head against the crossbar. But there was to be no reprieve as McKay remedied the error, sticking the ball away. It was the perfect end to a perfect day for the ex-Magpie.

On this performance, Sunderland clearly got the better of the deal with the player exchange of McKay and Thomson. The latter, at best, had a mediocre game but McKay was comfortably the man-of-the-match.

The Newcastle team had five forwards who had played reserve team football last season and their inexperience showed. To their credit, the Newcastle men had shown grit and determination and had not been beaten until the last ten minutes. But the failure of their defenders to play to the whistle had cost them three goals. Sunderland had played the better football in terms of skill and effectiveness. This was not really surprising as their defence included an English international goalkeeper and two top class full backs and their attack included four Scottish internationals.

Defeat meant that Newcastle were bogged down in a relegation position, two points ahead of bottom placed Bury who had two games in hand. It was a worrying time for Tyneside – a far cry from the league championship success only 18 months earlier.

Football League
Division 1
Newcastle United 4 Sunderland 3 (HT: 2-2)
9th March 1929
St James' Park
66,275

Newcastle: M Burns, A Maitland, R Thomson, R McKenzie, J Hill, J Harris, T Urwin [8], A Cunningham, H Gallacher [29 (pen), 87], T McDonald, T Lang; (og A Allan [60])
Sunderland: A McInroy, W Murray, E England, W Clunas, A Allan, A Andrews, G Robinson [17], R McKay [36], D Halliday, T McInally, A McLean [70]
Referee: G N Watson (Nottingham)

WITH TEN games to go Sunderland, four points adrift of league leaders Sheffield Wednesday, were still in contention for the championship. But, with two points for a win, they could not afford to drop many more points.

Most interest in the match surrounded the contrasting styles of Scotland's top two centre forwards, Hughie Gallacher and Dave Halliday. With Gallacher and Jack Hill back in their side, Newcastle were at full-strength. United had made quite a good recovery in the league since the last local derby when they had looked like relegation possibilities. The club was criticised for raising admission prices (to 1s 0d minimum) and banning wheelchairs from the ground, the latter on the basis that it would be too dangerous with such a massive crowd.

With Albert McInroy returning in goal for Sunderland, the visitors were also able to name a full-strength side so a close match was eagerly anticipated.

League Positions

		Pos	Pl	Pts		Pos	Pl	Pts
Before:	Sunderland	2nd	32	40	Newcastle	11th	31	29
After:	Sunderland	2nd	33	40	Newcastle	10th	32	31

143

This game was a classic derby. Fortunes fluctuated to and fro with goals aplenty to entertain the crowd. It started after eight minutes with Newcastle striking first, Tommy McDonald sending over a fine cross for Tommy Urwin to shoot home.

Sunderland made a spirited rally and deservedly equalised after 17 minutes although their goal was something of a gift. Adam McLean sent a good cross from the left which should have been intercepted. But it went right across the goalmouth to the unmarked George Robinson who slammed it into the net from point blank range.

Either Lady Luck or short-sighted match officials smiled on Newcastle as a home defender twice seemed to handle the ball in their penalty area but each time the visitors' claims for a spot kick were rejected, possibly on the grounds of lack of intent. But after 29 minutes when England handled in his penalty area, referee Watson spotted the offence, much to the chagrin of the Sunderland supporters. Up stepped Hughie Gallacher to beat McInroy from the spot.

Sunderland refused to give up and they drew level again nine minutes from half-time when Bob McKay took a well-judged pass from Dave Halliday and let fly with a cracking drive at goal. Burns leapt and managed to turn the ball up on to the underside of the bar but it still ended up in the net.

The game could have gone either way as the second half began. But it was United who regained the lead although, yet again, luck seemed to be in their favour. After an hour they forced a corner and a high, dropping ball was sent into the goalmouth. A group of three players, Allan, Hill and Cunningham, all went up for it and it was the Sunderland centre half who got his head to the ball first only to head it into his own net.

Ten minutes later Sunderland managed to equalise for a third time with a top-quality goal. Bob McKay cleverly drew the Newcastle defence before astutely passing to Adam McLean. He cut inside, cleverly tricking Maitland, before suddenly flashing home a stunning shot.

A draw would have been a fair result but Newcastle grabbed both points with a goal almost at the death. Tommy Lang centred beautifully from the left and the ball flew right across the goal to where Hughie Gallacher was lurking just beyond the far post. He darted forward to head the ball unerringly through the tiniest of gaps to net the winner. It was a heartbreaker for Sunderland who surely deserved something from a superb game.

This had been one of the all-time classic Tyne-Wear derbies. The consensus of opinion was that a draw would have been the fairest result. Most unbiased spectators thought Sunderland certainly deserved at least one penalty. On the other hand, others were heard to observe that if you concede a penalty and score an own goal, you don't deserve to take anything out of the match.

Before the game, many people were asking who should be Scotland's international centre forward – Gallacher or Halliday? On this performance the wee man in the black and white stripes won hands down – although he did not have Jack Hill up against him.

The defeat was a hammer blow to the Rokerites' title aspirations. They were in contention up until this game but were to win just two of their last ten matches and were to finish in an ultimately disappointing fourth place – yet just five points behind champions Sheffield Wednesday. A classic case of so near, yet so far.

Football League
Division 1
Sunderland 1 Newcastle United 0 (HT: 1-0)
19th October 1929
Roker Park
58,519

Sunderland: J C Bell, W Murray, E England, W Clunas, J McDougall, A Allan, W Eden, R McKay, D Halliday, A Wood, G Gunson [**12**]
Newcastle: A McInroy, A Maitland, R Thomson, R McKenzie, J Hill, J Harris, T Urwin, W Chalmers, H Gallacher, J McCurley, T Lang
Referee: H N Mee (Mansfield)

SUNDERLAND, WITH just one win so far this season, came into this game just one point above bottom club Portsmouth and one behind Manchester United although the Wearsiders had a game in hand over both. Nevertheless, the situation at Roker was serious. They had signed Billy Eden from Darlington during the week before the game and he made his debut for the club in place of Lawley. Gordon Gunson also took over from McLean on the left wing in the other change to the side that had drawn away to Sheffield Wednesday a week earlier.

Newcastle fielded arguably their strongest team with Roddy McKenzie returning from injury to replace Mathison in the half-back line although it was debatable as to whether Jock McCurley in place of McDonald at inside left actually strengthened the side. This was to be Hughie Gallacher's one and only appearance for Newcastle at Roker. An intriguing match was in prospect with Newcastle seeming to have the stronger team (especially in attack) but Sunderland the crucial home advantage.

League Positions		Pos	Pl	Pts		Pos	Pl	Pts
Before:	Newcastle	14th	10	10	Sunderland	21st	9	5
After:	Newcastle	18th	11	10	Sunderland	20th	10	7

The previous derby had been a classic. This was the opposite. To say it was mediocre would be an exaggeration of quality with tempers frayed on both sides. At least Sunderland played some good, open football in the first half. Newcastle relied far too much on Gallacher but he was well shackled by fellow Scot Jock McDougall. Wee Hughie did however have the ball in the Wearsiders' net early on but he was well offside and the referee's decision was not disputed.

The game's one goal came after 12 minutes, Sunderland deservedly going ahead when a long, high ball came down awkwardly for Maitland and bounced off his body. Gordon Gunson pounced quickly to take possession, cut inside and score from a narrow angle.

Sunderland continued to enjoy territorial superiority with Newcastle's play cramped and confined in their own half. United had Albert McInroy, back on his old stamping ground having been transferred earlier in the season, to thank for keeping the score down to a single goal up until half-time. Two of his saves bore the hallmark of a great goalkeeper – a low one from a McKay shot and a tip over the top to deny Halliday from close range. United were handicapped when McKenzie was injured after half an hour's play and had to switch to the right wing but the Rokermen still deserved to be more than one ahead at half-time.

But there was a transformation after the interval. Despite having a passenger on the wing, Newcastle began to take the game to Sunderland. They failed to dominate the game as much as the Red'n Whites had in the first half but the Magpies were certainly the better team in the second. The game was punctuated with a series of goals ruled out for offside. Gunson beat McInroy with a spectacular header only to have it disallowed – a disputed decision but probably correct. Similarly, Billy Eden had a goal ruled out, as did Gallacher and this last decision was fiercely contested by the Newcastle players. They contended that the ball had been played on by a home defender. If it had, then the goal should have been allowed but most impartial observers felt that the referee was right. In fact Mr Mee came in for some praise for his control of a potentially volatile match. The game ended with Sunderland hanging on. Jack Hill fired in the shot of the day that Jack Bell did well to hold and Gallacher drove over the bar just as he was grassed by three home defenders. But there was still one goal between the teams at the final whistle.

Newcastle supporters thought that their team had deserved a point for their second half rally and if McKenzie had not been injured, they may have got it. But the consensus of opinion was that Sunderland deserved the victory for their first half performance alone.

Despite the win, Sunderland were to sink to rock bottom in the league by the end of the month and Newcastle would not be far above them in 19th place. But the Rokermen were gradually to pull themselves away from the relegation zone and it was United who were to endure a struggle for survival as the 1920s came to an end.

Football League
Division 1
Newcastle United 3 Sunderland 0 (HT: 1-0)
22nd February 1930
St James' Park
49,304

Newcastle: A McInroy, J Richardson, R Thomson, G Mathison, J Harris, S Weaver, J Boyd [63], J Devine, D Hutchison [25], T McDonald, T Lang [59]
Sunderland: J C Bell, W Murray, H Shaw, W Clunas, J McDougall, A Andrews, T Urwin, R McKay, E Morrison, A Wood, A McLean
Referee: H N Mee (Mansfield)

THIS WAS a critical game for both sides with both of them in the bottom three. Only Grimsby Town, one point ahead of United, separated them. Once again Newcastle banned bath chairs (wheelchairs) from the ground, supposedly on the grounds of safety, and the directors also closed the boys' gate so youngsters had to pay full admission price.

Scotland were playing Ireland on the same day as the derby and Newcastle agreed to release Hughie Gallacher but the Scottish selectors, realising how critical the local derby was, said that it was up to him whether he played at Celtic Park or St James'. He chose country before club.

Both sides delayed team selection until the day. Newcastle had problems with their defence with Jack Hill injured and Dave Davidson also missing. Controversially Joe Richardson, who had made his first team debut a week earlier in a cup-tie against Brighton, was preferred to the more experienced Alf Maitland.

Sunderland also had defensive problems with goalkeeper Bob Robinson, injured in the midweek Cup defeat against Nottingham Forest, ruled out and reserve 'keeper Jack Bell deputising. Harold Shaw, signed a couple of days earlier from Wolverhampton Wanderers, came in for his debut. Intriguingly two former players from each side faced their old teams – McInroy and Thomson for Newcastle and Urwin and McKay for Sunderland.

League Positions

		Pos	Pl	Pts		Pos	Pl	Pts
Before:	Sunderland	20th	27	23	Newcastle	22nd	27	20
After:	Sunderland	20th	28	23	Newcastle	21st	28	22

After the travesty of a match at Roker earlier in the season, this game exceeded all expectations. It might not quite have reached the heights of the classic at St James' 11 months earlier but it was top class entertainment. Both sides went at it hammer and tongs right from the opening whistle. Sunderland had a distinct edge in the early stages but Albert McInroy made them rue selling him as he produced outstanding saves from McLean and Morrison. His full backs and half-backs also defended stoutly before United eventually began to relieve the pressure to mount some attacks of their own. In one of them after 25 minutes, Bell had to rush out to halt Hutchison only for the ball to break free to Boyd. The home supporters were already celebrating a goal as the winger shot towards an empty net but Harry Shaw appeared seemingly from nowhere to head the ball clear for a corner.

But the corner led directly to Newcastle's opening goal. Tommy Lang took it and Duncan Hutchison rose well to firmly head the ball beyond Bell's outstretched hands into the net.

There was still nothing between the teams. Sunderland were unlucky when Arthur Andrews tried a shot that rattled the bar and then McInroy held on to a rocket of a shot by Wood. United could so easily have increased their lead when Hutchison tussled with Bell for the ball to go just past the outside of a post. Yet Newcastle could count themselves lucky to be ahead at half-time. If it had not been for McInroy's heroics, they would not have been.

Fluctuating play continued in the second half but Sunderland no longer controlled the game. Still McInroy stood firm, a full length save from Morrison being as good as anything he had produced in the first half. But a second goal for Newcastle a minute before the hour totally changed the complexion of the match. Hutchison and Lang combined to open up the Wearside defence and it was Tommy Lang who put the finishing touch as Bell advanced from his goal.

There was no holding Newcastle now and it took them just a further four minutes to put the game out of Sunderland's reach. A feint by Laing out on the left created the chance for him to send over a centre and Jimmy Boyd was perfectly positioned to convert.

These goals broke Sunderland's spirit and they began to flag as Newcastle dominated the later stages. They could easily have increased their lead when Lang beat Bell but Harry Shaw blocked another certain goal. In the end, United were deserved winners but for the best part of an hour Sunderland had looked as good, if not better.

This was an amazing result for Newcastle considering that they had been without Gallacher (who scored twice for Scotland that day), Cunningham, Hill and Maitland. Yet it had been a personal triumph for the young players brought in. The win lifted United off the foot of the league, putting them ahead of Grimsby on goal average. Now they were just one point behind Sunderland.

No-one knew how valuable the win was to be for the Magpies. If they had lost (and the remainder of their results had gone the same way), they would have finished bottom of the league. Even if they had drawn, they would have been relegated on goal average. As it was, they scraped themselves clear to finish fourth bottom. Sunderland did even better, winning 10 of their next 12 games and finishing in the top half of the league.

Player of the Decade
1920s

Thomas Urwin

TOMMY URWIN belongs to that select band of players who have played competitive football for the North East's 'big three' clubs – Middlesbrough, Newcastle and Sunderland; and that was the order in which he played for them. He was not the first to achieve this distinction. Billy Agnew turned out for Newcastle 1902-04, Middlesbrough (1904-06) and Sunderland (1908-10).

Tommy was a County Durham man, born in Haswell in 1896. Although short of stature (he was just 5ft 6ins tall in his prime), even as a youngster he seemed destined to make his mark on the football field. He was an England Schoolboy international but started off playing as an amateur in local football. He soon progressed to the North Eastern League playing for Shildon Athletic. This was the league that the reserve teams of the 'big three' played in so there was ample opportunity to impress.

It was Middlesbrough who spotted him first and took him to Ayresome Park early in 1914. He was still an amateur but, realising his potential, Boro' quickly changed his status and persuaded him to sign professional forms.

The First World War meant that he had just one season of league football (1914-15) before the game ceased for the duration. But, even though he was a mere 18 years of age, he still managed to break through into the first team and chalk up seven league appearances before play was suspended. He saw service in the East with the Royal Artillery but he was back on Teesside to resume his career when football began again in 1919 and, now 23, he immediately established himself as a first team regular.

The speedy little winger was soon a favourite with the Teesside public and, equally at home on the left or the right wing, he established himself as a first team regular during the first five seasons after the war.

International honours also came his way although he was unfortunate not to be capped earlier. He had taken part in an international trial, the North v England XI, and was chosen as reserve to Jimmy Dimmock of Spurs for the game against Wales at Ninian Park in 1921. Dimmock eventually cried off but the FA were unable to contact Tommy in time for him to make the journey from the North East to Cardiff to play so Alf Quantrill of Derby County turned out instead. Tommy had to wait another couple of years before playing for England. He won three caps in 1923, two of them against Sweden and one against Belgium, all away from home.

But the 1923-24 season was one of unmitigated disaster for the Teessiders. Not only did they finish bottom of the league, they ended up a massive ten points adrift of second bottom Chelsea. However Urwin was never to taste Second Division football with the Boro'. After 200 league and cup appearances, he fell out with them over an expected second benefit payment. Benefit payments were normally payable after each completed period of five years service with a club. He had already received one but, as he had signed professionally with the club in 1914, he reasoned that he was now due another. As football had been suspended during the war, the club argued that he had not given them ten years service.

An impasse developed and number of clubs expressed an interest, including Sunderland, Everton and Manchester United. However he was persuaded to throw in his lot with the Magpies, a sizeable transfer fee of £3,200 changing hands. Newcastle had won the FA Cup in 1924 so it looked like he had just missed out on domestic honours but this was not the case. It took him a few games to get into the first team as United initially kept faith with the side that had won the cup for them a few months earlier. But once Tommy got in, he became very difficult to shift. Soon, as at Ayresome, he became virtually a permanent fixture in the side.

His first season at St James' was marred by a suspension when he was sent off at Anfield for throwing mud into the face of Liverpool's centre half Walter Wadsworth in retaliation for one scything tackle too many. The Merseysider proceeded to punch Urwin in the face and both players were dismissed and subsequently suspended for a month.

Tommy was a regular during his time at Gallowgate and never missed more than four matches a season over the next three campaigns. He was a key member of United's diminutive forward line when they won the league title in 1926-27, chalking up 39 (out of 42) league appearances that year, supplying the bullets for Hughie Gallacher from the right while Stan Seymour did likewise from the left.

He received his fourth (and final) cap for England in a 3-1 defeat against Wales at Selhurst Park. It was strange that the one time he tasted defeat in an England shirt was in his one home game for them

By the 1929-30 season, Tommy was 33 years old and his best years were behind him. It was perhaps fitting that his last league game for the Magpies should have been against former club Middlesbrough on Boxing Day 1929 (a 2-2 draw) although he did make one more appearance for United in an FA Cup tie against York City in January.

He was eventually transferred to Sunderland a month later for a nominal £525 fee to complete his round of the 'big three'. Sunderland were struggling at the time. They were fourth bottom when he joined them although they were still three points better off than Newcastle who were rock bottom. It was hoped at Roker that Tommy, by teaming up once again with former Magpie Bob McKay, would act as a catalyst in a recovery.

Two heavy defeats away from home in his first two games (one against Newcastle) did not augur well. But then Tommy switched inside from the right wing to replace McKay and Sunderland improved dramatically, winning their next five games. They eventually finished in the top half of the league and, although most of the credit quite rightly went to ace goalscorer Bob Gurney, the signing of Tommy Urwin was undoubtedly a success.

He made quite a few appearances for the Red'n Whites during his first two seasons with them, usually as inside right in support of Gurney. But, by the start *of the 1931-32 campaign, he was 35 years old and could no longer command a first team place. He still made a few appearances but retired from playing full time football at the end of the 1933-34 season. After joining the Roker coaching staff as an assistant trainer, he kept playing in a part-time capacity, occasionally turning out for Sunderland Reserves in the North Eastern League. He even made one final first team appearance in April 1935, coming out of virtual retirement to play away to Preston North End when he had reached the grand old age of 39, the oldest player ever to turn out for Sunderland in a league match.*

At the end of the following season when he took over responsibility for coaching the youngsters at Roker – a role he fulfilled for a number of years – he retired completely from playing. Contemporary reports refer to the good work that he did in that capacity while also praising his ability as a jazz pianist – "the best in football" was how he was described (although how many jazz pianists there were in football is open to conjecture).

He was at Roker long enough to receive a benefit payment and thus became the first man to receive benefits from all of the North East's 'big three'. After finishing with football he worked as an accounts clerk at the Sunderland Royal Infirmary before retiring to live out his days at his home in Monkseaton. He died, aged 72, in Tynemouth Infirmary in 1968.

His style of play was best summed up in the local press when he was transferred from Newcastle to Sunderland: "His fleetness along the touchline, perfect ball control and accurate centring transformed the Magpies' forward line from an average combination into one of the most brilliant in league football. There were long spells during which Urwin was simply idolised". But he was not a natural goalscorer. If his finishing had matched his approach work, he would have been a world beater.

Record

Newcastle	August 1924 – February 1930	
Football League	188 apps	23 gls
FA Cup	12 apps	1 gl
Total	200 apps	24 gls

Sunderland	February 1930 – May 1936	
Football League	50 apps	5 gls
FA Cup	5 apps	1 gl
Total	55 apps	6 gls

CHAPTER 5

1930s
Wearside on Top

IF EVER a decade illustrated the vagaries of football fortunes, it was the 1930s – at least as far as Newcastle and Sunderland were concerned. Despite the transfer of Hughie Gallacher to Chelsea at the very beginning of the decade, United met with success early on. They won the Cup in 1932 and finished in a very respectable fifth place in the league the following season. Then it all went horribly wrong with relegation in 1934 and Second Division mediocrity in the years that followed. In fact they avoided further relegation to the Third Division (North) in 1938 only on goal average.

Sunderland meanwhile enjoyed the antithesis of fortunes, rising to runners-up in the league in 1935 and winning the title in the following season. The overall highlight for Wearside, however, was FA Cup glory in 1937 with victory at Wembley against Preston North End. However by the time the Second World War curtailed league football in 1939, their glory years were behind them.

In terms of head-to-head meetings between Tyne and Wear during the decade, there was nothing to chose between the local rivals with both sides chalking up four wins apiece. Neither side was able to complete the double over their rivals in any one season.

League Meetings (8)

At Newcastle:	Newcastle – won 2	Drew 0	Lost 2
At Sunderland:	Sunderland – won 2	Drew 0	Lost 2

Scoring Substitutes

Newcastle
Peter Cartwright (29 Aug 1979)
Michael Chopra (17 Apr 2006)
Albert Luque (17 Apr 2006)

Sunderland
Roy Greenwood (14 Oct 1978)
Gordon Armstrong (18 Oct 1992)

Football League
Division 1
Sunderland 5 Newcastle United 0 (HT: 2-0)
22nd November 1930
Roker Park
24,120

Sunderland: R Middleton, W Murray, H Shaw, S Morris, J McDougall, A Hastings, W Eden [**11, 88**], T Urwin, R Gurney [**79**], J Leonard, J Connor [**29, 71**]
Newcastle: A McInroy, J Richardson, D Fairhurst, J Naylor, J Hill, S Weaver, D Hutchison, W Chalmers, D Lindsay, J Devine, J Wilkinson
Referee: E Wood (Sheffield)

NEITHER TEAM was doing particularly well in the league. Indeed, Sunderland were just one point ahead of Leeds United who were in a relegation position although Manchester United were well adrift at the bottom of the league with just three points.

Newcastle made a couple of changes after conceding seven at home to Portsmouth a week earlier, bringing in Davy Fairhurst and Willie Chalmers for former Sunderland man Bob Thomson (injured) and JR Richardson.

Sunderland had a change forced on them. Billy Clunas was expected to return to the side having missed their previous game (a draw away to Bolton Wanderers) but was confined to bed with a high temperature so the comparatively inexperienced Sam Morris was brought in. Torrential rain preceding the game deterred many from attending and the crowd was the lowest for many years.

League Positions

		Pos	Pl	Pts		Pos	Pl	Pts
Before:	Newcastle	14th	15	13	Sunderland	20th	15	11
After:	Sunderland	16th	16	13	Newcastle	17th	16	13

Newcastle began by playing the ball wide to the wings and their open play made them look quite useful in the opening stages. Yet it was Sunderland who started the scoring against the run of play after 11 minutes. Alex Hastings started the move with some clever play on his left wing near the half-way line but it was Jimmy Leonard who played the telling pass through for Gurney. Bobby's centre into the middle was inch-perfect for Billy Eden to head a glorious goal.

Alarmed at the setback, Newcastle switched tactics and adopted a close-passing game. They inevitably became bogged down and Sunderland, who maintained their long ball tactics, took control.

After 29 minutes Eden swung the ball into the Newcastle penalty area where Gurney cleverly feinted a header, allowing the ball to go on to the unmarked Jimmy Connor who made no mistake with his trusty left foot.

Sunderland's compact defence limited Newcastle to long-distance goal attempts although a couple of these looked useful. The first one by Hutchison brought a good save out of Bob Middleton and then a 30 yard effort by Sam Weaver did even better, striking a Sunderland post. But the Rokerites still led 2-0 at half-time – and deservedly so.

Sunderland's intelligent play suggested that they would score more goals but Newcastle's defence, where Jack Hill and Albert McInroy excelled, initially kept them out. However, after 71 minutes good play on the home right wing gave Sam Morris the opportunity to cross the ball into the middle. Naylor's attempt at kicking clear merely helped it on to Jimmy Connor and his hard left foot shot flew past McInroy.

Then another attack down the right wing ended with Eden turning a pass inside to Urwin. The former Newcastle man was allowed to take the ball forward unchallenged until he hit a firm pass to Bobby Gurney who deflected it into the net. Many people thought that Tommy's "pass" was a shot at goal.

Two minutes from time Gurney and Connor exchanged passes on the left before playing the ball into the middle. Billy Eden had drifted inside and was unmarked when the ball reached him. He made no mistake as he completed the rout; 5-0 – the biggest winning margin in a Tyne-Wear derby for 10 years.

Newcastle were reckoned to be the weakest side seen at Roker so far that season. Sunderland had been by far the faster team, both with the ball and without it. They had also adapted their play and tactics to the weather and playing conditions, something that Newcastle had singularly failed to do. United had been a well beaten team long before the end and the 5-0 scoreline did not flatter the Rokermen in any way.

The win saw Sunderland climb above United in the league although both teams were to endure a fairly undistinguished season.

Football League
Division 1
Newcastle United 2 Sunderland 0 (HT: 0-0)
28th March 1931
St James' Park
38,000

Newcastle: M Burns, J Nelson, D Fairhurst, J Naylor, D Davidson, S Weaver, J Cape, H Bedford [**88, 89**], D Lindsay, R Starling, T Lang
Sunderland: R Middleton, W Murray, H Shaw, S Morris, J McDougall, A Hastings, W Eden, T Urwin, R Gurney, J Devine, J Connor
Referee: E Wood (Sheffield)

SUNDERLAND HAD lost to Birmingham in the semi-final of the Cup a couple of weeks earlier and had also lost away to Grimsby in midweek so they made a couple of changes, dropping Keeton and Gallacher in favour of Devine and Connor. This meant their team included 10 of the 11 players who had defeated Newcastle 5-0 at Roker earlier in the season. The exception was Devine who had been in the United team on that day.

Newcastle, on the other hand, fielded only four players from that game. They retained the same side that had won away to Portsmouth a week before. Once again, they closed the (half price) boys' gate and advised supporters in bath chairs not to attend. Despite this, the city was besieged for the match with people converging from as far afield as Berwick and Carlisle. Little groups of enthusiasts walked from remote mining villages 10-15 miles distant. One Sunderland supporter even walked from Thirsk.

The LNER introduced special cheap excursion fares – 1s 7d from Sunderland and Monkwearmouth and 1s 0d from South Shields, High Shields and Tyne Dock – and thousands of supporters took advantage.

League Positions

		Pos	Pl	Pts		Pos	Pl	Pts
Before:	Newcastle	12th	34	32	Sunderland	16th	34	31
After:	Newcastle	11th	35	34	Sunderland	17th	35	31

Both defences were well on top, so much so that neither goalkeeper had much to do. The game itself was like a sandwich with Newcastle on top in the opening and closing stages but Sunderland clearly holding the upper hand in the middle. The standard of football was quite good to begin with but fell away as the game progressed. There was scarcely a shot worthy of the name apart from an effort by Tommy Lang that came back off a Sunderland post after 20 minutes play.

The visitors enjoyed their brightest spell just before the interval when Eden should have turned their advantage into goals. Twice he hit the side-netting and then missed the best chance of the game with a feeble effort following a clever feint by Bobby Gurney who let the ball run through his legs, completely deceiving the home defence.

'Mediocre' was the best way to describe play at the beginning of the second half – then it deteriorated. Both sides seemed intent on wasting time at every opportunity. Newcastle had better stamina and this gave them the upper hand in the closing stages. Nevertheless a nondescript stalemate seemed inevitable until the last couple of minutes. Then the unexpected happened – goals!

Two minutes from time a Lang centre was headed away by Hastings but only as far as Jimmy Naylor. He avoided a Hastings' challenge and crossed a low ball into the middle where Harry Bedford tried a shot at goal. His effort grazed McDougall and scraped just inside a post.

Sunderland were still suffering from the shock of conceding such a late goal when Newcastle struck again. It was the same combination with Tommy Lang's cross perfect for Bedford to head past the advancing Middleton.

Newcastle were lucky to win but this was the last success that their supporters had to cheer about this season. They were to pick up just two more points (from draws) from their last seven games and were to slip to 17th position by the end of the campaign.

Sunderland were to do exactly the opposite, winning no fewer than five of their last seven matches and leap-frogging their neighbours to finish in mid-table.

Football League
Division 1
Sunderland 1 Newcastle United 4 (HT: 0-3)
28th November 1931
Roker Park
34,580

Sunderland: J Thorpe, A Hall, W Murray, S Morris, H Shaw, J Devine [53], T Urwin, R Gurney, E J Vinall, P Gallacher, J Connor
Newcastle: A McInroy, J Nelson, D Fairhurst, R McKenzie*, D Davidson, S Weaver, J Boyd [88], J R Richardson [19], J Allen, H McMenemy [23], T Lang [34]
Referee: J Shaw (York)

SUNDERLAND HAD slumped badly in the league, picking up just one point from their last five games, and were now only three points above a relegation position. They had approached Celtic about forward Charles Napier, offering Patsy Gallacher in part-exchange. The bid, which was hardly conducive to encouraging Gallacher, was rejected. They delayed their team selection until the morning of the game, hoping for a belated new signing but had to make do with existing players although they made a number of changes from their last game (a 5-0 defeat away to Leicester City).

Newcastle had been thrashed 8-1 at Everton at the end of October but this had been their only defeat in their last seven games. They had not won at Roker since October 1920 but fielded an unchanged line-up for an eighth successive game when they travelled to Wearside.

League Positions		Pos	Pl	Pts		Pos	Pl	Pts
Before:	Newcastle	10th	14	17	Sunderland	17th	17	12
After:	Newcastle	9th	15	19	Sunderland	19th	18	12

The Sunderland players, as if attempting to justify their directors' team selection, went all out for an early goal. They nearly succeeded when a glorious Patsy Gallacher drive brought the best out of Albert McInroy. But once the Rokermen's early spell of aggression had been withstood, Newcastle's superior football took over. An Allen shot that flew just wide of the goal was a warning that the Wearsiders should have heeded.

After 19 minutes Jimmy Nelson took a free kick near the half-way line, placing the ball into the home penalty area where Jimmy Richardson played a pass to Tommy Lang before going on to take the return ball and scoring with a fine shot.

United's left wing caused problems for Hall and Morris and a corner forced on that flank soon led to a second goal. Lang curled a corner into the goalmouth where Harry McMenemy rose to reach the ball before Thorpe and head home.

Tommy Lang enjoyed a field day in the first half and poor Hall really struggled against him. So it was not surprising when the winger scored after 34 minutes. Harry McMenemy sent him through and Lang beat Hall for the umpteenth time before cutting inside and sending a curling shot over Thorpe into the far corner of the net.

Newcastle continued to dominate play and, with a 3-0 half-time lead, their supporters confidently looked forward to a comfortable victory.

But Sunderland realised the danger and instructed their full backs to switch flanks, much to the relief of Hall. Eddie Vinall was also moved to the right wing so that Gurney could spearhead the attack. The changes had the desired effect. Newcastle still enjoyed more of the play but no longer dominated it.

Vinall began to cause problems and this led to the goal of the match after 53 minutes. He forced a corner and the ball was headed clear only for Joe Devine to meet it perfectly and crash a thunderous shot from fully 25 yards. The ball flew over the heads of everyone in a packed penalty area into the far corner of the net.

There was still plenty of time for Sunderland to fight their way back into the game and they set about their task with gusto. Devine and Vinall shone and had Gallacher accepted the best chance of the match set up by the latter, they may have succeeded – but he scooped the ball over the bar from a great position. Undeterred, the Wearsiders kept up their scorching attack. McInroy was well beaten by an Urwin shot but Nelson cleared off the line.

Then a great drive by Vinall was touched on to a post by the 'keeper before the ball was scrambled away. United's luck held and they mounted some attacks of their own. Thorpe had good fortune on his side when he missed a cross by Lang but managed to get back to turn a follow-up shot around an upright.

It was Newcastle who struck near the end. Thorpe failed to gather a cross from the right and Jimmy Boyd was left with an easy chance that he gleefully accepted.

Newcastle deserved to win but the scoreline flattered them. Sunderland's defence had improved dramatically in the second half when Bill Murray had reverted to his old right back position and managed to keep Lang quiet after the winger had tormented Hall beforehand. Former Newcastle player Joe Devine had been made captain for the day and had scored the goal of the match but the defeat left the Wearsiders fourth bottom, just one point ahead of second bottom Blackpool. They were worrying times for the Rokermen.

Football League
Division 1
Newcastle United 1 Sunderland 2 (HT: 0-1)
9th April 1932
St James' Park
45,000

Newcastle: A McInroy, J Nelson, D Fairhurst, R McKenzie, D Davidson, J Naylor, J Boyd, J R Richardson, J Allen, H McMenemy, T Lang [56]
Sunderland: R Middleton, W Murray, H Shaw, A Hastings, J McDougall, D Edgar, J Temple, R Gurney, B Yorston [41], J Devine, P Gallacher [89]
Referee: R W Blake (Middlesbrough)

NEWCASTLE HAD reached the FA Cup Final and were scheduled to play Arsenal at Wembley in a couple of weeks. Sunderland, however, had defeated the Gunners (who were second top of the league) at Roker Park in mid-week so they fielded an unchanged team to try and do the double over both cup finalists.

United were unbeaten at home since the first game of the season but were slightly below strength for the derby game. Sammy Weaver was winning his first cap for England against Scotland at Wembley (England won 3-0) so Jimmy Naylor was brought in. Harry McMenemy, however, had recovered from an eye injury and replaced Ronnie Starling.

Once again, the Magpies closed the boys' gates for the game along with those for disabled (or 'cripples and invalids' in the vernacular of the time). The club claimed that this was for security purposes but many cynical supporters thought that it was to maximise income.

League Positions		Pos	Pl	Pts		Pos	Pl	Pts
Before:	Newcastle	10th	35	38	Sunderland	15th	38	34
After:	Newcastle	10th	36	38	Sunderland	14th	39	36

There was little derby atmosphere in this game, either on the terraces or on the pitch. Few spectators present, used to the normally fierce North East sporting rivalry, could remember such a poor exhibition. A strong, troublesome, cross wind did not help matters. Newcastle tried to play a close passing game to combat it but most of their play was on the left wing, leaving Boyd isolated on the other flank. They managed a few shots on goal but they were charged down before reaching Middleton. Sunderland played a more open, and slightly more effective, game. Newcastle were handicapped when McInroy had to go off for treatment and their centre forward, Jack Allen, went between the posts until he returned. But after the opening half hour, the 'keeper was unable to take the goal kicks.

It was Sunderland who opened the scoring shortly before the interval. The goal was the result of a misunderstanding between Fairhurst and McInroy who hesitated when McDougall punted a long ball forward into their penalty area. Benny Yorston had no such indecision and chased after it. McInroy managed to deflect his shot to the right but it was immediately returned back across the goal to where Patsy Gallacher was able to head it into the middle for Yorston to head home. In fact, McInroy dived across to punch the ball away but the referee ruled that it had crossed the line and allowed the goal.

Newcastle should have been level within a minute when they were awarded a penalty for a handling offence by Shaw but McKenzie blasted the spot kick over the bar.

Play was not much better after the resumption with neither team putting any passion into their play. Newcastle perhaps had an excuse with the Cup Final on their minds and they seemed to make a game of it after they managed to draw level 11 minutes into the second half. Tommy Lang met a corner kick first time and flashed a cross-shot past Middleton.

United now had the upper hand but play deteriorated even more. Patsy Gallacher, easily the best Sunderland player on view, was the one man on the field to enhance his reputation. He hit a post at one point but this ill luck was balanced when he grabbed a debatable winner a minute from time.

McMenemy gave the ball away to Murray and the Sunderland back played a long pass upfield. A tussle in the corner of the Newcastle penalty area ended with Yorston heading the ball on to Gurney. He crossed towards the far side of the goal where Gallacher had stolen his way forward. He had a simple task to tap the ball into the net but had looked well offside when Gurney played his pass. To Newcastle's horror, the referee allowed the goal and Sunderland won the game.

Perhaps Sunderland could regard themselves as slightly fortunate. Both their goals had been somewhat contentious with the second particularly doubtful. In truth, neither team had deserved to win a lack-lustre game. But the Rokermen were not worried; they were too busy celebrating their first win at Gallowgate since December 1923 and the fact that they had won three games out of three in the last eight days.

Newcastle's celebrations would come a fortnight later and would be even more ecstatic. They were to defeat Arsenal 2-1 at Wembley and win the Cup. Then it would be the Magpies' turn to gain the advantage of a strongly disputed goal. It was part and parcel of the game.

Football League
Division 1
Sunderland 0 Newcastle United 2 (HT: 0-1)
26th November 1932
Roker Park
40,000

Sunderland: J Thorpe, W Murray, H Shaw, C Thomson, J McDougall, J Devine, H Davis, P Gallacher, R Gurney, R Carter, J Connor
Newcastle: M Burns, J Nelson, D Fairhurst, R McKenzie, A Betton, J Murray, J Cape, J R Richardson, J Allen **[87]**, H McMenemy, T Lang **[11]**
Referee: R W Blake (Middlesbrough)

THERE WAS little between the teams when they met at Roker. Sunderland had a full fit squad to pick from with the notable exception of long term casualty Benny Yorston who was recuperating at his parents' home in Aberdeen. They fielded the team that had won away to Wolves a week earlier.

Newcastle, who had also won last weekend (2-0 at home to Manchester City), had Jimmy Boyd and Sammy Weaver absent through injury, but Jimmy Nelson returned at right back after missing that game so the Magpies were still able to field a strong team.

The gates were opened at noon for a 2.15pm kick-off and the early start was blamed for a rather disappointing crowd, it being claimed that many people could not get to Roker from work by kick-off time. Newcastle announced that the score at Roker would be posted up on their scoreboard at St James' Park (where the reserves were playing Durham in the North Eastern League) at half-time and at midway in each half.

League Positions		Pos	Pl	Pts		Pos	Pl	Pts
Before:	Newcastle	10th	14	16	Sunderland	11th	15	15
After:	Newcastle	7th	15	18	Sunderland	13th	16	15

This was not a great game. The gale force wind that blew from one goal to the other saw to that. Play was variously described as "grim" and "ding-dong". Sunderland won the toss and took advantage of the elements in the first half. Newcastle surprised everyone by adapting well to the conditions and the quality of their football in the first half earned praise. They retained possession whenever possible and kept the ball on the ground. Sunderland enjoyed territorial advantage, thanks to the wind, but the better football definitely came from Newcastle.

The opening goal came after 11 minutes from a move down the right wing. Harry McMenemy was given possession and he played Tommy Lang through. The winger tried to play an inside pass but the ball came back to him and he tried an attempt at goal himself. Fortunately for him, his shot went in off a post.

With the wind in their favour Sunderland were bound to have chances of their own. A Gurney header nearly did the trick but their best opening fell to Connor who found himself with the goal at his mercy. Unfortunately for him, he delayed his shot and Nelson and Betton combined to block him, not once, but twice. It was a blow for the Rokermen to be behind at half-time after having the wind behind them so far.

Sunderland improved significantly after the break as they redoubled their efforts. They forced a series of corners and Gurney broke through only to be foiled by the advancing Burns. At the other end both McMenemy and Allen had chances but put their efforts wide. There was little in the game until three minutes from time when the all-important second goal was scored.

Sunderland brought about their own downfall. Gallacher took the ball from a throw-in but his attempted cross-field pass to his left wing went straight to Jackie Cape. The Newcastle man cut inside and supplied Jack Allen who drove a right foot shot goalwards. Thorpe managed to get a touch but no more and was unable to stop it going past him.

The final scoreline flattered Newcastle. They probably deserved to win for their first half performance but there had been little between the teams after the interval. A couple of Sunderland's younger players had seemed a little overawed by the electric atmosphere.

There was praise for referee Blake who had always been in control of a somewhat heated encounter.

The result seemed to stir both sides as they proceeded on an impressive run of results. Sunderland lost just one of their next eight league games (although there were a couple of draws in the sequence). Newcastle did even better, winning six (and drawing one) of their next eight. Both were to climb the league as result.

A Short Career

Nigel Walker is one of the select band who have turned out for both Newcastle and Sunderland. But his time in the Sunderland first team was very brief indeed – a solitary substitute appearance, coming on in the 82nd minute at home to Watford in November 1983. This was his only game for the first team and, at the time, it set a record for the shortest Sunderland playing career. However it has since been broken (Simon Ramsden in January 2004).

Football League
Division 1
Newcastle United 0 Sunderland 1 (HT: 0-1)
8th April 1933
St James' Park
35,618

Newcastle: A McInroy, J Nelson, D Fairhurst, R McKenzie, A Betton, J Murray, J Boyd, J R Richardson, J Allen, H McMenemy, T Lang
Sunderland: J Thorpe, W Murray, H Shaw, C Thomson, J McDougall, D Edgar, H Davis, P Gallacher, R Gurney [5], J Devine, J Connor
Referee: R W Blake (Middlesbrough)

THE FORM book pointed to Newcastle as clear favourites to win this game. They were four points behind leaders Arsenal and three behind second placed Sheffield Wednesday although they had a game in hand over both teams. But games were running out and United could not really afford to lose any more. They fielded the side that had drawn away to Everton in mid-week.

Sunderland, on the other hand, had failed to win any of their last six matches and rung the changes in a re-shuffled forward line. Gurney and Connor were fit again so were brought back in to the team along with Devine who returned to face his former club. Yorston, Hastings and young Carter were all dropped or 'rested'.

League Positions

		Pos	Pl	Pts		Pos	Pl	Pts
Before:	Newcastle	3rd	35	45	Sunderland	13th	35	33
After:	Newcastle	3rd	36	45	Sunderland	11th	36	35

The crowd was well below expectations – and the football was the same. The one brilliant thing about the day was the weather. The sun shone unremittingly and the heat seemed to sap the vitality of the players. This was certainly the case as far as Newcastle were concerned. They made a disastrous start by conceding a goal after five minutes with a comedy of errors.

Fairhurst made a desperate attempt to keep the ball in play on the half-way line but succeeded only in giving possession to Sunderland as he landed on the ground out of position.

The ball was played up the visitors' right wing with Betton and Gurney in pursuit. The Newcastle man looked favourite to catch it but he fell over himself to leave Bob free. He closed in on goal along the byeline with McInroy setting himself for a cross. In doing so, however, he left his near post unprotected and Gurney shot home from a narrow angle.

Newcastle did most of the attacking for the rest of the first half but rarely looked like breaching a resolute Wearside defence in which Jock McDougall was outstanding. So effective was the visitors' rearguard that Thorpe almost enjoyed a day off.

Play continued in a similar vein in the second half. Only Jack Allen looked a potential threat. He at least went close with a brilliant low effort that flew inches wide. His enthusiasm also resulted in a nasty injury to McDougall who took a toe-cap in the mouth. He needed stitches after the game and was lucky not to lose a few teeth. United began to look dangerous in the closing stages and Richardson should have equalised just before the final whistle but somehow missed a sitter.

This summed up Newcastle's overall performance. It was way below expectations. Sunderland themselves were poor but they were undoubtedly better than United and were worthy winners.

Those supporters who stayed away showed good judgement as this drab game could hardly masquerade as entertainment. Sunderland at least had the victory to celebrate.

For Newcastle, defeat virtually extinguished any faint hopes they had of challenging for the title. The heart seemed to go out of them and they were to lose four of their last six matches to finish a disappointing fifth.

Sunderland were not to do any better but expectations at Roker had not been as high and they were probably happy to finish in mid-table.

Football League
Division 1
Newcastle United 2 Sunderland 1 (HT: 1-0)
21st October 1933
St James' Park
45,000

Newcastle: A McInroy, J Nelson, D Fairhurst, D Bell, A Betton, S Weaver [13, 88], J Boyd, J R Richardson, J Allen, J Murray, T Lang
Sunderland: J Thorpe, W Murray, H Shaw, A McNab, J McDougall [83], D Edgar, H Davis, R Carter, R Gurney, P Gallacher, J Connor
Referee: J H Perks (Tipton)

SUNDERLAND, AFTER a poor start to the season, were now emerging as genuine championship contenders and were clear favourites against a Newcastle side who were not only struggling in the league but were also plagued with injuries. They had been forced to call on no fewer than seven reserve players so far this season.

With just one win behind them to-date, they were only two points above bottom placed Chelsea and Sheffield United while Sunderland were three points behind leaders Tottenham and one adrift of second placed Arsenal. The visitors played in white shirts for this game.

League Positions

		Pos	Pl	Pts		Pos	Pl	Pts
Before:	Sunderland	4th	10	11	Newcastle	20th	10	7
After:	Sunderland	9th	11	11	Newcastle	20th	11	9

The standard of football varied between "high" and "outstanding" as both teams contributed towards a derby classic – one of the best ever encounters between Tyne and Wear. Sunderland played the better football in the first half and had more of the play although they came up against a resolute Newcastle defence. It was really against the run of play that United opened the scoring.

A cross from the right wing after 13 minutes was headed clear by a Sunderland defender but only as far as the edge of their penalty area where Sammy Weaver hit a rocket of a shot past Thorpe before the 'keeper could move.

The goal seemed to act as a spur to Sunderland who put the Tyneside defence under considerable pressure but they were foiled time and time again by their former favourite, Albert McInroy, in goal for Newcastle. Nevertheless, the Rokermen could have felt aggrieved to be behind at half-time.

Newcastle had attacked spasmodically in the first half but they improved after the interval. The crowd was kept on tenterhooks as the game entered its closing stages with Sunderland still on top. Both Dave Bell and Davy Fairhurst cleared off the line as United hung on.

Sunderland grabbed a deserved equaliser seven minutes from the end just as the Geordie supporters thought that they were going to hang on for a memorable victory. A corner from Bert Davis was met by Jock McDougall who headed first against a post and then reacted sharply to nod the rebound into the net.

Both teams seemed satisfied with a point with no risks taken until an unexpected, dramatic finale. With two minutes to go came the best move of the match – a superb bout of inter-passing between Sammy Weaver and Jimmy Richardson. It sliced open the exasperated Wearside defence before Sam beat Thorpe with a driving shot from 12 yards. The crowd erupted and Tyneside celebrations began.

Sunderland had been unlucky. They had shown undoubted skills and talent and had played the better football but dogged determination and a never-say-die attitude had given Newcastle victory. Even the United supporters, leaving the ground, were heard to admit (perhaps grudgingly) that the Rokerites were a good side.

Stay at home Tynesiders had missed their chance with this derby match. They were not to see Sunderland at Gallowgate in the league for another 14 years with Newcastle winning just four more games at St James' during the rest of the season as they slipped to relegation.

Football League
Division 1
Sunderland 2 Newcastle United 0 (HT: 1-0)
3rd March 1934
Roker Park
31,776

Sunderland: M Middleton, W Murray, H Shaw [**75** pen], C Thomson, R Johnston, A Hastings, H Davis [**5**], R Carter, R Gurney, P Gallacher, J Connor
Newcastle: W McPhillips, J Nelson, R Thomson, D Bell, D Davidson, S Weaver, J Boyd, J R Richardson, R Williams, R Dennison, T Lang
Referee: G Hewitt (St Helens)

ALTHOUGH THERE were only three points between them, Sunderland were clear favourites. They were able to field their strongest team and had been defeated just once at home so far this season (back in August).

Newcastle had not been playing with confidence recently and lined up with a couple of reserves in their side in Dennison and Thomson. The Magpies placed most of their hopes on the fact that the game was to be played in a gale force wind that could prove to be a great leveller.

League Positions

		Pos	Pl	Pts		Pos	Pl	Pts
Before:	Sunderland	9th	30	31	Newcastle	15th	30	28
After:	Sunderland	5th	31	33	Newcastle	16th	31	28

High winds undoubtedly spoiled the game, reducing play almost to a lottery. Sunderland initially had the elements behind them and did most of the attacking in the first half. Good football was at a premium, with far too many petty fouls disrupting the game. But the build-up to the opening goal after five minutes was brilliant, out of context with the general play. Alex Hastings began the move from deep in his own half and the ball was moved swiftly upfield via Patsy Gallacher and Bob Gurney before reaching Bert Davis out on the right wing. He cut inside before driving a low cross shot past McPhillips.

Sunderland continued to press forward but Newcastle's stubborn defence refused to yield. Willie McPhillips particularly stood out with a series of outstanding saves. Gallacher found the Newcastle net at one point although his effort was disallowed for offside – a close decision.

United should have drawn level when they were awarded a penalty after 12 minutes when Johnston fisted away a Boyd centre. Weaver took the kick but blasted the shot against the bar and the ball was scrambled away to safety. One goal did not seem enough at half-time and there was a feeling that if Newcastle could utilise the wind they could not only get something out of the game but possibly even win it.

Sunderland soon showed that they could be as determined (and dour) as Newcastle. But the Magpies were to blame for their failure to break through as they continually failed to take full advantage of the elements that were now in their favour. The Rokermen were more dangerous against the wind than their visitors had been in the first half despite the fact that Gallacher was struggling with injury.

Sunderland clinched the points with a second goal quarter of an hour from the end, this time from the penalty spot although there was a huge element of doubt about, and luck with, the penalty. It was awarded for a handling offence that almost everybody, apart from the referee, thought was accidental. Harold Shaw took the kick but blasted it straight at McPhillips. Geordie delight at the save was short-lived, however, with the referee indicating that someone had encroached inside the area and instructing that the kick should be retaken. This time Shaw was successful although the 'keeper almost saved, getting a hand to the ball but not enough to stop it from rolling into the net.

Although the second goal was lucky, Sunderland undoubtedly deserved to win a scrappy encounter.

Defeat for Newcastle was the beginning of the end. They were to win just one of their remaining eleven games as they slid to relegation.

Sunderland were to go in the opposite direction, finishing a comfortable sixth this season and going on to league and cup success in the next few years as United wallowed in Second Division obscurity.

Dismissals

Only three players have been sent off in Tyne-Wear derbies. All three were Sunderland men – Gary Bennett & Howard Gayle (both 1 Jan 1985) and Paul Hardyman (13 May 1990). Although no Newcastle player has been sent off, one has received a red card without being dismissed. On 23 October 2005, Scott Parker was mistakenly booked instead of Stephen Carr. Parker had his booking rescinded on appeal and the yellow card was switched to Carr who had already been booked. This meant that Carr was subsequently given a red card as a consequence of two yellows and was suspended for Newcastle's next game. As he was injured anyway, he would have missed the game in any event. Nevertheless, he had received a red card without being sent off.

Player of the Decade
1930s

Albert McInroy

IN MANY ways, as a footballer, Albert McInroy was a lucky man. He was born in 1901. Had he been born just two or three years earlier, he could easily have joined in the carnage of the First World War. If he had been born a few years before that, even if he missed out on trench warfare, his career would have been decimated by the suspension of football for the duration of 'the war to end all wars'. If he had been born ten years later than he was, his career would have been cut short by the second Armageddon. As it was, his birth date meant that he virtually managed to sandwich his whole professional playing career between the two global conflicts.

Born in Lancashire, he started his career, like many of his peers, playing in local minor leagues as an amateur. He even spent a short time (still as an amateur) at Preston North End when he was 20 although he never appeared in the first team.

He was with Leyland when Sunderland picked him up and took him to Roker Park just as the 1922-23 season ended. He was only 22 but it was just seven games into the following season when he was given the chance between the posts for the first team.

Once he got into the senior side, he was there to stay, playing a key part in a very effective defence that included Warney Cresswell, Ernie England and Charlie Parker. From his debut away to Manchester City in September 1923 he chalked up 78 successive appearances, a run interrupted only by an injury in April 1925 that saw him miss one solitary game (away to Blackburn). If it hadn't been for that one game, he would have recorded a full house of league and cup appearances during the '24-25 season. He was never to get as close to a complete season again.

Noted for his agility, he impressed as Sunderland finished in an impressive third place in the league in his first year at Roker, a feat that they repeated two years later (1925-26) and again in the following year (when Newcastle won the league). It was not surprising that he began to attract the attention of the England selectors. He was deservedly capped in October 1926, playing in a 3-3 draw against Ireland at Anfield. Unfortunately, by his own admission, he had a poor game in this, his one international appearance.

His understudy at Roker, John Stoneham, showed remarkable patience, waiting for an occasional first team run out. But Albert was consistency personified and John got into the team only when Albert was injured. Unfortunately, this did happen occasionally and seasons 1925-26 and 1927-28 were not particularly good ones with Albert suffering prolonged absences which saw him miss a dozen league and cup games in each campaign.

However, the last game of the 1928 season saw him enjoy his best game ever for Sunderland as he produced a proverbial blinder in a 3-0 win against Middlesbrough that sent the Teessiders down to the Second Division and kept Sunderland up.

By this time Paddy Bell had taken over as understudy from Stoneham and he was given some opportunities to show his goalkeeping skills although Albert missed just four games during the 1928-29 season when Sunderland again did well in the league, finishing fourth.

The following campaign, however, saw a radical change in fortunes. Albert was still only 28 and should have been in his prime as a 'keeper. However, six games into the season he lost his place between the sticks at Roker to Bell and, within a month, Albert was on his way – to St James' Park of all places.

To many people, it was something of a surprise when Albert joined Newcastle. United were in the middle of a goalkeeping crisis with first choice custodian Mick Burns a long term absentee due to injury. His deputy Albert Fidler was struggling at the top level and a new goalkeeper had become the prime objective for the Gallowgate directors.

Rumours circulated that they first approached their Roker Park counterparts for Bell but the Wearside hierarchy refused even to consider it. So instead Newcastle (supposedly) switched their attention to McInroy and submitted a derisory bid of £1,000 for him. This was rejected as quickly as their approach for Bell had been but the Newcastle men were back within 24 hours with a radically improved offer of £2,750. This was accepted and the clubs agreed terms although the fee was regarded in the press at the time as "cheap at the price".

But persuading Albert to switch from Wear to Tyne was a different matter. He was happy at Sunderland and was settled there. He was not keen to uproot and transfer his allegiance even 12 miles up the road. Or perhaps it was also a case of leaving one club where he had a battle on his hands for first team football to another where there would be similar competition when Burns recovered. Whatever the reason, it took more than an hour to persuade him to put pen to paper and join Newcastle.

His doubts seemed justified although he initially managed to fend off Burns' challenge for the first team shirt. Mick eventually took it off him in December although it was not for long. By the beginning of January Albert was back in the first team and there he stayed – at least to the end of the season.

Albert and Mick vied for the first team shirt for the next three seasons. Although Albert usually managed to retain it and made the most appearances, Mick also had prolonged periods as first choice 'keeper as the two battled it out for supremacy.

The one season that Albert virtually made the position his own was 1931-32 which, fortunately for him (or should that be partly because of him?), United embarked on a famous FA Cup run. He played in 38 of the 42 league matches that year and also all nine cup games as the Magpies marched on Wembley. During the cup run he never conceded more than one goal in any single game including the semi-final against Chelsea at Leeds Road and the final against Arsenal. His game against Chelsea was, arguably, the best of his career.

Hughie Gallacher, by then leading the Chelsea attack, drooled over Albert's performance. Victories by 2-1 in both the semi-final and the final saw Albert pick up a coveted FA Cup winners' medal and this became his greatest achievement.

Season 1933-34 was to be a disaster for him personally and Newcastle as a team. He appeared in the first 23 games of the campaign but a broken collar bone away to Portsmouth at the end of December saw his Newcastle career effectively end. Added complications with a poisoned finger saw amputation considered. Thankfully it was avoided but he never played for Newcastle again and was helplessly sidelined as United plunged from an apparently safe 12th position in February to second bottom by the end of the season and relegation.

When blame was apportioned by public and press for Newcastle's fall from grace just three players were exonerated – Jimmy Nelson, Davy Fairhurst and Albert McInroy.

By now Albert was 33 – not old for a 'keeper but no longer in his prime. But he still had a good few years left in him. So it was with surprise and consternation that the Tyneside public learnt that he was included on United's transfer list at the end of the season. Perhaps it was with a degree of cynicism that it was pointed out that he would have been due a benefit from the club if he had stayed on for a few more months. This quickly became the consensus opinion among supporters.

When he heard that he was transfer listed, Albert asked if he could be granted a free transfer to enable him to go to his club of choice. This was the least that the Gallowgate directors could do. Although he had always given of his best for the Magpies, there is little doubt that Albert's heart was still with Sunderland and he must have been delighted to rejoin them on a free transfer during the close season.

Sadly there was to be no fairy tale return to Roker. He stayed there for a year but never made it back into the first team where first Bob Middleton and then Jimmy Thorpe became first choice 'keepers. Albert eventually moved on to Leeds United at the end of the season.

At least at Leeds he was able to enjoy regular first team football. He spent two years in the First Division at Elland Road before returning to the North East to see out his league career with Gateshead in the Third Division (North). The fact that he turned out in a total of 140 league games for Leeds and Gateshead over the four years with the clubs showed that the veteran could still do a decent job between the posts.

Like a number of his contemporaries, Albert became a publican after his retirement from the game, initially on Tyneside but later in Houghton le Spring in his adopted homeland of County Durham. It was there that Albert passed away, aged 83, in January 1985.

Record

Sunderland	May 1923 – October 1929
	June 1934 – May 1935
Football League	215 apps
FA Cup	12 apps
Total	227 apps
Newcastle	October 1929 – June 1934
Football League	143 apps
FA Cup	17 apps
Total	160 apps

CHAPTER 6

*1940s
Rivalry Renewed*

THE SECOND World War brought competitive football to a close. Indeed, Sunderland closed down completely for a few months unlike Newcastle who, following a brief hiatus, continued playing friendly games and in the wartime North East Regional League followed by the North Regional League.

Competitive rivalry of sorts resumed during the 1941-42 season in the Football League – Northern Section and continued until the end of the war although these were not regarded as first class competitive games. Similarly, the first post war season (1945-46) saw both sides participate in the Football League North competition but the only first class games were in the FA Cup which resumed that season although initially ties were on a two-legged basis.

When peace time football fully resumed, both sides started off where they had ended in 1939 – Sunderland in the First Division and Newcastle in the Second.

But they did not have long to wait for Tyne-Wear derbies to recommence. Newcastle won promotion in the second post war season (1947-48) and soon proved that they were going to be a force to be reckoned with. So did Sunderland and the 1949-50 campaign ended with both of the North East rivals in the top five clubs in the First Division.

As the 1940s came to a close, Newcastle could boast the likes of Jackie Milburn, Joe Harvey, Frank Brennan and Bobby Mitchell while Sunderland paraded the silky skills of Len Shackleton alongside Dickie Davis, Willie Watson and Ivor Broadis. With both clubs averaging gates approaching 50,000, these were golden years for the Tyne-Wear rivals.

League Meetings (4)

At Newcastle:	Newcastle –	Won 1	Drew 1	Lost 0
At Sunderland:	Sunderland –	Won 0	Drew 2	Lost 0

Football League
Division 1
Sunderland 1 Newcastle United 1 (HT: 1-1)
9th October 1948
Roker Park
51,399

Sunderland: J Mapson, J Stelling, A Hudgell, W Watson, F Hall, A Wright, T McLain, J Robinson, R Davis, L Shackleton [25], T Reynolds
Newcastle: J Fairbrother, R Cowell, R Batty, J Harvey, F Brennan, N Dodgin, A Sibley, C Gibson, A Donaldson, E Taylor, G Hair [8]
Referee: G Sunderland (Barnsley)

THE NORTH EAST football supporting public welcomed the first Tyne-Wear league derby since March 1934 by turning out in force. Just one point separated the teams going into the game although Sunderland were slight favourites to win. Fittingly, there was a strong North East presence in both sides with each team fielding six players born in either Northumberland or Durham. But it was the Geordie who was missing from the Newcastle team that gave them most concern. Jackie Milburn was away on England duty.

Sunderland supporters were confident. Unbeaten at home, they were fresh from victory over Cup holders Manchester United and Newcastle had not scored in their last three games. United's supporters were quick to point out that they had conceded only one goal in those three, a narrow 1-0 defeat away to league leaders Portsmouth. But they fielded a much-changed team with Colin Gibson, Ernie Taylor and George Hair coming in for George Stobbart, Milburn and Tommy Walker. No-one knew what effect this would have. Sunderland made one change to their successful side, trying Tom McLain in place of Ronnie Turnbull.

The queues started outside Roker Park at 4.00pm on the Friday when three women from Birtley lined up in place of their husbands. By 6.00pm, men, boys and girls had joined the queue and the crowds increased during the night as workers from the shipyards, pits and factories joined in. The gates opened at 11.45am for the 3.00pm kick-off.

League Positions		Pos	Pl	Pts		Pos	Pl	Pts
Before:	Sunderland	5th	11	14	Newcastle	6th	11	13
After:	Sunderland	5th	12	15	Newcastle	7th	12	14

The match was packed with pace and excitement but possibly spoiled by over-eagerness on both sides. There was a cup tie atmosphere with plenty of 'needle' in the game and Newcastle were the main aggressors, Joe Harvey obviously deciding that the way to subdue danger man Len Shackleton was to

171

clobber him – hard. It worked. After a few crunching tackles, all he wanted to do was get rid of the ball although his distribution remained good.

The opening goal after eight minutes began with a clearance by Frank Brennan. Harvey played a long ball to Joe Sibley who played it out to Gibson. A low cross was headed goalwards by Andy Donaldson and Mapson was able only to parry the ball up for it to fall behind him where George Hair ran it into the net.

The goal spurred on Sunderland and they enjoyed their best spell of the game. A volley by Dickie Davis in the 17th minute beat Fairbrother but hit a post. It took another eight minutes but Sunderland's equaliser was well deserved. A long throw in by Arthur Wright saw Davis flick it on with his head and Len Shackleton hit an instinctive shot at goal from 20 yards out in the inside left position. Fairbrother was ideally positioned but he stood no chance as the ball curved away from him into the far corner of the net.

Newcastle now came back into the game and the 1-1 half-time scoreline seemed a fair reflection of play.

Newcastle held the upper hand in the second half with the Sunderland attack too easily subdued by a resolute visiting defence. The home wingers were hardly in the game and Brennan eventually had the beating of Davis. The Rokermen were also squeezed out of it in midfield and, although there were chances at both ends, United created more of them. Their play gave them an edge and they probably deserved more than a share of the points.

In many ways, the respective performances were to shape the remainder of the season for both teams. For Newcastle, their performance was more important than the result. It gave them confidence and they followed the Roker game with six consecutive wins that saw them climb to second place in the league.

It was the reverse for Sunderland who won only one of their next seven and plummeted down the table, their confidence undoubtedly affected by the game against Newcastle.

Magpie Idols in Red'n White

'Wor Jackie' Milburn was regarded as the Idol of Tyneside but few people know that he also played for Sunderland, guesting for them twice during the 1944-45 season. Newcastle goalscoring hero Albert Stubbins did even better when he guested for the Wearsiders during the 1941-42 season. He appeared and scored for them in the Wartime League Cup final against Wolves. Unfortunately Sunderland lost 6-3 on aggregate in the two-legged final.

Football League
Division 1
Newcastle United 2 Sunderland 1 (HT: 0-1)
5th March 1949
St James' Park
58,250

Newcastle: J Fairbrother, R Cowell, R Batty, J Harvey, F Brennan, N Dodgin, T Walker, G Robledo [64], J Milburn [46], G Lowrie, R Mitchell
Sunderland: J Mapson, J Stelling, A Hudgell, W Watson, W Walsh (inj 46), A Wright, L Duns, I Broadis, R Turnbull [16], L Shackleton, T Reynolds
Referee: H Holt (Rochdale)

BY THE time the two teams met at St James', Newcastle were second in the league and Sunderland were struggling. United were optimistic about the future with new signing Bobby Mitchell making his competitive debut and Chilean forward George Robledo playing in only his third league game for them. They also brought back Ron Batty, who had been rested for the recent friendly game against Liverpool, in place of Corbett.

Sunderland also had a new recruit in their forward line with Ivor Broadis making only his third league appearance for them. The big surprise in their team selection was when Len Duns and Ronnie Turnbull were preferred to Davis and Robinson as well as the choice of Billy Walsh at centre half instead of usual captain Fred Hall although he may have been carrying an injury.

The pitch was covered with a thin layer of snow and the field markings had to be cleared before the match could begin. The form book said that Newcastle should win – but the form book often went out of the window in derbies. This became more likely with the game played in a gale force wind and snow.

League Positions

		Pos	Pl	Pts		Pos	Pl	Pts
Before:	Newcastle	2nd	29	37	Sunderland	15th	29	28
After:	Newcastle	2nd	30	39	Sunderland	15th	30	28

Arthur Wright won the toss for Sunderland and took advantage of the elements with the snow and gale force wind in their favour. The Wearsiders proceeded to give Newcastle a lesson in the finer points of the game with their wing halves, Wright and Watson, aided and abetted by inside forwards, Broadis and Shackleton, taking control of the middle of the park.

They deservedly took the lead just after quarter of an hour when Ivor Broadis completely beat Harvey before trying a shot at goal. Fairbrother did well to block the effort but Ronnie Turnbull raced in to finish off the job.

The impressive Wearsiders continued to play the better football with neat inter-passing and understanding but, ominously for them, they failed to build on their lead before the interval with Brennan taking a grip in the middle of the Magpies' defence.

A sensational first minute of the second half really decided the match. George Robledo won the ball from Walsh and played a pass through to Jackie Milburn who took control before touching it past the oncoming Mapson. The ball was going just wide of the goal but Jackie caught it in time and tapped it in. Unfortunately for Sunderland, Walsh had sustained a ligament injury when tackled and he was carried off, leaving the visitors with only ten men and the next 44 minutes to face both an exuberant Newcastle and the gale.

Shackleton dropped back into the half-back line leaving Sunderland with just four forwards. Newcastle looked more and more dangerous as the game progressed with both Robledo and Milburn threatening. Fortunately for the Wearsiders, Johnny Mapson was in fine form, producing a series of outstanding saves.

The winning goal came when Tommy Walker centred the ball after 64 minutes and Mapson, seemingly with plenty of time to gather, fumbled, dropping it to allow George Robledo to shoot past Shackleton who was covering on the goal line.

Gallant Sunderland risked gaps at the back as they tried to hit back with counter attacks. They went near once or twice in the closing stages but, even with Fairbrother carrying an injury, Newcastle held out.

Newcastle won the points but Sunderland won the plaudits for their courageous performance in the second half. There is no doubt that the game had been spoilt by the injury to Walsh. He had just won his place in the first team in the game before the derby – now he was out for the rest of the season. Fairbrother recovered quickly from his leg injury and never missed a game as a consequence but Milburn, who had played on after sustaining a groin strain, missed United's next match.

Newcastle faded slightly towards the end of the season to finish in fourth place. Sunderland, on the other hand, were to lose just one more match this season (their next one) and finished a respectable eighth. They drew too many matches to seriously challenge their neighbours to the unofficial title of "Cock of the North" but it was a big improvement over their position in early March. The signing of Tommy Wright from Partick Thistle a few days after the derby game had a lot to do with their improvement.

Football League
Division 1
Newcastle United 2 Sunderland 2 (HT: 2-1)
15th October 1949
St James' Park
57,999

Newcastle: E Garbutt, R Cowell, A McMichael, J Harvey*, F Brennan, C Crowe, T Walker [32], T Thompson, G Robledo [27], F Houghton, R Mitchell
Sunderland: J Mapson, J Stelling, A Hudgell, W Watson, W Walsh, A Wright (inj. 45), T Wright [45], I Broadis, R Davis [60], H Kirtley, T Reynolds
Referee: H Holt (Rochdale)

JACKIE MILBURN and Len Shackleton missed the Tyne-Wear derby. They were playing for England against Wales in Cardiff, a game that was a personal triumph for the Newcastle man. He scored a hat-trick in a 4-1 win. George Robledo came into the United side to lead the attack in his absence, the one change to the side that had won away to Burnley a week earlier.

Nineteen-year-old Harry Kirtley deputised for Shack in the visitors' forward line with Billy Walsh taking over from Fred Hall at centre half, making two changes from the side that had drawn at home to Blackpool last week. Interestingly, Walsh had deputised for Hall at Gallowgate last season as well. This time, however, he was virtually to take over the pivot position on a long term basis.

Pre-match and half-time musical entertainment was provided by the 4th Battalion, Northumberland Fusiliers and one minute silence was observed before the kick-off for Colonel Joseph Prior, Chairman of Sunderland, who had died the previous weekend.

League Positions

		Pos	Pl	Pts		Pos	Pl	Pts
Before:	Newcastle	10th	11	11	Sunderland	13th	11	11
After:	Newcastle	10th	12	12	Sunderland	12th	12	12

Sunderland started well with their long cross-field passes, usually right to left, causing the Newcastle defence plenty of problems although Brennan generally had Davis under control.

United persevered and gradually gained the upper hand in midfield. Their wingers, Tommy Walker and Bobby Mitchell, were in inspired form and it was not really a surprise when the Magpies took the lead following some fine wing play. After 27 minutes Joe Harvey and George Robledo exchanged passes before releasing Tommy Walker down the right wing. Robledo had the presence of mind to run on into the penalty area and was on the spot to meet Walker's cross, making no mistake with his header.

United's second goal five minutes later was a gem and came from the other flank. Alf McMichael cleared a Sunderland corner off the line and Bobby Mitchell set off on a 60 yard run up the left wing before crossing to Tommy Walker 15 yards out. The No 7's half volley was perfection, giving Mapson no chance as it went in off the underside of the crossbar.

Mitchell should have made the points secure but he shot wide with just Mapson to beat and this miss was eventually to prove crucial.

Sunderland suffered a setback when Arthur Wright pulled a muscle and was forced to hobble out on the left wing. He had been their star man up until then but when outside left Tom Reynolds dropped back to cover for him, he proved to be just as good. In fact the visitors' strength in midfield was one of the telling factors in the game.

Sunderland made the crucial breakthrough seconds before the break. Tom Reynolds sent a free kick into the Newcastle penalty area where Tommy Wright headed towards goal. His luck was in because the ball gained a deflection off Brennan and left Garbutt wrong footed. The game was back in the melting pot.

Sunderland resumed the second half with ten men, Arthur Wright staying in the dressing room. Newcastle looked as if it was going to be only a matter of time before they scored again and made the points secure. But they failed to take account of Sunderland's never-say-die attitude. To the Rokerites' credit, they refused to panic and played composed and constructive football. Admittedly United did most of the attacking but they were over-anxious. Mitchell began to over-elaborate on the wing but he lacked support with Houghton subdued by Willie Watson. Tommy Thompson's thrusts occasionally looked dangerous and he was unfortunate when one of his headers hit the Sunderland bar. But the ball refused to go in and when it eventually did, it was at the other end!

After an hour Tom Wright dribbled through in the inside left position and an Ivor Broadis pass led to a scramble in the Newcastle box. Dickie Davis cheekily tried a back-heeler at goal that United cleared but the referee, standing 15 yards away, indicated that the ball had crossed the line. Newcastle protested vehemently. Goalkeeper Garbutt chased the referee outside the penalty area, claiming that the ball had not even been close to the line. "It was a foot short", he claimed. But he protested in vain. The referee was adamant. It was a goal.

The points were shared but Sunderland won most of the accolades. Newcastle really should have done better. They had enjoyed by far the more possession and had done most of the attacking but had failed to make either count. The one consolation for the Magpies was that they stayed above Sunderland in the league. But that was soon to change with Sunderland winning seven of their games by the turn of the year to United's four.

It was feared that Arthur Wright's injury would rule him out of action for some time but, in the event, he was to miss only one game.

Football League
Division 1
Sunderland 2 Newcastle United 2 (HT: 1-2)
4th March 1950
Roker Park
68,004

Sunderland: J Mapson, J Stelling, A Hudgell, W Watson, W Walsh, A Wright, T Wright, I Broadis [**52**], R Davis, L Shackleton [**27**]*, T Reynolds
Newcastle: J Fairbrother, R Cowell, R Corbett, J Harvey, F Brennan, C Crowe, T Walker, E Taylor [**30**], F Houghton [**11**], G Hannah, R Mitchell
Referee: H Holt (Rochdale)

THEY FLOCKED in their masses to Roker Park, setting a new attendance record for Tyne-Wear derbies, one that will almost certainly never be beaten. It was also a new ground record for a league game. This was a vital match for Sunderland's league title ambitions. They were three points behind joint leaders Manchester United and Liverpool as the end of season run-in approached. The Wearsiders were unbeaten at home so far this season and the form book clearly pointed to a Sunderland victory. But since when did the form book count in local derbies?

Newcastle recalled Sunderland-born Ernie Taylor in place of the out of form George Robledo. The Chilean had twice recently turned down a move to Sheffield Wednesday after Newcastle and the Owls had agreed a £25,000 fee. Sunderland, unbeaten in the league since the turn of the year, not surprisingly fielded an unchanged side.

League Positions

		Pos	Pl	Pts		Pos	Pl	Pts
Before:	Sunderland	3rd	30	37	Newcastle	12th	29	30
After:	Sunderland	3rd	31	38	Newcastle	11th	30	31

Joe Harvey won the toss for Newcastle and played with the wind in their favour in the first half. The elements were an advantage and United did most of the attacking with emergency centre forward Frank Houghton giving an impressive performance as a lively leader, forcing Walsh to do a lot of chasing, although Frank was not a natural finisher. Nevertheless, it was the Newcastle No 9 who shocked the Roker crowd with the opening goal after 11 minutes. The Sunderland defence was hesitant as they allowed him to cut inside to the inside left position and try a shot that left Mapson beaten.

An intriguing battle followed with neither side dominating but the wind giving United more of the play. So it was a bit of a surprise when Sunderland equalised just before the half hour. Len Shackleton was the scorer and he deserved all of the credit for the goal. He tried a shot from just outside the

177

penalty area that thundered off the underside of the crossbar into the net, giving Fairbrother no chance.

The Roker fans' joy at the equaliser was short lived because, within three minutes, United were back in front again and Mapson had to take some of the blame for the goal. He seemed to come out too early to collect a Harvey cross and dropped the ball. Ernie Taylor justified his selection by latching on to it and scoring.

Newcastle's work-rate and the elements ensured that they held the upper hand until the interval but they were still only one ahead at the break, leaving the Wearsiders with a chance.

Sunderland, as expected, came into the game more in the second half although the nippy Taylor and Hannah continued to impress going forward for Newcastle. They looked a much more cohesive unit than Broadis and Shackleton although these were two of Sunderland's better performers. Indeed, they both scored goals.

It was just seven minutes after the resumption when Ivor scored his equaliser. It was a close range affair. He showed good anticipation to race in and net from close range with Crowe and Corbett hesitating.

With the wind in their favour, Sunderland had more of the play in the second half but were not quite good enough to breach a tenacious Tyneside defence. Jack Fairbrother showed uncanny positional awareness, Frank Brennan was a impenetrable barrier through the middle and the determined Joe Harvey showed himself as the best half-back on the field.

The most exciting incident came in the closing stages when Sunderland came within a whisker of stealing both points. Dickie Davis, in midfield, for once by-passed Brennan, hooking a Watson pass around the big Scot. Broadis was on to it like a flash through the middle only to be up-ended on the edge of the penalty area. This began a heavy siege on the Newcastle goal. It ended when a Tom Reynolds shot hit Fairbrother, knocking him out. The ball hit the underside of the crossbar and was cleared. In the end, both sides felt that they should have won but a draw was probably a fair result.

Strangely, three of the four goalscorers in this game were to play for both of the Tyne and Wear clubs at some time during their careers; Frank Houghton was the exception.

The game had been one of better derbies although it was the third draw between these rivals in the four meetings since the war.

Both clubs embarked on a run of impressive results following the derby. Sunderland won four of their next six games (drawing the other two) to challenge for the championship before slipping up towards the end of the season and finishing an impressive third, just one point behind eventual champions, Portsmouth. If only they had not lost three of their last five games!

On paper, Newcastle's results were even more impressive. They were to lose only one of their last dozen games and almost caught their Wearside rivals. But they had to settle for fifth, two points behind Sunderland.

Player of the Decade
1940s

Leonard Francis Shackleton

IT WAS Pele who memorably described football as "the beautiful game". But it was Len Shackleton who had first demonstrated that the game could be that way a couple of decades earlier.

Leonard Francis Shackleton was the supreme ball artist. He could cajole a caseball with the consummate caress of a Casanova. He certainly seduced the supporters of Tyne and Wear during his time in both camps. He was a genius as far as football was concerned – but a flawed one. While he delighted the fans, he could leave the coaching and training staff in despair. Why else did he find himself out of favour at various times with both clubs and even with the England national team? He certainly deserved much more international recognition than a meagre five full caps.

The problem was that Shack would not conform and delighted at thumbing his nose at those in authority. His wicked sense of humour also told against him. It was not for nothing that he was known as the Clown Prince of Soccer. Part of the problem was that others did not share (or understand) his humour. Even when he wrote his autobiography and left a blank page for the chapter on 'What the Average Director Knows about Football', the publisher of the book had to partly spoil the joke by insisting that a footnote should be added explaining that the page had been left blank intentionally. Shack would probably have seen the irony of the explanation.

A Yorkshireman by birth, Len was naturally gifted at cricket as well as football and was good enough to play professional at the summer game at minor county level. In fact he later claimed that he was paid more for playing cricket in the North East than he was for playing football!

Rejected by Arsenal as a youngster, he always seemed to pull out a little bit extra when he later faced the Gunners to show them what they had missed. Ever the showman, he once sat on the ball during a game against them, challenging all and sundry to come and take it off him!

So it was back at his home town club of Bradford Park Avenue that he built his soccer career. Like many other players during the war, he guested for clubs and once famously played for both Bradford clubs in one day; for Park Avenue in the morning and City in the afternoon – and this was Christmas Day as well!

He came to the North East when Newcastle splashed out a club record fee of £13,000 for him in October 1946 and he repaid a sizable chunk of that money by scoring six goals on his debut in an epic 13-0 drubbing of Newport County. The legend of "Six Goal Shack" was born.

The Gallowgate crowds idolised him and he reciprocated the best way that he knew how – by entertaining them. No one could deny that he was ultimate crowd pleaser.

Unfortunately for the Magpie supporters, the club management did not see it that way. They wanted him to conform and to blend in with the team's style of play. But Len was not willing, or perhaps not able, to change. He was the supremely gifted individual and he played the way he wanted. Bob Stokoe was later to admit that if Len had been more of a team player than an entertainer, he would have been a world-beater.

A rift with management arose over promised club accommodation and led to a short-lived strike with skipper Joe Harvey joining Len over a similar grouse. This was quickly rectified but further problems with re-imbursement of expenses later raised its ugly head, a situation that was exacerbated by Shack's disillusionment with the management style at St James'.

He made the short journey down the road to Roker Park in February 1948, swapping promotion-chasing United for a club who had never played outside the top flight but were struggling to maintain that proud record. It is well-recorded that Sunderland won the battle for his signature when Colonel Joe Prior slapped in a bid of over £20,000 for him to frighten off the competition. It was just £50 over, but it did the trick. It was a record fee but it was to be money well spent.

With Len weaving his magical spell, Sunderland survived; but only just, finishing third bottom of the league. Within two years they were to finish third top, a 'talent money' position, as they once again became a power in the land.

Shack was idolised as much on Wearside as he had been on Tyneside – if not more so. One of the main reasons that he was so keen to go to Sunderland was that he could stay among the people of the North East, an area he had come to love. There may be intense rivalry between the rival fans in the region but Len appreciated that they were both among the very best in the country.

He was acutely aware that most of the money that came into football during the boom years after the war did not make its way through to the players. He was aggrieved that, when chosen to play for England against Scotland in front of 136,000 at Hampden Park in the Victory International, he received just £1 10s 0d (£1.50) plus a third class rail ticket.

He even tried (unsuccessfully) to get his pal Jackie Milburn to persuade the Newcastle team to go on strike before the 1951 Cup Final rather than play for a mere pittance. This was not borne out of jealousy of United but more a sense of injustice at how the £39,336 gate money was distributed. With the players receiving something like £12 a man, just £264 was paid to the stars of the show (no subs in those days). Shack had a point.

Len loved his time at Roker where he was the No 1 star in the famed Bank of England side. Yet his beloved Sunderland never won anything. Shack once refuted this, mischievously claiming that they once won a corner at Wolverhampton! Were there any regrets that his former team was reveling in Wembley glory with three Cup Final successes during his heyday on Wearside? Possibly – but Shack never showed it, preferring to pursue his philosophy that the game was more about entertainment than winning trophies or medals.

He could either make a player or break one. Jackie Milburn, a personal friend as well as team mate, fell into the former category. There is little doubt that Len provided the springboard to Jackie's international career. In an Inter-League game against the Irish League, he actually took the ball around the goalkeeper but rather than tap it into an empty net, he gently rolled it back for Jackie to blast home.

The reverse applied with his relationship with Trevor Ford at Sunderland. It was no secret that they did not get on. Shack reputedly used to place passes to the dynamic Welsh forward just too far for him to reach so that he would look bad. This may or may not be true but there was undoubtedly animosity between them.

Matters became so bad that Ford refused to play in the same team as him in September 1953. From that point onwards they never appeared together again as the club alternated from one to the other. Something had to go – and it was Fordy, transferred to Cardiff City a couple of months later. Len lasted until the first game of the 1957-58 season, the irony of a 1-0 home defeat against Arsenal was not lost on the veteran who, by now, was plagued with ankle injuries. He officially retired from the game at the end of that season when Sunderland were relegated for the very first time. But at least he was able to claim that he had never played for them outside the top flight.

He pursued a career in sports journalism after giving up the game, demonstrating his acerbic wit and making his astute observations for the Daily Express (which he enjoyed) and The People (which he didn't). But his most famous printed work was The Clown Prince of Soccer, published while he was still playing in 1955. Even today it is a fascinatingly entertaining (and controversial) read.

Len enjoyed his retirement at Grange-Over-Sands but sadly died in November 2000, not long after the publication of the long-awaited sequel to his autobiography. Broadcaster, journalist and fellow Yorkshireman Michael Parkinson provided the foreword to the book, The Return of the Clown Prince. It comprised literally one word followed by a signature. This time there was no need for a footnote. Parky obviously shared the same sense of humour as Shack.

Record

Newcastle	October 1946 – February 1948	
Football League	57 apps	26 gls
FA Cup	7 apps	3 gls
Total	64 apps	29 gls

Sunderland	February 1948 – May 1958	
Football League	320 apps	97 gls
FA Cup	28 apps	3 gls
Total	348 apps	100 gls

At the Double

Newcastle have done the league double nine times compared to Sunderland's six in Tyne-Wear derbies.

CHAPTER 7

1950s
United's Cup Years

THERE IS no doubt that the 1950s belonged to Newcastle. They won the FA Cup three times in five years during the first half of the decade and there was a school of thought that a league and cup double could easily have been achieved during the first of these years (1950-51). At the time, the Cup had greater prestige than the league and the players concentrated on picking up the pot at Wembley during the last few weeks of the season. They won just one of the 11 league games preceding the final but still finished fourth.

Sunderland, in contrast, had a poor decade, despite becoming known as the Bank of England club as they tried to emulate their neighbours by buying success. They had plenty of stars in their ranks but they rarely blended together as a team. A single finish in the top four of the league (once known as 'talent money' positions because clubs were permitted to pay an extra bonus over and above the maximum wage) was the best that they could manage (1954-55).

Newcastle also paid talent money for league 'success' just once. But they had Cup glory to celebrate. At least Sunderland had the satisfaction of completing a league double over the Magpies in 1954-55, the last of United's Cup seasons. But Newcastle finished higher in the league on five of the eight seasons that they played together in the '50s.

The Geordies completed a league double over the Wearsiders twice (in 1955-56 and in the following year). But as far as United were concerned, they lost the most important derby match of the decade when they were defeated by an overjoyed Sunderland side in the quarter-final of the Cup in 1956 – and this was at St James' Park!

The Red'n Whites reached the semi-final of the Cup in successive seasons, 1955 and '56, but never reached the final, losing first to Manchester City and then to Birmingham City.

Both sides fell away alarmingly in the latter half of the decade and finished in the bottom six in both 1956-57 and '57-8. It was in the latter of these that Sunderland tasted relegation for the first time and United at last found themselves in a higher league than their neighbours. Not that they had much to celebrate or gloat about. They had avoided relegation themselves only on goal average.

The clubs were not to be apart for long.

League Meetings (16)
At Newcastle: Newcastle – won 3 drew 4 lost 1
At Sunderland: Sunderland – won 3 drew 1 lost 4
Cup Meetings (1)
At Newcastle: Newcastle – won 0 drew 0 lost 1

Football League
Division 1
Newcastle United 2 Sunderland 2 (HT: 1-1)
23rd March 1951
St James' Park
62,173

Newcastle: J Fairbrother, R Cowell, R Corbett, J Harvey [4], F Brennan, C Crowe, T Walker, E Taylor, J Milburn [84], G Robledo, R Mitchell
Sunderland: J Mapson, J Hedley, A Hudgell, W Watson, F Hall, A Wright, T Wright [20], H Kirtley, T Ford [61], L Shackleton, T Reynolds
Referee: B J Flanagan (Sheffield)

UNITED CAME into this game quite high in the league, two points behind second placed Manchester United but seven adrift of clear leaders Tottenham Hotspur. Newcastle, however, had three games in hand over both so were still in the running as title contenders. Although in the lower reaches of the league, Sunderland were eight points clear of Aston Villa in the second bottom relegation position.

Thoughts on Tyneside were turning towards the Cup Final (still more than a month away) rather than the derby, although Newcastle fielded their full-strength cup team. Sunderland delayed team selection with injury doubts over Watson and Hudgell but both recovered in time to play.

The Good Friday fixture attracted a massive crowd with the gates closed at 2.00pm, over an hour before the scheduled 3.15 kick-off time. It was estimated that 20,000 late-comers were turned away at the turnstiles with 8,000 of them (supporters of both sides) staying on outside the ground to hear a commentary of the match broadcast over a loudspeaker system by Newcastle director, Alderman William McKeag.

League Positions		Pos	Pl	Pts		Pos	Pl	Pts
Before:	Newcastle	5th	30	39	Sunderland	15th	33	30
After:	Newcastle	4th	31	40	Sunderland	15th	34	31

A confident Newcastle tore at Sunderland straight from the kick-off with the exuberant Tyneside forwards, prompted by Joe Harvey and Ernie Taylor, sweeping through a seemingly wide open Wearside defence. Yet the opening goal, scored in one of the first attacks of the game, was a bit of a surprise. No-one was more shocked than United skipper Joe Harvey when after four minutes he found himself in possession just outside the visitors' penalty area. He decided to have a crack at goal and the shot surprised Mapson along with everyone else as the ball flew past the 'keeper into the net.

That was the incentive that Newcastle needed and they careered forward. Three times the ball ricocheted around the Sunderland goalmouth with a strong crosswind making control difficult. Mapson did well to palm away one effort and Robledo struck a Wearside upright when faced with an open goal. Then, totally against the run of play, Sunderland grabbed an equaliser after 20 minutes.

It was a goal out of nothing as Tommy Wright closed in to try a blast from fully 20 yards. The strong wind helped it on its way past the bemused Fairbrother and suddenly, despite their dominance, United found themselves pegged back to 1-1.

Time after time the Newcastle forwards swept through the Sunderland defence. There were many scrambles around Mapson's goal but the Magpies just could not put the ball in the net. Sunderland came into the game more as half-time approached but the whistle came with them having just one shot on target in the entire 45 minutes – but they had scored!

It was a different story after the interval when Sunderland moved the ball more freely with Kirtley, Ford and Tommy Wright causing the Tyneside rearguard real problems. It was not really a surprise when two of Wearside forwards combined to give the Rokermen the lead.

Local youngster Harry Kirtley, an increasing influence on the game, capped an impressive second half just after the hour when he whipped over a pass that Trevor Ford neatly glanced wide of Fairbrother's clutching left hand with his head. Sunderland were now playing the better football and they pushed forward to try and grab a decisive third goal. Twice Frank Brennan saved United, clearing the danger from a yard or so out following dangerous crosses from the bye-line. But it was United's turn to shock the opposition with a crucial goal six minutes from time. A punted clearance by Fairbrother was flicked on to Mitchell by Harvey and Bobby played a superb inside pass for Milburn. Jackie needed no second bidding and his vicious right foot shot from fully 22 yards screamed past Mapson just inside a post and hardly a foot off the ground.

Suddenly the game changed completely and Sunderland were hanging on. Both Crowe and Taylor shot just wide as the Wearsiders prayed for the whistle. Their prayers were heard because the scores were still level when it came. But, in truth, a draw was a fair result.

This was undoubtedly a setback to Newcastle's title ambitions although both sides seemed happy with a share of the points. The enormous crowd, which had seen a classic, fluctuating encounter, were convinced that they had seen, in Jackie Milburn and Trevor Ford, the two best centre forwards in the modern game. They were right. Few, however, knew that United had suffered an injury handicap. Skipper Joe Harvey had damaged his heel but had courageously battled on to turn in one of Newcastle's top performances. But he would now miss a couple of games. Injuries to key players were something

---

Football League
Division 1
Sunderland 2 Newcastle United 1 (HT: 2-1)
26th March 1951
Roker Park
55,150

---

that the Magpies did not want in the run in to the Cup Final.
Sunderland: J Mapson, J Hedley, A Hudgell, W Watson, F Hall, A Wright, T Wright, H Kirtley [17], T Ford [34], L Shackleton, T Reynolds
Newcastle: J Fairbrother, R Cowell, R Corbett, R Stokoe, F Brennan, C Crowe, T Walker, E Taylor, J Milburn, G Hannah, R Mitchell [28]
Referee: B J Flanagan (Sheffield)

NEITHER TEAM had done particularly well in the one game they had played since the derby at Gallowgate. Newcastle had dropped a point at home to Liverpool and Sunderland had gone down 3-0 away to Sheffield Wednesday.

Joe Harvey was still an absentee after damaging his Achilles tendon in the earlier game so Bob Stokoe still deputised. George Robledo also missed the Roker game. He was rested and George Hannah came in to take his place. Sunderland had several players in for treatment and were unable to name their team until the day of the game. Trevor Ford, with a foot injury, had the most serious injury but he (and everyone else) recovered to line up in an unchanged side over the three Easter games.

League Positions		Pos	Pl	Pts		Pos	Pl	Pts
Before:	Newcastle	6th	32	41	Sunderland	15th	35	31
After:	Newcastle	6th	33	41	Sunderland	10th	36	33

The first half saw total Sunderland domination with Cowell, Corbett and Brennan given a rough time as the Rokermen streamed forward. It was no surprise when the Wearsiders took the lead although there was an element of luck about the goal.

Len Shackleton pushed a pass through for Trevor Ford after 17 minutes but the Welsh centre forward scuffed his shot. Luckily for him the ball rolled to the side where Harry Kirtley ran in to shoot past Fairbrother.

Newcastle tried to fight back but their football was poor in comparison with the polished play of the home side. So it was a bit of a shock when United drew level against the run of play. The goal came out of nothing around the half hour. Newcastle were awarded a free kick on the edge of the Sunderland penalty area and Bobby Mitchell stepped up and with great precision lobbed a shot over the defensive line-up into the top corner of the net with Mapson well out of position. As free kicks go, it was just about perfect.

Nevertheless, Sunderland continued to command the game and they deservedly regained the lead six minutes later. It was a text book two-man move. Tommy Wright weaved his way inside from the right wing and tipped the ball on for Trevor Ford as Corbett tackled. The No 9 raced clear of Brennan and calmly placed a shot past the oncoming Fairbrother.

The Wearsiders continued to have the upper hand until half-time but failed to add to their score. Newcastle could perhaps regard themselves as lucky to be just one goal in arrears at the break but they felt that they had every chance of making amends when play resumed.

It was a different United who came out for the second half and it quickly became apparent that Sunderland had a fight on their hands. It was a mixture of desperation and determination but gradually the Magpies gained the upper hand. They almost drew level for a second time when Milburn ended a brilliant run by taking the ball around Mapson but shot into the side netting. Then, following a corner, a shot by Taylor seemed to be heading for the net when it struck Mitchell. Newcastle's supremacy did not last and Sunderland regained control in the closing stages.

Len Shackleton over-did his trickery at times otherwise Sunderland may have stretched their lead. A switch between the tiring Hannah and Walker on the Tyneside right wing had little or no effect. In fact, it was Sunderland who almost increased their lead in the closing seconds when a Tommy Wright effort beat Fairbrother but hit the foot of a post. No-one could deny that Sunderland were worthy winners. If anything, the final scoreline probably flattered Newcastle.

This was Sunderland's first competitive win over Newcastle since 1934 and in taking three points off United the Wearsiders virtually ended the Magpies' hopes of completing a league and cup double. Newcastle still had nine games to play but were now ten points adrift of leaders Spurs. Admittedly United had three games in hand but in those days of two points for a win, the lee-way was too much to make up.

It was thought at the time that they should concentrate on the Cup. This is what they did, winning just three of their remaining league games (to finish fourth in the table) but gloriously lifting the Cup at Wembley against Blackpool.

Sunderland were to lose just one of their remaining six games but draw three of them to finish disappointingly in mid-table.

Football League
Division 1
Sunderland 1 Newcastle United 4 (HT: 0-2)
25th December 1951
Roker Park
52,274

Sunderland: R Robinson, J Stelling, A Hudgell, W Watson, F Hall, G Aitken, W Bingham, H Kirtley, T Ford [62], L Shackleton, J McSeveney
Newcastle: R Simpson, R Cowell, A McMichael, J Harvey, F Brennan, E Robledo, T Walker, W Foulkes [27], J Milburn [41], G Robledo [48, 71], R Mitchell
Referee: B J Flanagan (Sheffield)

NEWCASTLE WERE in a very respectable sixth place but they were also only two points behind second placed Manchester United with a game in hand. League leaders Portsmouth were two points further ahead but the Magpies were clear top scorers, having netted 15 goals more than Pompey. Even high scorers Manchester had scored six less than the Geordies.

Sunderland, in contrast, were wallowing in the league. They were four points ahead of second bottom Fulham although the Rokermen had two games in hand. Nevertheless they were keen to start picking up points to avoid being sucked into a relegation campaign.

Neither side had any fresh injury problems and were able to field unchanged line-ups.

League Positions		Pos	Pl	Pts		Pos	Pl	Pts
Before:	Newcastle	6th	22	27	Sunderland	18th	21	17
After:	Newcastle	5th	23	29	Sunderland	18th	22	17

The standard of football was surprisingly good for such a vital derby. All too often emotions and endeavour outweighed soccer skills in Tyne-Wear games but the Christmas spirit seemed to calm aggression. Sunderland set the early pace but Newcastle kept cool and quickly gained the upper hand.

Thereafter the Wearsiders were never in the hunt with Newcastle skipper Joe Harvey setting a fine example in making the ball do the work as the visitors forced the local favourites back on defence. They were battened down by a much better United side in which George Robledo was outstanding.

The first goal came after 27 minutes. Bobby Mitchell gained possession on the left wing and centred to find Billy Foulkes unmarked on the edge of the six yard box and he had no difficulty in heading home.

The second goal, four minutes before half-time, was almost a repeat of the first. Mitchell crossed from the left and Foulkes' header beat Robinson but came back off an upright. The 'keeper dived to turn it away from the goalmouth but Jackie Milburn dashed in and angled a cross-shot from the corner of the six yard box into the net.

Newcastle continued where they had left off and extended their lead three minutes after the interval. Frank Brennan started the move, feeding his skipper Joe Harvey who placed a perfect through-pass to send George Robledo in on goal. His finishing was clinical.

To their credit, Sunderland refused to give up and long range shots by Shackleton and Ford raised the home supporters' hopes. Eventually they succeeded in pulling back a goal after 62 minutes when a Len Shackleton free kick created the opening for Trevor Ford to go through and reduce the lee-way.

But the Roker hopes were dashed within nine minutes when Newcastle scored again. A Tommy Walker corner was made to measure for George Robledo to turn into the net.

Both captains led by example. Joe Harvey's positional play and well-judged passes gave Newcastle an edge in midfield (although Sunderland's approach play was just as good) while Willie Watson's hard work and aggression ensured that the Wearsiders were always in with a chance until the closing stages. Up front, however, the Roker men struggled with their forwards showing very little bite. Kirtley and Aitken were particularly weak, often finding the pace of the game and the heavy going too much for them. At the other end Bobby Robinson produced a brilliant save, flinging himself to his left to turn a 25 yard effort from Milburn away for a corner.

The Geordies were jubilant with the win, especially with league leaders, Portsmouth, losing away to Arsenal. Newcastle were now only two points off top spot although there were three teams on level points – Portsmouth, Manchester United and Arsenal. Nevertheless, although it was just half-way through the season the Magpies were genuine championship contenders.

All Sunderland had to hope for was revenge at St James' Park on Boxing Day but their forwards would have had to improve significantly if this was to be realised.

Football League
Division 1
Newcastle United 2 Sunderland 2 (HT: 0-1)
26th December 1951
St James' Park
63,665

Newcastle: R Simpson, R Cowell, A McMichael, J Harvey, F Brennan, E Robledo, T Walker, W Foulkes, J Milburn [**46** (pen), **69**], G Robledo, R Mitchell
Sunderland: R Robinson, J Hedley, A Hudgell, W Watson, F Hall, G Aitken, W Bingham [**41**], L Shackleton, T Ford [**51**], A Wright, J McSeveney
Referee: B J Flanagan (Sheffield)

NEWCASTLE WERE cock-a-hoop following their comprehensive win at Roker on Christmas Day and it was no surprise when they fielded an unchanged side. Sunderland, however, had concerns. They had to combat the threat of Mitchell on Newcastle's left wing so they matched Hedley against the mercurial Scot in place of Stelling and also dropped Kirtley for Arthur Wright at inside forward, Shackleton switching from left to right to accommodate the change.

Once again, a massive bank holiday crowd squeezed their way into St James' making the attendance the biggest in the country by a considerable margin.

League Positions

		Pos	Pl	Pts		Pos	Pl	Pts
Before:	Newcastle	5th	23	29	Sunderland	18th	22	17
After:	Newcastle	4th	24	30	Sunderland	18th	23	18

The opening 20 minutes saw both sides produce some superb football with Sunderland faster into their stride. Unfortunately the standard of play soon declined under hard, no-quarter tackling. There was a great duel between Irish compatriots Alf McMichael and Billy Bingham with the Sunderland man eventually coming out on top.

Frank Brennan also had to battle hard against the pace and tenacity of Trevor Ford with the Welshman emerging to give a man-of-the-match performance. He gave a wonderful display, receiving tremendous support from Len Shackleton. Between them they seemed to slice open the Tyneside defence at will although the final touch always evaded them. At one point, McSeveney centred for Bingham but his effort hit McMichael's legs on the goal line.

It was not all one-way traffic. At the other end, Bobby Robinson did well to turn a Foulkes header around the post.

Sunderland deservedly went ahead four minutes before the interval when the tenacious Ford beat Brennan to supply McSeveney and the winger

189

played the ball inside for young Billy Bingham to open the scoring. No-one could deny that Sunderland were deserved leaders at the end of a stimulating first half.

Newcastle struck within a minute of resuming although they were distinctly fortunate. Tommy Walker tried a hard shot into the middle that struck Hall on the arm just inside the penalty area. The award of a spot kick seemed particularly harsh as the Sunderland defender had little chance of getting out of the way but Jackie Milburn was not going to look a gift horse in the mouth as he blasted the kick home.

If Lady Luck smiled on United for the equaliser, she favoured the Wearsiders five minutes later. Simpson took a goal kick but shot it straight at Trevor Ford, lurking almost on the 18 yard line. The ball rebounded three yards off him but he was on to it like a shot to flash a hard, low drive past the frustrated 'keeper.

Sunderland had more of the play but little territorial advantage. Ted Robledo was Newcastle's best player. He got better the longer the game went on.

Sunderland's experiment of playing Arthur Wright at inside left was not really a success. The two best chances that they created in this half fell to him but he failed to convert either. Gradually the visitors were forced back on defence as Newcastle began to take control.

Jackie Milburn missed a header in the crowded penalty area after 69 minutes but recovered to half turn as the ball bounced and hooked a left foot equaliser past the unsighted Mapson.

Newcastle dominated the last 20 minutes as Sunderland were forced to defend in depth. This almost brought about their downfall as they surrendered midfield to the Magpies who were allowed to move more freely and mount more attacks. There were some nerve-tingling escapes in the Sunderland penalty area and, in one scramble, left back Hudgell slashed an attempted clearance against his own post. But it was still 2-2 at the final whistle and, taken over the whole 90 minutes, a draw was probably a fair result.

Jackie Milburn's goals emphasised the rich vein of form that he was in. This game saw him notch up his 13th goal in his last 12 league games. The point lifted Newcastle to fourth place in the league, two points behind leaders Arsenal, Manchester United and Portsmouth but with a game in hand over the first two. However, Newcastle's challenge for the title was to evaporate as they embarked on another cup run that was to culminate with a second successive victory at Wembley.

Sunderland had no such distractions, going out in a Third Round replay. But they were to take the opportunity to consolidate themselves in the league and were to finish in a comfortable mid-table position.

Football League
Division 1
Newcastle United 2 Sunderland 2 (HT: 0-1)
10th September 1952
St James' Park
60,727

Newcastle: R Robinson, R Batty, A McMichael, T Casey, F Brennan, C Crowe, T Walker, R Davies [73], J Milburn, G Robledo, R Mitchell; (og J Stelling [49])
Sunderland: H Threadgold, J Stelling, J Hedley, G Aitken, F Hall, A Wright, T Wright [81], L Shackleton, T Ford, W Watson [44], G Toseland
Referee: T Seymour (Wakefield)

THE NORTH EAST rivals had suffered contrasting starts to the season. Sunderland had won three of their four games by a 2-1 margin, losing the other match. Newcastle had failed to win any of their opening four games and were just one point above bottom placed Sheffield Wednesday. All was not well in the United camp and they fielded only five of the side which had won the Cup in April. They intended to make a number of changes to their forward line, including dropping Milburn and Foulkes but Hannah had been injured in their last game so Jackie kept his place. Tommy Walker and Reg Davies were promoted from the reserves. Simpson was on military Z-training duty so Bobby Robinson, who had appeared in goal for Sunderland in both of last season's Tyne-Wear derbies and had made his Newcastle debut in their previous game against Burnley, was picked against his old club.

Sunderland delayed their team selection until a few hours before the game. Willie Watson had not returned to the club from cricket duty until the beginning of the week (this was a Wednesday evening game) so this was his first match of the season. Len Shackleton was rated highly doubtful with an ankle injury but he returned to the side after missing one game, Bingham dropping out of a reorganised forward line that saw Tommy Wright move to the wing.

League Positions		Pos	Pl	Pts		Pos	Pl	Pts
Before:	Sunderland	7th	4	6	Newcastle	21st	4	2
After:	Sunderland	8th	5	7	Newcastle	19th	5	3

A strong wind did not encourage fluent football but Newcastle started brightly. Soon, however, Sunderland took over largely due to Willie Watson's influence. He had the ability to take on and go through the home defence with good assistance from Arthur Wright whose passing defied the elements. Frank Brennan was a rock at the heart of the Newcastle rearguard. Neither team held back in the tackle and the robust challenges were not for the faint-hearted. Both trainers were kept busy.

191

Sunderland deservedly took the lead just before the interval. Len Shackleton hit a right wing corner to Watson who took the ball past Casey and stabbed it home just before Batty could get in his tackle.

Newcastle improved in the second half but their equaliser had more than an element of good fortune about it. Four minutes after half-time Tommy Walker, the pick of the Newcastle forwards, found Reg Davies with a pass and the Welshman slid the ball across the Sunderland penalty area. Stelling, running back to intercept, was horrified when the ball struck him and went straight past his 'keeper. It was the incentive Newcastle wanted and it soon became Fred Hall's turn to show his defensive abilities as the Rokermen were forced back. United could easily have taken the lead when good play by Davies led to George Robledo planting a shot from 20 yards against the bar.

They eventually took the lead in the 73rd minute when Milburn and Walker exchanged passes out wide on the right before the winger played the ball up for Reg Davies to run forward and beat Aitken to a 50/50 chance and head home with accuracy.

Newcastle really had their tails up and Threadgold had to be on his toes to keep out another effort by Davies who became a growing influence as the game progressed. Mitchell also tested the Wearside 'keeper with a 20 yard effort but United's main goalscorers, Robledo and Milburn, had left their shooting boots at home.

Ford and Tommy Wright battled away for Sunderland to ensure that the home defence could not relax. Both sides suffered a handicap in the second half with Crowe obviously carrying an injury and Watson having to receive prolonged treatment on the cinder track surrounding the pitch in the closing stages.

Sunderland grabbed their equaliser nine minutes from time. Tommy Wright topped an impressive display with a quality goal as he raced through the middle before letting fly with a rocket of a shot from fully 30 yards that tore into the top of the net.

Not surprisingly both sides ended with injuries. Crowe and Milburn were forced to miss Newcastle's next game with Jackie far from happy. He was to apply for a transfer just after the Sunderland match to go along with one submitted by Cowell just before. Shackleton had declared himself fit to face his old team but had probably come back too early and he was to miss the next few games. Other absentees from Sunderland's next match were Threadgold (who had been unable to take his own goal kicks for most of the match), Stelling and Hedley.

Although disappointed to share the points, the draw was enough to lift Newcastle away from a relegation position despite the fact that it was far too early in the season to be concerned about survival. Nevertheless, they now found themselves two points ahead of bottom placed Sheffield Wednesday and above both Manchester City and Derby County on goal average. Both sets of Tyne and Wear supporters looked forward to renewing acquaintance with each other with the return match at Roker a week later.

Football League
Division 1
Sunderland 0 Newcastle United 2 (HT: 0-1)
17th September 1952
Roker Park
59,665

Sunderland: H Threadgold, J Stelling, J Hedley, G Aitken, F Hall, A Wright, W Bingham, T Wright, T Ford, W Watson, T Reynolds
Newcastle: R Simpson, R Cowell, A McMichael, T Casey, F Brennan, C Crowe, T Walker, R Davies, G Robledo [20]*, G Hannah, R Mitchell [75]
Referee: T Seymour (Wakefield)

QUEUES OF upwards of 600 supporters had already formed over two hours before the scheduled 5.30pm kick-off time (this was a mid-week match before the advent of floodlights for league games). Both clubs were hampered by injuries and played their selection cards close to their chests. Newcastle seemed to be retaliating to Sunderland's tactics of a week earlier when they kept their line-up secret until the last moment and had belatedly included Len Shackleton who had been regarded as a non-starter.

The Wearsiders had lost 2-0 away to Blackpool in the interim and they eventually made six team changes (one of which was positional). The rearguard of Threadgold, Stelling and Hedley (all of whom had been injured at St James' Park) returned en-bloc. Bingham was back on the right wing with Tommy Wright moving inside to the exclusion of Kirtley. Reynolds had recovered from an ankle injury and he took over the left wing berth from Toseland. Shackleton (who had missed the Blackpool game) was a definite absentee.

Newcastle, who had beaten Preston North End at the weekend, brought in Cowell and Crowe for Batty and Ted Robledo as the only changes from Saturday. Simpson had already returned for the Preston game.

League Positions

	Pos	Pl	Pts		Pos	Pl	Pts
Before:	Sunderland 13th	6	7	Newcastle	14th	6	5
After:	Newcastle 12th	7	7	Sunderland	14th	7	7

Two well-matched sides made this game a thriller. Whole hearted endeavour with little quarter asked by either side was to be expected but football's finer arts were not entirely sacrificed. After initial probing, Sunderland enjoyed territorial advantage and battered away at their visitors' defence but the Tyneside rearguard held firm. Indeed, from the early stages, the Magpies threatened the home goal with break-away attacks. Robledo gave the Rokermen a warning when he headed wide from a Mitchell cross. But Sunderland failed to heed the warning and the Chilean was soon back to punish them.

193

After 20 minutes, Reg Davies tried a shot at goal that beat Threadgold and struck his crossbar. But there was to be no reprieve with George Robledo lurking nearby to nod the rebound into an empty net.

The game developed into an intriguing battle between Trevor Ford and Frank Brennan with the Scottish defender eventually coming out on top but not until after a titanic encounter.

Robledo was in the wars soon after his goal. He clashed with Reynolds after the Sunderland man grabbed his foot. The Chilean, unusually for him, retaliated by lashing out with his free foot and laid the Sunderland winger flat out. The Newcastle man was cautioned by the referee as Reynolds received attention. Robledo became a target for the boo-boys from that moment and largely disappeared from the game until the closing stages. Sunderland piled on more and more pressure only to find Ronnie Simpson outstanding in the visitors' goal. But the fact that Newcastle survived with their lead until the interval had as much to do with poor Sunderland finishing as much as United's defending.

It was all Sunderland as the second half got under way. Simpson denied Ford twice early on and then similarly stopped an Aitken header. The 'keeper was saved by Frank Brennan soon afterwards when a Tommy Wright header caught Ronnie out of position but the big centre half cleared off the line. It was not all one way traffic and Reg Davies had the ball in the Sunderland net only for it to be quite rightly ruled out for offside. But then, a quarter of an hour from time, came a second hammer blow for the Rokerites.

Robledo, virtually anonymous following his booking, started the move that led to United's second goal. He robbed Hedley and laid on the pass for Reg Davies whose shot hit the inside of an upright. Threadgold did well to get his hand to the ball and stop it from crossing the line but it rolled over to where Bobby Mitchell had the simple task of slotting it home.

The second goal destroyed Sunderland and Newcastle finished on top. They looked yards faster than their dispirited neighbours in the closing stages but 2-0 remained the final score. However, over the whole 90 minutes, it flattered United.

Scottish selectors were at the game and they could not help but be impressed by Frank Brennan and Ronnie Simpson. Many Sunderland supporters could not understand how they had lost the game having enjoyed so much territorial advantage. But Newcastle had shown poise and opportunism in front of goal and had been rewarded accordingly.

It was early in the league campaign and both sets of fans saw reason for optimism. Indeed, Sunderland embarked on a run of eight games unbeaten while Newcastle, although not quite as impressive, also gradually began to climb the league. Their fans were happy enough to have picked up three points out of four against their local rivals.

Football League
Division 1
Newcastle United 2 Sunderland 1 (HT: 1-1)
22nd August 1953
St James' Park
58,516

Newcastle: R Simpson, R Cowell, R Batty, J Scoular, F Brennan, C Crowe, J Milburn, R Davies, V Keeble [**61**], G Hannah, R Mitchell [**33** pen]
Sunderland: J Cowan, J Stelling, J Hedley, G Aitken, R Daniel, A Wright, T Wright, H Kirtley, T Ford, L Shackleton [**2**], J McSeveney
Referee: J H Clough (Bolton)

THE DERBY this year came virtually at the beginning of the season. This was Newcastle's first game although most First Division sides had played a mid-week match. Sunderland had suffered a particularly inauspicious start, conceding five goals away to Charlton Athletic (although scoring three). Big things were expected from the Rokermen this year with the recruitment of three internationals during the close season – Ray Daniel (Wales), Billy Elliott (England) and Jimmy Cowan (Scotland) – for a combined fee of nearly £70,000, a small fortune at the time.

Daniel was the new captain of the Red n'Whites and Newcastle also had a new skipper in their own close season record signing – Jimmy Scoular. He had taken over from Joe Harvey who had retired from first team football. With Walker, White and Foulkes all unfit, Newcastle played Jackie Milburn on their right wing with Vic Keeble leading the attack.

The Magpies obviously expected a big attendance for the game and announced that the gates would open "as soon as the club could get the gatemen assembled"! It was thought that this would be some time before 1.00pm (for a 3.15pm kick-off).

League Positions

	Pos	Pl	Pts		Pos	Pl	Pts
Before: Newcastle	13th	-	-	Sunderland	15th	1	0
After: Newcastle	9th	1	2	Sunderland	21st	2	0

The Wearsiders shaped up stronger in the early stages and stunned the majority of the massive crowd by grabbing the lead in the second minute. They were awarded a free kick just outside the Newcastle penalty area. The home defenders lined up to form a defensive wall – or a defensive fence to be more accurate as it had a gap in the middle. Len Shackleton was not going to waste such a chance and blasted the ball straight through it into the net.

United were under a handicap from these opening minutes with Scoular badly wrenching his knee in blocking a defender's attempted clearance. But the balding Scot was renowned as a hard man and he bravely played on. Shack impressed at his former club and Tommy Wright also looked good on the Sunderland right wing, going past Ron Batty with ease early on. But Batty battled away and gained the upper hand well before the interval.

With Frank Brennan soon dominating in defence and Ronnie Simpson as agile as ever, the visitors' attack was quickly subdued and the Magpies, confidence increasing all of the time, began to control play. Jackie Milburn, enjoying his first game on the right wing for two years, was the star of the show. His pace constantly had the visitors' defence in a panic and the crowd roaring. Jimmy Cowan showed why he was an international 'keeper when he somehow kept out a shot from Hannah with a wonderful fingertip save. Even when he was eventually beaten, from the penalty spot, the goal was a fluke.

The goal after 33 minutes came when a long ball was dropped into the penalty area where Keeble and Daniel were waiting. Instead of heading clear, the Sunderland centre half allowed it to go through. Keeble anticipated his ploy and it took a late, illegal tackle on the Newcastle man to stop him.

Referee Clough had no hesitation in pointing to the penalty spot. Bobby Mitchell stepped up to take the kick but stubbed his foot into the ground. He seemed to be aiming to Cowan's left and the 'keeper anticipated this with his dive. Unfortunately for Sunderland, the ball trickled over the line in the opposite corner. Mitch looked disgusted – but not as disgusted as Cowan.

Within a couple of minutes Sunderland had the ball in the Newcastle net again but, once more, fortune smiled on United. Johnny McSeveney sent in a curling corner kick that sailed straight into the net. Mr Clough initially signalled a goal but the Newcastle players drew his attention to his linesman who was flagging. After consultation, the referee changed his mind and gave the Magpies a free kick for a foul on Simpson by Tommy Wright as the corner was being taken. The first half ended with the Wearsiders striving to regain the lead but Simpson's trailing legs kept out a shot by Harry Kirtley.

The game could have gone either way but it was Newcastle who eventually edged in front. Just after the hour Jackie Milburn took a corner and placed it perfectly on the edge of the six yard box for Vic Keeble to storm in and rocket home a header. At least there was no fluke about this goal.

Jimmy Scoular deserved credit for his grit and determination in playing on through the game but his injury began to tell towards the end when Newcastle were forced to hang on. It seemed as if their efforts were in vain seven minutes from time when Sunderland threw everything forward. Trevor Ford blasted two shots goalward and, from a clearance, Kirtley rattled the underside of the Newcastle crossbar. A scramble in the penalty area ended with Cowell tackling the tiring Shackleton in the corner of the box. The referee pointed immediately to the spot but, once again, the linesman had his flag raised and, persuaded by the Newcastle players, referee Clough consulted him. This time he did not change his mind and he placed the ball on the spot again. Up stepped

Ford and seemed certain to score as Simpson dived to his left. But Ronnie's party piece was to save shots with his trailing legs and this is precisely what he did. St James' Park went wild as the rebound fell awkwardly for the visiting No 9 who was unable to put it away. It was the best chance of an eventful match and United still led 2-1 at the final whistle.

This had been a desperately close game with nothing between the sides. A draw would probably have been a fairer result. Although United were delighted to start their season with a win, they were very concerned about the injury to Scoular which it was feared could rule their new captain out of action for some time. In the event he was absent for just three weeks. But the injury situation at Gallowgate was soon to tell on the Magpies who were to win only one of their next nine matches in a season of mediocrity.

Sunderland were to suffer a similar league campaign and were to win only three of their opening 14 games although one of their victories was an amazing 7-1 victory over Arsenal. But the league campaign really confirmed what everyone thought after the August derby encounter – there was little between the North East rivals.

Football League
Division 1
Sunderland 1 Newcastle United 1 (HT: 0-0)
19th December 1953
Roker Park
49,922

Sunderland: J Cowan, J Hedley, A Hudgell, S Anderson [49], F Hall, G Aitken, T Wright, H Kirtley, R Daniel, L Shackleton, W Elliott*
Newcastle: R Simpson, R Cowell*, A McMichael, J Scoular, F Brennan, R Stokoe, J Milburn, I Broadis [66], A Monkhouse, G Hannah, R Mitchell
Referee: J H Clough (Bolton)

ALTHOUGH IT was just half-way through the season, these were desperate times for Sunderland who came into the game rock bottom in the league. But optimists on Wearside could point out that their favourites were just behind Liverpool on goal average and only one point behind Middlesbrough – and the Rokermen had a game in hand over both sides. Not that Newcastle were doing much better – they were just four points above the Wearsiders.

Sunderland had played Ray Daniel as an emergency centre forward at home to Charlton a week earlier and he had performed well, helping the

Rokermen to collect two valuable points; so the experiment was repeated against the Magpies.

Newcastle had also won their last game (away to Blackpool) and fielded an unchanged team, retaining Alan Monkhouse at centre forward with Jackie Milburn on the right wing. There were many intriguing personal battles to look forward to in this game: Daniel v Brennan; Shackleton v Scoular; Aitken v Broadis. There was even added spice in the return of Ivor Broadis to Roker for the first time as a Newcastle player.

League Positions

		Pos	Pl	Pts		Pos	Pl	Pts
Before:	Newcastle	15th	22	19	Sunderland	22nd	21	15
After:	Newcastle	17th	23	20	Sunderland	20th	22	16

This was a ragged, disjointed game, almost devoid of goalmouth excitement. Newcastle enjoyed more possession but it was Sunderland who looked more purposeful. Len Shackleton twice looked dangerous in the opening minutes but first he was foiled by Ronnie Simpson on the six yard line and then by Frank Brennan sticking out a boot at the crucial moment.

A long cross-cum-shot by Billy Elliott then went close, curling just outside a post. Alf McMichael tried a pot shot at the other end that bounced up on to the bar before Jimmy Cowan gathered safely. But it was Sunderland who went closest to scoring when an Elliott cross to the far post was met by Daniel two yards out but Simpson somehow scooped the ball away from under the bar.

Newcastle hit the woodwork again when Broadis received a Bob Stokoe pass inside the penalty area and half volleyed an effort against the bar. But it was Sunderland who eventually opened the scoring four minutes after half-time.

It was a first ever league goal for Stan Anderson as he forced a loose ball through several opponents before hitting a fine 12 yard shot past Simpson.

Once ahead, Sunderland played the one sustained spell of good football. Unfortunately for them, poor finishing let them down and they let Newcastle off the hook. United had to rearrange their forward line ten minutes into the second half when Monkhouse took a knock. He went out to the right wing with Milburn switching inside but Jackie had no more success against the outstanding Fred Hall than Monkhouse. Sunderland paid the consequences for not turning their superiority into goals when United grabbed an equaliser. Typically, it was a former Sunderland player who scored.

After 66 minutes George Hannah took a pass from Bob Stokoe but his attempt on goal seemed to stick in the mud. Ivor Broadis reached it just before Cowan or Hall and toe-poked the ball over the line as he was sandwiched by the Roker defenders.

Defenders took the main honours with Hall, Arthur Hudgell and Jack Hedley shining for the home side and Bobby Cowell doing just as well for the visitors.

Sunderland had a gilt-edged chance to settle the game two minutes from time. A Shackleton back-pass to Hall saw the central defender play the ball through the middle. It looked like Frank Brennan would clear but Harry Kirtley flicked it on to the unmarked Daniel eight yards out with just Simpson to beat. The Wearside No 9 showed that he was not a natural finisher by deciding to steady himself which allowed the 'keeper to come out quickly and narrow the angle. The shot eventually went just wide of the post and Sunderland had to settle for a share of the points.

Surprisingly the match statistics indicate that Newcastle did much more attacking than Sunderland, forcing 13 corners to the home side's one. Even the goal kicks were in United's favour (20-10). But the consensus of opinion was that if either side deserved to win, it was Sunderland. They had played the better football but had been let down by poor finishing. Nevertheless, their performance gave them encouragement in the league and they were to lose just two of their next seven league games to climb away from the bottom.

Conversely, Newcastle were to win just two of their next seven league games and the spectre of relegation raised its head before they, too, recovered to finish a couple of points above their rivals. But neither club could really be happy with their season.

Football League
Division 1
Sunderland 4 Newcastle United 2 (HT: 2-0)
9th October 1954
Roker Park
66,654

Sunderland: W Fraser, J Hedley, J McDonald, S Anderson, R Daniel, G Aitken, W Bingham [**39, 52**], L Shackleton, E Purdon [**33**], K Chisholm [**63**], W Elliott
Newcastle: S Mitchell, R Cowell, A McMichael, J Scoular, R Stokoe, C Crowe, L White, I Broadis, J Milburn [**47**], G Hannah, R Mitchell [**67** pen]
Referee: Arthur Ellis (Halifax)

THIS SEASON had seen a remarkable transformation in the fortunes of Sunderland AFC. The previous year they had flirted with relegation, finishing 18th. Now they were high-flying, championship contenders, one point behind leaders West Bromwich Albion and Manchester City and ahead of Chelsea on goal average. What was the reason for the change? After all, these were largely the same players who had struggled last term. There were a couple of changes – Willie Fraser had taken over in goal from Jimmy Cowan and Joe McDonald had replaced Arthur Hudgell as the regular left back (although both changes had really taken place in the latter stages of the previous season). The main reason for the improvement was that manager Bill

Murray had been able to field a settled team although he had injury doubts for this game. George Aitken and Ken Chisholm were doubtful, although both recovered to play.

Newcastle, meanwhile, had problems. They came into the derby on the back of three successive league defeats as well as a loss away to Plymouth Argyle in a friendly match. Changes were made to the side that had lost their last league fixture away to Cardiff, Alf McMichael, Ivor Broadis and George Hannah came in for Ron Batty, Vic Keeble and Stan Keery. United seemed to think that their problems lay with their attack but, in reality, defensive weaknesses were much more apparent. The fact that Frank Brennan (increasingly out of favour) and Ronnie Simpson (injured) were both absentees did not help. The one positive aspect that Newcastle could take into this match was that Sunderland had won one just of the 12 derbies since United had been promoted in 1948.

League Positions

		Pos	Pl	Pts		Pos	Pl	Pts
Before:	Sunderland	3rd	11	15	Newcastle	12th	11	11
After:	Sunderland	1st	12	17	Newcastle	12th	12	11

Newcastle surprised Sunderland by raising their game and making quite a fight of it. They played the better football in midfield in the opening 20 minutes with Charlie Crowe in particular doing well. But the Wearsiders' cavalier-style attacks eventually paid dividends. It was certainly great entertainment for the enormous Roker crowd. Sunderland relied heavily on the big boot upfield to Ted Purdon early on. The centre forward played well and received much more support than Jackie Milburn did for Newcastle. It was left to Len White on the Magpies' right wing to show the most threat.

The home wingers, Billy Bingham and Billy Elliott, both impressed and Len Shackleton showed a combination of skills and trickery although, as usual, he over-indulged at times. Bobby Mitchell was Newcastle's ball artist and he gave Jack Hedley a bit of a roasting although his final pass was always delayed just too long. It took Sunderland some time to breach the Magpies' defence but when they did they netted two goals in quick succession.

After 33 minutes, Bob Stokoe failed to clear and Bobby Cowell's back heeler spun the ball towards the bye-line where Ted Purdon somehow managed to nip between Cowell, Scoular and Stewart Mitchell to roll the ball in from an acute angle. Six minutes later Joe McDonald sent a free kick to Len Shackleton who touched it to Billy Bingham. The Northern Irish international's consummate dipping shot from 25 yards sailed over the 'keeper's head to go in just under the bar near the far post. Sunderland just about deserved their half-time lead.

Newcastle began the second half determined to fight back and they gained an early success, Jackie Milburn crashing home a wicked, angled drive from the right that Willie Fraser never saw.

Hopes of a full fight back were quickly dispelled when Sunderland restored their two goals advantage five minutes later. The goal came from one of several superb crosses by Billy Elliott – this one was met by Billy Bingham who nodded in at the far post.

Sunderland were still not satisfied and killed off their rivals with a fourth after 63 minutes. Stan Anderson played a pass inside to Shackleton who cheekily drew four defenders towards him as he danced over the ball. A shrewd forward pass set up the chance for the quick thinking Ken Chisholm who raced in to tap the ball home.

It was not quite over as the Geordies pulled another goal back from the penalty spot soon after. Joe McDonald headed a Milburn effort off the goal line but only as far as Len White. His shot back into the crowded penalty area was handled by George Aitken. Many thought that it was ball to hand rather than the other way round, but referee Arthur Ellis was adamant – it was a penalty. Up stepped Bobby Mitchell to confidently convert the kick, blasting the ball past Fraser.

That was the end of the scoring although Newcastle never ceased trying with Milburn, Mitchell and Broadis all going close. At the final whistle Sunderland still led 4-2 and deservedly picked up both points.

It had been a highly entertaining game with plenty of bite in the play although little or no viciousness. The firm control of referee Ellis went a long way to ensuring that it never got out of hand.

The win catapulted Sunderland to the top of the league and raised hopes of a championship contending campaign. But it was very close with the Rokermen just ahead of Manchester City on goal average and above Manchester United, Preston North End and West Bromwich Albion by one point. However it was still fairly early in the season and the winning post was a long way away yet.

Football League
Division 1
Newcastle United 1 Sunderland 2 (HT: 0-1)
26th February 1955
St James' Park
62,835

Newcastle: R Simpson, R Cowell, R Batty, J Scoular, R Stokoe, T Casey, J Milburn [46], I Broadis, V Keeble, G Hannah, R Mitchell
Sunderland: W Fraser, J Hedley, J McDonald, S Anderson, R Daniel, G Aitken, S Kemp, C Fleming [43, 90], E Purdon, K Chisholm, W Elliott
Referee: Arthur Ellis (Halifax)

BOTH SIDES were in the middle of cup runs when they met in late February. Sunderland had just won a Fifth Round replay against Swansea Town and were to face league leaders Wolverhampton Wanderers in the quarter-finals. Newcastle had a similar replay of their own lined up for two days after the derby with a home tie against Nottingham Forest. The Wearsiders, however, had their eyes on two trophies. They were three points behind Wolves with a game in hand and ahead of the chasing pack of Charlton Athletic (who had a further game in hand), Portsmouth and Manchester City who were all one point adrift. Certainly they had every incentive to win this derby apart from local prestige.

Newcastle had some unwelcome injuries going into this game with Brennan and Crowe out but they also made some extra team changes from the side that had drawn away to Forest in the cup. Out went Davies and White as in came Broadis, Hannah and Casey (for Crowe). But Sunderland had problems themselves with Bingham suffering from strained thigh muscles and Daniel doubtful until the day of the match (although he recovered to play). Controversially, however, Sunderland dropped Shackleton who had been particularly poor against Swansea and he lined up for the reserves against Blackhall Colliery at Roker Park as Purdon and Kemp (for only the third league game of his career) came into the side that faced the Magpies.

There was some doubt the match being staged due to heavy snow. An army of workers had cleared it from the pitch on the Wednesday and had lain straw to protect the surface. The terraces had been similarly cleared on the Thursday and Friday to ensure that went the game went ahead.

League Positions

		Pos	Pl	Pts		Pos	Pl	Pts
Before:	Sunderland	2nd	29	35	Newcastle	12th	28	28
After:	Sunderland	2nd	30	37	Newcastle	13th	29	28

Newcastle started well and were unlucky not to be awarded a penalty when Stan Anderson bowled over Vic Keeble. Then, soon afterwards, they should have scored the opener when a short cross by George Hannah was met by the No 9 just five yards out but he was unable to stoop low enough to get any leverage on his header. This allowed Willie Fraser to palm away the ball. Keeble went close again in the 20th minute but his header from a Bobby Mitchell cross went just over the bar. Then Fraser saved a long range effort from Jimmy Scoular before play switched to the other end where it took a brilliant save by Ronnie Simpson to foil Billy Elliott from eight yards.

It was Sunderland who snatched the lead just before the interval. Ron Batty did well to concede a corner, whipping the ball off Ted Purdon's toes close in but the respite was short-lived. The corner was only half cleared and Billy Elliott was able to send over a cross for Sam Kemp to head down to where Charlie Fleming shrugged off a challenge and whipped the ball home from the edge of the six yard box. The goal came at a bad time for United who could regard themselves as unlucky to be behind at the interval.

But they were far from dispirited and they came out for the second half determined to rectify matters.

They succeeded within a minute. Keeble touched the ball to Ivor Broadis at the kick-off and tried a dribbling run following a return pass only to be obstructed as he approached the penalty area. The foul took place 22 yards out from goal, just a nice distance for Jackie Milburn. Scoular rolled the ball to him and Fraser never even saw it as it screamed thorough the Wearside defensive wall and past him. At least one source timed the goal at six seconds from the restart but, based on the description, this would not be possible. Nevertheless it was a very quick goal.

The game was robust but was played in a sporting fashion which, coupled with good refereeing, kept play flowing. Both defences played well with Bob Stokoe having a particularly successful time against Purdon but Sunderland were challenging for the championship and their determination showed in their play. Both sides went close with Simpson finger-tipping an effort by Elliott over the bar and Keeble being unfortunate when a header from a Mitchell cross looked goalward bound but hit Fraser on his knee as he scampered along the goal line. Ron Batty cleared off the line from Elliott in the later stages and a lovely header by Fleming went just wide as the Wearsiders pushed for the winner.

Injury time was being played when the decisive goal was scored. Sunderland were awarded a free kick 40 yards from goal. Jack Hedley took it and sent the ball high into the home penalty area where Charlie Fleming, in the inside left position, met it with another header that eluded Simpson, diving high to his left.

The game was restarted but within two or three seconds the whistle was blown to end the match and Newcastle had no chance to mount another attack.

This had been another desperately close game. Although United could regard themselves as unlucky to concede a goal so late in the game, Sunderland had probably just deserved to win. Victory was certainly more important for them. They were now only a point behind Wolves (on level games) and two ahead of third placed Chelsea. But their challenge was soon to fade as they followed their success at Gallowgate with six games without a win. Ultimately, their fourth place finish (behind second and third placed Wolves and Portsmouth on goal average) was to be regarded as disappointing.

Newcastle, on the other hand, were to finish in a moderate eighth position in the league but were to go on to cup glory, winning the FA Cup for the third time in five years at Wembley ten weeks after the derby. To them went the ultimate glory.

Football League
Division 1
Sunderland 1 Newcastle United 6 (HT: 0-4)
26th December 1955
Roker Park
55,723

Sunderland: W Fraser, J Hedley, J McDonald, S Anderson, R Daniel, G Aitken,
L Shackleton, C Fleming [**48**], E Purdon, K Chisholm, W Elliott
Newcastle: R Simpson, R Batty, A McMichael, J Scoular, W Paterson, T Casey,
J Milburn [**14, 67**], R Davies, V Keeble [**2, 28**], W Curry [**18, 81**], R Mitchell
Referee: A Luty (Leeds)

CHRISTMAS WAS always one of the crucial times of the football year with
all First Division teams playing three games over the festive holiday. Before
Christmas Eve, Sunderland had been fourth in the league, only two points
behind leaders Manchester United with two games in hand. Newcastle, meanwhile, had been down in 15th position. A 4-0 defeat away to Huddersfield for
the Wearsiders and a 5-0 win at home for the Magpies however had begun to
change things.

The Newcastle supporters went to Roker full of confidence but they knew
that much depended upon recently reinstated centre half Bill Paterson and
their newly formed left wing triangle of Casey, Curry and Mitchell.

Sunderland brought back Ted Purdon at centre forward in place of youngster Derek Weddle although many thought that Purdon was not the answer to
their striking problems.

League Positions

		Pos	Pl	Pts		Pos	Pl	Pts
Before:	Sunderland	6th	21	26	Newcastle	13th	22	22
After:	Sunderland	7th	22	26	Newcastle	10th	23	24

Newcastle relied on the side that had demolished Preston on Christmas
Eve and shocked the Roker faithful by proceeding to do the same with Sunderland. After just two minutes Stan Anderson fouled Bobby Mitchell on the
Sunderland right flank and Tom Casey sent the resultant free kick into the
penalty area for Vic Keeble to run in and arrow a header past Fraser.

Twelve minutes later United went two up; Jackie Milburn took a square
pass from Reg Davies and dummied Joe McDonald in the corner of the penalty box before whipping home a low, left foot rocket that flashed under Willie
Fraser's dive.

Four minutes after that Bobby Mitchell played a firm, forward through-
pass for Bill Curry to turn a left footed shot into the net from close range.

It took another ten minutes before the fourth went in. A Milburn corner was met perfectly by Keeble who was allowed a free header that was so hard and deadly that Fraser scarcely saw the ball as it flew past him.

With four goals in the opening half an hour, this was becoming a massacre and the Roker Roar was silenced. In fact, the ground seemed to be filled with cheering Geordies. Yet, if the truth be told, Sunderland did as much of the attacking as Newcastle. The first half match statistics tell a more accurate tale than the scoreline: Sunderland forced seven corners to Newcastle's four while Fraser took just two goal kicks to Simpson's ten. The difference was that United's finishing had been deadly.

Fortunately for Sunderland, Mitchell sustained a recurrence of an ankle injury just before half-time and was effectively a spent force thereafter. Nevertheless, a 4-0 deficit looked like a lost cause for the Wearsiders. Yet Sunderland struck three minutes after the resumption to give their supporters a faint hope. Billy Elliott was obstructed by Ron Batty out on the wing and took the free kick himself. He placed it perfectly for Charlie Fleming who ran in from the right to head home.

Despite this goal, Newcastle continued to look the more dangerous side with Milburn, now hitting peak form, giving a vintage display and providing a rare treat – a headed goal (and a good one at that). Bill Curry beat Jack Hedley on the left wing but over-hit his cross. Reg Davies recovered it on the opposite flank and chipped the ball forward to where Jackie rose majestically to flick the ball past a helpless Fraser.

The sixth came nine minutes from time, Milburn burst past McDonald on the right before slinging the ball out to Mitchell on the left. Bobby's pin-point centre into the middle was met by Curry right in front of the posts and he nearly burst the net as he blasted the ball in.

The result equalled Newcastle's biggest win over Sunderland (at Gallowgate back in 1920) and there seemed little doubt that, if Mitchell had not been a virtual passenger for half of the game, the score could have even been worse for Sunderland – possibly even avenging the 9-1 massacre of 1908.

The Wearsiders responded to what was becoming a crisis immediately. Within a few hours of the final whistle they signed Burnley centre forward Bill Holden for £12,000 at a rendezvous in Ripon. He would make his Sunderland debut in the return fixture against Newcastle at St James' Park the following day.

Football League
Division 1
Newcastle United 3 Sunderland 1 (HT: 0-1)
27th December 1955
St James' Park
61,058

Newcastle: R Simpson, R Batty, A McMichael, J Scoular, W Paterson, T Casey, J Milburn [**55**], R Davies, V Keeble [**53**], W Curry, L White [**90**]
Sunderland: W Fraser, J Hedley, J McDonald, S Anderson, R Daniel, G Aitken, S Kemp, C Fleming, W Holden [**5**], W Elliott, L Shackleton
Referee: A Luty (Leeds)

ENCOURAGED BY the thrashing of Sunderland at Roker on Boxing Day, a magnificent crowd of 61,000 crammed into St James' Park the following day. Sunderland made wholesale changes to their forward line. Out went Ted Purdon and Ken Chisholm to be replaced by newly signed Bill Holden and Sam Kemp with Len Shackleton and Billy Elliott taking up different positions. At the time there were no newspapers printed over Christmas and TV was not widespread so when the name Holden was announced over the loudspeakers, the vast majority of spectators were puzzled. Who was Holden?

Newcastle made one change to their team and that was enforced on them, Len White taking over from the injured Bobby Mitchell.

League Positions		Pos	Pl	Pts		Pos	Pl	Pts
Before:	Sunderland	7th	22	26	Newcastle	10th	23	24
After:	Newcastle	6th	24	26	Sunderland	10th	23	26

The crowd were still mulling over the changes to Sunderland's forward line when the man at the centre of their bemusement made the ideal start to his Wearside career. After just five minutes Billy Elliott took the ball from Scoular with a sliding tackle and started a move that involved all five visiting forwards and ended with Sam Kemp trying a shot at goal. It was blocked but Holden was on hand to net the rebound and shock the Geordie crowd.

Newcastle now knew that they had a fight on their hands and the game that followed was one of the best ever matches between the two old rivals – a stirring and thrill packed affair. Sunderland were stronger and quicker on the ball in the first half and had a number of chances to increase their lead before the interval. But their finishing left something to be desired. Charlie Fleming, in particular, missed a golden opportunity. Bill Paterson had one of his best ever games for Newcastle in the centre of their defence which was just as well as Scoular had wrenched his knee and could play only at half pace.

Newcastle came into the game more in the second half and Sunderland were soon to rue missing their earlier chances.

After 53 minutes White tried a shot that Ray Daniel half cleared straight back to him. This time Len prodded it into the middle where Vic Keeble headed first against a post as Reg Davies distracted the 'keeper and then reacted quickest to tear in and slam the ball home.

Soon after this Elliott had to go off the field to receive treatment to a head wound and it was while Sunderland were temporarily down to ten men that Newcastle grabbed the lead. Ron Batty sent a free kick towards the visitors' goal and Davies managed to get in a shot. It was blocked but the ball came out to Jackie Milburn who hooked it in under the bar from 12 yards.

Elliott resumed on the left wing with Shackleton switching inside. Sunderland looked more dangerous with Shack lending his skills as a striker. Holden looked a good acquisition although he was a bit sluggish. It was touch and go as both teams went for the next crucial goal. Ronnie Simpson made two great saves from Fleming and Shackleton before a shot from White beat Fraser but hit a post.

There were just 30 seconds left to play when the decisive goal was scored. White supplied Curry near the half-way line and he played it out to Milburn. Jackie played a through pass for White who was bursting forward and his shot gave Fraser no chance.

This was Newcastle's Christmas. Including their 5-0 win over Preston on Christmas Eve, they had played three games and won all three, scoring 14 goals to 2 – their first Christmas treble since the 1932-33 season. Sunderland, on the other hand, had suffered three festive defeats starting with a 4-0 reverse at Huddersfield – 2 goals for and 13 against.

The Magpies double over the Rokermen saw the Geordies leap frog their neighbours in the league as they shot up from fifteenth to sixth. Tyneside was cock-a-hoop. But there was to be a sting in the tail because the teams were to meet again in the cup later in the season with a vastly different outcome.

A Unique Record

Newcastle achieved something at Roker Park that no other club has done – not even Sunderland. They won an FA Cup semi-final tie there, beating York City, 2-0, in March 1955. Sunderland, of course, are not allowed to play semi-final ties at home.

FA Cup
6th round
Newcastle United 0 Sunderland 2 (HT: 0-1)
3rd March 1956
St James' Park
61,474

Newcastle: R Simpson, R Batty, A McMichael, R Stokoe, W Paterson, J Scoular, J Milburn, R Davies, V Keeble, W Curry, R Mitchell
Sunderland: W Fraser, J Hedley, J McDonald, S Anderson, R Daniel, G Aitken, W Bingham, C Fleming, W Holden [**41, 83**], W Elliott, L Shackleton
Referee: R H Mann (Worcester)

CUP HOLDERS Newcastle, flying high in the league and having already completed a league double over the neighbours, were confident of completing a hat-trick of derby wins. But, ominously for their supporters, Tom Casey had failed a fitness test a couple of days before the game and Jimmy Scoular had to come back from a two month absence due to a knee injury in the strange position for him of left half.

Sunderland were doing very well themselves in the league and were only two points behind the Magpies with two games in hand. On top of that, they were not just unchanged but could now boast a growing reputation of having one of the best defences in the country.

Thousands of counterfeit tickets for the game were in circulation although holders were told that they could be detected at the gates. But valid tickets were also available on the black market at grossly inflated prices. Typically, 2s 6d ground tickets were going for 25s 0d while seat tickets were being snapped up at £5 0s 0d.

Men were employed on the morning of the match to clear the protective covering of straw from the pitch. Sunderland had an estimated 16,000 fans in the massive crowd. Newcastle had increased the admission prices for certain parts of the ground with the normal 3s 6d paddock tickets costing 4s 0d. Consequently a new ground receipts record of £9,600 was set for the game.

Both sides played in change strips but, after all of the pre-match hype, the game was a big let down with a troublesome wind spoiling most attempts to play constructive football. The tension also seemed to get to both sets of players and the game was littered with jittery play. Sunderland adapted better to the conditions although it was Newcastle who showed up well in the early stages. Soon, however, Billy Elliott and Charlie Fleming made their presence felt and the visitors gained the upper hand. Man-of-the-match Elliott gave Stokoe a torrid time and, with Bill Paterson particularly nervous, the Rokermen looked the more threatening side although there was not much between the teams in a fairly even first half. The breakthrough came not long before half-time.

A long through ball by Len Shackleton found Bill Holden ten yards out from the Newcastle goal line with his back to the goal. He gambled with a back header and caught Ronnie Simpson four yards off his line, the ball sailing over him to give Sunderland a half-time lead.

Perhaps Newcastle could have regarded themselves unfortunate to be behind at the interval but the goal gave Sunderland confidence and they were quite clearly the better team in the second half. Nevertheless, it was United who, once again, pressed early on. Jackie Milburn was particularly unlucky with a rocket of a shot that hit Ray Daniel on the head and deflected away for a corner. But Sunderland were soon in control. They forced 11 corners to Newcastle's eight and took ten goal kicks to United's 20, which shows how much attacking they did. But they knew that one goal was never going to be enough. Shackleton did not endear himself to his former supporters with his deliberate time wasting.

Such tactics were no longer required after the visitors deservedly went two up with seven minutes left. Paterson anxiously kept the ball in play but was robbed by Holden who kept his head as he dribbled in from the right and rolled the ball home from three yards as Batty desperately slid along the line.

Newcastle claimed that the wind had defeated them as much as Sunderland but, in truth, the Wearsiders had clearly been the better team. In fact, United had looked jaded and inexplicably produced their worst display in the Cup since the war. Defeat saw their glorious 1950s Cup era come to an end and Wembley glory was to be no more than a distant dream for a full generation of Geordie supporters.

The Sunderland fans, meanwhile, left Gallowgate with plenty to celebrate. They dreamed of beginning a cup era of their own but their hopes lasted only another two weeks before they crashed 3-0 to Birmingham City at Hillsborough in the semi-final.

Holden, however, could look back on his games against Newcastle with delight. By the time the Tyne-Wear cup tie ended, he had played a dozen games for Sunderland, scoring three goals – all against the Magpies. But this was to be the pinnacle of his career. Seven months, and four goals, later Sunderland were to sell him to Stockport County.

Football League
Division 1
Sunderland 1 Newcastle United 2 (HT: 0-1)
25th August 1956
Roker Park
51,032

Sunderland: J Bollands, J Hedley, J McDonald, W Morrison, R Daniel, G Aitken, J Hannigan, S Anderson, C Fleming, L Shackleton [**53**], W Elliott
Newcastle: R Simpson, R Batty, A McMichael, J Scoular, R Stokoe, C Crowe, R Davies [**87**], J Milburn [**39**], V Keeble, G Hannah, R Mitchell
Referee: H Webb (Leeds)

THIS GAME was very early in the season (which had started the previous weekend) and both sides were trying to find their feet. Nevertheless, even with just two games gone, they had both already lost their unbeaten records.

Sunderland relied on the side that had defeated Bolton Wanderers at Roker in midweek with Len Shackleton captaining the Wearsiders for the first time in a Wear-Tyne derby. Newcastle had lost 5-2 away to Cardiff in their last game when Ronnie Simpson had suffered his worst game yet for the Magpies. He gained a reprieve to keep his place at Roker but George Lackenby had been injured at Ninian Park and Ron Batty came into the side at full back to take his place.

The crowd at Roker was excellent considering the appalling weather conditions. As if heavy rain before the game was not enough to deter the fans, it become torrential during the match when thunder and lightning adding to the drama.

League Positions

		Pos	Pl	Pts		Pos	Pl	Pts
Before:	Sunderland	13th	2	2	Newcastle	14th	2	2
After:	Newcastle	9th	3	4	Sunderland	17th	3	2

After a quiet start, the first half undoubtedly belonged to Newcastle who surprised their supporters after their dismal display in South Wales. George Hannah was always too elusive for Morrison while Jimmy Scoular's class stood out. He was easily the best wing half on the field. Sunderland had Johnny Bollands to thank for keeping them in the game. He made two magnificent saves from Mitchell and Hannah as United tried to turn their superiority into goals. But they had to wait until six minutes before the interval until they eventually did so.

Reg Davies impressed for Newcastle in the first half and it was his diagonal cross into the middle that set up the chance for Jackie Milburn to score with a diving header from 15 yards. The Sunderland defence seemed intent on marking Newcastle's target-man, Vic Keeble, and (like Manchester City in the Cup Final last season) forgot about Milburn.

Perhaps the Rokermen had reason to disregard Jackie. He had sustained a groin injury in the 20th minute and was beginning to labour by the time the goal was scored.

If Newcastle had controlled the first half, it was totally different after the interval. The Roker rally began straight from the restart and the best move of the match ended with Fleming shooting just past the post. The standard was set for an amazing turn-around in fortunes as Len Shackleton took the game by the scruff of the neck. He turned on his full repertoire of skills and served up some delightful entertainment for the Roker masses. It was fitting that he should score the equaliser after 53 minutes.

Shack beat Scoular to a misplaced pass from Crowe and made up ground before cracking a superb shot from fully 25 yards that had Simpson beaten all the way as it flew into the top right hand corner. Now level, and with Shack in inspired form, Sunderland pressed forward eagerly. But although Sunderland created plenty of chances most of them fell to Charlie Fleming and the Cannonball had left his shooting boots at home. Some of his misses were appalling although many of them fell to his 'weaker' left foot. Eventually Shackleton had to try another long range effort himself. Once again he left Simpson helpless only to see the ball hit the crossbar. A Stan Anderson header also beat the Newcastle 'keeper but Ron Batty (a stalwart in the Newcastle defence) managed to head it over the bar. When Alf McMichael similarly nodded a fierce drive by Billy Elliott over the top as well, Sunderland must have known that it was not to be their day.

And so it proved. The game looked a certain draw when, against the run of play, Newcastle grabbed the winner with just three minutes left. Bobby Mitchell, who had been generally subdued by Jack Hedley, somehow managed to send over the sodden ball (by now dead-weight) from an awkward position out on the left. His cross to beyond the far post was perfect and Reg Davies was on hand to direct a downward header that bounced into the far corner of the net with Bollands out of position.

It was perhaps fitting that, if Newcastle had to win, it was Davies who should score the goal. But spare a thought for Len Shackleton who trooped off the field, poker-faced, at the final whistle, He had produced just about a perfect performance but had still finished on the losing side.

Despite their first half dominance, Newcastle had been lucky to win. Over the 90 minutes, Sunderland had been the better team. But United had one facet to their play that the Rokermen hadn't – they took their scoring chances. Sadly for the Red'n Whites, most of their's had fallen to Fleming who had a game to forget.

The end of the game was sadly marred by an unsavoury incident. Elliott seemed to butt Stokoe in the face as they left the field. Perhaps defeat was hard to take. But this should not detract from Len Shackleton's display. Even the Newcastle supporters were heard to mutter as they left the ground, "Thanks for the memory, Len". Sadly it was to be his last competitive appearance in front of his own crowd against his arch-rivals.

Football League
Division 1
Newcastle United 6 Sunderland 2 (HT: 3-1)
22nd December 1956
St James' Park
29,727

Newcastle: R Simpson, R Keith, R Batty, J Scoular, R Stokoe, T Casey [**70** pen],
L White [**7**], R Davies [**72**], A Tait [**21, 37, 56**], W Curry, W Punton
Sunderland: J Bollands, J Hedley, J McDonald, S Anderson, R Daniel, G Aitken,
W Bingham, D Revie, C Fleming [**41, 64**], L Shackleton, W Elliott
Referee: H Webb (Leeds)

BOTH SIDES were struggling in the league when they met for their pre-Christmas encounter on Tyneside. Indeed, Sunderland were second bottom – a relegation place – although it was still just half-way through the season. They were three points above tail-enders Charlton Athletic and one behind Portsmouth although the Roker men had a game in hand over the Addicks. But the Wearsiders had won their last two games without their schemer-in-chief Don Revie, who had been injured. Now he was fit again and returned in place of Alan Hope (who was later to change his name by deed poll to Alan O'Neill).

Newcastle relied on the side who had performed so well in picking up a point away to Portsmouth in their last game and so fielded an unchanged side for the first time since the beginning of September. Thus there was no place in the team for either Jackie Milburn or Bobby Mitchell.

The Saturday before Christmas was traditionally a bad time for football attendances but this year the Tyne-Wear derby crowd ducked under 30,000 for the first time since 1930 (since 1903 for a Gallowgate game). In this instance, however, it wasn't just the counter-attraction of Santa Claus to blame. Thick fog permeated the country and most people assumed that the game would be off. Visibility was so poor that thousands of spectators were kept waiting outside the ground until 35 minutes before the kick when referee Webb finally decided that it should go ahead. With the pitch also waterlogged, it seemed a strange decision. The North East was lucky. Six of the scheduled First Division matches country-wide were postponed. By the time this game had finished, the Sunderland supporters wished that this one had been as well!

League Positions		Pos	Pl	Pts		Pos	Pl	Pts
Before:	Newcastle	18th	21	18	Sunderland	21st	21	13
After:	Newcastle	16th	22	20	Sunderland	21st	22	13

The puny Gallowgate floodlights were switched on for this game but they did little to pierce the gloom. The fog and mud made playing conditions abysmal but Newcastle seemed to revel in them while Sunderland seemed as despondent as the weather. Initially they showed a complete lack of commitment (unforgivable in a Tyne-Wear derby) and Newcastle took full advantage. United's right half Jimmy Scoular produced a vintage display and Tom Casey, on the other flank, was almost as good. With captain Bob Stokoe leading by example between them, Sunderland never stood a chance. It did not take the inexperienced but effervescent United attack long to open their account.

After seven minutes, Johnny Bollands did well to push away Casey's 25 yards shot but all he did was knock the ball towards Len White who came racing in crash it into the empty net.

Newcastle continued to dominate and could have scored twice more in as many minutes. First Tait sent a header just over the bar and then Bollands tipped a White lob over the top.

But United were not to be denied and they went two up after 21 minutes when a White corner was helped on by Reg Davies to young Alex Tait who turned quickly to flash a shot home.

At last Sunderland began to show some much-needed improvement but they had little to show up front although Ronnie Simpson made one good save from Fleming. After 37 minutes a long, diagonal pass from Davies found White who centred from the right. Tait managed to get in a header that Bollands once again did well to block but, yet again, could not hold and, as the ball rolled towards the foot of a post, the United centre forward dashed in to apply the finishing touch.

Sunderland tried everything to try and get back into the game. They forced three corners in quick succession before eventually making a breakthrough four minutes before half-time. Even the Geordie supporters had to admit it was a class goal as Stan Anderson, Billy Elliott and Len Shackleton all combined to create an opening for Charlie Fleming to beat Simpson with a low drive.

Heartened, Sunderland attacked as the fog began to thicken. Simpson had to make two fine saves from Fleming and Revie to keep them at bay. But they tried to be too precise with their passing (clearly the wrong tactics on this waterlogged pitch) and when the next goal came, it was at the other end some 11 minutes after the restart.

Bill Curry's astute forward pass found Alex Tait unmarked just inside the visitors' half. He still had a lot to do as he raced forward towards Bollands. The 'keeper came out and defenders closed in on the young centre forward but he kept his head to coolly stroke the ball in and complete his hat-trick.

Sunderland now needed a miracle. Shackleton was reduced into trying long range pot shots, a couple of which went over the top but one hit the bar. But hopes were once again raised when they eventually managed to pull another goal back after 64 minutes. Don Revie played in Charlie Fleming and he chalked up his second goal with a powerful shot that beat Simpson all of the way.

Any hopes that Sunderland harboured about a rally were quickly snuffed out when United scored twice within the next eight minutes.

First, Ray Daniel, getting rattled by the baying of the Newcastle crowd, barged clumsily into Tait inside the Wearside penalty area. It was a spot kick and up stepped Tom Casey to make it 5-2.

It took just a further two minutes to kill off Sunderland. Len White raced almost to the bye-line before pulling the ball back for Reg Davies to demonstrate his sharp-shooting ability with a left foot effort from 15 yards that once again beat Bollands.

Shackleton fired against a post and Bingham headed over in the closing stages but it was Newcastle who finished on top.

The final scoreline did not flatter Newcastle in any way. They were clearly the better side and the defeat left Sunderland facing a very real threat of relegation although it was not yet Christmas. But all was not lost. They were still three points ahead of Charlton and one behind Portsmouth although Pompey now had a game in hand.

Rumours soon abounded that the Rokermen could turn to Tyneside for a Messiah with both Jackie Milburn and Bobby Mitchell said to be their targets. But these were merely rumours and nothing became of them. In fact Sunderland eventually rescued themselves, but only just. They displayed true northern grit by going seven games without defeat in the later stages of the season before losing their last three games, all away from home. But by then they had done enough to keep them out of a relegation spot – by one place!

Not that Newcastle did much better. They finished just four points above their neighbours. But Christmas 1956 saw the Geordie fans celebrate in style. Not only had they thrashed the old enemy, but in doing so had set up a record of four successive league wins in Tyne-Wear derbies. Needless to say this was Alex Tait's finest hour. His was the first hat-trick by a Newcastle player in a Tyne-Wear derby – not bad for a part-timer!

Football League
Division 1
Sunderland 2 Newcastle United 0 (HT: 1-0)
21st September 1957
Roker Park
45,718

Sunderland: W Fraser, J Hedley, J McDonald, S Anderson, G Aitken, W Elliott, W Bingham, D Revie [43], C Fleming, A O'Neill, C Grainger [52]
Newcastle: S Mitchell, R Keith, A McMichael, J Scoular, R Stokoe, T Casey, J Hill, R Davies, V Keeble, W Curry, R Mitchell
Referee: A W Luty (Leeds)

ALTHOUGH IT was still early in the season, Sunderland already seemed to have a relegation battle on their hands. They were one of four teams on four points and were just above bottom placed Birmingham City on goal average. They were also in disarray. A proposed move to Swansea for Ray Daniel fell through a couple of days before the derby due to a massive difference in the amount Sunderland wanted for him (£15,000 – down from £20,000) and what the Swans were willing to pay (£8,000 – up from £5,000). Daniel had 'flu but would have been in the reserves away to Darlington anyway.

But if the situation within the Wearside club was bad, it was worse at St James' Park. In fact, it would have been laughable if it had not been so serious. A selection committee of three directors (Chairman WB Taylor, Alderman WG McKeag and WE Hurford) made four changes to the team that had played in the previous game away to Portsmouth. This was the choice of the last two directors not the Chairman who objected. So did the players when the new team was posted up in the Gallowgate dressing room.

They felt that the selection was interference with the running of the team by directors against the man who they regarded as their boss, director Stan Seymour. He immediately discussed the situation with his arch-rival in the boardroom, William McKeag, and informed him that the team would be unchanged. And it was. It was a staggering situation with the two most powerful directors virtually tearing the club apart and the players effectively picking the team themselves.

League Positions

		Pos	Pl	Pts		Pos	Pl	Pts
Before:	Newcastle	13th	7	7	Sunderland	21st	8	4
After:	Newcastle	15th	8	7	Sunderland	19th	9	6

Despite getting their own way in team selection, the Newcastle players failed to perform at Roker. Their right wing partnership of Hill and Davies was hardly in the game and the playing conditions suited neither Keeble

215

nor Curry with the ball frequently skidding off the greasy turf. For some reason, Newcastle persisted in playing the ball along the ground to the two forwards whose strength lay in the air although they both missed golden chances to score.

Sunderland's forward power was far too much for a spiritless and sluggish Newcastle with the home right wing partnership of Billy Bingham and Don Revie shining. Joe McDonald also stood out in the Roker defence. Dick Keith was the pick of the United rearguard and Jimmy Scoular did well at right half. Bob Stokoe also more than held his own in the middle of the Tyneside defence although he was overworked at times with Charlie Fleming proving a real handful.

Sunderland were easily the better team although Bobby Mitchell made a sparkling start, tormenting the life out of Jack Hedley and anyone else who dared to approach the Bobby Dazzler in the opening stages. Soon, however, with little response from his fellow forwards, he drifted out of the game and Sunderland began to dominate. They should have opened the scoring as early as the sixth minute when Stewart Mitchell fumbled a shot by Stan Anderson and left young Alan O'Neill with an open goal and the ball at his feet but he somehow rolled it wide of an upright. Fleming was unlucky with a shot that beat the goalkeeper but came back off the crossbar. Stan Anderson and Billy Elliott controlled the middle of the park yet it was not until two minutes before the interval that the Rokermen made their superiority count.

Stewart Mitchell raced out to reach a through-ball from Stan Anderson and just beat Fleming. It ran loose to Don Revie who coolly lobbed the 'keeper. Unfortunately, Mitchell fractured one of his fingers during this incident when someone trod on his hand. It was an injury that Newcastle really did not need.

United opened the second half quite promisingly but found themselves further behind within seven minutes.

Billy Bingham was prominent in a move down the right and when Fleming eventually crossed the ball into the middle, Colin Grainger was there to head it goalwards, squeezing it in between Dick Keith and his unsighted 'keeper at the far post.

It almost became embarrassing for Newcastle as Sunderland proceeded to create chance after chance. Stewart Mitchell saved well, diving at Revie's feet, and when the Sunderland man did finally get the ball past him, Alf McMichael was there to clear off the line. Newcastle did manage to get briefly on top with 20 minutes to go, mainly through the determined drive of Jimmy Scoular, who was roundly booed by the Roker supporters every time he touched the ball. But Sunderland still led 2-0 at the final whistle and no-one could dispute that they had easily been the better team. In fact the scoreline flattered Newcastle.

League positions do not lie so this was a poor Sunderland side. But they had totally outplayed a Newcastle team that was a long way below its best.

Victory lifted the Red'n Whites out of a relegation position but they failed to build on it, winning just one of their next seven games, and were soon back in the mire. A long, desperate struggle against relegation lay ahead.

Newcastle were to struggle as well. They won only one of their next eight matches and joined their neighbours in the battle at the foot of the table. With Middlesbrough already in the Second Division, these were black days for football in the North East.

Football League
Division 1
Newcastle United 2 Sunderland 2 (HT: 2-0)
1st February 1958
St James' Park
47,739

Newcastle: S Mitchell, W McKinney, A McMichael, J Cooper, W Paterson, A Franks, A Tait [**23**], G Eastham, W Curry [**37**], R Davies, R Mitchell
Sunderland: W Fraser, J Hedley, J McDonald, S Anderson, C Hurley, W Elliott [**67** pen], W Bingham, A Fogarty, D Revie, A O'Neill [**71**], C Grainger
Referee: L J Tirebuck (Halifax)

BOTH CLUBS were in the middle of a relegation battle with Newcastle ahead only because of goal average. Both were one point above bottom placed Leicester City with Leeds United sandwiched between them.

Surprisingly Sunderland were the more confident side. Newcastle had been knocked out of the cup at home to Scunthorpe United from the Third Division (North) on the previous weekend and were in the midst of an injury/illness crisis. For various reasons (primarily a 'flu epidemic that was sweeping St James') they were without virtually a full side of first team players: Simpson; Keith, Batty, Scoular, Stokoe, Casey; Hughes, Hill, White, Hale, Punton.

Sunderland, on the other hand, had enjoyed a free Saturday on the previous weekend and the epidemic had missed Roker Park altogether so they had a full-strength squad to pick from. No wonder they were confident. To his credit, Newcastle's chairman, Alderman William McKeag, refused to request a postponement and sent a largely inexperienced side out to face their archrivals for a crucial relegation game.

League Positions

		Pos	Pl	Pts		Pos	Pl	Pts
Before:	Newcastle	18th	27	20	Sunderland	20th	27	20
After:	Newcastle	19th	28	21	Sunderland	20th	28	21

The Newcastle chairman was rewarded for his insistence on playing the game by an enthusiastic performance by his team. They were certainly a different class to their visitors in the early stages. This may have been due to the seemingly casual and almost careless approach adopted by the Rokermen. Yet it was Sunderland who went closest to scoring in the opening minutes when Billy Elliott sent Alan O'Neill away for him to shoot against the Newcastle 'keeper. Ambrose Fogarty was on hand to take the rebound and his shot beat Stewart Mitchell and looked a certain goal until Alf McMichael scrambled it off the line. Soon, however, it was Newcastle on the attack with Reg Davies and Bobby Mitchell sending efforts narrowly off target. So it was no surprise when Newcastle opened the scoring mid-way through the half.

Anderson failed to clear properly for Sunderland and Davies won possession. He beat two men before slipping a pass to Alex Tait whose shot from eight yards went in off Fraser.

Sunderland fought back for a time and had the home defence in some trouble but soon it was back to the other end where Tait and Mitchell had the Wearside rearguard reeling.

There was a touch of luck about United's second goal after 37 minutes. In chasing a ball out towards the corner flag, Tait appeared to push Hurley but got away with the foul and the ball. He had time to pick his spot for his cross into the middle where Bill Curry neatly headed in at the near post.

Both sides went close to scoring before the interval, Willie Fraser making a great save from Bobby Mitchell and the winger's namesake, Stewart, doing equally well to tip a Don Revie attempt over the bar.

Newcastle continued to slice open the visitors' defence in the early stages of the second half but, ominously for them, they failed to put their chances away. Revie, Sunderland's deep-lying centre forward, was the key man. He saw plenty of the ball and fed his team mates with a series of chips, lobs and passes. But Newcastle's workrate in midfield largely negated the much vaunted Revie Plan. Gradually, however, the stamina sapping pitch began to tell on the young Newcastle side and Sunderland began to look the stronger team. They eventually pulled a goal back midway through the half although there was a touch of controversy about it.

After 67 minutes Cooper challenged O'Neill to a bouncing ball inside the penalty area wide of the goal and it seemed as if any danger had been averted when the linesman suddenly began to wave his flag vigorously. He had spotted a handling offence by Cooper. Referee Tirebuck had been unsighted so he naturally sided with his assistant as Newcastle protested. The consensus was that Cooper had handled the ball but that it had looked accidental. Nevertheless, it was a spot kick and Billy Elliott made no mistake when he took it.

Sunderland now had their tails up and within four minutes they were level. This time there was no controversy. Jack Hedley spotted Paterson out of position and played a neat ball up to Allan O'Neill. Stewart Mitchell hesitated and Cooper failed to get up high enough as the Sunderland man steered home a header from no more than seven yards; 2-2. It was a great fightback and it set up the game for an exciting finish as both sides went for the winner. United did most of the pressing and, with a bit of luck, they may have snatched both points in the closing stages with Curry blazing over the top and Willie Fraser saving well from Albert Franks as the seconds ticked away. But it was still all square when the final whistle came to signal the end of an engrossing and exciting encounter.

Both sides seemed satisfied with the result – Sunderland for picking up their fifth away point of the season and also for coming back from two goals down to share the spoils; Newcastle for collecting a point despite fielding an undeniably weakened team. There is no doubt that their supporters would have settled for this result before the kick-off even if they were somewhat disappointed not to win after being two goals up at half-time and the better side for a large part of the game.

In the final analysis, the share of the spoils was to decide the immediate future of both clubs. Newcastle's point was to save them from relegation. They were to finish 19th (of 22 with the bottom two going down). Sadly for Wearside, Sunderland occupied one of those positions (21st). Goal average was to decide the fate of the one club in the country who, until then, had never played outside the top flight. Newcastle, Portsmouth and Sunderland were all to finish on 32 points (one ahead of Sheffield Wednesday). But the Rokerites' meagre 'goals for' total of 54 (as opposed to 73 for both the Magpies and Pompey) was to send them down and put an end to Tyne-Wear derbies for the next few years.

Most Consecutive Wins

Newcastle	Sunderland
5 wins:	3 wins:
24 Feb 2002/17 Apr 2006	24 Dec 1904/2 Sept 1905
(on-going)	11 Nov 1922/22 Dec 1923
4 Wins:	
29 Mar 1992/4 Sept 1996	

Player of the Decade
1950s

Stanley Anderson

"If you can meet with Triumph and Disaster
And treat those two impostors just the same"

SO MUSED Rudyard Kipling in his classic poem 'If'. The words could easily apply to Stan Anderson, a player who met with both 'impostors' and came through to succeed.

A product of the fertile soccer breeding ground of County Durham, Stan was not only a member of that select band who played for the North East's 'big three' (Sunderland, Newcastle and Middlesbrough) but went one better – he captained all three as well.

Born in Horden in 1934, Stan underwent a typical soccer childhood for a potentially talented footballer. As a youngster he progressed through his school team to the county line-up and ultimately to England Schoolboys. Although he always loved the game, as a child he did not envisage making a career out of football. But others did. His local big club, Sunderland, obviously thought so, signing him as an amateur at 15 but only after Middlesbrough had rejected him after trials.

Initially he played for the Sunderland 'B' team in the local Houghton & District League but impressed manager Bill Murray enough for him to sign the youngster on professional forms as soon as he reached the age of 17.

He quickly progressed through the reserve ranks to make his first team debut as an 18-year-old at home to Portsmouth in October 1952. It was the first of a record breaking 447 league and cup appearances for the Rokermen.

After turning out a few times for the first team that season (1952-53), he established himself during the following campaign and that was the way it stayed for the next ten years. He was the typical home grown boy in a team of imported crowd pleasers as Sunderland chased success with an open cheque book and became known as the Bank of England club.

But money could not buy a player like Stan. His watchwords were the three 'Ds' – discipline, diligence and determination. Just once did he let the first of these attributes slip. England Under-23 caps had already come his way and he was chosen to go on a tour of eastern Europe with the England 'B' team in 1957. It was in the game against Bulgaria 'B' that he was sent off after clashing with a niggling home winger who had been aggravating Stan throughout the game.

He did not play for the rest of the tour and was temporarily consigned to the wilderness as far as international recognition was concerned – a harsh penalty for an offence of which he was guilty only under extreme provocation. He was to eventually win two full caps for his country but had to wait five years to do so.

Back home his domestic career went from strength to strength. At Roker he was a model professional as Sunderland's all stars pulled in the crowds. Yet success always seemed to elude them. A top four finish in the league in 1954-55 and semi-final cup appearances in both that season and the one following was the nearest that they came to winning honours. At least in the latter season (1955-56) they had the satisfaction of knocking arch-rivals Newcastle out of the cup at the quarter-final stage.

But as the 1950s progressed, things began to turn sour for Sunderland. A scandal surrounding illegal payments shattered the club and they suffered relegation in 1958. Yet they so nearly avoided the drop, going down on goal average. So an unbroken period of top flight football on Wearside stretching back to 1890 came to an end; as did Sunderland's proud boast to have been the one team in the country never to have played outside the top division.

As a local boy, relegation hurt Stan more than most. But his determination and dedication came to the fore and he was at the forefront of rebuilding the club and launching a series of promotion campaigns. But it always seemed to be a case of so near yet so far. In the days when just the top two teams in the Second Division were promoted, Sunderland finished third in 1962 and again in 1963.

As captain, failure in 1963 was particularly galling for Stan. Even a draw at Roker in Sunderland's last game of the season over promotion rivals Chelsea would have been enough. Everyone was preparing for the celebrations. So it was heartbreaking when Chelsea managed to squeeze a 1-0 win to condemn the Rokermen to another season of Second Division football. It wasn't even as if it was a quick execution. The Pensioners still had one more game to play to pip Sunderland who could do nothing more than sit disconsolately in a promotion place waiting for the coup de grace. Needless to say, Chelsea won and scraped above them on goal average.

Season 1963-64 was to be third time lucky for the Rokermen – but not for Stan. Sunderland were among the pacesetters in the league in November when, out of the blue, came the news that stunned the North East. Stan was transferred to Newcastle. He was shattered that his beloved Sunderland had decided to dispense with his services – in this his benefit year. His benefit game was due later in the season and he insisted upon a guarantee that it would still take place before he would sign. So the weird situation arose whereby Roker Park staged a benefit match for a Newcastle player! But the Roker faithful did not desert him. They turned up in their thousands to thank a man who had given them 14 years dedicated service.

But once he changed his colours, he never gave less than 100% for the Magpies. He was quickly appointed captain of his new club and, although promotion in his first (part) season was beyond them, they soon mounted a challenge in 1964-65. The Newcastle half-back line of Anderson, McGrath and Iley was the foundation of a team that won the Second Division title. It was a great day for Stan when he at last led his team into the top flight. He played in all but one of the games that season and finished as joint third top goal scorer – no mean feat for a half-back.

But life has a habit of kicking you when you least expect it. So it was with Stan. He had settled down to enjoy First Division football and anticipated spending the rest of his career at St James' when suddenly, in mid-November, Newcastle transferred him to Middlesbrough.

Sunderland fans had been shocked when he had been sold at Roker and now the

Newcastle fans felt similar emotions. But his role at Ayresome Park was somewhat different. He went as a player-coach to a team struggling for survival in the Second Division. It was a battle against the odds and one that was to be eventually lost. So he went from captaining a side to the Second Division Championship in one season to taking another team down to the Third in the following one.

With relegation looking more and more likely that year, manager Raich Carter had resigned in mid-season to allow trainer Harold Shepherdson and Stan to take over control for the rest of the campaign. A last day defeat away to Cardiff City consigned Boro' to the drop and Stan thereafter became full time manager, quitting playing to concentrate on getting them back up again.

He succeeded in his very first season with the Teessiders finishing runners-up to champions Queen's Park Rangers. Stan remained at the helm for the next seven years and mounted promotion challenges back to the top flight on at least two occasions (1968-69 & 1969-70) without ever quite making it.

It was while in charge at Ayresome Park that he brought the likes of John Hickton, Hugh McIlmoyle, David Mills, Stuart Boam, Willie Maddren, Jim Platt, David Armstrong and, finally, Graeme Souness either to the club or through the ranks.

Stan was never quite able to take Middlesbrough up and he resigned early in 1973. It was left to Jack Charlton, using a nucleus of Anderson's players, to eventually take them to the promised land in the following season, winning the league by a massive 15 points.

But Stan was not finished with football by any means. A varied career followed with stints coaching in Greece, at Queen's Park Rangers and Bolton Wanderers as well as managing Doncaster Rovers and Bolton. On top of that he did scouting jobs for various clubs including Newcastle. Not bad for the boy who never thought about making a career out of football. That he did so is something that supporters on Wearside, Tyneside and Teesside should always be grateful.

Record

Sunderland	June 1949 (pro February 1951) – November 1963	
Football League	402 apps	31 gls
FA Cup	34 apps	4 gls
Football League Cup	11 apps	0 gls
Total	447 apps	35 gls

Newcastle	November 1963 – November 1965	
Football League	81 apps	13 gls
FA Cup	2 apps	1 gl
Football League Cup	1 app	0 gls
Total	84 apps	14 gls

CHAPTER 8

1960s Highs and Lows of Football

IF EVER there was a decade that illustrated the highs and lows of football, it was the 1960s. It began and ended with Newcastle on top but Sunderland had more than their fair share of supremacy in between.

United began the decade in the First Division while their neighbours wallowed in the Second. But the Magpies joined them at the end of the first season (1960-61), finishing 21st of 22 teams. Strangely, although Sunderland finished in a respectable sixth place in the Second Division, Newcastle comfortably scored more goals than them (86 compared to 75). The fact that the Geordies conceded 109 goals indicates where their weakness lay.

For the three seasons that they were in the Second Division together (1962-64), there is no doubt that Sunderland had the better of things. In six meetings between them, the Rokermen won two compared to Newcastle's one but, more importantly, the Red'n Whites finished higher in the league each time. Indeed, they were very unlucky not to gain promotion before they eventually did, finishing third in successive years (at a time when just the top two went up) before making it 'third time lucky' by finishing as runners-up to Leeds United in 1963-64.

Newcastle soon joined them, going one better by winning the Second Division title in the following season although they had four points less than Sunderland had the year before.

Once in the First Division both sides initially struggled. Indeed, Sunderland never finished above 15th place during a six year stay there. At least they had the satisfaction of completing the double over the Magpies in 1966-67 with 3-0 wins at both Roker and St James' Parks. That was the season that Newcastle avoided relegation by just one place (20th out of 22). But from that point onwards, the decade belonged to Newcastle as far as the North East was concerned.

During 1967-68 season they actually finished in the top half of the league in 10th place. This was enough to qualify them for Europe, the first North East team to do so. The rules of the Inter Cities Fairs Cup provided for "one city, one club". This meant that the likes of Everton, Tottenham Hotspur and Arsenal all missed out because their local rivals had already qualified and Newcastle scraped in via 'a back door entry'. Any jibes at such a qualification from Sunderland fans, however, were quickly quashed by Newcastle supporters who pointed out that the 'back door' had also been available for the Wearsiders.

If Newcastle had gained entry via the back door, they went out through the front by winning the tournament, 6-2 on aggregate, against Hungarians Ujpest Dozsa. Yet United still could not complete the double over Sunderland although the Magpies generally had the better of things, winning two and drawing four of their six meetings during the period 1967-70.

But as Newcastle slowly improved towards the end of the decade (10th, ninth and seventh positions saw them qualify for Europe in three successive seasons), Sunderland's fortunes slowly declined with 15th, 17th and 21st position finishes. The last one saw them relegated back to the Second Division to leave Tyneside clearly in the ascendancy as the clubs entered the 1970s. But that had been the situation at the start of the 1960s and who knew what the following decade had in store?

League Meetings (16)

At Newcastle:	Newcastle – won 4 drew 3 lost 1
At Sunderland:	Sunderland – won 4 drew 4 lost 0

Highest Goalscoring Ratios – Over 0.50
(minimum of 2 goals to qualify)

	Newcastle Player	Played	Scored	Ratio		Sunderland Player	Played	Scored	Ratio
1	A Tait	2	4	2.00	1	W Holden	2	3	1.50
2	H Bedford	1	2	2.00	2	C Suggett	4	5	1.25
3	P Beardsley	3	4	1.33	3	J Paterson	4	4	1.00
4	P Cannell	2	2	1.00	4	B Clough	3	3	1.00
	K Dyson	2	2	1.00	5	J G Coleman	2	2	1.00
	A Smailes	2	2	1.00		S Cummins	2	2	1.00
7	A Shepherd	10	8	0.80	7	H R Buckley	5	4	0.80
8	J Milburn	14	11	0.79	8	R McKay	4	3	0.75
9	H Gallacher	4	3	0.75	9	C Fleming	7	5	0.71
	L White	4	3	0.75	10	G Holley	22	15	0.68
11	G Robledo	7	5	0.71	11	R Hogg	6	4	0.67
12	V Keeble	7	4	0.57		K Phillips	6	4	0.67
					13	W Eden	3	2	0.67
						J O'Hare	3	2	0.67
					15	AS Brown	5	3	0.60
						A Hawes	5	3	0.60
					17	T Ford	7	4	0.57
					18	D Halliday	9	5	0.56

Football League
Division 2
Newcastle United 2 Sunderland 2 (HT: 1-0)
2nd December 1961
St James' Park
53,991

Newcastle: D Hollins, R Keith, A McMichael, B Wright, J McGrath, J Bell, G Hughes, I Allchurch, L White [**18**], J McGuigan [**67**], J Wilson
Sunderland: P Wakeham, C Irwin, L Ashurst, S Anderson, C Hurley, J McNab*, H Hooper, G Herd, B Clough [**66, 82**], A Fogarty, J Overfield
Referee: Vic James (York)

IT WAS an historic day when the arch-rivals met for the first time for nearly four years. This was the first league meeting between Tyne and Wear that had not taken place in the top league.

Newcastle were trying to adapt to life in the Second Division following their relegation the previous season and were a club in disarray with no fewer than eight players requesting transfers. New temporary manager Norman Smith had done his best to ease the tension at St James' and five of the players had subsequently withdrawn their requests (Hughes, Wright, Ferguson, Wilson and Stewart Mitchell).

The Board had, however, agreed to three requests (Scanlon, Harrower and Hodgson). United, with injury doubts regarding Hughes and Suddick and with Hale an absentee due to National Service duties, delayed their team selection. In the end, Hughes played but Suddick did not. John McGuigan had become a target of the boo-boys at Gallowgate and he came in for Hale with the Board appealing to the crowd to give him a fair crack of the whip.

In comparison, everything was going well in the Sunderland camp. With just one defeat in their last 11 league games, they were doing well in the league and their team virtually picked itself as they remained unchanged for their sixth successive game.

League Positions

		Pos	Pl	Pts		Pos	Pl	Pts
Before:	Sunderland	5th	19	22	Newcastle	11th	19	18
After:	Sunderland	5th	20	23	Newcastle	13th	20	19

Newcastle surprised the high-flying Wearsiders by taking the game to them straight from the kick-off and it was two of United's younger players who sparked off this impressive early showing – Jimmy Wilson and Sunderland-born Brian Wright. Sunderland soon recovered their composure and just as it seemed that they were going to get on top, Newcastle grabbed the opener after 18 minutes.

225

Wilson created it, taking a deft pass from McGuigan, feinting past Irwin and drawing Hurley and Anderson before slipping a pass inside to the unmarked Len White, ten yards out. He calmly scooped home a left foot shot beyond the outstretched arm of Wakeham.

Sunderland were shocked and were soon rocking as the exuberant Magpies tore at them. Peter Wakeham saved brilliantly from Jackie Bell, turning his shot over the bar, before Charlie Hurley somehow turned a point-blank Ivor Allchurch effort away for a corner. But they weathered the storm and by the time the interval arrived they were at least mounting as many attacks as Newcastle, much to the concern of the Geordies who had failed to turn their undoubted first half superiority into goals.

As the Newcastle fans feared, Sunderland were on top in the second half and it was soon United's turn to defend. The Rokermen brought Hooper into the game more and he proved himself a thorn in Newcastle's side. George Herd had a shot blocked, Dick Keith cleared off the line from Overfield, Alf McMichael did like-wise from Fogarty and then Keith, again, denied Anderson. When a Hooper goal-bound shot hit McGrath in the face it seemed as if Sunderland's luck was well and truly out. Until, that is, midway through the half when they eventually made a deserved break-through.

Fittingly, it was man-of-the-match Harry Hooper who set up the equaliser. With delightful ball control, he left McMichael near the half-way line, brushed past Bell and recovered from a weak McGrath sliding tackle before pulling a square pass across the face of the goal.

Hollins managed to get a touch but no more than that and there was Brian Clough to bundle the ball into the net from close in despite the challenge of Keith. The goal was the signal for hordes of Wearside youngsters to invade the pitch.

Newcastle retaliated virtually straight from the restart. Clough fouled White and McMichael took the kick, placing the ball to Allchurch. He astutely squared a pass to McGuigan who, unchallenged, was able to pick his spot from 20 yards out and slam the ball home. Even the Gallowgate barrackers cheered him and the Geordie youngsters showed that they could also stage a celebratory invasion.

Both sides went full out for the crucial, deciding goal with Sunderland having slightly the better of things. Harry Hooper was unlucky with a shot from 10 yards that deflected wide off Allchurch. But when Lady Luck did eventually show her favours, they were red and white.

With eight minutes to go, Allchurch was clearly brought down in full flight in a dribble through on the Sunderland goal but referee Vic James waved play on. The Wearsiders counter-attacked with devastating effectiveness.

Overfield played the ball to Hooper who chipped brilliantly over McMichael before nipping around him to pick it up again. His pass into the middle was perfection with Keith caught wrong-footed. The full back could not afford to touch the ball because it would have gone in so he had to let it go past and there was Clough again, on the spot at the far post, to score a simple goal. But that was the mark of an ace goalscorer – being at the right place at the right time.

The game could have gone either way in the last few minutes with Sunderland going closest to clinching the points. Hooper set off on an amazing 60 yard dribbling run three minutes from time but Dave Hollins saved the day for Newcastle, rushing out to force the winger to shoot wide. A goal would have been the icing on the cake for the Sunderland No 7 who enjoyed one of his best ever games in a red and white shirt despite being virtually starved of the ball in the first half. But, in truth, neither side deserved to lose a classic derby encounter.

The press and supporters were virtually unanimous in the view that this was one of the best local derby games seen for a long time. As one reporter said, "This was the best that three bob could buy"; except, of course, he got in for nothing!

Both sides could validly claim they deserved to win but a draw was a fair result. It confirmed the more methodical Sunderland as genuine promotion contenders while giving injury hit Newcastle a timely boost. They slipped to 13th position but their supporters were keen to point out that they were still only six points from the second promotion place.

Sunderland, however, were just two from that elusive spot, filled at that moment by Leyton Orient. The problem was that, even at this stage in the season, there seemed to be just one promotion place to go for. Liverpool were already six points clear at the top and, in those days of two points for a win, that was quite a lead.

Football League
Division 2
Sunderland 3 Newcastle United 0 (HT: 1-0)
21st April 1962
Roker Park
57,666

Sunderland: J Montgomery, C Irwin, L Ashurst, S Anderson, C Hurley, J McNab*, H Hooper, G Herd [**19, 82**], B Clough, W McPheat [**76**], J Overfield
Newcastle: D Hollins, R Keith, A McMichael, B Wright, W Thompson, G Dalton, W Day, J Kerray*, B Thomas, I Allchurch, J Fell
Referee: Arthur Luty (Leeds)

SUNDERLAND WERE genuine promotion contenders. Liverpool, well clear at the top of the league, were virtually uncatchable but the Rokermen were just three points behind second placed Leyton Orient and one behind Scunthorpe United with a game in hand over both. They also had an advantage over

Newcastle in that they went into this game fresh. It was played on Easter Saturday and they had enjoyed a day off on Good Friday, unlike United who had played (and defeated) Derby County.

The Wearsiders made two changes from the side that had won away to Luton Town a week earlier, Stan Anderson returning from international duty to replace Martin Harvey and Charlie Hurley, now fit, taking over from Dickie Rooks.

Newcastle also made two changes, veteran Alf McMichael replacing 18-year-old Colin Clish and Ivor Allchurch coming in for Ken Hale who had picked up a calf injury against Derby. Rain started to pour down two hours before the kick-off and never let up. It was obvious that the pitch was going to cut up and that the game would be as much a test of courage and stamina than skill.

League Positions		Pos	Pl	Pts		Pos	Pl	Pts
Before:	Sunderland	4th	38	46	Newcastle	11th	39	37
After:	Sunderland	3rd	39	48	Newcastle	11th	40	37

Despite the water-logged pitch, Sunderland looked a different class to Newcastle and dominated play. Only Welshmen Ivor Allchurch and Dave Hollins saved the Magpies from humiliation. United tried hard enough but determination and fighting ability were never going to be enough against an obviously superior Sunderland side. Yet the Magpies did reasonably well in the opening quarter of an hour. It was during that time that Jimmy Fell wasted two glorious chances created by Allchurch's long passes. Billy Day caught the eye with the odd solo run but Thomas was completely subdued by the imperious Charlie Hurley. Nevertheless passions were high and after unsavoury clashes between McNab and Kerray (both booked) and McPheat and Wright, referee Arthur Luty called both captains together to tell them to control their players.

The opening goal after 19 minutes was controversial. Brian Clough played a long through-pass to George Herd who hesitated, expecting an offside flag. But when it didn't come, he went on to slip the ball past Hollins as the Newcastle defence looked at the referee in disbelief. They claimed that Herd had been three or four yards offside. That may have been a bit of an exaggeration but the goal certainly looked doubtful.

Nevertheless, it counted and Newcastle's heads dropped from that point. Sunderland dominated both in attack and in defence and only the heroics of Hollins, who pulled off save after save, kept them in the game. But even he had to give way to Allchurch as the man-of-the-match for Newcastle. He was magnificent, performing wonders with skill and power. But none of his team-mates could take advantage of his work and the Rokermen continued to control the game.

By half-time the pitch was a quagmire but this made little difference to Hurley who mastered the conditions and never gave an inch in the middle of the home defence. Willie McPheat was always willing to drop back and help when the need arose and Jimmy McNab was tenacious in midfield. The pacey George Herd and Harry Hooper linked well with the grafting Brian Clough up front to cause plenty of problems for the Tyneside rearguard although the visiting defenders usually held their own.

Allchurch continued to try and perform miracles for United and was denied only by two tremendous saves by young Jim Montgomery who was already making a name for himself as a 'keeper of exceptional ability. At the other end Dave Hollins bravely kept out Anderson and Clough as United fought to stay in the game.

Any hopes that they had of a fightback died when Sunderland scored a second goal after 76 minutes. Once again, there was a touch of controversy about it. Allchurch was clearly pushed in the back as Sunderland won possession but the offence went unpunished by the referee. Instead it was Sunderland who punished Newcastle. Hooper brilliantly controlled an astute Stan Anderson chipped pass at speed before cutting inside to unleash a shot that beat Hollins but stuck in the mud on the goal line. It was left to Willie McPheat to race in and help it over the line. The record books show that Willie was the scorer but Harry deserved the most credit.

Newcastle tried to hit back and Jimmy Fell hit the Sunderland bar to remind the Rokermen that the game was not quite all over.

But a third Sunderland goal showed that it was and there was no controversy about this one. It was a superb strike by George Herd eight minutes from time. He fastened on to a ball from Jack Overfield and made ground before rocketing in a shot from the angle of the penalty area that beat Hollins all ends up.

It could easily have been worse for Newcastle a couple of minutes later when a spectacular headed clearance off the line by Alf McMichael kept out a thunderous shot from McPheat. There was no doubt at the final whistle who were the North East's top dogs – Sunderland.

Although the Rokermen were worthy winners, both sides deserved credit for serving up an entertaining game in such appalling conditions. In many ways the game was a classic and showed that no-one gave up the battle in a Tyne-Wear derby.

Victory elevated Sunderland to third and raised promotion hopes. They were now just two points behind Orient and one point ahead of Scunthorpe. With three games to go, Sunderland had a game in hand over the O's but the London club had a better goal average. Nevertheless hopes were high. The Rokerites gave it their best shot with a comfortable double over Rotherham in their next two games. But a 1-1 draw away to Swansea Town in their last game meant that they finished one point behind Orient in third place. Sunderland were not to know it at the time, but a two goal victory over the Swans would have edged them above Orient on goal average.

Newcastle were to end the season in mid-table as one of no fewer than eight teams on 39 points. United, by virtue of a superior goal average were to finish highest of the eight. Both sides looked forward to renewing their rivalry next season.

Football League
Division 1
Newcastle United 1 Sunderland 1 (HT: 1-1)
13th October 1962
St James' Park
62,262

Newcastle: D Hollins, R Keith, C Clish, B Wright, W Thompson, J Iley, D Hilley, A Suddick, B Thomas, J Kerray[**42**], J Fell
Sunderland: J Montgomery, C Nelson, L Ashurst, S Anderson, R Rooks, J McNab, J Davison, G Herd, B Clough [**30**], A Fogarty, G Mulhall
Referee: Harry Webb (Leeds)

WITH BOTH sides doing well in the league, huge crowds converged on St James' and the gates were locked with well over 10,000 outside clamouring to get in. Some estimates put the figure as high as 20,000! Fans clambered up trees overlooking the Popular Side and perched on rooftops of the houses in Leazes Terrace. Many broke into a new ten-storey office block behind the Gallowgate End and climbed on to the girders and scaffolding surrounding it. A squad of police took half-an-hour to clear them away.

On the field there was some doubt about team selections. Newcastle had hoped to sign a new left back, David Holt of Hearts, in time for the game but the Edinburgh club refused to sell. Instead, manager Joe Harvey brought in the Ns' (Junior team's) FA Youth Cup winning skipper Colin Clish, a former Roker supporter. United also included Sunderland-born Brian Wright as Alf McMichael and Duncan Neale were dropped. Jim Iley and Dave Hilley were doubtful for the game but responded to treatment and both turned out.

Sunderland were not so lucky with Charlie Hurley. He had sustained knee and ankle injuries in the Rokermen's previous game, a home win against Derby County. But despite intensive treatment he failed a fitness test and Dickie Rooks turned out in their one team change.

League Positions		Pos	Pl	Pts		Pos	Pl	Pts
Before:	Sunderland	4th	12	16	Newcastle	8th	13	15
After:	Sunderland	3rd	13	17	Newcastle	7th	14	16

The massive crowd was entertained by a tense, sporting and enjoyable derby game – one of the best ever between these old rivals. Sunderland seemed as if they did not have a single weakness in their side although Newcastle battled all of the way and displayed no mean football skills themselves. In fact United forced six corners to Sunderland's three but the visitors looked more composed. Jim Iley was Newcastle's star man although Jim Montgomery and Len Ashurst were every bit as good – if not better.

Alan Suddick also impressed with patches of sheer brilliance while George Mulhall shone on the Wearsiders' left wing. Stan Anderson and Jimmy McNab also caught the eye for the red and whites and both centre halves, Bill Thompson and Dickie Rooks, were resolute and steady throughout. Only a brilliant save by Montgomery when he turned a Barrie Thomas shot for a corner in the 25th minute kept Newcastle out. Dave Hilley then had a diving header cleared off the line from the resultant corner.

But it was Sunderland who grabbed the lead after half-an-hour although it was poor defending by Newcastle that gave the goal away. George Herd beat Iley to the ball and pushed a pass up to Jimmy Davison. He raced past Clish to the bye-line before sending over a low cross into the middle. Hollins failed to intercept it and Brian Clough was on hand to side-foot a simple goal from just two yards out.

Newcastle kept battling away and gained their reward three minutes before the break although there was an element of luck about the goal. Alan Suddick worked his way down the right before playing a diagonal pass forward to Jimmy Kerray who tried a shot at goal from ten yards. It looked as if the ball was going to go straight at Montgomery but it gained a slight deflection off Anderson to leave the 'keeper helpless and end up in the opposite corner.

Sunderland continued to play the more constructive football but, conversely, Newcastle carved out more chances. One was particularly unfortunate when a Thomas rocket seemed as if it was going in until it hit Rooks on the goal line. But the game hinged on a controversial incident eight minutes from time when Dave Hilley went down under challenge from McNab well inside the Sunderland penalty area. Newcastle appealed vociferously for a spot kick and even McNab stopped, half expecting the whistle, before carrying on.

At least one Sunderland director felt that it was a penalty but it would have been a travesty if his team had got nothing from this magnificent advertisement for Second Division football. A draw was probably a fair result but if either team deserved to win, it was Sunderland.

Both sides went up one place in the league as a result of the draw. Sunderland were now only a point behind second placed Bury although league leaders Huddersfield Town, having won at home to Chelsea, were now three points ahead of the Wearsiders. Like last season, hopes were high on Wearside of a promotion campaign. Sustaining consistency was to be the problem.

Perhaps expectations were not quite so high on Tyneside but Newcastle were just a point behind their neighbours (although they had played a game more) and there was still a long way to go.

Football League
Division 2
Sunderland 0 Newcastle United 0 (HT: 0-0)
2nd March 1963
Roker Park
62,420

Sunderland: J Montgomery, C Nelson, L Ashurst, S Anderson, C Hurley, J McNab, G Herd, A Fogarty, D Sharkey, J Crossan, G Mulhall
Newcastle: D Hollins, R Keith, C Clish, D Neale, W Thompson, J Iley, D Hilley, R McGarry, B Thomas, J Kerray, A Suddick
Referee: Kevin Howley (Middlesbrough)

ONCE AGAIN, Sunderland were challenging for promotion when they met their rivals. They were in second place but five points adrift of leaders Chelsea. However the Rokermen were ahead of Bury only on goal average with Plymouth Argyle a further two points behind. Many regarded this derby clash as a make or break encounter. A win would give Sunderland's promotion prospects a healthy boost while a defeat would be a major setback. On the other hand, a win for Newcastle would see them force themselves into the promotion race.

However, the game was in doubt due to the severe winter that had been totally disrupting football fixtures since before Christmas. Newcastle had not even played their Third Round FA Cup tie and that had been originally scheduled for early January. In fact, United had played only one game since the turn of the year. Sunderland themselves had managed just one league game in that time although three cup matches had ensured that there was a sharpness to their general fitness.

The referee passed the pitch fit at 10.30am and, despite the severe frost, queues began to form outside Roker Park well before noon for a 3.00pm kick-off. By the time the game began, well over 60,000 were inside the ground, giving Roker Park its first crowd over that level since Newcastle had played there in 1954. Sunderland had left braziers burning on the frozen pitch to try and thaw it out. It worked – at least on the pitch surface. Beneath the top layer, the ice held firm, particularly on the Clock Stand side of the ground where the bright sunshine that heralded a thaw did not reach.

League Positions		Pos	Pl	Pts		Pos	Pl	Pts
Before:	Sunderland	2nd	26	32	Newcastle	7th	25	28
After:	Sunderland	2nd	27	33	Newcastle	7th	26	29

Joe Harvey took his team to Roker intent on defence, playing Thompson as a third back between Keith and Clish in a 3-4-3 formation. Sunderland were clearly the better team. They had talent and confidence built on the foundations of a fine half-back line where Stan Anderson and Charlie Hurley were the stars. Yet Newcastle went desperately close in the opening seconds. Jimmy McNab slipped and Dave Hilley managed to get in a shot that deflected off Hurley and clipped the top of the crossbar before going behind.

Other than that, Newcastle had few chances. The home full backs were rarely troubled and the game consisted mainly of the Sunderland forwards playing stylish, entertaining but mostly abortive football as they tried to breach the Tyneside defence. Time and again the Rokermen worked their way into the Newcastle penalty area with apparent ease only to get bogged down in United's packed defence. Newcastle's heroes in a rearguard action were Jim Iley, Dave Hollins and Bill Thompson. A special word must be said about Jim who, as one reporter said, did everything but take the gate money! Even Sunderland reporters admitted that he was the man-of-the-match, just ahead of Wearside's Johnnie Crossan. Despite Sunderland's dominance, few shots got through to Hollins and those that did, he dealt with more than capably. The turning point of the game came in the 39th minute when Iley conceded a penalty. Up stepped Stan Anderson to take it but Hollins saved magnificently and it was still all square at the interval.

The second half was similar to the first – Sunderland attacking, Newcastle defending and doing it very effectively. It says much for Anderson's resilience and determination that he was not disheartened by his failure from the penalty spot. He proceeded to play a fine game. Sunderland should have been awarded a second penalty eight minutes into the second half when Iley bundled Mulhall off the ball well inside the box. But referee Kevin Howley awarded an indirect free kick that came to nought.

Newcastle's attempts at goal were few and far between: a strong drive by Jimmy Kerray that Jim Montgomery plucked down from just under the bar and an awkward centre that was turned for a corner. The crunch moment of the second half came 16 minutes from time when Hollins' cat-like reflexes again rescued Newcastle. A header by George Herd looked like a certain goal until the United 'keeper somehow dived low to palm the ball off the line. The Sunderland winger had to hold his head in disbelief that the ball had not gone in. But Hollins had already shown that he was in top form by keeping out a snap header by Jimmy Crossan and a Nick Sharkey shot near the foot of a post. The Rokermen realised that this was not going to be their day when Herd rushed in to meet a McNab centre and hit the ball first time but saw his effort strike Ambrose Fogarty and spin behind.

The Sunderland pundits reckoned that this was the most one-sided match seen at Roker Park this season. There was no doubt which set of players were happiest with the result as the Magpies trooped off at the final whistle with grins all over their faces. They had gone to Wearside looking for a point and had succeeded.

After dominating the game so much, Sunderland had to regard this as a point lost. Yet they had improved their standing in the league if not their position. Both Chelsea and Bury (first and third in the league respectively) had lost at home so Sunderland were now just four points behind the Pensioners with Bury and Plymouth Argyle a point behind. Hopes were high on Wearside that this could be promotion year despite the disappointing result against Newcastle.

With a valuable away point gained, Newcastle were mounting a promotion challenge themselves. They were certainly in contention, four points behind the Wearsiders with a game in hand. But their challenge never really materialised. They were to climb as high as fourth but then fade to seventh, five points from a promotion spot.

Sunderland were to suffer the ultimate heartbreak, finishing in third place just behind Chelsea on goal average with champions Stoke City one point ahead. One more point for the Red'n Whites would have done it and if they had turned their superiority into goals in either of the Tyne-Wear derbies this season, they could have been back in the First Division.

Football League
Division 2
Sunderland 2 Newcastle United 1 (HT: 1-1)
9th October 1963
Roker Park
56,903

Sunderland: J Montgomery, C Irwin, L Ashurst [43], M Harvey, C Hurley, J McNab, B Usher, G Herd [81], D Sharkey, J Crossan, G Mulhall
Newcastle: D Hollins, R Keith, G Dalton, A Burton, J McGrath, J Iley, A Suddick, D Hilley, B Thomas, R McGarry, C Taylor [14]
Referee: A Holland (Hailifax)

ALTHOUGH IT was still fairly early in the season, Sunderland were second just two points adrift of leaders Swindon Town and one ahead of both Leeds United (who had a game in hand) and Preston North End. The Wearsiders, who had lost only two of their opening 12 league fixtures, fielded the side that had won so dramatically away to Norwich City the previous Saturday. This meant that Stan Anderson was left out, thus missing his first Tyne – Wear derby since establishing himself in Sunderland's first team in 1953. Manager Allan Brown felt that he could not drop the impressive Martin Harvey who had been doing so well in Stan's normal right half position. No-one knew it but Anderson had played his last game for Sunderland and would soon be joining their arch-rivals.

Newcastle were also doing reasonably well considering they had been affected by injuries. Bill Thompson had hardly played so far and was already ruled out for this match. Then his deputy, Bob Moncur, sprained an ankle on the eve of the game and was eliminated as well. This meant that right back John McGrath had to switch to Moncur's position and Dick Keith, who had requested a transfer, was drafted in as his replacement.

League Positions

		Pos	Pl	Pts		Pos	Pl	Pts
Before:	Sunderland	2nd	12	17	Newcastle	8th	12	13
After:	Sunderland	2nd	13	19	Newcastle	8th	13	13

The game was played at a tremendous pace with plenty of exciting incidents to entertain and enthral the large crowd. The Sunderland men were confident of success but United seemed determined to run them off their feet with their pace and exuberance. They soon shocked the Wearside supporters by taking the lead after 14 minutes.

Jim Iley and Dave Hilley combined in a build-up which ended with Alan Suddick managing to send over a cross. The ball glanced off Charlie Hurley's head wide of Jim Montgomery to where Colin Taylor was waiting to crash a shot into the empty net.

Both goalkeepers saw plenty of action with Dave Hollins turning a terrific angled shot by Jimmy Crossan over the bar before saving a crisp low effort from George Mulhall and then hurling himself along the goal line to turn a Jimmy McNab rocket around a post. At the other end Montgomery flicked another Taylor effort over the bar before saving at the foot of a post from Burton. If anything, Newcastle had the upper hand for the first 35 minutes

But the home trio of Len Ashurst, Martin Harvey and Hurley were magnificent and eventually established control. Hurley sustained a bad cut above his right eye in a clash with Barrie Thomas five minutes before the interval.

The Sunderland captain was led off with blood streaming down his face to have three stitches put in the wound. However it was soon after this that Sunderland equalised.

This was Len Ashurst's 200th league appearance for Sunderland and he celebrated in the best way possible – with a spectacular goal against the old enemy. Suddick conceded a free kick 25 yards out from the Newcastle goal. United's defenders lined up expecting a pass but Len decided to have a pot at goal himself and slammed a shot through a gap in the defence straight into the net. It was only the second goal of his career.

The Sunderland supporters were delighted to see Hurley lead his men out for the second half despite his eye injury. More important, he led by example and turned in a man-of-the-match performance. Newcastle had been a little unfortunate to be pegged back just before the interval after their first half endeavours but it was a different story in the second half when the Rokermen took control of the game. It was one way traffic almost throughout. Only heroics by John McGrath and Jim Iley kept them at bay. The longer that the game went on, the more it became apparent that Newcastle were happy to settle for a draw and they very nearly got it despite all of the Sunderland pressure. But United paid the consequence nine minutes from time when George Mulhall sent a cross/pass through a gap in the packed Tyneside defence and George Herd ran on to send a shot well wide of Hollins and into the net.

There was no way back now for Newcastle and Sunderland nearly made it 3-1 when Nick Sharkey met a Harvey cross and beat Hollins with a header that struck the foot of a post and bounced clear. But a third goal would have flattered Sunderland who emerged worthy, if close, winners of an enthralling encounter.

This was almost a unique game – a Sunderland/Newcastle encounter where the result became almost of secondary importance to the skills, pace and entertainment put on by the players. It was justly referred to as a 'classic' and it was only after it was all over that many supporters realised how critical the result was to both teams. This was especially so for Sunderland as only goal average seperated them from league leaders Swindon Town (although the Wearsiders had played a game more). Leeds United were hot on their heels, a point behind and also with a game in hand.

Charlie Hurley's eye injury was causing concern but he was not to miss any league games because of it.

Barrie Thomas was not so fortunate for Newcastle. He had sustained a groin injury during the game and was to miss United's next four games – all of which they were to lose to plunge the Magpies into the lower reaches of the league and rule out any idea of them mounting a serious promotion challenge this season.

Football League
Division 2
Newcastle United 1 Sunderland 0 (HT: 1-0)
14th March 1964
St James' Park
27,341

Newcastle: G Marshall, D Craig, G Dalton, S Anderson, J McGrath, J Iley*, D Hilley, R McGarry [**34** pen], R Cummings, W Penman, A Suddick
Sunderland: J Montgomery, C Nelson, L Ashurst*, M Harvey, C Hurley, D Elliott, B Usher, G Herd, D Sharkey, J Crossan, G Mulhall
Referee: A Jobling (Morecambe)

BY THIS stage of the season an intriguing situation had arisen at the top of the league with three teams breaking clear. Sunderland led Leeds United by one point with Preston North End a further two points behind. With just two teams to be promoted, one of this unlucky trio would miss out. Sunderland, unbeaten in the league since Christmas (a run of nine games), were determined that it would not be them.

Although Newcastle were in a fairly healthy position in the league, they were not really promotion contenders, a spate of mid-season injuries had ruled out that possibility.

A great deal of controversy surrounded this game with Newcastle the unfortunate victims of an expensive hoax. Torrential rain swept the North East and many supporters set off to go to the match but returned home without even going to the ground. A notice was put up at the Central Station stating that the game was off and coach companies were also informed. This cost Newcastle (and their players) a small fortune.

They expected a gate in excess of 50,000 – instead just over 27,000 turned up. This meant a reduction in gate receipts of about £5,000, of which 80% would have gone to Newcastle. The players' contracts also included a match day bonus based on the crowd. Each player would receive £1 for every 1,000 above a base level of 30,000. So, if the size of the crowd had been 50,000, each player would get £20 bonus – quite a useful sum at the time. They all lost that. It was a cruel hoax.

League Positions

		Pos	Pl	Pts		Pos	Pl	Pts
Before:	Sunderland	1st	33	48	Newcastle	6th	32	36
After:	Sunderland	2nd	34	48	Newcastle	5th	33	38

The weather for this game gave credence to the rumours that the match was off – rain, wind and lashing sleet. It was also bitterly cold. Newcastle, with the elements in their favour in the first half, played long ball tactics and adapted better to the conditions. To say that the pitch was heavy was an understatement. It was a quagmire – certainly not suitable for a rather lightweight Sunderland side (who played in an all-white strip). There were plenty of thrills in the first half, nearly all of them around the visitors' penalty area. Jim Montgomery enhanced his reputation with an imperious performance in goal. He made a spectacular diving save from Willie Penman and then touched a tricky ball by Jim Iley just over the top. In between, Len Ashurst breasted a Bobby Cummings effort off the line. The surprising thing was that it took United so long to open the scoring. Even then it took a penalty to break down Sunderland's resistance 11 minutes from half-time.

Dave Hilley accelerated quickly past three defenders before neatly chipping the ball over Montgomery towards the gaping goal. It was almost over the line, head high, when Charlie Hurley raced across and dived full length to turn it away with his hand. He tried to argue that he had headed the ball away but referee Jobling adamantly pointed to the spot. Up stepped Ron "Cassius" McGarry to take the kick. Monty dived the right way but was beaten by the pace and accuracy of the shot.

No-one could deny that Newcastle were worth their half-time lead.

Sunderland had the elements in their favour in the second half but Newcastle had no intention of loosening their grip. The visitors did manage to mount a couple of dangerous attacks with a shot by Sharkey flooring George Dalton and Marshall having to be alert to catch a Hurley header. But that was about all. Young David Craig totally subdued George Mulhall and Dalton similarly gave Brian Usher little leeway.

Generally Gordon Marshall was shivering with inactivity with the action mainly at the other end. Hurley tired as the game went on and began to struggle against the non-stop graft of Bobby Cummings who often had the beating of the darling of Wearside in the air. Len Ashurst again cleared off the line and there was panic in the visitors' defence when Cummings twice went close with back-headers following Iley throw-ins. When a Hilley centre went cleanly across the front of the Sunderland posts untouched it seemed as if the Wearside goal bore a charmed life. But somehow Newcastle just could not score a second goal and there was just one goal in it at the final whistle.

Perhaps it was promotion jitters, but Sunderland had been comprehensively outplayed by Newcastle. United clearly played above themselves and the final scoreline flattered the visitors with the defeat knocking them off the top of the table. Leeds United, winners away to Middlesbrough, took over the leadership. Preston North End were still three points behind in third place but they now had a game in hand.

But Sunderland learned their lesson and never again allowed another team take the initiative from them this season. They were to remain undefeated in their last eight games to clinch promotion in style, admittedly finishing a couple of points behind Leeds, but leaving Preston in their wake five points adrift.

The win over Sunderland was, more or less, to be the peak of Newcastle's season. They were to lose five of their last nine games and finish in a respectable eighth place but nowhere near promotion. That was to come next year.

Most Substitute Appearances

Newcastle	Sunderland
Shola Ameobi – 4	Julio Arca – 3
Lee Clark – 3	Alex Rae – 2
Liam O'Brien – 2	George Kinnell – 2
Alan Shearer – 2	Niall Quinn – 2
Peter Cartwright – 2	
Michael Chopra – 2	

Football League
Division 1
Sunderland 2 Newcastle United 0 (HT: 0-0)
3rd January 1966
Roker Park
54,668

Sunderland: J Montgomery, J Parke, L Ashurst*, M Harvey, C Hurley (M Hellawell 39), J Baxter, G Herd [49], D Elliott, J O'Hare [66], G Moore, G Mulhall
Newcastle: G Marshall, D Craig, A Burton, R Moncur, J McGrath, J Iley, C Napier, A Bennett, W Thompson, D Hilley*, T Robson. Sub: W Penman (unused)
Referee: J E Carr (Sheffield)

THIS GAME had been scheduled originally for 27th December but Sunderland had left the Roker Park pitch unprotected despite forecasts of a heavy frost. Consequently there was a postponement, causing the club much criticism especially from their own supporters.

Both clubs had incurred heavy defeats on New Year's Day, Sunderland 5-1 at home to West Bromwich Albion and Newcastle 4-2 at Aston Villa. Sunderland had suffered an injury crisis recently with a number of players absent. But it was now easing with Jim Montgomery (out since mid-October with a broken ankle) and George Mulhall returning for this game and Cec Irwin and Jimmy McNab almost fit again.

There was a brief panic on Wearside when some (presumably Newcastle) supporters broke into Roker Park on the eve of the match and painted the goalposts black and white. Sunderland had to paint them white again on the morning of the match. This was probably the most notable thing that the Black and Whites did on the day!

League Positions

		Pos	Pl	Pts		Pos	Pl	Pts
Before:	Sunderland	16th	21	18	Newcastle	19th	22	15
After:	Sunderland	16th	22	20	Newcastle	19th	23	15

Neither club was doing well in the league but, on this performance, Newcastle looked like relegation fodder. Sunderland were on the attack from the start and forced United to defend in depth, often with eight, nine or ten men back. It was not pretty to watch but no-one could deny that it was fairly effective. They had Gordon Marshall to thank for some fine saves in the opening session, foiling John O'Hare and Mulhall as wave after wave of Wearside attacks were launched at his goal. He was beaten after 24 minutes when Gary Moore's header caught him out of position but luck was on Newcastle's side as the ball hit the bar before being scrambled clear. Sunderland totally dominated the opening half despite the fact that schemer in chief Jim Baxter was out of touch. They were

239

handicapped when captain Charlie Hurley had to be helped off with a damaged ankle after half-an-hour's play. Despite treatment, he was unable to resume and was eventually replaced by Mike Hellawell, the first substitute to be used in a Tyne-Wear (or Wear-Tyne in this case) derby. He took up his usual right wing position with Martin Harvey moving to centre half.

The Roker Park pitch had been covered with straw before the game to protect it from the frost. It had been quite playable in the first half but ice began to form after the break as temperatures tumbled and the playing surface quickly became treacherous.

Four minutes after half-time, Baxter eventually came good, creating the opening goal with a defence-splitting pass. Moore deserved credit for a clever feint that took Jim Iley out of the game, and allowed the ball to run to man-of-the-match George Herd. He took it forward before beating the advancing Marshall with a fine shot.

Sunderland continued to dominate. Newcastle threatened just once in the entire game. It was on the hour mark when a close range header by Dave Hilley struck Montgomery and rolled loose but Herd hooked clear.

The Magpies could have been awarded a penalty after 66 minutes when an effort from Bill Thompson was turned aside by Martin Harvey's shoulder. As the visitors appealed, Sunderland broke away to launch a quick counter attack. It ended with O'Hare blasting in a terrific shot from fully 30 yards that flicked off McGrath's shoulder to deflect well wide of Marshall into the net.

Newcastle now looked a well-beaten side and could easily have conceded a penalty four minutes from time when Moore beat McGrath but was clearly pulled back by the Newcastle man. It looked a definite spot kick but referee Carr seemed determined not to award one and waved play on. So Sunderland had to make do with just a two goal victory. It could, and perhaps should, have been more.

The final 2-0 scoreline flattered the Geordies, a point emphasised by the 5-1 corner count in Sunderland's favour. The result meant no change in their league positions but it set alarm bells ringing on Tyneside. Admittedly it was just halfway through the season but Newcastle had picked up just one point from their last 14. But they were to claw themselves away from the relegation zone with a string of quite good results, losing only one of the six league games before meeting Sunderland again in the return fixture at St James'.

The Rokermen were to do exactly the opposite, winning just one of their eight league games in the interim as well as losing an FA Cup tie. Indeed, by the return fixture, Newcastle had edged above Sunderland in the league. It was becoming an intriguing, although none too successful, season for the North East rivals.

Football League
Division 1
Newcastle United 2 Sunderland 0 (HT: 1-0)
5th March 1966
St James' Park
52,051

Newcastle: G Marshall, D Craig, F Clark, W Thompson, J McGrath, J Iley, A Bennett, D Hilley, A Burton (P Noble 22), K Kettleborough, A Suddick **[33, 83]**
Sunderland: J Montgomery, J Parke*, L Ashurst, M Harvey, C Hurley, D Elliott, A Gauden, N Martin, D Sharkey, J Baxter*, G Mulhall. Sub: G Moore (unused)
Referee: E Crawford (Doncaster)

BOTH SIDES were struggling in the league and with injuries. Newcastle's main problem lay with their attack. Ron McGarry was ruled out with a back injury and Pop Robson had strained a stomach muscle in a practice match. Manager Joe Harvey took a gamble by playing Ollie Burton at centre forward. He had turned out in that position in his Norwich days but it was still a risk in playing him there. Albert Bennett was also drafted into the team.

The situation at Sunderland was much worse. They had suffered four defeats in a row coming into this game and, tactically, had intended to rely heavily on George Herd who had missed the last three games due to a knee ligament injury. He underwent two fitness tests on the day before the game but was eventually ruled out.

The Wearsiders made six team changes from their last game although four of them were positional. Cec Irwin and Mike Hellawell were dropped with the former verbally requesting a transfer as a consequence. Into the side came Martin Harvey and Alan Gauden but the main tactical change was the pushing of Jim Baxter forward from wing half into an inside forward position.

Both sides were six points above a relegation position so a win would ease matters considerably for one team as the run in to the end of the season began.

League Positions

		Pos	Pl	Pts		Pos	Pl	Pts
Before:	Newcastle	16th	29	24	Sunderland	17th	30	24
After:	Newcastle	15th	30	26	Sunderland	17th	31	24

Newcastle looked clearly the better team in the early stages but they lacked sparkle. It was a dull game that exploded into life midway through the first half but for the wrong reason. A below form Hurley clattered Burton with a crunching tackle that left the Welshman writhing in agony clutching his knee. It was quickly realised that his injury was potentially serious and he was stretchered off after 22 minutes, substitute Peter Noble coming on to play on the right wing with Albert Bennett moving inside to lead the attack. This unsettled United but did not stop them from taking the lead 11 minutes after Ollie's withdrawal.

Dave Hilley began the move deep inside his own half, hitting a through-pass for Alan Suddick to follow in the inside left position. He moved forward before letting fly with a shot that flew across Jim Montgomery high into the net. It was a breathtaking goal that enlightened the tedium of the game.

Sunderland struggled to hold a Newcastle attack that often just consisted of two strikers. If Suddick and Hilley had been given some support up front, it could have been a rout. Albert Bennett looked quite good when he switched into the middle but the home defenders had very little to do with the Sunderland attack almost non-existent.

Newcastle remained well on top but led only by their single goal for most of the match. Frustration showed in Sunderland's play as they struggled to get into the game. Suddick was in a class of his own and it was his brilliance that eventually killed off any hopes that the Wearsiders had of getting anything out of the game.

With seven minutes to go there was a touch of mischief about the way Suddick back-heeled the ball to Dave Hilley out on the left wing to start off a bout of interpassing between the two men that bemused Parke and Harvey and left Suddick with the chance to place a low cross-shot from 12 yards that ended with the ball nestling in the net inside the far post.

So the final scoreline was 2-0 but it flattered Sunderland.

Victory was sweet revenge for Newcastle following their two goal defeat at Roker a couple of months earlier. But the atmosphere in the Newcastle dressing room was muted when the seriousness of Burton's injury was realised. He would be out for the rest of the season.

As expected, victory eased Newcastle's relegation worries but left Sunderland still hovering above the strugglers at the foot of the league. Eventually both of the North East rivals were to survive although there was just one point between them at the end of the campaign. Sunderland were to finish 19th (fourth bottom), three points above relegated Northampton Town.

Newcastle were to end up in a rather elevated (and flattering) 15th place with just one point separating seven clubs in the lower reaches of the league.

Football League
Division 1
Newcastle United 0 Sunderland 3 (HT: 0-2)
29th October 1966
St James' Park
57,643

Newcastle: D Hollins, J Craggs, F Clark, R Moncur, W Thompson, J Iley, B Robson, R McGarry, RW Davies, D Hilley, A Suddick. Sub (unused) K Kettleborough
Sunderland: J Montgomery, C Irwin, L Ashurst, C Todd, G Kinnell, M Harvey, G Herd, J O'Hare [80], N Martin [41], J Baxter, G Mulhall [7]. Sub (unused) D Elliott
Referee: Ken Stokes (Newark)

NEWCASTLE HAD been thrashed 6-0 away by bottom placed Blackpool a week earlier and manager Joe Harvey rung the changes for the derby match. He had just made a crucial breakthrough in the transfer market, signing Wyn Davies from Bolton Wanderers for £80,000. Albert Bennett was the player to make way and he immediately slapped in a transfer request.

Sunderland were below United in the league but were buoyant following a 2-1 midweek win over league leaders Stoke City. Manager Ian McColl naturally fielded an unchanged side although he also had unsettled players at the club. Martin Harvey wanted to get away and John Parke was threatening to quit the game if Sunderland did not make him available for transfer.

Even at this comparatively early stage of the season, the game was regarded as a struggle for survival by the North East's 'big two'.

League Positions

		Pos	Pl	Pts		Pos	Pl	Pts
Before:	Newcastle	17th	13	10	Sunderland	21st	13	9
After:	Sunderland	17th	14	11	Newcastle	20th	14	10

United's new centre forward raised high expectations among the Newcastle fans, evidenced by the excellent attendance. But it was Sunderland who shocked the Tyneside masses with a goal after seven minutes although there was a touch of luck about it.

George Mulhall roamed from one wing to the other. He popped up on the right and beat Frank Clark's challenge before crossing hard and low into the middle. It seemed to be no more than a centre but the ball beat Bill Thompson's outstretched foot and curled in past Hollins who was caught standing flat-footed.

Newcastle almost relied entirely on the aerial ability of their new signing who was well named 'Wyn the Leap'. He had the crowd gasping with amazement with his ability to climb high and seemingly hang in mid-air. But apart from Davies (and possibly Alan Suddick who at least showed some ball skills

243

for the opening hour), Newcastle were totally outclassed. Tactically they were a shambles with Moncur's enthusiasm getting the better of him. He pushed forward and left gaping holes at the back that Cec Irwin was quick to spot. United had no authority in midfield where Jim Baxter and George Herd were able to stroll around unchallenged, setting up chances for Neil Martin, Mulhall and John O'Hare.

Yet Newcastle almost stole an equaliser five minutes before the break when Pop Robson played the ball in from the right to Dave Hilley who lobbed Jim Montgomery only for George Kinnell to head clear before it crossed the line. Play quickly swept to the other end where the Wearsiders increased their lead.

Len Ashurst drove a long cross into the Newcastle box for Martin to run in unchallenged to head home with Thompson and Hollins giving passable imitations of statues.

Sunderland were well worth their 2-0 half-time lead.

Davies continued to amaze the crowd, displaying all manner of acrobatics (or should that be aerobatics?) to get his head to crosses from all angles. He looked great in the air and even had a headed goal disallowed but he had little support and Sunderland still looked the better team. Their football was simple but effective: powerful in defence and mobile in midfield.

Tyneside misery was completed when the visitors grabbed a third goal ten minutes from time. George Mulhall created the opening, leaving young John Craggs in his wake before rolling the ball back for John O'Hare to sidefoot home.

There was still time for Newcastle to add a touch of respectability to the score when Suddick created an opening for Moncur but he shot appallingly wide when it looked easier to score.

Newcastle had been well beaten. Director William McKeag did not endear himself to their fans when he declared, "We were walloped by a better side". But he was speaking no more than the truth. Neil Martin rubbed salt in Geordie wounds when he gloated, "We have had harder training matches at Cleadon!"

Press rumours said that Newcastle were willing to listen to offers for all but two of their 18 man first team squad but this was quickly refuted. The Magpies admitted, however, that they were willing to listen to offers for five players.

Sunderland fans could not have cared less about the problems at St James'. They were now above their rivals – and they were to stay there.

Football League
Division 1
Sunderland 3 Newcastle United 0 (HT: 0-0)
4th March 1967
Roker Park
50,442

Sunderland: J Montgomery, C Irwin, M Harvey, C Todd, G Kinnell, J Baxter, R Kerr [**56, 74**], J O'Hare, N Martin, G Herd, G Mulhall [**88**]. Sub (unused) A Gauden
Newcastle: G Marshall, D Craig, F Clark, D Elliott, J McNamee, R Moncur, B Robson, R McGarry, RW Davies, D Hilley, T Robson. Sub (unused) P Noble
Referee: L J Hamer (Bolton)

SUNDERLAND HAD half an eye on the FA Cup Fifth Round tie at Leeds United a week later. Newcastle were embroiled in a league survival battle and had no such distractions.

Sunderland's key player, Jim Baxter, had been troubled with strained calf muscles and had missed the previous week's game at West Bromwich. He passed a fitness test in the morning.

United had hoped to field the side that had beaten Arsenal a week earlier but were forced to make a late change when John McGrath dropped out with a groin strain, Dave Elliott coming in to face his former club. He had been substitute for Sunderland when the two teams had met at St James' earlier in the season.

League Positions		Pos	Pl	Pts		Pos	Pl	Pts
Before:	Sunderland	15th	29	27	Newcastle	21st	29	19
After:	Sunderland	15th	30	29	Newcastle	21st	30	19

Newcastle, wearing a change strip of white shirts and black shorts, came to defend and destroy rather than create. Sunderland attacked the Fulwell End and had United's defence at full stretch in the early stages. But Newcastle survived to adopt a no nonsense approach which degenerated into crude play at times. Sunderland were easily the better footballing side but rarely looked like turning their superiority into goals. The first half was deadly dull and brought more jeers than cheers from the crowd as it ended goalless.

The second half started in the way that the first had ended but eventually a goal was scored after 11 minutes when a bad mistake by McNamee opened the door for Sunderland. He tried an overhead back pass from a long ball down the middle into the Newcastle penalty area. The ball never looked like reaching Gordon Marshall and young Bobby Kerr raced in to delicately glance a header past the 'keeper.

The goal was the signal for Wearside. The Roker Roar turned up to full

245

volume as the red and white trickle quickly became a torrent with Sunderland pouring forward on the attack.

Sunderland deservedly went two up after 74 minutes with another Kerr goal. George Herd started the move, stretching the Newcastle defence before slipping a pass through to Neil Martin down the right wing. He hammered a shot that cannoned off Marshall at the near post and spun away past Moncur towards George Mulhall out on the opposite flank. He flashed a first time, low shot across the face of the goal where Bobby prodded it high into the net.

Newcastle were now a beaten team and began to look like relegation material. It soon became simply a matter of whether they could keep the score respectable.

With Sunderland totally in control, Jim Baxter showed his considerable array of skills and it was he who cheekily tried to slip the ball through the legs of a Newcastle defender two minutes from time. He didn't succeed but the ball ran to George Herd. He checked his shot as a tackle came in and played in Mulhall on his right. The winger's rocket from fully 20 yards hardly lifted off the ground as it flew into the net. Tyneside's despair was complete.

No one could deny that Sunderland deserved both points. Their win took their unbeaten run into double figures and they looked forward to the Cup encounter with Leeds with confidence. Yet it was the Cup that was to ruin their season. Their tie against Leeds was to go to a second replay before eventual defeat. Dispirited, they were to lose five of their next six league games and to win just three of the last twelve. Consequently they slipped to finish in a safe (but not exactly exalted) 17th position.

Defeat left Newcastle four points behind third bottom West Bromwich Albion but the Magpies were to improve over their last dozen games, winning half of them and drawing a couple of others, in their struggle against relegation. They were to survive, but only just, finishing in third bottom position although four points from relegation.

First Time Substitutes Used

Newcastle	Sunderland
5 Mar 1966	3 January 1966
Peter Noble	Mike Hellawell
(on for Ollie Burton – 22 mins)	(on for Charlie Hurley – 39 mins)

Football League
Division 1
Newcastle United 2 Sunderland 1 (HT: 1-1)
26th December 1967
St James' Park
59,579

Newcastle: G Marshall, A Burton, F Clark, D Elliott, J McNamee, R Moncur, J Scott, A Bennett [**70**], RW Davies [**23**], J Iley, T Robson. Sub (unused) G Winstanley
Sunderland: J Montgomery, C Irwin, J Parke, C Todd, C Hurley, M Harvey (G Kinnell 52), G Herd, C Suggett [**27**], N Martin, R Brand, G Mulhall
Referee: Vic James (York)

A DISASTROUS sequence of results had seen Sunderland slide down the league. They had picked up just two points from their last six league games (both draws) and had also been knocked out of the League Cup. Pressure was beginning to build up on manager Ian McColl and the sale of Jim Baxter to Nottingham Forest for £100,000 a couple of weeks earlier had met with a mixed reaction on Wearside. Many fans had regarded "Slim Jim" as a luxury Sunderland could not afford while others felt that, on his day, he was one of the most creative players in the country.

Newcastle, on the other hand, were sitting comfortably in the league and had few problems. Thousands were left locked outside St James' when the gates were closed just before the kick-off but an estimated at 5,000 frustrated fans were not to be denied and forced their way in. Such was the crush that six ambulances were called to the ground but only one person was detained in hospital, a Sunderland man with a broken leg.

League Positions		Pos	Pl	Pts		Pos	Pl	Pts
Before:	Newcastle	8th	22	24	Sunderland	17th	21	17
After:	Newcastle	6th	23	26	Sunderland	19th	22	17

Newcastle, with greater drive and a sharper edge than their neighbours, oozed confidence. All United's outfield players seemed to be involved continually in the game and were eager to press forward. John McNamee and Bob Moncur established early control and squeezed out any Roker menace through the middle.

The Tyneside attack was much better balanced with Jimmy Scott showing a zest for the ball and, together with the quick darting Tommy Robson, kept the Wearside defence on tenterhooks. Wyn Davies and Albert Bennett exerted additional stress as they pressurised the visitors' goal.

A Herculean display by Charlie Hurley kept the Magpies out. Jim Montgomery had to be alert to turn a Bennett header away for a corner but chances

247

for the visitors were few and far between. They did create a couple however, Hurley heading a George Mulhall corner back for Ralph Brand to shoot over and Mulhall running on to a ball from Herd to curl a header against the face of the Newcastle crossbar. But when the breakthrough eventually came, it was no surprise that it was at the other end. Unfortunately it came through a Montgomery error.

After 23 minutes Albert Bennett sent over a high, dropping cross that the 'keeper went up to collect. He seemed to take it but dropped it under challenge and Wyn Davies reacted quickest as he swivelled to touch the ball home. Monty objected, claiming that he had been elbowed by the Welshman but referee Vic James did not agree and awarded the goal amid Wearside protests.

Newcastle did not enjoy their lead for long with Sunderland hitting back four minutes later with a brilliant piece of opportunism by Colin Suggett, their best forward. He received the ball from Cec Irwin in the inside right position 35 yards out, took it forward past Clark and sent a raking, low shot wide of the advancing Marshall into the Newcastle net.

United quickly resumed command and Sunderland were forced to rely on the solid defending of Hurley and the breakaway attacks of Suggett. However the Magpies continued to build up pressure on the Wearside goal but the Rokerites' defence held firm.

Newcastle still did most of the attacking in the second half with Davies whipping a right foot shot narrowly wide and Montgomery doing well to catch an overhead effort from Robson. A goal had to come and it eventually did 20 minutes from time.

Frank Clark hit a long ball upfield to Tommy Robson who cleverly eluded Hurley's attempted tackle before slipping a short pass to Albert Bennett. He seemed to be hemmed in but managed to get in a curling shot from 20 yards just before Kinnell, on for Harvey earlier in the second half, managed to get in his tackle.

The bend on the shot was such that it deceived Monty. Some press reports referred to Bennett's "banana shot" but Albert was honest enough to admit that he had merely hit the ball as hard as possible; the 'bend' had been accidental.

Sunderland tried to hit back and Marshall had to dive full length to block a Mulhall effort. Then the United 'keeper lost the ball on the ground but Brand shot wide. It was too little, too late, and Newcastle emerged as deserved winners.

With Newcastle climbing to sixth as a result, and Sunderland dropping to 19th, it was a moment of boom on Tyneside and gloom on Wearside. The rival managers, perhaps not unnaturally, took different views of Newcastle's controversial opening goal. Ian McColl was adamant that it should have been a free kick to Sunderland. Joe Harvey, on the other hand, insisted that it was not a foul and that Monty had merely not taken the ball cleanly.

The fact remained that relegation was beginning to raise its ugly head for

Sunderland who were now only one point ahead of second bottom Sheffield United. The consolation for the Wearsiders was that the return fixture with Newcastle at Roker Park was to take place just four days later. So there was to be an early opportunity for revenge. Whether they would take it, however, was a different matter.

Football League
Division 1
Sunderland 3 Newcastle United 3 (HT: 2-1)
30th December 1967
Roker Park
46,030

Sunderland: J Montgomery, C Irwin, L Ashurst, C Todd, C Hurley (G Kinnell 60), I Porterfield, B Stuckey [47], C Suggett [31, 35], N Martin, R Brand, G Mulhall
Newcastle: G Marshall, A Burton [13 pen, 70 pen], F Clark, D Elliott, J McNamee [87], R Moncur, J Scott, A Bennett, RW Davies, J Iley, T Robson. Sub (unused) G Winstanley
Referee: Kevin Howley (Billingham)

SUNDERLAND HAD played in all-red at Gallowgate four day earlier. Here they reverted to their traditional red and white stripes while Newcastle wore an all-blue strip.

The Wearsiders made three changes to the side that had lost at Gallowgate, bringing in Ian Porterfield (signed from Raith Rovers on the previous evening) in place of the injured Martin Harvey, Len Ashurst for John Parke (also injured at St James') and Bruce Stuckey for George Herd.

Newcastle had also made a breakthrough in the transfer market since the earlier game, recruiting Jackie Sinclair from Leicester City. But, with a six match unbeaten run behind him, manager Joe Harvey decided not to disrupt his team.

League Positions

		Pos	Pl	Pts		Pos	Pl	Pts
Before:	Newcastle	6th	23	26	Sunderland	19th	22	17
After:	Newcastle	6th	24	27	Sunderland	19th	23	18

Sunderland reserved their best display of the season for this game, showing skill and determination throughout. But this supremely confident Newcastle team was a match for anyone. However the Wearsiders had the man-of-the-match on their side in Colin Suggett who celebrated his 19th birthday with a magnificent performance. Sunderland actually started off rather apprehensively but, taking their lead from the youngster's example, they soon took the game to United. So it was bit of a surprise when the Magpies scored first.

After 13 minutes, Wyn Davies went past Porterfield, cutting inside from the left, and took on Hurley only to be sent crashing to the ground by the Irish centre half who totally mistimed his tackle. It was an obvious spot kick and Ollie Burton made no mistake, blasting the ball home.

Sunderland pressed forward but were unable to unlock the Newcastle defence. United also mounted their fair share of attacks and both goalkeepers had to be alert. Overall, the football was not of as high a standard as at St James' but the excitement generated was every bit as good. Burton sustained a badly gashed leg in a tackle from Ashurst and needed prolonged treatment. Substitute 'Tot' Winstanley stripped off his tracksuit and actually stepped on to the pitch before being ordered off again by trainer Ron Lewin who was treating Burton. It was while Newcastle were temporarily down to ten men that Sunderland equalised.

Ralph Brand supplied the crucial pass to Colin Suggett after 31 minutes and his hooked shot, chest high, flew past Marshall high into the Newcastle net. Newcastle had hardly recovered from this setback when he struck again four minutes later. It was another lethal piece of opportunism inside the visitors' penalty area. The ball ping-ponged around the box as Newcastle tried to clear but Suggett darted in among a mass of blue shirts to prod it over the line.

Once ahead, Sunderland's confidence grew. Nevertheless, Newcastle could regard themselves as unlucky to be a goal down at the interval.

The Roker Roar resounded loud and clear as Sunderland went at Newcastle again straight from the restart. The noise reached a crescendo when, within a couple of minutes, the Red'n Whites increased their lead. Bruce Stuckey was the scorer, crashing an unstoppable shot past Marshall to put the Rokermen well and truly on top.

Most supporters (of both persuasions) thought that it was all over – but the Newcastle players didn't. They threw caution to the wind and furiously attacked the Sunderland goal. So, instead of cruising to victory as most people expected, the Wearsiders found themselves under siege. A deciding moment came when on the hour mark when Sunderland lost star centre half Charlie Hurley due to injury. George Kinnell was a capable substitute but there is no doubt that the home defence was weakened. By now Newcastle were in full flow and they pushed the home side further and further back on defence. Panic began to set in although the decision to award Newcastle a second spot kick was, perhaps, a trifle harsh.

With 20 minutes to go former Sunderland man Dave Elliott went down under challenge from Ralph Brand and Referee Howley pointed to the spot, much to the dismay of the Roker masses. Burton was rewarded for his determination to play on after his earlier injury when he lashed in his second penalty of the match; 3-2 and the game was back in the melting pot.

Sunderland's earlier confidence had now gone and they were hanging on. Their players began to clock watch as the minutes ticked away. Jim Iley took a corner nine minutes from time and, with everyone watching Wyn Davies, John McNamee powered in a header that Jim Montgomery stopped with an incredible save. Roker breathed a collective sigh of relief but it was a warning that the Sunderland rearguard should have heeded.

Three minutes to go and another Iley corner. Once again McNamee was left unmarked and this time he made no mistake, bulleting a header into the net. The way he swung on the crossbar in celebration became etched in Tyne-Wear folklore.

The Sunderland fans were obviously disappointed in having victory snatched from their grasp in the dying moments but even they had to admit, albeit grudgingly, that Newcastle's fightback had been something special. Newcastle's star man, Jim Iley, had his own theory regarding Sunderland's collapse. He reckoned that they should remove the clocks from the 'stands at Roker Park because their players spent too much time watching them! But he was not doing himself or his team mates justice. He had been the man who had inspired the determined Magpies' fightback.

Sunderland had really needed both points. They at least had the consolation of knowing that in Suggett, Todd, Stuckey and new man Porterfield, they had a quartet bursting with promise.

They also knew that they had a relegation fight on their hands but it was one that they were eventually to win rather comfortably eventually finishing in 15th position, five points above the drop zone. Newcastle on the other hand were to do even better. They were to qualify for Europe albeit from 10th position thanks to the one-city, one-club qualification rule for the Inter Cities Fairs Cup.

Football League
Division 1
Sunderland 1 Newcastle United 1 (HT: 0-1)
31st August 1968
Roker Park
49,807

Sunderland: J Montgomery, M Harvey, L Ashurst (C Palmer 45), C Todd, C Hurley, I Porterfield, G Herd, G Harris, B Stuckey, C Suggett [70], G Mulhall
Newcastle: W McFaul, D Craig, F Clark, T Gibb, J McNamee, A Burton, J Scott, B Robson [20], RW Davies, D Elliott, G Allen (J Iley 85)
Referee: Kevin Howley (Billingham)

ALTHOUGH IT was still August, both teams were on to their seventh game of the season. Both had also had similar starts and were tied in the league.

Sunderland manager Alan Brown had a few injury problems with Cec Irwin ruled out due to an ankle injury and George Kinnell just recovering from a knee injury and not yet in full training.

It was expected that Newcastle manager Joe Harvey would rely on the same starting line up that had been unbeaten in their last three games. But he shocked everyone by dropping £70,000 Jackie Sinclair and bringing in Jimmy Scott, a player he was willing to sell and who wanted to leave the club.

League Positions		Pos	Pl	Pts		Pos	Pl	Pts
Before:	Newcastle	10th	6	6	Sunderland	10th	6	6
After:	Newcastle	9th	7	7	Sunderland	9th	7	7

Both sides realised who the opposition's danger man was in attack – Colin Suggett for Sunderland and Pop Robson for Newcastle. Both felt that, if these men could be blocked, the effectiveness their side could be nullified. But this was easier said than done. United, once again playing in an all blue strip, were the much sharper side in the first half. Their rapier like attacks had Sunderland in trouble on a number of occasions early on so it came as no surprise when they took the lead.

Tommy Gibb, bringing a much needed touch of class to Newcastle's midfield, set up the chance after 20 minutes when he crossed from the bye-line to where Pop Robson shook off the attentions of Colin Todd and slid the ball home.

Newcastle thought that they had extended their lead just after the half hour mark when Dave Elliott played a through pass that deflected off Todd to Jimmy Scott who beat Jim Montgomery to find the net.

The referee initially pointed to the centre circle but Newcastle's natural celebrations were cut short by a linesman's flag for an offside decision against Scott. Most reporters though that the goal was valid but the decision was to be critical despite the Magpies evident control of the game until the half-time whistle.

They should have built up a comfortable lead but Davies had a game to forget. He was usually well shackled by Charlie Hurley but when he did get away from him in the second half, he wasted three good chances by putting the ball over or wide of the target when each time it looked easier to score. Colin Suggett, frail looking but always in the thick of things, was the one man who looked capable of breaching the visitors' defence. But even he missed a couple of golden opportunities. Perhaps it was not fair to blame him for the misses. Iam McFaul deserved credit for saving them although his second stop, with his foot, had more than a touch of luck about it. But you can't keep a good man down (or 'out' in this case) and Newcastle eventually paid the consequences.

The goal came in a classic counter-attack, Sunderland's best of the game, with 20 minutes left. Gordon Harris resolutely brought the ball out of defence to mount an across-field raid. He managed to play the ball through to George Mulhall who cracked over a low cross into the middle where Suggett (who else?) did the rest.

Suddenly Sunderland were on top and it was Newcastle's turn to defend. Suggett went desperately close to giving his side the lead just five minutes after his goal when he dived to head a short lob from Stuckey against the top of a post. The Rokermen went for their visitors and certainly finished the stronger. Suggett was everywhere and only a courageous dive by McFaul at the Washington teenager's feet five minutes from time denied him the winner. In truth, however, a draw was a fair result.

Both managers were satisfied with a share of the points but this game forced Joe Harvey to change his mind about one of his players. Only a week earlier he had agreed to let Scott go and promised he would help him to find a club. But the skilful Scot had now played himself out of a move. As Harvey said, "He stays at Newcastle. I couldn't let him go after that performance!"

Obviously both teams were still level in the league although Newcastle's attention was soon to switch to more cosmopolitan targets as their first foray into Europe began.

Football League
Division 1
Newcastle United 1 Sunderland 1 (HT: 1-0)
22nd March 1969
St James' Park
48,588

Newcastle: W McFaul, J Craggs, F Clark, T Gibb, A Burton, R Moncur, J Sinclair [12], B Robson, RW Davies, J Scott, A Foggon (A Horsfield 78)
Sunderland: J Montgomery, M Harvey, L Ashurst, B Heslop, R Pitt, C Todd, G Harris, C Palmer, M Moore, C Suggett [83], D Tueart. Sub (unused) W Hughes
Referee: Kevin Howley (Billingham)

ALTHOUGH THERE was little between the two teams in the league, despondency ruled on Wearside if not on Tyneside. Newcastle had four games in hand and Sunderland were in the midst of a financial crisis. They had approached their bankers to request funding to buy new players just before the transfer deadline (on the previous weekend) but had been rebuffed. Club chairman Syd Collings explained, "We had our financial worries at the beginning of the season but have just not been drawing big crowds". He was right. Attendances at Roker had steadily declined throughout the campaign from 30,000 at the start to less than 20,000 in recent games.

It was acknowledged that manager Alan Brown had inherited a king-sized headache but the chairman expressed full confidence in him before flying off to Majorca for a month's rest on the eve of the derby! Brown had injury problems with both Charlie Hurley and Gary Moore having to undergo fitness tests on the morning of the match. Crucially, the former failed his and 17-year-old Richie Pitt had to continue at the heart of their defence.

Psychologically, with a ten day break behind them, Newcastle were in much better shape. They had reached the quarter-final of the Inter Cities Fairs Cup and had a 5-1 home leg lead to take to Vitoria Setubal during the following week. For once, the game against Sunderland was not uppermost in their minds.

League Positions		Pos	Pl	Pts		Pos	Pl	Pts
Before:	Newcastle	15th	30	28	Sunderland	16th	34	27
After:	Newcastle	16th	31	29	Sunderland	17th	35	28

This game was claimed to be robbery with violence; robbery by Sunderland and violence by Newcastle. Every derby game generates extra keenness but there is a difference between determination and downright dirty play and there was an unpleasant ruthless streak in Newcastle's approach.

They took the lead after 12 minutes with a strike of genuine class. A free kick from Frank Clark from near the half-way line saw Wyn Davies let the ball run on to Pop Robson in the inside right position just inside the penalty area. He stabbed a pass forward to Jackie Sinclair who turned, ten yards out, and shot for goal. There was no real power in his effort but it was perfectly placed and the ball trickled into the net just inside a post with Montgomery motionless.

Despite taking the lead, Newcastle continued with their dirty play. Burton was particularly rough and, at one point, had two Sunderland players stretched out on the ground at the same time. There were a couple of Newcastle players who were exceptions to the rule. John Craggs gave a polished display at right back and Jimmy Scott wove some delightful patterns in midfield.

But the star men in this game played for Sunderland. Jim Montgomery enjoyed a proverbial blinder between the sticks and Colin Todd exuded skill as he minimised the threat of Newcastle danger man Robson. Yet United were clearly the better team, enjoyed territorial advantage and had considerably more efforts on goal.

Only Montgomery stopped Newcastle from racking up a cricket score. He produced a string of superb saves and it was thanks to him that Sunderland were still in the game when the equaliser came. United had brought on Arthur Horsfield for Alan Foggon to try and grab an all-important second goal but the ploy failed and seven minutes from time they paid the consequences for not turning their advantage into goals.

It was a scrappy goal, Colin Suggett forcing the ball home in a goalmouth scramble. The consensus was that Sunderland did not deserve to score. Yet, in many ways, it was not surprising. Suggett had a habit of scoring against Newcastle and this goal meant that he had done it five times in his last four games against them.

Even then Newcastle were desperately unlucky not to grab both points. Robson looked as if he had done it in the very last minute when he finally beat Monty but had to look on in disbelief as his apparent winner hit an upright and came out.

So Newcastle failed to capitalise on their obvious superiority over their rivals. Yet they had only themselves to blame. They had to learn to temper their aggression and turn their skills into goals.

Alan Brown expressed the view that his team had deserved a point but his comments were really for public consumption on Wearside. This had been plain robbery. The Wearsiders were to survive in the league, finishing in 17th place, four points above relegated Leicester City. Newcastle were to go on to European glory, winning the Inter Cities Fairs Cup in a two-legged final in the summer. By then, the point dropped against Sunderland in March had long been forgotten.

Football League
Division 1
Newcastle United 3 Sunderland 0 (HT: 1-0)
8th November 1969
St James' Park
56,317

Newcastle: W McFaul, D Craig, F Clark, T Gibb, A Burton, R Moncur, B Robson, K Dyson [**42, 87**], RW Davies [**61**]*, P Arentoft, J Sinclair. Sub (unused) J Scott
Sunderland: J Montgomery, C Irwin, L Ashurst, C Todd*, B Heslop, M McGiven, G Harris*, W Hughes, J Baker, W Kerr, D Tueart. Sub (unused) C Symm
Referee: Vic James (York)

LESS THAN half of the season had gone but bottom placed Sunderland were already in the middle of a relegation fight. Three successive draws had given them some hope that the drop could be avoided but the trip to St James' had assumed critical importance. Manager Alan Brown relied on a primarily youthful unchanged team.

Joe Harvey, on the other hand, went for experience, recalling Benny Arentoft and Jackie Sinclair in place of youngsters John Cowan and Jimmy Thomson. Both Ollie Burton and Wyn Davies pulled out of Wales' trip to Italy for a World Cup Qualifier during the week preceding the derby 'due to injuries'. Wyn was touch and go for the derby but both eventually recovered to turn out. United had embarked on another European campaign but the local derby against the old enemy was every bit as important.

League Positions		Pos	Pl	Pts		Pos	Pl	Pts
Before	Newcastle	13th	18	16	Sunderland	22nd	18	11
After:	Newcastle	13th	19	18	Sunderland	22nd	19	11

Despite the disparity between the two in the league, Sunderland claimed that there was nothing between them in terms of ability. Newcastle set out to prove otherwise. However, in the first half especially, it seemed that the Wearsiders' claim was justified. Newcastle had an edge but it was a fine one and the visitors made them fight all of the way. Gradually United gained the upper hand as the Rokermen struggled to contain the hard working Arentoft in midfield and over-lapping full backs, David Craig and Frank Clark.

With Bobby Moncur imperious as a sweeper, Iam McFaul had little to do in the Newcastle goal. Not so Jim Montgomery who, once again, was in magnificent form for the visitors. The way he kept out efforts by Pop Robson, Davies and Tommy Gibb showed that he was a goalkeeper at the top of his game. But even the best of 'keepers can be beaten and Newcastle managed to do this just before the interval although they had a huge slice of luck with the goal.

Keith Dyson was credited with the goal. Three minutes before half-time he let fly with a shot from fully 25 yards that glanced off Brian Heslop's head and deflected away from Montgomery who was left flat-footed as the ball flew past him. It was a bad time to concede a goal and the Sunderland fans feared the worst at the turn-round.

Their team had enjoyed the advantage of a blustery wind in the first half but it was a different proposition facing it in the second. It proved too much for them and they folded virtually without a fight although Colin Todd and Gordon Harris were honourable exceptions. Even they were booked in a goal-mouth melee along with Davies who had asked for trouble when he felled Montgomery. The two Sunderland men jostled the Welshman who retaliated and all three ended up being booked. Harris was the one man to go close to scoring, his shot early in the second half shaving a Newcastle upright.

But it was Davies who scored United's second goal just after the hour to virtually put the game beyond Sunderland's reach. A cross from Moncur created the opening and Wyn made no mistake as he whipped the ball home.

By this time the visitors' defence was in tatters and they kicked anywhere and anything as United swarmed forward with Tommy Gibb and Jackie Sinclair buzzing in midfield. Sunderland were almost played off the park with Joe Baker totally subdued by Ollie Burton. The surprising thing was that Newcastle led only by the two goals as the closing minutes ticked away.

A third Newcastle goal three minutes from the end gave the scoreline a more realistic look. It was a classic strike, Dyson latching on to an Arentoft header and cracking the ball on the turn past Montgomery before the overworked goalkeeper could move.

Even with this late third goal, the scoreline flattered Sunderland. They ended up a well beaten team and the threat of relegation loomed even larger.

Sadly, there was an unsavoury aftermath to this game. After the match hundreds of Newcastle fans made their way to the Central Station to jeer the opposition. The situation escalated and then got out of hand. A train window was smashed as it waited at the platform to leave. There was also trouble on one train that was stopped several times because of hooligans and the police had to be called in twice (at East Boldon and Seaburn Stations) before the train arrived at Sunderland 45 minutes late. The spectre of hooliganism that was to plague football throughout the 1970s was growing.

As far as the game itself was concerned, Newcastle had shown in no uncertain terms that there was a class gap between the two teams. Yet Sunderland soon had a chance for revenge. A testimonial match for Len Ashurst at Roker Park on the following Wednesday saw a Sunderland XI take on a North East XI which consisted largely of Newcastle players (so much so that the team was also billed as a 'Newcastle United XI'). The Rokermen exacted a modicum of revenge with a 4-2 win although it was regarded by most people as a fun game. With diminutive Bobby Kerr in goal in the second half and Jim Montgomery in the forward line, it could hardly be taken seriously. But the Sunderland fans were happy to put one over on their Tyneside neighbours no matter what the game was. Sadly just 6,470 turned up to pay tribute to a loyal club servant, an indication of the level of despondency on Wearside among football supporters.

Football League
Division 1
Sunderland 1 Newcastle United 1 (HT: 0-0)
27th March 1970
Roker Park
51,950

Sunderland: J Montgomery, C Irwin, M Harvey, C Todd, B Heslop, M McGiven, R Park [**75**], R Kerr, W Hughes, G Harris, D Tueart. Sub (unused) C Symm
Newcastle: W McFaul, D Craig, R Guthrie, T Gibb, A Burton, R Moncur, B Robson, K Dyson, RW Davies, J Smith [**51**], A Foggon. Sub (unused) D Elliott
Referee: Maurice Fussey (Retford)

THIS WAS the 100th competitive Tyne-Wear derby and, on paper, it looked like a foregone conclusion. It was a matter of the team lying bottom of the league and with the poorest scoring record in the division against the side who had the best organised defence.

But there were two factors that hinted towards an upset. Sunderland had been given a bit of a lift with a good draw away to Coventry in mid-week (a match which most pundits felt that they had been unlucky not to win). In addition, Newcastle were recovering from an injury crisis in the run up to the game with no fewer than eight first team squad players either injured or on the road to recovery. In the event, most of them recovered with Craig, Guthrie, Moncur and Smith all coming back into the side so that only two obvious choices, Clark and McNamee, were eventually ruled out.

For Sunderland, Len Ashurst was the main absentee. It really was a must-win game for them with matches running out. They had just five left and were three points behind the three teams immediately above them. The Rokermen had a game in hand over one of them (Crystal Palace) but, significantly, had the worst goal average of the four.

League Positions		Pos	Pl	Pts		Pos	Pl	Pts
Before:	Newcastle	6th	37	41	Sunderland	22nd	37	21
After:	Newcastle	6th	38	42	Sunderland	22nd	38	22

There was only one star in this game: Jim Montgomery. He was absolutely magnificent. Without him Sunderland would have been hammered out of sight. His lightning reflexes and cat-like agility kept his side in the game when they should have been dead and buried well before half-time.

Otherwise this was Newcastle's game. They defied a blustery wind to serve up some delightful and imaginative football with pin-point passing and superb running off the ball. Pop Robson and Tommy Gibb continuously sliced open the home defence down their left flank. The first flash-point in the game came in the 26th minute when Ron Guthrie swung in a free kick from near the half-way line that Monty clutched to his chest. Big Wyn Davies came charging in to bundle the 'keeper into the back of the net. Years later, when goalkeepers were to be protected like an endangered species, this would clearly have been regarded as a foul. But in 1970 the interpretation of the laws of football was that if the 'keeper had both feet on the ground (which Monty had) and the charge was shoulder to shoulder (which it apparently was), then it was not a foul. As Monty went hurtling into the net, referee Maurice Fussey looked questioningly at his linesman who made no response. In such a volatile atmosphere, Fussey erred on the side of caution and gave Sunderland a free kick. It was a controversial incident at the time. Colin Todd did well to hold Newcastle at bay but it took a brilliant save by Montgomery late in the first half to keep United out. It was soon after this that Sunderland managed their first real effort on goal, a powerful Dennis Tueart header that Iam McFaul did well to pull down high to his right.

Sunderland had the wind in their favour in the second half and opened quite brightly. McFaul had to be alert as he rushed out to kick clear after Bobby Park burst through to the edge of the penalty box. But Newcastle soon regained control and it was no surprise when they eventually opened the scoring.

Ollie Burton broke up a Sunderland attack six minutes into the second half and mounted a counter offensive, shrugging off the attentions of Tueart on the way. He plied Jimmy Smith who swung the ball out to Keith Dyson on the far right before racing in towards the Sunderland penalty area. The return ball was perfect for the Newcastle No 10 to crash in a volley in full flow and the ball flew through the crowded area to bulge the net. The Roker Roar was silenced.

Surprisingly for a delicate ball player, Smith seemed to relish the physical aspects of the game. But Newcastle's real heroes were Tommy Gibb, Alan Foggon and (especially) Pop Robson who seemed to cover every blade of grass to impress his fellow Wearsiders. But one goal is never enough, especially in local derbies, and Newcastle paid the consequences for some slip-shod covering a quarter of an hour from time.

The wind caught a cross from the right by Bobby Kerr and the ball sailed over both Moncur and Burton to Tueart who quickly played it back to Park. He blasted in a shot from 16 yards that thudded against the underside of the Newcastle crossbar and came out. Tueart reacted quickest and nodded the loose ball past McFaul into the net. Most people felt that the No 11 had scored and some match reports said that he had done so but Alan Brown insisted that Park's effort had crossed the line and he was credited with the goal.

The scoreline stayed at 1-1 until the final whistle but Newcastle felt that this was a point lost after dominating the game for so long.

The draw meant that, rather neatly, the Tyne-Wear rivals were on equal standing after 100 derbies with 36 wins apiece and 28 draws. This was Newcastle's seventh successive draw away from home in the league and it consolidated them in sixth place.

But a draw was not enough for Sunderland. They really had to win games to stand any chance of avoiding relegation. They were now tottering on the brink, two points from safety after having played a game more than the other strugglers. Alan Brown seemed upset to see that virtually all match reports heaped praise on Montgomery. The Sunderland manager emphasised that his team had ten other players as well and he thought that Monty had enjoyed a quiet game! He had seen a different game to everyone else.

Joe Harvey was nearer the mark when he said that he found it incredible that Monty was not in the England squad for the World Cup. Most of the Sunderland fans gave up after the local derby and some 33,000 less turned up on the following day to see the home game against Derby County. Yet their team made a bit of a fight for First Division survival, losing just one of their last six games (including the Newcastle match). The trouble was that they drew four of the others and were eventually relegated by one point. Their weakness clearly lay in attack where their 30 league goals was the second lowest in the entire Football League.

Player of the Decade
1960s

Robert Moncur

THERE ARE three essential attributes for a good captain: a willingness to shoulder responsibility, the capacity to motivate players and the ability to lead by example. Bobby Moncur displayed all of these in abundance at both Newcastle United and Sunderland.

Bob, of course, guaranteed his immortal place in Newcastle's history with his goals in the Inter Cities Fairs Cup Final of 1969. But goalscoring was not his forte. In fact, many fans still think that his efforts against Ujpest Dozsa were his first goals for the club. In reality they were not even his first cup final goals for the Magpies. He had already scored for them in a cup final, grabbing the winning goal against Wolverhampton Wanderers Youths in the second leg of the FA Youth Cup Final in 1962.

Bobby was born in Perth in 1945 but learned his trade on Tyneside. He ended up in Newcastle purely because he liked the place and the people. He had played for Scotland Schoolboys and even appeared at Wembley when he was just 15. He became one of the most sought after youngsters north of the border and had trials at a number of English clubs. In fact, both Manchester United and Wolverhampton Wanderers (then a massive club) wanted to sign him. But once he came to Newcastle for a trial, he knew that this was the place for him. Everyone was friendly and, as he has often said, it felt like home right from the start.

It was a long learning process as he developed his skills through the juniors and the reserves. In his first season with the club (1960-61), young Bobby mainly played in the local district league against the likes of Longbenton Juniors and Wallsend Juniors although towards the end of the season he made a few appearances in the Northern Intermediate League for United's main junior side.

By the next season he was a regular for the juniors' first team which was known as the N's (the Newcastle, Northumberland and North Durham Nursery) and even made three appearances for the reserves in the Central League towards the end of the campaign. This was the season that Newcastle won the FA Youth Cup.

The following season (1962-63) saw a big breakthrough. He started off in the Ns but quickly became established in the reserves and did so well that he was promoted into the first team away to Luton Town towards the end of the year. He made three first team appearances before the season ended. 1963-64 saw him once again play mainly in the reserves. Matt Busby saw him play against Manchester United Reserves at Old Trafford and forecast that he had seen a future Scotland captain play for the Magpies that day. Did Sir Matt have a crystal ball?

That year Bobby made another three first team appearances but the following season (the year United won the Second Division Championship) he played in 12

games (11 of them in the league). Gradually he was beginning to establish himself as a first team player although, for him, not quickly enough. He very nearly
joined Norwich City at one point and only City's refusal to cough up an extra
£5,000 prevented him from changing his plumage from a Magpie to a Canary.
Instead he stayed at Gallowgate and by early 1967 had made himself a permanent fixture in the first team. Not only that but, within five months, he was taking
over as acting captain in the absence of Jim Iley due to injury.

1967-68 was the big year for Bob – a permanent place in Newcastle's first team
and a job as acting skipper for the first time with caps for Scotland at both Under-
23 and full international levels. Not bad! It was even better during the following
season when he took over the United captaincy on a permanent basis as they
made their first foray into Europe – a campaign that ended in ultimate glory.

Many people believed that Bob modelled himself on his manager, former United
skipper Joe Harvey. This was partly true. Joe undoubtedly influenced him but,
during his early days on Tyneside, the youngster learned a lot from his first captain there, fellow Scot Jimmy Scoular. Joe and Jimmy were not bad role models
for any aspiring skipper.

No-one should under-estimate the influence that Bobby had on Newcastle at this
time. But it was in the Fairs Cup Final that he had his finest moment. United
were struggling to break down a resolute Ujpest Dozsa defence in the first leg at
Gallowgate. Everyone knew that the Magpies needed a lead to take to Hungary
and there they were, inside the last half hour, and it was still 0-0. But cometh the
hour, cometh the man – and that man was Bobby Moncur. Uncharacteristically,
for a player who had developed into a defender par excellence, he pushed up to
help his attack. Incredibly he grabbed two goals to spark off a 3-0 first leg win.

But better was to follow in the second leg. Ujpest had United on the rack and had
pulled two goals back before half-time. Even Bob's head was down in a despondent dressing room during the half-time break. Until, that is, Joe Harvey took a
hand. The cagey old warhorse sensed how dispirited his side was and reminded
them that they were still ahead on aggregate and if they could score a single goal
"the foreigners would collapse like a pack of cards".

He was right. Incredibly it was Bob who proved it by grabbing the all important
goal in the first minute of the second half. Ujpest did indeed collapse and it was
a proud Bobby Moncur who went up to collect the trophy from FIFA president
Sir Stanley Rous.

He continued to captain Newcastle for the next five years and also captained his
country. But all good things must come to an end and in Bob's case it was a disastrous one. Wembley 1974 – and the day that United fans had looked forward
to with so much excitement and anticipation ended with disaster. Liverpool 3
Newcastle 0 – and the scoreline flattered the Magpies!

But none of the Newcastle fans realised as they disconsolately trooped back to
Tyneside that this had been Bobby's last competitive game for their team. They
could not believe it when Bob Stokoe secured his transfer to Sunderland during
the close season for a £30,000 fee.

To the Wearsiders' credit, they realised Bobby's qualities as a leader and made
him captain immediately. He was an ever-present during his first season at Roker

and must have felt quite at home with former Newcastle team-mates Pop Robson and Ron Guthrie in his side. Sunderland finished a creditable fourth in the league, just missing out on promotion behind Manchester United, Aston Villa and Norwich City.

It was a different story during the 1975-76 season. Sunderland made a shaky start to the campaign and Bob was surprisingly relieved of the captaincy, Tony Towers taking over. It says volumes for Moncur's professionalism that he never complained and continued to give 100%. The fans appreciated this and voted him as their Player of the Season.

Sunderland were in contention from the end of August onwards and were top of the division for most of the year. No-one managed to play in every league game but Bob managed to get in 39 matches (out of 42) with only former skipper Bobby Kerr and Pop Robson (with 40) playing more. Sunderland clinched the title by three clear points from Bristol City and West Bromwich Albion.

Sadly Bob did not last long back in the First Division, losing his place in the team six games into the new season (five in the league and one in the League Cup). He never played for the Red'n Whites again. In October, Stokoe resigned and a month later Moncur followed him out of the door, joining Carlisle United as their player-manager.

It seemed a natural progression for a man with a proven track record of leadership. To be truthful, his managerial career did not reach the high levels many expected of him although he did enjoy some success. He joined a Carlisle side struggling in the Second Division and was unable to keep them up although they went down by the narrowest of margins – goal difference. He quit playing to become full time manager and managed to mount a promotion challenge in 1978-79 although it could not be maintained.

One claim to fame while he was at Brunton Park was that it was he who gave Peter Beardsley his break in league football. But Bob left early in 1980 to take over at Heart of Midlothian. It was there that he enjoyed his main success as a manager, Hearts winning the Scottish First Division a few months later. But immediate relegation in their first season back in the Premier League saw Bob move on again, this time to Plymouth Argyle.

Further success eluded him and, after two years in the South West, he returned 'home' to the North East and became involved in local non-league football. A further stint with Hartlepool United in the late 1980s was his last involvement in full time management. In recent years, apart from occasionally being involved socially at St James' Park, he has pursued a variety of business interests including running a squash club, working in local radio and involvement with his real passion – sailing, including running a luxury boat hire company in the Caribbean.

He always maintained that his two proudest moments in football were captaining his country for the first time and skippering United to European success. A third 'moment' could be added – when the Sunderland supporters voted him their Player of the Year. Fans on Tyne and Wear always appreciate class.

Record
Newcastle

	Apprentice October 1960	
	(pro April 1962) – June 1974	
Football League	293 (3 sub) apps	3 gls
FA Cup	18 apps	1 gl
Football League Cup	10 apps	-
Europe	22 apps	4 gls
Others	15 apps	2 gls
Total	358 (3 sub) apps	10 gls

Sunderland

	June 1974 – November 1976	
Football League	86 apps	2 gls
FA Cup	7 apps	-
Football League Cup	3 apps	-
Others	5 apps	-
Total	101 apps	2 gls

Most Appearances in Derby Matches (Top 20)

Newcastle United

		Lge	Cup	Total
1	J Lawrence	22	5	27
2	F Hudspeth	21	3	24
	W Low	21	3	24
	W McCracken	19	5	24
5	C Veitch	18	5	23
6	J Rutherford	17	2	19
7	A Gardner	17	1	18
	R Mitchell	17	1	18
9	A Aitken	16	1	17
10	J Carr	15	1	16
	T McDonald	16		16
	G Wilson	11	5	16
13	A McMichael	14	1	15
14	J Milburn	13	1	14
15	R Cowell	13		13
	G S Seymour	13		13
17	F Brennan	12		12
	R McKenzie	12		12
	P McWilliam	10	2	12
20	J Hay	8	3	11
	W Hibbert	8	3	11
	J Howie	9	2	11
	M Kingsley	10	1	11
	T Lang	11		11
	R Simpson	10	1	11
	A Shearer	9(2)		9(2)

Sunderland

		Lge	Cup	Total
1	G Holley	17	5	22
	W Hogg	19	3	22
3	C Buchan	18	3	21
4	A Bridgett	18	2	20
5	J Mordue	13	5	18
	C Thomson	13	5	18
7	E England	17		17
8	L Shackleton	15	1	16
	H Low	11	5	16
	J Hedley	15	1	16
11	J Montgomery	15		15
	H Martin	12	3	15
13	S Anderson	13	1	14
	L Ashurst	14		14
	J Watson	13	1	14
	W Murray	14		14
	G Aitken	13	1	14
18	J E Doig	12	1	13
	F Cuggy	10	3	13
	C Parker	13		13

CHAPTER 9

*1970s
Success and Failure*

TO SUNDERLAND fans, the 1970s meant just one thing – the glorious day in 1973 when they won the FA Cup! The image of Bob Stokoe rushing across the Wembley pitch to embrace goalkeeping hero Jim Montgomery is one that will be engraved in the hearts and memories of true Black Cats everywhere for as long as the game of football is played. What is often forgotten, however, is the fact that Sunderland spent nine seasons in the Second Division during the decade; and in the one season that they spent in the top flight (1976–77), they were relegated.

Newcastle, on the other hand, spent no fewer than eight seasons in Division One. Admittedly, they were not great years with 1972–73 being their most successful (if ninth place can be called 'success'). But success is relative and the fact that United finished higher in the league than Sunderland in eight of the ten seasons indicates that they were the better team.

Head-to-head encounters, however, do not necessarily support this assertion. There was nothing between the clubs in league meetings, both winning and losing two apiece with the other two drawn. But when it came to cup encounters, Sunderland had a definite edge, albeit mainly in miscellaneous tournaments. Both meetings in the League Cup ended as draws although Sunderland were ultimately victorious in a penalty shoot-out. But the Magpies succumbed to the Rokermen when they met in the Texaco and Anglo-Scottish Cups in the mid-70s. The fact that it was Newcastle who went on to win the Texaco Cup in 1975 when the clubs had met in the preliminary qualifiers is forgotten on Wearside.

In any event, these sponsored tournaments are not officially regarded as first class fixtures although they were first team games. Attendances for these games were significantly less than normal and some clubs took the opportunity to experiment with their teams. On one infamous occasion in 1976 Newcastle were even fined and disqualified from the Anglo-Scottish Cup for fielding a reserve side against Ayr United.

Most record books disregard these games. However, for the sake of completeness, detailed match reports of the Tyne-Wear encounters in these tournaments are included in this chapter although they are excluded from the players' statistics as they were not first class games.

If 1973 was the zenith for Sunderland in terms of 'success', 1974 was the nadir. This was because at the end of the '73–'74 season both Middlesbrough and Carlisle United were promoted to join Newcastle in the top flight. For the first time in their history, the Rokerites were no longer one of the top three clubs in the far north of England.

But it was Sunderland who finished on top at the end of the decade as far as Tyne-Wear rivalry was concerned. Newcastle had joined them in the Second Division in 1978 but, once there, they had been left behind. The Rokermen missed promotion by one point (fourth place finish) in 1979 but clinched runners-up spot to Leicester City in the following season. Newcastle were left to stew all alone in the Second Division until a Messiah called Keegan was to arrive. But that is a story for the 1980s.

League Meetings (6)
At Newcastle: Newcastle – won 2 drew 0 lost 1
At Sunderland: Sunderland – won 1 drew 2 lost 0
League Cup Meetings (2)
At Newcastle: Newcastle – won 0 drew 0 lost 1*
At Sunderland: Sunderland – won 0 drew 1 lost 0
*although the game at Newcastle finished as a draw, Sunderland won the penalty shoot-out.
Miscellaneous Cups (2)
At Newcastle: Newcastle – won 0 drew 0 lost 1
At Sunderland: Sunderland – won 1 drew 0 lost 0

Most Consecutive Games Undefeated

Newcastle	Sunderland
9 games 26 Dec 1967 – 14 Oct 1978	
7 games 21 Apr 2001 – 17 Apr 2006 (ongoing)	7 games 21 Sept 1957 – 9 Oct 1963
6 games 25 Dec 1951 – 19 Dec 1953 17 Nov 1991 – 5 Apr 1997	6 games 26 Dec 1903 – 30 Dec 1905 8 Apr 1985 – 17 Nov 1991 5 Apr 1997 – 26 Aug 2001

Texaco Cup
Qualifying group
Sunderland 2 Newcastle United 1 (HT: 0-0)
3rd August 1974
Roker Park
28,738

Sunderland: J Montgomery, R Malone, R Guthrie, S Ternant, D Watson, R Moncur, R Kerr [**65**], W Hughes, V Halom [**51**] (T Finney 72), B Robson, M A Towers
Newcastle: W McFaul, D Craig, A Kennedy, T McDermott, G Keeley, P Howard, M Burns, T Cassidy, M Macdonald (J Smith 72), J Tudor [**75**], T Hibbitt
Referee: A W S Jones (Ormskirk)

THE QUALIFYING round of the Texaco Cup was played in pre-season and was based on a group competition with the four strongest teams in the far north of England grouped together: Carlisle United, Middlesbrough, Newcastle and Sunderland. With the recent promotion of Carlisle, the first three clubs were all in the First Division while Sunderland were in the Second (they had finished just two points behind the Cumbrians last season albeit in sixth place).

The Wearsiders were the underdogs but were determined to prove themselves as good as their neighbours, especially Newcastle, who were the holders of the Texaco Cup. Although this was not regarded as a first class match, the fact that it was a competitive game added some spice to the fixture and ensured that a more than respectable crowd (over 10,000 more than any other game in England) turned up.

It was strange for Newcastle fans to see Bobby Moncur, who had captained United at Wembley in the Cup Final just three months earlier, lining up for the opposition. Both sides fielded virtually full-strength sides.

Pride and prestige ensured that this game was hotly contested. Both sides were determined with Sunderland, relishing their roles as underdogs, perhaps putting a little bit more effort into their game. This just about tipped the scales in their favour. Most eyes were on Moncur and his replacement in the United side, Glen Keeley. Both were successful in giving their respective goalkeepers plenty of cover. Micky Burns had a lively game for Newcastle on the right wing but Malcolm Macdonald got little or no change out of the impressive Dave Watson in the middle of the home defence. Most of the action in the first half was in midfield where both teams battled to gain supremacy. Neither really succeeded and half-time arrived with the scoresheet blank.

The turning point of the game came with two incidents within a minute early in the second half. After six minutes Macdonald let fly with a cracking right foot shot that seemed destined for the net with Jim Montgomery going the wrong way. But somehow Jim stuck out his legs to deflect the ball away and Sunderland broke up field. Terry Hibbitt should still have cleared the danger on the edge of his penalty area but he paid the consequences for dwelling on the ball. He was dispossessed by the bustling Vic Halom who inter-passed with Billy Hughes before veering to the left and hitting a fine shot from 16 yards that flew inside the angle of bar and post.

The goal was the spur that Newcastle needed and they stepped up a gear to force Sunderland back in defence. Monty kept his side ahead with a combination of astute positioning and fine reflex saves. One, from a powerful Macdonald header, was outstanding. Yet, despite this pressure, it was Sunderland who scored again.

After 65 minutes an attack down the home left flank involving Halom and Tony Towers ended with the ball being played in to Bobby Kerr and the diminutive No 7 curled in a beautiful first time shot to put Sunderland two up.

Macdonald switched flanks to attack down the right and had more success, creating a couple of chances for Tudor but Supermac's timing in front of goal needed sharpening up. Billy Hughes looked very sharp and fit for Sunderland and was probably the most impressive player on the pitch. Macdonald took a knock and was replaced by Jimmy Smith. Bob Stokoe also made a substitution, bringing on Tom Finney for Halom. The Newcastle substitute made a big difference and it was he who created United's goal. With 15 minutes left Jinky Jim sent over an inch-perfect cross into the penalty area where John Tudor, storming in at the far post, rocketed a shot into the net.

Newcastle poured forward on the attack but Dave Watson and Bobby Moncur stood firm. It still took another great save by Montgomery in the dying minutes to deny Terry McDermott and ensure a memorable victory for the underdogs.

The Sunderland fans were delighted to have beaten their old foes. However two 'fans' invaded the pitch and thought that they had just to clamber into the Clock Stand paddock to escape capture from the authorities. They found that the real fans there would not let them in, obviously deciding to make a small contribution to stamp out any kind of hooliganism at Roker Park.

Although the honours (and the points) went to Sunderland on this occasion, it was Newcastle who were to progress through to the knockout stages of this sponsored tournament. The Wearsiders were to pick up just one point from their remaining two games (losing to Middlesbrough and drawing with Carlisle).

Newcastle were to draw away to the Cumbrians and with only one point from their first two games, effectively looked out of the competition. But a resounding victory at home to Middlesbrough in the last qualifying game saw United progress. The rules of the group stages of the tournament awarded a bonus point to any team who scored three or more goals in a game. The 4-0 victory over Middlesbrough was to prove conclusive. Newcastle were to go on to win the cup, defeating Southampton with an aggregate score of 3-1 over the two-legged final.

Anglo-Scottish Tournament
Qualifying group
Newcastle United 0 Sunderland 2 (HT: 0-2)
6th August 1975
St James' Park
20,088

Newcastle: W McFaul, I Nattrass, G Nulty, P Howard, G Keeley, T Hibbitt, P Cannell, T Cassidy, M Macdonald, A Gowling, A Bruce. Subs (unused) 12 M Burns, 14 M Mahoney
Sunderland: T Swinburne, J Ashurst, J Bolton, T Gibb, J Clarke, R Moncur, R Kerr, D Longhorn (12 T Finney 85), V Halom [**44**], B Robson [**36**], I Porterfield. Sub (unused) 14 J Montgomery
Referee: Dave Richardson (Blackburn)

TEXACO'S SUDDEN withdrawal from football sponsorship was a bitter blow but the Football League quickly stepped in to organise a similar tournament to the Texaco Cup which saw the same four far north clubs which had competed in last year's pre-season Texaco qualifiers, meet again.

This was Gordon Lee's first game in charge at St James' Park and, although he realised that preparation for the new league campaign was the prime objective, this was a game he wanted to win. With Middlesbrough having already virtually clinched the top spot in the group, having won both of their qualifying games to-date and picking up two bonus points (for scoring three goals in a game) in the process, neither Newcastle nor Sunderland had much to play for except local pride. But that was enough in these games.

Neither side was at full-strength. Lee had pledged to give every member of his first team squad at least a full 90 minutes run out in the tournament to show him their capabilities before the league season started. But he was also beset with injury problems with the likes of Kennedy, Barrowclough, David Craig, Tudor and Smith all ruled out. Bob Stokoe had problems of his own and Sunderland were forced to take the field without Tony Towers and new striker Mel Holden. Bob also played young Trevor Swinburne in goal, giving Jim Montgomery a rest. Trevor's father (Tommy) had played between the posts for Newcastle before, during and after the Second World War.

Newcastle started at a breakneck pace that they could not hope to maintain especially on such a hot and sticky night. Sunderland, more controlled in their play, were content to sit back and let United over-elaborate and run into blind alleys. Consequently it was the Wearsiders who created the better openings. Former Newcastle favourite Pop Robson looked very sharp and it was he who eventually opened the scoring.

After 36 minutes Geoff Nulty was put into trouble by Glen Keeley and lost possession to Robson who quickly played a pass to Bobby Kerr. Iam McFaul did well to block Bobby's shot but Pop reacted sharply to follow up and finish it off.

Encouraged, Sunderland began to show more ambition and forced Newcastle back. Another Wearside goal a minute before the interval really put United in trouble. The Geordies conceded a free kick in a dangerous position when Irving Nattrass fouled Ian Porterfield. Denis Longhorn took it and sent the ball firmly into the home penalty area where Newcastle's marking was virtually non-existent as Vic Halom ran in to rocket it home.

New Newcastle striker Alan Gowling had a quiet debut and it was left to Malcolm Macdonald to create his side's best chance early in the second half. Terry Hibbitt played a delightful through-ball into Supermac's path and he went on to round goalkeeper Swinburne and shoot for goal. It must have been galling for him to see his former captain Bobby Moncur get back and block his effort. In fact all three former Newcastle players – Moncur, Robson and Gibb – enjoyed good games on their return to their old stamping ground and caused uncertainty in the home defence. This almost led to a third Sunderland goal when Robson stole in to meet a superb crossfield pass only to be stopped by the diving McFaul. It was not until the closing stages that Newcastle managed to exert any kind of sustained pressure on the Sunderland defence and two outstanding saves by the young Sunderland 'keeper kept out Macdonald. No-one could deny that Sunderland were worthy winners.

Gordon Lee was not particularly enamoured with pre-season sponsored football. He regarded the tournament merely as preparation for the forthcoming league campaign but dearly wanted a win in his first game in front of his new supporters. Yet, even with his injury situation, he could hardly have been happy with what he had seen.

Second Division Sunderland looked much better prepared for the new season. But this was to be the Wearsiders' sole success in the Anglo-Scottish Tournament this season. They had already lost away to Middlesbrough and were to lose their third (and last) game at home to Carlisle United to finish second bottom of the group. But they were to finish above Newcastle (who were to collect just one point with a draw at Middlesbrough in their final game) and the Roker fans were happy with that. They were to be happier still nine months later with the Second Division Championship under their belts.

Football League
Division 1
Newcastle United 2 Sunderland 0 (HT: 1-0)
27th December 1976
St James' Park
50,048

Newcastle: M Mahoney, I Nattrass, A Kennedy [**83**], T Cassidy, A McCaffery, G Nulty, S Barrowclough, P Cannell [**41**], M Burns, A Gowling, T Craig.
Sub (unused) D Craig
Sunderland: B Siddall, R Malone, J Bolton, MA Towers, J Clarke, J Holton, R Kerr, W Hughes, R Lee (T Gilbert 64), A Brown, G Rowell
Referee: Pat Partridge (Durham)

THE OLD rivals met for their Christmas holiday game with radically contrasting fortunes and expectations. Newcastle, who had been written off as relegation candidates at the start of the season, were now outside title hopefuls and were clear favourites over bottom placed Sunderland.

Second Division Champions Sunderland had been a big disappointment in their return to the top flight. New Roker manager Jimmy Adamson tried to raise Wearside morale by pointing out that anything could happen in derby games and, historically, there was nothing between the teams.

Newcastle were relieved that Irving Nattrass, who had broken his wrist in an accident in the gym, was allowed to play wearing a special safety strapping in place of his plaster cast.

League Positions		Pos	Pl	Pts		Pos	Pl	Pts
Before:	Newcastle	5th	18	22	Sunderland	22nd	18	9
After:	Newcastle	5th	19	24	Sunderland	22nd	19	9

The game was played in a white hot atmosphere but, even from the early stages, Sunderland played like a team without heart. They were reluctant to undertake even the simplest of moves and Mick Mahoney in the Newcastle goal had one of the quietest games of his career. The surprising thing was that it took United so long to take the lead.

The goal came four minutes before half-time. Stewart Barrowclough floated a free kick from near the right wing corner into the middle where it skidded off the heads of Clarke and Alan Gowling to Micky Burns. He intelligently chipped the ball back in front of goal for Paul Cannell to launch himself at it and head past Barry Siddall. The 1-0 half-time scoreline undoubtedly flattered Sunderland.

Newcastle continued to dominate the game although this was more due to Sunderland's short-comings than the fact that the Magpies played particularly well. The Wearsiders' expensive striker Bob Lee failed to justify his price tag and made no impact on the game. Eventually he was replaced by young substitute Tim Gilbert who made his first team debut. Yet surprisingly, considering how one-sided the game was, there was just one more goal scored and that was near the end.

Seven minutes from the end Alan Gowling shook off his shadow, Jim Holton, and drove for goal. Siddall dived to divert the ball away but Alan Kennedy swooped as others dithered and calmly stroked in a shot from an unbelievable angle that squeezed between the 'keeper and a post.

The goal was the sign for a mass exodus among the 10,000 Roker supporters in the crowd. By the end of the game, the Newcastle fans, intent on rubbing salt on the remaining visiting supporters' wounds, were taunting them with chants of "Where's the Roker Roar?" and "You're going down again".

It was a despondent Sunderland who left Tyneside. They now had five successive defeats behind them and were three points behind second bottom West Bromwich Albion and four behind Tottenham Hotspur and Bristol City with the bottom three going down. A quick return to the Second Division was now becoming a probability rather than a possibility.

Newcastle manager Gordon Lee offered them a crumb of comfort when he said that they could still escape but ominously added that time (or the lack of it) was not on their side. Yet there was still over half of the season to go! Jimmy Adamson insisted that they were not going to throw in the towel.

United were now just five points behind leaders Liverpool with two games in hand. Lee confidently expressed the view that their team spirit and character would give them a chance of winning of the title. Team spirit obviously did not extend to him as he was to desert the club a month later to take over at Everton!

Football League
Division 1
Sunderland 2 Newcastle United 2 (HT: 1-0)
8th April 1977
Roker Park
46,056

Sunderland: B Siddall, M Docherty, J Bolton, K Arnott [**41**], S Elliott, J Ashurst, R Kerr, D Collins, M Holden, R Lee [**55**], G Rowell. Sub (unused) M Coady
Newcastle: M Mahoney, I Nattrass, A Kennedy, T Cassidy, A McCaffery, G Nulty, S Barrowclough, P Cannell [**70**], M Burns*, A Gowling, T Craig [**86**]. Sub (unused) R Blackhall
Referee: Bob Matthewson (Bolton)

NEWCASTLE HAD compiled a a seven match unbeaten run. Only four points behind league leaders Liverpool and two behind second placed Ipswich, they were now in an UEFA Cup qualifying position. Not unexpectedly, they were unchanged.

Sunderland, on the other hand, were embroiled in the middle of a relegation battle. They were in second bottom place, just one point ahead of West Ham and behind Bristol City on goal average. But both of these teams had three games in hand. With three sides to be relegated, things were looking black for the Rokermen. Colin Waldron was suspended for this game. Perhaps surprisingly, manager Jimmy Adamson decided not to bring back club captain Tony Towers but opted for Doug Collins instead.

League Positions		Pos	Pl	Pts		Pos	Pl	Pts
Before:	Newcastle	4th	33	41	Sunderland	21st	33	23
After:	Newcastle	4th	34	42	Sunderland	20th	34	24

The first half of this game can be summed up in one word – 'abysmal'. Play plunged to new levels of boredom before a huge Good Friday crowd. By half-way through the session, chants of "What a waste of money" rang around Roker. Newcastle harried the home team, restricting their chances, and actually had more shots at goal. Paul Cannell even had the ball in the net at one point but had his goal disallowed because Alan Gowling was adjudged to have fouled the 'keeper.

After 41 minutes there was at last a goal to relieve the tedium. Cannell half cleared the ball straight to Kevin Arnott, the youngest player on the field. He opted to run at the Newcastle defence before sending a swerving shot past Mahoney, high into the net.

The goal gave Sunderland confidence and they started the second half with passion in their play. Ten minutes after half-time a rare slip by Geoff Nulty led to the Rokermen going two up. He tried to play himself out of trouble but lost possession to Bobby Kerr. The ball was played to Mel Holden who shot for goal. Mahoney managed to parry the effort but the loose ball fell to Bob Lee who wasted no time in putting it away.

Now two goals ahead, confidence began to sweep through the ranks of the home supporters who took up the chant, "We're going up the league". Holden almost made it three when he was put through on his own but Alan Kennedy recovered the situation for Newcastle.

It was Kennedy's pace with 20 minutes left that brought Newcastle back into the game. He raced past two defenders before crossing low into the middle for Micky Burns to slam in a shot that Siddall managed to block with his legs only for Paul Cannell to crash in the rebound.

Four minutes from time Shaun Elliott conceded a free kick outside the penalty area and as the Sunderland defence tried to organise a wall, Burns quickly rolled the ball to Tommy Craig who blasted the ball home from 25 yards.

A draw was probably the fairest result from a boring game that neither team deserved to win. Although to achieve only a draw after holding a two goal lead against the old enemy was a devastating setback for Sunderland. Jimmy Adamson tried to be optimistic when he said, "Half a loaf is better than none". The point lifted his team one place in the league, but relegation was now staring them in the face. Arguably, the loss of this point was to cost them First Division survival. They were to go down in third bottom place, just one point from safety.

The draw lifted Newcastle to within three points of leaders Ipswich with eight games to go. But a poor finish to the season (when they lost four of their last five games) saw United finish fifth – a little disappointing after promising so much but enough to qualify for the UEFA Cup.

Football League
Division 2
Sunderland 1 Newcastle United 1 (HT: 0-1)
14th October 1978
Roker Park
35,405

Sunderland: B Siddall, M Henderson, J Bolton, M Docherty, J Clarke, S Elliott, G Chisholm (R Greenwood 60 [74]), A Brown, W Entwhistle, R Lee, G Rowell
Newcastle: S Hardwick, P Kelly, J Brownlie, K Mitchell, J Bird, D Barton, C Suggett, N Walker, P Withe [13], T Hibbitt, J Connolly. Sub (unused) M McGhee
Referee: Terry Morris (Leeds)

TYNE AND WEAR Council fixed a capacity of 47,000 for this game and decreed that it should be all-ticket. In the event, the attendance was well below this limit largely because of the fear of violence that pervaded football at the time. Pub landlords and shopkeepers around Roker were advised to close unless they were confident that they could cope with the derby crowds.

The fears were well grounded as hooligans embarked on an orgy of vandalism on the train journey from Newcastle to Wearside. A total of 13 railway carriages were wrecked – windows smashed, toilet doors wrenched from hinges, seats slashed and wooden panels ripped away. The police expressed the view that it was the worst display of vandalism ever seen on British Railways.

Team selection news paled in comparison although both sides had injury problems. Sunderland were missing both Mick Buckley (recovering from a broken jaw) and Roly Gregoire (yet to play this season due to knee ligament trouble). Initially it looked even worse for Newcastle but John Brownlie and

Peter Kelly recovered after being doubtful for the game. However both John Blackley and long term absentee Irving Nattrass were ruled out.

League Positions

		Pos	Pl	Pts		Pos	Pl	Pts
Before:	Newcastle	6th	9	11	Sunderland	11th	9	10
After:	Newcastle	6th	10	12	Sunderland	10th	10	11

This game was a superb advertisement for local derby football. It was played with passion, pride and fluctuating fortunes. The tension on both the pitch and terraces was almost tangible. Newcastle showed the early composure and flair and had the advantage of an early lead.

After 13 minutes Jeff Clarke conceded a free kick by bringing down Nigel Walker and was still on his way back into the middle after receiving a lecture when the young midfielder centred the ball. With Clarke out of position, Peter Withe was unmarked as he moved in to meet the cross at the near post and send a downward header into the net.

Strangely, once ahead, United adopted a more cautious approach and failed to give much support to their front men from midfield. This gave the initiative to the Rokermen who forced them onto the back foot. Fortunately for Newcastle, John Bird was in commanding form in the middle of defence and Steve Hardwick confidently dealt with most of the crosses into the box. Nevertheless Sunderland managed to get the ball into the Tynesiders' net ten minutes before the break when Alan Brown and Wayne Entwhistle worried the ball away from Hardwick and young Alan touched in the ball. Their celebrations were short-lived, however, with the referee indicating a free kick for an illegal challenge on the 'keeper. Hardwick then made an incredible reaction save from a close-in effort by Gary Rowell following a Mick Docherty corner just before the break which arrived with the game delicately balanced.

Newcastle could easily have put the game out of Sunderland's grasp five minutes after the resumption when Walker broke clear of Clarke down the right. His cross into the middle was met perfectly by John Connelly whose shot easily beat Siddall only for Bob Lee to get back and somehow head clear from under the crossbar. Sunderland's first half fire seemed to have been quenched but they gradually forced their way back into the game. Their play picked up further when Roy Greenwood was introduced for Gordon Chisholm. Newcastle were forced back once again and, although their defence did great work, an equaliser always looked likely.

It eventually came after 74 minutes when Joe Bolton broke up a visitors' attack and sent Gary Rowell clear. His cross-field pass found Mick Docherty in acres of space and, although Hardwick did well to block his shot, the 'keeper was unable to hold the ball and Greenwood pounced to net the rebound.

Now it was anybody's game and Roker was no place for the faint-hearted as both sides went for the winner. A Kenny Mitchell cross had the home defence in all kinds of trouble while Hardwick pulled off top quality saves at the other end from Mick Henderson and Gary Rowell. At the end a draw was just about the fairest result.

It was just sad that the antics of so-called fans off the field grabbed the headlines rather than the engrossing game on it. There were a total of 25 arrests inside the ground and 15 outside with a further 60 ejected from the terraces. Fortunately there was little trouble after the game.

The draw meant that Sunderland remained unbeaten at home in the league so far this season (won 3, drew 2) and that Newcastle were now undefeated in their last eight league games. No wonder both managers were satisfied that the game had ended with honours even.

Football League
Division 2
Newcastle United 1 Sunderland 4 (HT: 0-2)
24th February 1979
St James' Park
34,733

Newcastle: S Hardwick, J Brownlie*, I Nattrass, M Martin, J Bird*, J Blackley (K Mitchell 45), A Shoulder, N Walker, P Withe, T Hibbitt, J Connelly [50]
Sunderland: B Siddall, M Henderson, J Bolton, K Arnott* (M Docherty 75), J Clarke, S Elliott, G Chisholm, W Rostron, W Entwistle [72], R Lee*, G Rowell [6, 25, 62 (pen)]
Referee: Pat Partridge (Durham)

SUNDERLAND HAD high hopes of promotion, just three points behind the top three teams (Brighton, Crystal Palace and Stoke). Manager Billy Elliott kept faith with his youngsters, retaining teenager Gordon Chisholm and 20-year-old Kevin Arnott in his team despite the availability of the more experienced Mick Docherty and Mick Buckley, both having recovered from injury.

Newcastle were a bit dispirited having been knocked out of the Cup (1-0 in a replay at Wolverhampton) two days earlier. Manager Bill McGarry relied largely on experience although an injury to Jim Pearson at Molyneux upset his plans.

League Positions

		Pos	Pl	Pts		Pos	Pl	Pts
Before:	Sunderland	5th	26	30	Newcastle	12th	25	25
After:	Sunderland	5th	27	32	Newcastle	15th	26	25

Tensions were high with so much at stake and it was soon apparent that mistakes would be punished. They were – and it was Newcastle who made them. After six minutes Jeff Clarke sent a free kick in to the middle from far out on the right for Gordon Chisholm to head on into a crowded goalmouth. There was an almighty scramble with flailing legs trying to make contact before the ball came back off Wilf Rostron to Gary Rowell and his instinctive strike found the net. It was a scrappy goal but, in view of what was to follow, was of critical importance.

Newcastle tried to fight their way back into the game and Sunderland had Barry Siddall to thank for maintaining their advantage. Twice he denied Peter Withe, first tipping his header from a Nigel Walker cross on to the top of a post and then dropping on another header when John Brownlie set up the big striker. But Newcastle looked distinctly vulnerable at the back, failing to pick the Sunderland forwards up when they pushed forward.

After 25 minutes there was no-one anywhere near Rowell when he took a great pass through the middle by Kevin Arnott. If Gary's first goal had been scrappy, this one was sublime as he calmly waited for Hardwick to advance before driving a shot just wide of the 'keeper's left hand from outside the penalty area.

Rowell was now confidence personified and he could easily have notched up his hat-trick before half-time. The ball flicked off Blackley's head to leave him with a free run on goal but this time he opted to place his shot and Hardwick saved comfortably. At last, prompted by young Nigel Walker, United began to force their visitors back. For the ten minutes before the break Newcastle were on top and gave their supporters at least some hope but the Wearside defence comfortably nullified their attacks and Siddall was never really troubled as they held on to their two goal lead.

Newcastle replaced John Blackley with Kenny Mitchell after the break and renewed their efforts to try and claw their way back into the game. For a time, albeit briefly, Sunderland seemed to lose their composure and it was no real surprise when United scored.

Five minutes after half-time John Connolly was brought down by Mick Henderson out on the left and went into the middle to let Walker take the free kick. The youngster placed it perfectly and Connolly brilliantly headed wide of the groping Siddall to make it 1-2.

At last it looked as if Newcastle were going to make a game of it – at least temporarily. Then Sunderland struck again just after the hour. Rostron started the move that sent Henderson scurrying into the Newcastle penalty area. It looked as if he had pushed the ball too far ahead but that was of no consequence when Mitchell clearly brought him down. A penalty! Not surprisingly, up stepped Gary Rowell to make spot kicks look easy and complete his hat-trick.

Newcastle were now a beaten team and it simply became a question of 'how many?' Sunderland soon charged up field from defence and Bob Lee shot home. It seemed rough justice that the referee had already blown his whistle to give Sunderland a free kick outside the Newcastle penalty area for a foul by Hardwick on the effervescent Rowell.

The Rokermen were not to be denied and after 72 minutes they grabbed their fourth when Rowell expertly took the ball to the bye-line before looking up and chipping Hardwick for Wayne Entwistle to nod in at the far post.

By now Sunderland were akin to thoroughbreds while disjointed Newcastle more closely resembled selling platers. To say that the Magpies were relieved to hear the final whistle was an understatement.

For 21-year-old Gary Rowell this was the stuff that dreams are made on. He was not joking when he said, "This is the happiest day of my life". Billy Elliott, the Sunderland manager, added, "I don't like picking out individuals after a team show like that but Gary really was magnificent".

Bill McGarry, now under pressure as Newcastle's slide down the league gathered momentum, also acknowledged "Rowell is, quite simply, a gift – and Sunderland must be in with a great chance of promotion". They were, especially as they were to win eight of their next ten league games (and draw one of the others). Inexplicably, however, they were to lose two of their last three home games and miss promotion by one point.

Newcastle were to improve slightly to finish in a fairly respectable eighth place but their season had been ruined by the thrashing at home at the hands of the old enemy.

Football League Cup
2nd round (1st leg)
Sunderland 2 Newcastle United 2 (HT: 1-0)
29th August 1979
Roker Park
27,658

Sunderland: B Siddall, S Whitworth, J Bolton, J Clarke, S Elliott*, G Chisholm, K Arnott, W Rostron [19], W Entwistle, B Robson [73 pen], A Brown.
Sub (unused) G Rowell
Newcastle: S Hardwick*, J Brownlie, I Davies* [76], M Martin, D Barton, J Bird*, A Shoulder*, T Cassidy, P Withe*, T Hibbitt, G Nicholson (P Cartwright 71 [83])
Referee: Norman Glover (Chorley)

ALTHOUGH BOTH sides were in the Second Division and the league campaign had just started, the pairing of the North East rivals in the Football League Cup captured the imagination locally. It was confidently felt that demand for tickets would be high and the match was designated as an all-ticket affair. So it was a bit of a disappointment that the crowd at Roker Park was well under 30,000, especially with Sunderland, equal fourth, making quite a good start to the season. Some blamed the increased admission prices for the poor attendance.

Bill McGarry had hoped to sign Stuart Boam from Middlesbrough for this game but the financial negotiations could not be concluded in time so Newcastle fielded the same starting eleven that had drawn away to Charlton in their last game.

Sunderland also fielded an unchanged line-up although in their case it was a winning one, having defeated Fulham at home the previous weekend. Gary Rowell had missed that game with an ankle injury but he had recovered enough to be named as substitute against Newcastle.

Although the crowd was not very big, passions still ran high – as much on the pitch as on the terraces. Crunching tackles from both sides punctuated the early play as commitment to attack seemed to be the order of the day. Sunderland created more clear cut chances in the opening exchanges but both Wilf Rostron and Shaun Elliott blasted opportunities high and wide respectively. Newcastle looked dangerous on counter-attacks but it was Sunderland who made the first breakthrough.

Young Scot Gordon Chisholm played a superb ball down the right wing after 19 minutes to find Wayne Entwistle in full flight. He was in the team only because Rowell was not fully fit but he made the most of his opportunity, sending over a perfect cross for the unmarked Rostron to head home from 12 yards.

The goal sparked a series of goalmouth incidents at both ends. Within a minute, former Newcastle favourite Pop Robson almost made it 2-0 but his fierce drive was well saved by Steve Hardwick. Within another minute John Bird almost levelled matters but he lifted his first time shot under pressure over the bar. Play swung from end-to-end. Alan Brown drove over the Newcastle bar and then Alan Shoulder sent a header over the top at the Sunderland end. Hardwick earned his wages with two outstanding saves, tipping over a venomous drive from Brown and then holding on to a sharp, low shot from Robson. Soon play was back at the other end and Barry Siddall was able to show off his goalkeeping skills, saving well from Gary Nicholson and then from Ian Davies in first half injury time. The whistle went to end a cracking opening session with Sunderland just about deserving their slender lead.

Newcastle came out for the second half determined to wipe out the deficit. They almost did it in the 54th minute when a Peter Withe header from a John Brownlie cross beat Siddall only for Steve Whitworth to come to the rescue and head off the line. But United looked a vulnerable at the centre of their defence and they were lucky to escape when a Joe Bolton cross almost reached Brown but the ball was hacked away at the last second. Newcastle brought on Peter Cartwright for the limping Nicholson but he had hardly time to settle in to the pace of the game when Sunderland increased their lead.

In the 73rd minute Alan Brown's pace took him past both John Bird and David Barton and into the Newcastle penalty area. He tried to take the ball around Hardwick but was brought crashing to the ground by the 'keeper. Referee Norman Glover immediately pointed to the spot, brushing aside Hardwick's vehement protests (and booking him for dissent). Amid all of the mayhem, Robson stood patiently waiting with the ball on the penalty spot and, when the referee eventually indicated that the kick should be taken, Pop calmly sent the goalie the wrong way to score.

Sunderland, fans and players alike, were in raptures but they were caught stone cold as Newcastle struck within three minutes to reduce the leeway.

Brownlie created the goal, catching out Brown and sending Ian Davies scampering unmarked into the Sunderland penalty area where he stroked the ball away as if scoring goals was second nature. It was, in fact, his first goal for Newcastle.

Suddenly Sunderland found themselves under pressure. It now became a matter of whether they could hold on until the final whistle. They couldn't.

With seven minutes left Mick Martin took an indirect free kick awarded just inside the Sunderland penalty area and found Cartwright, totally un-marked in front of goal. He made no mistake as he headed past the stunned Siddall. The Roker crowd was just as stunned but it could have been even worse in the closing minutes when Cartwright burst into the Sunderland area and was denied by a brave, last gasp save by Siddall.

The only losers from this fascinating game were those fans who had stayed away. They had missed a classic. The game had everything – passion, commit-ment, skill and (ultimately) great drama.

Newcastle had probably deserved the draw for their determination not to give in, even when they were two goals down with a quarter of an hour to go. They left Wearside feeling as if they had won and there was a similar view in the Roker camp where assistant manager Frank Clark moaned, "We played like amateurs for the last hour".

Former trainee civil engineer, Peter Cartwright, plucked from non-league obscurity at North Shields a couple of months earlier, was obviously ecstatic. "I have only scored two headed goals in my life", he enthused. As he was just 5ft 6ins tall, this was not perhaps surprising although it says volumes about the Sunderland marking for the equaliser.

But the tie was not over yet. It was just half-time in this two-legged fixture and the two rivals had to meet again at St James' Park a week later when even more drama was in store.

Football League Cup
2nd round (2nd leg)
Newcastle United 2 Sunderland 2 (HT:0-0) [aet]
(Aggregate score 4-4 – Sunderland won 7 – 6 on penalties)
5th September 1979
St James' Park
30,533

Newcastle: S Hardwick, J Brownlie, I Davies, M Martin*, D Barton, S Boam [**80**], A Shoulder [**84**], J Pearson, P Withe, T Hibbitt*, G Nicholson (P Cartwright 78)
Sunderland: B Siddall, S Whitworth, J Bolton, J Clarke, S Elliott, J Ashurst, M Buckley, W Rostron, A Brown [**74, 90**], B Robson, G Rowell (G Chisholm 102)
Referee: Pat Partridge (Cockfield, Co Durham)

THE SIDES had encountered mixed fortunes in their games since the first leg meeting at Roker Park. Newcastle had won at home to Chelsea but Sunderland had lost away to Oldham Athletic. Consequently United had leap-frogged the Wearsiders in the league.

But Newcastle had injury worries. Tommy Cassidy was ruled out as a result of an injury to his instep sustained in the Chelsea game and Mick Martin turned out only after passing a test on a leg strain.

Tom's absence saw a less than fully fit Jim Pearson come into the side. John Bird was also an absentee due to an ankle injury but he had also missed the Chelsea game. However Bill McGarry had managed to complete his signing of Stuart Boam from Middlesbrough soon after the first leg game at Sunderland and he was a ready made replacement in the middle of the Tyneside defence.

Sunderland had injury problems as well. Kevin Arnott was out with a thigh injury but this was more than compensated for by the return of Gary Rowell, the man Newcastle feared, to the starting line-up. Barry Siddall had sustained a hand injury against Oldham that had required three stitches but he was still able to turn out. Newcastle allocated 10,000 tickets to Sunderland but, sadly, just 3,500 visiting fans made the short trip to St James' (compared to about 6,000 Newcastle fans at Roker). Ken Knighton criticised his supporters for staying away but obviously most of them thought that it was a lost cause.

Sunderland made the early running only for Pop Robson to put a header wide and Steve Hardwick to save well from Mick Buckley. Suddenly an atrocious back pass by Clarke let in Peter Withe who burst clear on goal.

Fortunately for Sunderland, Siddall was alert to the threat and he raced out of his area to block the big centre forward's shot with his body. Withe then went close again with a shot that rattled the side-netting as United stepped up a gear. Both Withe and Pearson went close again with shots that flew just wide and Newcastle ended the first half on top.

The restart was delayed until a smoke bomb, thrown into Siddall's goal-mouth, was removed. Withe continued to threaten the visitors' defence who suffered an anxiety attack every time he came forward. He almost created the opener when he headed on a free kick for the unmarked Pearson to head against the Sunderland bar from inside the six yard box. The Wearsiders breathed a sigh of relief as the ball was scrambled away. But it wasn't all Newcastle and it took a wonder save by Hardwick to keep the visitors out when he tipped over a deflected shot by Jackie Ashurst midway through the half. The Newcastle 'keeper came to the rescue again a couple of minutes later, saving bravely at the feet of Robson, taking a full blooded shot square in the face in the process. But he was eventually beaten 16 minutes from normal time.

Wilf Rostron floated in a free kick from out on the wing and Hardwick could only push away the ball. It fell perfectly for Alan Brown who, although at an acute angle, headed over the packed home defence into the net. The small Sunderland contingent went wild.

With time running out, Newcastle redoubled their efforts. Withe again went close with a header from a Terry Hibbitt free kick that flew agonisingly wide. Peter Cartwright eventually came on to a hero's welcome in place of Nicholson and within seconds of his introduction United equalised although he was not involved in the goal which came with ten minutes remaining. A corner taken by Alan Shoulder found Stuart Boam inside the penalty area and the big central defender glanced in his first goal for his new club.

If the Newcastle fans were delighted with that goal, they were delirious with the next, four minutes later. It came from another corner, this time taken by Hibbitt. The ball was nodded on by Mick Martin to Alan Shoulder, un-marked at the far post, and his header put the Geordies ahead.

Now it was Sunderland's turn to frantically push up in search of an equal-iser. The Newcastle fans were anxiously looking at their watches when the goal came with virtually the last kick of the game. Boam was caught out by a long ball and Alan Brown darted in to turn the home rearguard and blast a shot past Hardwick. Apart from the 3,500 ecstatic Sunderland fans, St James' Park was stunned.

Fitness was to be a critical factor in this epic tie but both sides showed in extra time that they were at least physically well prepared. The bustling Withe caused problems for the visitors' defence as he weaved into their penalty area but Siddall was equal to his attempt on goal. The goalkeeper similarly foiled Shoulder after the little striker had broken clear. By this time Sunderland had replaced Rowell with Gordon Chisholm and the tension built up both on the terraces and on the pitch.

Cartwright almost stole a goal for Newcastle but Siddall managed to scram-ble the ball away for a corner. But the nearest to the decisive breakthrough came at the other end. Mick Buckley broke down the right before supplying a perfect cross for Robson at the far post. His header beat Hardwick and looked like a certain goal but the Sunderland man could held his head in disbelief as the ball rebounded off the far post.

With the scores still level at the end of half an hour's extra time, the tie went to a penalty shoot out and the tension that had gone before was nothing compared to what was to follow. Both managers joined their teams in the centre circle to quickly decide the sequence for their penalty takers. Sunderland went first

Sunderland		Newcastle	
Robson	Scored (1-0)	Shoulder	Scored (1-1)
Rostron	Scored (2-1)	Withe	Scored (2-2)
Buckley	Scored (3-2)	Martin	Scored (3-3)
Ashurst	Scored (4-3)	Davies	Scored (4-4)
Whitworth	Scored (5-4)	Brownlie	Scored (5-5)
Chisholm	Scored (6-5)	Barton	Scored (6-6)
Brown	Scored (7-6)	Pearson	Shot saved (7-6)

So it was Sunderland who went through to the next round.

Management reaction from the rival camps was exactly the opposite to their opponents. Jubilant Ken Knighton enthused, "This was a tremendous display from us. The match was a credit to both sides".

Bill McGarry could not even face the press and it was his chief coach, Willie McFaul, who gave his reaction, "The boss is sick – just as we all are. We had much of the play but we simply did not have an end product. I think it is a bit of a farcical way to end a game".

But that was what the rules stipulated and it was Sunderland who went through to defeat Manchester City at the second attempt in the next round before going out to West Ham United in a Fourth Round replay.

Football League
Division 2
Newcastle United 3 Sunderland 1 (HT: 1-1)
1st January 1980
St James' Park
38,322

Newcastle: S Hardwick, J Brownlie, I Davies, T Cassidy [56], D Barton, S Boam, A Shoulder [58 pen], P Cartwright [38], P Withe, W Rafferty, T Hibbitt. Sub (unused) J Connelly
Sunderland: C Turner, S Whitworth, J Bolton, J Clarke, S Elliott, M Buckley, K Arnott, C Marangoni, J Hawley, B Robson (G Rowell 67), S Cummins [25]
Referee: David Richardson (Great Harwood)

ALTHOUGH THERE were just four points between the teams, table-topping Newcastle came into this game as clear favourites. After all, they had dropped only one point at home so far this season. But Bill McGarry had injury worries. Mick Martin was a long term absentee (and would be out for the rest of the season) and, even worse, Peter Withe was a doubtful starter. He had missed the last couple of games with a badly gashed shin that had required six stitches and four days in hospital. But he emphasised his determination to play against Sunderland when he said, "Even if I have to turn out on crutches, I will try and play". He had to have a late fitness test before he did eventually return to lead the United attack in front of the biggest English crowd of the day.

The Newcastle players spent New Year's Eve in an hotel to facilitate team bonding. The more cynical supporters thought that this was more to ensure that they did not overdo their new year celebrations.

Sunderland boss Ken Knighton's main doubt was Stan Cummins. He had missed their last game, a first away win of the season (at Fulham), due to a recurring knee injury that he had originally sustained at the beginning of December. But he also recovered to take his place in the side, displacing Gary Rowell who had enjoyed his finest hour with a hat-trick at St James' Park just over ten months earlier. This time he had to be satisfied with the substitute's shirt.

League Positions

		Pos	Pl	Pts		Pos	Pl	Pts
Before:	Newcastle	1st	23	31	Sunderland	5th	23	27
After:	Newcastle	1st	24	33	Sunderland	6th	24	27

A tricky playing surface caused problems but it seemed (in the early stages at least) that Sunderland adapted to it better. Mick Buckley and Cummins, in particular, did not find much difficulty. But the visitors were given a warning when, despite their early superiority, Newcastle were the first to go close, Peter Cartwright cracking a 20 yard effort that flew just the wrong side of an upright.

It was Sunderland who took the lead after 25 minutes when a long clearance by goalkeeper Chris Turner was carried upfield into the Newcastle penalty area by the strong wind. The bounce beat Brownlie and Cummins was alert enough to dart in and shoot past Hardwick, the ball going in off the inside of the near post.

Sunderland turned the screw and Newcastle were lucky not to concede further goals in the following five minutes. First Jeff Clarke rose well to meet a Kevin Arnott free kick only to steer his header past a post. Then Cummins stole in to try another shot at goal but saw his effort deflected for a corner. This was soon followed by a horrendous miss by Pop Robson who somehow volleyed over when he had the goal at his mercy. The Rokermen were to rue those misses.

It was Peter Cartwright, who had endeared himself to Newcastle fans when he had scored after coming on as substitute at Roker in the League Cup back in August, who put United back in the game after 38 minutes. He picked up an attempted clearance from Clarke and chipped in a shot from 20 yards that completely bamboozled Turner and squeezed just inside a post.

Boosted by this goal, Newcastle took over. With Cartwright's energetic running stretching the Wearsiders' defence and Withe's belligerence unsettling them, Sunderland were forced back. Terry Hibbitt went closest to scoring when, just before half-time, he thudded in a free kick that Chris Turner, at full stretch, just managed to turn around a post.

Newcastle very nearly grabbed the lead in the first minute of the second half but Tommy Cassidy failed to punish a slip by Shaun Elliott. However a piece of magic by United's Northern Ireland midfield maestro soon turned the tables decisively in their favour.

After 56 minutes Claudio Marangoni headed out a cross by the hard working Hibbitt but merely sent the ball 25 yards to where Cassidy was waiting. He was coolness personified as he chested it down before smashing in a rocket of a shot that gave Turner no chance. This was a First Division goal in everything but name.

Sunderland were shocked at the quality of the strike. But shock turned to despair when United increased their lead two minutes later.

An inexplicable handball by Elliott as he challenged Billy Rafferty for a high ball inside the penalty area saw referee David Richardson point to the spot. Up stepped Alan Shoulder to take it and his kick was perfection – just inside the diving Turner's right hand post.

In desperation, Ken Knighton sent on Rowell for Robson midway through the half but, by now, some of his players were disheartened and had virtually given up – an unforgivable sin in a local derby. Newcastle's class shone through and Shoulder almost made it 4-1 in the closing minutes when he stole in on the blind side but had to watch as Turner deflected his shot around a post.

At the final whistle, Withe saluted the Newcastle crowd with exhausted delight. He knew what the game had meant to them.

Derby defeats hurt. But Ken Knighton was not disheartened. "It was a magnificent game, a credit to both teams and to football in general. There's no way that we're out of the promotion race", he claimed. Bill McGarry agreed with him, "Overall, it was superb entertainment, a tremendous game – and no-one should rule Sunderland out". He never spoke a truer word.

He should have been more concerned about his own team because, incredibly, table topping Newcastle were to win only two of their last 18 league games and were to plummet down the league. Sunderland, on the other hand, lost just one of theirs and were to power their way towards promotion.

Football League
Division 2
Sunderland 1 Newcastle United 0 (HT: 0-0)
5th April 1980
Roker Park
41,752

Sunderland: C Turner, S Whitworth*, J Hinnigan*, J Clarke, R Hindmarch, S Elliott*, K Arnott, G Rowell, A Brown, B Robson, S Cummins [73]. Sub (unused) B Dunn
Newcastle: S Hardwick, S Carney, I Davies*, T Cassidy*, S Boam, D Barton, A Shoulder, P Cartwright (N Walker 77), P Withe, T Hibbitt, R Shinton
Referee: Ken Walmsley (Blackpool)

THIS WAS an all-ticket match and Newcastle were allocated 8,000 at £1.30 each. Although they were above Sunderland in the league, the Wearsiders felt supremely confident. After all, they were undefeated at home in the league this season and United had chalked up just two wins out of 18 away league games (and the last of those was in November). On top of that, the Rokermen were only a point behind the Magpies and had two games in hand.

Incredibly, Ken Knighton named a squad of 20 players for this match (to show the strength in depth at Roker Park). Gary Rowell made a timely return to the starting line-up replacing £320,000 signing Claudio Marangoni. Gary had come off the bench to replace the Argentinian in the recent win away to Notts County.

Injury problems did not help Newcastle's confidence. Both John Brownlie (ankle) and John Bird (groin) had been injured and had struggled in the recent home draw with Notts County so Steve Carney and David Barton were drafted into the side. With games running out, Bill McGarry realised that this game was almost make or break.

League Positions

		Pos	Pl	Pts		Pos	Pl	Pts
Before:	Newcastle	5th	36	42	Sunderland	7th	34	41
After:	Sunderland	5th	35	43	Newcastle	7th	37	42

Newcastle looked the more settled side right from the kick-off with Tommy Cassidy's composure standing out in a tense midfield battle. He received good backing from Peter Cartwright whose non-stop running was a feature of the game. Their passing was more accurate than the home side's although the Wearsiders forced more corners in the first half. One of these caused a real panic in the visitors' penalty area as the Magpies' defence struggled to scramble the ball away. But most of the action was at the other end where Sunderland's back four had to graft hard to keep United at bay. Young sweeper Rob Hindmarch was their most impressive performer.

The game was so competitive in midfield that some 27 minutes elapsed before the first shot on target. This was soon followed by a piece of sublime skill by Cassidy that saw him go past three defenders before chipping a shot over Chris Turner but just clearing the bar. United continued to dominate with Cartwright volleying just wide and an Alan Shoulder header bringing a fine save out of Turner.

But Sunderland showed that they were still a force to be reckoned with when Kevin Arnott force a full stretch save out of Steve Hardwick with a delightful 20 yard free kick. As the half-time whistle was blown, there was a feeling that Newcastle would regret not turning their first half superiority into goals.

The second half was much more even with Sunderland showing up more as an attacking force. It took a goal line headed clearance by Stuart Boam direct from an Arnott corner on the hour mark to keep them out. Cassidy and Boam missed from good openings before a run by Stan Cummins down the left saw Pop Robson test Hardwick with a neat flick. A goal had to come and, when it did, it was Sunderland who scored it after 73 minutes.

It seemed as if Newcastle had repelled the attack but Steve Whitworth knocked the ball wide to Arnott on the right. He had time to spare to pick his spot with a right foot cross that beat both Hardwick and Robson, who was right in front of goal. Fortunately for him, Cummins half anticipated the miss and slid in at the back post to force the ball home.

Newcastle desperately went for the equaliser with substitute Nigel Walker replacing Cartwright in the last quarter of an hour. They pressed in the closing stages but Sunderland held firm to collect both points.

This was Sunderland's first league win over Newcastle at Roker since 1967 and they could not have produced it at a more crucial time. Not only did they go above Newcastle in the league but they were now just three points behind the top two sides (Birmingham City and Chelsea) with one and two games in hand over them respectively. They were also only one point behind third placed Luton Town (with a game in hand over them as well) so, with the top three going up, the Rokermen found themselves in an excellent chance of promotion. Ken Knighton declared himself to be delighted but admitted that it had been a poor match.

Bill McGarry was naturally far from happy, declaring that the result "was a travesty of justice… we were a different class". Perhaps he was overstating things but there was a degree of truth in what he was saying. Newcastle had managed 11 efforts on goal (compared to Sunderland's eight) but had managed just two of them on target (Sunderland four). A draw would have been a fairer result. The Wearsiders had an additional cause for celebration. – the match had brought in record ground receipts. But the celebrations really started a month later when they clinched promotion, finishing second to Leicester City.

Player of the Decade
1970s

Bryan Stanley Robson

BRYAN 'POP' ROBSON was the lad from Sunderland who learned his trade and made his name at Newcastle before eventually returning to play for his home town team not once, not twice but three times and then to return later again as a coach and even, briefly, as acting manager. He was an itinerant player who always seemed to be drawn back to the North East and to Sunderland in particular.

Sunderland were always his team as a boy. This is not surprising considering he was born, Bryan Stanley Robson, right next door to Roker Park in Westburn Terrace in 1945. His first football jersey was red and white and as a youngster he used to collect avidly the Sunderland players' autographs.

Even when his family moved away from Sunderland to Prudhoe on the banks of the Tyne, the Wearsiders remained his first love. But it was Newcastle who first picked him up, spotting him playing for a local team, Clara Vale. It was at the beginning of the 1962-63 season that 'Pop' (as he had always been known since boyhood) became a fledgling Magpie.

Only 16 years old when he joined United, he played as an amateur until he was 17 and was able to sign professional forms. He followed the time-honoured route through the ranks although he soon had an early run out with the reserves. Naturally he scored on his Central League debut in a 3-0 win over Blackburn Rovers Reserves.

His first season at St James', however, was mainly spent playing for the junior side in the Northern Intermediate League or the 'A' team in the Northern Alliance. It was not until the following year (1963-64) that he earned himself a regular place with the second team and it was the season after that before he made his league debut for the first team. He was still just 18 when he turned out at Charlton and scored the only goal of the game in a 1-0 Newcastle win.

He played on the right wing at the time and became an important member of the first team squad that year, making 20 appearances and scoring seven valuable goals as United stormed to the Second Division title. Pop was the youngest member of the team.

He had a similar campaign in the first season back in the First Division (23 league appearances and nine goals). Although he became a first team regular during the 1966-67 campaign (37 league appearances although only ten goals), by the following year he was back to being a fringe player with just 12 league starts. His career was stagnating if not going backwards. Part of the problem was that Pop was also a very good golfer with a handicap in low single figures. He won the Professional Footballers' Golf Championship with a record score of 70 and even thought about becoming a full time professional golfer.

Joe Harvey, his manager at Newcastle, advised him to give up golf if he wanted to make the grade at the top level in football. But it was his future father-in-law Len Heppell, a former ballroom dancing champion, who took him aside and taught him the importance of balance in any sport. Cutting back on his golf and taking on board the advice given him, Pop trained throughout the summer of 1968 and his improvement when the players reported for duty was there for all to see.

Switching to inside forward and playing as a twin striker alongside Wyn Davies, Pop looked a different player. United took Europe by storm, winning the Inter Cities Fairs' Cup (the forerunner of the UEFA Cup) at the first time of asking despite a so-called back door entry.

Pop scored 21 league goals that season plus three in domestic cup tournaments, but it was his half dozen in Europe that stick in the memory almost 40 years after the matches. Spectacular strikes against Sporting Lisbon and Real Zaragoza were particular gems.

By now Pop had been capped three times at Under-23 level and a step up to full international status was the logical progression. But it never came despite his 25 goals during the following year.

It was during the 1970-71 season that things began to go wrong for him at Newcastle. A third successive campaign in Europe ended somewhat ignominiously with elimination via a penalty shoot-out at the hands of Hungarian minnows Pecsi Dozsa. Deeply disappointed, Joe Harvey was quick to criticise some of his players – among them Robson.

Within days, Pop rocked Newcastle by calling a press conference in the city and publicly claiming that he was being unfairly victimised and that he was unhappy at St James'. Worse still as far as the club was concerned, he condemned the set-up at Gallowgate as "unprofessional".

His action seemed out of character for someone who was regarded as the quiet man at the club. Both Harvey and club chairman Lord Westwood expressed disappointment that he had not raised his grievances with them first. The more cynical supporters pointed out that his contract would expire at the end of the current season and his action was tantamount to demanding a transfer without actually submitting a request for one. Had he done so, he would have had to forego his percentage of any transfer fee.

Initially it seemed that life was going to continue as normal with Harvey continuing to play him in his first team. But the die had been cast and he was transferred to West Ham (without formally requesting a transfer) three months later for a fee of £120,000. He signed off for Newcastle the same way that he had started, by scoring the only goal of the match (against Spurs) in a 1-0 win.

Pop plied his wares at the Boleyn Ground for three seasons and the goals continued to flow. During the 1972-73 season he netted 28 times to finish as the top scorer in the Football League. But still his avowed aim of international recognition failed to materialise.

In the summer of 1974 he was on the move again and this time he joined the club that he had always dreamed of playing for – Sunderland. They splashed out £145,000 to bring him to Roker Park and it was to be money well spent. Joining up again with his old Newcastle skipper Bobby Moncur, Pop spearheaded the Rokerites' attack as they mounted a concerted campaign to return to the First Division.

Narrow failure in 1975 (fourth place) was rectified in the following year when the Second Division Championship was won, Sunderland finishing three points clear at the top of the league. Pop was top scorer in both seasons with 21 and 15 goals respectively (although, with cup goals included, Mel Holden tied with Pop in the latter season).

But he was soon on his way again, ironically back to West Ham who needed a proven goalscorer to help them fend off the threat of relegation. Sunderland were bottom of the league and the Hammers second bottom when he left in October. Manager Bob Stokoe had to raise funds to finance his team rebuilding programme but it seemed strange to sell your top scorer when you are struggling.

In the event, Pop's 14 goals at Upton Park kept the Hammers up, finishing two points ahead of relegated Sunderland.

By 1979, Pop was 33. But, although his sharpness was not quite what it was in days of yore, he still had a natural goalscorer's touch although he often played in midfield. He was once again seen as the man to shoot Sunderland to promotion and returned to Roker that summer. Yet again, he did not disappoint. His 20 league goals in 1979-80 saw him again finish as top scorer as the Red'n Whites once again fought their way into the top flight, this time finishing as runners-up to Leicester City.

But 1980-81 was a bad year for the veteran. For the first time since he was a youngster he found that he was no longer an automatic first team choice. He made as many appearances as substitute as he did in the starting line-up and at the start of March he was on his way again, this time to Carlisle. Another sojourn in London (with Chelsea) followed as well as a loan spell back at Brunton Park.

By now he was a player-coach. But there was to be yet another return to Sunderland. He came back to Roker for the 1983-84 season, this time on a free transfer and was still good enough to make a few appearances in the First Division for his home town team in his 38th year.

He went back to Carlisle at the end of that season to take up a post as assistant manager and, briefly, as manager before returning to Tyneside in non-league football.

His playing days now over, he stayed in the game in minor managerial posts as well as scouting and coaching. Not unexpectedly, these included yet another return to Sunderland in the mid-1990s.

It is a travesty that Pop did not receive greater international recognition than he did. He was able to score goals at every level he played – and to score plenty of them as well – 265 to be precise. A mere three Under-23 caps and a Football League XI appearance were scant rewards for a striker with his natural scoring prowess.

Record

Newcastle	August 1962 (pro November 1962) – February 1971	
Football League	205 (1 sub) apps	82 gls
FA Cup	10 apps	4 gls
Football League Cup	4 apps	2 gls
Europe	24 apps	9 gls
Total	243 (1 sub) apps	97 gls

Sunderland	June 1974 – October 1976	
	June 1979 – March 1981	
	July 1983 – July 1984	
Football League	146 (8 sub) apps	60 gls
FA Cup	8 apps	4 gls
Football League Cup	10 (2 sub) apps	3 gls
Other	8 apps	1 gl
Total	172 (10 sub) apps	68 gls

Most Successful Players - Performance Percentages (Top 20)

The obvious way to measure success is to base it on results. The following performance percentages are calculated on the basis of full marks for a win, half for a draw and none for a defeat. Players who turned out in only a few derbies will have an advantage in obtaining a high percentage. Therefore a minimum number of six games (including substitute appearance) are needed to qualify.

Newcastle United					Sunderland			
Pos	Player	Played	%		Pos	Player	Played	%
1	L Clark	6	91.67		1	E Rhodes	6	66.67
2	S Ameobi	6	83.33		2	J W Farquhar	10	65.00
3	S Given	8	75.00			A McCombie	10	65.00
4	R Simpson	11	72.73		4	W Fraser	7	64.29
5	G Robledo	7	71.43		5	G Herd	11	63.64
6	R Batty	10	70.00		6	Sh Elliott	8	62.50
	R Davies	10	70.00			J Gemmell	12	62.50
8	A Shearer	11	68.18			L R Roose	8	62.50
9	J Finlay	6	66.67		9	C Irwin	9	61.11
	A Hughes	6	66.67		10	J Watson	14	60.71
	C Spencer	6	66.67		11	W Hogg	22	59.09
	S Weaver	6	66.67			R Jackson	11	59.09
	N Solano	9	66.67			A Milton	11	59.09
14	T Casey	7	64.29		14	R Hogg	6	58.33
	J Harvey	7	64.29			A McAllister	12	58.33
	R Lee	7	64.29			J Mordue	18	58.33
17	F Brennan	12	62.50			K Phillips	6	58.33
	K Scott	8	62.50			J Richardson	6	58.33
19	A Higgins	9	61.11			B Siddall	6	58.33
	T Walker	9	61.11		20	J Clarke	7	57.14
						G Rowell	7	57.14

CHAPTER 10

1980s
Fluctuating Fortunes

WAS THERE ever a decade that illustrated the fluctuating fortunes of football teams than the 1980s as far as Newcastle and Sunderland were concerned? United started and ended it in the Second Division but enjoyed a few years in the top flight in between and also revelled in the cavalier days of Kevin Keegan (as a player) on Tyneside.

But if the Magpies rejoiced/endured the vagaries of fortunes, what about the Rokermen? They began the decade by lording it in the First Division but were hardly in a position to gloat over their neighbours as they never really looked comfortable there and never managed a top half finish. Even worse, they suffered the indignity of relegation to the Second Division and the Third before rising, Phoenix-like, from the ashes to achieve the ultimate reward – promotion to back to the top at the expense of the Geordies. And at St James' Park as well!

Yet the 1980s started so mundanely with Newcastle just squeezing into a top half finish in the Second Division followed by a slight improvement in 1981-82 before the club shocked the whole football world with an audacious (and for many fans unbelievable) signing of England captain Kevin Keegan.

To many, he signed away his international career when the joined United in the Second Division but in return he was idolised on Tyneside as he led his team of entertainers back to the elite during two years of flair and fantasy football. Alongside the emerging talents of Chris Waddle and Peter Beardsley, KK filled grounds all over the country. Admittedly, Newcastle gained promotion only at the second time of asking in 1984 (and in third place at that) but it was a wonderful time for Geordie supporters. They knew, however, that when King Kevin flew away in a helicopter from St James' Park that it was an end of an era.

Sunderland had to look on in envy as media attention focused on the ground 12 miles up the road. Yet it was they who were in the First Division although, admittedly, they were hardly setting the world alight there. They even finished just one place and two points above relegation in '82.

They changed managers regularly to try and find a winning formula as Ken Knighton, Alan Durban and Len Ashurst all had stints in the hot seat (as well as a couple of short term/caretaker appointments in Mick Docherty and Pop Robson) but all to no avail. Their crowds declined while Newcastle's increased.

At the start of the decade, Sunderland's attendances (at well over 26,000) were well above Newcastle's (over 17,000) but once Keegan arrived at St James', crowd levels changed dramatically. His arrival meant an average increase at the gate of 7,000 in his first year with an additional 5,000 in his second (promotion) year. At Roker the reverse happened. Indeed, by the time Newcastle were promoted, the Wearside gates were just above the 16,000 mark despite the attraction of First Division football.

They had high hopes that the appointment of Lawrie McMenemy in 1985 would change matters. It did – for the worse! Eventually the legendary Bob Stokoe was brought back (too late!) as temporary manager in 1987 to try and salvage things as Sunderland finished third bottom of the Second Division and subjected their fans to the traumatic torture of the play-offs. Crowds at Roker had plunged to an average of 13,600 by this time but a semi-final second leg game against Gillingham attracted a healthy attendance 25,470 although this figure included more than a few Mags supporters who were backing the Gills. It was they who went home happy with a 4-3 Sunderland win condemning the Wearsiders to the Third Division for the first time on the away goals rule.

On Tyneside, Newcastle had failed to build on the feel-good factor left by Keegan. Manager Arthur Cox left straight after him and big Jack Charlton took over. Gradually, however, the stars left with Waddle and Beardsley eventually departing for pastures new as United's barren years (in terms of winning a trophy) continued. The emerging talent of the precocious Paul Gascoigne briefly gave hope for the future. He blossomed after former goalkeeper Willie McFaul took over the hot seat from big Jack but did not stay long, heading for the bright lights of London like Waddler before him.

Remarkably Newcastle's crowds remained healthy. Not unnaturally, they fell away following the heady days of Keegan but they remained well above 20,000 despite relegation to the Second Division in 1989. Meanwhile, Sunderland, under the guidance of Denis Smith, soon put the nightmare of the Third Division behind them by winning the title in their one and only season there.

With the rivals spending just two seasons together in the same division throughout the whole decade, Tyne-Wear derbies were few and far between. So when the clubs did meet, the clashes meant much more than normal. None more so than their meetings at the end of the 1989-90 season when the potential prize was so high – possible promotion to the First Division.

The meetings were the semi-finals of the Second Division play-offs. The fact that Newcastle, under manager Jim Smith, had finished third in the league and Sunderland sixth counted for nothing in a couple of highly charged meetings. The first, at Roker, ended goalless amid much controversy with Sunderland's Paul Hardyman sent off in the closing minutes. But the return leg at St James' reached the zenith in terms of passion, tension and incident as Sunderland merged victorious by virtue of a deserved 2-0 win. It also plunged the depths in terms of sportsmanship as a crowd of mindless morons among the Magpie fans tried to cause a riot.

Sunderland went on to lose to Swindon Town in the play-off finals at Wembley but, with even more controversy, managed to gain promotion after the Robins were found guilty of financial misdemeanours and demoted without even kicking a ball in the top flight.

So the decade ended in the way it had started, with Sunderland in the First Division and Newcastle in the Second. But both Tyneside and Wearside knew that such a situation could be transitory and that things could change very quickly. The 1980s had shown that.

League Meetings (including play-offs) (6)
At Newcastle: Newcastle – won 1 drew 1 lost 1
At Sunderland: Sunderland – won 0 drew 3 lost 0

Penalty Failures (excluding penalty shoot-outs)

Newcastle (8)	Sunderland (9)
24 Dec 1904 – Appleyard (shot wide)	10 Mar 1909 – Brown (Lawrence saved)
20 Mar 1907 – McCracken (shot wide)	10 Apr 1909 – Holley (Lawrence saved*)
25 Dec 1914 – Hudspeth (shot wide)	13 Sep 1913 – Low (Lawrence saved)
5 Nov 1927 – McDonald (shot wide)	26 Dec 1913 – Mordue (Mellor saved)
9 Apr 1932 – McKenzie (shot over)	26 Dec 1914 – Best (shot wide)
3 Mar 1934 – Weaver (hit bar)	9 Oct 1920 – Hobson (Lawrence saved)
1 Jan 1985 – Beardsley (Turner saved)	22 Aug 1953 – Ford (Simpson saved)
18 Nov 2000 – Shearer (Sorensen saved)	2 Mar 1963 – Anderson (Hollins saved)
	13 May 1990 – Hardyman (Burridge saved)

*Although Lawrence saved the penalty, blocking the shot, Holley followed up and netted the loose ball. But as this goal was not scored directly from the penalty kick it is recorded as a 'save'.

Football League
Division 1
Newcastle United 3 Sunderland 1 (HT: 1-0)
1st January 1985
St James' Park
36,821

Newcastle: K Carr, M Brown, W Saunders*, P Heard, J Anderson, J Clarke, G Megson, K Wharton, I Baird*, P Beardsley [**15, 48** (pen), **80**], N McDonald.
Sub (unused) S Carney
Sunderland: C Turner, B Venison, N Pickering, P Daniel, G Bennett #(87), S Berry*, H Gayle** #(48), D Hodgson*, C West* [**71**], M Proctor (J Cooke 82), C Walker
Referee: David Scott (Burnley)

NEW YEAR'S Day brought a crucial clash of the old rivals. Both sides were struggling in the league on the same number of points and were undergoing bad runs. Newcastle had picked up just one point out of their last five matches and had to take the field minus star forward, Chris Waddle, who missed his first game of the season with a hamstring injury. Glenn Roeder and David Mc-Creery were also absentees due to injury.

Sunderland's run was not much better with five defeats in their last six league games. They were missing Shaun Elliott and Gordon Chisholm but were at least able to welcome back speed merchant (and former Newcastle player) Howard Gayle after a two match absence due to a stomach injury.

League Positions		Pos	Pl	Pts		Pos	Pl	Pts
Before:	Sunderland	15th	22	26	Newcastle	18th	22	26
After:	Newcastle	17th	23	28	Sunderland	18th	23	26

A frenetic opening was littered with reckless tackles on the sleet-lashed playing surface and these helped to inflame the vociferous passions on the terraces. But among all the mayhem Peter Beardsley kept his head and it was he who scored the opener after quarter of an hour. A corner by Pat Heard was half cleared by Gary Bennett but only as far as Beardsley. As the Sunderland defence raced out to try and catch Ian Baird offside, the Newcastle No 10 decided to try a shot for goal and slotted it low through the narrowest of gaps at Chris Turner's right.

The rest of the first half was fairly even with a Kevin Carr save from Steve Berry and a Gary Megson shot blocked by Peter Daniel being the best efforts for each side.

The game was effectively decided after just three minutes of the second half in Newcastle's first meaningful attack of the session. A rash challenge by Gayle on Wes Saunders as he raced into the Sunderland penalty area chasing a ball from Baird saw the referee point to the penalty spot. The visiting winger received his marching orders when he was booked for a second time in the match for losing his temper and arguing too long over the award. Beardsley stepped up to take the kick and calmly sent Turner the wrong way from the spot.

Peter had a great chance to complete his hat-trick when Newcastle were awarded a second penalty kick just before the hour. This was awarded when Daniel brought down United's stand-in skipper Kenny Wharton. Up stepped Beardsley again but this time Turner guessed right with his dive and saved the kick.

Newcastle failed to take full advantage of their numerical superiority and Sunderland matched them all of the way although the visitors clocked up a series of bookings with their over-committed play as they did so.

The Wearsiders came storming back into the game after 71 minutes with a goal of genuine class. Colin West took the ball off Dave Hodgson's toes following a corner from Clive Walker but was forced away from the Newcastle goal. Suddenly he whipped around and chipped a perfect shot over the surprised Carr into the Newcastle net.

But Beardsley completed his hat-trick ten minutes from time. Daniel lost the ball on the edge of his area and Megson pounced to play Peter clean through on goal. He was calmness personified as he drilled the ball low past the exposed Turner.

There was still a final sting in the tail as passions boiled over both on the pitch and on the terraces. Sunderland finished the game with just nine men after Bennett was sent off following a bad challenge on Saunders near the end.

Discipline was becoming a problem for Sunderland. They had now had six men sent off so far this season as well as a glut of bookings. These would naturally lead to suspensions that they could ill afford. However, manager Len Ashurst insisted that they were not a dirty side, merely competitive. Former Sunderland defender Jackie Ashurst summed up the passion in a Newcastle v Sunderland derby perfectly when he said, "World War III could start during a Tyne-Wear derby match and fans wouldn't be interested".

The win gave Newcastle confidence and they slowly began to climb the league. Defeat for Sunderland meant that they were just four points clear of a relegation spot. A struggle for survival beckoned.

Football League
Division 1
Sunderland 0 Newcastle United 0 (HT: 0-0)
8th April 1985
Roker Park
28,246

Sunderland: C Turner, B Venison, N Pickering, G Bennett*, G Chisholm, S Elliott, P Lemon, I Wallace, J Moore, S Berry, C Walker. Sub (unused) S Cummins
Newcastle: M Thomas, M Brown, J Anderson, D McCreery*, J Clarke, G Roeder, N McDonald, A Cunningham, G Reilly*, P Beardsley, P Heard.
Sub (unused) P Gascoigne
Referee: Keith Hackett (Sheffield)

SUNDERLAND HAD lost all three league games since facing Norwich City in the Milk Cup Final at Wembley and came into this game on the precipice of relegation. Their situation was not helped by an ongoing injury crisis with Dave Hodgson (groin strain) and Reuben Agboola (knee ligaments) both missing from this game and Mark Proctor out for the rest of the season.

Newcastle had just beaten West Bromwich Albion to ease their relegation fears. They were missing Chris Waddle with a knee injury. It was well known that he was going to join Tottenham at the end of the season so his departure meant that he never faced Sunderland, the club he had supported as a boy, while playing for Newcastle. Gary Megson (thigh injury) was also ruled out for them which meant that young Paul Gascoigne was named as a first team substitute for the first time.

League Positions		Pos	Pl	Pts		Pos	Pl	Pts
Before:	Newcastle	15th	34	41	Sunderland	18th	33	34
After:	Newcastle	15th	35	42	Sunderland	20th	34	35

A hostile atmosphere pervaded Roker Park with early trouble between rival factions of supporters at the Fulwell End. The game itself left little for the purist or non-committed supporter to enthuse over. Both sides were clearly apprehensive over their First Division survival. Newcastle, playing in rather drab all grey strips, were clearly the better team in the first half but they had little penetration up front where both Tony Cunningham and George Reilly caused problems but lacked the killer touch. Chris Turner was in top form for Sunderland and pulled off two top drawer saves from Pat Heard and Cunningham in the opening half.

Sunderland showed up briefly as an attacking force in the first few minutes of the second half. But they were obviously lacking confidence and soon Newcastle were back on top although they were unable to break through. Turner again performed heroics to keep the scoresheet blank. One save in particular was magnificent. He somehow climbed to claw away a soaring header that came off Gordon Chisholm's head when the defender began to buckle under aerial pressure. Peter Beardsley tormented the Roker defence, setting up a series of scoring chances, mainly for Cunningham, all of which went a-begging. Jeff Clarke and Glenn Roeder were resolute at the heart of the visitors' defence and made it an arduous 90 minutes for the Wearside attack.

The draw was a much better result for Newcastle than Sunderland. In fact, with fellow strugglers Luton and Ipswich both winning, the Wearsiders slipped into a relegation position (bottom three) for the first time this season. They had just eight games to go and the future looked bleak. Sadly, they were to win only one of these matches and were to be relegated in 21st place, ten points adrift of safety.

Newcastle survived, finishing in a relatively comfortable 14th position.

Football League
Division 2
Sunderland 0 Newcastle United 0 (HT: 0-0)
24th September 1989
Roker Park
29,499

Sunderland: T Carter, R Agboola, P Hardyman, G Bennett, J MacPhail, G Owers, P Bracewell, G Armstrong, E Gates, M Gabbiadini, C Pascoe.
Subs (unused) 12 A Cullen, 14 T Hauser
Newcastle: G Kelly, J Anderson, M Stimson, K Dillon, K Scott, A Thorn*, J Gallacher (12 G Brazil 78), K Brock, M Quinn*, M McGhee, B Kristensen.
Sub (unused) 14 R Ranson
Referee: Roger Dilkes (Mossley)

THIS WAS the first Tyne-Wear derby (or Wear-Tyne as it was now more correctly known) for more than four years and the police, fearing public disorder, decreed that the game should be switched to a Sunday with a noon kick-off. This upset Newcastle manager Jim Smith who complained, "If Manchester United v Manchester City and Liverpool v Everton can play on a Saturday, then surely Sunderland v Newcastle can".

He had hoped to have signed goalkeeper John Burridge from Southampton in time for the derby game but called off the deal (at least temporarily) after it was leaked to the press. A 3-1 defeat away to Third Division Reading in a Littlewoods Cup tie (first leg) had left him far from happy with his team. He dropped Ray Ranson and replaced him with John Anderson but delayed his team selection until 45 minutes before the kick-off in the hope that Wayne Fereday would recover from a groin injury. However the former QPR man failed a late fitness test and Bjorn Kristensen was drafted into the side.

Sunderland manager Denis Smith fielded an unchanged side from his last couple of league games although since then Sunderland had played a Littlewoods Cup tie against Fulham. Paul Bracewell, who had returned to Roker on loan from Everton, had not been allowed to play in that game because the Toffees did not want him cup-tied. He came back into the side in place of John Cornforth as did Marco Gabbiadini who took over from Thomas Hauser in attack.

League Positions		Pos	Pl	Pts		Pos	Pl	Pts
Before:	Sunderland	6th	6	11	Newcastle	10th	6	10
After:	Sunderland	4th	7	12	Newcastle	7th	7	11

The height of Newcastle's ambition in this game seemed to be to get a draw. They fielded an unusual 4-1-3-2 formation with Kristensen operating just in front of the back four. Their approach stifled attacking football and it soon became a matter of whether Sunderland had enough guile and penetration to break them down.

Bracewell provided the former and was the main inspiration in midfield for the Rokermen while Kevin Brock made an increasing contribution to Newcastle's midfield battle. The much-anticipated confrontation between rival strikers Marco Gabbiadini and Micky Quinn just did not materialise with scoring chances kept to a minimum by two resolute rearguards. The Wearsiders did most of the running and enjoyed plenty of possession but rarely looked like scoring.

Their best chance came midway through the first half when Mark Stimson slipped and allowed Colin Pascoe a clear shot. He put his effort over the top. In fact, the closest to a goal in this half was at the other end just before the interval when Mark McGhee cracked in a searing right foot shot that stand-in 'keeper Tim Carter did well to block.

It was more of the same in the second half. Sunderland once again had territorial advantage but, conversely, Newcastle created the better openings – at least what there were of them! Carter again distinguished himself with a fine save from McGhee. Gary Kelly, on the other hand, was hardly tested in the Newcastle goal.

However he did have a touch of good fortune when he missed a Gordon Armstrong corner and Stimson cleared off the line, the referee dismissing Sunderland claims that the full back had used his hand. The final chance fell five minutes from time when Quinn managed a close range header only to see the ball hit Carter's body and rebound to safety.

A goalless draw had always looked on the cards and that is how it finished. Newcastle were obviously happier with the draw than Sunderland. In fact, encouraged by this result, they went on to win five of their next six league games and climbed to second in the table.

Sunderland were also to embark on a decent run of results, winning five of their next eight league games – not as good a sequence as Newcastle but the league campaign was a marathon not a sprint and there was a lot of football to be played yet.

Football League
Division 2
Newcastle United 1 Sunderland 1 (HT: 0-0)
4th February 1990
St James' Park
31,572

Newcastle: J Burridge, D Bradshaw, M Stimson, R Aitken, K Scott, B Kristensen (14 J Anderson 62), J Gallacher, K Dillon, M Quinn*, M McGhee [**77**], P Sweeney (12 K Brock 69)
Sunderland: A Norman, J Kay, P Hardyman*, R Agboola, J MacPhail, G Owers*, P Bracewell, G Armstrong (14 A Cullen 76), E Gates, M Gabbiadini [**49**], B Atkinson. Sub (unused) 12 T Hauser
Referee: Jim Ashworth (Luffenham, Leicestershire)

THERE WAS nothing between the teams when they met for this critical promotion fixture. Sunderland were ahead in the league, but only just – and they had started to look a bit jaded. They had not won a game since Boxing Day and manager Denis Smith had given them a complete rest from training during a break in Blackpool. It seemed to do the trick with them returning totally refreshed. However, they had selection problems. Captain Gary Bennett was out through suspension and there were doubts about John MacPhail and Richard Ord; McPhail was to make it but Ord missed out. Welsh international goalkeeper Tony Norman was recalled and took over from Tim Carter between the posts.

For once, the local derby was not uppermost on supporters' minds on Tyneside. Cup fever was building up with the Magpies due to meet Manchester United in the Fifth Round of the FA Cup two weeks hence. They also had injury problems. Ray Ranson was ruled out with a groin injury and both Roy Aitken (hamstring) and Kevin Brock (knee) were doubtful. John Anderson was an obvious replacement for Ranson but he had broken his wrist and had to wear a plaster.

Much depended upon whether the referee would allow him to play with his plaster on. In the event, Aitken was deemed fit enough to start the game and Brock and Anderson were named as substitutes. Darren Bradshaw was drafted into the starting line-up at right back in place of Ranson.

League Positions

		Pos	Pl	Pts		Pos	Pl	Pts
Before:	Sunderland	5th	27	43	Newcastle	6th	26	41
After:	Sunderland	5th	28	44	Newcastle	6th	27	42

The weather was awful – a howling gale that swirled the length of the pitch. It made good football almost impossible. Yet blue-shirted Sunderland, playing with whole-hearted endeavour and aggression laced with an astute short-passing style, adapted to it well. They made it clear that, aided by the wind in the first half, they were prepared to shoot on sight and an early dipping volley by Paul Bracewell tested the diving John Burridge to the full. The fact that a linesman's flag was raised was immaterial. The effort was a warning for Newcastle.

The visitors saw much more of the ball and used it well. But they rarely threatened Burridge. They were limited to long distance shots with efforts by Paul Hardyman and Gordon Armstrong that drifted wide of their target. Newcastle managed just one decent effort in the first half, John Gallacher managing a shot at goal from a frantic scramble in the Sunderland penalty area that Tony Norman clawed away. When half-time came with the scoresheet blank, most Newcastle supporters were confident that, with the elements in their favour in the second half, their side would take control. They were to be mistaken.

The Wearsiders surprised the Gallowgate faithful by coping with facing the elements much better than Newcastle had in the first half. They adopted the simple tactic of keeping the ball on the ground and their midfield quartet of Armstrong, Bracewell, Owers and Atkinson stood out.

The opener came within four minutes when Marco Gabbiadini flicked the ball out to Eric Gates on the left and he sliced open the Tyneside rearguard with a perfect return ball that sent Gabbiadini haring past Bjorn Kristensen and Mark Stimson into the penalty area. He already had 17 goals to his credit so far this season and he made it 18 as he shot low past Burridge from eight yards. The 'keeper managed to get the slightest of touches but nowhere near enough to keep it out.

The goal gave Sunderland confidence (if they needed it) and this grew as the game progressed. Newcastle tried to push forward but they found John MacPhail and Reuben Agboola in no mood to surrender in the centre of the visitors' defence. United brought on John Anderson for the disappointing Kristensen and this improved matters slightly. Nevertheless, 20 mins of the second half had elapsed before United's ace goalscorer Mick Quinn managed his one shot of the game, an effort from 16 yards that went over the top. But Newcastle began to look increasingly dangerous as the game entered its final stages. Tony Norman twice pulled off superb saves to deny headers from Roy Aitken and Anderson and it looked as if Sunderland were going to survive. But their hopes were dashed a couple of minutes later when Newcastle finally snatched the equaliser after 77 minutes.

Paul Hardyman conceded a free kick just outside the Sunderland penalty area on the right and Kevin Brock, by now on for Paul Sweeney, floated the ball over to the far post where Mark McGhee stole in to rise unchallenged and head down into the net from inside the six yard box.

Newcastle, sensing blood, poured forward but Tony Norman, handling the ball impeccably, was rarely troubled again and Sunderland comfortably held out for a share of the points. Any worse result would have been a travesty.

If either team emerged from this game with credit, it was Sunderland. Despite being underdogs, they had demonstrated that they were at least the equals of their neighbours – if not better. Surprisingly, this result was not to have any great effect on their future performances. They were to win only one of their next five games and were to slip out of a play-off position – although all was to come good at the end.

Newcastle were to do exactly the opposite, They were to avoid defeat in their next seven league games and were to lose just three (of 19) games until the end of the league campaign to finish in third place in the league.

But it was not to be enough. Third meant involvement in the play-offs where they had to meet sixth placed Sunderland. It was all to go horribly wrong for the Geordies – much to the delight of Wearside. At least Stan Anderson, who had captained both sides with distinction in the 1960s (and was now scouting for Newcastle in Yorkshire), got it spot on when he predicted after the February encounter that both clubs would reach the play-offs.

Football League
Division 2 Play-offs Semi-final (1st Leg)
Sunderland 0 Newcastle United 0 (HT: 0-0)
13th May 1990
Roker Park
26,641

Sunderland: A Norman, J Kay, P Hardyman # (90), G Bennett, J MacPhail, G Owers*, P Bracewell, G Armstrong, E Gates, M Gabbiadini, R Agboola.
Subs (unused) 12 K Brady, 14 T Hauser
Newcastle: J Burridge, K Scott, M Stimson*, R Aitken*, J Anderson, R Ranson* (12 L O'Brien 35*), K Brock, W Askew, M Quinn*, M McGhee, B Kristensen.
Sub (unused) 14 K Dillon
Referee: Vic Callow (Solihull)

NEWCASTLE HAD finished a comfortable six points ahead of the other play-off teams, Swindon Town and Blackburn Rovers, who both had 74 points along with Sunderland. It was only the fact that Sunderland had the poorest goal difference of the three that the extra North East derbies came about at this stage.

A Sunday noon kick-off was decreed and just 4,000 tickets were allocated to Newcastle fans in a bid to minimise trouble. Arrangements were made to broadcast the game live at the Newcastle City Hall and Whitley Bay Ice Rink but, in the event, the attendance at Roker Park was disappointing. In fact, it was the lowest at Roker Park for a competitive Wear-Tyne derby since the war. Even the Texaco Cup game in 1974 had attracted a bigger crowd. This was possibly because the Rokermen were rated as 7-2 outsiders to win the play-offs with Newcastle odds on favourites. Sunderland rested their hopes on the fact that Newcastle had not won at Roker for 34 years, a total of 15 league and cup matches. Newcastle, however, could point out that eight of the last nine games there had ended as draws!

Jim Smith took his team for a relaxing break in Ireland prior to the match, returning on the Friday. Most of the fans on both sides eagerly anticipated the clash of both sides' top scorers – Marco Gabbiadini of Sunderland and Mick Quinn of Newcastle. The latter was nursing a knee injury but was in full training and was never really in doubt for the clash.

The game, strewn with a series of niggling fouls, was a poor advert for North East football. Few fans had expected a classic but this travesty of a match plunged the depths. Newcastle, playing in yellow and green, naturally adopted a defensive approach allowing Sunderland to shade the exchanges in terms of possession. They also enjoyed territorial advantage but found Kevin Scott and John Anderson solid at the heart of the Tyneside defence. Certainly they gave the astute Eric Gates and the pacey Marco Gabbiadini little scope.

Players on both sides rarely hesitated in committing reckless fouls and hurling both physical and verbal abuse at their opponents. Few men stood out among the morass of mediocrity although two exceptions were the cultured Bjorn Kristensen for Newcastle and the industrious Gordon Armstrong for Sunderland. The former even maintained his standards when he was switched to right back to replace the injured Ray Ranson after 35 minutes. There were just two real scoring chances in the first half, both created by Sunderland. First Gabbiadini blasted in an effort that just cleared the crossbar and then, two minutes before the break, only a courageous save by John Burridge denied Armstrong.

It was more of the same in the second half when Sunderland, once again, enjoyed territorial advantage. The Rokermen had a great chance to break the deadlock early in the half but Gabbiadini, normally a lethal finisher, for some reason opted to lay a pass off to Paul Hardyman when he had just the exposed Burridge to beat. Then Armstrong missed a great chance when he carelessly headed wide following a Hardyman right wing corner.

Newcastle hardly bothered Tony Norman at all until the very last minute. It was then that the game erupted. Gary Bennett saved the day when he desperately blocked a goal-bound Mark McGhee effort and the Wearside men charged up the field on a final counter-attack. They poured forward into the Newcastle penalty area where a clumsy tackle by Mark Stimson brought Gabbiadini crashing to the ground.

The United players were furious when the linesman on the Clock Stand side of the ground flagged for a penalty and referee Vic Callow pointed to the spot. All arguments duly rejected, up stepped Paul Hardyman to take the kick. His shot was well-placed but weakly hit and John Burridge guessed correctly, diving to his right to save and hold on to the ball. Hardyman lost control as he tore furiously forward to kick at the ball and struck the prostrate 'keeper instead. Pandemonium followed as players piled in either to break things up or join the fracas. At the end, referee Callow had no option but to show Hardyman a red card and end his participation in the play offs. The referee must have been delighted to blow his whistle soon afterwards. The adrenalin might have been flowing at last but for the wrong reason.

Newcastle were obviously happier with the draw than Sunderland and were confident that they could finish the job in the second leg at St James' Park four days later. The Rokermen would then, of course, be without Hardyman who was automatically suspended for the second leg. But, in truth, this had been a game to forget, memorable just for the last minute penalty and its aftermath.

The real winners on the day were the police. Their heavy presence around Roker and along the route from Seaburn Station to the ground had kept trouble to a minimum – at least outside the stadium. There had been some scuffles inside. Perimeter fencing, to keep fans from encroaching on to the playing area, had been taken down throughout the country in the wake of the Hillsborough disaster. But the fencing at Sunderland had been removed earlier as a reward for good behaviour to the fans at Roker. The absence of these barriers had allowed trouble makers to spill over on to the pitch and the police and stewards had been left with an almost impossible task to keep them at bay.

The players had to take some blame for any trouble inside the ground. Their irresponsible attitude on the pitch undoubtedly stoked the fires of rivalry on the terraces. But it was to be even worse, much worse, at St James'.

Most consecutive draws

4 games: 8 April 1985 – 13 May 1990

Football League
Division 2 Play-offs Semi-final (2nd Leg)
Newcastle United 0 Sunderland 2 (HT: 0-1)
[Aggreg: 0-2]

16th May 1990
St James' Park
32,199

Newcastle: J Burridge, K Scott, M Stimson, R Aitken, J Anderson, D Bradshaw (12 K Dillon 45), K Brock, W Askew (14 L O'Brien 77), M Quinn*, M McGhee*, B Kristensen
Sunderland: T Norman, J Kay*, R Agboola, G Bennett, J MacPhail, G Owers, P Bracewell, G Armstrong, E Gates [13], M Gabbiadini [85], W Hawke.
Subs (unused) 12 K Brady, 14 T Hauser
Referee: George Courtney (Spennymoor)

HAVING DRAWN at Roker and done what appeared to be the hard part of this two-legged play-off encounter, Newcastle were fairly confident about the home leg. Manager Jim Smith was co0nvinced that his side was the better footballing team although he needed his players to keep calm. "Cool it", he demanded.

Sunderland boss Denis Smith was equally adamant that his team would emerge victorious. He believed that in the three encounters between these traditional rivals this season, Sunderland had shown themselves to be the better team but had just failed to make their superiority count. He insisted that there would be no mistake this time.

Both sides had to make one change although it was due to different circumstances. Ray Ranson, certainly one of Newcastle's most experienced and best players, was ruled out due to injury so Darren Bradshaw was drafted into the defence. Paul Hardyman, of course, was suspended for Sunderland following his dismissal at Roker Park but Reuben Agboola dropped back to take his place in defence with youth team product Warren Hawke stepping in for only his second start of the season. The all-ticket game was virtually a sell-out but, sensing trouble, some 550 police officers were on duty. Sadly, they were to be needed.

The atmosphere was taut and intimidating – no place for the faint-hearted. There was just too much at stake. The Newcastle fans were confident and the early exchanges supported their optimism with Mark McGhee striking the outside of Tony Norman's right hand post. But Sunderland quickly subdued the home crowd by displaying determination and taking the game to Newcastle. Nevertheless, the opening goal after 13 minutes was a shock.

It came in Sunderland's first real attack. A John Kay throw-in saw Marco Gabbiadini hook the ball on for Gary Owers to chase down the right wing. He took the ball to the bye-line before crossing low and hard into the middle where Eric Gates forced it into the net from close range.

The goal gave the Wearsiders confidence. Newcastle fought hard but struggled to get on terms and their one-paced defence always looked vulnerable. Fortunately the ugliness that had permeated the first leg was missing from this encounter. At least it was missing on the pitch. Hostility on the terraces remained high. On the field, Sunderland maintained the offensive and only an excellent one-handed save by John Burridge kept out Owers after Gabbiadini had put him through. The visitors were on top for most of the first half but Newcastle at last showed up in attack as the interval approached and the visitors' goal seemed to bear a charmed life as goal-bound shots by Mick Quinn and Roy Aitken were blocked.

Newcastle replaced the out of touch Darren Bradshaw with Sunderland born Kevin Dillon at the interval but the change hardly improved matters and it took another brilliant save by Burridge to deny Gabbiadini. But one goal was never going to be enough and tension built up, both on the pitch and on the terraces, as the second half progressed. United were desperate for the equaliser while Sunderland were equally determined to hang on to their lead.

Gates stood out as the best player on the field although he received good support from his team mates who, man for man, seemed superior to the increasingly despondent Magpies. Just Kevin Brock, steady in midfield for United, seemed capable to matching the Wearsiders. Owers should have wrapped things up in the 69th minute when a mistake by Kevin Scott left the Sunderland man with the goal at his mercy only for Mark Stimson to come from nowhere with a last gasp tackle.

Quinn seemed totally out of touch up front although he had been nursing a knee injury for the last five weeks. A second Newcastle substitution, Liam O'Brien for the ineffective Billy Askew in the 77th minute, highlighted the fact that time was running out for Newcastle. Then it happened – a second Sunderland goal.

With five minutes to go Warren Hawke started the move out on the left wing, sliding the ball inside to Gabbiadini. He took it forward to play a short pass to Gates before running on into the penalty area to take a superb return ball and shoot left footed across Burridge into the far corner from 10 yards.

It was all too much for many of the Newcastle fans. They poured over the low wall surrounding the pitch and charged on to the field in fury. Referee George Courtney, who had kept perfect control throughout, managed to clear them away with the help of the club stewards and police. But the reprieve was temporary and a second pitch invasion was much more menacing as St James' became a cauldron of hate and insanity.

In 1969, Glasgow Rangers fans had stormed on to this pitch in the semi-final of the Inter Cities Fairs Cup in an attempt to have the game abandoned. A significant hooligan element among the Newcastle fans now did exactly the same. And, like Rangers, this was no minor invasion. Massed hordes poured on to the field, intent on mayhem and determined to reach the Sunderland fans housed in the Gallowgate End of the ground. To the Wearsiders' credit, they stood their ground. They had a lot more to lose by retaliating – but they were also completely outnumbered. Mr Courtney had no choice but to take the players off. It was a night of shame for Newcastle United as a thin blue line of policemen prevented the moronic masses from reaching the 'enemy'. English teams were suspended from European competition because of the thuggish behaviour of supporters. This episode merely confirmed that the ban would be extended. It took 18 minutes for the pitch to be cleared to let the teams go through the motions for the last three minutes and complete the game. Sunderland deservedly went on to the play-off finals at Wembley.

The pitch invasion dominated the headlines. The *Newcastle Journal* newspaper splashed it across its front page: "Mad Minority's Night of Shame and Violence". There had been 66 arrests with 12 police officers (and 11 spectators) injured. Newcastle chairman Gordon McKeag spoke of his club's shame at the incident as Sunderland celebrated.

This was Wearside's night and, as their supporters began their trek across the Tyne joyously singing and anticipating their trip to Wembley, misery ruled on Tyneside. Many Geordie fans left the stadium in tears, not only at the humiliation heaped on them by their fellow fans but moaning at the injustice of finishing third in the league, six points above their neighbours, yet missing out to sixth placed Sunderland. But these were now the league rules and everyone knew this before the season began.

Sunderland had now won seven of their last eight away games and manager Denis Smith was quick to point out that the play-off final at Wembley was also away from home. If he was trying to give his side a psychological edge, it didn't work because there they faced Swindon Town and were well beaten although the score was only 1-0.

But this season of controversy was not yet over. Swindon were being investigated by the Football League and were found guilty of making illegal payments under a previous administration. The unprecedented result was that they were demoted from the First to the Third Division without even kicking a ball in the top flight and Sunderland were consequently promoted.

Newcastle? They had to go back to square one in the Second Division and Tyne-Wear derbies were over for the time being.

Player of the Decade 1980s

Jeffrey Derrick Clarke

IT IS probably fair to say that few Sunderland supporters were particularly en-amoured when Jeff Clarke joined Sunderland. He was merely the makeweight in a deal that took defensive hero Dave Watson to Manchester City and not many Red'n White fans knew much about the 21-year-old who came to Roker to try and fill his boots. Watson had been the defensive lynchpin in the team that had gloriously won the Cup in 1973 and had established himself in the England team in the years that followed despite playing in the Second Division.

But by the summer of '75, he was 28 years old and needed First Division football to maintain the momentum of his international career – something Sunderland could not guarantee, missing out on promotion by a mere two points in both years since their Wembley success.

Manager Bob Stokoe had little choice but to let him go that summer, for a report-ed £175,000 fee plus City's reserve centre half Jeff Clarke. Ian McFarlane gave the former England schoolboy and youth international a glowing recommendation and Bob did not hesitate in accepting the youngster as part of the deal. It was to be a shrewd piece of business by the Roker boss.

Jeffrey Derrick Clarke was a Yorkshireman, born in Hemsworth near Barnsley in January 1954. But it was a Lancashire club, Manchester City, who first gave him his chance in the game. He joined them as a 17-year-old apprentice at the start of the 1971-72 season and signed his first professional contract on his 18th birthday.

He followed the time-honoured route through the junior and reserve sides, learn-ing his trade. But progress into the first team was blocked by the not inconsiderable presence of Tommy Booth and it was not until the start of the 1974-75 season that Jeff managed to make his league debut. He turned out 13 times in the league for City that season but Manchester felt that they needed an established international star at the centre of their defence – Dave Watson – and were willing to let Jeff go to Sunderland as part of the deal.

Just as Dave craved First Division football, Jeff needed first team action. Bob Stokoe was able to give him this at Roker. So everyone was happy with the situa-tion – except perhaps the Roker fans. But they soon warmed to the young central defender

He certainly impressed during his first season on Wearside as the Red'n Whites mounted a determined promotion challenge. He was an ever present in the side until he sustained a broken bone in his foot away to Orient in mid-March that ruled him out for the rest of the season. Such was his determination to continue that, although he sustained the fracture in the first half, he played on until the final whistle. It was during a precautionary visit to hospital a day or so after the match that the extent of the injury was ascertained. By an ironic co-incidence, a back injury suffered by Dave Watson at Manchester City saw his campaign end on the same day.

So Jeff missed the run in to the end of the season that saw the Rokermen clinch the title by three clear points from Bristol City and West Bromwich Albion. But, having played in 31 of the 42 league games, he still won a coveted championship medal.

He was back in action when the Red'n Whites started off their First Division campaign a few months later. This time, however, it was to be a battle for survival in the top flight – a battle that was to be ultimately lost. But, once again, Jeff was not to see out the season. This time he was crocked in the 4-0 home win against Middlesbrough in mid-February. The injury was serious – medial ligament damage in his right knee.

He was out of action for the best part of a year, returning at the beginning of December. This time he kept himself injury free for the rest of the season but by now questions were being raised as to whether he was injury prone or, worse still, jinxed. The problem was that when he got injured it was invariably serious and meant a long time out.

He failed to see out the season in 1978-79 as well although this was nothing to do with injuries. Sunderland were in the middle of another promotion battle and there were just seven games to go when Jeff was suspended. Jack Ashurst made the most of his recall in his place and, with manager Billy Elliott reluctant to change his defence during the run-in, Jeff could only sit on the sidelines and watch his team miss out on promotion by one point, finishing fourth.

Promotion eventually came in 1980 which, mathematically, was Jeff's best season in terms of freedom from injury. He turned out in 39 of the 42 league games. But in many ways it was the worst insofar as the injury jinx was concerned. A freak collision with team mate Joe Hinnigan away to Cardiff City in the penultimate game saw him carried off with yet another knee injury – and this one was the most serious of the lot. Sunderland drew at Ninian Park that day. A win would have seen them pip Leicester City for the Second Division title.

Jeff's career was now in jeopardy. He spent the following season fighting a recovery battle – which he was eventually to win. To his credit, he tried to use the countless days, weeks and months in the treatment room productively. He was fascinated with the work of Johnny Watters, the respected Sunderland physiotherapist. A seed was sown that was to have a profound effect on Jeff's life in later years.

Jeff had one more year at Roker (1981-82). But, once again, it was not injury free although he did not have to suffer the trauma of the interminable months in the treatment room. Nevertheless, at the end of that season manager Alan Durban decided to let him go – and on a free transfer at that.

Jeff's former coach at Sunderland, Arthur Cox, was now manager at Newcastle and he snapped up Jeff, reasoning that, at 28, the big central defender should have been at his peak and still had a good few years ahead of him. Arthur had helped to mould Jeff's career at Roker and felt that if he had been based in London or Manchester, he would have played for England. The player appreciated the confidence expressed in him and had no hesitation in signing.

His arrival in the summer of 1982 was quickly forgotten when, a few weeks later, Keeganmania hit town. Newcastle signed Kevin Keegan and all eyes (and cameras) were focused on the England captain. He carried the burden of the hopes and aspirations of the Geordie masses. Any Toon fan who was at the opening game of the season at home to QPR will proudly proclaim that he (or she) was there when Keegan made his debut. Few will remember that Jeff Clarke made his debut in the same match (as did Steve Hardwick) and John Craggs was also back from an 11 year exile on Teesside.

With everyone watching United's effervescent attack, few paid much attention to their defence. But at the heart of the rearguard, Jeff went about his business in a competent and professional manner. He remained largely injury-free in his first season at Gallowgate, playing 39 of the 42 league games. But Newcastle missed out on promotion, finishing fifth, three points behind Leicester City who went up in third place.

When it became known that the following season (1983-84) was to be Keegan's last, the pressure to make it successful was immense. Success was to be achieved with United going up, albeit in third place behind Chelsea and Sheffield Wednesday. But it was not a particularly successful year for Jeff. He played just a supporting role, managing just 14 games in another injury wrecked campaign. At least this year they were not all knee injuries. A broken nose sustained in a game against Chelsea ruled him out of the run in to promotion. He had refused to go off in that game, playing on to dominate in the air despite his injury, prompting Arthur Cox to shake his head in disbelief at his courage and determination.

With Cox gone and Jack Charlton in charge at Gallowgate, Jeff was loaned out briefly to Brighton at the start of the 1984-85 season. But he soon returned to reclaim his place in the Newcastle team only for his injury jinx to strike again – at Roker Park of all places. He celebrated the 300th league and cup game of his career in the local derby at Easter and typically broke his nose again, this time in an accidental collision with team mate defender Glenn Roeder.

The following year (1985-86) was a good one for him as he missed just one of Newcastle's 46 league and cup games. The jinx had been buried. But by now he was almost a veteran and he knew that his first class career would soon be coming to an end. Manager Willie McFaul was actively looking for a replacement as the next season began, significantly declaring that he was looking for a young Jeff Clarke.

When he signed Peter Jackson to play alongside Glenn Roeder at the heart of his defence, Jeff knew that his days were numbered at Gallowgate.

He moved on a free transfer at the end of that season to spend a few months playing in Turkey and it was there he ended his playing days. He soon returned to the North East and eventually, late in 1988, found himself back at St James' working in the Football in the Community Scheme. Manager Kevin Keegan persuaded him to go into the coaching side of the game and he enjoyed his stints coaching the reserves and the juniors. But he always thought back to the interminable months spent chatting to Johnny Watters in the treatment room at Roker and decided to become a physiotherapist. It took four years commuting back and forth to Salford University, taking advantage of a PFA scheme, before he became fully qualified

He always reckoned that physiotherapy was a more stable profession than coaching and so it proved when, amid general upheaval at St James' in the summer of 1997, Jeff found himself out of a job. He had brief spells back at Sunderland and also at Leeds United before finally moving north of the border to settle as physio with Dundee United.

At least in that role Jeff could appreciate fully the frustration felt by professional sportsmen when they are sidelined due to injury for any length of time. He certainly had enough experience of it in his time as a player. If he hadn't, who knows what personal achievements he might have attained. Many Sunderland and Newcastle fans felt that international recognition should have come his way.

Record

Sunderland	June 1975 – July 1982	
Football League	178 (3 sub) apps	6 gls
FA Cup	15 apps	-
Football League Cup	14 apps	-
Others	8 apps	-
Total	215 (3 sub) apps	6 gls

Newcastle	July 1982 – May 1987	
Football League	124 apps	4 gls
FA Cup	5 apps	-
Football League Cup	5 apps	1 gl
Total	134 apps	5 gls

Top Ten Attendances

1	68,004	4 Mar 1950	Sunderland 2 Newcastle 2 (Roker Park)
2	67,211	19 Mar 1927	Newcastle 1 Sunderland 0 (St James' Park)
3	66,654	9 Oct 1954	Sunderland 4 Newcastle 2 (Roker Park)
4	63,665	26 Dec 1951	Newcastle 2 Sunderland 2 (St James' Park)
5	62,835	26 Feb 1955	Newcastle 1 Sunderland 2 (St James' Park)
6	62,420	2 Mar 1963	Sunderland 0 Newcastle 0 (Roker Park)
7	62,262	13 Oct 1962	Newcastle 1 Sunderland 1 (St James' Park)
8	62,173	23 Mar 1951	Newcastle 2 Sunderland 2 (St James' Park)
9	61,761	29 Nov 1919	Newcastle 2 Sunderland 3 (St James' Park)
10	61,474	3 Mar 1956	Newcastle 0 Sunderland 2 (St James' Park)

Although seven of the top ten attendances at Tyne-Wear derbies have been at St James' Park, Newcastle have only won one of them. They also failed to win any of the other three at Roker Park!

CHAPTER 11

1990s Tyneside Resurgence

SEASON 1989–90 had ended with joy on Wearside and despair on Tyneside as Sunderland climbed into the First Division following a play-off victory over Newcastle at St James' Park. The Rokerites' defeat by Swindon Town in the play-off final at Wembley became of little consequence when an investigation into the affairs of the Robins saw them demoted from the top flight without even playing a single game there.

But a decade is a long time in football. Sunderland were to fail to make the most of their somewhat fortuitous promotion and, after one season in the higher echelons, were to find themselves back in the same league as Newcastle. Both teams' stay in the Second Division was to be brief because, within a year, the Premier League was formed and the 'Second Division' was renamed the 'First'.

Newcastle were to be the first champions of this league, Sunderland avoiding further relegation into the 'new' Second Division by one point as the gulf between the two clubs widened again. The Wearsiders were not to rejoin their neighbours until 1996 when they once again briefly tasted high-life in the top flight only to go down again after their first season. By this time Newcastle had become a force in the land and, before the decade was over, they were to finish twice as runners-up in both the Premiership and the FA Cup although silverware of any kind proved elusive.

Meanwhile Sunderland were becoming a bit of a yo-yo club. They underwent the trauma of the play-offs again in 1998, suffering the agony of defeat in a penalty shoot-out at Wembley against Charlton Athletic following a monumental encounter that ended in a 4-4 draw after extra time. But ecstasy was to follow agony a year later as the Wearsiders walked away with the Nationwide Football League Division 1 title, lifting the trophy by a massive 18 points over runners-up Bradford City while establishing a record points total of 105 – a magnificent achievement.

Peter Reid had taken over as manager at Roker Park in the mid-1990s, the last manager to do so because it was during his tenure that the club left their traditional home of the last 99 years. They did not move very far, just to the mouth of the Wear where they had built an impressive, brand new stadium which they named the Stadium of Light.

However the relocation from Roker to Wearmouth meant that the club's old nicknames of the Rokerites or the Rokermen were no longer appropriate. The club consulted its supporters about a new nickname and, by a sizeable majority, they opted for 'The Black Cats', reflecting a traditional association that dated back to the early 19th century and the Black Cat gun battery that was located near the mouth of the Wear. The club had adopted the Black Cat as an emblem before the First World War and the Supporters' Club had similarly done so in the 1960s.

So it was with a deep-rooted sense of tradition that contemporary supporters chose the club's new nickname.

Up on Tyneside, Newcastle were to rely on a number of high profile managers during the decade with Kevin Keegan, Kenny Dalglish and Ruud Gullit each taking turns at the helm. It was the last of these who was to give Sunderland a much-needed morale boost when, in a torrential downpour, the Black Cats defeated the Magpies in one of the most controversial derbies of the century. It was the Wearsiders' one victory over United in the entire decade but it was a success that was to see Gullit vacate the St James' Park hot seat and Bobby Robson return to his native North East to guide Newcastle into the new century.

League Meetings (8)

At Newcastle:	Newcastle – won 2 drew 1 lost 1
At Sunderland:	Sunderland – won 0 drew 2 lost 2

Hat-trick Heroes

Newcastle	Sunderland
A Tait – 22 Dec 1956	R Hogg – 23 Dec 1899
P Beardsley – 1 Jan 1985	W Hogg – 5 Dec 1908
	G Holley – 5 Dec 1908
	R Best – 25 Dec 1914
	G Rowell – 24 Feb 1979

Football League
Division 2
Sunderland 1 Newcastle United 1 (HT: 1-0)
17th November 1991
Roker Park
29,224

Sunderland: A Norman, J Kay, A Rogan, G Bennett, I Sampson, P Davenport [21] (12 G Owers 71), P Bracewell, D Rush (14 T Hauser 81), G Armstrong, J Byrne, C Pascoe
Newcastle: T Wright, D Bradshaw (12 S Watson 52), M Stimson, L O'Brien [59], K Scott, M Appleby, D Roche, G Peacock, S Howey, A Thompson (14 L Makel 86), A Hunt
Referee: John Lloyd (Wrexham)

THERE WAS no doubt that recently relegated Sunderland were favourites going into this game. Struggling Newcastle had not won at Roker Park since 1956 and they were badly hit by injuries. The main problems were at right back and left midfield where youngsters Steve Watson and Alan Thompson were on standby owing to doubts about Darren Bradshaw and Kevin Brock. Following fitness tests, Bradshaw made it but Brock didn't. The likes of Pavel Srnicek, Micky Quinn and Lee Clark were also missing from the United line-up and manager Ossie Ardiles admitted that his side were the underdogs, claiming "Sunderland have home advantage, a more settled squad and more points than us".

But Sunderland also had problems. They had not won a home Wear-Tyne derby for 11 years and an injury to Kevin Ball prevented them from fielding the side that had lost narrowly away to Bristol City in their last game. Ian Sampson deputised in a line-up that was also without Paul Hardyman and Richard Ord. Goalscoring hero Marco Gabbiadini had also been sold to Crystal Palace a few weeks earlier and although the club had bought John Byrne, they had not yet replaced the former fans' favourite.

Newcastle turned out in their change strip of yellow shirts and green shorts.

League Positions

	Pos	Pl	Pts		Pos	Pl	Pts
Before: Sunderland	14th	17	22	Newcastle	21st	17	18
After: Sunderland	14th	18	23	Newcastle	21st	18	19

Far from being overwhelmed by the Roker Park atmosphere, Ossie Ardiles' youthful Newcastle side took the game to Sunderland straight from the kick-off and Gavin Peacock flashed a shot just wide of Tony Norman's post in the very first minute. The 'keeper was also in the right place to take another

Peacock effort in the 14th minute as United tried to turn their early attacks into goals. The turning point came soon afterwards, however, when Gary Bennett managed to overhaul Steve Howey after the young centre forward looked as if he was breaking clear following a David Roche through-ball. It was Sunderland who opened the scoring, against the run of play, in one of their first serious attacks of the game.

After 21 minutes Gordon Armstrong launched an attack with Paul Bracewell playing the ball out to the left where Anton Rogan took it past Roche before swinging over a cross. This was partly headed clear thanks to Armstrong's challenge in the middle and the clearance fell straight to Peter Davenport ten yards out. His first time volley flew past Tommy Wright and deflected off Matty Appleby on the goal line into the roof of the net.

Buoyed by the goal, Sunderland assumed control and, with Byrne playing some nice touches up front, they threatened to increase their lead. Fortunately for Newcastle, Wright was in fine form and twice in the space of five minutes he pulled off top class saves to deny Armstrong. Sunderland were clearly on top when the half-time whistle was blown.

The Wearsiders continued where they had left off when the game resumed. It seemed as if it would just be a matter of time before they would score again to finish Newcastle off. United brought on 17-year-old Steve Watson for Bradshaw to try and add additional young legs to their play. Then, just as the Rokerites had struck against the run of play in the first half, Newcastle did likewise in the second.

Nearly an hour had gone when Steve Howey and Alan Thompson combined to dispossess Armstrong in the middle of the Sunderland half and the ball broke nicely to Liam O'Brien. He spotted Tony Norman off his line and advanced a few yards before sending a delightful chip shot from 25 yards over the 'keeper who managed to get a touch but not enough to keep it out.

Surprisingly, the goal took the wind out of Sunderland's sails and their confidence evaporated. Conversely, the goal inspired O'Brien and he began to dominate midfield. Appleby and captain Kevin Scott proved a formidable barrier to any Sunderland counter-attacks but most of the activity was at the other end. Watson should have done better with a header as the Wearsiders were forced to defend in depth. The combative Gary Owers was brought on for Davenport to try and ignite some spark up front for Sunderland but it was to no avail. Yet they could have snatched a late winner when John Kay had a great chance but delayed his shot and allowed Mark Stimson to get in his tackle. At the final whistle the scores were still level and both sides had to be satisfied with a point apiece. But Newcastle, who had gone into this game fearing the worst, felt that they had won a moral victory.

The 4,000 Newcastle fans packed in the Roker End were ecstatic at the final whistle and even injured stars Micky Quinn and Lee Clark came on to the field on their crutches to join in the post match celebrations.

Although the result made no difference to either club's league position, Sunderland were naturally disappointed, perhaps a natural consequence when expectations are not realised. But some of their experienced international players such as Bracewell, Pascoe and Davenport had just not done enough during the game. Sunderland went on to lose five of their next seven league games before the turn of the year and slide down the league. Newcastle were to do even worse, winning just two of their next twelve.

Before the two clubs were to meet again in the spring they were both to change their managers, Malcolm Crosby taking over from Denis Smith at Roker and Newcastle replacing Ossie Ardiles with a man who was already almost a legend on Tyneside from his playing days – Kevin Keegan. A new era was about to start – at least it was on Tyneside.

Football League
Division 2
Newcastle United 1 Sunderland 0 (HT: 1-0)
29th March 1992
St James' Park
30,306

Newcastle: T Wright, S Watson, M Stimson*, L O'Brien, B Kilcline, K Scott, M Quinn, G Peacock, D Kelly [33], K Sheedy, K Brock.
Sub (unused) 12 D McDonough, 14 L Clark
Sunderland: T Carter, J Kay, A Rogan, K Ball, P Hardyman, D Rush*, P Bracewell, P Davenport (12 B Mooney 58), G Armstrong, J Byrne, B Atkinson.
Sub (unused) 14 I Sampson
Referee: Ian Hendrick (Preston)

THE ATTRACTION of Tyne-Wear derbies proved as strong as ever with the encounter drawing a sell-out crowd to the reduced capacity St James' Park despite the fact that both teams were languishing near the relegation zone. In fact the crowd was the biggest so far in the Second Division this season.

Both teams had injury problems. For Sunderland, goalkeeper Tony Norman had damaged his shoulder in the game against Bristol City a week earlier and was ruled out at the last minute, Tim Carter deputising. On top of that, both Gary Bennett and Don Goodman were missing after picking up injuries in a midweek reserve game. The bright side for manager Malcolm Crosby was the return of Paul Hardyman from a hamstring injury. He replaced Richard Ord in defence.

Newcastle boss Kevin Keegan had problems of his own but his were more of selection choice than injuries. He opted for Republic of Ireland international Liam O'Brien in preference to recent signing Darren McDonough and any thoughts that he had of bringing Bjorn Kristensen into the side following a long lay off due a knee injury had to be shelved when the Dane broke down in training. Sunderland also had their eyes on the FA Cup where they had reached the semi-final. Kevin Keegan had no such distraction as he tasted the unique emotions of a Tyne-Wear derby for the first time. He could not help but compare it with Liverpool v Everton encounters. "On Merseyside" he said, "it isn't uncommon to get Liverpool and Everton fans in the same family and the two sets of supporters even go to games together. Not here!"

League Positions		Pos	Pl	Pts		Pos	Pl	Pts
Before:	Sunderland	17th	35	43	Newcastle	18th	38	43
After:	Newcastle	17th	39	46	Sunderland	18th	36	43

Perhaps Sunderland had on eye on the FA Cup semi-final (their next game) because they certainly put less than 100% effort into this match and allowed Newcastle to gain the ascendancy early on. United could easily have grabbed the lead in the 12th minute when the impressive Steve Watson, who had recently celebrated his 18th birthday, rattled the visitors' crossbar with a left foot rocket from 30 yards.

The Rokermen rarely threatened Tommy Wright as United continued to control play. Tim Carter did well to push away a point blank header from Mick Quinn following a teasing cross by Gavin Peacock from the left wing on the half hour mark. But the reprieve was short-lived and the Magpies were back soon afterwards to take a deserved lead after 33 minutes.

United forced a left wing corner and Kevin Brock played a short pass to Kevin Sheedy. His left foot cross was a shade behind David Kelly but the No 9 did very well to reach it, diving backwards in a crowded penalty area to steer the ball goalwards with a header from just outside the six yard box. There was not much power behind his effort but it was perfectly placed, just inside the post, as Carter and Hardyman tried in vain to keep it out.

Sunderland were either unable or unwilling to retaliate and a combative Newcastle side continued to see more of the ball for the rest of the half without really creating any more scoring opportunities. Nevertheless, the one goal lead at the interval was not a true reflection of Tyneside superiority in the opening session.

The critical moment in the second half came just four minutes after the resumption when Lady Luck undoubtedly smiled on Sunderland. Another perfect Gavin Peacock cross was met by Mick Quinn and his close range header easily beat Carter and looked to have crossed the line before Anton Rogan hastily hacked the ball away.

Referee Ian Hendrick waved play on and was immediately surrounded by the incensed Newcastle players. They appealed in vain although it was evident that Rogan was standing well behind the line when he cleared the ball. Perhaps the referee was not in a perfect position to make a judgement but his linesman certainly was.

Television replays later indicated that the ball was over the line and that Sunderland had had a lucky escape. But Newcastle did not need a second goal against their disappointing visitors for whom only the assured John Kay and the determined Kevin Ball emerged with any credit. The substitution of Brian Mooney for Peter Davenport during the second half had little or no effect as United strolled to a comfortable victory.

The Newcastle fans were delighted with the win but, if they were honest with themselves, this was a game to forget. In fact it was one of the worst in the long series of Tyne-Wear derbies.

Victory saw United leap-frog Sunderland in the league and left Malcolm Crosby to puzzle why his side could play so well in the Cup but so poorly in the league. Sunderland had now lost three games in a row but, even more worrying, had just won one of their last eight in the league.

The Wearsiders still had games in hand over all of the other sides near the drop zone but they were now just two points above a relegation place. Success in the FA Cup semi-final against Norwich City merely papered over the cracks as a struggle for survival developed. They succeeded – and even finished above Newcastle for whom games were running out after the derby match.

In the end one point separated the rivals. But 18th and 20th in the Second Division was hardly a satisfactory situation for the North East's self-perceived big two especially as Middlesbrough finished second top and became founder members of the new Premier League.

Football League
Division 1 (new)
Sunderland 1 Newcastle United 2 (HT: 0-1)
18th October 1992
Roker Park
28,098

Sunderland: T Carter, J Kay, A Rogan, G Owers, G Bennett*, K Ball, S Cunnington, D Goodman*, P Davenport, B Atkinson, D Rush (12 G Armstrong 65 [69])
Sub (unused) 14 J Colquhoun
Newcastle: T Wright, B Venison, J Beresford*, L O'Brien* [76], K Scott, S Howey, R Lee, G Peacock, D Kelly, L Clark, K Brock. Subs (unused) 12 M Quinn, 14 B Kilcline; (og Owers [12])
Referee: Stephen Lodge (Barnsley)

TABLE TOPPING Newcastle returned from a break on the Isle of Man fully refreshed and relaxed, apart from the half dozen players who had been away on international duty. The Magpies could boast a 100% record in the league and were almost able to field a full-strength side, Kevin Sheedy being the one absentee due to injury. Kevin Brock was a more than capable deputy.

Sunderland, on the other hand, came into the game with their confidence severely shaken following a 6-0 thrashing at West Ham. Malcolm Crosby named a 15-man squad for the game but the determination of his players was epitomised by the attitude of Don Goodman who insisted on playing despite having eight stitches in a head wound. The one thing in Sunderland's favour was the fact that Newcastle had not won on Wearside for 36 years. On the other hand, a Newcastle win would equal the club's unbeaten start to a season (set up in 1950).

League Positions		Pos	Pl	Pts		Pos	Pl	Pts
Before:	Newcastle	1st	10	30	Sunderland	16th	10	11
After:	Newcastle	1st	11	33	Sunderland	17th	11	11

Despite a relatively small crowd in the reduced capacity Roker Park, the atmosphere inside the ground was magnificent. Emotions among fans boiled over a couple of times but did not mar an enthralling contest: the determination of Sunderland against the finesse of Keegan's cavaliers. There was little in it during the opening exchanges and it took an own goal to break the deadlock. Barry Venison started a move down Newcastle's right flank after 12 minutes that ended with him playing the ball in to Gavin Peacock whose delightful flick sent Robert Lee away on the right. He almost reached the goal line before he pulled a cross low into the middle where Gary Owers, under pressure from Kevin Brock, slid the ball into his own net from close range.

Newcastle's crisp, inter-passing play really caught the eye as they built their moves from the back but battling Sunderland hustled them and prevented them from establishing their normal rhythm. The home defence kept a tight grip on David Kelly and Gavin Peacock and Brian Atkinson shadowed Lee Clark all over the pitch. Sunderland showed that they were still a force to be reckoned with when Gary Owers clipped the top of the bar with a free kick and Gary Bennett had a headed goal disallowed for a foul on Kelly.

One goal was never going to be enough and Newcastle strove for a second. They nearly got it when Steve Howey broke through the middle to put in Peacock but he blazed over the bar. Sunderland gradually began to stifle United's creativity and then shocked them with the equaliser with 21 minutes to go. An Owers' corner from the right was not cut out and the ball fell to the feet of Newcastle-born Gordon Armstrong, a substitute who had been on the pitch for only four minutes. He rifled home a low shot from eight yards. He directed his celebrations to the Sunderland dugout, indicating that he felt that he should have been in the starting line-up.

Now there was little in it and Sunderland probably deserved to be level for their endeavour and commitment. But this Newcastle team were always capable of conjuring up something out of nothing – and so it proved. Seven minutes after the equaliser, Atkinson conceded a free kick 20 yards out from the Roker

End goal where the Newcastle fans were massed. Liam O'Brien stepped up to take it and swerved a spectacular, curling effort into the top left hand corner of the net – a truly great strike worthy of winning any game.

The goal was a hammer blow and home heads went down allowing Newcastle to coast home. In fact they could easily have increased their lead with Peacock chipping an effort just over the bar and Tim Carter producing a breathtaking save to keep out a curling shot by Clark. But a bigger margin would have been harsh on the Wearside warriors.

Although they lost the match, Sunderland restored their lost pride in this game. Perhaps predictably, there were cries for Malcolm Crosby to be sacked but Kevin Keegan sprang to his defence, "There is no way that Malcolm's job should be under threat when his side can play with this level of commitment". But Crosby was to hang on to his job only until the beginning of February when the club, just above a relegation place, took drastic action.

Newcastle had now won 13 successive league games (including two from the previous season) and needed one more to equal the record jointly held by Manchester United (1904-05), Bristol City (1905-06) and Preston North End (1950-51). A win in their next game against Grimsby Town at St James' Park would do it but they surprisingly failed, losing 0-1. Their fans were not too upset. The first win at Roker since 1956 and the fact that they were ten points clear at the top of the league saw to that.

Football League
Division 1
Newcastle United 1 Sunderland 0 (HT: 1-0)
25th April 1993
St James' Park
30,364

Newcastle: P Srnicek, B Venison, J Beresford, P Bracewell, K Scott, S Howey, R Lee, A Cole, D Kelly, L Clark, S Sellars [10]. Subs (unused) 12 M Robinson, 14 B Kilcline
Sunderland: A Norman, J Kay (14 Martin Gray 59), Michael Gray, J Colquhoun (12 P Davenport 78), T Butcher, K Ball, S Cunnington, D Goodman, M Harford, B Atkinson, G Armstrong*
Referee: Keith Hackett (Sheffield)

THIS DERBY took place on a Sunday with a 12.00 noon kick-off to accommodate live television coverage, the first for a Tyne-Wear derby. Newcastle had temporarily been deposed at the top of the league by Portsmouth on the Saturday. Nevertheless they came into the game as clear favourites over their struggling neighbours.

Both sides tried to take pressure off themselves with Kevin Keegan pointing out, "Bookies don't always get it right". Sunderland player/manager Terry Butcher's view was somewhat different, "If you look at the league form and table, we should be in for a right stuffing". Derby games, however, were regarded as great levellers and appalling weather also made the game a bit of a lottery.

Andy Cole, seven goals in the last seven games, was looked upon as the danger man as far as Sunderland were concerned. The fact that they had picked up just two points out of the last 18 had left the Wearsiders in dire straits but Newcastle had not done a double over them for 36 years.

League Positions

		Pos	Pl	Pts		Pos	Pl	Pts
Before:	Newcastle	2nd	42	84	Sunderland	19th	42	47
After:	Newcastle	1st	43	87	Sunderland	21st	43	47

The groundsmen performed miracles to get the game staged following torrential rain although at the kick-off the pitch resembled a paddy field. The fact that it was televised seemed to have a lot to do with their efforts. Despite the atrocious conditions, the Football League's biggest crowd of the season crammed into St James'. They were served up with a typical blood and guts derby. Newcastle displayed all of the creative play but, as at Roker earlier in the season, this was largely offset by Sunderland's passion and commitment.

The game was settled after ten minutes. When Terry Butcher was adjudged to have unfairly climbed over Kevin Scott, Newcastle were awarded a free kick just outside the Sunderland penalty area in front of the visiting fans packed in the Leazes End. Liam O'Brien, who had scored in similar circumstances at Roker in October, was not playing so Scott Sellars took the kick. Every Sunderland player, with the exception of Tony Norman, was on or around the penalty spot but the result was the same as at Roker as the ball flew past the defensive wall. It thudded against a post before it ended in the net and most of St James' Park erupted.

The goal acted as a boost to Newcastle who, with Lee Clark and former Roker favourite Paul Bracewell dominating midfield, soon began to control the game. David Kelly and Robert Lee could easily have increased the Tyneside lead with Sunderland restricted to just one attempt on goal, a Mick Harford header that Pavel Srnicek palmed over.

The ball frequently stuck in puddles and both sides had to resort to the long boot up the middle. Sunderland showed up quite well in the first 10 minutes of the second half but it was soon back to Tyneside supremacy. Rob Lee went close a couple of times, as did Steve Howey, but Sunderland hung on until the closing stages when they went full out for an equaliser. They never really looked like getting it and no-one could deny that Newcastle, who had dominated possession throughout, were worthy winners. To the Wearsiders' credit, they had battled hard. Their attitude and commitment had been first rate. But they had hardly bothered Newcastle and the final scoreline flattered them.

Defeat left Sunderland just one place and one point above relegation with three games to go. The problem was that two of those three were away from home. Newcastle Chairman Sir John Hall expressed his wish about his Wearside neighbours, "I hope Sunderland stay up and get promoted next year".

The first half of his wish was to come true; they were to finish fourth bottom, one point above a relegation place. But promotion to the Premiership was not to come until 1996. Newcastle were to win their last three league games and finish as the inaugural champions of the new First Division by eight clear points.

The 80ft x 30ft 'Toon Army' banner that had been passed along and over the heads of the supporters in the East Stand at half-time was an indication of the exciting years that lay ahead for the Geordies.

Premier League

Sunderland 1 Newcastle United 2 (HT: 1-0)

4th September 1996
Roker Park
22,037

Sunderland: 1 A Coton, 2 D Kubicki, 3 M Scott [**20** pen], 4 P Bracewell, 5 K Ball, 6 A Melville, 7 M Gray, 8 R Ord, 17 N Quinn*, 10 P Stewart (9 C Russell 82), 11 S Agnew (15 A Rae 76). Subs (unused) 30 L Perez, 12 G Hall, 19 M Bridges
Newcastle: 1 P Srnicek, 19 S Watson, 26 R Elliott*, 4 D Batty, 6 S Howey, 5 D Peacock, 7 R Lee*, 8 P Beardsley [**52**], 9 A Shearer, 10 L Ferdinand [**63**] (20 L Clark 76), 14 D Ginola. Subs (unused) 15 S Hislop, 11 F Asprilla, 27 P Albert, 18 K Gillespie
Referee: Jeff Winter (Stockton-on-Tees)

UNDEFEATED SUNDERLAND had enjoyed an encouraging start to the season although they had failed to score in five of their last six league games (including last season). New signing Alex Rae had been suspended for the first three games of this campaign but he was now available. Manager Peter Reid, however, relied on the side that had ground out a goalless draw away to Liverpool and Rae had to be satisfied with a place on the subs' bench.

The same fate befell Tino Asprilla who had returned from South America on the day before the derby. Kevin Keegan, fearing jet-lag, decided the leave his Columbian marksman (who had scored a hat-trick against Chile on the previous weekend) on the bench as well. He was joined, perhaps surprisingly, by Philippe Albert as Keegan rang the changes to combat the aerial threat of 6ft 5ins Niall Quinn, bringing in Darren Peacock to man mark him. Club skipper Peter Beardsley, now 35 and in the twilight of his illustrious career, was brought in to make his first Premiership start of the season.

But the real controversy surrounding this match concerned the supporters. Initially it was decided, on safety and security grounds, to bar visiting fans from Roker Park. But then, somewhat belatedly, Sunderland (and Northumbria Police) decided to allow just over 1,000 Newcastle supporters to attend the game. Newcastle had already made arrangements to beam the match live back to the Newcastle Arena (8,000 seats) and to the Platinum Club and Bar 1892 (700) at St James' Park. Both venues were sold out and the club rejected the Sunderland offer of tickets for Roker much to the disgust of the Geordie fans.

United's Chief Executive Freddie Fletcher tried to ward off criticism but merely succeeded in fanning the flames before the match by publicly denouncing the Wearside club. "When you've got a ground like Roker Park, you're bound to have problems. So it came as no surprise when we were asked to give up the chance of selling tickets for this game. For Sunderland FC to say that Northumbria Police were involved in all of this is utterly wrong. The police were contacted once everyone agreed and they supported the decision. It stinks. But don't blame Newcastle. Don't blame Northumbria Police. Blame Sunderland!" His comments were hardly conducive towards promoting a harmonious relationship between the two clubs.

League Positions

		Pos	Pl	Pts		Pos	Pl	Pts
Before:	Sunderland	6th	3	5	Newcastle	14th	3	3
After:	Newcastle	8th	4	6	Sunderland	10th	4	5

A few – very few – Newcastle fans managed to obtain tickets for Roker Park illicitly but they kept quiet throughout the game. Not that they had much to enthuse about anyway in the first half when Sunderland, prompted by the inspirational Paul Bracewell in midfield, clearly had the upper hand. They made a mockery of United's multi-millionaire status as they dominated possession and took the game to the Magpies. The visitors, playing in a pale blue strip, were forced on to the back foot. Michael Gray was a constant threat down the left flank and he found an eager partner in Martin Scott. Pavel Srnicek had to punch clear from a Scott free kick but his clearance fell to Bracewell whose follow-up volley flew just wide. Driven on by a fanatical crowd, a goal had to come. But when it did, it was from the penalty spot.

After 20 minutes skipper Kevin Ball played the ball wide to Steve Agnew who cut inside before attempting to go around Robbie Elliott only to be brought down just inside the box. The Newcastle full back was lucky to stay on the field having already been booked. Scott was coolness personified as he sent Srnicek the wrong way (to his right) from the spot to send the Roker faithful wild with delight.

Newcastle were now hanging on with the goal giving Sunderland an undoubted boost. Srnicek kept the Geordies in the game with an acrobatic save from a spectacular Paul Stewart scissors kick that seemed destined for the top corner until the 'keeper somehow managed to get across and palm the ball away. He was on the spot again just before half-time to block a Michael Gray effort and Sunderland had to make do with a single goal lead at the interval. There was a nagging feeling that it may not have been enough.

It seemed that these fears were justified as Newcastle came out for the second half in a much more positive and determined state of mind. Robert Lee and David Batty showed their battling abilities to get a grip on the middle of the park and Les Ferdinand began to look increasingly dangerous up front. The Roker Roar quietened significantly at this change in fortune and was silenced completely when Newcastle grabbed the threatened equaliser seven minutes after the restart.

Ferdinand created the opening, powering his way through two tackles in the inside right position before cleverly chipping a pass over to Peter Beardsley who was standing unmarked on the penalty spot. There was not much power behind the Newcastle skipper's header but he placed it perfectly, across the 'keeper and into the net off his left hand post.

The game was now back in the melting pot and the confidence seemed to drain out of Sunderland who found it impossible to regain their first half momentum. Newcastle now looked the more dangerous side and a dipping shot by Ferdinand from well out side the penalty area went just over the top. The Wearside defence looked increasingly worried and Richard Ord seemed to panic when he conceded a corner with Alan Shearer moving in on him. This led to Newcastle taking the lead after 63 minutes.

David Ginola's flag kick was perfect for the towering Ferdinand to out-leap Ord and power in a header that was a goal from the moment it left his head. Never had a goal at Roker been met with such silence although the noise in the Newcastle Arena more than compensated.

It was Ferdinand's first goal of the season but it was destined to be the last goal ever scored by a Newcastle player at Roker Park. He was also, arguably, Newcastle's best player on the night, although he limped off with a quarter of an hour to go to be replaced by Lee Clark. Peter Reid sent on Rae for his Sunderland debut in place of Steve Agnew at the same time in the hope of pulling something out of the bag. Stewart sent a header just over the bar and Rae had a drive deflected wide. But it was too little, too late, and the Rokermen paid the penalty for not turning their first half superiority into goals. Newcastle went off the field as deserved winners.

It had been a game of two halves. Sunderland had clearly been the better side in the first but had been outfought, outmanoeuvred and, ultimately, outclassed in the second. Keegan's tactics of bringing in Peacock to nullify the threat of Quinn had worked perfectly.

This had been the first time since before the First World War that Newcastle had come from behind at half-time to win at Roker. They went above both Sunderland and North East neighbours Middlesbrough as a result and the parting of the ways was to continue with United eventually finishing as runners-up in the Premiership to Manchester United and both of the other local clubs being relegated. Middlesbrough, however, were rather unfortunate, going down only because of a three point penalty imposed by the Premier League for their failure to fulfil a fixture against Blackburn Rovers.

Premier League
Newcastle United 1 Sunderland 1 (HT: 0-1)
5th April 1997
St James' Park
36,582

Newcastle: 15 S Hislop, 2 W Barton, 5 D Peacock, 19 S Watson, 26 R Elliott, 18 K Gillespie, 7 R Lee (20 L Clark 28), 4 D Batty, 14 D Ginola, 10 L Ferdinand (11 F Asprilla 45), 9 A Shearer [**77**]. Subs (unused) 1 P Srnicek, 8 P Beardsley, 3 J Beresford
Sunderland: 30 L Perez, 12 G Hall, 14 L Howey*, 8 R Ord, 2 D Kubicki, 26 A Johnston (16 D Kelly 62), 5 K Ball, 4 P Bracewell, 7 M Gray [**31**] (19 M Bridges 67), 10 P Stewart (17 N Quinn 82), 25 C Waddle. Subs (unused) 32 C Woods, 33 J Eriksson
Referee: Paul Durkin (Portland)

HIGH FLYING Newcastle were clear favourites which was not surprising considering they had scored more goals at home in the Premiership (42) than any other team and that Sunderland had suffered more defeats and also conceded more goals than any other team away (33) in that league. It was no wonder that the bookies rated United as 8-13 favourites and Sunderland as 7-2 outsiders. Considering derby games are one-off affairs and often great levellers, the odds against Sunderland seemed worth a flutter.

It seemed strange for many Newcastle fans to see Chris Waddle line up against them. He had recently joined the Rokermen from Bradford City. This was his first taste of a competitive Tyne-Wear derby as he had never turned out in the league or cup for the Magpies against the Wearsiders. With Paul Bracewell also in the Sunderland starting line-up and David Kelly on the visitors' bench, there seemed to be a feeling of an old boys' reunion about the game.

International calls had disrupted manager Kenny Dalglish's preparations for the game. Tino Asprilla arrived back from Paraguay (where he had been playing for Colombia) on the evening before and Pavel Srnicek (Czech Republic) and Keith Gillespie (Northern Ireland) had also been away. Only the Ulsterman made the starting line-up. Philippe Albert was suspended for the game but Alan Shearer returned to lead the attack after six weeks absence having just recovered from a groin injury.

Peter Reid also had problems although his were more long term. A broken leg ruled out Tony Coton and Martin Scott also had a leg injury. Andy Melville

324

had just undergone an Achilles operation and was ruled out for the rest of the season. The one silver lining was the return of Niall Quinn who had been out since the autumn following a knee operation. He had played a couple of reserve games and was able to take his place on the bench.

There was a ban on away fans at St James' but Sunderland arranged to beam the match back live to Roker Park where a giant screen had been erected on the pitch. They opened only the main stand but this was quickly sold out and 6,000 fans settled down to enjoy the weird experience of watching a local derby played 12 miles away.

League Positions

		Pos	Pl	Pts		Pos	Pl	Pts
Before:	Newcastle	4th	30	52	Sunderland	16th	32	33
After:	Newcastle	4th	31	53	Sunderland	15th	33	34

The gap between the teams in the league was significant. But Sunderland, playing in white shirts with red trimmings, made up for an apparent difference in class by sheer determination and will power. They fought for every ball and battled right until the final whistle. Yet, roared on by a partisan home crowd, Newcastle started as if they were intent on sending the Rokermen back to Wearside with their tails between their legs as they launched raid after raid on the visitors' goal. As early as the sixth minute Lionel Perez saved brilliantly as he turned a Les Ferdinand rasper around a post. Seconds later the French 'keeper was there again, this time to deny a long range Robert Lee effort, tipping the ball over the bar. Ferdinand was soon back again to power a David Ginola cross goalwards but Perez pulled off another great save.

Within a minute Lionel again denied Les as Newcastle threatened to run riot. All of this happened in the opening quarter of an hour but, having survived the onslaught, Sunderland gradually clawed their way into the game. Soon Shaka Hislop found himself in action, saving from Michael Gray. But Newcastle should really have took the lead when Ferdinand found himself with a gilt-edged opportunity after being put through by Lee. But he fired over the bar when it looked easier to score. Lee was soon forced to go off with a head injury, Lee Clark coming on to take his place. Within a couple of minutes of the substitution the unthinkable happened for the Gallowgate masses – Sunderland broke away to score.

After 31 minutes Waddle took the ball diagonally across the field before playing it out to Gray on the left. He cut eagerly inside a static Newcastle rearguard before cracking a right foot drive from 15 yards past Hislop and in at the near post. St James' Park was briefly stunned by this goal while the Sunderland fans watching the beam back at Roker Park went wild with delight. Back at Gallowgate, boos of frustration accompanied the Newcastle players off the pitch at the half-time whistle.

Ferdinand paid the penalty for his first half profligacy when he was replaced at the interval by Asprilla. United began the second half in much the same way as they had the first, by throwing everybody forward to try and breach the Wearside defence. Clark, Batty and Shearer all went close and Sunderland found themselves pegged back into a rearguard action. Waddle was booed every time he touched the ball yet Kelly received a hero's welcome from the Newcastle fans when he came off the bench to replace the tiring Allan Johnston. Gray was later replaced by Michael Bridges as the Rokermen began to look increasingly likely to hold out for a shock victory. But then, with just 13 minutes to play, Alan Shearer struck.

Ginola had looked particularly bright and dangerous in the early stages of the game but had been virtually ignored since then. Suddenly he found himself in possession on the left wing. He tantalised the visitors' defence before curling over a right-footed, pin-point cross that found Warren Barton on the far side of the six yard box. His header picked out Shearer, who criminally had been left unmarked close in. This was the kind of chance he dreamed about and he lashed the ball home.

Encouraged by the goal, the fans came alive and roared on Newcastle. But it was Sunderland who almost snatched victory. Niall Quinn replaced Paul Stewart with just eight minutes to go. However he was not involved when, a couple of minutes later, skipper Kevin Ball lashed a shot goalwards. Shaka Hislop first blocked it and then recovered his position to take a shot from the rebound full in his face – but he kept it out. There was still time for Perez to earn his wages with yet another top drawer save as he denied Ginola a last gasp winner.

With Newcastle fighting for a place in Europe and Sunderland hoping to stave off relegation, the draw seemed to do no-one any good. Peter Reid was happy that his tactic of playing with one out and out striker (Stewart in a 4–4–1–1 formation) worked. But he must have been torn between the satisfaction of coming to St James' as out and out underdogs and getting a point and the fact that his team had held the lead for half of the game only to concede a late equaliser. Kenny Dalglish thought that a draw was a fair result but felt that it was better for Sunderland than his side.

Yet it was not to be enough for the battling Rokermen. They were to lose three of their last five games and were to be relegated by one point.

Newcastle were to avoid defeat in their last seven games (although they drew three of them) and were to finish as runners-up to Manchester United in the Premiership although ahead of Arsenal and Liverpool only on goal difference. Shearer's goal ultimately had been crucial. Seldom can a single goal in Tyne-Wear derbies have had such dramatic and (bearing in mind that this had effectively qualified them for the European Champions' League) profitable repercussions.

Premier League

Newcastle United 1 Sunderland 2 (HT: 1-0)

25th August 1999
St James' Park
36,420

Newcastle: 32 T Wright, 2 W Barton, 5 A Goma*, 34 N Dabizas, 4 D Domi*, 15 N Solano, 7 K Dyer [28], 19 J McClen*, 11 G Speed, 10 S Maric (9 A Shearer 72), 28 P Robinson (20 D Ferguson 57). Subs (unused) 13 S Harper, 31 S Green, 18 A Hughes

Sunderland: 1 T Sorensen, 2 C Makin, 3 M Gray, 5 S Bould, 6 P Butler*, 7 N Summerbee, 16 A Rae, 20 S Schwarz (4 K Ball 69), 21 G McCann*, 9 N Quinn [64], 10 K Phillips* [74]. Sub (unused) 28 J Oster, 13 A Marriott, 12 D Dichio, 8 T Helmer

Referee: Graham Poll (Hertfordshire)

NEWCASTLE MANAGER Ruud Gullit refused to become embroiled in the hype that preceded this derby encounter. He clearly did not realise how important the game was to the fans and was quoted as saying, "I have been involved in derbies in Milan. It is sometimes even worse when teams from the same city play. This is just about being the best in the region. I am very calm about it". This was not what Newcastle fans wanted to hear especially after such a dreadful start to the season when their team had picked up just one point from the opening four games. The dreadlocked Dutchman also had problems in his dressing room. He had a long list of injuries to contend with but he had alienated himself from some of the club's senior players. Rob Lee was not even in the squad and Gullit was in open conflict with club captain Alan Shearer.

Out injured were Ketsbaia, Dumas, Marcelino (as usual), Glass and Howey. Seemingly the only good news was that Duncan Ferguson was on the road back to fitness. He had managed half an hour in the previous game against Wimbledon but was not yet 100% fit.

Bearing this in mind, it seemed incredible that Gullit should leave out Shearer in favour of an untried youngster. Shearer had been suspended for the Wimbledon game and 20-year-old Paul Robinson had deputised. But it was a shock for everyone when the youngster kept his place for the crucial Sunderland match and Shearer joined Ferguson on the bench in a £23 million substitute strike force. Shearer was later to say, "It was bad enough being left out of the team. But to find out that I wasn't starting the match by looking at a notice board an hour before the game really hurt".

Gullit claimed that he was "down to the bare bones". Some Bones! He certainly had goalkeeping problems. Shay Given had a long term injury, former Sunderland 'keeper Lionel Perez was totally out of favour and John Karelse was carrying a knee injury. It looked like Steve Harper was the one option available until, on the eve of the match, Newcastle signed Tommy Wright on a month's loan from Manchester City and it was the veteran former United 'keeper who was preferred against Sunderland.

In contrast Peter Reid had few problems. Paul Butler, who had sustained a badly gashed leg just four days earlier against Leeds, recovered to play and Steve Bould, who missed that game with hamstring problems, returned. Club captain Kevin Ball, now nearing the end of a distinguished Sunderland career, dropped down to the substitutes' bench as Peter Reid was able to name virtually a full-strength team.

League Positions		Pos	Pl	Pts		Pos	Pl	Pts
Before:	Sunderland	16th	4	4	Newcastle	18th	4	1
After:	Sunderland	11th	5	7	Newcastle	19th	5	1

The heavens opened well before the kick-off and torrential rain lashed down throughout. Sunderland opened brightly and soon had the home defence on the rack. Most of the action was in and around the Newcastle penalty area. Niall Quinn just failed to connect with a Kevin Phillips' cross at the far post and then Phillips himself tried a cheeky scissors kick following a Nicky Summerbee centre but directed the ball straight into Wright's arms. United survived this early pressure and gradually Gary Speed and Keiron Dyer began to make their presence felt in midfield. By the time the deadlock was eventually broken Newcastle had gained the upper hand.

The opener came just before the half hour. Silvio Maric had little influence on the game but it was he who started the move. He cut in from the right and played the ball to Paul Robinson. The youngster spotted Dyer and slid a delightful pass for him to run on to and confidently beat the offside trap and the advancing Thomas Sorensen.

The goal deflated Sunderland and Newcastle controlled play from then until the interval although they failed to create any clear cut chances. Nonetheless they went in for the half-time break satisfied with a job well done.

But it was Sunderland who came back out into the deluge for the second half to seize the initiative. Soon Newcastle were forced back and a last gasp tackle by Nicos Dabizas foiled Phillips as he chased a flick on from the towering Quinn. Gullit decided to introduce a bit more experience up front but it was Ferguson who replaced Robinson rather than Shearer. The change made little difference because, by now, Sunderland were in control and Newcastle rarely showed up in attack. Summerbee was proving to be a constant worry to the home rearguard especially with his skill at dead ball situations. It was from one of these free kicks after 64 minutes that the Black Cats equalised.

Summerbee's cross from out on the right was made to measure for Quinn who neatly steered a glancing header across and past Wright at the near post. It was a goal that had been coming ever since the second half had started.

The downpour increased in ferocity and playing conditions deteriorated badly. Both sides made substitutions as a possible abandonment looked increasingly likely. Interestingly they both brought their captains on, Sunderland replacing Stefan Schwarz with Kevin Ball and, soon afterwards, Shearer taking over from Maric as the chants for him from the 'stands reached a crescendo. His introduction did not have the effect that the Toon Army expected because, within two minutes, Sunderland took the lead.

Summerbee was again instrumental in creating the goal. He played a superb cross-field pass to Phillips who broke clear with water spraying off the ball as he moved forward. Tommy Wright did well to keep out his first shot but SuperKev was not to be denied. Despite the driving rain and sodden surface, he tore out to the left hand side of the penalty area and spun around to chip an incredible shot over the 'keeper into the far corner of the net. The Toon Army was stunned into silence as those Mackems present went wild.

Having chanted for Shearer, the Geordies fans now turned their attention to Lee (who was not even at the ground), showing their dissatisfaction with Gullit's team selection policy. Many people felt that if the visitors had not taken the lead, referee Graham Poll might have abandoned the match so farcical had the conditions become. But once either side was in the lead, such a decision looked less and less likely. Sunderland tried to remain calm but began to wilt in the closing stages. Nobby Solano wasted a glorious chance in the 88th minute, shooting wide from inside the penalty area but it was in injury time that the real decisive moment came. Kevin Ball launched a determined tackle on Ferguson 30 yards out only for the ball to loop over his stranded goalkeeper and hit the bar. At that moment the Toon Army knew that they were beaten – and so it proved.

The delirious Mackems celebrated in style during the short trip over the Tyne on their way home as the death knell sounded over Gullit's reign at St James' Park. The *Newcastle Evening Chronicle* filled virtually the whole back page with the banner headline 'It Doesn't Get Any Worse Than This' – and they were not talking about the weather!

The manager exacerbated the situation with his two star strikers, Shearer and Ferguson, in an astonishing post-match interview by implying they were to blame for the defeat. His logic was based on the fact that United were winning until he began to change his starting line-up. This lost him most of his remaining support in the dressing room and his position became untenable. His team sheet for the game was later described, with more than an element of truth, as a 'suicide note'. Three days after the game, he resigned.

However his departure speech was gracious as he thanked the players for their efforts and professionalism (although, years later, he was to launch a scathing verbal attack on Shearer). He went on to thank the St James' Park staff for their assistance, his personal secretary, the hotel he had stayed in on Tyneside (Malmaison) and the restaurants he had dined in "for their marvellous food and hospitality". He specifically mentioned chairman Freddy

Shepherd and chief executive Freddie Fletcher for their support. The claustrophobic close-knit community on Tyneside had just become too oppressive for him – that and the disastrous start to the season. Just one point out of the opening 15 was the worst in Newcastle's history. The chairman also added his voice to the sorry affair by praising Ruud as a man of honour. To his credit, Gullit never made any claim for compensation.

Both Shearer and Ferguson were restored to the starting line-up for the next game, away to Manchester United but a 5-1 defeat did not augur well for the future. Veteran former England manager Bobby Robson was a popular choice as the next manager and, after a narrow defeat away to Chelsea in his first game in charge, he began to turn things round. An 8-0 win over Sheffield Wednesday in his first home game was a good start.

Never has the winning team in a North East derby received so little recognition for their achievement. But the win over Newcastle was just a start for Sunderland. They went on to chalk up a ten match unbeaten run in the league, winning seven of them. By Christmas they were to reach the heady heights of third in the Premiership. But they flattered to deceive and were not able to maintain the pace in the later stages of the campaign.

Premier League
Sunderland 2 Newcastle United 2 (HT: 1-2)
5th February 2000
Stadium of Light
42,192

Sunderland: 1 T Sorensen, 2 C Makin, 3 M Gray, 6 P Butler, 17 J Craddock, 20 S Schwarz*, 21 G McCann, 7 N Summerbee (31 M Reddy 75), 4 K Kilbane, 9 N Quinn, 10 K Phillips **[22, 83]**. Subs (unused) 13 A Marriott, 14 D Holloway, 16 A Rae, 29 E Roy
Newcastle: 13 S Harper, 2 W Barton, 36 A Pistone (18 A Hughes 36), 34 N Dabizas*, 39 Helder Cristovao **[21]**, 37 R Lee* (D Gavilan 88), 11 G Speed, 4 D Domi **[11]** (32 K Gallacher 88), 7 K Dyer, 20 D Ferguson, 9 A Shearer. Subs (unused) 1 S Given, 38 Fumaca (ie J Antunes)
Referee: Dermot Gallagher (Banbury)

THE RIVAL managers succinctly summed up the importance of the local derby. Peter Reid stated simply, "This is a bigger game than Manchester United". Bobby Robson expressed similar sentiments in a different way, "There is much more to running Newcastle United than getting a win against Sunderland but you can forget everything else this week".

Although Sunderland were well above Newcastle in the league, they had started to slip lately and had lost four of their last five league games (with the other one drawn). Changes were made from their last game with Chris Makin, Nicky Summerbee, Niall Quinn and Jody Craddock all returning although captain Steve Bould was missing due to suspension.

Robson made one change to his revitalised team, opting for Didier Domi in place of Kevin Gallacher with Nobby Solano still absent due to injury. Nicos Dabizas fuelled the derby fires by claiming, "Sunderland's strikers are predictable – a series of long, diagonal balls into the box for Quinn to flick on to Phillips". Significantly, however, he added, "But they are both strong players and sometimes it is not enough to know the oppositions' game".

This was the first Wear-Tyne derby to be played at the Stadium of Light but just 2,000 Newcastle fans were allowed in for the all-ticket clash. More than 10,000 watched beam back transmissions at the Telewest Arena in Newcastle and at St James' Park with both venues sold out. Added spice to the game was the anticipated clash between the top two scorers in the Premiership, Kevin Phillips (20 goals) and Alan Shearer (14).

League Positions

		Pos	Pl	Pts		Pos	Pl	Pts
Before:	Sunderland	5th	23	38	Newcastle	15th	23	27
After:	Sunderland	6th	24	39	Newcastle	13th	24	28

Both sides opted for a standard 4-4-2 formation but it was Newcastle, playing in striped shirts but white shorts, who took command in the first half when Keiron Dyer and Domi dictated midfield. They nearly grabbed an early lead when Duncan Ferguson powered a header goalwards following a Dyer corner only for Thomas Sorensen to pull off an amazing save, finger-tipping the effort over the bar. But it was a short-lived reprieve because United were back to open their account within a minute.

After 11 minutes Dyer started the move, cutting inside from the right to slip a pass to Ferguson who neatly played it on to Domi. The French midfielder tried a first time shot at goal and had luck on his side as the ball clipped Quinn and deflected past the helpless Sorensen.

Sunderland tried to hit back immediately, Gavin McCann flashing a free kick just wide. But soon Sorensen was back in action again, brilliantly keeping out a shot by Dyer although perhaps Ferguson should have scored from the rebound. Sunderland were being run ragged and it was no surprise when United scored again ten minutes later.

This goal also came from a Dyer set-piece – this time a free kick conceded by Makin on the Sunderland right flank. Dyer swung the ball into the middle where Helder was, incredibly, allowed a free header at goal. The Stadium of Light was stunned into silence – apart from the small section of 2,000 Geordies.

Once again Sunderland tried to hit back immediately – and this time they succeeded. As Dabizas had forecast, Sunderland attacking tactics were predictable – but stopping them was a different matter. A minute after Newcastle's goal, Chris Makin sent a high free kick into the Newcastle penalty area where Niall

Quinn rose high to flick the ball on for Kevin Phillips. SuperKev was able to run unimpeded into the Newcastle penalty area to joyfully steer the ball home between Harper's legs as the 'keeper tried to close him down.

Now the game was back in the melting pot and everything that was good (and bad) about English Premier League football was there for all to see with the spice of a critical derby to give it added flavour. It was a pulsating affair and the atmosphere was electric. Jody Craddock cleared off the line from Ferguson as Newcastle went for a crucial third goal. What United later claimed to be the turning point of the game came ten minutes before half-time when Pistone was blatantly tackled from behind by Summerbee and went down obviously badly hurt. Incredibly, referee Dermott Gallagher did not even give a free kick although the Italian had to be stretchered off with a broken leg. Aaron Hughes quickly came on in his place and did not let Newcastle down but the momentum had been lost. Indeed, the Black Cats could easily have been level by half-time when only an incredible save by Steve Harper denied Makin, the 'keeper somehow touching the ball on to the bar when the full back let fly with a terrific curling shot.

Newcastle had undoubtedly been the better team in the first half but it was a different story after interval as Sunderland forced their visitors back. United were under siege for long periods and it soon became a matter of whether they could hold out in the face of increasing pressure. Makin had never scored for Sunderland but it he seemed determined to rectify this statistic as he pushed forward to lend support to his strikers. But Harper was equally determined to stop him and Makin could hardly believe it as the 'keeper denied him yet again with another stupendous save on the hour mark. With a quarter of an hour to go, Peter Reid decided to change tactics to try and breach the Tyneside rearguard. He sent on Michael Reddy in place of Summerbee to add firepower up front and his ploy worked.

Time seemed to be running out for Sunderland when Kevin Kilbane arced a cross into the Newcastle penalty area. Phillips timed his dart forward to perfection as he stroked the ball home from close range. Newcastle claimed that he was offside and TV replays proved inconclusive but it's the referee's decision that counts and referee Gallagher indicated a goal. The Stadium of Light erupted in a tidal wave of delirium as the anxiety exploded and SuperKev found himself swamped by team mates and fans alike.

There were still seven minutes to go (plus injury time) and the game was not over yet. The initiative had clearly passed to Sunderland and there seemed as if there was going to be just one winner as they pushed forward to try and grab the clinching third goal. Another great save by Harper, this time from a McCann free kick, increased tensions even more. Bobby Robson eased the pressure and slowed the tempo of the game by making a couple of late substitutions and this did the trick. The scores were still level at the final whistle as players and supporters alike ended the game emotionally and physically exhausted.

In terms of the eagerly awaited clash between the Premiership's top scorers – Alan Shearer and Kevin Phillips – there is no doubt that the Sunderland man came out on top in this game. Big Al may have been the more prolific scorer over his career but SuperKev, with his two goals, showed that he was the current man in form. His display brought forth a clamour from Wearside and beyond for him to be given further chances in the England team. He was to continue this form and finish as top scorer in the Premiership with 30 goals and was consequently to be included in England's Euro 2000 squad during the following summer but was not to be given a run out. Nevertheless he was to be named as the Carling Player of the Year.

Shearer (who was to finish with 23 Premiership goals) was to retire from the international scene after the tournament. Intriguingly, both forwards were selected as the twin strikers in the *Rothmans Football Yearbook* Team of the Season.

Most Derby Goals Scored (Top 20)

	Newcastle United	Lge	FA Cup	Total		Sunderland	Lge	FA Cup	Total
1	J Milburn	11	0	11	1	G Holley	13	2	15
2	A Shepherd	7	2	8	2	A Bridgett	9	0	9
3	G Robledo	5	0	5		C Buchan	8	1	9
	J Rutherford	4	1	5	4	W Hogg	7	0	7
5	P Beardsley	4	0	4		J Mordue	4	3	7
	N Harris	4	0	4	6	D Halliday	5	0	5
	W Hibbert	4	0	4		C Fleming	5	0	5
	V Keeble	4	0	4		C Suggett	5	0	5
	T Lang	4	0	4	9	H R Buckle	4	0	4
	T McDonald	4	0	4		J Paterson	4	0	4
	R Mitchell	4	0	4		G Herd	4	0	4
	R Orr	3	1	4		R Hogg	4	0	4
	GS Seymour	4	0	4		K Phillips	4	0	4
	A Tait	4	0	4		L Shackleton	4	0	4
	G Wilson	2	2	4		T Ford	4	0	4
16	J Boyd	3	0	3	16	A Hawes	3	0	3
	W Curry	3	0	3		B Clough	3	0	3
	R Davies	3	0	3		W Bingham	3	0	3
	H Gallacher	3	0	3		A S Brown	2	1	3
	J Howie	3	0	3		W Holden	1	2	3
	T Urwin	3	0	3		R McKay	3	0	3
	C Veitch	2	1	3		T Wright	3	0	3
	L White	3	0	3		G Rowell	3	0	3
	A Shearer	3	0	3		R Marshall	3	0	3
						R Best	3	0	3

Player of the Decade
1990s

Paul William Bracewell

PAUL BRACEWELL was a player who enjoyed immense success as well as heart-breaking failure. Some of that success came on both Wearside and Tyneside but it was on Merseyside that he enjoyed his greatest years. Yet the FA Cup was to prove his nemesis – four appearances in the final and four defeats. It doesn't come any more heart-breaking than that. Yet he rose again and again to prove he was resilience personified.

Born in Heswall on the Wirral (then part of Cheshire) in 1962, Paul began his career as a 16-year-old apprentice with Stoke City, signing as a full time professional two years later. He made his league debut as a 17-year-old and soon became a permanent fixture in the Potters' first team, missing just three games in the next three seasons and being capped at Under-21 level in the process.

He was obviously destined for bigger things and so it proved when Sunderland splashed out £250,000 to take the young midfielder to Roker in the summer of 1983. He had won four Under-21 caps by the time Sunderland signed him and he soon added to that total (eventually being capped 13 times at that level). He quickly made an impact for the Rokermen who did not take long to realise they had unearthed a gem. But so did other teams and his first stay on Wearside did not last long. He moved to Everton at the end of his first season. At least Sunderland made a tidy profit on the deal with £425,000 changing hands.

He just missed Everton's success in the 1984 Cup Final but was able to help them win the Charity Shield in his first competitive game. There are not many better ways in making your debut for Everton than a 1-0 win over Liverpool in front of 100,000 at Wembley.

Things soon got even better with the League Championship winging its way to Goodison Park in his first season there as well as the European Cup Winners' Cup (a 3-1 win against Rapid Vienna). But there was also failure with defeat against Manchester United, 1-0, in the FA Cup Final.

Another defeat in the final of the following year, 3-1 against Liverpool, proved football can be a cruel mistress. But things were to take a sudden turn for the worse for Paul after that. A career threatening ankle injury ruled him out of action for over two years and he took no part in Everton's League Championship success of 1986-87. He returned to action in December 1988 and played, once again, in the Cup Final that season (another defeat by Liverpool, 3-2). Although by now a full international, having been capped three times in 1985 and '86, his ankle injury had undoubtedly affected him.

He returned to Wearside at the beginning of the 1989-90 season, initially on loan. This soon became a permanent arrangement and he became a key player in Sunderland's historic promotion campaign. Victory over Newcastle in the play-offs was especially sweet for all concerned with the Red'n Whites although eventual promotion, after losing to Swindon in the play-off final at Wembley, was achieved only after the Robins were demoted as punishment for a breach of league rules involving irregular payments to players.

Sadly Paul was not able to prevent Sunderland slipping straight back down into the Second Division although he was an ever present that season (1990-91). He captained them to the FA Cup Final in the following year, his fourth final, but once again he had to be satisfied with a losers' medal. For the third time it was Liverpool who proved to be his undoing. As someone born near Merseyside, and an ex-Toffee, this must have been hard to take.

The Cup Final turned out to be his last game during this stint at Roker because he was soon on his way again. His contract expired that summer but Wearside fans were as stunned as those on Tyneside when Newcastle manager Kevin Keegan swooped to sign him, seeing the experienced midfielder as the ideal man to steady the Magpies' engine room in a concerted challenge for promotion.

He scored the opening goal of a campaign that was to eventually end in success with the 'new' First Division Championship coming to St James'. But an ankle injury sustained in that very first game was to sideline him and set the standard for the whole season. Liam O'Brien quickly claimed the midfield berth and made a success of it as Paul struggled against injury. Consequently he missed more games than he played. However O'Brien succumbed to injury himself in the later stages of the campaign and Paul was able to step into the breech for the run in to the title.

He was the anchor man in midfield when United finished third in their first season back (1993-94). But disaster struck during the following summer. He had already undergone two recent groin operations when it was disclosed that a serious pelvic complaint would require prolonged rest and that he could be out of action for the full season. But his 'complaint' was much worse than that – a cancer scare. Yet he overcame this setback as well and his will power and determination saw him back in action by the turn of the year and back in Newcastle's first team.

By the end of the 1994-95 season, he was approaching his 33rd birthday and it was time for him to look beyond playing. So when the opportunity came for him to join his former Everton team mate Peter Reid, newly appointed as Sunderland's manager, he was more than happy to sign for a third time for the Rokermen, this time as a player/coach.

If anyone thought that Paul's career as a player was coming to an end, he certainly proved them wrong. In his first season back on Wearside he was a regular in midfield as he helped to guide Sunderland to the First Division title, thus completing a North East double.

Sadly the following year (1996-97) was to see them slip out of the Premiership again but at least they made a fight of it, going down in third bottom place by a very narrow margin with five clubs within two points above them. But there was personal satisfaction for Paul this season as he managed to chalk up a full set of league appearances.

But time catches up with everyone and by the start of the 1997-98 campaign he was 35 and clearly in the veteran stage of his career. He was to make just one more league appearance for Sunderland, as a substitute in a 4-0 win away to Bradford City in

September, although he played in both legs of a second round Coca Cola Cup tie against Bury as well (both wins). By the time Sunderland faced Middlesbrough in the third round in mid-October (a 2-0 defeat away from home), Paul had left the club to join his former boss Kevin Keegan as player/coach at Fulham for a £75,000 fee.

As if to prove that there was life in the old dog yet, Paul missed just one league game from his Fulham debut in October until the end of the season as he helped to guide the Cottagers into the Division 2 play-offs. Unfortunately there was to be no fairy tale ending with Fulham losing out to Grimsby Town. But success came during the following season (1998-99) when Fulham stormed to the Second Division title, finishing a massive 14 points ahead of Walsall. Paul, by now 37, stopped playing on a regular basis in February although he made one final appearance as a substitute in the penultimate game of the campaign.

Just over a week later, Keegan was appointed as full time England coach and Paul found himself in the hot seat as his successor at Craven Cottage. He did reasonably well during his first year in charge with a top half finish in the league. But this was not good enough for owner Mohammed Al Fayed who replaced him with Frenchman Jean Tigana before the season ended.

The Shay was Paul's next port of call with the remit to keep struggling Halifax Town in the Football League. Relegation was avoided (only just) in 2000-01 but a bad start to the following campaign saw him become the first managerial casualty of the season as he and the club parted 'by mutual consent' before the end of August.

He worked for two years as a national coach with the Football Association with him playing a key role with the England youth teams. But, by early 2004, he felt that it was time to move on to face other challenges.

These challenges obviously include coaching – as Walsall could testify – but what the long term future holds for Paul remains to be seen. One thing is certain, if he enjoys half as much success as a coach as he did as a player, some clubs are going to grateful for his experience and ability.

Record

Sunderland	June 1983 – May 1984	
	August 1989 – June 1992	
	May 1995 – October 1998	
Football League	226 (2 sub) apps	6 gls
Play Offs	3 apps	-
FA Cup	15 apps	-
Football League Cup	21 apps	-
Others	3 apps	-
Total	268 (2 sub) apps	6 gls
Newcastle	June 1992 – May 1995	
Football League	64 (9 sub) apps	3 gls
FA Cup	6 (2 sub) apps	-
Football League Cup	3 (1 sub) apps	1 gl
Other	2 apps	-
Total	75 (12 sub) apps	4 gls

CHAPTER 12

2000s
A Tale of Two Cities

THE QUEEN had marked the 40th anniversary of her accession to the throne in 1992 by bestowing 'City' status upon Sunderland in recognition of its efforts to overcome the decline and disappearance of its traditional heavy industries and its endeavours at reconstruction. The Stadium of Light was to become symbolic of this reconstruction, at least from a sporting point of view. So when the new century dawned, Sunderland AFC were welll established in their new home and the rivalry between the Tyne and the Wear was really a tale of two ctities in sporting conflict.

The new millenium started well for Sunderland. Not only did they chalk up a prestigious win over the Magpies at St James' Park (drawing the return fixture at the Stadium of Light) but they were able to lord it over their neighbours in terms of a Premiership finishing position as well. A very respectable seventh place in 2001, four places above Newcastle, was exactly the same as in the previous season.

But for many Wearside fans, seventh place was something of a disappointment. They had hoped the previous year would be a springboard to success and so it had seemed for a while with their favourites lying second to long time leaders and eventual champions Manchester United in mid-January. Instead this was to be their zenith in the Premiership and they were never even to claim a place in Europe by virtue of their league position.

The following season (2001-02) saw decline set in as the Magpies became top dogs in the North East again. Indeed, Newcastle briefly topped the Premiership around Christmas time although they had to settle for fourth place. The Geordie fans were more than satisfied with this, especially as Sunderland embarked on a downward spiral in the latter half of the season. Defeat at home to the Mags in late February was the start of a horrendous sequence of defeats with the Black Cats winning just two of their last twelve games to finish in a worrying 17th position, only one spot above relegation.

But it was to get worse, much worse, in the following season. 2002–03 was to be one of the worst in Sunderland's history. They started off reasonably well, losing just one of their first four games. But by the time they met Newcastle at St James' Park in September, the rot had well and truly set in. Decline quickly became disaster as defeat followed defeat with monotonous regularity.

Incredibly they picked up only one point out of 57 in the second half of the season to finish in rock bottom place, 26 points from safety. To make matters worse, Newcastle completed a league double over them. By the time the return fixture took place, Mick McCarthy had taken over the hot seat from Peter Reid but by then the battle for Premiership survival had been lost.

United again briefly topped the Premiership in mid-season but were never really in contention for the title and most fans were happy with a third place finish and qualification for the potentially lucrative European Champions League for 2003–04. Their enjoyment of this elite tournament was to be short-lived although participation in the UEFA Cup as compensation was to see them reach the semi-final only to succumb to a crippling injury situation and Olympique Marseille.

Mick McCarthy eventually turned things around at Sunderland and the Black Cats mounted a decent, although ultimately unsuccessful, challenge for promotion in 2003-04. They finished third and had to face sixth-placed Crystal Palace in the semi-final of the play-offs. Wearside fans had to endure the trauma of a penalty shoot-out elimination at home. There was little sympathy from Newcastle fans who thought back to their own elimination at the hands of the Black Cats in similar circumstances in 1990.

When Newcastle had won at the Stadium of Light in April 2003, Sunderland had already been condemned to relegation. At the end of the game the Black'n White fans had taunted their Red'n White counterparts en masse with the classic Second World War song:

"We'll meet again
Don't know where
Don't know when
But I'll know we'll meet again
Some sunny day".

The 'sunny day' for Wearside came two years later when Sunderland stormed to the Coca Cola Football League Championship title, finishing a comfortable seven points clear of second placed Wigan Athletic. By an ironic quirk of fate, on the very day that they collected the trophy, Dame Vera Lynn was on stage with Katherine Jenkins in Trafalgar Square joining in the community singing of the wartime anthem as part of the celebrations to mark the 50th anniversary of VE Day.

Meanwhile, on Tyneside, the reign of local hero Sir Bobby Robson had come to a controversial end. His two predecessors, Kenny Dalglish and Ruud Gullit, had resigned under pressure but Sir Bobby was made of sterner stuff and the club had to sack him to get rid of him. All three had left in August with little time for their successors to draft in new players before the transfer deadline. Few fans wanted Graeme Souness as their new manager and he had problems on his hands as his first season in the St James' hot seat was marred by player confrontation. Top scorer Craig Bellamy was initially sent into exile in Scotland (to Celtic) before finally being transferred to Blackburn.

Others were also shown the door as the new boss tried to clear the decks to bring in his type of player. Great things had been expected of Patrick Kluivert but he had failed to deliver and was released. With dead ball specialist Laurent Robert also leaving Gallowgate, many fans wondered where the goals were going to come from in 2005-06, even with Alan Shearer deciding to defer his retirement and sign for another year.

A semi-final appearance in the FA Cup and the quarter-final of the UEFA Cup in 2005 merely papered over the cracks and showed the lack of depth in terms of quality at the club as injuries once again took their toll. Most fans and pundits pointed to a 14th place finish in the Premiership as a more accurate indication of Newcastle's fall from grace. Sir Bobby had been sacked for finishing only fifth the previous season.

To describe the start to the 2005-06 season for both North East giants as 'inauspicious' would be an understatement; 'horrendous' would be a better description.

By the end of August, Newcastle had been eliminated from the Inter-Toto Cup and had failed to find the net in any of their opening four league games. They found themselves wallowing in second bottom place in the Premiership with just one point out of a possible twelve and only a goalless draw at home to West Ham to show for their efforts.

Yet things were even worse at Sunderland with the Black Cats propping up the Magpies in the league. Expectations had not been high on Wearside, despite Sunderland comfortably winning the Coca Cola Championship in the previous season, but this was a rude awakening.

Both Newcastle and Sunderland were heavily in debt. United's was greater but most of it was long term and it was the Wearsiders who had immediate funding problems. The club had been forced to sell their star players (and thus the highest wage earners) like Kevin Phillips and Thomas Sorensen after relegation in 2003. Overall, they had managed to half the wage bill but it also meant McCarthy had to operate on a comparative shoestring.

Such was the financial situation at the Stadium of Light that he had limited funds to try and build a Premiership standard team. He gambled on a series of bargains and free transfers from the lower leagues rather than splash out on one big name player. His gamble misfired with Sunderland failing to pick up a single point from their opening five games.

Graeme Souness had no such funding problems, splashing out on Emre (£4.5m), Scott Parker (£6.5m) and Albert Luque (£9.5m). When that was not enough he was able to invest a further £16.5m on Real Madrid's England striker, Michael Owen. The purchase of Owen alone was four times the amount that McCarthy had been able to spend. His signing of Jon Stead (£1.8m), Kelvin Davies (£1.25m), Andy Gray (£1.1m) and Daryl Murphy (£100,000) were small beer in comparison. However some astute free transfers and loan signings in the shape of Tommy Miller, Nyron Nosworthy, Alan Stubbs, Christian Bassila, Justin Hoyte and Anthony Le Tallec supplemented the squad. Yet the Black Cats' fans were not fooled. They knew that a season of struggle lay ahead although they put a brave face on things. Survival was their target.

By the time the two sides met in late October, matters had improved somewhat, particularly for Newcastle. Despite an appalling record of mainly muscle related injuries, they had slowly clawed their way up the league. Sunderland, also afflicted by a lengthy injury list, had also managed to drag themselves off the bottom.

But both sides were forced to field weakened teams in the Tyne-Wear derby. The absence of Owen from the United line-up undoubtedly gave the Black Cats hope. The teams may have been weakened but the entertainment in this game was magnificent. The match had pace, power, pride and passion and was emotionally exhausting for players and fans alike. Newcastle won by the odd goal in five because they had one thing that Sunderland did not have – luck!

But Graeme Souness was anything but 'lucky' after this and hopes of a European qualifying campaign quickly evaporated as the injury situation deteriorated. When Michael Owen sustained a broken bone in his foot at Tottenham on New Year's Eve, United suddenly found themselves slipping towards the relegation zone.

Mick McCarthy had enjoyed a vote of confidence by the fans in a newspaper poll run by the local press on Wearside. But Souness, who had never been a popular choice as manager on Tyneside, found that a wave of unrest was building up.

By the beginning of February, the North East's 'big three' found themselves in the bottom six in the league and disillusionment growing among all three groups of fans. By now, even the Sunderland supporters were beginning to doubt McCarthy.

Newcastle were the highest placed of the 'big three' but it was Souness who was sacked, academy manager and former captain Glenn Roeder taking over as caretaker manager with club captain Alan Shearer acting as his assistant. This happened early in February following protests at St James' Park but there was an immediate upturn in fortunes with Newcastle setting off on a run of half a dozen games undefeated, five of them wins.

Sunderland's supporters had been much more tolerant, perhaps appreciating McCarthy's success in getting the club back into the Premier League last season coupled with sympathy for Mick, feeling he had been hamstrung by inadequate funding. Most of the fans' anger was aimed at those higher up in the club with chairman Bob Murray being the main target of their wrath. When the latter sacked McCarthy early in March with Sunderland firmly in bottom place and relegation inevitable, the fans' ire turned on the chairman.

Murray took a leaf out of Freddie Shepherd's book at Newcastle by appointing a former captain and club academy coach as caretaker boss. Kevin Ball was undoubtedly popular but injury-ridden Sunderland were in a much more parlous state than Newcastle and there was to be no similar improvement on Wearside.

With 22 defeats from 28 games, most supporters had accepted the inevitability of relegation long before McCarthy's departure. Even avoiding the wooden spoon seemed an unrealistic target. But there were two objectives as the run-in to the end of the season began: avoiding setting a new all-time low Premier League points haul of 19 (set by themselves in 2003) and, more importantly, beating Newcastle at the Stadium of Light on Easter Monday.

Sunderland were mathematically relegated on Good Friday despite a magnificent defensive performance away to Manchester United when the Black Cats became the first team to stop the Red Devils from scoring at Old Trafford this season. But a 0-0 draw was not enough and the Red'n Whites were already relegated by the time they welcomed the Magpies to the Stadium of Light.

If anything, Newcastle's injury situation was worse for this game than it had been for the match at St James' back in October. But, unlike Souness, Glenn Roeder refused to use the injuries as an excuse for inadequate performances. In any event, Sunderland had injuries of their own.

This season had been unbelievably cruel on the Wearside supporters and this was encapsulated in this game as Newcastle came from a half time deficit to hit the home side with devastating effectiveness. Two goals in 90 seconds shattered the Black Cats and the Magpies rubbed salt in the wounds with two further goals as they chalked up a 4-1 victory. Even the loss of skipper Alan Shearer to an injury that would curtail his career with just three games to go could not take the gloss off the Geordies' celebrations.

So Sunderland (who failed to reach their 19 points target) went back down to the Championship with, statistically, the worst record ever in the Premiership. But they knew that they would be back 'some sunny day' (as the Newcastle fans reminded them with a further rendition of "We'll Meet Again").

The only redeeming feature of their brief sojourn in the top flight this time round had been their fans. They had earned the praise and admiration of the football world with their loyalty and devotion. With one of the best stadiums in the country and some of the best supporters, it could only be a matter of time before they would regain their rightful place in the top flight. Then fans from both sides of the great North East divide could again cheer their favourites on against their arch rivals with the traditional call...

"HA'WAY/HOWAY THE LADS"

League Meetings (8)

At Newcastle:	Newcastle – won 2 drew 1 lost 1
At Sunderland:	Sunderland – won 0 drew 1 lost 3

Premier League

Newcastle United 1 Sunderland 2 (HT: 1-0)

18th November 2000
St James' Park
52,030

Newcastle: 1 S Given, 30 S Caldwell, 7 R Lee*, 18 A Hughes, 15 N Solano, 6 C Acuna (2 W Barton 77), 10 C Bassedas (20 L Lua Lua 56), 11 G Speed [4], 4 D Domi, 8 K Dyer, 9 A Shearer. Subs (unused) 13 S Harper, 12 A Griffin, 17 D Cordone
Sunderland: 1 T Sorensen, 2 C Makin (33 J Arca 66), 36 Emerson Thome*, 17 J Craddock, 3 M Gray*, 4 D Hutchison* [67], 18 D Williams, 16 A Rae, 11 K Kilbane, 9 N Quinn [75] (12 D Dichio 85), 10 K Phillips. Subs (unused) 30 J Macho, 28 J Oster, 32 S Varga
Referee: Graham Poll (Tring, Hertfordshire)

SUNDERLAND HAD not won away in the league so far this season and manager Peter Reid was now under pressure. Bookmakers were offering odds of 14-1 on him being sacked after the weekend but he remained upbeat about the situation and fielded an unchanged team from the side that had drawn at home to Southampton. Stefan Schwarz and Gavin McCann were on the road back from long term injuries and had turned out for the reserves but were not ready for the first team yet.

Bobby Robson had slightly more serious injury problems, particular in defence. Nicos Dabizas and Marcelino had been out since the first couple of games of the season and Alain Goma failed a late fitness test so 20 year old Steve Caldwell was brought in for his first league start. Carl Cort was also a long term injury but Nobby Solano returned from a one game absence due to a pulled hamstring, Andy Griffin dropping down to the substitutes' bench.

Robson called his foreign players together to explain the importance of the game, comparing it with AC Milan v Inter, Roma v Lazio and even Real Madrid v Barcelona. Interestingly Newcastle and Sunderland were captained by a Geordie (Alan Shearer) and a Mackem (Michael Gray) for the first time in modern times.

The pre-match talk from the Newcastle camp was about how they were going to gain revenge for last season's defeat by their arch-enemies. Last year there had been an excuse – Newcastle had been a club in turmoil and the game had been played in ridiculous monsoon conditions. Today there could be no excuses.

League Positions		Pos	Pl	Pts		Pos	Pl	Pts
Before:	Newcastle	7th	13	20	Sunderland	12th	13	17
After:	Newcastle	8th	14	20	Sunderland	9th	14	20

Newcastle started off as if revenge was their's for the taking as they swarmed all over Sunderland. They should have taken the lead after only 20 seconds. Didier Domi played a through-ball to Gary Speed, who found himself in unbelievable space on the edge of the Sunderland penalty area only to panic and scuff a miserable shot well wide. But he was to make amends after four minutes. Robert Lee started the move with a superb pass out to the over-lapping Solano wide on the right. His cross found Speed rushing into the penalty area. At first it looked as if he had missed again as his header thudded against the left hand post but the ball deflected off Don Hutchison's back to the Welshman who was prostrate on the ground on the edge of the six yard box. He was alert enough to hook the ball home and the crowd went wild.

Newcastle continued to dominate the opening exchanges and they almost scored a second a couple of minutes later when Solano curled a free kick from the left to where Acuna came diving in to send his header into the side-netting from a narrow angle at the far post. But Sunderland also had the odd chance, Niall Quinn forcing Shay Given into a back-peddling, finger-tip save with a delicate lob from just outside the penalty area. But this was a rare excursion by the visitors into Newcastle territory. Yet Sunderland could easily have been awarded a penalty when Shearer tugged at Jody Craddock's shirt following a left wing cross and the Sunderland man, blatantly impeded, managed only to direct his header straight at Given. United were soon back on the offensive and a couple of minutes later Speed stole behind the Sunderland defence to meet another Solano free kick and power in a downward header that goalkeeper Thomas Sorenson saved well, low down to his right.

Slowly but surely, however, the Wearsiders battled their way back into the game in midfield. They showed up dangerously when Alex Rae dispossessed Lee and broke towards the Newcastle goal. Sunderland had numerical advantage – three on to two – but Steve Caldwell rose to the occasion and halted Rae with a superb tackle. Yet another Speed effort, this time from 20 yards, flashed narrowly wide of the right hand post. A frenetic first half played in a white hot atmosphere, ended with Sunderland pouring forward but failing to create a single clear cut chance. This was largely due to heroic defensive work by United's young central defenders, Aaron Hughes and Caldwell. The Scot, in particular, seemed to relish the physical elements of the game. There is no doubt that Newcastle deserved to be ahead by more than their single goal at half time but there was an uneasy feeling among some of their supporters that they could be made to pay for their missed chances.

This proved to be the case although they had a good chance to increase their lead a couple of minutes into the second half when Acuna broke into the penalty area to send in a header following good work by Christian Bassedas and Solano. However his hurried effort sent the ball wide of the target with just the 'keeper to beat. The pace of the game in the second half was slower than the first although tensions built up among the crowd. This became worse as Sunderland pushed forward and Newcastle were forced to defend. Given made a superb diving save to keep out a Quinn header but the reprieve was short-lived because the Wearsiders were back within a minute to grab the equaliser after 67minutes.

Kevin Phillips had hardly been in the game when he received the ball out on Sunderland's left wing. However he sprung into life as he turned Hughes inside out before crossing low into the middle where Hutchison arrived late at the far post to plant a left foot shot from just inside the six yard box into the net. Now it was the turn of the Sunderland fans, perched high up in the north west corner of the stands, to go wild.

To their credit, Newcastle responded positively and were very unlucky not to regain the lead three minutes later when Solano blasted in a free kick from nearly 30 yards out. His shot easily beat the motionless Sorenson but agonisingly hit the inside of a post and came out. If that was hard to bear, much worse was to follow for the Newcastle fans when, with fifteen minutes remaining, Sunderland skipper Michael Gray broke down the left and crossed perfectly. The towering Quinn met the ball with his head from near the penalty spot and it looped over Given into the Newcastle net.

The atmosphere was now white hot as both sets of fans screamed their teams on. Suddenly, in the 82nd minute, Newcastle received a lifeline. Robert Lee burst into the Sunderland penalty area on the left and was needlessly up-ended by a reckless challenge by Quinn – it was a penalty! Up stepped Shearer to blast the spot kick on target but Thomas Sorenson guessed correctly and dived to his left to block the effort. Newcastle knew then that they had lost. The final whistle went with Sunderland's fans screaming "We beat the scum 2-1".

As the disconsolate Newcastle fans streamed away, the stadium announcer perkily broadcast a message to the effect that "Freddy Shepherd and the Board thank you for your support and hope that you enjoyed the game and have a great weekend". For most Newcastle fans this result had ruined their year – and he was talking about having a great weekend! The comment emphasised the gulf between some of the people who ran the club and the supporters.

But it certainly was a great weekend for the Sunderland fans who, for the second year in succession, went back over the Tyne with the three points in the bag. And this time the Geordies could have no excuses about the defeat.

For Sunderland, this was just the start of an encouraging campaign. They now embarked on a very impressive run in the league when they lost only one and drew one of ten successive Premiership games. This was to lift them to second top of the league by mid-January although they were not able to maintain this standard in the later stages of the season.

Newcastle? A season of mid-table mediocrity was to follow but things would get better – eventually.

Premier League

Sunderland 1 Newcastle United 1 (HT: 0-0)

21st April 2001
Stadium of Light
48,277

Sunderland: 1 T Sorensen, 5 P Carteron [**66**], 3 M Gray*, 17 J Craddock, 36 Emerson Thome, 20 S Schwarz*, 4 D Hutchison*, 8 G McCann, 9 N Quinn*, 10 K Phillips*, 33 J Arca. Subs (unused) 30 J Macho, 21 P Thirlwell, 18 D Williams, 11 K Kilbane, 32 S Varga
Newcastle: ! S Given, 2 W Barton*, 14 W Quinn, 34 N Dabizas, 5 A O'Brien [**78**], 15 N Solano (12 A Griffin 76), 6 C Acuna* (17 D Cordone 76), 11 G Speed*, 10 C Bassedas*, 32 K Gallacher (23 S Ameobi 76), 16 C Cort.
Subs (unused) 13 S Harper, 18 A Hughes
Referee: Mike Riley (Leeds)

THE GAME started at 5.15pm on a Saturday to accommodate a live Sky TV broadcast, a time that was heavily criticised as it meant that many fans would spend the day drinking, giving concerns about safety. Sunderland manager Peter Reid appealed for calm.

Newcastle bussed their supporters from St James' Park to avoid conflict between the rival factions and this tactic largely worked although over 40 fans (of both persuasions) were still arrested before the kick off because everyone did not take up the offer of free transport.

The game was sold out with Newcastle being allocated 3,000 tickets. With both Don Hutchison (groin) and Gavin McCann (ankle) recovering from injuries, Reid had a full strength squad to pick from apart from long term absentee Alex Rae. But the Wearsiders were having a bad run of results and their European qualification aspirations were disappearing fast. They were now four points behind sixth placed Liverpool who had two games in hand. Peter admitted, "We're going through a terrible spell at the moment. This is when you find out about people".

Robert Lee was not able to turn out for Newcastle despite intensive treatment on a knee injury although Warren Barton declared himself fit enough to play even though he had lasted just nine minutes of United's last game due to an Achilles tendon injury. But he summed up the determination in the Magpie camp when he said, "My foot would have to be chopped off before I missed this match". Sunderland had not beaten Newcastle on Wearside for 21 years and this was their first chance to complete the double over them for 34.

Neither team had been in form recently with Newcastle winning just one of their last eight games. Sunderland were even worse with one win in their last eleven. But these statistics stood for nothing as far as the fans were concerned. To say that passions were high for this match would be an under-statement. They were at frenzy level, both on the pitch and in the crowd. There was so much at stake.

League Positions		Pos	Pl	Pts		Pos	Pl	Pts
Before:	Sunderland	8th	34	49	Newcastle	13th	32	42
After:	Sunderland	8th	35	50	Newcastle	13th	33	43

This was always going to be a physical encounter and no quarter was asked nor given by either side. Referee Mike Riley booked no fewer than nine players as passions overflowed. Newcastle showed up first on attack but Sunderland weathered the early storm and gradually gained the upper hand with the impressive Julio Arca causing the visitors all sorts of trouble on their right flank. This was the main difference between the teams. It was one of a number of perfect crosses by him after 37 minutes that almost broke the deadlock.

Emerson Thome met the ball perfectly with a free header that powered against Shay Given's right hand post with the 'keeper nowhere in sight. Within another couple of minutes, Arca was back again. Another centre caused chaos in the Newcastle penalty area until Andy O'Brien relieved his lines by slicing the ball away for a corner. It was still level at half time but Sunderland had looked the more likely scorers in the first half after the early Newcastle flurry. Fortunately for them, Nicos Dabizas had Niall Quinn well shackled and Andy O'Brien had the ace Sunderland striker, Kevin Phillips, under control.

Newcastle had come back into the game as an attacking force just before the interval and they continued where they had left off when play resumed. But soon Sunderland were back on the attack. Arca (again) and Hutchison combined to set up a Kevin Phillips' header but Given pulled off a superb save. He did even better to deny Phillips a few minutes later when he tipped another effort over the bar.

Sunderland's pressure eventually paid off with a classic goal mid-way through the half. Emerson brought the ball out of defence and picked up Hutchison with a pass out to the right. The Gateshead born Scottish international played a perfect pass forward and inside for Patrice Carteron to run on to. He raced into the box from the right before firing low under Given's despairing dive and the Stadium of Light erupted.

Now came Newcastle's test of character. After defending so valiantly for so long, could they fight their way back? Carl Cort certainly thought so because he soon sent in a towering header that Sorensen just managed to tip over the top – a superb save. From the resultant corner, Dabizas managed to get a header on target but it was cleared by Carteron. Bobby Robson tried his three card trick a quarter of an hour from time, bringing on his three substitutes at once and his ploy paid dividends almost immediately.

After 78 miutes Andy Griffin sent over a cross beyond the far post where Cort stole in to turn the ball back inside for Andy O'Brien who stabbed it home from just inside the six yard box. Now it was the Geordie fans', located behind Sorensen's goal, turn to go wild.

Newcastle could even have wrapped up all three points near the end. First Speed almost clinched it with a half chance but his effort from the edge of the box was well saved. Then, right at the death, Ameobi hesitated when he could have gambled with a shot. But defeat for Sunderland would have been a travesty. They had dominated the game for long spells and had deserved to get something out of it. It was not for nothing that Shay Given was rated as United's top performer on the day. Yet it was the Magpies who won the corner count, 8 – 4, so a draw was probably a fair result.

Although the match ended all square, only one set of supporters celebrated as the crowds left the Stadium of Light – Newcastle's. Their team had vindicated itself by coming from behind and at the same time seemed to have delivered a major body blow to Sunderland's European aspirations. In the event, it made little difference. The Black Cats were to win two of their least three games and draw the other one but a final 7th position in the league was not to be good enough for European qualification.

Newcastle were to finish six points behind their neighbours in mid-table. Both clubs knew that they should have done better.

Premier League
Newcastle United 1 Sunderland 1 (HT: 1-1)
26th August 2001
St James' Park
52,021

Newcastle: 1 S Given, 2 W Barton*, 3 R Elliott (5 A O'Brien 38), 34 N Dabizas, 18 A Hughes, 4 N Solano, 7 R Lee, 11 G Speed (6 C Acuna 41), 32 L Robert*, 17 C Bellamy [43], 23 S Ameobi (9 A Shearer 74). Subs (unused) 13 S Harper, 20 L LuaLua
Sunderland: 1 T Sorensen, 2 B Haas*, 3 M Gray, 6 Emerson Thome, 17 J Craddock, 20 S Schwarz (16 A Rae 90), 4 D Hutchison (15 D Bellion 69), 8 G McCann*, 9 N Quinn, 10 K Phillips [34], 11 K Kilbane. Subs (unused) 24 G McCartney, 30 J Macho, 33 J Arca
Referee: Mike Riley (Leeds)

THE DERBY took place on a Sunday, a week into the season, with a 4.00pm kick off. Newcastle had taken part in the Inter-Toto Cup pre-season and probably had an edge in match fitness. On the other hand, they had injury problems with Alan Shearer, Kieron Dyer and Carl Cort all out of action although the former England captain was named as a substitute for this game. Sunderland were looking for a hat-trick of Gallowgate wins having beaten United 2-1 in the two previous seasons.

Both clubs had strengthened their sides during the summer with Newcastle recruiting Laurent Robert, Craig Bellamy and Robbie Elliott. Sunderland's only new face in their starting line-up was Bernt Haas. Their big summer signing, Lilian Laslandes, was not even named as a substitute although free transfer recruit David Bellion was.

League Positions

		Pos	Pl	Pts		Pos	Pl	Pts
Before:	Sunderland	13th	2	3	Newcastle	16th	1	1
After:	Sunderland	10th	3	4	Newcastle	14th	2	2

The atmosphere was electric and, as usual, passions were high as both teams made a tentative start to the game. A clash between Haas and Elliott ended with the Sunderland man staggering off the pitch to have stitches inserted in a head wound.

Two minutes after Haas returned to the fray in the 32nd minute, Sunderland opened the scoring. Stefan Schwarz sent over a perfect cross into the Newcastle penalty area and Kevin Phillips, one of the smallest men on the field, caught the home defence ball watching as he beat everybody to it and flicked home a header from close range.

The goal raised Sunderland's confidence and for a while it looked as if they were going to condemn Newcastle to a third successive home derby defeat, especially when the Magpies lost both Robbie Elliott and Gary Speed in quick succession due to injuries. But just as the visitors seemed to be gaining the ascendancy, Newcastle struck back with a goal of absolute quality.

It came two minutes before half-time. Laurent Robert weighted a perfect 40 yard through ball from the centre circle for Craig Bellamy to chase. His blistering pace took him clear of the Wearside defence and, without breaking his stride, he blasted a rocket of a shot that Sorensen managed to touch but could not stop. The goal gave Newcastle the upper hand and they controlled most of the second half. Robert Lee, whose testimonial game had been a couple of weeks earlier, was particularly outstanding in midfield as the Magpies took the game by the scruff of the neck.

Thomas Sorensen proved to be his usual barrier to Tyneside aspirations and a mixture of great saves by him and poor finishing by Newcastle (Solano in particular) kept Sunderland in the game. Alan Shearer came on to a tremendous welcome from the home supporters for the last quarter of an hour or so but none of the chances fell to him. Manager Peter Reid and most of the Sunderland fans were relieved to hear the final whistle and leave Tyneside with a point.

Sunderland were undoubtedly happier with the draw than Newcastle. But United had only themselves to blame for not turning their second half superiority into goals. Peter Reid was particularly happy with his side's team spirit and never-say-die attitude.

Bobby Robson realised that this was very early in the campaign and he felt that he had seen enough in his team's performance to be quite optimistic about the season ahead. The biggest plus for Newcastle was the successful return to action after a six month absence by Alan Shearer.

Premier League
Sunderland 0 Newcastle United 1 (HT: 0-0)
24th February 2002
Stadium of Light
48,290

Sunderland: 1 T Sorensen, 2 B Haas, 3 M Gray, 12 J Bjorklund, 17 J Craddock, 20 S Schwarz (26 T Butler 70), 16 J McAteer*, 4 C Reyna, 11 K Kilbane*, 9 N Quinn (7 P Mboma 45*), 10 K Phillips. Subs (unused) 30 J Macho, 18 D Williams, 24 G McCartney
Newcastle: 1 S Given, 18 A Hughes, 24 S Distin, 5 A O'Brien, 34 N Dabizas [63], 4 N Solano, 7 J Jenas, 11 G Speed, 32 L Robert (23 S Ameobi 89), 17 C Bellamy*, 9 A Shearer. Subs (unused) 13 S Harper, 3 R Elliott, 6 C Acuna, 20 L Lua Lua
Referee: Graham Barber (Tring)

DURING A week in which Bobby Robson celebrated his 69th birthday, Sunderland manager Peter Reid led calls for the veteran Newcastle boss to be knighted. Peter summed up the importance of this derby match when he recalled, "I have played in both Merseyside and Manchester derbies – games that are massive – but they don't come any bigger than this. The atmosphere it generates is second to none."

He had a good record in North East derbies, having lost just one out of seven against Newcastle during his time on Wearside. But this did not stop a section of Sunderland fans turning against him after a string of poor results. Many accused him of lacking ambition in the transfer market. Newcastle had just signed top teenage prospect Jermaine Jenas from Ipswich for £5million and had Alan Shearer (£15m), Laurent Robert (£10m) and Craig Bellamy (£6) in their ranks. Sunderland had yet to break the £5million barrier with their signings with Cameroon striker Patrick Mboma their most recent recruit and he was only on loan from Parma until the end of the season. He had yet to play although they had high expectations of him. So it was a bit of a surprise when he was named only as one of the substitutes.

Both sides had players absent due to injury but Sunderland's situation was much worse than Newcastle's. McCann (knee injury), Thirlwell (ankle) and Emerson Thome (knee) were all ruled out for the Black Cats but only Dyer (foot) was a first choice absentee for the Magpies.

United came into the game riding high in the league, five points behind

349

leaders Manchester United with Arsenal and Liverpool between them. But with this being a Sunday match, the Geordies had games in hand over the teams above them, two in the case of Manchester and Liverpool and one over Arsenal.

The game kicked off at 1.00pm to minimise potential crowd trouble.

League Positions		Pos	Pl	Pts		Pos	Pl	Pts
Before:	Newcastle	4th	26	52	Sunderland	13th	26	31
After:	Newcastle	2nd	27	55	Sunderland	14th	27	31

The form book can go out of the window in local derbies and this seemed to be the case when Sunderland started as the brighter side. O'Brien had to be alert to clear an early Reyna effort and Phillips fired over the top from six yards soon afterwards. But Craig Bellamy quickly demonstrated what everyone knew – that his pace would worry any defence. He burst clear in the 16th minute to run on to an Aaron Hughes' pass and drive the ball past the exposed Sorenson. To Sunderland's relief, an offside flag came to their rescue although TV replays later showed that the referee's assistant had erred as Bellamy had been fractionally behind the ball at the moment it was played to him.

Five minutes later the speedy Welshman once again had the Wearsiders holding their breaths. Shearer out-jumped Bjorklund to glance on a back-header and Bellamy hit a half volley first time that just cleared the bar and clipped the top of the net. Not that Newcastle had it all their own way and Sunderland could very well have taken the lead in the 25th minute. A high centre by Michael Gray saw Speed head the ball into his own box and Kevin Kilbane pounce. He managed to reach the ball just before Given but lifted his effort over the top from six yards as he hurried his shot. United seemed to be enjoying more possession but were being allowed very little time on the ball and it was the Wearsiders who created the better chances in the closing stages of the half. Shay Given made a brilliant save to deny Kevin Phillips when the Sunderland striker darted between two defenders to reach a flicked-on header from Quinn. His shot was hard and accurate but Given parried the effort and it was scrambled away. Then, seconds before the half time whistle, Shay did even better, showing remarkable reflexes when Kilbane unleashed a vicious, low shot that arrowed straight towards the bottom corner. Until, that is, the 'keeper somehow got down to push it around the post. So half time came with the scoresheet blank.

Sunderland sent on Patrick Mboma for Niall Quinn and the Cameroon star was given a rousing reception by the home fans. But it was Newcastle who looked the more likely scorers in the opening stages of this half and the Sunderland goal had a remarkable escape in the 53rd minute. Bellamy sent over a perfect centre to the far post where Nicos Dabizas turned a shot in at goal from close range but the ball came back off Sorensen's legs when the 'keeper apparently knew nothing about it. Nevertheless it was a crucial save. Sunderland tried to counter-attack but most of the action was at the other end where the Geordie fans were massed. They almost had a goal to cheer after 58 minutes when Dabizas, pushing forward to lend support to his forwards, managed to get in a first time shot on an awkwardly bouncing ball. His effort was close, glancing off the angle of the crossbar before travelling on into the crowd. But he did not have long to wait for a goal

Perhaps incongruously, it came from Mboma's first meaningful contribution to the game. He fouled Hughes out on Newcastle's right in the 63rd minute, earning a yellow card in the process, and it was from the resultant free kick that Newcastle scored. Laurent Robert lifted the ball into the Sunderland penalty area where Alan Shearer managed to get the deftest of flick-ons with his head. The ball went on to Nicos Dabizas at the far post and the Greek headed home from close range as the Geordie fans behind the goal went into ecstasy.

The goal encouraged Newcastle and they pushed forward for a second killer goal. Sunderland tried to steady the ship by bringing on Thomas Butler in place of Steffan Schwarz but United could easily have increased their lead a couple of minutes later. Shearer fed Bellamy close in but the Welshman directed his header straight at Sorensen. But the final critical moment came at the other end six minutes from time. Kevin Phillips spotted Given a little way off his line and curled in a superb shot from just outside the box that looked a goal all of the way until Shay managed to arch his back and somehow touch the ball away from the top angle. It was a save worthy of the entrance money alone (if you were a Newcastle fan) and it finished off the Black Cats.

It had not been a great game – derbies seldom are – but the result was of paramount importance as it confirmed Newcastle as genuine title contenders. However two consecutive defeats by fellow challengers, Arsenal and Liverpool, quickly showed that United were not quite Championship material and they eventually had to settle for fourth place in the league.

No-one could deny that Shay Given had been the man of the match. He had produced a faultless performance. But this was primarily a team effort on a day of Tyneside delight. Even Bobby Robson threatened to join his players on a night out in the clubs and bars on the Quayside to celebrate. He was, of course, only joking.

For Sunderland, a season of struggle continued and just two further wins in the run in to the end of the campaign meant that there was always an outside threat of relegation. They survived, but only just, finishing four points and one place above a relegation spot. The disparity between Tyne and Wear was growing.

Premier League
Newcastle United 2 Sunderland 0 (HT: 2-0)

21st September 2002
St James' Park
52,181

Newcastle: 1 S Given, 12 A Griffin, 18 A Hughes, 34 N Dabizas, 5 A O'Brien, 4 N Solano (7 J Jenas 64), 8 K Dyer, 11 G Speed, 32 L Robert* (45 H Viana 77), 10 C Bellamy* [2] (23 S Ameobi 84), 9 A Shearer [39]. Subs (unused) 13 S Harper, 19 T Bramble
Sunderland: 1 T Sorensen, 2 S Wright*, 3 M Gray, 5 P Babb, 12 J Bjorklund* (18 D Williams* 71), 8 G McCann*, 16 J McAteer (29 N Quinn 45), 7 M Piper, 11 K Kilbane, 4 C Reyna, 9 T A Flo (31 M Stewart 86). Subs (unused) 26 T Myhre, 15 D Bellion
Referee: Mike Riley (Leeds)

THE FACT that both teams were in the bottom three of the league merely added spice to an already critical fixture. Although it was early in the season, both sides were in relegation positions with United a mere three points above tail enders West Ham United.

Newcastle had not had the best of preparations for the game with a midweek visit to Dynamo Kiev in the European Champions' League where they had suffered a 2-0 defeat. Alan Shearer had picked up a bad head wound there but he still played in a derby that Sir Bobby Robson regarded as critical. "Even the visit of Juventus does not compare with this", he declared and proved it by resting both Solano and Robert from the starting line-up in Kiev to ensure that they were fit to face the Wearsiders.

Sunderland welcomed back Gavin McCann after missing four games through injury (although he had been one of the substitutes in the last of them against Fulham). But they were still weakened due to the long term absences of Kevin Phillips and Emerson Thome. Peter Reid decided to play five men in midfield to try and control of the centre of the park. A fleet of coaches conveyed Sunderland fans from the Stadium of Light to St James' for the 12.15pm kick off.

This was a game that neither side could afford to lose although Peter Reid refuted suggestions that his future as Sunderland manager rested on the result. Newcastle were 4-6 favourites to win with Sunderland at 7-2 and odds of 23-10 for the draw.

League Positions		Pos	Pl	Pts		Pos	Pl	Pts
Before:	Sunderland	18th	6	5	Newcastle	19th	5	4
After:	Newcastle	13th	6	7	Sunderland	19th	7	5

Unfortunately for Reid, his tactics of packing midfield lay in ruins within the first two minutes. Shearer took a clearance from Given and neatly rode a tackle by Bjorklund before spinning superbly and feeding Kieron Dyer. The midfielder barely broke stride before sending Craig Bellamy racing away, leaving Babb and Wright in his wake before slipping the ball beneath and beyond the advancing 'keeper from eight yards. Just 83 seconds had passed.

From that point onwards Sunderland were up against it. They held their own – but no more. In fact the game developed into a bit of a stalemate. Until, that is, the 38th minute when the visitors almost grabbed an undeserved equaliser. It was almost a moment of supreme embarrassment for Given who tried to kick the ball clear but saw it charged down by Flo, albeit with his hands, with the rebound bouncing towards the Newcastle goal. Fortunately for Shay (the referee did not blow up for handball although he later admitted that he would not have allowed a goal) he managed to get back and gather it again. From this escape Newcastle broke away to grab a second goal.

Alan Shearer, his head heavily bandaged to protect the wound sustained against Kiev in midweek, was clumsily tackled by McAteer on the edge of the Sunderland penalty area. Nobby Solano took the resultant free kick, rolling the ball sideways to tee-up Shearer for a shot. His right foot pile-driver arrowed towards goal, through the defensive wall, and Sorensen stood no chance.

And that was that. Sunderland's collective heads went down. There was one exception – Claudio Reyna. He displayed not only some neat and tidy football but was also a steadying influence to his crumbling team. He was Sunderland's top man by a mile, twice setting up chances for Flo but each time the towering forward headed over. Half time came with Newcastle comfortably ahead and the cheers from the Geordies throughout the ground contrasted sharply to the silent visiting supporters high up in the corner of the Milburn and Sir John Hall 'stands.

Sunderland introduced Niall Quinn for the unhappy McAteer at half time and the veteran Irishman, although his best years by now well behind him, at least gave the visitors some hope. In fact he set up Sunderland's best chance of the match eight minutes into the second half but Reyna's effort brought a sharp save out of Given. After that, Newcastle took control although they failed to hit the heights. They should have been awarded a penalty just after the hour mark when Bellamy broke on a quick-silver counter attack but was fouled by Piper inside the box. Mike Riley, however, deemed that Craig had dived although TV replays indicated that Piper had pushed the darting striker. But Bellamy was still booked for 'ungentlemanly conduct'. Both sides made substitutions during the second half but these had little real impact on the game. The Wearsiders looked a well beaten side long before the end – a sorry rabble of dropped heads and slouched shoulders - and the Newcastle fans were celebrating well before the final whistle.

After this dispirited performance it was little wonder that Peter Reid kept his players in their changing room after the match. He emerged a frustrated and angry man and, for the first time, lambasted them to the press afterwards. Normally he shielded them from criticism but he knew that this meek surrender in a Tyne-Wear derby was totally unacceptable.

But it was too late as far as he was concerned. The writing was on the wall and a couple of weeks later he was sacked.

Things were much better for Newcastle. Victory had seen them shoot up the league. Their fans felt that matters were to get even better – and they were right.

Yet the game cost Newcastle money - £50,000 to be exact. That was the sum that they had to pay Stoke City as an additional fee for Andy Griffin because he had now chalked up his 50th appearance for United. This was, of course, in addition to the £1.5million paid to the Potters when he had joined them in January 1998. United probably thought that it was money well spent.

Premier League
Sunderland 0 Newcastle United 1 (HT: 0-1)
26th April 2003
Stadium of Light
45,067

Sunderland: 1 T Sorensen, 18 D Williams*, 3 M Gray, 12 J Bjorklund*, 17 J Craddock, 15 D Bellion, 24 S Thornton, 32 M Proctor* (36 R Ryan 76), 11 K Kilbane, 33 J Arca (9 T A Flo 84), 19 K Kyle*. Subs (unused) 40 M Poom, 27 G McCartney, 25 B Clark
Newcastle: 1 S Given, 12 A Griffin*, 18 A Hughes, 5 A O'Brien (30 S Caldwell* 19), 27 J Woodgate, 4 N Solano [**43** pen], 8 K Dyer*, 7 J Jenas, 45 H Viana* (35 O Bernard 72), 10 C Bellamy, 9 A Shearer (23 S Ameobi 26).
Subs (unused) 13 S Harper, 20 L LuaLua
Referee: Steve Bennett (Orpington)

THERE CAN rarely have been such a contrast between these two traditional rivals as they faced each other. Sunderland, deep in financial trouble and without a league win since before Christmas, were floundering at the foot of the table and already relegated. Newcastle, despite picking up just one point out of their last twelve, were fourth top and pushing for a place in the European Champions' League.

The Wearsiders, bereft of most of their 'star' players through injuries and suspensions, looked no match for the star-studded United line-up – at least on paper. But derby games are great levellers and it was upon this time honoured adage that most Sunderland supporters built their hopes. The Geordie fans took comfort in the fact that their twin attack of Shearer and Bellamy had scored more goals in the Premiership this season than the entire Sunderland squad put together including their (absent) top scorer Kevin Phillips.

League Positions

		Pos	Pl	Pts		Pos	Pl	Pts
Before:	Newcastle	4th	35	62	Sunderland	20th	35	19
After:	Newcastle	3rd	36	65	Sunderland	20th	36	19

The game was packed with incident, including two crucial refereeing decisions at the very beginning and very end – both of which referee Steve Bennett ruled in favour of the defending side. The first came in the second minute following a cross into the Sunderland penalty area from Nobby Solano out on the right. Alan Shearer, his head swathed in a bandage from a previous injury, bustled his way behind Darren Williams to nod the ball into the net only to have his effort disallowed for pushing.

Tensions built up on the pitch and in the stands as Sunderland matched Newcastle's undoubted class with passion and commitment to make it an intriguingly even contest. Shay Given had to be on his toes to keep out a searing left foot drive from the pacey David Bellion but Thomas Sorensen similarly foiled Craig Bellamy with an equally heroic save although it took a crucial block by Jody Craddock to deny the Welshman's second snatch at goal.

Quarter was neither asked nor given with play flowing from one end of the pitch to the other. Newcastle were soon forced to make changes due to injuries. They first lost Andy O'Brien after Kevin Kyle caught him in the face with his boot, the United defender going off with a broken nose. Then, crucially, the Magpies lost Shearer, although his injury was largely self-inflicted as he went in heavily with a tackle on Sean Thornton. Newcastle seemed to gain the upper hand but they were lucky to escape four minutes before the break when Hughes headed against his own bar. This was followed a minute later by a sensational save by Given who again denied Bellion from point-blank range, the rebound bouncing off Jonathan Woodgate to trickle past the upright with the United 'keeper helpless. Yet it was Newcastle who went straight up to the other end and scored two minutes before the interval.

Craig Bellamy's pace always troubled the Wearside rearguard and his surging run into the home penalty area in the inside right position proved too much for Kevin Kilbane whose lunging tackle took the man instead of the ball. It was a clear penalty. The one question was who was going to take it in the absence of Shearer? Nolberto Solano was just about the only calm man in the ground as he stepped up to send Sorensen the wrong way (to his left) and stick the penalty into the opposite corner.

Newcastle had a great chance to put the match out of Sunderland's reach before half time when Bellamy, not for the first time, burst through to face a one to one with Sorensen but the great Dane came out on top again.

Newcastle realised that one goal would probably not be enough and they strove for a second. Bellamy, once again, was denied by Sorensen and Solano missed a good chance to wrap things up. Gradually, however, United realised that their constant pushing forward could leave them exposed at the back and they were forced into a more containing, if not defensive, mode. Both sides made substitutions, Sir Bobby Robson replacing Hugo Viana with Olivier Bernard and Mick McCarthy bringing on an untried youngster, Richie Ryan, for his league debut in place of Michael Proctor.

As the game entered its closing stages, Sunderland were definitely on the offensive. Twice Sean Thornton went close before Tore Andre Flo came on for Julio Arca. Two incidents in the final minutes encapsulated the game. With three minutes to go Sorensen yet again denied Bellamy but the real drama was at the other end a minute later. Darren Williams sent a speculative cross into the Newcastle penalty area where the towering Kevin Kyle aggressively charged in to loop a header over Given into the Newcastle net. Delight for the Sunderland supporters and despair for Newcastle's quickly switched around as referee Bennett adamantly pointed to the edge of the six yards box indicating a free kick. He was one of the few people in the ground who had noticed, in the prevailing passion, that Flo had barged into Given thus preventing him from reaching the ball. The final whistle soon followed and Bennett left the pitch to a cacophony of whistles and boos from the Wearside faithful.

Not surprisingly, McCarthy was incensed at the disallowed goal forgetting, in the emotions of the moment, that Newcastle had, just as contentiously, had a goal disallowed in the opening minutes. But television replays showed that the referee had probably been right on both occasions.

A draw would probably have been a fairer result. It would certainly allowed the Sunderland supporters to go down into the First Division with pride. Instead they were forced to watch the gloating Magpie supporters holding cards aloft proclaiming "Let's All Laugh at Sunderland" and regaling their unfortunate neighbours with choruses of the Second World War classic "We'll Meet Again". But gloating is transient and everyone knew that, sooner or later, these two giants of North East football would indeed meet again – and the tables could be turned.

Sunderland lost their last two games and were duly relegated in bottom place in the league. They had collected just one solitary point from the 57 available in the second half of the season. It really was a time of trial and tribulation for their loyal supporters. Newcastle, on the other hand, went on to finish in third place in the league and qualify for the European Champions' League. There were exactly 50 points between Tyne and Wear at the end of the season, the biggest margin ever in over a century of soccer rivalry between the Magpies and the Black Cats.

But perhaps the last word should be left to Newcastle manager Sir Bobby Robson who expressed the view that if Sunderland had shown the passion, commitment, effort and determination throughout the season that they had shown against Newcastle in this game, they would never have been relegated. He was right.

Premier League

Newcastle United 3 Sunderland 2 (HT: 2-2)

23rd October 2005
St James' Park
52,302

Newcastle: 1 S Given, 2 S Carr**, 6 J-A Bousmong, 27 S Taylor, 26 P Ramage, 4 N Solano (21 L Clark 80), 17 S Parker, 5 Emre Belozoglu [**63**] (15 A Faye 81), 14 C N'Zogbia, 23 S Ameobi [**33, 37**] (28 M Chopra 79), 9 A Shearer.
Subs (unused) 24 A Caig, 39 M Brittain
Sunderland: 1 K Davis, 12 N Nosworthy, 5 G Breen (22 A Stubbs 43), 6 S Caldwell, 32 J Hoyte, 7 L Lawrence [**35**], 8 D Whitehead*, 14 T Miller*, 11 A Welsh (33 J Arca 45), 10 S Elliott [**41**], 18 A Gray (17 A Le Tallec 79). Subs (unused) 13 B Alnwick, 4 C Robinson
Referee: Rob Styles (Waterlooville)

BOTH SIDES had made horrendous starts to the season and by the end of August they had occupied the bottom two Premiership places. But by the time they met in late October, matters had improved somewhat, particularly for Newcastle. Despite an appalling record of mainly muscle related injuries (Dyer, Emre and Bramble had all managed a mere two starts each so far and Solano had yet to appear since rejoining the club at the end of August), they had slowly clawed their way up the league.

Sunderland, also afflicted by a length injury list, had also managed to drag themselves off the bottom although this was as much to do with the inadequacies of Everton (three points from eight games) as anything else. But there was no doubt that the absence of McCartney, Bassila, Piper, Stubbs, Wright, Kyle and Healy was a savage blow to the Wearsiders' derby hopes. At least there was the prospect of Julio Arca, arguably their best player, returning to action against Newcastle after (hopefully) recovering from a fractured toe. In the event, it was thought that it would be too much of a risk for him to start the game. So he was on the substitutes' bench as Sunderland fielded an unchanged side from the one that had performed so well (but lost) at home to Manchester United in their last game.

Newcastle's main injury concern was Michael Owen, a victim of a hamstring injury sustained in training. He was also ruled out and his absence was a body blow for Tyneside although the first appearance of Nobby Solano since his return from Aston Villa and the return of Emre to the starting line-up raised spirits. But the absence of Dyer, Bowyer, Babayaro and Elliott meant that United, like Sunderland, were not able to field anywhere near their strongest team.

In fact young Peter Ramage had to be drafted in for just the third competitive start of his Newcastle career and his first appearance of the season – a baptism of fire if ever there was one.

Sunderland came into the game as underdogs (Newcastle were 8-13 favourites) but with some optimism. Their fans felt that if they could give the same level of commitment as they had shown against the Red Devils in their last game, they could surprise Newcastle.

The 1.30pm Sunday kick-off to accommodate Sky TV ensured that there was little or no drunken behaviour before the match, especially with the Sunderland fans bussed to St James' from Wearside. But there was to be plenty of time for mayhem afterwards.

League Positions

		Pos	Pl	Pts		Pos	Pl	Pts
Before:	Newcastle	13th	9	9	Sunderland	19th	9	5
After:	Newcastle	11th	10	12	Sunderland	19th	10	5

The game turned out to be a classic – the best derby for many a year. Dean Whitehead set the tone after just 36 seconds with a crunching tackle from behind on Emre, earning a booking in the process. The Turkish international's response was a break from midfield to unleash a fearsome left foot shot that Kelvin Davis did well to parry clear.

Newcastle maintained the offensive and Sunderland's increasingly maligned goalkeeper showed why Mick McCarthy rated him so highly with a great one-handed save, diving low down to his left, to deny Shola Ameobi. The Nigerian-born, Newcastle Academy product had also suffered more than his fair share of criticism from his own fans with less than convincing performances as a striker in the past, but today he seemed fired up to prove the doubters wrong.

It was Ameobi who made the breakthrough after 33 minutes. Emre showed his accuracy with a left wing corner that was made to measure for Shola to give a passable imitation of Alan Shearer as he powered in a header from outside the six yard box. The marking left a lot to be desired but the finishing was superb.

The Newcastle fans had hardly finished cheering when Sunderland struck back with devastating effectiveness. It was a goal out of nothing as Liam Lawrence picked the ball up from a Tommy Miller pass in midfield. The United defence backed off as the Sunderland man skipped inside around Scott Parker and unleashed a raking shot from 25 yards that seared low, across Given into the far corner. Now it was the 3,500 manic Mackems, high up in the corner between the Milburn stand and the Leazes End (Sir John Hall stand), who went mad. Two goals in 90 seconds had set this game alight.

Yet it was to be just a further two more minutes before Newcastle struck again and it was that man Ameobi who was to do the damage again. Stephen Carr did brilliantly to accelerate past Andy Welsh before crossing the ball from the right to beyond the far post to where Charles N'Zogbia hooked it back into the middle. This time Steve Caldwell was there to cover Ameobi but the gangling striker was the more determined man as he forced in his header from the end of the six yard box. It gained a deflection off the Scottish defender and left Davis with no chance. Most people gave the goal to Ameobi and a Premiership Dubious Goals Committee later confirmed this view but, at the time, the jubilant Geordies did not care who had scored. All that mattered was that they were ahead again.

But they hardly had time to start up their chants of derision at their rivals when the Black Cats retaliated again. And, if anything, this goal was even better than their first. Stephen Elliott collected the ball and switched inside and outside Jean-Alain Boumsong, avoiding a Parker challenge in between, before suddenly letting fly with a left foot strike of stunning effectiveness from 20 yards. The ball screamed past the outstretched arm of the diving Given before bulging the net. No wonder the Wearsiders went wild. It looked a contender for a goal of the season and even a few Newcastle fans were seen to applaud a goal of genuine quality.

The half-time whistle went four minutes later and both team left the field to a standing ovation. This was what football was all about – breathtaking, exhilarating and emotionally exhausting.

Sunderland skipper Gary Breen had been forced to go off injured three minutes before half-time, Alan Stubbs taking his place in defence with Caldwell taking over the captain's arm band against his old club. The half-time break also saw Julio Arca return to action, coming on in place of Welsh.

The second half could not match up to the first – at least not in terms of goals. But it did as far as passion, excitement and incidents were concerned. If Newcastle had a slight edge in the first half, it was Sunderland who started the second in an adventurous and determined mood. Whitehead had a shot deflected just wide off Boumsong before Shay Given palmed behind a low shot from Stephen Elliott.

But it was another shot of genuine quality that restored Newcastle's lead 18 minutes after the resumption. Caldwell was penalised for fouling Ameobi 10 yards outside the Sunderland penalty area in the middle of the park. Up stepped Emre to take the kick and his shot was perfection, curling away from Davis to clip the inside of the 'keeper's left hand post before nestling in the net; 3-2. Emre rushed to embrace Graeme Souness in celebration.

Steve Taylor almost put the game out of Sunderland's reach with a close range header soon after but Davis was equal to the task, saving low down. The visitors had a good claim for a penalty turned down when Liam Lawrence clearly tripped over N'Zogbia's leg inside the penalty area but referee Rob Styles waved on play. Did the Sunderland man drag his leg intentionally to make contact? Or should it have been a penalty? Your viewpoint depended upon which team you supported. But Newcastle knew that they had been lucky.

Both managers used up their substitutes in the space of three minutes with ten minutes to go but the decisive moment of the game came a couple of minutes later when Stephen Elliott almost wrote his name in Wearside folklore. He despatched an exquisite lob from just outside the penalty area over Given but saw his effort hit the crossbar and come out for Boumsong to clear the danger.

A last ditch tackle by Taylor denied Elliott a tap in equaliser as Sunderland piled forward and United hung on. The final whistle was greeted with a roar of relief as much as jubilation. It could not have been any closer and it had undoubtedly been a classic.

If ever there was a game where the losing team deserved to get some reward, this was it. Perhaps Newcastle had a slight edge in quality but the Wearside warriors had more than compensated for this by their fire and determination. Yet Newcastle, with six 'local lads' on the field at some time or other during the game, had matched the Black Cats with effort all of the way, particularly in those nerve-shredding final minutes.

The penalty claim against N'Zogbia had not been the only contentious refereeing decision. A case of mistaken identity had seen Parker booked for a foul on Welsh instead of Stephen Carr. When Carr was booked later on for a vicious tackle on Arca, a second yellow card would have seen him sent off. Parker's caution was later rescinded and the booking was transferred to Carr who was subsequently suspended. It was another reason for Sunderland fans to bemoan the injustice of it all.

The Newcastle fans went on the town to celebrate, culminating in trouble as drink-fuelled mayhem broke out in the Bigg Market some four hours after the final whistle. About 300 'supporters' were involved with 20 of them arrested (making a total of 56 arrests on the day) as the police closed down several pubs and cordoned off streets in the city centre.

The Sunderland fans were totally innocent. They had headed home over the Tyne well before the outbreak with their heads held high but moaning about their luck. But there were to be unwelcome repercussions for Wearside as well – and these were to be much more far-reaching.

The two defeats against Manchester United and Newcastle, when Sunderland had played well but had gained no reward, seemed to affect their confidence and there was a sense of déjà vu as defeat followed defeat with monotonous and heart-breaking regularity. It was like the 2002-03 season all over again – but worse. Then the Black Cats had picked up just 18 points by Christmas. This season, nine successive league defeats (including the derby game at St James') saw them accumulate a meagre five points by the festive break. Sunderland fans had no reason to celebrate.

Newcastle, on the other hand, gradually climbed the table although a distinct anti-Souness mood among a sizeable section of support prevailed. They were eventually to get their wish.

But the derby game in October was best summed up by Newcastle's match-winner Emre who observed, "I have played in Milan (for Inter) in the big derby against AC Milan, but I have never seen anything like this. The fans were incredible". Welcome to Tyne-Wear rivalry.

Premier League

Sunderland 1 Newcastle United 4 (HT: 1-0)

17th April 2006
Stadium of Light
40,032

Sunderland: 1 K Davis, 32 J Hoyte [**32**], 6 S Caldwell, 15 D Collins, 3 G McCartney*, 7 L Lawrence, 8 D Whitehead, 14 T Miller, 26 D Murphy (33 J Arca 64), 9 J Stead (16 K Kyle 68), 20 C Brown. Subs (unused) 30 J Murphy, 5 G Breen, 23 G Leadbitter

Newcastle: 1 S Given, 2 S Carr, 18 C Moore, 19 T Bramble*, 33 C Babayaro, 4 N Solano, 15 A Faye, 21 L Clark* (28 M Chopra 59 [**59**]), 14 C N'Zogbia [**66**] (6 J-A Boumsong 88), 7 K Dyer, 9 A Shearer [**61** pen] (20 A Luque 71 [**87**]). Subs (unused) 12 S Harper, 26 P Ramage

Referee: Chris Foy (St Helens)

BY THE time the sides met on Easter Monday, momentous changes had been made at both clubs since their October meeting. Both managers had been sacked and replaced by their respective academy coaches as caretaker bosses. By a strange co-incidence, both Graeme Souness and Mick McCarthy had lost their jobs after defeats away to Manchester City.

Souness had pointed persistently to the crippling injury situation at St James' Park for the failure of his club to make an impression in the Premiership. His replacement, Glenn Roeder, refused to give similar excuses/reasons although his side was undoubtedly handicapped with arguably his best forward (Michael Owen), midfielder (Scott Parker) and defender (Steven Taylor) all missing due to injuries for the fixture on Wearside. This meant that £16.5 million signing Owen had failed to appear in either of the Tyne-Wear derbies this season. Newcastle fans were not happy that most of the media attention was focused on whether he would recover from his broken metatarsal in time to play for England in the World Cup in the summer. They really wanted him on the pitch for United, and against Sunderland in particular. Further injuries suffered not long before the derby game further handicapped the Magpies with Emre, Lee Bowyer and Shola Ameobi also ruled out. So it was a much weakened team that Roeder took to the Stadium of Light.

But the Black Cats had injury problems of their own although, admittedly, they were not as critical as Newcastle's. Stephen Elliott and Rory Delap were their main absentees with Julio Arca, as with the game at St James' Park, just returning from injury and having to make do with a place on the substitutes' bench. Elliott's absence, together with that of both Emre and Ameobi for Newcastle meant that three of the four goalscorers from the game at St James' Park were sidelined. Liam Lawrence was the exception.

Sunderland's fans had suffered a nightmare of a season with just two wins (and six draws) from 33 league games. Also those two wins had been away from home so they were facing the ignominy of becoming the first Premiership side ever to go through an entire season without a win at home. A win over Newcastle, who had not lost on Wearside for 26 years, would go some way towards easing the pain of relegation.

This had been mathematically confirmed three days earlier at Old Trafford. Ironically, it had come after Sunderland's best display of the season, a magnificent rearguard action that resulted in a 0-0 draw and more or less destroyed the Red Devils' lingering hopes of mounting a belated challenge to Chelsea for the Premiership title. The Black Cats also became the first visiting team this season to keep a clean sheet at the Theatre of Dreams.

With that game following hot of the heels of an away draw at Everton, there was some optimism on Wearside that Sunderland could break their home duck against the Mags. It would not redeem the season but it would make it decidedly more bearable.

But there was also confidence in the Newcastle camp. They had won their last three games, including the derby fixture away to Middlesbrough, and were mounting a belated challenge for a place in Europe, albeit probably via the InterToto Cup.

League Positions		Pos	Pl	Pts		Pos	Pl	Pts
Before:	Newcastle	9th	34	48	Sunderland	20th	33	12
After:	Newcastle	7th	35	51	Sunderland	20th	34	12

A blustery wind was not conducive to good football but that which was played came from Sunderland who clearly seemed to have the bigger appetite for the game. With Liam Lawrence, Dean Whitehead and Tommy Miller, buzzing in midfield, it looked like lethargic Newcastle were going to be over run. The Black Cats forced six corners in the opening 20 minutes but a lack of a cutting edge up front meant they came to nothing. A deflected header by captain and central defender Steve Caldwell from one of the corners was the nearest that they came to breaching the Magpies' defence. Nevertheless, the visitors were kept on the back foot in a first half that clearly belonged to the Black Cats. Yet the football played, even by Sunderland, could hardly be called dynamic. Indeed, until the opening goal, most of the entertainment in the first half came from the rival sets of fans who gleefully traded colourful insults.

The much deserved breakthrough came after 32 minutes with a counter attack of devastating effectiveness. Charles N'Zogbia slipped and lost possession in the Sunderland penalty area and Justin Hoyte broke from defence up the home right wing almost as far as the half way line. There he played a pass forward to Jon Stead and his acceleration left Titus Bramble struggling for pace as he raced towards the Newcastle corner flag. His pass inside found Dean Whitehead inside the penalty area but still with a lot to do. His quick twist and spurt to the bye-line left Craig Moore for dead and the way he pulled the ball back inside to the fast approaching Hoyte was perfection. Justin made goalscoring look easy as he sidefooted the ball home from the edge of the six yard box right in front of the posts. He had run about 80 yards to score. It was a beautifully worked goal – a fact that was to be forgotten in the mayhem that was to follow – and the home fans celebrated in style, seemingly intent on taking the roof off the stadium with the noise.

Sunderland proceeded to dominate the rest of the first half and a curling shot by Lawrence was deflected high and wide off Bramble as they pushed forward. A Nobby Solano free kick that was directed straight at Kelvin Davis was the best that Newcastle could muster but this was matched by a Lawrence free kick that curled just over the top on the verge of half-time.

The Black Cats clearly deserved the standing ovation accorded them as they left the field at the interval with their fans goading Alan Shearer with chants of "Shearer, Shearer, what's the score". In truth, Sunderland deserved more than a single goal lead at this stage but, significantly, that is all they had.

Newcastle had shown apathy rather than passion in the opening 45 minutes and Glenn Roeder, normally a calm and controlled man, laid into his players during the half-time interval, letting them know in no uncertain terms what he thought of their performance. They managed to step up the tempo when play resumed but Sunderland refused to relinquish control.

Something had to be done if Newcastle were to get back into the game and Roeder did it with an inspired substitution just before the hour mark. Former Sunderland player Lee Clark had been booed throughout by the Wearside faithful and it was he who made way for Michael Chopra. No-one could have foreseen what the next few seconds had in store. Michael ran on to the pitch from the half way line and made a bee-line for the Sunderland goal. Bramble, meanwhile, launched a long ball upfield from his own half. No-one seemed to realise that Chops was there as he chased the ball into the Sunderland penalty area. Caldwell let it go over his head, expecting Davis to come out and collect. The 'keeper tried to do this but he either did not react quickly enough or the wind fractionally held the ball up. The end product was that he failed to hold on to it and spilled it as Chopra came in. The young striker had the simple task of shooting home from only a foot out to record his first ever Premiership goal – just 13 seconds after coming on. Statisticians were left to examine the record books to see if this was the quickest goal ever by a substitute in the Premier League history. It certainly was as far as Wear-Tyne derbies were concerned. Michael, a Geordie born and bred, did not care as he celebrated as wildly as the Newcastle fans behind the goal.

Sunderland now had to regroup and recompose themselves – quickly. Instead they seemed to fall apart. They were still trying to come to terms with losing the lead after controlling the game for so long that they failed to deal with a Solano chip forward that was flicked on by Faye into their penalty area. N'Zogbia twisted around Hoyte to get goalside of the full back only for the defender to haul him to the ground. Referee Chris Hoy had no hesitation in pointing to the spot. Shearer had suffered the ignominy of having had a penalty saved against Sunderland at St James' Park back in November 2000. He claimed six years of anguish were in the venomous spot kick as he lashed the ball past the helpless Davis. The 'keeper dived the right way (both figuratively and literally) but such was the ferocity of the shot that he had no chance of saving it. Now "Shearer, Shearer, What's the score" resounded from the Newcastle end.

In 90 seconds the game had been turned on its head. The 3,500 Geordie fans, behind the goal where all of the action was, had suffered the derision of the home supporters in the first half with chants of "1-0 to the Champions League". Now they responded with "2-1 to the Premier League". Sportsmanship goes out of the window in local derbies.

The Sunderland fans began to fear the worst as Newcastle, urged on by their fanatical followers, began to take control of the game. Kevin Ball tried to resurrect the situation by sending on fans' favourite Julio Arca for Daryl Murphy. But the damage had been done and the Red'n Whites' confidence visibly seemed to evaporate.

They went further behind in the 66th minute with a goal of sublime artistry. Charles N'Zogbia was increasingly imposing his presence on the game and his solo goal had all neutrals drooling. He picked up a short pass from Keiron Dyer 35 yards out and twisted and turned as he jinked his way past Hoyte, Miller and Collins into the penalty area before slotting the ball low into the bottom right hand corner; 3-1 and it was the signal for some Sunderland fans to make for the exits. The introduction of Kevin Kyle for Jon Stead midway through the half made little difference in a game that had somehow been thrown away.

Nineteen minutes from time came the moment which spoiled the day for Newcastle. Shearer went down heavily under a challenge from Arca and was forced to hobble off. He sportingly exonerated Julio from all blame for the injury. Albert Luque, an expensive signing from Deportiva La Coruna early in the season who had failed to justify the huge fee paid for him, was sent on to replace his captain and it was he who put the final nail in Sunderland's coffin with a fourth goal three minutes from time. An awkward bounce left Collins and Caldwell wrong footed and gave the Spaniard a clear run on goal. He gave a glimpse as to why Souness had paid so much for him with a coolly taken goal, as he raced into the area and dinked the ball over the advancing Davis.

Many of the Sunderland fans had long-departed before this comedy of errors and the goal was the signal for a further exodus. It was now 1-4 and Sunderland's misery was complete – a sad day for all of those in Red and White.

It was hard to remember a game in the entire history of Wear-Tyne (or Tyne-Wear) football where there had been such an incredible change in fortunes. Surprisingly, however, turning a half-time deficit into victory away from home was not that unusual. Indeed, it had happened three times in the last ten years, with Sunderland chalking up back-to-back recoveries at St James' as recently as 1999 and 2000 and Newcastle doing the trick at Roker Park in 1996.

But these had been 2-1 wins. To rattle in four goals after being behind at half-time was unique. Not that a 4-1 away win had never been achieved. Sunderland had done it in 1979 when Gary Rowell had scored a hat trick. But they had led 2-0 at half-time and it was not a recovery.

The score at the Stadium of Light was Newcastle's biggest win on Wearside for half a century (since a 6-1 win in December 1955) and the biggest win anywhere since a 6-2 victory at St James' a year later. The record for the biggest away win of all time, of course, still lay with Sunderland. Their 9-1 victory in 1908 will probably never be beaten.

Other records were also broken at the Stadium of Light. Chopra's 13 second goal shattered the former four minutes record held by Gordon Armstrong in 1992. On top of that, the 4-1 win had seen two substitutes score for the first time in a derby. This was not surprising as only three substitutes had ever scored in such games before.

Strangely, until Newcastle had come back from a goal down at home to Wigan Athletic a couple of days before the Sunderland game, they had never won this season where they had fallen behind. Now they had done it twice over the Easter weekend.

Both clubs still had something to play for (although their ambitions were widely different) over the last few games of the season. Victory had seen Newcastle grab a potential European qualification spot in the league. But could they hang on to it without the talismanic leadership of Alan Shearer?

The answer was 'yes'. They were to qualify for the InterToto Cup by virtue of a last day win over champions Chelsea, pipping Bolton Wanderers for the coveted seventh place in the Premier League – a finish that was beyond anyone's wildest dreams when Souness was sacked. Glenn Roeder's reward for this minor miracle was to be appointed as permanent manager at the end of the season although chairman Freddy Shepherd had to overcome considerable opposition to appoint him, most notably from the League Managers Association. They objected because Roeder did not possess the required UEFA Pro Licence although Glenn had signed up for the course when in charge at West Ham only for a life-threatening brain tumour to prevent him pursuing it. He intended to re-apply so Shepherd obtained a vote from Premier League chairman to clear the way for Roeder's appointment, thus over-ruling the LMA.

Sunderland's 'ambitions' had been much lower – to win at least one home league game this season (they only had two left to play) and to pass (or at least reach) the Premiership all time lowest points haul of 19 (set by themselves three years earlier).

They had partial success. They avoided the mortification of becoming the first team to go through an entire season without a home win by beating Fulham 2-1 (amid much euphoria) in their last home match of the campaign. But they were to end up with just 15 points, not only failing to reach their Premier League target but just matching Stoke City's all-time low of 15 for top flight football (since three points for a win were awarded). With Reading also breaking Sunderland's Championship points total of 105 (set in 1999), the Black Cats were setting and losing the wrong type of records.

Morale was low. As they went down into the Championship, there was a feeling on Wearside that they may not come back as quickly as they had last time. Yet most pundits felt that they had the nucleus of a good, young side who, with the right coaching and experience, could develop into a promotion challenging team. The fans placed most of their hopes for the future on the take-over fronted by Black Cats' legend Niall Quinn. Certainly in terms of their stadium, support, and training facilities, they are a Premiership team in everything but name. They will return – of that there can be no doubt.

Newcastle went back to Tyneside with the bragging rights for the immediate future secured but their feeling of euphoria was marred by the injury to Shearer. He had sustained medial knee ligament damage which was to curtail his illustrious career only three games from the end of his last season. Alan, who until this game had never scored for Newcastle on Wearside, seemed upbeat about it all, explaining that he wanted to end with his final game at St James' Park "But if I had to finish, it's not a bad way to do it – coming to your local enemies and scoring a goal that helps you get a 4-1 win". Such is the importance of Tyne-Wear derbies.

Most Wins in Derby Matches (6 or more)

	Newcastle United	Wins		Sunderland	Wins
Pos					
1	W McCracken	11	1	W Hogg	10
2	J Lawrence	10	2	G Holley	9
	W Low	10		A Bridgett	9
4	F Hudspeth	8	4	J Mordue	8
	G Wilson	8		C Buchan	8
6	R Simpson	7	6	J Watson	6
7	C Veitch	6		J Gemmell	6
	R Mitchell	6		H Low	6
	T McDonald	6		E England	6
	J Milburn	6		C Thompson	6
	G S Seymour	6		W Murray	6
	T Lang	6			
	R Batty	6			
	R Davies	6			
	A Shearer	6			

Player of the Decade 2000s

Stephen Caldwell

NO-ONE would regard Steve Caldwell as one of the all time greats. But as an honest player, always giving of his best and showing commendable loyalty to his club, he is up there with the very best of them. He was a young Scots lad who came down to England to learn his trade and become a professional footballer. He succeeded but the road was long and hard.

He was born in Stirling in September 1980, 19 months before his brother Gary who was to join him at Newcastle as a junior player. Indeed, for a number of years it seemed that a sibling rivalry developed between the two youngsters as they leap-frogged each other in the development stakes with both playing in the centre of defence.

Steve first appeared as a schoolboy triallist for Newcastle's Under-17 side as a mere 15-year-old, making his debut (by a strange co-incidence) in the Northern Intermediate League away to Sunderland in April 1996.

He was a success and he returned to Tyneside to play a number of games for the juniors during the following year and was taken on in the summer of 1997 as a two year Youth Training Scheme apprentice. A key member of the side, he played alongside Gary in the team which won the Northern Intermediate League title in 1997-98.

By the following year, Steve had moved up to the Under-19 side which he captained. It was this season (1998-99) that he also graduated into the reserve side in the Pontins' League Second Division, albeit as a substitute. Both of the brothers were still eligible for the FA Youth Cup and they both appeared in all nine games Newcastle played to reach the semi-final where they lost to Coventry City. Unfortunately, skipper Steve was sent off in the first leg for a professional foul.

By 1999-2000, the brothers were appearing together for the Under-19 side and also the reserves. But suddenly it seemed that Steve's career was about to collapse. It was Gary who was allocated a first team squad number, not Steve, and it was the younger brother who was named as substitute for a couple of early season Premier League games and even away to Roma in the UEFA Cup. He never got on the pitch but it must have been galling for Steve to see his young brother pass him in the pecking order.

Things went from bad to worse when Steve was placed on the transfer list in March 2000. To his credit, he realised that it was make or break time in his career as a professional footballer and, by his own admission, he knuckled down. He was quickly rewarded with a one year's contract and his name was taken off the list. Even better, he was awarded a first team squad number himself as the season drew to a close.

Things improved even more early in the next season. He won his first Under-21 Cap and, soon afterwards, found himself on the bench for a Worthington Cup tie away to Leyton Orient. He was not called upon but he had only four more days to wait before tasting first team action, coming on as substitute at Manchester City.

It was another month before his first start, when he scored in a 4-3 win at home to Bradford City in the Worthington Cup. His first Premiership start, a 2-1 home defeat by Sunderland, came in mid-November and by this time he could regard himself as a first team squad player.

He wasn't a regular but by the end of the season he had chalked up ten first team competitive appearances although four of them were from the subs' bench. It was progress.

But the road to success is neither straight nor easy. If Steve thought that 2001-02 was to see further progression, he was to be sadly mistaken. He came off the bench three times in the early season Inter-Toto Cup games but soon found himself farmed out on loan to gain first team experience. Brother Gary was to suffer similar 'development'. In fact Gary was to spend most of his Newcastle career out on loan. He never appeared for Newcastle in a competitive first team game although, strangely, was capped four times for Scotland as (officially) a United player.

In Steve's case, he was loaned out to Blackpool and Bradford City. At least he could claim to have helped Blackpool to win a cup, scoring a crucial goal in a narrow 3-2 win over Stoke City in the First Round of the LDV Vans Trophy. This was his only involvement in the competition and he had long gone by the time the Tangerines lifted the trophy by beating Cambridge United at the Millennium Stadium in March 2002.

He had to wait until the following season before he managed to force himself back into Newcastle's first team. This was to be his most successful year at Gallowgate. Newcastle finished third in the Premier League and he managed 14 competitive starts and three substitute appearances. But, although he made more appear-ances in the first team than he did in the reserves, he still could not regard himself as a first team regular.

Nevertheless he managed his first senior international start that season. He had made one substitute appearance for Scotland away to Poland in 2001 but it was a proud day for the young Scot when he turned out at Hampden Park to face the Republic of Ireland in February 2003. Little did he realise that facing him in the green shirt of Ireland was Gary Breen with whom he was to form such an effective partnership on Wearside in the near future.

To many, it seemed only a matter of time before the Caldwell brothers lined up together for Scotland. They had both played at Under-21 level against Belgium in March 2001 and they both turned out at Easter Road for Scotland's first team against Trinidad & Tobago in May 2004 – but they did not appear together. Steve came on as substitute to replace Gary. The long-awaited appearance alongside each other happened a few months later in October when Scotland drew 1-1 away to Moldova in a World Cup Qualifier, Steve's first cap as a Sunderland player. By this time, Gary was back in Scotland with Hibernian.

In the English Premiership, a product of a club's youth system is always going to struggle for recognition over high priced superstars. So Steve had to take a back seat when Newcastle signed Jonathan Woodgate in the latter part of the 2002-03 season. Yet the Scot was to end the campaign in Newcastle's first team after coming on for the injured Andy O'Brien against Sunderland at the Stadium of Light and then starting the last two matches with first O'Brien and then Woodgate ruled out. He proved himself a more than capable deputy but the writing was on the wall for him at St James' with his contract due to expire at that summer.

He signed a new one year contract eventually but his final season at Newcastle was to see him only make sporadic first team appearances. Once again he was farmed out on loan, this time to struggling Leeds United. He made more appearances for the Yorkshire club (13 consecutive Premiership games) than he did for Newcastle (just five in the league – and two of them were as substitute). Yet when the call came from the Magpies, he responded. Newcastle found their playing resources stretched as his loan period with Leeds came to a close and asked him to return to Tyneside to help out. Loyalty was one of Steve's strongest attributes and he was only too willing to assist his parent club. So Steve once again finished the season in United's first team.

But his Newcastle career was over although he did not have far to go to continue as a professional footballer. Mick McCarthy was trying to build a team to get Sunderland back into the Premier League having just missed out in the 2004 Nationwide Division One play-offs. He saw Steve (now with four caps to his name but available on a free transfer) as one of the players who would fit the bill.

So it proved as he quickly established himself at the Stadium of Light to become a lynchpin of the Wearside defence alongside Gary Breen. Steve played in 41 of the 46 league games (with Gary turning out in just one less) as Sunderland walked away with the newly named Coca Cola Championship in 2004-05. The quality of his performances this season matched the quantity with a series of impressive displays. The Black Cats' clinched the title by seven clear points from Wigan Athletic. To Steve fell the glory of scoring the goal that secured promotion, a perfect header against Leicester City at the Stadium of Light.

But no-one on Wearside was under any illusions about the monumental task that lay ahead for Sunderland even to retain their Premiership status. McCarthy had very little funds available to build a team of Premiership standard – and what he had, was not enough. Despite whole-hearted endeavour from the likes of Steve, the team was found wanting and the defeat followed defeat with monotonous regularity. It was a season of disaster and the Black Cats, with just six points to their name by the turn of the year, seemed virtually doomed to relegation by the halfway mark. Their total of 15 points was the lowest in Premiership history.

Steve had already shown that he was one of the best defenders outside the Premiership in England. He would have to do it all again if he was to prove that he was up to the task of playing at football's top table. It would be a rash man who would bet against him if, or when, the chance comes again.

Record

Newcastle	April 1996 – June 2004	
Football League	20 (+ 8 sub) apps	1 gl
FA Cup	-	-
Football League Cup	3 apps	1 gl
Europe	1 (+ 5 sub) apps	-
Total	24 (+13 sub) apps	2 gls

Sunderland	June 2004 –	
Football League	64 apps	4 gls
FA Cup	1 apps	-
Football League Cup	4 apps	1 gl
Total	69 apps	5 gls

Most Games Undefeated in Derby Matches

	Newcastle United	Wins	Draws	Total		Sunderland	Wins	Draws	Total
1	G Robledo	3	4	7	1	H R Buckle	4	1	5
2	J Harvey	2	5	7	2	G Chisholm	2	3	5
3	L Clark	5	1	6		J McNab	2	3	5
4	S Ameobi	4	2	6	4	W Grimshaw	3	1	4
5	A O'Brien	3	2	5	5	R Agboola	1	3	4
6	C Bellamy	3	1	4		M Gabbiadini	1	3	4
	S Howey	3	1	4		E Gates	1	3	4
8	R McIntosh	2	2	4		J MacPhail	1	3	4
	S Watson	2	2	4	9	A Fogarty	0	4	4
10	T Gibb	1	3	4	10	J O'Hare	3	0	0
	J McDonald	1	3	4	11	C Makin	2	1	3
	W McFaul	1	3	4		W Rostron	2	1	3
	J Scott	1	3	4	13	B Clough	1	2	3

Note that David Kelly was also undefeated in four derby matches (three wins with Newcastle and a draw with Sunderland). He therefore had a 100% success record with United, as did Jermaine Jenas and goalkeeper Mick Burns (both with three wins). John O'Hare also achieved this distinction for Sunderland.

STATISTICS & RECORDS

NEWCASTLE UNITED PLAYERS - APPEARANCES AGAINST SUNDERLAND

NAME	League Apps	Sub	Tot	Gls	Major Cups (FA & FL) Apps	Sub	Tot	Gls	Total Apps	Sub	Tot	Gls	Result Won	Drew	Lost
Acuna C	2	1	3				0		2	1	3	0		2	1
Agnew W B	2		2				0		2		2	0	1		
Aitken A	16		16		1		1		17		17	0	5	5	7
Aitken W	8		8	1			0		8		8	1	3	2	3
Aitken R	3		3				0		3		3	0		2	1
Allchurch I	2		2				0		2		2	0		1	
Allen J	5		5	1			0		5		5	1	3		2
Allen G	1		1				0		1		1	0		1	
Ameobi S	2	4	6	2			0		2	4	6	2	4	2	
Anderson A	3		3	1	1		1		4		4	1	1	2	1
Anderson S	1		1				0		1		1	0	1		
Anderson J	5	1	6				0		5	1	6	0			
Appleby M	1		1				0		1		1	0		4	5
Appleyard W	9		9	1			0		9		9	1	3	1	1
Arentoft P	2		2				0		2		2	0	1		1
Askew W		1	1				0		0	1	1	0		1	
Asprilla F	1		1				0		1		1	0	1	1	
Babayaro C	1		1				0		1		1	0	1		
Baird I	2		2				0		2		2	0		1	2
Barrowclough S	3		3		2		2		5		5	0	1	2	2
Barton D	5		5				0		5		6	0		4	1
Barton W	2		2				0		2		2	0	1		
Bassedas C	2		2				0		2		2	0		1	2
Batty R	9	1	9		1		1		10		10	0	6	2	2
Batty D	2		2				0		2		2	0	1	1	
Beardsley P	3		3	4			0		3		3	4	1		1
Bedford H	1		1	2			0		1		1	2		1	
Bell D	2		2				0		2		2	0			2
Bell J	1		1				0		1		1	0		1	
Bellamy C	4	1	4	2	1		1		4		4	2	3		1
Bennett A	4		4	1			0		4		4	2	2	1	1
Bennie R	2		2				0		2		2	0	1		1
Beresford J	2		2		1		1		2		2	0	2	1	
Bernard O							0						2		
Betton A	3		3				0		3		3	2		2	
Bird J	2		2				0		3		3	1			1
Birnie E	1		1				0		1		1	0		1	
Blackley J	1		1				0		1		1	0			1

NAME	LEAGUE				Major Cups (FA & FL)				Total				Result		
	Apps	Sub	Tot	Gls	Apps	Sub	Tot	Gls	Apps	Sub	Tot	Gls	Won	Drew	Lost
Blake S	2		2				0		2	0	2	0	1		2
Boam S	1		1				0		1	0	1	0	1		1
Booth C	1		1				0		1	0	1	0			
Boumsong J-A	7		7		2		0	1	7	0	7	0	2		4
Boyd J	7		7	3			0		7	1	7	3	3		
Bracewell P	1	1	2				0		1	0	3	0	1		
Bradley W	8		8				0		8	0	8	0	2	2	4
Bradshaw D	3		3	1			0		3	0	3	0	3	2	1
Bramble T	1		1				0		1	0	1	0	1		
Brazil G		1	1				0			1	1	1	1		
Brennan F	12		12				0		12	0	12	0	4	1	
Broadis I	3		3				0		3	0	3	0		7	
Brock K	5		6				0		5	0	6	0	2		2
Brown H	1		1				0		1	0	1	0			
Brown M	2		2				0		2	0	2	0		3	
Brownlie J	3		3	2	2		2		3	0	5	0	1		2
Burgess C	2		2				0		2	0	2	0	1	2	
Burns M T	3		3				0		3	0	3	0	3	1	
Burns M E	3		3				0		3	0	3	2	1	2	
Burridge J	2		2				0		2	0	9	0	3	4	
Burton A	9	1	9		1		1		9	0	1	0	1	1	
Caie A	1		1		1		1		1	0	2	0			
Caldwell W (EE)											2	0	1		1
Caldwell S	2		2				0		2	0	2	0	1		2
Cannell P	2		2		1		1		2	0	2	0	2		
Cape J	1		1				0		1	0	1	0		1	
Carney S	15		15		1		0		16	0	16	0	5	4	
Carr J	1		1				1	1	1	0	1	0	1		
Carr K	2		2	1			0		2	0	2	2	2		
Carr S	2		2	1			0		2	0	2	0		1	7
Cartwright P	7		7		1		1		7	0	4	0	2	1	2
Casey T	4		4		2	2	2		4	2	7	2	4		1
Cassidy T	3		3				0		3	0	5	1	2	2	3
Chalmers W	2		2				0		2	0	3	1			
Chandler A	2		2				0		2	0	2	0		2	
Chopra M		2	2				0			2	4	0	2	2	
Clark JR	4		4				0		4	0	8	0			
Clark F	8		8	1			0		8	0	6	1	3	3	2
Clark L	3	3	3	1			0		3	3	2	0	5	1	2
Clarke J	2		2				0		2	0	2	0	1		
Clish C	2		2				0		2	0	2	0		2	

NAME	LEAGUE Apps	Sub	Tot	Gls	Major Cups (FA & FL) Apps	Sub	Tot	Gls	Total Apps	Sub	Tot	Gls	Result Won	Drew	Lost
Cole A	1		1		1		0		1	0	1	0			1
Collins J (EE)	2		2	1			0		2	0	2	1	1		1
Connolly J	1		1				0		1	0	1	0		1	
Cooper E	3		3				0		3	0	3	0	1	2	
Cooper J		1	1				0			1	1	0		1	
Corbett R	3		3	1			0		3	0	3	1			1
Cordone D	1		1				0		1	0	1	0			1
Cort C	4		4	1			0		4	0	4	1	4	2	3
Cowan W	13		13				0		13	0	13	0		6	1
Cowell R	2		2				0		2	0	2	0	3	2	2
Craggs J	7		7				0		7	0	7	0	1	1	
Craig D	2		2	1			0		2	0	2	1			2
Craig T	9		9		1		1		9	0	9	0	3	4	
Creilly R (EE)	1		1				0		1	0	1	0	1		
Crowe C	1		1				0		1	0	1	0		1	5
Cummings R	9		9	3	1		0		9	0	9	3	2	2	2
Cunningham A N	5		5	1			1		6	0	6	3	3		1
Cunningham A E	6		6		1		0		6	0	6	1	2	3	2
Curry T	3		3				0		3	0	3	0	1		1
Curry W	2		2	3			1		3	0	3	3			2
Dabizas N	4		4	2			0		4	0	4	2	2	2	2
Dalton G	9		9				1	1	10	0	10	3	6	4	2
Davidson T	8		8				0		8	1	8	2	2	1	2
Davidson D	2		2				2		4	0	4	0	1		2
Davies R	1		1		2		0		1	0	1	0			1
Davies W	1		1				0		2	0	2	0		2	1
Davies I	2		2				0		2	1	3	0	1		
Day W	3		3				0		3	0	3	0			1
Dennison R	1		1				0		1	0	1	0	1	2	1
Devine J	3		3	1			0		3	0	3	1			
Dillon K	2		2		2		2		2	0	2	0	1		2
Distin S	3		3				0		3	0	3	0		1	
Dixon E S	3		3				0		7	0	7	1	2	1	1
Dodgin N	5		5	1			0		6	0	6	0	3	1	
Domi D	6		6	2			0		2	0	2	0	3	1	4
Donaldson A	2		2				0		1	0	1	0	3	1	2
Douglas A	1		1				0		1	0	1	0			
Duncan A S	2		2				0		2	0	2	0			
Dyer K	3		3				0		3	0	3	0			
Dyson K	2		2				0		2	0	2	0			
Eastham G	1		1				0		1	0	1	0			

NAME	LEAGUE Apps	LEAGUE Sub	LEAGUE Tot	LEAGUE Gls	Major Cups (FA & FL) Apps	Major Cups (FA & FL) Sub	Major Cups (FA & FL) Tot	Major Cups (FA & FL) Gls	Total Apps	Total Sub	Total Tot	Total Gls	Result Won	Result Drew	Result Lost
Elliott D	4		4				0		4		4	0	1	2	1
Elliott R	3		3	1			0		3		3	1	1	2	
Emre B	1		1				0		1		1	0	1		
Evans T	1		1				0		1		1	0			1
Fairbrother J	5		5				0		5		5	0	4	1	3
Fairhurst D	7		7				0		7		7	0	2	3	1
Faye A	1		1				0		1		1	0			
Fell J	2		2				0		2		2	0			2
Ferdinand L	2	1	2	1			0		2	1	2	1	1	1	
Ferguson D	6		6				0		6		6	0		1	
Finlay J	2		2				0		2		2	0		1	
Foggon A	2		2	1			0		2		2	1	4		2
Foulkes W	2		2	3			0		2		2	3		2	1
Franks A	1		1				0		1		1	0	1		
Fraser J	4		4				0		4		4	0		1	
Gallacher H	4		4				0		4		4	0	3	2	3
Gallacher J	2		2				0		2		2	0		2	9
Gallacher K	1	1	1				0		1	1	1	0		1	
Garbutt E	5		5				0		5		5	0	1		3
Gardner D	17		17		1		1		18		18	0	4	5	9
Gardner A				2			0					2			3
Gavilan D	6		6				0		6		6	0		1	
Ghee T	4		4				0		4		4	0	2	3	
Gibb T	8		8				0		8		8	0	1	3	
Gibson W	1		1				0		1		1	0	2	1	
Gibson C	1		1				0		1		1	0			
Gillespie K	2		2				0		2		2	0	1	1	1
Ginola D	8		8				0		8		8	0	5	2	1
Given S	2		2				0		2		2	0			6
Goma A	9		9				0		9		9	0	1		
Goodwill T	2		2				0		2		2	0	2	1	
Gosnell A	3		3				0		3		3	0	1	1	
Gowling A	1		1	1			0		1		1	1	2		
Griffin A	2		2				0		2		2	0	1	1	
Guthrie R	1		1				0		1		1	0	2	2	
Hagan A	2		2				0		2		2	0		1	
Hair G	1		1				0		1		1	0			
Hall T	4		4				0		4		4	0			2
Hampson W	7		7	1			0		7		7	1	2	2	3
Hannah G	8		8	1			0		8		8	1	4		3
Hardinge H	1		1	1			0		1		1	0	3	2	1

NAME	LEAGUE Apps	Sub	Tot	Gls	Major Cups (FA & FL) Apps	Sub	Tot	Gls	Total Apps	Sub	Tot	Gls	Result Won	Drew	Lost
Hardwick S	4		4		2		2	0	6	0	6	0	1	2	3
Harper S	10		10	4					10	0	10	4	4	3	3
Harris N	5		5						5	0	5	0	3	1	1
Harris J	7		7	1					7	0	7	1	2	2	3
Harvey J	8		8		3		3	0	11	0	11	0	5	5	1
Hay J	2		2						2	0	2	0	1		1
Heard P	1		1	1					1	0	1	1			1
Helder C															
Henderson D (EE)					1		1	0	1	0	1	0		1	
Hewison R	4		4						4	0	4	0	1		3
Heywood F	1		1		3		3	0	4	0	4	0		1	3
Hibbert W	8		8	4	3		3	0	11	0	11	4	3	2	6
Hibbitt T	4		4		2		2	0	6	0	6	0	2	1	3
Higgins W	2		2						2	0	2	0		1	1
Higgins A	7		7	2	2		2	0	9	0	9	2	5	1	3
Hill J H	4		4						4	0	4	0	1		3
Hill J M	8		8						8	0	8	0	2	2	4
Hilley D	1		1						1	0	1	0			1
Hislop S															
Hoban T (EE)															
Hollins D	6		6	1					6	0	6	1	3		3
Horsfield A	1	1	2						2	0	2	0		2	
Houghton F	4		4	3					4	0	4	3		1	
Howey S	9		9	1	2		2	0	11	0	11	1	3	2	6
Howie J	21		21		3		3	0	24	0	24	0	8	8	8
Hudspeth F															
Hughes G	5		5						5	0	5	0	3		1
Hughes A	2		2	1					2	0	2	1		2	
Hunt A	10		10						10	0	10	0	3	4	3
Hutchison D	2		2						2	0	2	0	1		1
Iley J	2	1	3						3	0	3	0	1		1
Jackson J															
Jenas J	6		6						6	0	6	0	3	2	3
Jobey G	7		7						7	0	7	0	4		3
Keeble V	6		6	4					6	0	6	4	1		
Keith R					1		1	0	1	0	1	0			
Kelly P	1		1						1	0	1	0			1
Kelly G															
Kelly D	3		3	1					3	0	3	1			3
Kelsey W															
Kennedy A	2		2	1					2	0	2	1	1	1	1

NAME	LEAGUE				Major Cups (FA & FL)				Total				Result		
	Apps	Sub	Tot	Gls	Apps	Sub	Tot	Gls	Apps	Sub	Tot	Gls	Won	Drew	Lost
Kerray J	3		3	1			0	0	3	0	3	1		2	1
Kettleborough K	1		1				0	0	1	0	1	0	1		
Kilcline B							0	0		0		0			
King J	2		2				0	0	2	0	2	0	1		1
Kingsley M	10		10	1	1		1	0	11	0	11	1	3	3	5
Kristensen B	4		4				0	0	4	0	4	0		3	1
Lang T	11		11	4			0	0	11	0	11	4	6		5
Lawrence J	22		22		5		5	0	27	0	27	0	10	7	10
Lee R	7		7				0	0	7	0	7	0	3	3	1
Liddell R							0	0		0		0			
Lindsay W	4		4				0	0	4	0	4	0	2		2
Lindsay D	2		2				0	0	2	0	2	0	1		1
Little R							0	0		0		0			1
Loughlin J	1		1				0	0	1	0	1	0			1
Low W	21		21		3		3	0	24	0	24	0	10	6	8
Low J	3		3				0	0	3	0	3	0	2		1
Lowes T							0	0		0		0	1		
Lowrie G	1	1	1				0	0	1	1	1	0	1	1	
Lua lua L		1	1	1			0	0		1	1	1			1
Luque A							0	0	0	0	0	0			
Macfarlane A	5		5				0	0	5	0	5	0	1	1	3
Mahoney M	2		2				0	0	2	0	2	0	1	1	
Maitland A	7		7				0	0	7	0	7	0	3	1	3
Makel L		1					0	0	0	1		0			
Maric S	1		1				0	0		0		0			
Marshall G	6		6				0	0	6	0	6	0	3	1	2
Martin M	1		1		2		2	0	3	0	3	0		1	2
Mathison G	1		1				0	0	1	0	1	0	1		
McCaffery A	2		2				0	0	2	0	2	0	1	1	
McClarence J							0	0		0		0		1	
McClen J	1		1				0	0	1	0	1	0	1		
McColl RS	4		4	1			0	0	4	0	4	1	1	2	1
McCombie A	7		7				0	0	7	0	7	0	1	2	5
McCracken W	19		19		5		5	0	24	0	24	0	11	5	8
McCreery D	1		1				0	0	1	0	1	0		1	
McCurley J	2		2				0	0	2	0	2	0		1	1
McDonald J	2		2		2		2	0	4	0	4	0	1	3	
McDonald T	16		16	4			0	0	16	0	16	4	6	5	5
McDonald N	2		2				0	0	2	0	2	0	1	1	
McFaul I	4		4				0	0	4	0	4	0	1	3	2
McGarry R	5		5	1			0	0	5	0	5	1	1	1	3

NAME	LEAGUE				Major Cups (FA & FL)				Total				Result		
	Apps	Sub	Tot	Gls	Apps	Sub	Tot	Gls	Apps	Sub	Tot	Gls	Won	Drew	Lost
McGhee M	4		4	1			0		4	0	4	1		3	1
McGrath J	5		5				0		5	0	5	0	2	1	2
McGuigan J	1		1	1			0		1	0	1	1		1	
McInroy A	7		7				0		7	0	7	0	3		4
McIntosh R	4		4	1			0		4	0	4	1	2	2	
McKay R	3		3	1			0		3	0	3	1	2	1	
McKenzie R	12		12				0		12	0	12	0	5	2	5
McKinney W	4		4	1			0		4	0	4	1	2		2
McMenemy H	14		14		1		1		15	0	15	0	5	6	4
McMichael A	4		4	1			0		4	0	4	1	1	2	1
McNamee J	1		1				0		1	0	1		1		
McPhillips W	2		2		2		2		4	0	4	0			2
McTavish J	10		10	1	2		2		12	0	12	1	4	2	5
McWilliam P	1		1				0		1	0	1	1	1	3	
Megson G	13		13	11	1		1	1	14	0	14	11	6	4	4
Mellor W					1		1		1	0	1	0			1
Milburn J	13		13				0		13	0	13	0	6		
Miller H (EE)	3		3				0		3	0	3	0		3	5
Mitchell T	17		17	4	1		1		18	0	18	4	6	7	2
Mitchell R	3		3				0		3	0	3	0			1
Mitchell S	3	1					0		8	0	8	4		1	3
Mitchell K	1		1				0		1	0	1	0			
Moncur R	8		8				0		8	0	8	0	2	3	2
Monkhouse A							0		1	0	1	0		1	
Mooney E	5		5	1			0		5	0	5	0	1	2	2
Moore C	1		1				0		1	1	1	0	1		
Mordue T							0		1	0	1	0			
Muir A (EE)					1		1		1	0	1	0			1
Mulvey M (EE)					1		1		1	0	1	0	2	1	1
Murray J	3		3				0		3	0	3	0			
Mutch A	1		1				0		1	0	1	0			1
Napier K							0			1	1	0			
Nattrass I	3		3				0		3	0	3	0	1	1	1
Naylor J	3		3				0		3	0	3	0	1		2
Neale D	1		1				0		1	0	1	0			
Nelson J	7		7		2		2		7	0	7	0	4		
Niblo T	4		4				0		4	0	4	0		1	3
Nicholson G							0		2	0	2	0		1	3
Noble P	2		2				0		2	0	2	0	1		1
Nulty G	2		2				0		2	1	2	0	1		
N'Zogbia C	2		2	1			0		2	0	2	1	2		

NAME	LEAGUE				Major Cups (FA & FL)				Total				Result		
	Apps	Sub	Tot	Gls	Apps	Sub	Tot	Gls	Apps	Sub	Tot	Gls	Won	Drew	Lost
O'Brien L	3	2	5	2			0		3	2	5	2	2	2	1
O'Brien A	4	1	5	1			0		4	1	5	1	3	2	
Orr R	7		7	3	1		1	1	8		8	4	2	3	3
Ostler J	1		1				0		1		1		1		
Pailor R	1		1				0		1		1		1		1
Park O	2		2				0		2		2			2	
Parker S	1		1				0		1		1		1		
Paterson W	3		3		1		1		4		4		1	1	1
Peacock G	3		3				0		3		3		2	1	
Peacock D	2		2				0		2		2		2	1	2
Pearson J							1		1		1				
Peddie J	5		5	2	1		1		6		6	2	3	1	1
Penman W	1		1				0		1		1		1		
Pistone A	1		1				0		1		1			1	
Pudan R	2		2				0		2		2		1		1
Punton W	1		1				0		1		1		1	1	
Quinn M	5		5				0		5		5			3	2
Quinn W	1		1				0		1		1		1	1	
Rafferty W	1		1				0		1		1		1		1
Ramage P	1		1				0		1		1		1		
Ramsay A	2		2				0		2		2			1	
Ranson R	1		1		1		1		2		2		1	1	
Raylstone J (EE)							0								
Reilly G							0								1
Richardson J	1		1	1			0		2		2	1			3
Richardson J R	2		2				0		6		6		3	1	
Robert L	6		6				0		3		3		2	1	
Roberts R	3		3	1			0		3		3		1		2
Robinson R	2		2				0		2		2				1
Robinson R W	2		2		1		1	1	1		1		1	1	
Robinson P	1		1				0		1		1				
Robledo E	2		2				0		2		2		1	1	2
Robledo G	7		7	5			0		7		7	5	3	4	2
Robson T	3		4				0		4		4		1	1	
Robson B	6		6	1			0		6		6		1	3	
Roche D	1	1	1				0		1		1	1		1	
Roeder G	1		1				0		1		1			1	
Rogers J	4		4				0		4		4				
Roxburgh R	2		2				0		2		2		2	2	2
Russell S	1		1				0		1		1				
Rutherford J	17		17	4	2		2	1	19	0	19	5	4	8	7

NAME	LEAGUE				Major Cups (FA & FL)				Total				Result		
	Apps	Sub	Tot	Gls	Apps	Sub	Tot	Gls	Apps	Sub	Tot	Gls	Won	Drew	Lost
Saunders W	1		1						1	0	1	0	1		
Scott J G	4		4	1					4	0	4	1	1	3	
Scott J	8		8						8	0	8	0	3	4	1
Scott K	9		9						9	0	9	0	5	1	4
Scoular J	13		13						13	0	13	0	1	3	4
Sellars S	9	2	11	1					9	2	11	1	6	3	2
Seymour G S	7		7	4					7	0	7	4	6		1
Shearer A	7		7						7	0	7	0	1	4	2
Sheedy K	3		3						3	0	3	0	3		
Shepherd A	7		7	6	3		3	2	10	0	10	8	1		3
Shinton R	1		1	1				1	1	0	1	2			1
Shoulder A	3		3		2		2		5	0	5	0	3		3
Sibley A	1		1						1	0	1	0			
Simpson R	10		10	1	1		1		11	0	11	1	7	2	2
Sinclair J	2		2	2					2	0	2	2	2		
Smailes A	2		2						2	0	2	0		1	1
Smith J (EE)	1		1		1		1		1	0	1	0			
Smith J	9		9	1					9	0	9	0	5	2	2
Solano N	7		7	1					7	0	7	0	2	3	2
Speed G	3		3						3	0	3	0		2	1
Speedie F	6		6	1					6	0	6	0	3		1
Spencer C	2		2						2	0	2	0	2		
Srnicek P	1		1						1	0	1	0	1		
Starling R	1		1						1	0	1	0		1	
Stenhouse H					1		1		3	0	3	0	1	1	
Stevenson J	3		3		3		3		2	0	2	0		2	2
Stewart W	6		6	2	3		3		9	0	9	2	4	4	
Stewart J	6		6						6	0	6	0	2	1	
Stimson M	8		8						8	0	8	0	1	2	5
Stokoe R	6		6						6	0	6	0	2	1	2
Stott J	6		6						6	0	6	0			
Suddick A	1		1						1	0	1	0	1		
Suggett C	6		6	2					6	0	6	2		2	
Sweeney P	1		1						1	0	1	0		1	
Tait A	4		4	4					4	0	4	4	1	1	1
Taylor E	1		1	1					1	0	1	1			1
Taylor C	1		1	1					1	0	1	1			
Taylor S	3		3						3	0	3	0	1	3	
Templeton R	4		4						4	0	4	0	1		1
Thomas B	1		1						1	0	1	0		2	1
Thomas M	1		1						1	0	1	0		1	2

NAME	LEAGUE Apps	Sub	Tot	Gls	Major Cups (FA & FL) Apps	Sub	Tot	Gls	Total Apps	Sub	Tot	Gls	Won	Drew	Lost
Thompson T	1		1				0		1	0	1	0	1	1	
Thompson W	6		6				0		6	0	6	0	2	1	3
Thompson A	−		−				0		−	0	−	0			
Thomson R	5		5				0		5	0	5	0	1	1	3
Thorn A	1		1				0		1	0	1	0		1	
Tildesley J	2		2				0		2	0	2	0		1	1
Turner A	2		2				0		2	0	2	0			2
Urwin T	9		9	3			0		9	0	9	3	3	4	2
Veitch C	18		18	2	5		5	1	23	0	23	3	6	8	9
Venison B	2		2				0		2	0	2	0	2		
Viana H	1	1	2				0		1	1	2	0			2
Walker T	9		9	1			0		9	0	9	1	3	5	1
Walker N	2	1	3				0		2	1	3	0	1		2
Ward E	2		2	1			0		2	0	2	1	1	1	
Wardrope W	1		1	1			0		1	0	1	1	1		
Watson S	3		3				0		3	0	3	0	2		1
Watts C	2		2				0		2	0	2	0		2	
Weaver S	6		6	2	2		2		6	0	6	2	2	1	2
Wharton K	−		−				0		−	0	−	0	1		
White L	4		4				0		4	0	4	0	4		
Whitson T	6		6	3	2		2		8	0	8	3		1	2
Wilkinson J	3		3				0		3	0	3	0		2	1
Williams R	1		1				0		1	0	1	0	1	1	
Wills D	4		4				0		4	0	4	0	2		2
Wills T	2		2				0		2	0	2	0			2
Wilson G	11		11	2	5		5	2	16	0	16	4	8	3	5
Wilson J	1		1				0		1	0	1	0		1	
Wilson W (1920s)	7		7				0		7	0	7	0	2	3	2
Wilson W (1900s)	1		1				0		1	0	1	0		1	
Withe P	4		4	1	2		2		6	0	6	1	1	2	3
Woodgate J	1		1				0		1	0	1	0	1		
Wright B	3		3				0		3	0	3	0		2	1
Wright T	4		4				0		4	0	4	0	2	1	1
Young W (EE)					1		1		1	0	1	0			1

381

SUNDERLAND PLAYERS - APPEARANCES AGAINST NEWCASTLE UNITED

NAME	LEAGUE				Major Cups (FA & FL)				Total				Result		
	Apps	Sub	Tot	Gls	Apps	Sub	Tot	Gls	Apps	Sub	Tot	Gls	Won	Drew	Lost
Agboola R	4		4					0	4	0	4	0		3	1
Agnew S	13		13		1		1	0	14	0	14	0	4	3	7
Aitken G	3		3					0	3	0	3	0	1		2
Allan A					1										
Allan T	2		2					0	2	0	2	0	1		1
Allen T	13		13	1	1		1	0	14	0	14	1	5	5	4
Anderson S	11		11					0	11	0	11	0	4	2	5
Andrews A	2	3	5					0	2	3	5	0	1	1	3
Arca J	7	1	8					0	7	1	8	0	2	4	3
Armstrong G	4		4	1	1		1	1	5	0	5	1		4	1
Arnott K	14		14	1				0	14	0	14	1	4	7	3
Ashurst L	4		4					0	4	0	4	0	2	1	1
Ashurst J					1		1	0	1	0	1	0		1	
Atkinson B			1					0	1	0	1	0			1
Babb P															
Bach P	5		5					0	5	0	5	0	1	1	
Baker J	5	1	6					0	5	1	6	0	2		4
Ball K	4		4					0	5	0	5	0	3	1	2
Barrie A		1						0	4	0	4	0			1
Baxter J	3		3					0							
Becton T				1				0							
Bell E	2		2					0	3	0	3	0		1	2
Bell JC	7		7					0	7	0	7	0		1	
Bellion D	2	1	2					0	2	1	2	0	1		2
Bennett G	11		11	3				0	11	0	11	3	2	4	1
Berry S	7		7	3	1		1	3	8	0	8	3	3	2	7
Best R	3		3		1		1	0	3	0	3	0		2	3
Bingham W	3		3					0	3	0	3	0			3
Bjorklund J	2		2					0	2	0	2	0			3
Bollands J	5		5		2		2	0	7	0	7	0	2	3	2
Bolton J	1		1		2		2	2				0			1
Bonthron R	8		8					0	8	0	8	0		5	
Bould S	2		2					0	2	0	2	0	1	1	
Bracewell P					1		1	0				0	1		2
Brand R	1		1		1		1	0	1	0	1	0			1
Breconridge W								0				0			
Breen G		1	1					0	1	0	1	0		1	
Bridges M								0	0	1	1	0			

NAME	LEAGUE Apps	Sub	Tot	Gls	Major Cups (FA & FL) Apps	Sub	Tot	Gls	Total Apps	Sub	Tot	Gls	Result Won	Drew	Lost
Bridgett A	18		18	9	2		2		20	0	20	9	9	4	7
Broadis I	3		3	1			0		3	0	3	1	1	1	1
Brown AS	3		3		2		2		5	0	5	0	2	2	2
Brown A	3		3	1	2		2	2	5	0	5	3	2	1	2
Brown C	1		1				0		1	0	1	2		2	1
Buchan C	18		18	8	3		3	1	21	0	21	9	8	6	7
Buckle H R	5		5	4			0		5	0	5	4	4	1	
Buckley M	1		1		1		1		2	0	2	0	1		1
Butcher T					1		1		1	0	1	0			1
Butler J	3		3		3		3		6	0	6	0	2	2	2
Butler P	2		2				0		2	0	2	0	1	1	
Butler T		1	1				0			1	1	0			1
Byrne J	2		2				0		2	0	2	0		1	1
Caldwell S	2		2				0		2	0	2	0			2
Carter R	3		3				0		3	0	3	0	1		2
Carter T	3		3				0		3	0	3	0		1	2
Carteron P	1		1				0		1	0	1	0			1
Chisholm K	3		3	1			0		3	0	3	1	2		1
Chisholm G	3		3	1	1	1	2		5	0	5	1	2		1
Clark W	3		3				0		3	1	4	0		3	1
Clarke J	5		5		2		2		7	0	7	0			2
Clough B	3		3	3			0		3	0	3	3	3	2	
Clunas W	3		3				0		3	0	3	0	1	3	4
Coleman JG	11		11	2			0		11	0	11	2	4	3	4
Collins D	2		2				0		2	0	2	0	1	1	
Collins JD	1		1				0		1	0	1	0			1
Colquhoun J	1		1				0		1	0	1	0			1
Common A	2		2				0		2	0	2	0	1		
Connor J	2		2	2			0		2	0	2	2			4
Cooke F R	7		7				0		7	0	7	0	3		
Cooke J	1		1				0		1	0	1	0			1
Coton A	1		1				0		1	0	1	0		1	1
Cowan J	2		2				0		2	0	2	0	1	3	1
Cowell J	1		1				0		1	0	1	0	1	2	
Craddock J	6		6				0		6	0	6	0	1		2
Craggs J	3		3				0		3	0	3	0	1	3	
Crawford J	2		2				0		2	0	2	0	1	2	
Cresswell W	8		8				0		8	0	8	0	3	3	2
Cringan W	5		5				0		5	0	5	0	1		1
Crossan J	3		3				0		3	0	3	0	1	1	1

NAME	LEAGUE Apps	Sub	Tot	Gls	Major Cups (FA & FL) Apps	Sub	Tot	Gls	Total Apps	Sub	Tot	Gls	Result Won	Drew	Lost
Crossley C	10	-	10	-	3	-	3	-	13	-	13	-	5	3	5
Cuggy F	-	1	1	-	-	-	-	-	-	1	1	-	-	1	-
Cullen A	2	-	2	2	-	-	-	-	2	-	2	2	1	-	1
Cummins S	2	-	2	-	-	-	-	-	2	-	2	-	-	-	2
Cunnington S	8	-	8	-	1	-	1	-	9	-	9	-	3	1	5
Daniel R	-	-	-	-	1	-	1	-	1	-	1	-	-	-	1
Daniel P	4	-	4	1	-	-	-	-	4	-	4	1	2	1	3
Davenport P	4	-	4	2	-	-	-	-	4	-	4	2	-	-	2
Davis H	2	-	2	1	-	-	-	-	2	-	2	1	-	-	2
Davis K	3	-	3	-	-	-	-	-	3	-	3	-	-	-	-
Davis R	1	-	1	1	-	-	-	-	1	-	1	1	1	-	-
Davison A	-	-	-	-	1	-	1	1	1	-	1	1	-	-	1
Davison J	3	-	3	2	-	-	-	-	3	-	3	2	2	-	1
Daykin T	5	-	5	1	-	-	-	-	5	-	5	1	1	1	3
Death W	5	-	5	-	-	-	-	-	5	-	5	-	2	3	-
Devine J	0	1	1	-	-	-	-	-	0	1	1	-	1	-	-
Dichio D	3	-	3	-	-	-	-	-	3	-	3	-	1	2	-
Docherty M	12	-	12	2	1	-	1	-	13	-	13	2	5	4	4
Doig JE	2	-	2	-	-	-	-	-	2	-	2	-	1	-	1
Donaldson A	1	-	1	-	-	-	-	-	1	-	1	-	-	-	1
Duns L	3	-	3	-	-	-	-	-	3	-	3	-	2	-	1
Eden W	3	-	3	1	-	-	-	-	3	-	3	1	1	2	-
Edgar D	8	-	8	-	2	-	2	-	10	-	10	-	2	4	4
Elliott W	6	-	6	1	2	-	2	-	8	-	8	1	3	4	1
Elliott Sh	1	-	1	-	-	-	-	-	1	-	1	-	1	-	-
Elliott St	3	-	3	-	-	-	-	-	3	-	3	-	1	-	2
Elliott D	6	-	6	-	-	-	-	-	6	-	6	-	3	-	3
Ellis W	17	-	17	1	-	-	-	-	17	-	17	1	6	5	6
England E	2	-	2	-	1	-	1	-	3	-	3	-	1	2	-
Entwhistle W	10	-	10	-	-	-	-	-	10	-	10	-	4	3	3
Farquhar JW	7	-	7	-	1	-	1	-	8	-	8	-	3	1	4
Ferguson M	6	-	6	5	1	-	1	-	7	-	7	5	3	2	2
Fleming C	-	-	-	-	1	-	1	-	1	-	1	-	-	-	1
Flo T-A	1	1	2	-	-	-	-	-	1	1	2	-	-	1	1
Fogarty A	2	-	2	4	2	-	2	-	4	-	4	4	1	3	-
Ford T	7	-	7	4	-	-	-	-	7	-	7	4	3	3	1
Ford P	1	-	1	-	-	-	-	-	1	-	1	-	-	-	1
Forster H	6	-	6	-	2	-	2	-	8	-	8	-	3	2	3
Foster J	1	-	1	-	-	-	-	-	1	-	1	-	-	-	1
Fraser W	6	-	6	-	1	-	1	-	7	-	7	-	4	1	2

NAME	LEAGUE				Major Cups (FA & FL)				Total				Result		
	Apps	Sub	Tot	Gls	Apps	Sub	Tot	Gls	Apps	Sub	Tot	Gls	Won	Drew	Lost
Fullerton W	2		2	1					2		2	0	1		1
Fulton W	4		4	2					4		4	1	1	3	3
Gabbiadini M	6		6	1					6		6	2	3	3	
Gallacher P	4		4	1					4		4	1	1		1
Gates E	1		1						1		1	1			3
Gauden A	1		1						1		1	0	1		1
Gayle H												0			
Gemmell J	11		11	2	1		1		12		12	2	6	3	3
George W	1		1						1		1	0	1		1
Gibson W												0			
Gilbert T									1		1	0			
Gladwin C	2	1	2		1		1		5		5	0	2	2	1
Goodman D	2		2						2		2	0			2
Grainger C	1		1	1					2		2	0	1	1	
Gray A	1		1		3		3		1		1	0			
Gray Martin	11		11						11		11	1	2	4	1
Gray Michael	4	1	4						4		4	0	3	1	2
Greenwood R	1		1						1		1	0	1		1
Grimshaw W	10		10	1					10		10	0	5		5
Gunson G	2		2						2	1	2	5			
Gurney R	8		8	2					8		8	0	1	5	
Haas B	1		1						1		1	0			2
Hall A	1		1						1		1	0			1
Hall F	9		9						9		9	0	3	3	3
Hall M	1		1						1		1	0			1
Hall T	4		4						4		4	0		3	1
Hall G	3		3	1					3		3	0			1
Halliday D	1		1						1		1	0	1	1	
Hannigan J	4		4						4		4	0			1
Hardyman P	10	1	10						10	1	10	0	4	3	3
Harford M	4		4						4		4	0	3	3	1
Hargreaves L												0			
Harper G												0			
Harris G	5		5	3					5	1	5	3	4	1	
Harvey M	1		1						1		1	0	3	1	1
Hastings A	1		1						1		1	0			
Hauser T												0			1
Hawes A												0			
Hawke W												0			
Hawley J												0			1

NAME	LEAGUE Apps	Sub	Tot	Gls	Major Cups (FA & FL) Apps	Sub	Tot	Gls	Total Apps	Sub	Tot	Gls	Result Won	Drew	Lost
Hedley J	15		15		1		1		16		16		5	5	6
Hellawell M		1	1							1	1		1		
Henderson G	1		1						1		1		1	1	
Henderson M	2		2						2		2		1	4	2
Herd G	11		11	4					11		11		5	2	2
Heslop B	3		3						3		3		1	2	
Hewitt J	3		3						3		3			2	1
Hindmarch R	1		1						1		1		1		
Hinnigan J	9		9						9		9		3		6
Hobson B	19		19	7	3		3	2	22		22	7	10	6	2
Hodgson D	5		5	4	1		1		6		6	4	3	1	1
Hogg W	1		1	1					1		1	3	1	1	3
Hogg R	17		17	13	5		5	2	22		22	15	9	6	7
Holden W	1		1						1		1		1	1	1
Holden M	2		2						2		2				2
Holley G	9		9						9		9		1	6	
Holton J	3		3						3		3	1	3	1	3
Hooper H	2		2						2		2			1	1
Howey L	2		2	1					2		2		1	1	2
Hoyt J	9		9						9		9			6	3
Hudgell A	3		3						3		3		1	1	1
Hughes W	2		2						2		2				2
Hunter G	11		11	1				1	11		11		3	5	3
Hurley C	3		3						3		3		1	2	
Hutchison D	9		9						9		9		4	3	2
Irwin C	11		11		1		1		11		11	1	5	3	3
Jackson R	9		9		1		1		5	1	5		2	3	
Jarvie G	10	1	10	2					1		1	2	1		2
Jobling J	4		4											1	
Johnson A	1		1						6		6		1	6	
Johnston B	6		6						7		7		2	1	3
Kasher J	7		7						2		2				1
Kay J	2		2						2		2	1	1		2
Kelly R	2		2						5		5		1	2	
Kelly D	5		5	2					6		6	2	1		1
Kemp S	6		6						4		4		2	1	2
Kerr R	2	1								2				2	3
Kilbane K		2	2							2	2				1
Kinnell G	6		6						5		5		1	1	2
Kirkley W	2		2		1		1	1	6		6		1		3
									2		2			1	1

NAME	LEAGUE Apps	Sub	Tot	Gls	Major Cups (FA & FL) Apps	Sub	Tot	Gls	Total Apps	Sub	Tot	Gls	Result Won	Drew	Lost
Kirtley H	6		6				0		6	0	6	0		3	2
Kubicki D	2		2				0		2	0	2	0		1	1
Kyle K	1	1	2	1			0		1	1	2	1			2
Lawrence L	2		2				0		2	0	2	0			2
Le Tallec A		1	1				0			1	1	0			1
Lee R	4		4	1			0		4	0	4	1	1	2	1
Lemon P	1		1				0		1	0	1	0	1		
Leonard J	1		1				0		1	0	1	0	2	1	
Leslie J	4		4	2			0		4	0	4	2	2		2
Livingstone G	2		2	1			0		2	0	2	1			2
Low H	11		11	2	5		5		16	0	16	2	6	5	5
MacPhail J							0		4	0	4	0	1	5	
Makin C	4		4				0		3	0	3	0	2	3	
Malone R	3		3				0		1	0	1	0		1	1
Mapson J							0		6	0	6	0			1
Marangoni C	6		6	3			0		1	0	1	0	1	4	
Marples E A	1		1				0		8	0	8	3			3
Marshall R							0		1	0	1	0			1
Martin IG	8		8		3		3		15	0	15	0	5	5	5
Martin N							0		5	0	5	0	2	1	2
M'boma P	12		12				0		12	0	12	0		5	1
McAllister A	5		5	1	1		1		2	0	2	1	5	1	3
McAteer J							0		5	0	5	0	1		2
McCann G	11		11		1		1		10	0	10	0		4	1
McCartney G	2		2	1			0		2	0	2	1			
McCombie A	5		5				0		1	0	1	0	5		3
McConnell E	9		9				0		9	0	9	0	1	3	2
McCulloch D R	2		2				0		8	0	8	0			1
McDermid R	1		1				1		1	0	1	0	4		
McDonald J							0		9	0	9	0	1	3	2
McDougall J	8		8	1			0		8	0	8	0	4		1
McGhie J	8		8				1		1	0	1	0	4		
McGiven M	1		1				0		2	0	2	0	1	1	2
McGorian IM							0		3	0	3	0		2	1
McInally T	2		2				0		2	0	2	0	1		
McInroy A	3		3				0		1	0	1	0	1		3
McIntosh A	2		2				0		2	0	2	0	4	4	
McKay R	1	1	2				0		4	0	4	0	2		
Mclain T	4		4	3			0		1	0	1	0	2	1	2

NAME	LEAGUE Apps	Sub	Tot	Gls	Major Cups (FA & FL) Apps	Sub	Tot	Gls	Total Apps	Sub	Tot	Gls	Result Won	Drew	Lost
McLatchie C	7		7	1	1		1		8	0	8	1	4	1	3
McLaughlan H	1		1						1	0	1	0	1		
McLean A	3		3	1					3	0	3	1		3	
McNab A	1		1						1	0	1	0	1		
McNab J	5		5						5	0	5	0	2	1	2
McNeil R	4		4	1					4	0	4	1	2	1	1
McPheat W	3		3						3	0	3	0	1		2
McSeveney J	1		1						1	0	1	0			1
Melville A	3		3		1		1		4	0	4	0	2		2
Middleton R	1		1						1	0	1	0			1
Middleton M	6		6						6	0	6	0	2	3	1
Millar J	2		2						2	0	2	0			2
Miller T	7		7						7	0	7	0	5	1	1
Milton A	15		15						15	0	15	0	5	6	4
Mitton J					4		4		4	0	4	0	1		3
Montgomery J	1		1						1	0	1	0	1		
Mooney B		1	1						1	0	1	0		1	
Moore G	1		1						1	0	1	0			1
Moore M	1		1						1	0	1	0			1
Moore J	1		1						1	0	1	0	1		
Mordue J	13		13	4	5		5	3	18	0	18	7	8	3	7
Morris S	3		3						3	0	3	0	1		2
Morrison E	1		1						1	0	1	0			1
Morrison W	11		11						11	0	11	0	4	4	3
Mulhall G	14		14	2					14	0	14	2	6	1	7
Murray W	1		1						1	0	1	0			1
Murphy D	3		3						3	0	3	0	1	2	
Naisby T	3		3						3	0	3	0		3	
Nelson C	5		5						5	0	5	0	1	1	3
Ness H	5		5						5	0	5	0	1	3	1
Norman T	1		1						1	0	1	0			1
Nosworthy N					1		1		1	0	1	0			1
Oakley JE	3		3						3	0	3	0		1	2
O'Donnell D	3		3						3	0	3	0	3		
O'Hare J	3		3	2					3	0	3	2	1		2
Oliver J	1		1	1					1	0	1	1	1		
O'Neill A	2		2						2	0	2	0			2
Ord R	2		2						2	0	2	0	1	1	
Overfield J	2		2						2	0	2	0	1		1
Owers G	5	1	6						5	1	6	0		4	2

NAME	LEAGUE Apps	Sub	Tot	Gls	Major Cups (FA & FL) Apps	Sub	Tot	Gls	Total Apps	Sub	Tot	Gls	Result Won	Drew	Lost
Palmer C	1		2	1			0		1	0	2	1		2	2
Park R	1		1				0		1	0	1	0	1	1	4
Parke J	3		3				0		3	0	3	0	4	5	
Parker C	13		13				0		13	0	13	0		2	1
Pascoe C	2		2	4			0		2	0	2	4			
Paterson J	4		4		1		1		4	0	4	0	3		1
Peacock A	1		1				0		1	0	1	0	1		
Perez L	2		2	4			0		2	0	2	4		1	1
Philip G	6		6	1			0		6	0	6	0	2		
Phillips K	2		2	4			0		2	0	2	0		1	1
Pickering N	1		1				0		1	0	1	0		3	1
Piper M	1		1				0		1	0	1	0		1	
Pitt R	8		8				0		8	0	8	0		2	
Poole J	2		2				0		2	0	2	0	3	2	3
Porterfield I	3		3				0		3	0	3	0			
Prior J	1		1				0		1	0	1	0			1
Proctor M A	3		3	1			0		3	0	3	1			
Proctor M G	7		9	2			0		7	2	9	0			
Purdon E	2	2	4				0		2	2	4	1	2	4	3
Quinn N	1		1				0		1	0	1	2	2	1	1
Rae A	4		4				0		4	0	4	0	2		
Raine JF	2		2				0		2	0	2	0	2		2
Raisbeck W	2		2				0		2	0	2	0	1		1
Ramsay S		1	1		3		3			3	3	0	2		2
Raybould S	3		3	1			0		3	0	3	0			
Reddy M	2		2				0		2	0	2	1	1	1	1
Revie D	7		7				0		7	0	7	0			
Reyna C	6		6	1			0		6	0	6	0			
Reynolds T	3		3		2		2		3	0	3	0	1	4	1
Rhodes E	1		1				0		1	0	1	0	4		1
Richardson J	1		1				3	1	1	0	1	1	2	3	1
Robinson R S	2		2		3		3		2	0	2	0			
Robinson G	2		2				0		2	0	2	0			1
Robinson J	1		1				0		1	0	1	0			1
Robinson R	1		1				0		1	0	1	0	1	1	1
Robson E	2		2		2		2		2	0	2	0	2		
Robson B	2		4				0		2	2	4	0			
Rodgers J	3		3	1			0		3	0	3	1		1	1
Rogan A	1		1				0		1	0	1	0			
Rooks R							0						2	1	2

NAME	LEAGUE				Major Cups (FA & FL)				Total				Result		
	Apps	Sub	Tot	Gls	Apps	Sub	Tot	Gls	Apps	Sub	Tot	Gls	Won	Drew	Lost
Roose L R	6		6		2		2		8		8	0	4	2	2
Rostron W	5	1	6	3	2		2	1	3		3	1	2	2	2
Rowell G	3		3		1		1		6		7	3	3	1	1
Rush D	1	1	1						3		3	0			1
Russell C		1									1	0			1
Ryan R	1		1						1		1	0	1		
Sampson I	5		5	1					5		5	0		1	1
Schwarz S											3	0	1	3	2
Scott M	3		3						3		3		1		3
Scott W	6		6	1					6		6	0	3	2	7
Scott L	15		15	4					16		16	4	1	6	2
Shackleton L	4		4		1		1		4		4	0		1	
Sharkey D											1	0			5
Shaw Jos	9		9	1					9		9	0	4		1
Shaw H	1		1								1				3
Shore A V	4		4		2		2		6		6	0	2		
Siddall B	8		8						8		8	0	2	3	4
Sorensen T											1	0	1		
Spain J	1		1		1		1		1		1	0			1
Stead J	8		8						8		8	0	1	2	1
Stelling J	2		2						2		2	0		3	
Stephenson J	2		2						2		2	0		1	1
Stewart P		1								1		0	2		
Stewart M	2	1							2	1	2	0		1	
Stubbs A	4		4	1					4		4	0	1	2	6
Stuckey B	2		2	5					4		4	5	4		
Suggett C	10		10		2		2		12		12	0	1		1
Summerbee N											1	0	1	2	7
Tait T S	3		3						3		3	0		5	1
Temple J	1		1						1		1	0	6	1	
Thome E	13		13		5		5		18		18	0	2		
Thompson J W	3		3						3		3	0			1
Thomson C B											1	0	1		3
Thomson C M											1	0			1
Thomson R	4		4						4		4	0		1	
Thornton S	2		2						2		2	0	2	4	2
Thorpe J	8		8						8		8	0		1	
Threadgold H	1		1						1		1	0			
Todd C												0			
Toseland G												0			

NAME	LEAGUE Apps	LEAGUE Sub	LEAGUE Tot	LEAGUE Gls	Major Cups (FA & FL) Apps	Major Cups Sub	Major Cups Tot	Major Cups Gls	Total Apps	Total Sub	Total Tot	Total Gls	Result Won	Result Drew	Result Lost
Towers A	1	0	1				0		1	0	1	0	2		1
Travers B	4	0	4	2			0		4	0	4	2	1	2	2
Troughear W	6	0	6				0		6	0	6	0		2	3
Tueart D	3	0	3				0		3	0	3	0			1
Turnbull R	1	0	1	1			0		1	0	1	1	1	1	
Turner C							0					0	1		1
Urwin T	4	0	4				0		4	0	4	0	1		2
Usher B	4	0	4				0		4	0	4	0		1	3
Venison B	2	0	2				0		2	0	2	0			1
Vinall E	2	0	2				0		2	0	2	0		1	1
Waddle C	1	0	1				0		1	0	1	0		1	
Wakeham P	1	0	1				0		1	0	1	0		1	
Walker C	1	0	1				0		1	0	1	0		1	
Wallace I	2	0	2				0		2	0	2	0		2	1
Walsh W	1	0	1				0		1	0	1	0	1		
Ward R	3	0	3				0		3	0	3	0			
Watson J	13	0	13		1		1		14	0	14	0	1	5	1
Watson W	10	0	10	1			0		10	0	10	1	6	6	1
Waugh J	1	0	1				0		1	0	1	0	1		3
Webb I	2	0	2				0		2	0	2	0			3
Welsh A	1	0	1				0		1	0	1	0			1
West C	1	0	1	1			0		1	0	1	1	2	1	
Whelan W	1	0	1				0		1	0	1	0			1
Whitehead D	2	0	2				0		2	0	2	0	2		2
Whitworth S	2	1	3				0		2	1	3	0		1	1
Wilks A	1	0	1		2		2		3	0	3	0	1	1	2
Williams D	3	0	3				0		3	0	3	0	2		2
Willis D	3	0	3				0		3	0	3	0	1		1
Wilson H	4	0	4				0		4	0	4	0	1	1	2
Wood A	2	0	2				0		2	0	2	0			1
Wright D	2	0	2	3			0		2	0	2	3			1
Wright A	2	0	2				0		2	0	2	0	1		1
Wright T	10	0	10				0		10	0	10	0	1	6	3
Wright S	8	0	8	1			0		8	0	8	1		5	2
Yorston B	1	0	1				0		1	0	1	0	1		1
Young R	2	0	2	1			0		2	0	2	1	2		

East End/Newcastle United v Sunderland
Friendly Games

3 Nov 1883, Byker, 0-3 (0-0)
East End: J Broughton, J Fenwick, M K Hiscock, W Wilson, W Blackett, R Lightfoot, R Findlay,
J Armstrong, W Findlay, J Speight, J P Cook
Sunderland: D Stewart, J Hall, WM Allan, J Elliott, Anderson, Atkinson, J R Allan, F Woodward,
J McMillan, J McDonald, H Brown *(Sunderland 'A' team)*

25 June 1884, Newcastle Town Moor, East End 1, Sunderland 3 (2x30 mins)
 – *Temperance* Festival Final.

7 Nov 1885, Newcastle (Byker), 0-1 (0-1)
East End: E McClen, S Ryder, R Lightfoot, W Blackett, J Armstrong, E Hiscock, Hart, T Hoban, J P Cook,
P O'Brien, D Scott
Sunderland: W Kirkley, J Elliott, J Hall, J McMillan, H Brown, F Dale, J Hunter, J Spain, J Smart,
Hosking, W Marshall

20 Feb 1886, Abbs Field (Fulwell) 1-1 (0-1), 1,500
Sunderland: W Kirkley, W Marshall, J Elliott, J McMillan, J Smart, J R Allan (1), C H Jobes,
J T Summers, J Hunter, W Erskine, R Smith
East End: A McDougall, R Lightfoot, J Fenwick, W Blackett, A H White, J Wilson, D Scott, P O'Brien,
D Lord, W Muir (1), T Hoban

4 Dec 1886, Newcastle Road, 1-1 (0-1) (2x40 mins)
Sunderland: W Kirkley, J Elliott, W Erskine, F Dale, J Smart, J McMillan, R Smith (1), P Rooney, H Lord
A Davison, J R Allan
East End: E McClen, G Goulding, J Ferguson, R Lightfoot, A H White, W Blackett, D Scott, P O'Brien
(1), W Muir, T Hoban, E Hiscock

22 Dec 1888, Chillingham Rd, 1-1 (1-1), 3,000 (2 x 30 mins)
East End: D Henderson, R Creilly, J Miller, W Young, T Hoban, J Coupe, J Collins, J Smith, P Mack (1),
F Blackett, M Mulvey
Sunderland: W Kirkley, R McDermid, J Oliver, D McKechnie, H McLauchlan, W Gibson, A Davison,
J Smith, J N Breconridge, A Peacock, W Peacock (1)

16 Nov 1889, Chillingham Rd, 0-4, (0-3), 6,000
East End: M Scott, A Sawers, Tinn, R Creilly, A McCurdie, J Coupe, J Miller, R Watson, L Wood,
J Collins, M Mulvey
Sunderland: W Kirkley, T Porteous, J Oliver, J Stevenson, J R Auld (1), W Gibson, J Harvie, J Smith (1),
J Campbell (1), D Hannah, J Scott, scrimmage (1)

30 Apr 1891, Chillingham Rd, 0-3, (0-1), 3,000
East End: M Scott, P Watson, J Miller, A McMurdie, R Creilly, J McKane, M Mulvey, J Collins, J Sorley,
J Wallace, T McInnes
Sunderland: J E Doig, T Porteous, J W Murray, W Gibson, J R Auld, H Wilson, J Harvie (1), J Smith
(1), J Campbell (1), D Hannah, J Millar

7 Sept 1891, Chillingham Rd, 2-0, (2-0), 3,500. (Abandoned 60 mins (darkness)
East End: M Scott, P Watson, W Wilson, R Creilly, J Spence (1), J McKane, H Reay, T Crate (1),
W Thompson, J Sorley, J Wallace
Sunderland: J E Doig, T Porteous, J Oliver, W Gibson, J R Auld, Dow, J Smith, J Millar, J Campbell,
J Logan, J Scott

26 Sept 1891, Newcastle Rd, 2-0, (0-0), 5,000
Sunderland: J E Doig, J Oliver, D Gow (1), W Gibson, J R Auld, J W Murray, J Hannah, J Millar,
J Logan, D Hannah (1), J Scott
East End: M Scott, P Watson, J Miller, R Creilly, W Wilson, J McKane, H Reay, T Crate, W Thompson,
J Sorley, J Wallace

9 Jan 1892, Chillingham Rd, 4-6, (4-1), 5,000
East End: M Scott, P Watson, J Miller, R Creilly, J Spence, J McKane, H Reay (1), T Crate (1),
W Thompson (2), J Sorley, J Wallace
Sunderland: J E Doig, T Porteous, D Gow, H Wilson, J R Auld, J W Murray, J Hannah (1), J Smith,
J Campbell (3), D Hannah (1), J Scott (1)

11 Apr 1892, Chillingham Rd, 1-4, (0-2), 4,000
East End: M Scott, W Wilson, J Miller, R Creilly, J Spence, J McKane, H Reay, J Barker (1),
W Thompson, J Sorley, J Wallace
Sunderland: J E Doig, T Porteous, J Oliver, H Wilson, W Gibson, J W Murray, J Hannah (1),
D Hannah, J Campbell (1), J Millar (1), J Scott, og (Miller 1)

7 Sep 1892, Chillingham Rd, 2-2, (2-2), 6,000
East End: D Whitton, H Jeffrey, J Miller, R Creilly, W Graham, J McKane, J Collins, T Crate (1),
W Thompson, J Sorley, J Wallace (1)
Sunderland: J E Doig, T Porteous, R Smellie, J Dalton, J R Auld, W Gibson, Jas Gillespie (1), Brand,
D Hannah (1), J Millar, J Hannah

25 Feb 1893, St James' Park, 1-6, (0-3), 7,000
Newcastle Utd*: D Whitton, H Jeffrey, J Miller, R Creilly, W Graham (1), J Collins, H Reay, T Crate,
W Thompson, J Sorley, J Wallace
Sunderland: J E Doig, T Porteous, John Gillespie, W Dunlop, J R Auld, W Gibson, Jas Gillespie (1),
D Hannah (1), J Campbell (4) (incl 1 pen), J Millar, J Scott
East End became Newcastle United in Dec 1892

12 Apr 1893, St James' Park, 0-4, (0-3), 3,000
Newcastle Utd: F McCabe, H Jeffrey, J Miller, R Creilly, W Graham, J McKane, H Reay, T Crate,
J Sorley, J Collins, J Pattison
Sunderland: J E Doig, T Porteous, R Smellie, W Gibson, W Dunlop, H Wilson, J Hannah, J Harvie,
J Millar (2), D Hannah (2), J Scott

6 Sep 1893, St James' Park, 1-3, (0-3), 3,000
Newcastle United, A Ramsay, H Jeffrey, J Miller, JW Barr, W Graham, J McKane, J Bowman, T Crate,
W Thompson (1), R Creilly, J Wallace
Sunderland, M Scott, T Porteous, P Meehan, W Dunlop, J R Auld, J Dalton, J Gillespie (1), J Harvie
(1), D Hannah (1), J Millar, J Scott

5 Apr 1894, St James' Park, 1-2, (0-2), 5,000
Newcastle United, W Lowery, H Jeffrey, T Rogers, T Crate, W Graham (1 pen), J McKane, C Quinn,
R Willis, W Thompson, J Wallace, J Law
Sunderland, J E Doig, P Meehan, D Gow, J Dale, W Gibson, H Wilson, J Hannah (1), J Harvie,
J Millar, D Hannah (1), J Scott

21 Apr 1894, St James' Park, 4-1, (1-1), 7,500
Newcastle United, J Ryder, H Jeffrey, T Rogers, R Creilly, W Graham, J McKane, T Campbell (1),
C Quinn (1), R Willis (1), T Crate (1), J Law
Sunderland, J E Doig, P Meehan, H Wilson, J Dale, J R Auld, D Hannah, J Gillespie, J Harvie, J Millar
(1), T Hyslop, J Scott

30 Apr 1894, St James' Park, 1-3, (0-2), 6,000
Newcastle United, W Lowery, H Jeffrey, T Rogers, R Creilly, W Graham, J McKane, C Quinn, T Crate
(1), R Willis, J Wallace, J Law
Sunderland, J E Doig, D Gow, T Hyslop, Dow, J R Auld, H Wilson, J Gillespie, J Harvie, J Millar,
D Hannah, J Scott (2), Rushed thro' (1)

5 Sep 1894, St James' Park, 1-4, (0-2), 4,500
Newcastle United, WA Ward, H Jeffrey, T Rendell, R Creilly, W Graham, J McKane, T Campbell,
R Willis, W Thompson, J Smith (1), J Wallace
Sunderland, J E Doig, P Meehan, J McNeil, W Dunlop, J R Auld, J McNaughton, G Goodchild (1),
J Harvie, T Hyslop (2), D Hannah, J Scott, Rushed thro' (1)

19 Jan 1895, St James' Park, 1-4, (1-3), 8,000
Newcastle United, J Hynd, H Jeffrey, (sub W Beattie), R McDermid, R Creilly, W Graham, T Rendell, W Thompson, R Willis, J Smith (1), P G O'Brien, C Dickson
Sunderland, J E Doig, R McNeill, H Johnston, W Dunlop, A McCreadie, (1 pen), H Wilson (1), J Gillespie (1), J Millar, J Campbell (1), T Hyslop, J Scott

22 Apr 1895, St James' Park, 1-0, (0-0), 3,500
Newcastle United, W A Ward, P G O'Brien, R McDermid, J Smith, W Graham, T Rendell, W Milne, J Wallace, W Thompson (1), J McNee, C Dickson
Sunderland, J E Doig, R McNeill, D Gow, A McCreadie, J R Auld, H Johnston, J Gillespie, J Harvie, J Campbell, J Millar, A McNeil

11 Sep 1895, Newcastle Rd, 5-3, (2-2), 5,000
Sunderland, F Thompson, W Gibson, D Gow, W Dunlop, A McCreadie (1), H Wilson, J Harvie (Inj 45), W Cowan (1), J Campbell, J Hannah (2), A McKenzie (1)
Newcastle United, J Henderson, R McDermid, , R Foyer, W Miller, W Graham (1), J Stott, W Wardrope, A Aitken, J Logan, Mackay (1), C Quinn, Scrimmage (1)

30 Nov 1895, St James' Park, 0-4, (0-1), 11,000
Newcastle United, J Henderson, R McDermid, R Foyer, W Miller, W Graham, J Stott, M Lennox, J Collins, W Thompson, A Aitken, W Wardrope
Sunderland, J E Doig, W Gibson, D Gow, H Wilson, A McCreadie, , H Johnston, J Hannah, J Millar (1), J Campbell, J Harvie (1), J Gillespie (1), Scrimmage (1)

29 Feb 1896, St James' Park, 2-2, (2-2), 6,000
Newcastle United, J Henderson, R McDermid, R Foyer, W Miller, W Graham, G Adams, M Lennox (1), J Collins, W Thompson, A Aitken (1), J Stott
Sunderland, J E Doig, W Gibson, D Gow, H Wilson, W Dunlop, H Johnston, J Gillespie, J Harvie, J Campbell (2), J Millar, J Hannah

30 Apr 1896, St James' Park, 3-3, (3-0), 3,000
Newcastle United, J Henderson, R McDermid, R Foyer, W Miller, W Graham, G Adams, M Lennox, J Collins (1), W Thompson (1), A Aitken (1), W Wardrope
Sunderland, F Thompson, J Knowles, W Gibson (1), H Wilson, D Gow, W Dunlop, J Campbell (1), A McKenzie, J Hartley (1), W Cowan, Wilford

2 Sep 1896, St James' Park, 2-2, (0-2), 8,000 (2 x 35 mins)
Newcastle United, C Watts, J White, R Foyer, W Miller, W Graham, J Stott, W Thompson, J Collins, R Smellie (1), A Aitken (1), W Wardrope
Sunderland, J E Doig, R McNeill, D Gow, M Ferguson, W Dunlop, H Johnston, J Gillespie (1), J Wilson, J Campbell (1), J Hartley, R Johnston

23 Sep 1896, Newcastle Rd, 1-1, (0-1), 3,000 (2 x 35 mins)
Sunderland, J E Doig, R McNeill, D Gow, H Wilson, W Dunlop, H Johnston, J Wilson (1), J Campbell, R Johnston, J Hartley, J Hannah
Newcastle United, C Watts, J White, R McDermid, W Miller, J Stott, G Adams, M Lennox, A Aitken, R Smellie, Nicholson, W Wardrope (1)

31 Mar 1897, St James' Park, 5-2, (3-0), 3,000
Newcastle United, C Watts, G Stewart, J White, W Miller, W Graham, J Stott, M Lennox (2), J Collins, W Thompson (2 – 1pen), A Aitken (1), W Wardrope
Sunderland, Stevenson, R McNeill, P Boyle, M Ferguson, F Dale, T Lee, J Wilson, W Cowan, J Campbell (1), H Morgan, O'Brien, Scrimmage (1)

28 Apr 1897, St James' Park, 3-0, (2-0), 4,000
Newcastle United, C Watts, G Stewart, J White, G Adams, J Ostler (1), J Stott, M Lennox, J Connell, R Smellie, A Aitken (2), W Wardrope
Sunderland, J E Doig, P Boyle, H Wilson, M Ferguson, J Campbell, A McAllister, J Gillespie, W Cowan, H Morgan, R Johnston, A Hamilton

1 Sep 1897, St James' Park, 1-3, (0-1), 10,000
Newcastle United, C Watts, G Stewart, J White, T Ghee (1), J Ostler, J Jackson, R Allan, J Harvie,
J Campbell, A Aitken, W Wardrope
Sunderland, J E Doig, P Bach, P Boyle, M Ferguson, A McAllister, H Wilson, T Bradshaw, J Leslie (1),
J Brown, H Morgan (2), J Chalmers

19 Mar 1898, St James' Park, 1-1, (1-1), 16,000
Newcastle United, C Watts, W Lindsay, J Jackson, J Carr, T Ghee, J Stott, M Lennox, A Aitken,
J Peddie, W Smith, W Wardrope (1)
Sunderland, J E Doig, R McNeill, P Boyle, M Ferguson, A McAllister, W Dunlop, H Morgan, J Leslie,
J Brown (1), H Wilson, A Saxon

1 Sep 1898, Newcastle Rd, 1-1, (1-0), 15,000 (2 x 30 mins)
Sunderland, J E Doig, M Ferguson, R McNeill, W Raisbeck, A McAllister, W Dunlop, J Crawford,
J Leslie, H Morgan (1), H Wilson, J Chalmers
Newcastle United, M Kingsley, W Lindsay, J Jackson, T Ghee, W Higgins, A Aitken, J Rogers,
T Niblo, J Peddie (1), W Smith, W Wardrope

14 Feb 1899, Roker Park, 3-4, (2-1), 5,000
Sunderland, J E Doig, P Bach, R Jackson, M Ferguson, A McAllister, W Dunlop, J Crawford,
J W Farquhar, J Brown, W Fulton, C McLatchie (3)
Newcastle United, M Kingsley, W Higgins, J Jackson, T Ghee, C Veitch, J Stott, J Harvie, J Stevenson
(1), J Peddie (2), A Macfarlane, T Niblo (1)

21 Feb 1903, St James' Park, 1-0, (1-0), 4,000
Newcastle United, M Kingsley, J Tildesley, W Agnew, Alex Gardner, P McWilliam, E McIntyre,
A D Turner, R Orr, J Rutherford (1), R S McColl, Andrew Gardner
Sunderland, J E Doig, A McCombie, J Watson, A Barrie, A McAllister, W Robinson, W Hogg,
G Harper, J Gemmell, W Maxwell, A Bridgett

23 Apr 1904, Roker Park, 3-0, (1-0), 3,000
Sunderland, T S Rowlandson, E Rhodes, J Watson, J W Farqhar, W Fullarton, R Jackson, J Craggs,
A Bridgett (1), W Hogg (2), W Wardle, H R Buckle
Newcastle United C Watts, A McCombie, J Carr, A Gardner, E Birnie, A Aitken, J Rutherford,
J Howie, W Appleyard, R Orr, R Templeton

27 Sep 1904, St James' Park, 1-2, (1-1), 18,761
Newcastle United, C Watts, W McCracken, T Wills, A Gardner, E Birnie, E McIntyre, J Rutherford,
J Howie, W Appleyard (1), C Veitch, R Templeton
Sunderland, T S Rowlandson, E Rhodes, J Watson, JW Farqhar, W Fullarton, R Jackson, W Hogg,
A Common, J Gemmell (1), A Bridgett (1), HR Buckle (inj), [J Watson (Jnr)]

9 Oct 1907, Stanley, Co Durham, 2-0, (1-0), 10,000 (North'land & Durham Aged Miners' Homes)
Newcastle United, Purvis, W McCracken, Henderson, Middleton, J McCormack, T Niblo, A Gardner,
J Howie, W Appleyard, J Soye (1), G Hedley (1)
Sunderland, R Allan, R Bonthron, Spence, H Low, T Grey, Ledger, C Thompson, Wilkinson, T Brown,
W Montgomery, Muir

25 Oct 1911, St James' Park, 1-0, (0-0), 11,372 Archibald Cup (Newcastle & Sunderland Hospitals Cup)
Newcastle United, J Lawrence, W McCracken, J Hay, D Willis, W Low, J Finlay, J Rutherford,
J Stewart (1), J Fleming, A Higgins, G Wilson
Sunderland, W Scott, W Troughear, H Ness, E Hodkin, C Thompson, G Jarvie, J Mordue, R Healey,
C Buchan, J Gemmell, A Bridgett

23 Oct 1912, St James' Park, 0-1, (0-0), 7,000 Archibald Cup (Newcastle & Sunderland Hospitals Cup)
Newcastle United, J Lawrence, W McCracken, F Hudspeth, J Hay, W Low, J Finlay, J Rutherford,
J McTavish, W Hibbert, W J Hughes, G Wilson
Sunderland, J Butler, C Gladwin, A Milton, F Cuggy, C Thompson, H Low, J Mordue, G Holley (1),
T Hall, W Tinsley, H Martin

15 Oct 1913, Roker Park, 1-0, (0-0), 5,000 Archibald Cup (Newcastle & Sunderland Hospitals Cup)
Sunderland, J Butler, B Hobson, H Ness, F Cuggy, C Thompson, W Cringan, R Best, C Buchan (1), J Lane, G Holley, H Martin
Newcastle United, J Lawrence, F Hudspeth, T Whitson, J Hay, W Low, J Finlay, E Cooper, T Lowes, T Hall, W Hibbert, T Goodwill

23 Sep 1914, St James' Park, 0-1, (0-0), 6,738 Archibald Cup (Newcastle & Sunderland Hospitals Cup)
Newcastle United, J Lawrence, W Hampson, F Hudspeth, R Hewison, W Low, J Hay, A Douglas, A Higgins, W Hibbert, C Booth, T Goodwill
Sunderland, L Scott, C Gladwin, H Ness, F Cuggy, C Thompson, H Low, J Mordue, C Buchan, G Philip (1), C Crossley, H Martin

6 May 1916, St James' Park, 1-1, (0-1), 3,299 For Military Charities
Newcastle United, J Lawrence, W Hampson, F Hudspeth, J Spink, W Low (1), A Fenwick, (West Ham), E Cooper, R Hewison, Rutherford, T Hall, W Hibbert
Sunderland, J Boe, Cooke (Sheffield Utd), Williamson, F Cuggy, W Hopkins, H Low, J Mordue, C Buchan, R Best, G Holley (1), H Martin

*4 May 1918, St James' Park, 1-3, (0-2), 6,000. Advertised teams, *= played. National Football War Fund*
Newcastle United, J Lawrence, W McCracken, J English, (Sheffield Utd), T Curry, W Low, Hopkinson, Thompson, Linford, T Philipson* (1), Wilson, Featherstone
Sunderland, J Hugall, Charlton, Rogerson, F Cuggy, W Hopkins, H Low, Williams, C Buchan* (2), Leonard, Batty, G Holley* (1)

*31 Aug 1918, St James' Park, 0-4, (0-1), 5,000. Advertised teams. *= played. National Football War Fund*
Newcastle United, J Lawrence*, W McCracken*, Milne*, T Curry*, Barry/Bavey*, J Clarke*, J Donnelly, Thornley, Chambers, T Hall, W Hibbert
Sunderland, J Hugall, Rogerson, Charlton, F Cuggy, H Low, Hunter, Williams* (1), C Buchan, Batey, G Holley* (1), Cook, Leonard* (2)

*21 Dec 1918, St James' Park, 4-0, (0-0), 20,000. Advertised teams, * = played. For Comrades of the Great War Fund*
Newcastle United, J Lawrence*, W McCracken*, English*, J Finlay, Barnshaw, Harvey, Bond, S Bloomer* (1), E Cooper* (2), Higgins, Clarke* (1), Thornley
Sunderland, J Hugall, Rogerson, Charlton, F Cuggy*, W Hopkins, H Low*, Williams*, G Holley*, R Best, C Hafecost*, Cook*

26 Dec 1918, Roker Park, 1-0, (1-0), -
Sunderland, J Hugall, Charlton, Rogerson, F Cuggy, W Hopkins, H Low, Williams, C Hafecost, Philips (1), G Holley, R Best
Newcastle United, Robson, W McCracken, Bell, J Finlay, T Curry, Harvey, C Farrier, E S Dixon, E Cooper, C Booth, Clarke

*17 May 1919, Roker Park, 3-2, (2-0), 16,000. * = played. Footballers' National War Fund*
Sunderland, L Scott*, B Hobson, N Smith*, F Cuggy, H Sherwin*, H Low, R Best*, C Buchan*, B Travers*, J Mordue* (2), Keenleyside* (1)
Newcastle United, W Bradley, W McCracken, F Hudspeth, E S Dixon, Robinson, A Hagan (2), J Wilson, W Hibbert
Full Newcastle team unknown. Advertised Sunderland team only

30 Mar 1940, St James' Park, 2-0, (0-0), 15,000. Journal & North Mail War Fund
Newcastle United, T Swinburne, B Craig, R Ancell, J Gordon, J Denmark, JD Wright, J Park, H Clifton, W Scott (2), A Stubbins, T Pearson
Sunderland, A Heywood, J Gorman, R Rodgerson, C Thomson, A Lockie, A Hastings, J Spuhler, R Gurney, C Whitelum, R Carter, E Burbanks

13 Apr 1940, St James' Park, 3-2, (2-0), 8,666. Journal & North Mail War Fund
Newcastle United, T Swinburne, B Craig, J Law, J Gordon, J Denmark, S Green, J Park, H Clifton, W Cairns, A Stubbins (3), T Pearson
Sunderland, A Heywood, J Gorman, A Hall, C Thomson(1 pen), R Johnston, A Hastings, J Spuhler, H Thompson, C Whitelum (1), R Carter, E Burbanks

21 Dec 1940, St James' Park, 3-1, (0-0), 3,226
Newcastle United, C Theaker, B Craig, R Ancell, J Gordon, T Hutton, N Dodgin, R Birkett (1),
A Stubbins (1), H Billington (1) (Luton Town), F Osborne (guest), L Nevins (inj 1st)
Sunderland, B Bircham, J Gorman, J Eves, W Hewison, A Lockie, A Hastings, Maguire, J Spuhler,
R Gurney (1), Heslop, H McMahon

*14 Apr 1941, St James' Park, 3-4, (1-3), 4,700 Advertised teams * = played.*
Newcastle United, C Theaker, J Richardson, D Graham, A Price*, T Smith*, N Dodgin* (1),
W Cairns*, A Gilholme*, L Duns (Sunderland), J Short* (1) (Leeds Utd), R Birkett, L Nevins* (1)
Sunderland, A Heywood*, J Gorman, Richardson, A Housam, A Lockie, A Hastings*, J Spuhler,
R Gurney* (1), R Carter* (1), Allen* (1), S Bradwell* (1)

15 Aug 1942, St James' Park, 2-4, (0-1), 2,000. (2 x 40 mins)
Newcastle United, C Theaker, W Hughes, D Graham, A Price, T Smith, W Hart, T Walker (1),
J T Dixon, A Stubbins (1), R S Donaldson, , G McQuade
Sunderland, J Clark, J Gorman, J Eves, A Housam, W Hewison, A Hastings, J Spuhler* (1),
Richardson, C Whitelum (1), R Gurney, G H Robinson (1) (Charlton Ath), Allen (1)

6 Sep 1961, Roker Park, 0-1, (0-1), 18,239. 'Cock of the North' Tournament
Sunderland, P Wakeham, C Nelson, L Ashurst, S Anderson, C Hurley, J McNab, H Hooper, A Fogarty,
B Clough, W McPheat, J Overfield
Newcastle United, D Hollins, D Keith, A McMichael, B Wright, G Heslop, G Dalton, L White,
I Allchurch, J McGuigan, K Leek (1), L Tuohy

25 Oct 1961, St James' Park, 2-1, (1-1), 12,230. 'Cock of the North' Tournament
Newcastle United, S Mitchell, D Keith, R Ferguson, B Wright, J McGrath, J Bell, G Hughes, C Woods,
L White (2), J McGuigan, A Scanlon
Sunderland, P Wakeham, C Irwin, L Ashurst, S Anderson, C Hurley, J McNab, G Herd (1), A Murray,
B Clough, A Fogarty, J Overfield

12 Nov 1969, Roker Park, 4-2, (1-1), 6,470. Len Ashurst's Testimonial game (Newcastle United XI)
Sunderland, J Montgomery (B Kerr), C Irwin, L Ashurst, C Todd (M Harvey), B Heslop, M McGiven, ,
G Harris, B Hughes, J Baker (C Symm), B Kerr (J Montgomery(1 pen)), D Tueart (2), (F Clark (1og))
Newcastle United, W Whigham, (Middlesbrough), D Craig, F Clark, D Elliott, J McNamee, R Moncur
(1), J Scott (1), J Barnwell (Nottingham Forest), C Suggett (West Bromwich Albion), G Eastham (Arsenal),
A Foggon

23 Jan 1971, St James' Park, 1-1, (0-0), 16,650
Newcastle United, W McFaul, D Craig, R Guthrie, D Young, J McNamee, R Moncur (1),
S Barrowclough, B Robson, W Davies (G Hindson), J Smith, A Foggon (I Nattrass)
Sunderland, J Montgomery, C Irwin, M Harvey, C Todd, R Pitt, I Porterfield, (B Park), B Chambers,
(M Horswill), B Kerr, B Hughes (1), G Harris, D Tueart

14 May 1973, St James' Park, 2-1, (1-0), 35,873. Ollie Burton's Testimonial game
Newcastle United, M Burleigh, I Nattrass, F Clark, T McDermott (T Gibb), P Howard, R Moncur,
T Cassidy (1), J Smith, J Tudor (1) (K Robson), T Hibbitt (T Green), S Barrowclough
Sunderland, J Montgomery, D Malone, R Guthrie (1), M Horswill (D Young), D Watson, R Pitt
(M Horswill), B Kerr, B Hughes, V Halom (R Ellison), I Porterfield, D Tueart (J Bolton)

13 May 1974, Roker Park, 2-3, (1-2), 29,625. Jim Montgomery's, Testimonial game
Sunderland, J Montgomery, D Malone, R Guthrie (J Bolton), M Horswill (Manchester City)
(D Longhorn), D Young, R Belfitt (1), B Kerr(T Towers), B Hughes (1), V Halom, I Porterfield, D Tueart
(Manchester City)
Newcastle United, J Platt (Middlesbrough) (T Swinburne (Sunderland)), J Craggs, (Middlesbrough),
A Kennedy (Inj 33) (D Crosson), T McDermott (2(1 pen)), P Howard, D Laughton, A Bruce (1), B Robson,
(West Ham United), J Tudor(Inj 8) (P Cannell), A Foggon, T Hibbitt (S Barrowclough)

28 Apr 1975, Roker Park, 3-2, (2-1), 13,654. Martin Harvey's Testimonial game
Sunderland, J Montgomery, D Malone (J Ashurst), J Bolton, R Moncur (1), R Pitt, I Porterfield (1),
B Kerr, B Hughes, R Belfitt (1), B Robson, T Towers
Newcastle United, W McFaul, I Nattrass, A Kennedy, T Gibb (1), F Clark, P Howard (G Keeley),
S Barrowclough, G Nulty, A Bruce (J Tudor), M Burns (1), T Craig (T Hibbitt)

30 Apr 1975, St James' Park, 5-3, (2-0), 21,280. David Craig's Testimonial game
Newcastle United, W McFaul, D Craig (I Nattrass), F Clark (A Kennedy (1)), T Craig, G Keeley,
P Howard, S Barrowclough, T Gibb, M Macdonald (2), M Burns (1) (J Tudor (1)), T Hibbitt (A Bruce)
Sunderland, J Montgomery, D Malone, J Bolton, R Moncur, R Pitt(J Ashurst), I Porterfield, B Kerr (1),
B Hughes (R Mitchell (1)), R Belfitt (T Finney), B Robson (1(Pen)), T Towers (D Longhorn)

28 Apr 1976, St James' Park, 6-3, (2-3), 19,974. Frank Clark's testimonial game
Newcastle United, R Jones (M Mahoney), I Nattrass (R Blackhall), F Clark, R Hudson, A McCaffrey,
G Oates, M Burns (2), A Kennedy (2), M Macdonald (1), A Gowling (A Guy (1)), T Craig
Sunderland, T Swinburne, J Craggs (Middlesbrough), J Bolton, D Longhorn, J Ashurst, R Moncur
(S Elliott), B Kerr (R Mitchell), R Train, M Holden (2), B Robson (1), B Hughes

18 Aug 1981, St James' Park, 1-1, (1-1), 9,982
Newcastle United, K Carr, J Brownlie (P Haddock), I Davies, J Trewick, D Barton, B Halliday,
N Walker, B Shinton (1), A Shoulder (K Todd), K Wharton (M Martin), C Waddle
Sunderland, C Turner, J Hinnigan, I Munro, G Chisholm (M Buckley), J Clarke, R Hindmarch, K Arnott,
T Ritchie (1), J Hawley (J Cooke), G Rowell, N Pickering (B Dunn)

22 Aug 1981, Roker Park, 2-1, (1-1), 10,032
Sunderland, C Turner, J Hinnigan, I Munro, M Buckley, S Allardyce (1), J Clarke, K Arnott, T Ritchie,
J Hawley (1), G Rowell, N Pickering (B Dunn)
Newcastle United, K Carr, J Brownlie (P Haddock), I Davies, J Trewick, D Barton, B Halliday,
N Walker, K Shinton (K Todd), A Shoulder (1), K Wharton, C Waddle

Newcastle United v Sunderland
First World War Games

25 Jan 1919, St James' Park, 4-3, (2-3), 18,000
Newcastle United, J Lawrence, W R McCracken, F C Hudspeth (1 pen), T Curry, F Reed, J Finlay (1),
C Farrier, ES Dixon, C Booth (2), G Fulthorpe, J W Donnelly
Sunderland, J C Hugall (Clapton Orient), B Hobson, Wood, Wilson, F Cuggy, Thompson, R Best,
B Travers, Johnson, G H Holley, J Mordue (3 incl 1 pen)

22 Mar 1919, Roker Park, 2-1, (1-1), 20,000
Sunderland, J J Baverstock (Bolton Wanderers), B Hobson, R T Young, F Cuggy, H Sherwin, H F Low,
J Mordue (1), C M Buchan (1), R R Parker, G H Holley, R Best
Newcastle United, J Lawrence (Inj), F C Hudspeth, G A Bell, T Curry, W L Low, J Finlay, E Cooper,
E S Dixon (in goal 2nd half), J Doran (1), C Booth, H Cummings

Second World War Games

25 Oct 1941, St James' Park, 1-1, (1-0), 22,000. Football League North
Newcastle United, C A Theaker, J Richardson, D Graham, A Price, T Smith, N Dodgin, R J E Birkett,
J D Short (Leeds Utd), A Stubbins, C Wayman (1), S Peppitt (Stoke City)
Sunderland, A E Heywood, J Gorman, R Rodgerson, A Housam, A J Lockie, A C Hastings, J O Spuhler
(1), G H Robinson, (Charlton Athletic), C Whitelum, S Bradwell, H McMahon

1 Nov 1941, Roker Park, 3-2, (1-0), 12,000. Football League North
Sunderland, A E Heywood, J Gorman (1), J R Eves, A Housam, A J Lockie, L Wheatman, J O Spuhler,
G H Robinson, (Charlton Athletic), C Whitelum (1), S Bradwell, H McMahon (1 pen)
Newcastle United, C A Theaker, J Richardson, D Graham, W R Hart, T Smith, A Price, R J E Birkett,
J D Short (Leeds Utd) (1), A Stubbins (1), C Wayman, S Peppitt (Stoke City)

10 Jan 1942, Roker Park, 2-2, (0-2), 10,459 . Football League War Cup
Sunderland, A E Heywood, J Gorman, J R Eves, W J Hewison, A J Lockie, A Housam, J O Spuhler,
G H Robinson (1), (Charlton Athletic), C Whitelum, H S Carter (1), H McMahon
Newcastle United, C A Theaker, J Richardson, D Graham, W R Hart, P H Taylor (Liverpool),
N Dodgin, R J E Birkett, J D Short (Leeds Utd) (1), A Stubbins (1), J Balmer (Liverpool), C Woollett

17 Jan 1942, St James' Park, 2-1, (0-1), 19,728. Football League War Cup
Newcastle United, C A Theaker, J Richardson, D Graham, P H Taylor (Liverpool), T Smith, W R Hart, R J E Birkett, J D Short (Leeds Utd)(1), A Stubbins (1), J Balmer (Liverpool), H Eastham (Liverpool)
Sunderland, A E Heywood, J R Eves, R Rodgerson, W J Hewison, A J Lockie, A Housam, J O Spuhler, G H Robinson (1), (Charlton Athletic), C Whitelum, F Smallwood (Reading), H McMahon

25 May 1942, St James' Park, 2-2, (2-0), 5,000. Football League North
Newcastle United, R King, J Richardson, D Graham, A Price, T Smith, W R Hart, T J Walker (1), R S Donaldson, J D Short (Leeds Utd)(1 pen), S Howden, G McQuade (Annan)
Sunderland, J Clark, W Walsh, T Slack (1), O H Burns (Burnley), A J Lockie, W A Curzon, W S Lloyd, R Gurney, E Ireland (1), D Milsom, R G Ramsey

5 Dec 1942, Roker Park, 3-5, (2-2) , 7,000. Football League North
Sunderland, B Bircham, J Gorman, J R Eves, S Bradwell, WJ Hewison, A C Hastings, J O Spuhler (1) , G H Robinson), (Charlton Athletic), C Whitelum , H J Potts (Bury) (1), F Smallwood (Reading) (1)
Newcastle United, N H Tapken (Manchester Utd), J Richardson, D Graham, J Gordon, R D Sales, W R Hart, T J Walker (1), J D Short (Leeds Utd), A Stubbins (4), E M Carr (Arsenal), J Mullen (Wolves)

12 Dec 1942, St James' Park, 3-3, (1-2), 15,115. Football League North
Newcastle United, N H Tapken (Man Utd), J Richardson, D Graham, J Gordon, R D Sales, W R Hart, N Coyde (Southend Utd), J D Short (Leeds Utd), A Stubbins (2), E M Carr (Arsenal) (1), J Mullen (Wolves)
Sunderland, B Bircham, J Gorman, J R Eves, A Housam, A J Lockie, A C Hastings, J O Spuhler (1 pen), H J Potts (Bury), C Whitelum (2), H S Carter, F Smallwood (Reading)

6 Feb 1943, Roker Park, 3-3, (2-2), 12,000. Football League War Cup
Sunderland, B Bircham, J Gorman, W E Nicholson (Spurs), F Laidman, A J Lockie, A C Hastings, J O Spuhler (1), G H Robinson (Charlton Ath), C Whitelum, H S Carter (2), F Smallwood (Reading)
Newcastle United, T V Rutherford, J Richardson, D Graham, J Gordon, R D Sales, J Woodburn, D S Hamilton, J D Short (Leeds Utd) (1), A Stubbins (1 pen), E M Carr (Arsenal) (1), J Mullen (Wolves)

13 Feb 1943, St James' Park, 2-3, (1-2), 20,500. Football League War Cup
Newcastle United, T V Rutherford, J Richardson, R F D Ancell, J Woodburn, R D Sales, R S Donaldson, D S Hamilton, J D Short (Leeds Utd) (1), A Stubbins (1), E M Carr (Arsenal), J Mullen (Wolves)
Sunderland, N H Tapken (Manchester Utd), J Gorman, J R Eves, S Bradwell, A J Lockie (1), A C Hastings, J O Spuhler (1) , T Johnson (Gateshead), C Whitelum, H S Carter (1), G H Robinson (Charlton Athletic)

6 Nov 1943, Roker Park, 4-2, (2-1), 16,000. Football League North
Sunderland, J Clark, J Gorman, E Hindmarch, A Housam, A J Lockie, A C Hastings, J O Spuhler, F Laidman (2), C Whitelum (2), L Wensley, S Bradwell
Newcastle United, T V Rutherford, R G Cowell, W E Nicholson (Spurs), J Woodburn, T Smith, R S Donaldson, E Copeland, J T Dixon, A Stubbins (2), J E T Milburn, L Lightfoot

13 Nov 1943, St James' Park, 3-1, (2-1), 24,241. Football League North
Newcastle United, R King, J Richardson, R G Cowell, R S Donaldson, T Smith, P B Woods, E Copeland, E Taylor (1), A Stubbins (1) (# 65), J E T Milburn (1), L Lightfoot
Sunderland, J Clark, J Gorman (# 65), J R Eves, S Bradwell, A J Lockie, A C Hastings, G E Collins (Wrexham), F Laidman, J O Spuhler (1), L Wensley, E Hindmarch

27 Dec 1943, St James' Park, 4-2, (2-2), 26,272. Football League War Cup
Newcastle United, D S Cumming (Middlesbrough), J Richardson, W E Nicholson (Spurs), R S Donaldson, R D Sales, J Woodburn, E Copeland, J T Dixon, A Stubbins (2), J E T Milburn, C Woollett (1), (AJ Lockie) (1og)
Sunderland, B Bircham, L Wheatman, R Scotson, E Hindmarch, A J Lockie, A C Hastings, J Spuhler (1), F Laidman, C Whitelum (1), L Wensley, G E Collins (Wrexham)

1 Jan 1944, Roker Park, 3-0, (1-0), 14,000. Football League War Cup
Sunderland, B Bircham, R Scotson, J Bell, E Hindmarch, A J Lockie, A C Hastings, J O Spuhler, F Laidman (1), C Whitelum, L Wensley, G E Collins (Wrexham)(2)
Newcastle United, D S Cumming (Middlesbrough), J Richardson, W E Nicholson (Spurs), R S Donaldson, R D Sales, P B Woods, E Copeland, J T Dixon, A Stubbins, E Taylor, C Woollett

15 Apr 1944, Roker Park, 0-3, (0-1), 7,000. Tyne-Wear-Tees Cup & Football League (North)
Sunderland, J Clark, J Gorman, J R Eves, E Hindmarch, A J Lockie, A C Hastings, J O Spuhler,
F Laidman, K Walshaw, H D Bell, G E Collins (Wrexham)
Newcastle United, D S Cumming (Middlesbrough), J Richardson, R G Cowell, R S Donaldson,
T Smith, R Scarr, H B Henderson, J E T Milburn, A Stubbins (1), R Rutherford (2), C Woollett

22 Apr 1944, St James' Park, 5-2, (2-1), 12,106. Tyne-Wear-Tees Cup & Football League (North)
Newcastle United, D S Cumming (Middlesbrough), J Richardson, R G Cowell, J Gordon, T Smith,
R S Donaldson, L Porter, J E T Milburn (1), A Stubbins (3), R Rutherford, C Woollett, (J R Eves) (1og)
Sunderland, B Bircham, J Gorman, J R Eves, E Hindmarch, A J Lockie, A C Hastings, J O Spuhler,
D Milsom (1), N Robb (1), H D Bell, J Kilgallon (Blackpool)

23 Sep 1944, Roker Park, 2-0, (0-0), 18,000. Football League North
Sunderland, A E Heywood, J Gorman, J R Eves, H Wallbanks (Fulham), A J Lockie, A C Hastings,
J O Spuhler, F Laidman, C Whitelum (2), W S Lloyd, K Walshaw
Newcastle United, D S Cumming (Middlesbrough), D R Harnby, R G Cowell, J Gordon, T Smith,
R S Donaldson, L Porter, J E T Milburn, A Stubbins, E M Carr (Arsenal), C Woollett

30 Sep 1944, St James' Park, 1-5, (1-1), 28,693. Football League North
Newcastle United, D S Cumming (Middlesbrough), D R Harnby, R G Cowell, J Gordon, T Smith,
R S Donaldson, L Porter, J E T Milburn (1), A Stubbins, E M Carr (Arsenal), C Woollett
Sunderland, A E Heywood, J Gorman, J R Eves, H Wallbanks (Fulham), A J Lockie, A C Hastings,
J O Spuhler (1), F Laidman, C Whitelum (3), H D Bell, K Walshaw (1)

26 Dec 1944, St James' Park, 3-1, (2-0), 40,311. Football League North
Newcastle United, D S Cumming (Middlesbrough), J Richardson, R G Cowell, T D Gray (Dundee),
T Smith, R Duffy (Celtic), J E T Milburn , E M Carr (Arsenal), A Stubbins (2), C Wayman (1), T U Pearson
Sunderland, B Bircham, J Gorman, J R Eves, H Wallbanks (Fulham), A J Lockie, A C Hastings,
J O Spuhler, F Laidman , C Whitelum (1) , H Bell, K Walshaw

30 Dec 1944, Roker Park, 4-3, (1-1), 19,000. Football League War Cup
Sunderland, B Bircham, J Gorman, J R Eves, A Housam, A J Lockie, A C Hastings, H Wallbanks
(Fulham), F Laidman (1), C Whitelum (3), K Walshaw, W E Burbanks
Newcastle United, D S Cumming (Middlesbrough), J Richardson, R G Cowell, R S Donaldson,
R D Sales, R Duffy, J E T Milburn, E M Carr (Arsenal), A Stubbins (2-1 pen), C Wayman (1), T U Pearson

2 Apr 1945, St James' Park, 0-3, (0-0), 13,000. Football League War Cup
Newcastle United, G A Wood, R G Cowell, R Corbett, P B Woods, J Richardson, R S Donaldson,
J Sloan, J E T Milburn, A Donaldson, C Wayman, G Hair
Sunderland, B Bircham, J Gorman, J G S Stelling, A Housam, A J Lockie, W R Scott (Brentford),
J O Spuhler (1), C Brown (Brentford) (1), C Whitelum (1), J W R Taylor, T Reay

9 May 1945, St James' Park, 5-0, (3-0), 10,217. Victory game
Newcastle United, G A Wood, R G Cowell, R Corbett, J Gordon, T Smith, R S Donaldson,
J E T Milburn (1), E M Carr (Arsenal), A Stubbins (1), C Wayman (3), G Hair
Sunderland, B Bircham, J G S Stelling, J R Eves, J S S Fleck, A J Lockie, J Wallbanks (Reading),
H Hetherington, A Housam, C Brown (Brentford), T White, K Walshaw

20 Apr 1946, Roker Park, 1-0, (1-0), 37,000. Football League North
Sunderland, J Mapson, J G S Stelling, J E Jones, C K Willingham, A J Lockie, A Housam, A E Gray,
T White, C Whitelum, K Walshaw, W E Burbanks (1)
Newcastle United, T A Swinburne, D Graham, RG Corbett, J Harvey, T Smith, J D Wright,
J E T Milburn, E C Brown, A Stubbins, C Wayman, G Hair

27 Apr 1946, St James' Park, 4-1, (1-0), 29,564, Football League North
Newcastle United, T A Swinburne, D Graham, R G Corbett, J Harvey, T Smith, J Woodburn,
J E T Milburn (1), E C Brown (1), A Stubbins (1), C Wayman, T U Pearson (1)
Sunderland, J Mapson, J G S Stelling, J E Jones, C K Willingham, A J Lockie, A Housam, L Duns (1),
C Brown (Brentford), C Whitelum, E Dunn, W E Burbanks

Newcastle United 'A'/Res v Sunderland 'A'/Res
Competitive Games – Results

Northern Alliance

1892-93
22 Oct
East End 'A' 4   Sunderland 'A' 1 (3-0)
Dodds, Coupar,   *Scrimmage*
Wilde, Simm
24 Dec
Sunderland 'A' 3   Newcastle 'A' 0 (1-0)
Hunter, Ledger 2

1893-94
16 Sep
Sunderland 'A' 4   Newcastle 'A' 2 (4-1)
D Hannah, Hunter,   *og, Quin*
Scott, Curry
14 Oct
Newcastle 'A' 1   Sunderland 'A' 4 (0-3)
Stokoe   *Scrimmage, J Hannah,*
   Gillespie 2

1894-95
13 Oct
Sunderland 'A' 2   Newcastle 'A' 2 (2-1)
Brand, Ledger   *Bell, Laverick [pen]*
2 Jan
Newcastle 'A' 1   Sunderland 'A' 2 (1-1)
Veitch   *Callighan, Brand*

1895-96
26 Oct
Sunderland 'A' 4   Newcastle 'A' 1 (3-1)
og, Hartley, Brand,   *Carr*
Ledger
28 Dec
Newcastle 'A' 2   Sunderland 'A' 3 (1-2)
Bell, og   *Goodchild 2, Brand*

1896-97
Sunderland 'A' did not play in the Northern
Alliance this season.

1897-98
4 Sep
Sunderland 'A' 1   Newcastle 'A' 2 (1-2)
Simpson   *Gillespie 2*
25 Dec
Newcastle 'A' 1   Sunderland 'A' 0 (0-0)
Gillespie

1898-99
31 Dec
Newcastle 'A' 1   Sunderland 'A' 0 (0-0)
og
31 Mar
Sunderland 'A' 1   Newcastle 'A' 1 (0-1)
Carmichael   *Milne*

1899-1900
16 Sep
Newcastle 'A' 2   Sunderland 'A' 0 (2-0)
Milne 2
30 Dec
Sunderland 'A' 0   Newcastle 'A' 1 (0-0)
   Collins

1900-01
25 Dec
Sunderland 'A' 1   Newcastle 'A' 1 (0-0)
J Hogg   *Pattison*
8 Apr
Newcastle 'A' 3   Sunderland 'A' 1 (0-1)
Littlefair, Bruce, Veitch   *Leslie*

1901-02
25 Dec
Newcastle 'A' 3   Sunderland 'A' 0 (1-0)
Veitch 2, Birnie
2 Jan
Sunderland 'A' 1   Newcastle 'A' 1 (0-0)
Craggs   *Bruce*

Northern League

1902-03
25 Dec
Sunderland 'A' 3   Newcastle 'A' 2 (3-0)
Robertson, Wardle,   *Richardson, Wilson*
Prince [pen]
17 Jan
Newcastle 'A' 4   Sunderland 'A' 3 (2-1)
Gardner, Veitch 2,   *Barrie, Murray, Robinson*
McIntyre

1903-04
16 Jan
Sunderland 'A' 3   Newcastle 'A' 3 (2-1)
Hewitt, Wardle,   *Roberts, McIntyre, Fraser*
Robinson
1 Apr
Newcastle 'A' 2   Sunderland 'A' 0 (1-0)
McClarence, Innerd

1904-05
24 Sep
Newcastle 'A' 3   Sunderland 'A' 0 (1-0)
Graham 2, McClarence
26 Dec
Sunderland 'A' 2   Newcastle 'A' 1 (2-0)
Robertson, Dixon   *McClarence*

1905-06
26 Dec
Sunderland 'A' 2   Newcastle 'A' 1 (0-1)
Hindmarch 2   *Dodds*
13 Apr
Newcastle 'A' 0   Sunderland 'A' 1 (0-0)
   Prince

North Eastern League

1906-07
8 Dec
Newcastle 'A' 1   Sunderland 'A' 1 (0-0)
McClarence   *McIntosh*
26 Dec
Sunderland 'A' 5   Newcastle 'A' 1 (1-1)
McIntosh 2, Hurdman, Hardinge
Foster, Brown

19 Jan (Newcastle Infirmary Cup)
Newcastle 'A' 2   Sunderland 'A' 0 (1-0)
McClarence, Dodds
23 Mar (Sunderland Shipowners' Cup)
Newcastle 'A' 1   Sunderland 'A' 3 (1-1)
McClarence   *Brown, Allan, Hurdman*

1907-08
14 Sep
Sunderland 'A' 3   Newcastle Res 1 (0-0)
Huggins 2, Ledger *McClarence*
5 Oct
Newcastle Res 3   Sunderland 'A' 1 (1-0)
Hardinge, Soye,   *Brown*
McClarence
4 Apr (Newcastle Infirmary Cup Final)
Newcastle Res 1   Sunderland 'A' 1 (1-0)
Whitson   *Brown*
15 Apr (Newcastle Infirmary Cup Final replay
Sunderland 'A' 1   Newcastle Res 1 (1-1)
Morley   *Soye*
28 Apr (Newcastle Infirmary Cup Final – 2nd
replay) – Trophy shared
Newcastle Res 1   Sunderland 'A' 1 [aet] (0-1)
Higgins   *Montgomery*

1908-09
25 Dec
Sunderland 'A' 2   Newcastle Res 3 (1-2)
Hope, Montgomery *Hall, Waugh pen, Allan*
9 Apr
Newcastle Res 5   Sunderland 'A' 1 (2-0)
Randall, Metcalfe 3, *Pearson*
Duncan

1909-10
11 Sep
Sunderland 'A' 2   Newcastle Res 5 (0-3)
Hunter, Agnew [pen] *Allan, Randall 3, Higgins*
16 Oct
Newcastle Res 8   Sunderland 0 (4-0)
Allan 3, Randall 3,
Metcalfe 2

1910-11
26 Dec
Sunderland 'A' 1   Newcastle Res 0 (1-0)
Hall
2 Jan
Newcastle Res 3   Sunderland 'A' 1 (2-1)
Willis [pen],   *og*
Metcalfe, Allan

1911-12
26 Dec
Sunderland Res 3   Newcastle Res 1 (1-0)
McCulloch, Hall, *Hewison*
Cringan
8 Apr
Newcastle Res 3   Sunderland Res 0 (1-0)
Fleming 2, Metcalfe

1912-13
25 Dec
Sunderland Res 2   Newcastle Res 1 (0-0)
Ness, Connor   *Little*

26 Dec
Newcastle Res 3   Sunderland Res 5 (2-1)
Lowes, Fleming 2 *Tinsley 3, Connor, McCulloch)*

1913-14
20 Sep
Newcastle Res 5   Sunderland Res 2 (2-1)
Pyke 5   *Moore, Connor*
25 Oct
Sunderland Res 1   Newcastle Res 2 (1-2)
Lane   *Hardy, Little pen*

1914-15
25 Dec
Sunderland Res 1   Newcastle Res 1 (0-1)
Seed   *Dixon*
26 Dec
Newcastle Res 4   Sunderland Res 0 (3-0)
Dixon 2, Soulsby 2

1919-20
27 Sep
Newcastle Res 2   Sunderland Res 1 (1-0)
Rutherford 2   *Power*
4 Oct
Sunderland Res 0   Newcastle Res 1 (0-1)
Rutherford

1920-21
22 Sep (Ingham Infirmary Cup)
Newcastle Res 3   Sunderland Res 0 (1-0)
Phillipson, Mitchell,
Swan
27 Dec
Newcastle Res 1   Sunderland Res 2 (0-1)
Dixon   *Power 2*
1 Jan
Sunderland Res 4   Newcastle Res 2 (2-1)
Power 3, Travers *Pyke [pen], Gray*

1921-22
26 Dec
Newcastle Res 1   Sunderland Res 2 (1-0)
Swan   *Young, Forster*
2 Jan
Sunderland Res 2   Newcastle Res 1 (1-0)
Clark, Stealey   *Partridge*

1922-23
7 Oct
Sunderland 0   Newcastle Res 2 (0-0)
                   Smailes, Clark

17 Mar
Newcastle Res 2   Sunderland Res 0 (0-0)
Clark, Keating

1923-24
22 Sep
Sunderland Res 1   Newcastle Res 2 (0-1)
Stannard [pen]   *Cowan, Mitchell*
29 Sep
Newcastle Res 1   Sunderland Res 0 (1-0)
Summerson

1924-25
30 Aug
Sunderland Res 3   Newcastle Res 1 (1-0)
Prior, Coglin, Death *Keating*

6 Sep
Newcastle Res 1   Sunderland Res 2 (0-2)
Mitchell pen   *Marshall 2*
1925-26
10 Mar
Sunderland Res 4   Newcastle Res 2 (2-0)
Gurney 2, Heyes,   *Mordue [pen], Robson*
Grimshaw
10 Apr
Newcastle Res 2   Sunderland Res 1 (2-0)
Mordue [pen], og   *Prior*
1926-27
16 Oct
Newcastle Res 0   Sunderland Res 1 (0-1)
                    Gurney
3 Jan
Sunderland Res 3   Newcastle Res 1 (1-1)
McGorian 2 [1 pen], *Clark pen*
Coglin
4 Apr (North Eastern League Cup [semi-final])
Newcastle Res 4   Sunderland Res 0 (3-0)
Loughlin, Clark,
Lang, Low
1927-28
26 Nov
Newcastle Res 0   Sunderland Res 3 (0-1)
                    Wood, Death, Ramsey
7 Apr
Sunderland Res 5   Newcastle Res 1 (3-1)
Kelly, McGorian,   *Halliday*
Wood, Hargreaves 2
1928-29
15 Sep
Newcastle Res 0   Sunderland Res 4 (0-3)
                    Gurney 2, Wood, Aris
26 Jan
Sunderland Res 3   Newcastle Res 1 (3-1)
Gurney 2, Cresswell *Wilkinson*
23 Mar
(North Eastern League Challenge Cup [4th Round])
Sunderland Res 1   Newcastle Res 1 (1-1)
Wright   *Carr*
2 Apr
(North Eastern League Challenge Cup [4th Round replay])
Newcastle Res 3   Sunderland Res 1 (2-0)
Chalmers 2, Carr   *Gurney*
1929-30
5 Oct
Newcastle Res 1   Sunderland Res 3 (0-2)
JR Richardson   *Allan, Wood 2*
8 Feb
Sunderland Res 1   Newcastle Res 4 (1-3)
Morrison   *Boyd 2, Chalmers 2*
1930-31
1 Jan
Sunderland Res 5   Newcastle Res 4 (2-0)
Morrison, Gallacher 2, *Devine 2 (1 pen), Lang,*
Keeton, Lawley   *Cape*

4 Apr
Newcastle Res 8   Sunderland Res 0 (6-0)
Hutchison 3, McDonald 3,
JR Richardson, Chalmers
1931-32
14 Nov
Newcastle Res 2   Sunderland Res 0 (2-0)
Ford, Bedford pen
25 Dec
Sunderland Res 3   Newcastle Res 1 (1-1)
Poulter 2, Wallace *Hutchison*
1932-33
19 Nov
Sunderland Res 0   Newcastle Res 0 (0-0)
2 Jan
Newcastle Res 1   Sunderland Res 2 (0-0)
Gallantree   *Yorston 2*
1933
Newcastle Res resigned from the North Eastern League to join the Central League. Sunderland Res did not join them there until 1983.

Central League – Division 1
1983-84
14 Sep
Sunderland Res 0   Newcastle Res 1 (0-0)
                    Saunders
18 Jan
Newcastle Res 1   Sunderland Res 2 (1-0)
Hedworth   *Wardrobe, West*
1984-1986
Newcastle played in the Central League Division 1 while Sunderland were in Division 2.

Central League - Division 1
1986-87
10 Sep
Newcastle Res 1   Sunderland Res 3 (1-1)
Bogie   *Moore, Corner, Cornforth [pen]*
27 Jan
Sunderland Res 2   Newcastle Res 0 (1-0)
Curran, Buchanan
1987-88
Sunderland played in the Central League Division 1 while Newcastle were in Division 2.

Central League – Division 1
1988-89
26 Apr
Newcastle Res 2   Sunderland Res 3 (2-1)
Gourlay, Mirandinha *Brady 2 [1 pen], Hawke*
9 May
Sunderland Res 3   Newcastle Res 2 (3-1)
Cullen, Hauser 2   *Lormor, Howey*
1989-90
Newcastle played in the Central League Division 1 while Sunderland were in Division 2.

Pontins' Central League – Division 1

1990-91

30 Aug
Newcastle Res 0 · Sunderland Res 1 (0-0)
· *Hauser*

18 Mar
Sunderland Res 1 · Newcastle Res 3 (1-3)
Cornforth pen · *Clark, Sloan, Askew*

1991-92

21 Aug
Sunderland Res 4 · Newcastle Res 2 (1-1)
Hawke 2, Davenport, · *Hunt, Gourlay*
Sampson

8 Jan
Newcastle Res 1 · Sunderland Res 1 (1-0)
Roche · *Gaughan*

Pontins' League – Division 1

1992-93

20 Aug
Newcastle Res 3 · Sunderland Res 2 (1-0)
McDonough, · *Atkinson, Davenport*
M Appleby,
Thompson

10 Feb
Sunderland Res 4 · Newcastle Res 0 (3-0)
L Howey, Brodie,
Mooney, Russell

1993-94

29 Sep
Newcastle Res 0 · Sunderland Res 0 (0-0)

23 Mar
Sunderland Res 3 · Newcastle Res 0 (1-0)
Brodie, Smith, Angel

1994-99

In different divisions of the Pontins' League:
1994-95 Sunderland – Div. 1
Newcastle – Div. 2
1995-96 Newcastle – Div. 1
Sunderland – Div. 2

1996-97

Newcastle withdrew from reserve league football.

1997-98

Sunderland – Div. 1
Newcastle – Div. 3

1998-99

Sunderland – Premier Div.
Newcastle – Div. 2
(Finished as champions of their respective divisions).

FA Premier Reserve League (North)

1999-2000

19 Oct
Sunderland Res 1 · Newcastle Res 1 (0-1)
Wainwright · *Marcelino*

10 Apr
Newcastle Res 3 · Sunderland Res 1 (1-1)
McMahon, Robinson, · *Nunez*
Gall

2000-01

11 Sep
Newcastle Res 0 · Sunderland Res 1 (0-1)
· *Thirlwell*

19 Feb
Sunderland Res 3 · Newcastle Res 1 (2-1)
Lumsden, McCartney, · *Bonvin*
Proctor

2001-02

17 Dec
Newcastle Res 2 · Sunderland Res 4 (1-3)
English, McMahon · *Kyle 2, Butler, Marchant*

11 Feb
Sunderland Res 0 · Newcastle Res 2 (0-0)
· *McMenamin, Cort*

2002-03

16 Sep
Sunderland Res 1 · Newcastle Res 0 (1-0)
Bellion

10 Feb
Newcastle Res 0 · Sunderland Res 1 (0-0)
· *Bellion*

2003-04

22 Oct
Sunderland Res 1 · Newcastle Res 3 (1-2)
Proctor · *Chopra, Dabizas, Orr*

13 May
Newcastle Res 3 · Sunderland Res 1 (1-1)
Ferrell 2, Guy · *Toft*

2004-05

24 Jan
Newcastle Res 1 · Sunderland Res 1 (1-0)
Guy [pen] · *Brown*

25 Apr
Sunderland Res 2 · Newcastle Res 1 (2-0)
Bridges [pen], · *McClen*
Thornton

2005-06

23 Nov
Sunderland Res 1 · Newcastle Res 1 (1-0)
Hartley · *Huntington*

3 Apr
Newcastle Res 3 · Sunderland Res 2 (2-1)
Finnigan, Carroll, · *og, Le Tallec*
Smylie

Sunderland v West End
Competitive Games

30 Oct 1886, Newcastle Road, FA Cup, (1st Round), 2-1 [aet], (1-1), 4,500. Declared void - darkness.
Sunderland, W Kirkley, I Elliott, W Oliver, J McMillan, J Smart, F Dale, P Rooney, W Erskine, R Smith, J Lord (2), A Davison
West End, R A Oldham, J Duns, J Waggott, A Campbell (1), JA Mather, J Chalmers, T K Dobson, J Welford, J Angus, R Aitken, J Barker
Ref: J Reed, (Cleveland Association)

13 Nov 1886, St James' Park, FA Cup, (1st Round replay), 1-0, (0-0), 4,000
West End, R A Oldham, J Taylor, J Duns, J Waggott, JA Mather, J Chalmers, TK Dobson, A Campbell, J Angus (1), R Aitken, W Tiffin
Sunderland, W Kirkley, W Oliver (Inj 40), J Elliott, J McMillan, J Smart, F Dale, P Rooney, W Erskine, R Smith, J Lord, A Davison
Ref: Mr Darley, (Blackburn Rovers)

5 Nov 1887, Newcastle Road, FA Cup, (2nd Round), 3-1 [aet], (0-1), 8,000
Sunderland, W Kirkley, T Halliday (1), J Oliver, J Richardson, P Ford, F Dale, S Stewart (2), R Smith, A Hastings, G Monaghan, A Davison
West End, T Fyfe, J Duns, J Chalmers, W Swinburne, J Raylstone, J Smart, J Barker, D McColl (1), T Nicholson, J Angus, J McDonald
Ref: J C Stacey

28 Apr 1888, St James' Park, Northumberland & Durham Cup Winners Challenge Match, 0-2, (0-2), 6,000
West End, T Fyfe, R McDermid, "R S Haig" (Hunter), W Swinburne, J Raylstone, J Grant, J Barker, D McColl, T Nicholson, A Brady, J McDonald
Sunderland, W Kirkley, G Oliver, G Moor, J Richardson, J Spain, F Dale, A Davison, G Gloag (1), A Hastings, S Stewart (1), J Kilpatrick
Ref: Dr Wilson (Birtley)

Sunderland v West End
Friendly Games – Results

Date	Match		Attendance	(half time)
1885-86				
13 Feb	Sunderland 1	West End 0	-	(0-0)
	Erskine			
9 Mar	Sunderland 2	West End 1	-	(1-1)
	Erskine, Hunter	Mather		
1886-87				
27 Nov	Sunderland 1	West End 0	6,000	(-)
	Smith			
1887-88				
8 Oct	West End 2	Sunderland 3	2,000	(1-3)
	Raystone, McDonald,	Davison, Hastings, Richardson		
11 Feb	Sunderland 2	West End 3	3,000	(1-0)
	Davison, Gloag	Nicholson, Raylstone, og		
1889-90				
7 Sep	Sunderland 3	West End 0	9,500	(2-0)
	og., Campbell, McLaughlan			
26 Apr	West End 1	Sunderland 4	5,000	(1-1)
	Raylstone	Scott, Hannah, Campbell, scrimmage		
1890-91				
29 Nov	Sunderland 5	West End 0	-	(3-0)
	Campbell 2, Millar 2, Gibson			

20 Apr	West End 1	Sunderland 1	5,000	(0-0)
	Wood	*og*		

1891-92

2 Sep	West End 1	Sunderland 8	3,000	(0-5)
	Hutchinson	*Scott, Logan 5, Millar, Gibson*		

East End v Sunderland Albion
Northern League Fixtures

26 Dec 1890, Blue House Field, 7-0, (2-0), 5,000
Sunderland Albion:, R Roberts, R Macfarlane, J Rae, G King, W Wardrop, P McCracken, J Hannah (1), W Crozier (1), H Boyd (3), R McLellan (1), Smith, [Miller (1og)]
East End, M Scott, W Wilson, J Miller, A McCurdie, A H White, J McKane, J Collins, R Creilly, W Thompson, M Mulvey, T McInnes
Ref: Mr Hardisty (Middlesbrough)

18 Apr 1891, Chillingham Rd, 1-0, (1-0), 4,000
East End, M Scott, P Watson, J Miller, A McCurdie, W Wilson, J McKane, J Wallace (1), J Collins, J Sorley, M Mulvey, T McInnes
Sunderland Albion:, R Roberts, R Macfarlane, J Rae, G King, W Wardrop, Lawson, J Gillespie, W Crozier, Moore, J Millar, J Oswald
Ref: Mr Grey (Darlington)

5 Mar 1892, Blue House Field, 0-3, (0-2), 3,000
Sunderland Albion:, W Kirkley, J Dewar, J Rae, G King, W Crozier, P McCracken, J Gillespie, J Strachan, R Buchanan, Watson, J Burns
East End, M Scott, W Wilson, J Miller, R Creilly (1), J Spence (1), J McKane, H Reay, T Crate, J Sorley (1), J Wallace, J Barker
Ref: Mr Grey (Darlington)

2 Apr 1892, Chillingham Rd, 1-0, (0-0), 3,000
East End, M Scott, P Watson, J Miller, W Wilson, J Spence, J McKane, H Reay, T Crate, W Thompson, J Sorley (1), J Wallace
Sunderland Albion, W Kirkley, J Dewar, J Rae, G King, W Crozier, P McCracken, J Gillespie, R Buchanan, J Mackie, J Strachan, J Burns
Ref: Mr Kemp (Redcar)

East End v Sunderland Albion
FA Cup Fixtures

6 Dec 1890, Final Qualifying, Chillingham Rd, 2-2, (1-1), [aet – 7 mins], 5,000
East End, M Scott, W Wilson, J Miller, A McCurdie, A H White, J McKane, R Creilly, J Collins (1), W Thompson, M Mulvey (1), T McInnes
Sunderland Albion, R Roberts, R McFarlane, J Rae, P McCracken, W Wardrop, G King, J Hannah (1), W Crozier, H Boyd (1), Smith, J Millar
Ref: CS Craven (Member of Council)

20 Dec 1890, Final Qualifying (Replay), Chillingham Rd, 0-2, (0-0), 4,000
East End, M Scott, W Wilson, J Miller, A McCurdie, A McLaughlin, J McKane, R Creilly, J Collins, W Thompson, M Mulvey, T McInnes
Sunderland Albion, R Roberts, R McFarlane, J Rae, P McCracken, W Wardrop, G King, J Hannah, W Crozier, H Boyd (1), R McLellan (1), Smith
Ref: H Grey (Darlington)

East End v Sunderland Albion
Friendly Results

Date	Match	Attendance	(Half time)
1888-89			
5 Mar	Sunderland Albion 4	East End 1	1,500 0-1)
	Stewart, scrimmage, McLellan, McFarlane	*Mulvey*	

23 May	Sunderland Albion 0	East End 1	-	(0-0)
		Mulvey		
30 May	East End 1	Sunderland Albion 0	2,000	(1-0)
	Barker			

1889-90

4 Sept	Sunderland Albion 1	East End 2	-	(0-1)
	Brand	*Mulvey 2*		
4 Apr	Sunderland Albion 1	East End 1	10,000	(0-0)
	Kinnaird	*scrimmage*		
26 Apr	Sunderland Albion 3	East End 1	6,000	(1-1)
	Kinnaird, Smith, Sawers	*Collins*		
26 May	East End 3	Sunderland Albion 1	2,000	(1-0)
	Thompson, Smith, scrimmage	*McLellan*		

1890-91

| 28 Feb | Sunderland Albion 1 | East End 0 | 4,000 | (1-0) |
| | *Crozier* | | | |

1891-92

| 2 Jan | East End 3 | Sunderland Albion 1 | 2,500 | (2-1) |
| | *Sorley, Thompson, Crate* | *Mackie* | | |

Sunderland Albion v West End
Northern League Fixtures

15 Apr 1891, St James' Park, 1-4, (0-4), 2,000
Newcastle West End, W Ryder, H Jeffrey, P Dowling, J Wardropper, Byrne, J McCann, R Patton, M McCrory, S Wood (1), E McCann, R Calderwood
Sunderland Albion, R Roberts, R McFarlane, J Rae, G King, W Wardrop, P McCracken, J Gillespie (2), W Crozier (1), J Moore (1), J Oswald, R McLellan
Ref: Mr Grundy (Whitburn)

25 Apr 1891, Blue House Field, 3-1, (2-0), 800 – 2,000
Sunderland Albion, R Roberts, R McFarlane, J Rae, G King, J Richardson, P McCracken, J Gillespie, W Crozier (1), J Moore (1), J Oswald (1), J Millar
Newcastle West End, W Ryder, H Jeffrey, P Dowling, J Ryder, Byrne, J McCann, R Patton (1), M McCrory, E McCann, R Calderwood, Heslop

16 Sep 1891, Blue House Field, 5-1, (3-1), 500
Sunderland Albion, R Roberts, J Dewar, J Rae, G King, W Crozier, P McCracken (1), J Gillespie, R Buchanan (1), R McLellan, J Burns (3), J Strachan
Newcastle West End, W Ryder, H Jeffrey, J Taylor, R McLeod, R Ferguson, I Ryder, T McNichol, J Collins, W Hutchinson (1), W McFarlane, J Gilmour
Ref: Mr Hardisty (Middlesbrough)

12 Mar 1892, St James' Park, 1-7, (1-3), -
Newcastle West End, D Whitton, H Jeffrey, P Dowling, M McCrory, R Ferguson, J Wardropper, R Willis, T Nicholson (1), J Connolly, W McFarlane, J Collins
Sunderland Albion, W Kirkley, J Dewar, J Rae, G King, W Crozier, P McCracken, J Gillespie (3), R Buchanan (2), J Strachan (1), J Mackie (1), J Burns
Ref: Mr Hardisty (Middlesbrough)

Sunderland Albion v West End
FA Cup

27 Oct 1888, Second (Divisional), St James' Park, 3-5, (2-1), 4,500
Newcastle West End, W Jardine, H Jeffrey, J Taylor, R Kelso, W Swinburne, D McKechnie, J Barker, D McColl (1), R Davison (2), J McDonald, J Stanger, *West End objected to Gloag (not qualified (Sustained))*
Sunderland Albion, J Angus, J Munro, J Moore, J Stewart, A Hastings, J Richardson, J Kilpatrick, S Stewart (2), R McLellan (1), R Gloag (1), G Monaghan (1)
Ref: Mr RS Gossen (Southport)

10 Nov 1888, Second (Divisional) replay, St James' Park, 1-2 [aet], (1-1), 4,000
Newcastle West End, W Jardine, H Jeffrey, J Taylor, R Kelso, W Swinburne, T Sadler, J Barker, D McColl, T Nicholson (1), J McDonald, T Stanger
Sunderland Albion, J Angus, J Munro, J Moore, J Stewart, A Hastings, J Richardson (1), J Kilpatrick, S Stewart (1), R McLellan, J Millar, J Allan
NB Gloag was one of the umpires
Ref: Mr Hastie (Lancashire Assoc.)

15 Nov 1890, Third Qualifying, St James' Park, 0-3, (0-1), 3,000
Newcastle West End, D Whitton, H Jeffrey, P Dowling, D Walker, R Ross, A Graham, R Patton, W Kennedy, W Dempsey, T McKenzie, R Calderwood
Sunderland Albion, R Roberts, R McFarlane, J Rae, J King, W Wardrop, P McCracken, J Hannah (2), Hall, H Boyd, Smith, J Millar (1)
Ref: Mr Hardisty (Middlesbrough)

Sunderland Albion v West End
Friendly Games – Results

Date	Match		Attendance	(Half time)
1888-89				
23 Feb	West End 1	Sunderland Albion 1	3,000	(1-1)
	McColl	*Brand*		
9 Mar	Sunderland Albion 4	West End 1	4,000	(3-0)
	McLellan, Brand, scrimmage, S Stewart	*McColl*		
1889-90				
21 Dec	West End 0	Sunderland Albion 3	3,000	(0 - 2)
		Brand, Weir, Hannah		
1891-92				
21 Nov	West End 2	Sunderland Albion 1	2,000	(0-0)
	Collins, Hutchinson	*Mackie*		

NB This game was the first at which turnstiles were used at St James' Park.

Newcastle Rangers v Sunderland
Northumberland & Durham Challenge Cup

12th February 1881, St James' Park 5-0 (3-0)
Newcastle Rangers G M Blake, J A Lochhead (1), A H White, J Campbell, G Hall, J Hetherington, R S Bain (1), W Simms (2), W V Mitchelson (1), N G P Herdman, J Wakinshaw
Sunderland J Graystone , R Singleton, J Sewell, W C Chappell, J C Taylor , R Roberts, J Allan, J Anderson, W E Elliott, E G Watson , J Coates

Stars in (both) Stripes

The following is a complete list of those players who have played for Newcastle and Sunderland and have appeared in the first team for both sides. It excludes those who have played in the first team for one side only and also those who have appeared as 'guests' (such as in war-time football).

	Newcastle		**Sunderland**	
	Apps (Subs)	*Goals*	*Apps (Subs)*	*Goals*
Agnew, William Barbour	May 1902/June 1904		May 1908/Sept 1910	
(1880/1936)	League 43	0	28	0
	FA Cup 1	0		
	Total 44	0	28	0
Anderson, Stanley	Nov 1963/Nov 1965		Feb 1951/Nov 1963	
(1934 -)	League 81	13	402	31
	FA Cup 2	1	34	4
	FL Cup 1	0	11	0
	Total 84	14	447	35
Auld, John Robertson	Oct 1896/June 1897		May 1889/Oct 1896	
(1862/1932)	League 14	3	99	6
	FA Cup 1	0	16	0
	Total 15	3	115	6
Bedford, Henry	Dec 1930/Jan 1932		Jan 1932/May 1932	
(1899/1976)	League 30	17	7	2
	FA Cup 2	1		
	Total 32	18	7	2
Bracewell, Paul William	June 1992/May 1995		June 1983/May 1984	
(1962 -)	League 64 (9)	3	38	4
	FA Cup 6 (2)	0	2	0
	FL Cup 3 (1)	1	4	0
	Misc 2	0		
			Sep 1989/June 1992	
	League		112 (1)	2
	Play Offs		3	0
	FA Cup		10	0
	FL Cup		9	0
	Misc		3	0
			May 1995/Oct 1997	
	League		76 (1)	0
	FA Cup		3	0
	FL Cup		8	0
	Total 75 (12)	4	268 (2)	6
Bridges, Michael	Feb 2004/May 2004		Feb 1995/July 1999	
(1978 -)	League 0 (6)	0	31 (48)	17
	FA Cup		2	0
	FL Cup		8 (3)	5
	Euro 1 (2)	0		
			Sept 2004/July 2005	
	League		5 (14)	1
	FA Cup		0 (2)	0
	Total 1 (8)	0	46 (67)	23
Broadis, Ivan Arthur	Oct 1953/July 1955		Jan 1949/Oct 1951	
(1922 -)	League 42	15	79	25
	FA Cup 9	3	5	2
	Total 51	18	84	27

Brown, Alan (1959 -)

	Nov 1981/Jan 1982 (loan)		Sep 1976/July 1982	
League	5	3	87 (26)	21
FA Cup			2 (2)	0
FL Cup			7	4
Misc			3	0
Total	**5**	**3**	**99 (28)**	**25**

Caldwell, Stephen (1980 -)

	Apr 1996/July 2004		July 2004 -	
League	20 (8)	1	64	4
FA Cup			1	0
FL Cup	3	1	4	1
Europe	1 (5)	0		
Total	**24 (13)**	**2**	**69**	**5**

Campbell, John Middleton (1870/1906)

	May 1897/Oct 1898		cs 1889/May 1897	
League	23	9	186	136
Tests	3	1	4	0
FA Cup	3	2	25	18
Total	**29**	**12**	**215**	**154**

Clark, Lee Robert (1972 -)

	cs 1988/June 1997		June 1997/July 1999	
League	153 (42)	23	72 (1)	16
Play offs			3	0
FA Cup	14 (2)	3	4	0
FL Cup	17	0	4 (1)	0
Europe	3 (5)	0		
Misc	4	1		
	July 2005/			
League	8 (14)	1		
FA Cup	2	0		
FL Cup	0 (1)	0		
Total	**201 (64)**	**28**	**83 (2)**	**16**

Clarke, Jeffrey Derrick (1954 -)

	July 1982/cs 1987		June 1975/July 1982	
League	124	4	178 (3)	6
FA Cup	5	0	15	0
FL Cup	5	1	14	0
Misc			8	0
Total	**134**	**5**	**215 (3)**	**6**

Devine, Joseph Cassidy (1905/1980)

	Jan 1930/Jan 1931		Jan 1931/May 1933	
League	22	11	68	7
FA Cup			9	0
Total	**22**	**11**	**77**	**7**

Dowsey, John (1905/1942)

	June 1924/May 1926		Nov 1927/Feb 1929	
League	3	0	11	1
FA Cup				
Total	**3**	**0**	**11**	**1**

Elliott, David (1945 -)

	Dec 1966/Jan 1971		1961/Dec 1966	
League	78 (2)	4	30 (1)	0
FA Cup	2 (1)	0	4	0
FL Cup	3	0	1	0
Euro	3 (1)	0		
Total	**86 (4)**	**4**	**35 (1)**	**0**

Ellison, Raymond (1950 -)

	May 1968/Feb 1973		Feb 1973/May 1974	
League	5	0	2	0
FL Cup	1	0		
Misc	1	0		
Total	**7**	**0**	**2**	**0**

Foggon, Alan
(1950 -)

	Aug 1965/Aug 1971		Sept 1976/July 1977	
League	54 (7)	14	7 (1)	0
FA Cup	4	0		
FL Cup	1 (1)	0	2	0
Euro	10 (3)	2		
Total	69 (11)	16	9 (1)	0

Gayle, Howard Anthony
(1958 -)

	Nov 1982/Jan 1983 (loan)		July 1984/May 1986	
League	8	2	39 (9)	4
FA Cup			1 (2)	0
FL Cup			6 (2)	1
Misc			2	0
Total	8	2	48 (13)	5

Gibb, Thomas
(1944 -)

	Aug 1968/June 1975		July 1975/May 1977	
League	190 (9)	12	7 (3)	1
FA Cup	8 (3)	0		
FL Cup	12	1		
Euro	24	3		
Misc	17 (5)	3	2 (1)	1
Total	251 (17)	19	9 (4)	2

Given, Seamus John James
(1976 -)

	July 1997 –		Jan/Apr 1996 (loan)	
League	291	0	17	0
FA Cup	27	0		
FL Cup	7 (1)	0		
Euro	54	0		
Total	379 (1)	0	17	0

Grey, Thomas J
(1885 - ?)

	Nov 1910/Oct 1919		May 1907/Sept 1909	
League	1	0	1	0
Total	1	0	1	0

Guthrie, Ronald George
(1944 -)

	July 1963/Jan 1973		Jan 1973/June 1975	
League	52 (3)	2	66	1
FA Cup	0 (1)	0	7	1
FL Cup	2	0	2	0
Euro	3 (2)	0	2 (1)	0
Misc	3	0	3	0
Total	60 (6)	2	80 (1)	2

Hall, Thomas
(1891 - ?)

	May 1913/cs 1920		Jan 1909/May 1913	
League	54	15	30	8
FA Cup	4	1		
Total	58	16	30	8

Hardwick, Stephen
(1956 -)

	Dec 1976/Feb 1983		Aug 1987/Sept 1987 (Loan)	
League	92	0	6	0
FA Cup	4	0		
FL Cup	3	0	2	0
Euro	2	0		
Total	101	0	8	0

Harford, Michael Gordon
(1959 -)

	Dec 1980/Aug 1981		Mar 1993/July 1993	
League	18 (1)	4	10 (1)	2
	Mar 1982 (temporarily)			
	Did not appear in 1st team			
Total	18 (1)	4	10 (1)	2

Harvie (Harvey), John
(1867 - 1940)

	May 1897/cs 1899		1889/Jan 1891	
League	26	6	15	1
Tests	4	2		
FA Cup	5	2	3	1
			cs 1892/May 1897	
League			80	11
Tests			2	0
FA Cup			9	2
Total	35	10	109	15

Kelly, David Thomas
(1965 -)

	Dec 1991/June 1993		Sept 1995/Aug 1997	
League	70	35	32 (2)	2
FA Cup	5	1	3	0
FL Cup	4	2	2 (1)	0
Misc	4	1		
Total	83	39	37 (3)	2

Kennedy, Alan Phillip
(1954 -)

	July 1971/Aug 1978		Sept 1985/May 1987	
League	155 (3)	9	54	2
Play offs			2	0
FA Cup	21(2)	0	4	0
FL Cup	16	0	2 (1)	0
Euro	2	0		
Misc	16 (1)	1	4	1
Total	210 (6)	10	66 (1)	3

Logan, James
(1870/1896)

	Sept 1895/Jan 1896		Aug 1891/Nov 1891	
League	7	5	2	0
FA Cup	2	3		
Total	9	8	2	0

McCombie, Andrew
(1876/1952)

	Feb 1904/Apr 1910		Dec 1898/Feb 1904	
League	113	0	157	6
FA Cup	18	0	7	0
Misc			1	0
Total	131	0	165	6

McDermid, Robert
(1870 - ?)

	Oct 1894/Feb 1897		cs 1888/1889	
League	56	2		
FA Cup	8	0	2	0
Total	64	2	2	0

McInroy, Albert
(1901/1985)

	Oct 1929/June 1934		May 1923/Oct 1929	
League	143	0	215	0
FA Cup	17	0	12	0
			June 1934/May 1935	
			Did not appear in 1st team	
Total	160	0	227	0

McKay, Robert
(1900 - ?)

	Nov 1926/Oct 1928		Oct 1928/Dec 1930	
League	62	22	49	17
FA Cup	4	1	2	0
Total	66	23	51	17

Moncur, Robert
(1945 -)

	Oct 1960/June 1974		June 1974/Nov 1976	
League	293 (3)	3	86	2
FA Cup	18	1	7	0
FL Cup	10	0	3	0
Euro	22	4		
Misc	15	2	5	0
Total	358 (3)	10	101	2

Raine, James Edmundson
(1886/1928)

	1905/Dec 1906 (amateur)		Dec 1906/Apr 1908	
League	4	1	25	6
FA Cup			3	1
Total	4	1	28	7

Robinson, Raymond Wilson
(1895/1964)

	May 1919/Aug 1920		Aug 1920/May 1921	
League	27	4	10	2
FA Cup	2	0		
			June 1922/Oct 1922	
			Did not appear in 1st team	
Total	29	4	10	2

Robinson, Robert
(1923 -)

	Aug 1952/June 1954		Feb 1947/Aug 1952	
League	5	0	31	0
FA Cup			2	0
Total	5	0	33	0

Robson, Bryan Stanley (Pop)
(1945 -)

	August 1962/Feb 1971		June 1974/Oct 1976	
League	205 (1)	82	90	34
FA Cup	10	4	7	4
FL Cup	4	2	6	1
Euro	24	9		
Misc			6	1
			June 1979/Mar 1981	
League			49 (3)	23
FA Cup			1	0
FL Cup			4 (1)	2
Misc			2	0
			July 1983/July 1984	
League			7 (5)	3
FL Cup			0 (1)	0
Total	243 (1)	97	172 (10)	68

Rowlandson, Thomas Sowerby
(1880/1916)

	1905/1906 (amateur)		Dec 1903/Dec 1904 (amateur)	
League	1	0	12	0
Total	1	0	12	0

Scott, Matthew
(1867 - 1897)

	Aug 1889 - Oct 1892 (East End)		Oct 1892/May 1897	
League			1	0
Nth League	42	0		
FA Cup	10	0		
Misc	5	0		
Total	57	0	1	0

Shackleton, Leonard Francis
(1922/2000)

	Oct 1946/Feb 1948		Feb 1948/May 1958	
League	57	26	320	97
FA Cup	7	3	28	3
Total	64	29	348	100

Smith, John
(? - 1911)

	Aug 1888/May 1889 (East End)		Aug 1889/May 1893	
League			24	2
FA Cup	3	3	8	2
Misc	7	2		
	cs 1894 - 1896			
League	25	10		
FA Cup	2	0		
Total	37	15	32	4

Spence, John

	July 1891/cs 1892 (East End)		Oct 1889/July 1891	
League			5	2
Nth League	12	3		
FA Cup	5	1		
Total	17	4	5	2

Suggett, Colin
(1948 -)

	Aug 1978/June 1981		July 1964/July 1969	
League	20 (3)	0	83 (3)	24
FA Cup			3	1
FL Cup	1	0	4	0
Total	21 (3)	0	90 (3)	25

Taylor, Ernest
(1925/1985)

	Sept 1942/Oct 1951		Dec 1958/Nov 1961	
League	107	19	68	11
FA Cup	10	2	3	0
Misc	26	7		
Total	143	28	71	11

Thomson, Robert W
(1905 - ?)

	Oct 1928/July 1934		Apr 1927/Oct 1928	
League	73	0	19	0
FA Cup	7	0	3	0
Total	80	0	22	0

Urwin, Thomas
(1896/1968)

	Aug 1924/Feb 1930		Feb 1930/May 1936	
League	188	23	50	5
FA Cup	12	1	5	1
Total	200	24	55	6

Venison, Barry
(1964 -)

	July 1992/June 1995		May 1979/July 1986	
League	108 (1)	1	169 (4)	2
FA Cup	11	0	7 (1)	0
FL Cup	9	0	21	0
Euro	1	0		
Misc	3	0	3	1
Total	132 (1)	1	200 (5)	3

Waddle, Christopher Roland
(1960 -)

	July 1980/July 1985		Mar 1997/June 1997	
League	169 (1)	46	7	1
FA Cup	12	4		
FL Cup	9	2		
Total	190 (1)	52	7	1

Walker, Nigel Stephen
(1959 -)

	Apr 1977/May 1982		Dec 1982/Jan 1983 (trial)	
League	65 (5)	3	Did not appear in 1st team	
FA Cup	3	0		
FL Cup	1	0		
			July 1983/June 1984	
League			0 (1)	0
Total	69 (5)	3	0 (1)	0

Whitehurst, William
(1959 -)

	Dec 1985/Oct 1986		Sept 1988/Dec 1988	
League	28	7	17	3
FA Cup	1	0		
FL Cup	1 (1)	0		
Misc			1	0
Total	30 (1)	7	18	3

Willis, David Lalty
(1881/1949)

	May 1907/May 1913		cs 1901/May 1903	
League	95	3	1	0
FA Cup	12	1		
Misc	1	0		
			cs 1904/May 1907	
League			47	2
FA Cup			4	0
Total	108	4	52	2

Young, David
(1945 -)

	Sept 1964/Jan 1973		Jan 1973/July 1974	
League	41 (2)	2	24 (6)	1
FA Cup			4	0
FL Cup	4	0	3	0
Euro	5 (1)	0	3 (1)	0
Misc	2 (1)	0		
Total	52 (4)	2	34 (7)	1

Analysis of Attendances

	Newcastle			Sunderland		
League games						
Decade	Aggregate	Average	No of seasons with higher attendance	Aggregate	Average	No of seasons with higher attendance
1890s	46,000	23,000	0	52,000	26,000	2
1900s	389,131	38,913	5	317,500	31,750	4
1910s	310,377	51,729	6	207,148	34,525	0
1920s	550,790	55,079	7	453,386	45,339	3
1930s	163,618	40,905	3	130,476	32,619	4
1940s	116,249	58,125	1	119,403	59,702	1
1950s	446,440	55,805	6	436,138	54,517	2
1960s	417,772	52,222	3	429,886	53,736	5
1970s	123,103	41,034	1	123,213	41,071	2
1980s	68,393	34,197	2	57,745	28,873	0
1990s	133,672	33,418	3	121,551	30,388	1
2000s	208,534	52,134	4	181,666	45,417	0
Totals	2,974,079	47,208	41	2,630,112	41,748	21
Play-offs	32,199	32,199	1	26,641	26,641	0
Cup games						
FA Cup	243,898	48,780		61,623	20,541	
Lgue Cup	30,533	30,533	1	27,658	27,658	0
Totals	3,280,709	46,867	43	2,746,034	40,383	21

Note that the FA Cup games have been omitted from the higher attendances comparison as they were not on a home and away basis (unlike the League Cup tie or the play-off games)

Analysis of Results

Newcastle
(League Results)

	Home					Away				
	W	D	L	F	A	W	D	L	F	A
1890s	0	0	2	2	5	2	0	0	5	3
1900s	3	1	6	11	24	2	4	4	12	15
1910s	2	2	2	11	12	3	0	3	9	10
1920s	7	2	1	23	10	1	4	5	10	17
1930s	2	0	2	5	4	2	0	2	6	8
1940s	1	1	0	4	3	0	2	0	3	3
1950s	3	4	1	20	14	4	1	3	18	12
1960s	4	3	1	12	8	0	4	4	6	15
1970s	2	0	1	6	5	0	2	1	3	4
1980s	1	1	0	4	2	0	2	0	0	0
1990s	2	1	1	4	3	2	2	0	7	5
2000s	2	1	1	7	5	3	1	0	7	2
League Totals	29	16	18	109	95	19	22	22	86	94
Play offs			1	0	2		1		0	0
FA Cup	1	2	2	5	9	1	1	1	3	2
League Cup*			1	2	2		1		2	2
Grand Totals	**30**	**18**	**22**	**116**	**108**	**20**	**25**	**23**	**91**	**98**

Sunderland
(League Results)

	Home					Away				
	W	D	L	F	A	W	D	L	F	A
1890s	0	0	2	3	5	2	0	0	5	2
1900s	4	4	2	15	12	6	1	3	24	11
1910s	3	0	3	10	9	2	2	2	12	11
1920s	5	4	1	17	10	1	2	7	10	23
1930s	2	0	2	8	6	2	0	2	4	5
1940s	0	2	0	3	3	0	1	1	3	4
1950s	3	1	4	12	18	1	4	3	14	20
1960s	4	4	0	15	6	1	3	4	8	12
1970s	1	2	0	4	3	1	0	2	5	6
1980s	0	2	0	0	0	0	1	1	2	4
1990s	0	2	2	5	7	1	1	2	3	4
2000s	0	1	3	2	7	1	1	2	5	7
League Totals	22	22	19	94	86	18	16	29	95	109
Play offs	0	1	0	0	0	1	0	0	2	0
FA Cup	1	1	1	2	3	2	2	1	9	5
League Cup *	0	1	0	2	2	1	0	0	2	2
Grand Totals	**23**	**25**	**20**	**98**	**91**	**22**	**18**	**30**	**108**	**116**

* Although the League Cup game at Newcastle ended as a 2 – 2 draw, Sunderland won the penalty shoot-out and therefore the tie, so the game has been recorded as a Sunderland victory.

Newcastle	Wins	50	Goals for	207
Sunderland	Wins	45	Goals for	206
	Draws	43		